1001
Dreams

1001 Dreams

THE COMPLETE BOOK OF DREAM INTERPRETATIONS

CASSANDRA EASON

STERLING ETHOS
New York

This book is dedicated to my beloved children, Tom, Jade, Jack, Miranda, and Bill, and my dear grandchildren, Freya, Oliver, Holly, and Sophie, all of whom keep me sane and my refrigerator empty. I also dedicate this book to Konnie Gold, my inspiration, dearest friend, and touchstone. This work has been a pure joy to write.

STERLING ETHOS
New York

ISBN 978-1-4549-4846-9
ISBN 978-1-4549-4847-6 (e-book)

Library of Congress Control Number: 2023934376

For information about custom editions, special sales, and premium purchases, please contact specialsales@unionsquareandco.com.

Printed in China

2 4 6 8 10 9 7 5 3 1

unionsquareandco.com

Cover design by Gina Bonnano and Melissa Farris
Interior design by Gina Bonnano and Gavin Motnyk

Picture credits appear on p. 541

Contents

Introduction

It's unbelievable to think that as we sleep, we are tapping into a treasure trove of advice, resources, and knowledge—a powerful connection to the psychic as well as the psychological world that is just waiting to be accessed. That is the remarkable potential of a dream: to make life more understandable so that we can gain (or regain) control over our waking world.

1001 Dreams is aimed at explaining and exploring the significance and practical use of dreams for everyone who has ever dreamed—and that is all of us— or tried to guide loved ones, particularly children and teens, with their dreams. When we become open to exploring the complexities of dreams, sleep becomes a pleasurable experience, not one to be feared.

About *1001 Dreams*

This book is more than a dream-meaning reference: it offers an insight into 1001 different dreams through the words of those who experienced them. This includes a description of the dream, the background of daily events or deep-seated worries that led to the dream, and popular fortune-telling significances relevant for every dreamer on each included topic. Each topic listed in this book has had a practical purpose for everyone who has dreamed of them. These meanings are based on a mix of traditional significance through the ages and modern everyday applications, so the dream symbols in this book have as much meaning in the twenty-first century as when analysis of dreams began among the Ancient Egyptians and Greeks.

Finally, each dream describes how the dreamer used the dream for changing their life for the better, though some dreamers choose to ignore dream warnings. These sections illuminate how daily decisions that seem unclear can be made with the help of the subconscious. Some examples are dramatic—predicting international disasters or guiding the dreamer to healing remedies—while others are more commonplace, such as enabling the dreamer to offer support to a relative who is suffering fears alone, who may call out for help in the dream but remains silent in the everyday world.

Using This Book

As well as 1001 dreams taken from all lands and people, from the very young to those in their nineties, this book briefly but clearly describes how dreams can be recalled, recorded, and acted upon as a guide if we tap into the unconscious radar we all possess. This often-underused intuitive sense can warn of danger and opportunity for ourselves and loved ones, allowing us to receive messages from spirit guardians, angels, and beloved ancestors.

There are techniques for knowing when you are dreaming during sleep, traveling anywhere in sleep, changing defeat to triumph through your subconscious, and changing fears to power by using the world of dreams to rehearse success in the days ahead. This book also considers past-life or recalled-memory dreams from ancestors, where on the dream plane we can learn the source of current phobias and how to overcome them, develop telepathic communication between lovers and loved ones, and reach out to those who may be estranged. We can even call in people that we have not yet met. Finally, dreams can be powerful tools to overcome nightmares and night terrors.

Remembering Your Dreams

In psychology, a "flashbulb memory" is when something vivid imprints on your memory like a photographic image. This often happens during particularly significant moments in history, such as the death of Princess Diana, or 9/11. Because of the significance of the moment, we are able to recall in detail what we were doing when we heard the news. Vivid dreams can be imprinted on our memory in the same way as these flashbulb memories.

But for many other dreams the details can fade within a few minutes once daily life intrudes. What's more, our memory can tidy up details as our conscious mind tries to rationalize or, if uncomfortable, explain away the dream experience.

Since dreams are often a source of hidden information, recalling them can make sense of seemingly unresolvable choices or others' reactions to a daily occurrence about which you dreamed. Once you start recalling and recording dreams, spontaneous dream recall also increases.

Recalling Dreams

◆ Keep a notebook and pen at your bedside or, if you prefer, record your immediate memories of the dream on your phone.

◆ As soon as you wake from a dream or nightmare, whether it's the middle of the night or the morning, write down or say aloud any details you can recall.

◆ Include dream characters who are part of your daily life. Feelings as to whether or not you are happy about a dream scenario can be crucial to unraveling your true emotions. This takes only a minute and can help you to return to sleep free from the dream, especially if it was a nightmare.

◆ If the dream was good and you want to return to it, picture one of the last or strongest pleasurable images or scenes that you liked, or imagine a path leading back to a place in the dream.

◆ If you do not want to go back into a particular dream or want to calm down after a nightmare, picture yourself floating on fluffy pink clouds through a starlit sky or enclosed in a warm, dark blanket.

The Significance of Bad Dreams

Bad dreams frequently remind us of oversights in daily life that need remedy, or unfinished business. A car crash dream where you have a tire burst on the freeway is not a psychic warning of a bad accident. Rather, it is a way of telling you what your automatic radar has picked up: that one of the tires on your car needs attention, that you haven't checked your tire pressure for a while, or that you've become distracted while driving. Sometimes anxiety dreams where everything goes wrong can signal stress overload and indicate that it's time to step back from trying to fix the world or working 24/7.

More positively, you can, by visualizing the point in the dream where everything went wrong, consciously change the ending of the dream in your semi-waking state. In doing so, you can take forward to your day happy successful energies of how you overcame the crisis on the dream plane or escaped from the monster. This is especially true of negative past-life dreams.

Creative Dreaming or Dream Incubation

Creating beautiful dreams has been practiced in different cultures for thousands of years. The Ancient Egyptians were the first dream experts and actively directed their dreams not only to bring peaceful sleep but also to find the answers to questions they wanted to know. The creative and inspirational part of the mind is largely unconscious and in sleep we can often find creative solutions to problems or recognize opportunities that our waking, more logical, brain had not thought about. Like the Greeks, the Egyptians had special dream temples—or sleep temples—which only priests were allowed to enter. Ordinary people would sit in a cave or other dark place and look into the light of an oil lamp to relax their mind before sleep.

◆ If you have a special question or dilemma, rather than letting it keep you awake, put a few drops of lavender oil beneath your pillow and complete the following steps.

◆ While in total darkness, light a battery-operated candle, nightlight, or shaded lamp and recite your question, or the area of your life in which you need guidance, seven times softly and continuously.

◆ Half close your eyes and focus on the halo around the light.

◆ Softly recite the question seven times more, quieter each time until your words fade into the silence.

◆ Extinguish the light and go to sleep, visualizing yourself walking into the golden light of the candle or lamp.

◆ The answer should come in the dream, perhaps in symbolic form, but if it does not, repeat the exercise the next night. Within two or three attempts, the dream answer will come.

◆ As you become experienced in creative dreaming, you may not even need to light the candle, only needing to recite the question several times before sleep or to write it down and place it under your pillow.

Lucid Dreaming: Awareness That You Are Dreaming

This is probably the most useful dream technique, as by knowing you are dreaming you can go anywhere, do anything, and overcome any potential hazard, transforming a nightmare into a challenge to overcome on the dream plane and in the waking world. Start with visualizing exotic or unusual scenarios to stimulate the all-important imagination.

◆ Just before sleep, lie in bed and close your eyes. Create your ideal dream scene—a tropical shore, a house by a lake, a castle or palace—with you as the central character, hero, or heroine, starring in your very own production.

◆ Imagine yourself interacting in this world—walk through the golden palace rooms, swim with multicolored fish beneath the ocean, or do whatever you desire in your particular dream scene.

◆ Now create a symbol in this dream setting that will remind you that you are dreaming when you see it in sleep. Choose something exotic and memorable—a rainbow-colored bird, a gigantic multicolored butterfly, or a golden peacock studded with gems, for instance—and rerun the imagined dream scene in your mind, letting the symbol appear five or six times so it fills the screen of your dream. As you picture it, say to yourself: "When I see the multicolored butterfly, I will know I am dreaming and anything is possible."

◆ When you are ready, drift into sleep, focusing on the image so it fills your mind.

◆ Be patient; the first night you may see only a few details of your visualized symbol, or nothing at all, and you may not recall you are dreaming.

◆ Repeat the technique every night until you see the symbol or simply recall that you are dreaming during sleep and can visit wherever and whoever you want, past, present, or future.

◆ Rehearse the words you need or want to say in real life, change the dream ending by overcoming your demons, and wake refreshed and full of power.

Psychic Dreams

In dreams, the barriers of time and space are not as fixed as they are in our waking lives when logic dominates our awareness of opportunity or danger. In sleep, our unconscious radar replaces conscious thought, offering warnings or advice about events that will soon come into our lives. If heeded, this can help us to avert hazards or to wait at the front of the line of opportunity. Parents and children of all ages link telepathically in sleep and a new parent can be alerted to a child's distress. These premonition dreams are different from nightmares or anxiety dreams.

◆ True predictive dreams have been described as more real than even a vivid dream and remain with us long after we would have forgotten an ordinary dream. The dream scene in premonitions is usually three-dimensional, very detailed, and, when we wake from it, we are fully awake and not at all sleepy or confused. These premonition dreams can also connect you with a twin soul on the dream plane and draw you to the place where you will meet each other.

◆ Unlike a predictive dream, a regular dream often involves waking with nagging anxiety rather than urgency, which suggests you are feeling jittery about life. The more you trust your dreams, the less anxious you become.

Ghosts in Dreams

The most common contact with deceased family members comes in dreams. There is nothing to fear if a loved grandmother or grandfather comes to you or a child in sleep and talks to you or cuddles you if you are lonely or sad.

It may be the mind's way of healing grief at the death of a loved one. If your relation died some years ago, such a dream will recall memories of the love and reassurance they offered you in their lifetime, perhaps when you were a child. These dreams often occur at a time in your present world when you are feeling vulnerable.

However, some people do believe that a person's essential personality lives on after death and can speak to us in dreams. Sometimes, particularly if you did not have the chance to say goodbye, or if the relative died with ill feeling between you, a dream can bring necessary reconciliation. Afterward, most people say that they feel a great sense of peace, especially if the person died suddenly or after a prolonged illness in which they suffered a great deal.

Past Lives

1001 Dreams also records what seem to be past-life or recalled-memory dreams from ancestors, where, on the dream plane, we can learn the source of current phobias and how to overcome them. When a dreamer knows nothing of their past heritage, perhaps because of adoption, a dream can rekindle clues of severed connections that can be explored in daily life if the ancestors, or maybe an unknown living relative, wants to make contact.

Dreams as Tools for Making Life Better

Every dream is a snapshot into real people's lives, allowing the reader to share the dream and see how the world of sleep can transform the waking world for the better. Key periods of life—pregnancy, childhood, adolescence, the twenties and thirties, bereavement, sorrow, and times of major change—feature strongly, as these periods are when psychic powers are at their height and the world at its most confusing. Use this book as a beacon of light to transform the sleep plane into a rich treasure trove of potential. Finally, of course, this book is relevant to those who are looking for a specific dream meaning or a recurring dream theme.

Dreams are your mind's way of making sense of the world, unencumbered by mundane worldly limitations that hold us back in our waking lives.

American Edgar Cayce (1877–1945), founder of the Association for Research and Enlightenment, said, "Dreams are today's answers to tomorrow's questions." In this book there is ample evidence he knew what he was talking about.

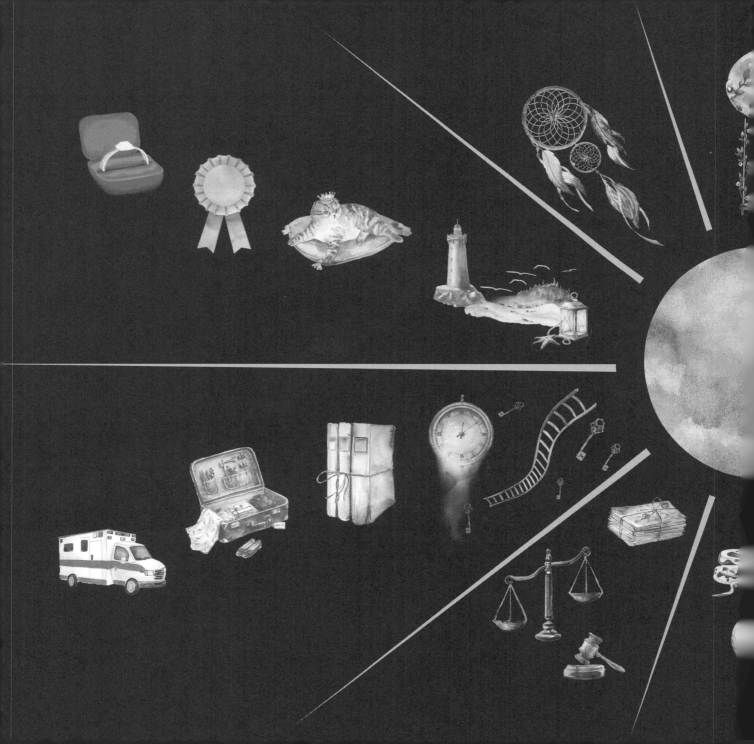

Dreams A to Z

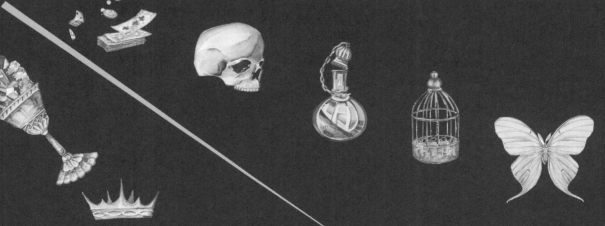

Abandonment

Maisie, twenty-eight, dreamed she was a young child selling fruit from a heavy basket in the streets of old London. She realized she had wandered farther than usual and was totally lost. Maisie sat on the bridge, crying. A well-dressed woman and two little girls said she could go home with them and they would care for her. She climbed into their beautiful carriage and was wrapped in a blanket. It was a fairy-tale ending.

DREAM BACKGROUND AND MEANING

Maisie had grown up in foster care and had been moved from foster home to foster home. Now she had met a guy with a wonderful family who totally pampered her. So why was she not happy? Abandonment dreams, especially past-life ones, tend to be compensatory and involve putting right past wrongs in the present world.

INTERPRETATIONS AND FORTUNE-TELLING MEANINGS

★ If you find yourself abandoned in a dream, is there something or someone in your present situation that is making you feel insecure?

★ If you are abandoning others, you may have an unacknowledged dissatisfaction with the reality of present relationships, or find home and family life overwhelming.

★ Fears of being abandoned in a dream can reflect doubts about your self-worth, especially if you are in a relationship where a partner constantly threatens to leave.

★ If you are rescued in the dream and cared for, you may need more nurturing in your current relationships if you are generally the nurturer.

★ Does the dream have a happy ending? In that case it may be that you are prepared to sacrifice independence for a sense of being protected, perhaps by entering a committed relationship or secure career.

★ If you don't mind being abandoned, consider the advantages versus drawbacks.

OUTCOME OF MAISIE'S DREAM

Maisie often felt stifled by her fiancé's family and by him. Maisie decided to move out for a while. She realized it was the secure life and not the people that she loved.

Abscess, Boil

Joseph, fifty-five, dreamed he had a painful abscess on his tooth. When he went to the dentist, the dentist said he was imagining it and not to waste his time. Joseph, a mild-mannered man, was furious and, picking up a sharp instrument, lanced his own abscess. The abscess burst and the pain was gone.

DREAM BACKGROUND AND MEANING

Joseph was continually undermined at work by his manager. When Joseph complained, the manager said the problem was in Joseph's mind and if he could not take the pressure he should leave. Joseph began to doubt himself. Abscess dreams should not be ignored, as they are warning of a problem that will not go away if ignored.

INTERPRETATIONS AND FORTUNE-TELLING MEANINGS

★ If you dream about having a painful abscess, or a boil without a head, you are resentful of an injustice but are trying to keep your feelings from spilling over.

★ If the abscess is swelling or coming to a head, you are feeling overwhelmed by a problem not acknowledged by others that needs bringing into the open.

★ If the abscess bursts, toxic emotions will be cleared and you will receive justice.

★ Depending on where the abscess is, it indicates the area of life where you need to take action. A tooth abscess shows you are not being listened to, and a limb or neck abscess signifies you are holding back from acting at the cost of your own health and harmony. A face abscess warns that someone is being two-faced, and a back abscess says you are being stabbed in the back.

★ The lancing of an abscess indicates that decisive action will clear the problem that the perpetrator is denying.

★ If you dream you lance an abscess yourself, the remedy is in your hands.

OUTCOME OF JOSEPH'S DREAM

Joseph went to his manager's boss and offered proof of the manager's intimidation. Joseph was moved to another department and the manager severely reprimanded.

Absent Friends and Family

Prudence, twenty-five, dreamed she was thousands of miles from home on the eve of her birthday and was feeling homesick. She dreamed of being with her family and their toasting her in champagne as they did every birthday. Her mother said, "Your special gift will arrive tomorrow. We miss you." Prudence woke hugging her family. She was so sad that the dream had ended.

DREAM BACKGROUND AND MEANING

Prudence was working as a nurse in Australia and missed her family. In the dream her family was at an unknown noisy bar. Dreams offer space between worlds where love can make it possible to see and even feel loved ones.

INTERPRETATIONS AND FORTUNE-TELLING MEANINGS

* Dreaming of a friend who is not in your life right now indicates telepathic communication. They are probably thinking about you.
* If an absent friend or family member is telephoning or mailing you in your dream, you will hear from them soon.
* If you see the absent friend or family member in a specific setting, this may be a form of clairvoyance where you see what absent friends are doing at a specific time.
* Alternatively, you may astrally project or mind-travel in the dream, or they may visit you on the dream plane.
* If you connect with a deceased friend or relative in a place you both loved, you may feel they are close when you visit that location.
* If you dream of a friend or family member in distress, contact them. They are hiding a worry.

OUTCOME OF PRUDENCE'S DREAM

On her birthday, Prudence received a photo of her family at the airport in Boston, saying they were on their way, bringing her gifts. They were toasting her at the airport bar. The link of love is one of the most powerful forces to make psychic connections and renew fractured communication.

Abyss, Chasm

Claudia, fifty, dreamed she was pushing her mother in her wheelchair with all her mother's bags strapped to the back. In the dream her mother was moving in with Claudia. Suddenly a huge dark hole appeared in front of them and her mother insisted that Claudia carry the wheelchair across the hole. Claudia knew they would both fall in. Her mother became angry and pushed Claudia into the hole. Claudia woke up shaking.

DREAM BACKGROUND AND MEANING

Although Claudia's mother was unable to look after herself, she refused to go into a retirement home, insisting she move into Claudia's home. The old lady said Claudia's sister, Tina, who did nothing to help, was far too busy. Abyss dreams indicate being swallowed up by unfair demands.

INTERPRETATIONS AND FORTUNE-TELLING MEANINGS

* If a large hole opens in front of you, beware of pitfalls ahead and don't take chances.
* An abyss can reveal issues with a dominating mother figure or older female relative.
* If you avoid or jump over the hole, a risky venture or a passionate love affair will turn out well.
* If you are teetering on the edge, you may be afraid of confronting deep negative, albeit justifiable, emotions.
* If someone pushes you in, beware treachery.
* A dream abyss can give advance warning that your position in life is insecure, especially concerning property or finance. You ignore this at your peril.

OUTCOME OF CLAUDIA'S DREAM

Claudia told her sister they had to find a retirement home for their mother or Tina would have to take her in, as Tina did not work, whereas Claudia, a single parent, had to work full-time. Tina persuaded their mother to go to a retirement home. On Tina's persuasion, their mother cut Claudia out of her will.

Accident

Heidi, twenty-one, dreamed she was standing at the top of a snowboarding slope. She launched herself after her boyfriend and went past him, but missed the slope and fell into the air, somersaulting until she reached the bottom. "You really did it this time," she thought.

DREAM BACKGROUND AND MEANING

Heidi had always been accident-prone, dropping, spilling, falling, and injuring herself. Now her boyfriend wanted her to go snowboarding with him. Heidi did not want to miss out and, despite never having previously snowboarded, she agreed to go. The nature of accident dreams reflects the problems behind the accident: accidents in water, becoming overwhelmed by emotion; plane crashes, overextending your resources; and those involving fire, becoming too passionately involved and careless.

INTERPRETATIONS AND FORTUNE-TELLING MEANINGS

★ Accident dreams can be advance warnings of what your subconscious has noticed as potential hazards regarding your health, domestic, and personal safety.

★ If you dream about a traffic accident, you may be anxious about your physical health, because a vehicle is a common symbol for the body, and you should take more care of your own well-being.

★ If you crash head-on, you may be worried about unavoidable conflict.

★ If there is a rescuer present in any kind of accident, you may be relying on the protection of others to get you out of trouble.

★ To dream of slipping or falling suggests you may say something unwise or commit to a risky action unless you are ultracautious.

OUTCOME OF HEIDI'S DREAM

The week she was due to go snowboarding, Heidi had some masonry drop on her foot as she passed a building site, breaking her foot. Some say accidents occur because we subconsciously know that a situation could be dangerous. Accident dreams can be based on an existing likelihood; it was not the building accident but the snowboarding that Heidi's unconscious was warning her against.

Accomplice

Derek, sixteen, dreamed he was leader of a crime syndicate, and the others at high school were acting as his accomplices. He masterminded crimes, and his accomplices carried them out. In his dreams he was unstoppable.

DREAM BACKGROUND AND MEANING

Derek, though quiet and studious, hung around with the school rebel gang. They said if he acted as lookout and drove the car while they robbed a service station, he could join them. But it went wrong. They ran away and Derek was left behind but escaped before police arrived. Accomplice dreams represent enlisting others to carry out actions that you would not dare perform in real life, the part of your ego you may repress.

INTERPRETATIONS AND FORTUNE-TELLING MEANINGS

★ If you are acting as an accomplice in a dream crime, you may be going along with a plan in the workplace or community in which you do not believe.

★ If in a dream you are seeking an accomplice for a crime, you may need support for an idea you know is unpopular.

★ If you dream you are arrested as an accomplice, you may feel guilty about an undiscovered omission or commission.

★ If you dream you are an accomplice driving a getaway vehicle after a bank robbery, you may be tempted to go along with other people's get-rich-quick schemes.

★ If you enjoy being an accomplice in a crime, you may want to take more chances in life but may be scared to go against the status quo.

★ If you feel guilty about being an accomplice, you may not actually want to take risks but are being pressured by others.

OUTCOME OF DEREK'S DREAM

Derek realized he was not a tough guy. Some of the gang were expelled and put in youth detention for minor crimes, and Derek put all his energies into study. Accomplice dreams can be wish-fulfillment, acting out a rebellious streak that can be diverted into accomplishing something worthwhile.

Accusations

Molly, thirty-five, dreamed she was a child of about ten, standing before the judge in a courtroom, accused of stealing fruit. She was innocent, but her mother, who had stolen the fruit, could not take the blame, as she was pregnant. Their father had run off, and Molly's mother had the other children to care for. Molly was terrified, as she knew the punishment would be severe, and she awoke shaking.

DREAM BACKGROUND AND MEANING

Money had been disappearing from the cash register at work, and Molly and her best friend Ginny were the only ones with access. Molly had suspected for some time that her friend had been stealing. Ginny was a single parent with two small children, relying entirely on her wages. To lose her job and possibly be prosecuted was unthinkable. But Molly did not want the accusation of being a thief on her own record. Accusation dreams may take dramatic forms to alert the dreamer to deal with unresolved obligations from different periods of life, and even from different lifetimes.

INTERPRETATIONS AND FORTUNE-TELLING MEANINGS

* If you dream of being unfairly accused of a crime, an old injustice may still rankle you and need to be put right or let go.
* If you are denying a mistake in real life that is invading your dreams, consider how it can be put right with the least damage.
* If you dream someone unknown is accusing you, they may be trying to divert attention from themselves. Identify who.
* If in your dream you are being accused in a present- or past-life courtroom, you may be denying a problem that needs confronting—if necessary, with official help.
* If you are defending someone against an unfair accusation, you may be trying to compensate for a personal action about which you feel guilty, maybe from the past.

OUTCOME OF MOLLY'S DREAM

Molly realized that she could not blight her own reputation. She offered to pay the stolen money back if Ginny confessed. As a result, Ginny was not prosecuted but lost her job. Accusation dreams are a good basis for deciding what is viable as well as ethical.

Acorns

Sue-Ellen, forty-five, dreamed that a beautiful oak forest was chopped down and nothing remained but fallen branches and acorns. But a new forest of tall green trees instantly grew and was filled with the wildlife that had either fled or been killed. She woke knowing life could still be good.

DREAM BACKGROUND AND MEANING

Sue-Ellen's home was due to be foreclosed on because of the economic downturn. She was leaving her beloved forest of oak trees where she gathered acorns to make flour and coffee that helped with her allergies. She packed her possessions and desperately searched for a new home she could rent where she could see the trees.

INTERPRETATIONS AND FORTUNE-TELLING MEANINGS

* Acorns are one of the luckiest dream symbols for the gradual growth of whatever is desired.
* They are a symbol of fertility and prosperity coming into your life.
* Dreaming of seeing small oaks springing up indicates that any projects you start now will succeed and grow.
* Since the acorn protects its seed within, if many acorns grow on trees, it promises freedom and safety from attack or intrusion.
* Since acorns are used for food by wild animals as well as by humans, acorns lying on the ground predict that you will receive a modest but much-needed bonus.
* Making foodstuffs from acorns in a dream says you should adapt existing resources in any area of your world, as the smallest acorn can grow into the mightiest tree.

OUTCOME OF SUE-ELLEN'S DREAM

Sue-Ellen found a tiny house with a huge outbuilding on the other side of the forest. She had been asked to make acorn flour and coffee for friends with allergies, and she converted her outbuilding into an acorn workshop from which she could start a small-scale acorn products and recipe book business. Because acorns are slow to grow, rapid growth in a dream indicates you already have the seeds to making your fortune.

Actor

Juliet, twenty, dreamed she was appearing in the starring role in the school play. However, she had not learned her lines and was relying on the prompter. Eventually people started leaving. Juliet shouted that the play was useless. She made a long, impassioned speech that had everyone cheering and returning to their seats.

DREAM BACKGROUND AND MEANING

Even when she was at school, Juliet had realized there was more to learning than repeating other people's words and opinions. She was having the same problem at college. Juliet was considering quitting college, but without qualifications she knew she would not be taken seriously.

INTERPRETATIONS AND FORTUNE-TELLING MEANINGS

★ If you are starring in a dream play, you may want more recognition for your hard work and talents from those around you.

★ If you forget your words, you may be relying on others in life generally to speak for you.

★ If you are continually checking the script or waiting for a prompt, you may be worried about others finding out your inadequacies.

★ Acting a part purely for the purpose of impressing, for example at a dream interview, may fail to achieve its purpose in real life.

★ If you are unwilling to step to center stage or in the spotlight in the dream, you may be being pushed to take a more public or higher profile role for which you are not ready.

★ If you dream you are taking a number of parts in a play, you may be showing different aspects of yourself to different people at the cost of being your true self.

OUTCOME OF JULIET'S DREAM

Juliet decided to change her major to creative writing. She has written several plays for the drama society. She is applying for an internship for scriptwriters in a theater company, and earning money in the evenings while she establishes herself.

Adoption

Linda, forty, dreamed she was in a labor ward with a blonde, blue-eyed woman who was giving birth to a beautiful boy. Linda woke shaken by the intensity of the dream and noted the date and time of the dream birth.

DREAM BACKGROUND AND MEANING

Linda and her husband, Richard, were waiting to be assigned an adoptive child at the time of the dream. Dreams can link telepathically with the child at birth or soon after, to reassure the adoptive parents that the adoption is meant to be.

INTERPRETATIONS AND FORTUNE-TELLING MEANINGS

★ If you dream of your adoptive child before the adoption, and if you have been waiting a while, you know that the child is near.

★ If you were expecting to adopt a baby but dream of two children, perhaps siblings, they will bring happiness.

★ If you consistently dream of much older generations who you do not know when you first meet your adoptive child, the birth family ancestors may be giving their blessing to the adoption.

★ If you suspect you are adopted and consistently dream of another family or location, you may be picking up vibes of a birth family that wants to enter your life. Make the necessary inquiries with the relevant authorities.

★ If you dream you are adopted but 100 percent know you are not, you may resemble an ancestor who also felt different, who may contact you in dreams.

★ If you dream of your adopted child being in danger or difficulty, this is the maternal or paternal radar kicking in, which exists even without a genetic link.

OUTCOME OF LINDA'S DREAM

When Linda and her husband were given the baby three months later, the birth date and time of baby Ivan's birth exactly matched the dream time and date. He was the boy Linda had seen in her dream. They felt Ivan was their special child since Linda had shared in the birth.

You may have been with your adopted child in a past world and so instantly feel the psychic link.

Adult Sex Toys

Dinah, sixty-four, dreamed of entering an adult store and selecting a range of adult sex toys, many of which she had seen advertised on late-night cable television. But she saw her thirty-four-year-old daughter, Trinny, peering in through the door. Dinah put the toys on the counter and ran out of the store. Her daughter said she was disgusting at her age to be in such a place.

DREAM BACKGROUND AND MEANING

Dinah had been happily married to George for forty-four years. But recently she had wanted to spice things up in the bedroom. But was she, as a mother and grandmother, too old to be fantasizing about more erotic sex? Dreams about sex toys can indicate a desire for more excitement at any age or stage of a relationship, not only in the bedroom but in life generally.

INTERPRETATIONS AND FORTUNE-TELLING MEANINGS

* If you dream of buying adult toys but are seen by a family member or neighbor, you may feel guilty about revealing your sensual, passionate nature, especially if you are of mature age.
* If in the dream you are buying adult toys without your partner or are without a partner, you may be uncertain about fulfilling your sexual needs.
* If you dream of erotic lovemaking with adult toys, the key is with whom you are sharing the experience—an unexpected partner may reveal an unacknowledged passion or temptation.
* If you dream of your partner producing sex toys and the idea is a turnoff, you may need more romance or tenderness in the relationship.
* If you dream of finding your partner's hidden sex toys, you may have doubts about their fidelity.

OUTCOME OF DINAH'S DREAM

After the dream, Dinah initiated more adventurous lovemaking, and to her surprise her husband started bringing home sex toys and booked a romantic cruise. Dreams can stimulate fantasies that then can be expressed, although they may have been denied earlier as not appropriate.

Adventure

In a recurring dream, Vera, sixty-one, was trekking through Peru with a small group of fellow travelers, visiting ancient ruins like Macchu Picchu. She was loving every minute of it. She woke feeling sad it was only a dream, but wondering if perhaps one day it could become a reality.

DREAM BACKGROUND AND MEANING

Vera lived in the same house in which she was born in a village in the United Kingdom. Vera never married and has worked in the same job as a librarian for thirty years. She recently learned that she was being given early retirement. Vera was aware that life was slipping by. But dare she go on the adventure of a lifetime? Adventure dreams are reminders there is a whole world waiting to be explored.

INTERPRETATIONS AND FORTUNE-TELLING MEANINGS

* If a recurring dream takes you to the same location time and again, this may have past-life significance for you, especially if it is about an ancient culture that fascinates you.
* If the dream adventure is exciting, you are ready for a life change very different from your present lifestyle.
* If the dream doesn't seem possible, explore ways you can make it happen, even in a modified form.
* If the dream adventure takes you to an unknown location or one you had never considered, see what clues the dream offers, as the destination or activity may hold hidden benefits.
* If the adventure dream is frightening, take time to consider the advantages of change to achieve unfulfilled desires.
* Even if you do not want a major adventure, your unconscious is prompting you to try new activities and maybe a new holiday location if life is stagnant.

OUTCOME OF VERA'S DREAM

Vera visited Peru on a specialized tour for older people with a degree of luxury, and on returning she enrolled in a university course on South American ancient history. Adventure dreams can open all kinds of doors of hidden potential.

Advertisement, Commercial

Becky, thirty, dreamed her face was on billboards everywhere, advertising her starring role in a new Broadway musical. On social media too there were commercials for opening night and information about her. People were recognizing her and asking for her autograph as she walked down Broadway. She had arrived.

DREAM BACKGROUND AND MEANING

It was a wish-fulfillment dream. Becky had at last broken into advertising and was the face of a new herbal shampoo, which financially was a great relief and raised her profile. But her ambition was for the stage. So far, success was confined to a few supporting roles with a theater company that traveled around the states. Her agent said advertising was the way to get herself known. But Becky was worried she would be typecast into advertising beauty products, which might prevent her from being considered a serious actor. Advertising in the modern age can transform a relative unknown into a household name, and so dreams about advertising are almost always positive.

INTERPRETATIONS AND FORTUNE-TELLING MEANINGS

★ If you dream you are creating or producing an advertisement, some aspect of yourself or your life needs bringing out, often shown by the nature of the dream advertisement.

★ If you are writing a jingle for an advertisement, you need to communicate your abilities and opinions more persuasively.

★ If in a dream you appear in an advertisement, it will highlight a coming change of image.

★ If you see a clear advertisement in your dream, it represents an unfulfilled ambition that is moving into the realm of possibility.

★ A faded or ripped advertisement speaks of ambitions or plans that now must be followed in a new way.

OUTCOME OF BECKY'S DREAM

Becky's agent was right. As a result of a whole series of advertisements, she was offered auditions, at first for television bit parts and then for her main love, the theater. Advertising dreams do herald an improving image if that recognition is used wisely.

Aging

Charlie, seventy-five, dreamed he was driving along the highway when a man darted out in front of him. Charlie swerved but hit the car traveling alongside, and the driver was badly injured. The police were called. Because Charlie was unlicensed, he was arrested.

DREAM BACKGROUND AND MEANING

Charlie had been driving since he was seventeen without an accident. But because of his age and deteriorating eyesight, he had not been granted a license renewal. He felt old and useless, and was thinking of risking driving unlicensed. Sometimes a dream involving aging can issue warnings that we need to take more care, and that we ignore signs of aging at our peril.

INTERPRETATIONS AND FORTUNE-TELLING MEANINGS

★ Often experienced by the over sixty-fives, aging dreams reflect fears, not predictions, of losing faculties.

★ If certain aging conditions appear in a dream, they are inner promptings to get a health check so problems can be fixed early.

★ As you get older, dreaming of a new interest or location is a direction to explore new activities or places that will offer alternative benefits.

★ If you see your children making future arrangements in your dreams that would not suit you, it's time to sort out your finances, preferred home area, and home.

★ If you see yourself young again, identify ambitions you had at the dream age that are still to be fulfilled, albeit modified.

OUTCOME OF CHARLIE'S DREAM

After the shock of the dream, Charlie realized that there was much he could do. As a young man he'd loved boats, but had let his old interest fade. Now he bought a motorboat and is enjoying new explorations, feeling younger every day. If aging is seen as bringing a new chapter, the extra leisure can open new doors or reopen old ones to provide a different but equally fulfilling way of life.

Air Raids

John, twenty-eight, had a recurring dream that he was piloting a bomber in World War II, fighting off enemy planes over London, which were coming each night to destroy the city. He saw an enemy plane too late and felt searing pain, turning over and over, and then darkness.

DREAM BACKGROUND AND MEANING

John had always experienced a terror of flying and, despite tranquilizers and desensitizing therapy, could not board a plane. Now he was due to go on his honeymoon to the Maldives and did not want to let his new wife down.

A number of people who fear flying have recurring air-raid dreams, either of being shot down in a plane during an air raid or as civilians being buried under their home during a raid.

INTERPRETATIONS AND FORTUNE-TELLING MEANINGS

∗ If you dream of a wartime aircraft bombing tragedy or your home being bombed, these may either be past-life trauma or free-floating memories acquired from a restless spirit by a psychic person.

∗ If you escape from an air raid in any land or war, an attack on your reputation or threat to your job or finances will be avoided.

∗ If you are helping to free others from air-raid wreckage, you may be asked to help a friend or family member who has run into major difficulties.

∗ If you dream you hear air-raid sirens, you should not ignore warning signs that you are taking unnecessary risks.

∗ Seeking refuge in an air-raid shelter advises you to wait for a confrontation or action until matters have calmed down.

∗ If you dream you are leading a bombing raid, there are matters to confront head-on at work or with hostile neighbors.

OUTCOME OF JOHN'S DREAM

John talked over the dream with a therapist who regressed him to relive the dream and so leave the trauma behind. John traveled to the Maldives, not 100 percent happy, but calmly. Past-life dreams are a spontaneous form of past worlds.

Airbrushing

Vicky, sixteen, dreamed she was at a photo shoot and her makeup artist joked, "As always, nothing needs changing." After the photos were released, social media was jammed with girls asking how Vicky could always look so perfect. She woke smiling—until she saw herself in the mirror.

DREAM BACKGROUND AND MEANING

Vicky always airbrushed her pictures before posting them online. She hated the shape of her nose, her weight, and her hair for not being blonde enough. She had been asked out by a gorgeous guy she met online. However, she was scared he would not like how she really looked. Airbrushing images in dreams can suggest insecurity about how others see you.

INTERPRETATIONS AND FORTUNE-TELLING MEANINGS

∗ If you dream of being contacted by dozens of admirers after posting your latest airbrushed image online, you are worried the real person will not be liked.

∗ If you dream you put the un-airbrushed you online by mistake, and no one contacts or likes you, you are relying on image to win friends.

∗ If someone you meet in person in your dream rejects or does not recognize you from the airbrushed version, you may discover that, in life, they are shallow.

∗ If in your dream you are airbrushed out of a photo, you may be feeling left out because you do not fit with others' views of the way you should act and appear.

∗ If in the dream the airbrushed and real versions of yourself are identical, be confident you can succeed.

OUTCOME OF VICKY'S DREAM

Vicky almost walked straight past the guy she was meeting, because he had also airbrushed his image. However, his real self was even nicer, and he told Vicky she was more beautiful than her picture. They are still dating. Airbrushing dreams reflect pressures by social media and society to present an ideal image.

Airplane

Tom, thirty-five, dreamed he was in a plane on his way to take up a new post in another state. He was invited into the cockpit and allowed to fly the plane. Then Tom realized the pilot and copilot had left the cockpit. The plane started to plunge, but Tom landed the plane smoothly on the airstrip below, and woke feeling totally confident.

DREAM BACKGROUND AND MEANING

This is a reassurance dream. In his waking life, Tom was considering applying for a new job involving a promotion and relocation, but doubted his ability to succeed, as he lacked experience. The dream confirmed that Tom could rise high in his chosen field if he seized the initiative.

INTERPRETATIONS AND FORTUNE-TELLING MEANINGS

* Dreaming of piloting a plane and landing smoothly is always a sign of success, being awarded a promotion, and rising to the top of a chosen career.
* Flying solo augurs well for launching a one-person initiative or business.
* A jet plane overhead heralds unexpected advantageous visitors or online overseas connections.
* Being asked to fly a plane alerts you to a major unexpected opportunity coming your way, most likely involving relocation.
* If you are flying a plane for the first time, be prepared to act in a more senior position in an emergency at work.
* Missing a plane warns you to be alert for opportunities that may pass you by and tells you not to hesitate about a forthcoming sexual experience that would bring happiness.
* Dreaming of a plane crash suggests that there is no secure basis for ambitions. Wait till you have the necessary resources in place.

OUTCOME OF TOM'S DREAM

A few days after the dream, Tom was offered a job in another state with a higher salary, which required learning new skills fast. He accepted and is already in line for promotion.

Alarms

Cynthia, thirty-five, dreamed she was in the front row on the first night of a new production, and her phone alarm kept ringing. She tried to turn off the alarm, even took out the battery, but it kept ringing. The audience and performers were becoming furious, and her boyfriend, also her boss, was embarrassed. She left the theater, but he did not follow. Once outside, the alarm stopped.

DREAM BACKGROUND AND MEANING

Cynthia had loved her boss for months, but he had only recently separated from his wife. Although they had met secretly many times, he promised they could appear together in public, though this had not yet happened. She knew things were not settled and he spent weekends at home with the children, sleeping in the spare room. Alarms of any kind ringing in dreams are inevitably a warning or wake-up call and may be triggered by an external noise source such as a car alarm outside the window.

INTERPRETATIONS AND FORTUNE-TELLING MEANINGS

* Dreams of alarms that will not stop ringing are persistent subconscious messages to be wary in the situation where they are ringing.
* Alarm clocks not ringing in dreams can indicate free-floating anxiety about being late or are a reminder of an unfulfilled obligation.
* Domestic burglar alarms are an alert to check security arrangements, as you may have unconsciously noticed something broken or amiss; also, anxiety about the family that is not acknowledged.
* Fire alarms in the workplace reflect underlying tensions or a potentially explosive situation escalating.
* Smoke alarms warn to be careful of subterfuge.
* Car alarms are linked with impulsive behavior and the potential sexual hazards of giving way to temptation.

OUTCOME OF CYNTHIA'S DREAM

Cynthia noticed that since he was apparently free, her boss had cooled toward her, and she heard his wife was pregnant and they were reunited. Alarms give warning signals in dreams before the dreamer has become aware of potential pitfalls.

Alien, Extraterrestrial

Julia, fifteen, dreamed that a huge saucerlike craft with brilliant white lights landed in the garden. Julia ran outside, not at all afraid. A tall blond man and woman dressed in white came down the ramp. They took her hands and led her into the craft. She watched through the windows as the craft sped across the galaxy toward a brilliantly illuminated star. The couple said this was her home planet and they were her star parents. She woke in her bed with a sense of belonging.

DREAM BACKGROUND AND MEANING

Julia had always felt like she was different from the rest of her family and her peers. She had from a young age been fascinated by the stars. Extraterrestrial dreams often involve astral or out-of-body travel.

INTERPRETATIONS AND FORTUNE-TELLING MEANINGS

★ Seeing a spaceship landing or overhead foretells someone new coming into your life with whom you will feel kinship.

★ If you encounter Nordics—wise, tall, blond figures—in a dream, you may be given wise advice.

★ If the dream is scary, involving abduction by aliens, you may be feeling alienated from others around you, or that you are not fitting into a new situation or environment.

★ If you willingly enter the craft, you are ready to spread your wings and explore a new location or environment.

★ If you believe you are a star soul from another galaxy, extraterrestrial experiences that seem more than dreams can be experiences from another dimension.

★ If there are a number of spacecraft and extraterrestrials who welcome you, seek like-minded people who share your life view and develop your unique talents, especially those connected with astrology or astronomy.

OUTCOME OF JULIA'S DREAM

Julia explored the concept of star souls online and decided to follow her ambition to become an astroscientist. She never had another extraterrestrial dream.

Alligator, Crocodile

Josh, twenty-five, dreamed he was camping alone near the shoreline of a deep, cloudy creek. He had seen a sign warning of alligators but pitched his tent anyway. When he woke in the morning, he realized his tent was surrounded by alligators snapping their jaws. He closed his eyes, and when he opened them again he saw watching eyes submerged in the river mud.

DREAM BACKGROUND AND MEANING

Josh had an offer from a friend living in Hawaii to move there and invest his savings in a turtle conservation and diving business. Josh trusted his friend, but did not know the main investor, an older man. Alligator or crocodile dreams signify a primal fear of being swallowed up by a risky situation or a powerful but not necessarily benign person.

INTERPRETATIONS AND FORTUNE-TELLING MEANINGS

★ If you dream that the alligator or crocodile is half-submerged in water, be alert to emotional betrayal or acts of spite from someone close.

★ If the alligator or crocodile is half-submerged in mud, beware that a business deal may not be all it seems.

★ An alligator or crocodile guarding eggs says you will be protected by a maternal figure. The eggs are a fertility omen for healthy babies.

★ An alligator or crocodile sunning on the riverbank is a potency sign for men, or for a strong sexual attraction in either sex, trading security for excitement.

★ Large fighting alligators or crocodiles represent ruthless or risky business deals where gains are potentially great if won.

★ Being surrounded by alligators or crocodiles backing away signifies overcoming powerful opposition. If they are moving closer, guard against unwise charismatic company.

OUTCOME OF JOSH'S DREAM

Josh persuaded his friend to go to Hawaii with him to investigate the potential business. The older man was a fast talker but had no suitable land or licenses. Josh pulled out, but his friend went ahead and lost money. Alligator or crocodile dreams suggest hidden factors in any venture, which need checking out, as they represent either great gain or great loss.

Alphabet

Phoebe, thirty-two, dreamed she was outdoors, and alphabet letters like snowflakes were falling, forming the initials AE in the sky, which made no sense. Then the alphabet formed the words "You will find me."

ABCDEFG

DREAM BACKGROUND AND MEANING

Phoebe's fiancé's initials were not AE. However, a new guy, Alan Edwards, had started working in the office and had asked her out. She had turned him down. After the dream, she was fearful that her marriage to her fiancé was not meant to be. Dream incubation, which she practiced before her dream, involves concentrating on a question immediately before sleep, such as *Who will I marry?* Alphabet letters give the answer.

INTERPRETATIONS AND FORTUNE-TELLING MEANINGS

* If particular letters form initials, be alert for a significant person or event with those initials.
* If falling alphabet letters surround you, there is never enough time to talk to people or a particular person to whom you have much to say.
* If letters are jumbled, there may be miscommunication. Rearrange the letters to discover a significant name or message.
* If you are trying to read a foreign alphabet, there may be alternative viewpoints to consider.
* If in your dream the alphabet letters fade on an email or document, use intuition to fill in the gaps.
* If you are trying to interpret an ancient alphabet such as hieroglyphics or Ancient Greek, look for the answer using traditional wisdom or, if it is a past-life dream, within the dream itself.

OUTCOME OF PHOEBE'S DREAM

Phoebe and her fiancé saw a house for sale that they loved. They applied to buy it. The name of the house was Acacia End, the initials in the dream. Then she recalled that she had been thinking as she went to sleep of finding the ideal house, not of who was right in love. With dream incubation, focus on what you want to know, or you may initially be taken off track.

Altar

Paula, twenty-five, dreamed she was handing her dish of offerings to a Hindu priest, who placed it on the altar. She was in a temple in India, wearing a beautiful garland of flowers around her neck, gold bracelets, and a fabulously embroidered sari. Behind her were many others waiting, and she was pushed outside the golden gates, feeling cheated. Paula walked down to the banks of the Ganges to an open altar and set her garlands and bracelets on it and felt the presence of the river goddess Ganga. She felt connected with divinity.

DREAM BACKGROUND AND MEANING

Paula had spent her savings on a trip to India to connect with its spiritual energies. But after several months of meditation, chanting, and making offerings at many different altars, she felt she lacked any personal connection. Altars can be either a gateway to connecting with divinity or a barrier to personal spiritual communication.

INTERPRETATIONS AND FORTUNE-TELLING MEANINGS

* If you dream you are praying at an altar, there will be an unexpected resolution of a seemingly insoluble problem.
* If you are creating or setting up an altar, you will discover a new form of healing or divination.
* If the intervention of a priest or priestess prevents your reaching the altar, you may feel out of touch with your life purpose.
* An unfamiliar altar with ancient robed priests and priestesses may be a past-life dream, and spiritual insights may emerge spontaneously that can later be verified.
* If the altar is unprepared for ceremony, you may be moving beyond your former beliefs or current form of spirituality.

OUTCOME OF PAULA'S DREAM

After the dream, Paula spent the rest of her time in India visiting outdoor altars in places of natural beauty. We can make altars anyplace or anytime, but, as in the dream, nature may offer the finest altar to divinity.

Ambulance

Paddy, fifty-five, dreamed regularly that he was driving through town and an ambulance flashing red lights was following him. No matter how often he pulled over or signaled to the ambulance to pass him, the ambulance remained close behind and eventually directed him through the hospital gates. It stopped behind Paddy outside the emergency room and the paramedics told him to lie on the waiting stretcher. Paddy refused and accelerated away.

DREAM BACKGROUND AND MEANING

Paddy had a high-powered job and an unhealthy lifestyle despite the efforts of his wife, Laura. He had repeatedly postponed his annual health checkup as he had been getting tired and breathless and was scared something serious was wrong. Ambulance dreams may be warnings if the dreamer is taking too many risks, whether driving or in hazardous activities.

INTERPRETATIONS AND FORTUNE-TELLING MEANINGS

* If you dream you are trailing an emergency ambulance, you may be worrying too much about your health or that of a loved one.
* A dream where the ambulance is filled with much older people suggests there are long-standing bad habits, addictions, or a continuing unhealthy lifestyle the dreamer has been living for a long time, which may be creating longer-term health issues.
* If you are in an ambulance going to a hospital, you may be in stress overload and need to relax to avoid burnout.
* If you are a dream paramedic, you are a source of advice and help for others in your life.
* If you see an ambulance racing through town or along the freeway and it passes you, a danger or problem (not necessarily medical) will be averted.
* If an ambulance crashes, you should not rely on others coming to your rescue but plan your own coping strategies.

OUTCOME OF PADDY'S DREAM

The dreams scared Paddy and, along with his wife's constant reminders, motivated him to go for his health checkup. Paddy had a minor heart problem, fixed with a small operation. Ambulance dreams are ways our unconscious mind alerts us to the need for a medical checkup, if only for reassurance that all is well.

Ambush

Tony, forty-two, had what seemed like a past-world dream. He and his teenage son, Trevor, were wearing World War I uniforms in the trenches. They were cold, wet, and muddy. Tony's regiment had to get over the ridge before dawn. At the order they ran as fast as they could, guns loaded. Suddenly they realized they had been ambushed by a nest of machine guns. His son fell. Tony put his son over his shoulder and staggered in the opposite direction. The dream ended with them flying through the air, away from the battle.

DREAM BACKGROUND AND MEANING

Tony's son had become involved with a bad crowd. Trevor was due to go to a rave with friends who were taking and selling heavy drugs. There was a danger he would be arrested. Ambush dreams indicate a situation where you will find yourself out of your depth.

INTERPRETATIONS AND FORTUNE-TELLING MEANINGS

* If you dream you are setting an ambush, you may be angry at double-dealing or spite and may be building toward effective retaliation.
* If you are ambushed, you may fear that you may be caught out over an indiscretion.
* If you avoid an ambush, swift action is necessary for personal safety.
* If you escape or help someone to escape, you can overcome bad influences and potential danger.
* If you see an ambush ahead but keep going toward it, it is a warning that there are people you should not trust who will lead you into trouble.
* If you are ordered toward what you suspect is an ambush, you may need to go your own way rather than blindly following others who cannot see the danger.

OUTCOME OF TONY'S DREAM

Tony knew he had to save his son, whatever the cost. Tony drove his son several hundred miles to stay on Tony's brother's remote farm. His brother was ex-special forces military. Ambush dreams warn that you or someone close is ignoring danger signs.

Anchor

Jay, seventy-five, dreamed he was sailing around the world in a brand-new yacht. The first time he dropped anchor, he realized it had become detached from the yacht. He knew he should return to the harbor before venturing into the open ocean. But if he did, he would be admitting defeat. So he tied the boat to a buoy and rowed the tender to the town for dinner. When he returned, the boat had drifted away and smashed on the rocks. He went home defeated.

DREAM BACKGROUND AND MEANING

Jay wanted to spend a year traveling through the wilderness, his lifetime dream, and he had no family. But his surgeon wanted him to have a minor heart operation before he went. Jay was impatient to leave right away as he had just sold his business. Anchors represent a stabilizing influence with something that really matters.

INTERPRETATIONS AND FORTUNE-TELLING MEANINGS

* If you dream an anchor is steadying a boat, someone close to you or coming into your life will bring you emotional security.
* A broken or missing anchor indicates fears of betrayal in someone you trust.
* To dream of a boat pulling up anchor and setting sail foretells travel, whether a spontaneous vacation, an adventure, or a relocation overseas.
* If a boat breaks from its anchor, events may move faster than you had hoped.
* An anchor tangled with seaweed or with its chain caught around it says you need to disengage from a person or situation that is holding you down.
* If you have anchored off a beautiful cove in a calm sea, you will enjoy a calm period in your life and don't need to worry about the future.

OUTCOME OF JAY'S DREAM

After the dream, Jay realized he was getting breathless. He delayed the trip while he had his operation and was 100 percent fit when he finally set off. Anchors can be restricting but are essential for security in any uncertain ventures.

Ancient Egypt

Since she was a child, Leticia, twenty, had had recurring dreams of being a slave girl in Ancient Egypt and dropping her featureless cloth doll in the sand. She became a favorite of the Pharaoh's daughter, who was about her age. The dream ended when the princess died and Leticia was to be entombed with her mistress. She ran away.

DREAM BACKGROUND AND MEANING

Leticia, who had an irrational fear of enclosed spaces, had been fascinated by Ancient Egypt from a young age, and as she grew older would visit the Ancient Egyptian section in her local museum. Leticia was saving to visit Egypt for her twenty-first birthday. Ancient Egypt is the land most recalled in recurring dreams.

INTERPRETATIONS AND FORTUNE-TELLING MEANINGS

* If you dream of an affinity with Ancient Egypt, this may be past-world recall.
* If you have a seemingly irrational fear of enclosed spaces, this may relate to experiences in the dream.
* If you subsequently visit Ancient Egypt, you may be drawn to and recognize particular locations from your dreams.
* If you dream of hieroglyphics or particular deities, try to research them when you wake, as they may hold particular significance for you.
* If you dream of Egypt only once but the dream is very vivid, there may be a person or situation that relates to the days after the dream, perhaps a warning.
* If you continually dream of a partner in Ancient Egypt, you may be encountering your twin soul.

OUTCOME OF LETICIA'S DREAM

Leticia went to Egypt for her twenty-first birthday and instantly felt at home. She recognized a doll in Cairo Museum like the one in her dream. She found the courage to enter a pyramid and, on leaving, overcame her fear of enclosed spaces. She has yet to encounter her twin soul. We do not understand why some places and times call us, but often they hold insights and the means to overcome irrational fears.

Anesthetic

Kimberley, sixty-five, dreamed she was in a hospital, waiting for an operation. The anesthetist refused to give her anesthetics, saying it was her own fault she was having the operation and she needed to face the consequences. Kimberley leaped off the operating table and ran out of the hospital, pursued by the doctor, nurse, and anesthetist. She ran home, locked the door, and would not answer though they were hammering on it. She woke feeling relief that she had escaped.

DREAM BACKGROUND AND MEANING

Kimberley was marrying Kevin, a widower. He was paying for her to have a gastric band operation so she would lose weight in time for the wedding. He complained that she was weak-willed to have put on weight in the first place. Anesthetic dreams talk about a desire to temporarily escape from daily worries.

INTERPRETATIONS AND FORTUNE-TELLING MEANINGS

* If you dream you are refused anesthetic, is help or relief being withheld as a means of control?
* Being given or being under anesthetic can indicate a desire to escape from difficult people who cause you pain.
* To wake under anesthetic in the middle of an operation, unable to move, suggests you are feeling powerless to escape from hurtful comments or people who won't listen.
* If you are fighting against being given an anesthetic, someone is trying to silence or override your wishes, and you should resist.
* If you are given anesthetic but it does not work, you may be trying to postpone decisions that need making.
* If you are taking excessive painkillers, you are not facing the causes of your problems.

OUTCOME OF KIMBERLEY'S DREAM

Kimberley realized she did not want the operation, but wanted to lose weight in her own way and time. Kevin had started to diminish her confidence and control her. She postponed the wedding as she realized that her weight prob-lems had occurred since meeting Kevin. She was using food as an anesthetic against his criticisms. Anesthetic dreams can say that sometimes life's pain has to be faced, not dulled.

Angels

Linda, seventy-one, dreamed she was driving home from bingo, her former regular Tuesday-evening activity. Unusually, Linda left early as she was having no luck. As she neared home, she saw a beautiful golden-haired angel sitting in the back seat. The angel said, "Linda, go back. Play the last game." Linda looked again in the mirror, but the seat was empty. Puzzled, she turned the car around and reached the bingo hall in time for the last game. She came up with the winning card.

DREAM BACKGROUND AND MEANING

Linda was having serious financial problems, as the roof on her house was badly leaking and the insurance would not pay. She had given up bingo to save money. But the day after the dream, Linda went along in time for the last game. Angel dreams don't just bring spiritual messages but can help at times when we have earthly problems seemingly impossible to solve.

INTERPRETATIONS AND FORTUNE-TELLING MEANINGS

* Angels act as messengers in dreams to advise or warn when most needed.
* If you see the same angel in subsequent dreams, that is your guardian angel.
* If you see an angel in ordinary clothes except for a light shimmering around it, you will receive practical help from a stranger in the days ahead.
* Even if you do not believe in angels, their appearance is a way of alerting you to information that your subconscious has picked up.
* If you dream of a host of angels or visit angelic realms, you are protected. Look for signs of angels the day after the dream.
* If you are drowning in daily demands, angel dreams are a reminder to get in touch with your spiritual side and listen to your intuition.

OUTCOME OF LINDA'S DREAM

Linda won enough money to fix her roof. She never saw her angel in dreams again. Angel dreams are always a good omen of good fortune coming.

Animal Cruelty

Ian, twenty-eight, dreamed he reported his neighbor to an animal-welfare organization for cruelty to his dogs. The organization refused to come and told his neighbor that Ian had complained. The neighbor threw bricks through his window and threatened to release the dogs on him. Ian woke to the unceasing barking from next door and knew something must be done.

DREAM BACKGROUND AND MEANING

Ian lived next door to a man with six German shepherd dogs who were starved and left chained up outdoors without shelter in all weather. Ian was scared of his neighbor and the dogs, but he knew he ought to report them. However, if he did, Ian feared the neighbor would know it was Ian. Dreams can express anxieties about consequences for taking actions we know are right to protect the vulnerable.

INTERPRETATIONS AND FORTUNE-TELLING MEANINGS

★ If you dream of actual animal cruelty, the dream prompts you to act regardless of consequences.

★ If you dream of animal cruelty you have not witnessed, you may be picking up psychic distress signals from an abused creature nearby. Stay alert.

★ If you dream of poachers killing endangered species or cruelly treating creatures overseas, an unexpected environmental issue may impact your life.

★ If you dream you are rescuing cruelly treated animals, you may be called upon to protect a vulnerable person or animal in your life.

★ If in the dream you are running an animal-rescue center and it is your ambition, a chance will come to enter this world.

★ If you dream you are unhappy running an animal-rescue center, one too many needy people are demanding your time.

OUTCOME OF IAN'S DREAM

Ian made an anonymous complaint; the dogs were removed, and the neighbor was given a summons. The neighbor believes his ex-wife reported him. Animal-cruelty dreams predict we may become involved, albeit unwillingly, in an altruistic concern where we can make a difference.

Animal Forewarnings

Bruce, twenty-five, dreamed that all the stray cats and dogs ran out of town and those with owners began howling and yowling. Hours later he heard a rumble, and the earth shook. Houses and cars were destroyed, and people were hit by falling debris. He was rushing from house to house, warning people to secure their properties, but they just laughed at him.

DREAM BACKGROUND AND MEANING

Bruce had learned from his zoology studies that certain creatures reacted to impending quakes, tsunamis, and even volcanic eruptions before sensitive machines could pick up the energies. But so vivid was his dream that he knew there was danger. Dream warnings tend to be even earlier than the disturbed-animal phenomenon and occur with those who are naturally in tune with the animal kingdom.

INTERPRETATIONS AND FORTUNE-TELLING MEANINGS

★ If you have a dream about an impending disaster shown by strange animal behavior, you are tapping into your psychic powers. Take precautions.

★ If in your dream you see fish leaping out of the water, this may be a forewarning of a disaster.

★ If you frequently have these dreams, consider working with animals or seismic monitoring.

★ If you sense the dream is symbolic and not an actual warning of a disaster, your dream animals may be alerting you to an insecure situation to be avoided.

★ If fish are leaping from water or snakes emerging from holes but there is not the immediacy of an actual prediction, beware of a huge emotional outburst by someone close.

★ If in your dream you sense the animals are escaping to a particular area, that is generally a safe place.

OUTCOME OF BRUCE'S DREAM

Bruce had moved to a safer area by the time the official warnings occurred. Though everyone said it was coincidence, Bruce knew that he had acted wisely in listening to his dream. No one fully understands how animals can be aware of impending disasters, but humans who are psychically sensitive can pick up the advance warnings in dreams.

Animal Sanctuary, Rescue Pets

Serena, fifty-five, dreamed her garden was filled with rescue animals, from goats and donkeys to dogs, cats, and exotic birds. She hated the noise and the mess and went inside, barring the door. At last, to her relief, they went away.

DREAM BACKGROUND AND MEANING

A surprising dream. It had been Serena's lifetime ambition to open an animal rescue center, and at last she had the resources. All her life she had cared for waifs and strays of the animal and human world. A dream can reveal how our desires and ideals can change over time, and they should be recognized.

INTERPRETATIONS AND FORTUNE-TELLING MEANINGS

⋆ If you dream you feel fulfilled being surrounded by animals needing care, it indicates that it may be possible to open or work at an animal sanctuary before too long.

⋆ If you are horrified at the prospect, you may be overwhelmed by the demands of others in your life.

⋆ Choosing a pet at a rescue center says your nurturing side is emerging, whether for an abandoned animal, fostering, or volunteering with children in need.

⋆ If you find a lost pet and take it home, you may be ready to add to your family, whether with a baby or a pet.

⋆ If you are pampering a rescued animal, especially if pressured to start a human family, you may certainly for now be happier adopting a furry baby.

⋆ If you dream your pet is lost and you find it in a rescue center, you may need help dealing with all the demands on you.

OUTCOME OF SERENA'S DREAM

Serena sponsored her local animal charity and made plans to travel overseas to photograph different sanctuaries for endangered species to create a blog and online resource base. Listening to dreams can alert us to what we truly want, and not what we think we ought to want.

Ant

Andrea, thirty-five, dreamed she was trying to stop flying ants from entering her home. But though she closed the windows and doors, they still found a way inside. She then realized they did not want to settle, and when she opened the doors and windows they flew away.

DREAM BACKGROUND AND MEANING

Andrea had moved back home with her children as her marriage had broken down. The house was very cramped and tempers were flaring. Andrea knew she had to move on. Should she go back to a marriage that was not working? Flying ants in dreams and actuality are queen ants looking for new mates to start colonies. They represent a chance to strike out for independence.

INTERPRETATIONS AND FORTUNE-TELLING MEANINGS

⋆ If you dream you see ants in a line carrying leaves and sticks back to their nest, you will need to cooperate with others to achieve a goal.

⋆ Ants scurrying to and fro say you have hard work ahead that will build from small beginnings.

⋆ Ants crawling everywhere in your home and over food means that you are feeling overwhelmed by small irritations or problems that have built up and need drastic action.

⋆ An abandoned anthill can indicate minor health worries you should tackle.

⋆ Killing ants that invade your home says you may have frequent unwelcome visitors, especially interfering relatives or neighbors you need to deter.

⋆ If you are trying to kill ants but fail, you may need to start conserving resources and accept the restrictions temporary frugality causes.

OUTCOME OF ANDREA'S DREAM

Andrea had been postponing decisions about the marriage, but after the dream realized action was necessary. She decided to not go back to the marriage. The house where her husband was still living was sold amicably. Andrea was able to buy a condo with a garden. Ant dreams indicate the need for action, not waiting for life to resolve itself.

Approval

Vicky, fifteen, was learning French online in her dream. She had achieved top marks and had been saving her results to show her mother, Sara. As she revealed them, someone else added twenty points to their score and Vicky dropped to sixth place. Her mother said, "Oh, you are useless at everything. I don't know why you bother," and went to get tea for Vicky's young brother, David.

DREAM BACKGROUND AND MEANING

Before David was born, everything Vicky did was praised by her mother. But now everything she achieved was ignored or dismissed. Vicky had been offered a place on a special trip to France, but she did not even mention it at home. If previous approval is withdrawn in a dream, this usually reflects the reality and changes in circumstances that have pushed the dreamer off the radar.

INTERPRETATIONS AND FORTUNE-TELLING MEANINGS

* If you dream of receiving approval in the form of a tangible reward at work or in a performing or creative art, you are on track to success.
* If you dream regularly that your efforts are unappreciated and you give up, it's a warning sign of becoming depressed, so find a sympathetic ear.
* If you buy an item on approval with the option of returning it if not right, you may feel constantly on trial to please others.
* If an official document gets a stamp or seal of approval in a dream, an application or examination will be successful.
* If you hesitate in approving the actions or words of someone demanding support, you may be picking up a false front that hides ulterior motives.

OUTCOME OF VICKY'S DREAM

Vicky's French teacher contacted Sara to ask why her star pupil was not going on the trip. Sara asked Vicky why she had not mentioned it. Vicky said her mother was no longer interested in her. Vicky's mother explained that she found David hard to parent and felt incompetent, so she had tried, maybe too hard, to not favor Vicky. Lack-of-approval dreams reflect the dreamer's lack of self-esteem, created by others' withholding deserved appreciation, sometimes because of their own feelings of inadequacy.

Aquarium

Dexter, twenty-five, dreamed he was swimming in a huge tank of fish in the city oceanarium. He noticed the fish were piranha, flesh eaters, and there was a large white shark. He banged on the glass, but people were walking by and the exit door was closed. The fish were encircling him. He knew he was trapped. Dexter woke shaking but unable to call out.

DREAM BACKGROUND AND MEANING

Dexter, who was shy, had been caught by a colleague viewing pornographic sites during work time. His colleague was threatening to tell everyone, including the boss, unless Dexter paid him every week. The amounts were going up, and Dexter knew there was a trace on his computer to prove his lapse. Aquarium dreams often represent a sense of being trapped because of a lack of meaningful relationships.

INTERPRETATIONS AND FORTUNE-TELLING MEANINGS

* If you dream you are trapped in a small aquarium, you are not able to freely express your emotions or may be in a restrictive love match.
* If you are swimming with small sharks in a large tank in a public aquarium or are in a submerged cage in a tank of large sharks, you may long for freedom but fear the risks.
* If dead fish are floating on the surface, you may need to free yourself from guilt and obligation.
* If the tank has only a few or dull-colored fish, it is time to widen your social life and activities.
* If there is an aquarium in your dream but you are not interested in it, you may feel detached from the lives of those around you.

OUTCOME OF DEXTER'S DREAM

Dexter realized how empty his life had become and left work without giving notice, knowing his computer would be wiped clean for the next employee. Dexter made a fresh start in his hometown's oceanarium and is paid to swim with the fish. Aquarium dreams talk of locked potential and the need to expand horizons before boredom leads to carelessness (see "Goldfish," p. 224).

Argument, Quarrel

Betty, sixty-five, dreamed she was arguing with her best friend, Gloria, over a film Betty wanted to see. Gloria refused and said the film was garbage and had bad reviews. For once, Betty stood up for herself. Gloria became furious, abused Betty for her selfishness, and stormed off, saying the friendship was over. Betty nearly ran after her friend and apologized, as usual, but instead took herself to the cinema.

DREAM BACKGROUND AND MEANING

Betty had known Gloria since school. Gloria was always criticizing Betty, dismissing Betty's opinions and wishes. Betty went along with the criticisms for a quiet life. Sometimes the dreamer can quarrel with someone in a dream when she would be unwilling or afraid to confront them in life (see "Shouting and Swearing," p. 431).

INTERPRETATIONS AND FORTUNE-TELLING MEANINGS

★ If in a dream you are quarreling with a friend, family member, or partner, you may have strong opinions or resentments that you are suppressing, even from yourself.

★ If you are a child quarreling with a sibling or a parent in a dream, you may have unresolved family issues, even with someone deceased.

★ If you do not know the person you are quarreling with in the dream, this may be an aspect of yourself in conflict with the way you are acting outwardly.

★ If you resolve an ongoing argument in a dream, this may be the way to resolve anger or estrangement in real life.

★ A dream argument can sometimes clear the air of decades of resentment if the wrong cannot be righted but you must still regularly see the person.

OUTCOME OF BETTY'S DREAM

Betty quietly stood her ground with her friend the next time they met. When Gloria tried to control Betty, first with silence and then with anger, and the silent treatment did not work, Betty left. Gloria has since stopped being so critical. Dream arguments can be a good dress rehearsal to build up the courage to speak.

Arrows

Melinda, thirty-five, dreamed she was on top of a hill in what seemed a Norman battlefield. Suddenly she saw a spear and arrows coming toward her and realized she could jump and fly away from trouble. Instantly she flew to the bottom of the hill. The spear and arrows did not touch her.

DREAM BACKGROUND AND MEANING

Melinda, a successful television presenter, was from an early age aware that she could control her dreams (see "Creative Dreaming or Dream Incubation," p. 10). This meant she was able in her dream to jump over the spears and arrows and escape from any hazards thrown her way. In dreams, we can rehearse real-life situations and, by winning in our dreams, carry that confidence into the waking world.

INTERPRETATIONS AND FORTUNE-TELLING MEANINGS

★ If the arrows directed toward you in a dream do not have a bow, spite or envy toward you will have no effect.

★ If in an archery dream your arrows are hitting the target every time, you know that you are on the right track for success and recognition.

★ If Cupid or Eros appears in your dreams, shooting toward someone you love or would like in your life, you are making an impression but may need to take the initiative.

★ If Cupid's arrows are coming toward you and they touch you, you have an admirer or a lover who will become ever more ardent.

★ If you are in a medieval battle fighting with arrows, this may be a past-world dream, indicating that you should speak out against gossip and against anyone attempting to threaten your reputation or trying to tempt away your lover.

OUTCOME OF MELINDA'S DREAM

The awareness of being able to influence the outcome of a dream had proven a valuable strategy in Melinda's life because, as she was beautiful and talented, she had experienced more than her share of dream and metaphorical arrows of spite and jealousy.

Arthritis

Rick, sixty-two, dreamed he was backing a famous singer on his guitar when his fingers seized up and he could not play a note. The singer covered for him but told Rick he would not be using him again. Rick woke, worried this could be the beginning of the end of his career.

DREAM BACKGROUND AND MEANING

Rick, a highly accomplished guitarist, was in great demand for studio work and had played with some of the biggest names in the business. Lately he had been experiencing intense pain and stiffness in his fingers when playing the guitar. His physician had diagnosed arthritis. Arthritis dreams in a person who values physical prowess above all other things can be leading the dreamer to explore alternative aspects of life.

INTERPRETATIONS AND FORTUNE-TELLING MEANINGS

★ If your career or business relies mainly on physical dexterity and mobility, your dreams are alerting you to consider longer-term career options.

★ If you dream of being temporarily or permanently incapacitated and are experiencing even mild arthritic symptoms, the dream is expressing anxiety.

★ If you dream of being unable to walk with arthritis, even if you have no symptoms, you may have fears of aging and incapacity generally.

★ If you dream someone you love has arthritis, they may be experiencing emotional difficulties they find hard to express.

★ If you have pain and stiffness in your fingers, knees, hips, or toes, ask yourself what unresolved resentment or sorrow is holding you back from reaching for opportunities and moving forward.

★ If in a dream you are being pushed in a wheelchair, you may be pressured to follow the wrong life path.

OUTCOME OF RICK'S DREAM

It was not so much a forewarning as a worst-case scenario that may not happen. However, Rick did open a studio in his extensive outbuildings for musicians to rent. Based on his reputation, he acted as an agent for the more promising and organized small music festivals. Arthritis dreams can represent anxiety or fear of change and almost always suggest expanding one's field of expertise to develop additional skills.

Artificial Suntan

Madison, eighteen, dreamed she looked in horror in the mirror at her bright orange skin and refused to get into a limo with her friends, which was taking them to the prom. She scrubbed her face, but the hideous color remained and had even stained her dress.

DREAM BACKGROUND AND MEANING

Madison was upset because her friends had made bookings at tanning salons so they would be bronzed for the forthcoming prom. But she had been told by the salon that, because she has red hair and freckles, tanning would not work and could be dangerous. She had bought an expensive instant-tanning lotion but hesitated to apply it. Dreams about beauty treatments going wrong reflect insecurities about not fitting in with the current fashion and can be a subconscious warning.

INTERPRETATIONS AND FORTUNE-TELLING MEANINGS

★ If you are sitting on an exotic shore getting naturally tanned, you can with patience and perseverance attain a positive image boost in the area of life most desired.

★ If in a dream you see yourself incredibly glamorous and toned, are you surrounded by admirers and others equally gorgeous, or feeling isolated and acting a part?

★ If you dream of reacting badly to any short-term beauty treatment, you may be uncomfortable about going along with outside pressures to appear what you are not.

★ If you get burned from excessive sunbed treatments in the dream, changing an image fast may have negative as well as positive results.

★ If your new tan instantly fades, quick changes in any part of life will only be short-lived and fool no one.

OUTCOME OF MADISON'S DREAM

Madison's boyfriend said he disliked women who used artificial enhancements and that she looked beautiful as she was. She danced all night, while her tanned friends looked too sophisticated and unapproachable.

Artificial tanning dreams, substituting an outer for inner change, present an image that may mask true charisma (see "Body Image," p. 62, and "Cosmetic Surgery," p. 116).

Assassination

Lorraine, thirteen, dreamed the phone rang and a voice said, "You know what you have to do." She took her knife and hid it in her sleeve and went to the park. In total darkness, a female figure was sitting on a park bench. Lorraine slipped the knife out of her sleeve, but the woman slumped over. Lorraine realized another assassin had reached her first.

DREAM BACKGROUND AND MEANING

Lorraine was deeply troubled by Penny, a girl in her year at school who constantly told the other girls Lorraine was trying to steal their boyfriends. Lorraine's best friend told her to spread rumors about Penny in retaliation so Penny would know what it was like. Lorraine was very tempted.

INTERPRETATIONS AND FORTUNE-TELLING MEANINGS

* If in your dream you are threatened with assassination, seek the identity of the enemy in real life and try to uncover their motives.
* If you dream you are assassinating someone, you may need to be more assertive in a difficult situation and prepare your response.
* If someone is trying to persuade you to join them in assassinating someone you care for, they may be causing trouble in the relationship.
* If you witness a famous person being assassinated, a much-loved celebrity may become the subject of accusations by the press.
* If you witness the assassination of someone who resembles you, a bad habit may need quitting, as it is damaging your lifestyle and reputation.
* Dreaming of surviving an assassination says you will overcome gossip and spite.

OUTCOME OF LORRAINE'S DREAM

Lorraine realized from the dream that character assassination was not her style. Before long Penny, who had made many enemies, was falsely accused of sending anonymous threats to staff members, and Lorraine tried to help her. Assassination is not without consequences to the assassin as well as the victim, and dreams can warn when it is time to let karma take its course.

Assisted Living Facility

Maureen, eighty, dreamed she was in a spotlessly clean, empty assisted living facility. No one was around, no residents, staff, or visitors. Maureen left and walked along a grassy path to a smaller stone house with fading paint, where she was instantly made welcome. A room was ready for her and music played from the cozy lounge room.

DREAM BACKGROUND AND MEANING

Maureen was aware she needed assisted living and had narrowed the choice to two. Her daughter preferred a state-of-the-art purpose-built facility, but Maureen thought it too impersonal. Maureen's best friend was in an older facility with small independent studios along with the care.

INTERPRETATIONS AND FORTUNE-TELLING MEANINGS

* Dreams of assisted living facilities are emotional, fraught with fears and doubts, and should be shared.
* If you are older but still independent and dream of being abandoned in a jail-like assisted living facility, explore different possibilities, especially if relatives are trying to influence your decision.
* If you are young and having nightmares of being trapped in an assisted living facility for much older people, this reflects anxiety about the future.
* If you dream of abuse toward a relative in an assisted living facility, whether they are older or disabled, these dreams may warrant careful investigation, as you may be picking up your relative's distress.
* If you are seeking care for yourself or a relative and you have recurring dreams of the same assisted living facility, try to locate it, as it will have the right energies.
* If you dream of your relative being neglected in an assisted living facility, though they are still at home, check to see if they are all right.

OUTCOME OF MAUREEN'S DREAM

After the dream, Maureen had a trial month at the more homelike facility. It was filled with laughter and kindness, and Maureen moved in. Dreams may pick up unconscious signals that make one place resonate with the dreamer.

Astroturf, Artificial Turf

Ted, sixty-five, dreamed that everywhere he looked there was hill upon hill of artificial turf, smoothing over the rocky paths. People were contentedly picnicking or walking, but he hated the conformity and pseudo-perfection. He returned to his car and drove home.

DREAM BACKGROUND AND MEANING

Ted's wife insisted that now they were older she wanted to Astroturf their huge lawn. Ted was adamant that he was not sacrificing the naturalness for the fake, even though he admitted it was harder to care for now that he had an artificial knee, but to lose his garden as well as openly acknowledge the loss of his former mobility was unthinkable. Astroturf in dreams represents replacing nature with a low-maintenance substitute at the cost of losing direct connection with the earth.

INTERPRETATIONS AND FORTUNE-TELLING MEANINGS

★ If in your dream a local sports stadium is covered with Astroturf, performance, competition, and results may predominate over a previously more leisurely attitude in your workplace.

★ If a love partner seeks to replace a living garden with artificial in the dream and you disagree, you may need to compromise over your plans and priorities in your future lifestyle.

★ If the dream Astroturf gets torn or develops holes, a superficial answer to a problem may prove only temporary.

★ If in the dream weeds start to grow up through the Astroturf, underlying issues will reemerge unless they are resolved.

★ If you dream of your garden being replaced with artificial grass and flowers against your will, there may be worries about your health and mobility that need acknowledging rather than resisting their effects.

OUTCOME OF TED'S DREAM

Ted compromised with his wife, as he knew he was not as able to tend the garden as he used to be. Dreams of Astroturf cast up questions of convenience versus spontaneity and are a reminder that artificial and unblemished, whether in people or life, should not be a substitute for what is genuine.

Atlantis

Juliana, forty, often dreamed she was in the lost world of Atlantis, looking up at the huge golden statue of Poseidon and walking through streets with buildings studded with precious metals and blossoming exotic fruit trees and flowers. There was a rumbling. The azure waters surrounding Atlantis flooded the land. The dream ended. Juliana never knew if she survived.

DREAM BACKGROUND AND MEANING

Juliana had possessed psychic powers from childhood and frequently dreamed of growing up in Atlantis. When she read accounts of the ancient Greek Plato and the twentieth-century visionary Edmund Cayce, the details matched her dreams. However, in adulthood she did not have the confidence to practice spiritual arts, although her adult Atlantean dreams showed her working as a healer and prophetess. If you dream regularly of Atlantis, you are connecting with a powerful inner source of wisdom and healing powers.

INTERPRETATIONS AND FORTUNE-TELLING MEANINGS

★ If you dream of meeting your spirit guide, one of the golden-haired wise demigod rulers, meditate or use channeled writings to recall forgotten knowledge.

★ If you witness the flooding of Atlantis in your dreams, you may be suppressing emotions of an actual family loss, whether recent, in childhood, or in love.

★ If you are with a twin soul in Atlantis, you may find them again in this life and instantly know them.

★ Dreaming of a daily life in Atlantis says you need to make your present life more spiritually focused to be more fulfilled.

★ If you practice healing, crystals, or prophecy in your dreams, let them reemerge in your present world.

OUTCOME OF JULIANA'S DREAM

Juliana realized she was not using her spiritual powers. She advertised on the Internet for others connected with Atlantis and created a magical group that shared dreams, visions, and insights into the lost world.

Whether factually accurate or not, lost worlds like Atlantis represent a state of enlightenment that the dreamer needs to work toward revealing so its wisdom is restored.

Attorney, Lawyer

Iris, fifty, dreamed she was in a courtroom being quizzed by a prosecutor about every aspect of her life. Her answers were pulled apart by the prosecutor until her head was spinning. At last, she looked directly at the prosecutor and said, "I will answer to no one." She realized the prosecutor was the man she was about to marry.

DREAM BACKGROUND AND MEANING

Iris had escaped from a controlling marriage and had met a man through a dating site. But as they grew closer, Victor started questioning her spending and the time she devoted to her family. Increasingly, she felt on trial. The identity of a prosecutor or defense lawyer may alert you to who judges and who helps.

INTERPRETATIONS AND FORTUNE-TELLING MEANINGS

* If in your dream you consult an attorney or lawyer, read the small print or take advice before signing a contract or finalizing an agreement.
* If you dismiss a dream lawyer, consider if you have the right representation in any actual court case or tribunal.
* If you see your lawyer taking money from your adversary, it does not mean dishonesty; rather, they may be extending the case to make extra money.
* If you dream you are the lawyer arguing a marital, workplace, or official dispute and one does not exist in real life, this alerts you to hidden dissension, resolvable through logic and reason.
* If you dream a lawyer in court accuses you and you have no defense counsel, you may be feeling unnecessarily guilty about an official, workplace, family, or marital matter.
* A prosecutor questioning your personal life suggests a partner or family member who may be overcritical or playing the guilt card to control you.

OUTCOME OF IRIS'S DREAM

Iris realized her trusting, pliable nature attracted controlling men to her. She ended the relationship with Victor and is now careful whom she dates. Dream attorneys reveal a great deal about our own feelings of responsibility or others' problems.

Auction

William, fifty-eight, dreamed he was at an auction, bidding for jewelry for his antique jewelry store. When the auction began, he was captivated by an elaborate jet-black Victorian necklace worn by mourners. He bid far more than he knew it was worth and woke happy.

DREAM BACKGROUND AND MEANING

William had recently auctioned family jewelry he had inherited, which had belonged to his great-grandmother, who he hardly knew. But afterward he regretted it. He inquired on the auction circuit and tracked down the buyer, another dealer, who had split the collection. For William, auctions had always been about profit and not sentiment. Now he was wondering about his family, with whom he had lost touch. Auction dreams are often signs of increasing profit through buying and selling or financial speculation and contain an element of chance.

INTERPRETATIONS AND FORTUNE-TELLING MEANINGS

* Bidding for goods or a house in an auction says you should sometimes be prepared to take more risks in daily life and business.
* If you are auctioning unwanted goods, focus on profit rather than sentiment.
* If you dream you are forced to auction your goods, your achievements are undervalued by others. Do not underrate what you have achieved and still can achieve.
* If you pay more than an item is worth at an auction, something may be of emotional rather than financial value.
* If an item does not reach its reserve price at an auction, the dreamer should be prepared to compromise.
* If you withdraw from auctioning your goods in the dream, this is not the right time to quit a venture.

OUTCOME OF WILLIAM'S DREAM

After the dream, William trawled auction sites and found the memorial necklace. He bought it and contacted the family, who he had not seen for years. He gave the necklace to a niece who loved Victoriana for her twenty-first birthday, and she is now learning her uncle's business. Auction dreams sometimes reflect conflict between money and emotions, and emotions can win.

Automation

Kenneth, seventy-six, dreamed of taking an empty dish to a local charity shop once a day to be given food. He knew he had money in the bank, but fierce dogs were guarding the door, and he dropped his dish of food.

DREAM BACKGROUND AND MEANING

Kenneth lives in a small town in New South Wales, Australia, and his closest banking facilities are closing. His nearest bank will now be seventy miles from his home. He has always dealt in cash and doesn't own a credit card, nor does he have a computer or smartphone. Dreams of being unable to cope in an increasingly digital world can become more frightening if the problem is not tackled head-on.

INTERPRETATIONS AND FORTUNE-TELLING MEANINGS

* If you dream of your computer crashing, your fears are blocking your ability to cope with technology.
* If you go into your bank and speak to talking robots asking difficult-to-answer questions you cannot answer, you should not be intimidated by an unfamiliar system or discouraging techno-speak.
* If you dream your job adopts new technology and you do not understand how it works, it is a signal for you to stay ahead of the game.
* If you are dreaming of reading a manual on modern technology, written in a strange language, search till you find someone who will interpret the jargon.
* If you dream you have a smartphone and the keyboard keeps disappearing, purchase one, but seek a course or savvy relative to explain the technology.

OUTCOME OF KENNETH'S DREAM

Kenneth went into his local post office before it closed forever and explained his fears. The clerk put him in touch with an age-related charity, which was setting up workshops in the town to teach new technology. Afterward, Kenneth formed a self-help club. Problem dreams involving newfangled technology are common, and it is advisable to seek face-to-face support rather than panicking.

Baby

Jessica, forty-two, dreamed she was in a café in a run-down part of the city. The woman running the café handed her a newborn baby, and the baby snuggled into her. Jessica could hear the baby's soft breathing and was reluctant to hand the baby back. When she asked whose baby it was, the woman replied, "It's your granddaughter."

DREAM BACKGROUND AND MEANING

Jessica had located her daughter squatting in an abandoned city warehouse but was reluctant to visit, since her daughter had told her to stay out of her life as her boyfriend was caring for her. Jessica was worried, as the boyfriend was heavily into drugs. A baby, newly born or unborn, can telepathically link to a grandparent as well as link a mother to the infant in dreams.

INTERPRETATIONS AND FORTUNE-TELLING MEANINGS

* To dream of a newborn baby is a sign of growing abundance and prosperity.
* If you are trying to conceive a baby, dreaming of holding a newborn is often a premonition of a future child.
* If you are holding an unknown baby in a dream, it may be that your adult daughter or a close female relative is pregnant.
* If you dream of having a baby, though you are beyond childbearing years, a new opportunity regarding a creative talent will present itself.
* If you are comforting a crying baby, a younger person in your family may be telepathically asking for your support.
* If you dream of adult or teenage children as babies, you may be worried you can no longer protect them.

OUTCOME OF JESSICA'S DREAM

After the dream, Jessica went to the warehouse where her daughter was squatting and found she was alone and heavily pregnant. Jessica took her daughter home, and the baby was born safely. It appears that an unborn baby, in this case one who Jessica had no prior knowledge of, can call out for help via the link of family love through dreams.

Back (Body Part)

Ted, twenty-five, dreamed he was competing in a wheelchair in the Summer Paralympics and winning his race. Everyone was cheering. With huge effort he stood up, pushed the chair out of the way, and sped across to where the Summer Olympic races were taking place. He easily won.

DREAM BACKGROUND AND MEANING

Ted had been an aspiring athlete. But in an accident during a race, he had seriously damaged his spine and was confined to a wheelchair. He was paralyzed from the waist down, though there was a slight chance he could recover spontaneously within two years, and he had adapted well to a new way of life. An operation could return full mobility, but if it failed it would leave him permanently and more severely paralyzed.

INTERPRETATIONS AND FORTUNE-TELLING MEANINGS

* If in the dream your back is hurting or injured, you have been trying too hard to hold back your feelings of frustration or anger.
* If you keep dreaming of a specific accident—for example, falling off a ladder—take care if you use ladders. If not, accept it as a potential avoidable fall from favor that could set you back materially.
* If you dream you are stabbed in the back, beware of false friends and jealous colleagues.
* If someone turns their back on you and walks away, be wary of their seeming friendship and support.
* If a friend or family member is supporting your back with their hand or patting your back, they are loyal and indicate you will get the backing you need.

OUTCOME OF TED'S DREAM

The dream showed Ted he desperately wanted to run again, and he made the decision to take a chance on the operation. Back dreams can pick up subconscious signals about health and prognosis, and indicate the willpower to get back into the action, which Ted did after a successful operation.

Back Door

Ross, twenty-nine, dreamed he was a footman at a big house. He was in love with the landowner's youngest daughter. Ross would meet her outside the back door when he had finished his work. He wanted to marry her and said he could work in his father's forge, which one day would be his. But she would not give him an answer. He often saw her greeting a young man and his family at the front door, and the cook told Ross they were pledged by the families to marry.

DREAM BACKGROUND AND MEANING

Ross was a welder, aiming one day to have his own business. Ruby was the business owner's daughter. She would only allow him to pick her up from the back door of her house. He had been told that she was going to marry the son of the owner of another welding company. Ruby denied it and said she would invite Ross to meet her family soon. Maybe a past-life dream, a back-door dream can reveal perceived differences in status between two people, symbolized by one being required to enter the other person's life secretly through the back door.

INTERPRETATIONS AND FORTUNE-TELLING MEANINGS

* Choosing to exit through the back door in a dream indicates trying to avoid issues or confrontation.
* Entering by the back door suggests you are reluctant or unable to show support openly for the owner of the door.
* Being admitted or shown out the back door says the owner may be trying to conceal your relationship or your influence in their life.
* A locked back door, if you are outside, warns you may have to directly confront risky but necessary matters.
* If you can't open the back door from the inside or the door is broken, an avoidance tactic will no longer work.

OUTCOME OF ROSS'S DREAM

After the dream, Ross knocked at the front door unexpectedly. Ruby was shocked and shut the door hastily, ushering him around the back, which told him he would never be accepted. Back doors in family life can suggest a warm informality, but not if used to keep secret a love considered inferior.

Backpacking

Graham, sixty-eight, dreamed he was camping on a cliff top. The rain was pouring down, but he was dry in his tent. A huge gust of wind blew away the tent, and Graham was propelled toward the cliff edge. The final words he heard as he plunged into darkness were, "No fool like an old fool," spoken by his older sister.

DREAM BACKGROUND AND MEANING

Graham was planning to backpack around the coast of mainland United Kingdom. He had never backpacked but was very fit. His sister, his only relative, told him to go on organized tours where he would have proper accommodation. But Graham desperately wanted to be free after years of working in a bank. Backpacking dreams represent the essentials we need in life, occurring at a time to clear emotional and sometimes actual clutter.

INTERPRETATIONS AND FORTUNE-TELLING MEANINGS

* If you dream of backpacking to a desired location, you are ready to break free of daily restrictions.
* If in the dream your backpack is too heavy, you may need to shed obligations that weigh you down.
* If you dream that a teen or adult child is trekking, you may suffer parental anxiety dreams; but if it is an urgent premonition of danger, act on the dream.
* If you dream of being robbed or attacked while you are backpacking, take extra precautions, as this may be a warning.
* If in your dream you are backpacking through an unknown land, try to identify it. It may have positive significance, even on a conventional vacation.

OUTCOME OF GRAHAM'S DREAM

Graham joined an online backpacking organization for seniors and went on several organized treks with like-minded people. When he felt confident, he set off on his solo backpacking trip. Backpacking dreams may act as guides to sensible precautions and not deterrents to adventure.

Backward, Back to Front

In her dream, Claire, forty, was watching a movie of her life that began in old age, with Claire and her husband living by the ocean, surrounded by great-grandchildren, which had been their dream. Then the movie ran backward, and the reel broke at the point where she was forty and leaving with the children.

DREAM BACKGROUND AND MEANING

Claire and her husband were going through a bad patch as her husband had been having an affair, and she also had planned to move out to be with her recently met lover. The backward dream, however, offered an alternative ending, in which her husband still played a part. Dreams of events running backward often occur at a crossroads in life.

INTERPRETATIONS AND FORTUNE-TELLING MEANINGS

* Dreaming of walking backward indicates you are impatient with the inertia or uncooperative attitudes of others.
* If you are retracing your steps in the dream, you will discover you already have the answer to an important question.
* If you are wearing clothes back to front, it is a lucky sign that good times and opportunities wait ahead, though in ancient times this was considered a sign of protection.
* If writing is backward, someone close is deliberately obscuring words to mislead.
* If the ending of a movie in the dream that relates to your life precedes the intervening stages, results of a different major decision to the one currently on offer may be revealed.
* If in the dream you are rearranging anything that has been presented back to front, the future is more in your control than you thought.

OUTCOME OF CLAIRE'S DREAM

After the dream, which seemed so vivid, Claire decided to have one more try to save her marriage. She and her husband are working toward a future with potential to have the happy ending seen in the backward movie. Seeing life backward in a dream opens the possibility of an entirely different ending from that expected.

Bad Behavior

Gordon, twenty-five, dreamed he was attending an incredibly boring meeting he knew would achieve nothing. He started making paper airplanes from the official minutes, deliberately spilled water on the conference table, and walked out the door, down the stairs, and into the sunshine. He felt totally liberated.

DREAM BACKGROUND AND MEANING

Gordon had always obeyed the rules and was aiming for a partnership at his firm, with a lucrative salary. But recently he had an irrational desire to do something totally irresponsible and shock people. Bad behavior in dreams can act as a warning of an inner restlessness toward a conventional path that may sabotage the future if not checked.

INTERPRETATIONS AND FORTUNE-TELLING MEANINGS

★ If you dream of a badly behaved dog, you may be finding others' spontaneity hard to deal with if you are naturally restrained.

★ If you dream about badly behaved children disturbing a journey or meal, you have been keeping your own emotions under control because you fear others' disapproval.

★ If you dream your own children are being badly behaved, you may be under pressure by a disapproving relative about the way you run your life.

★ If in the dream you are a badly behaved child and are being reproached or punished, you may be afraid to go against the status quo.

★ If you dream you are an adult behaving out of character under the influence of drink or drugs, you are finding it difficult not to speak your mind.

★ If in a dream you are trying to enforce rules and facing a rebellion, consider if you are on the right side or if it is the rules that are wrong.

OUTCOME OF GORDON'S DREAM

Gordon's mentor, noticing Gordon's frustration, suggested he take a break from company law working with big corporations, and he transferred to their little-known outreach division, helping individuals fighting against corrupt companies seeking to evict them. Gordon loved the work and focused his efforts onto righting injustices. Bad-behavior dreams can suggest the need to channel self-destructive trends into worthwhile causes.

Bail

Barry, fifty-six, dreamed he was in a courtroom, accused of illegal financial dealings. The judge offered bail, but none of the colleagues he asked, though they were responsible for the fraud, would put up the bail money. His wife, whom he was too ashamed to ask, had already paid the bail bond and freed him.

DREAM BACKGROUND AND MEANING

Three of Barry's colleagues had asked him to lend them a large sum from his wife's recent inheritance, as they said he would make a huge return on a foolproof investment. His wife refused, as she did not trust them. Barry was furious with her and said she was disloyal and lacked faith in him. The person who bails you out in the dream is the one who will remain loyal to you, which you may not have appreciated.

INTERPRETATIONS AND FORTUNE-TELLING MEANINGS

★ If you are granted bail in a courtroom dream, you will get temporary relief from financial or official problems.

★ Whoever stands bail for you is trustworthy and will stick by you emotionally as well as financially long-term.

★ If you bail yourself out in a trial, you have the personal resources and initiative to solve your own problems.

★ If you are refused bail, you may feel trapped by circumstances and need alternative ways or alternative help to extricate yourself.

★ If you are bailing water out of a sinking boat, you may need to make the best of a situation and put in extra effort rather than give up.

OUTCOME OF BARRY'S DREAM

After the dream, Barry realized where his loyalties lay. He had been considering taking the money secretly, as he had access to his wife's funds. On further inquiry, however, he discovered that if the scheme failed, it would leave him to take the blame legally. He bailed out just in time, before signing the incriminating paperwork. Bail dreams, if you are contemplating anything even slightly illegal or financially risky, are a warning that you may end up on the wrong side of the law.

Bait

In her dream, Juliana, twenty-five, was fishing, which she hated. The fish with hooks in their mouths were older businessmen she had signed up for deals with her company. The fishing lines were linked through her. She struggled to be free but tore her lips. The lines were taken by her bosses, and she was cast aside when the bait was no longer needed.

DREAM BACKGROUND AND MEANING

Juliana was given a job with a prestigious finance company. Her role was to entertain prospective clients and refer them to the senior executives, who closed the deals. She was given a good salary and expense account. However, being the bait for deals was not what she'd had in mind when she joined the firm. Bait dreams invariably ask who or what is the bait.

INTERPRETATIONS AND FORTUNE-TELLING MEANINGS

★ If you dream a fish is taking the bait, you will have success in love and/or financial matters.

★ If you see baited animal traps, beware of someone trying to trick you, usually the person baiting the traps.

★ If you react badly to provocation, step back, use logic, and be aware you are being fed the bait.

★ If a baited trap poisons or catches a creature for which it is not intended, you may find yourself caught up in others' quarrels.

★ If someone takes the bait, be sure you can deliver what you promise.

★ If you dream your bait is ignored and was intended for a rodent or pest, you may not find it easy to remove an infestation.

OUTCOME OF JULIANA'S DREAM

After the dream Juliana realized there were several other attractive, personable young men and women luring lonely older men and women to give their business to the company. Juliana is now working for a lower-paying organization but has job satisfaction. Bait dreams can occur if the dreamer suspects they are being valued only for their superficial qualities.

Balcony

Mal, twenty-eight, dreamed he was a medieval troubadour, standing beneath a balcony. He was serenading his perfect woman with a lute, but she was ignoring him. He saw flowers growing below the balcony, picked six red roses, and climbed the greenery to present them. Then he slipped, dropping his lute and the flowers, and the subject of his admiration did not even notice and closed the balcony doors.

DREAM BACKGROUND AND MEANING

Mal was constantly falling in love with beautiful starlets in the show-business world where he worked on the fringes, and he showered them with flowers and gifts. But they mostly ignored him. Romantic balcony dreams can suggest the dreamer is aiming for an unattainable love rather than finding someone who would appreciate him.

INTERPRETATIONS AND FORTUNE-TELLING MEANINGS

★ If you dream you are waving to others below from a balcony, you will soon get promotion or success at work, or public acclaim.

★ If you are royalty or with royalty or a celebrity acknowledging the crowds below, you have high ambitions to rise above the crowd.

★ When a balcony breaks, it means that someone's promises to you may not be fulfilled.

★ If you are climbing up to reach a balcony, you may need to take risks and use an unconventional approach to gain recognition.

★ A dream balcony can signify the desire to return to a mother or nurturing female's breasts and gain support, rather than having a sexual meaning.

★ Falling off a balcony suggests you may be aiming too high, too quickly.

OUTCOME OF MAL'S DREAM

After the latest rejection, when a starlet laughed in his face when he suggested he might take her to dinner, Mal realized that he was seeking to bask in a partner's prestige, rather than finding true love. He now dates a woman from production, and they are planning a life together. Balcony dreams may show ways of advancing, but if the balcony acts as a barrier, consider aiming for the attainable, not fantasy.

Ball Game

Mitch, twenty, dreamed he was watching a basketball championship game at college. The star player was hit in the face with a ball. Mitch rushed onto the court and took his place, scoring several times, and was carried off the court in triumph. He did not bother to tell his parents.

DREAM BACKGROUND AND MEANING

Mitch came from a multigenerational sporting family. Because Mitch had been ill as a child, he had missed the intense family coaching. Though he won a prestigious scholarship in physics, he was underrated by his family.

INTERPRETATIONS AND FORTUNE-TELLING MEANINGS

* If you dream you are playing ball or a ball game with others, you will remain secure in your present situation and relationships.
* If you are bouncing a ball alone rhythmically, your life is in balance. You do not need others to validate you.
* Two people kicking or throwing a ball to each other speaks of harmony between them, unless one is deliberately throwing it out of range to test the other.
* Three or more people playing ball bring an element of competition and rivalry. Resist attempts to undermine or interfere in your relationship.
* If you drop a ball and it goes over a fence or hits you, quarrels or misunderstandings may be caused by distractions and taking your eye off the main chance.
* If you are not playing ball or are never passed the ball, you may feel excluded from the happiness of others.

OUTCOME OF MITCH'S DREAM

Mitch started playing basketball for the college team and found he did have talent. Having proved it to himself, he now focuses on his real love, science, and is already being marked for awards. Skill in ball games can sometimes obscure other worthwhile talents and should not be used solely as a hallmark of attainment.

Ballet

Ruth, sixteen, dreamed she discovered an old music box with a dancing ballerina in an antique store. When she wound it up, Ruth herself started pirouetting. The music became faster and Ruth pirouetted faster. The music did not stop, and neither could Ruth. At last, she slammed the lid shut, the glass top shattered, and the music ceased.

DREAM BACKGROUND AND MEANING

Ruth had studied ballet from childhood and at last she had been offered a place training with a major American school of ballet. Yet though it had been her lifetime ambition, she hesitated, as it would require a huge commitment and she might get no further than the chorus. Ballet dreams contain great promise for dancers and nondancers alike of a life with beauty and harmony, but at a price.

INTERPRETATIONS AND FORTUNE-TELLING MEANINGS

* Dreaming of practicing ballet, whatever your age, indicates that you are focusing on moving into alignment with yourself.
* Dancing across a stage says you seek to rise above routine and mundane daily life.
* If you fall while practicing or performing, you are striving too hard to gain or regain harmony and balance.
* If in your dream you are in the chorus and have ambitions to rise higher, you may have to dedicate yourself without guarantees of stardom.
* If you are in the starring role and you are involved in dance in the real world, you can achieve the heights with total dedication.
* If you are watching a ballet, you may envy others their harmony but should seek it in your own way.

OUTCOME OF RUTH'S DREAM

The dream reminded Ruth that if she accepted the offer it would involve total dedication instead of enjoying relaxed years at college. She did go to ballet school and is finding it hard, as there is huge competition. Ballet dreams represent grace and harmony that may be missing in the dreamer's current life.

Balloons

Anastasia, sixty, dreamed she was a child again, following a balloon she had accidentally released. She chased it, even dashing across a road with a car narrowly missing her. Then the breeze caught it and it flew higher and disappeared. She was very disappointed and, though she knew there were other balloons, that was the only one she wanted.

DREAM BACKGROUND AND MEANING

Anastasia, quite happily married for forty years, always regretted the man who got away. Now she had found his name on social media and was tempted to contact him, as he appeared single. Was it too late? Balloons are by their nature transitory and often in dreams represent a lovely memory that should remain as such.

INTERPRETATIONS AND FORTUNE-TELLING MEANINGS

★ A sky filled with toy balloons indicates a releasing of worries and responsibilities.

★ Helium balloons decorated with symbols or messages suggest that an event or occasion will exceed expectations.

★ Inflating balloons suggests putting your hopes in an uncertain venture.

★ A deflated or broken balloon indicates disappointment and shattered hopes.

★ Being a child playing with balloons suggests daily life is becoming routine and you need to build in more leisure.

★ Water balloons or a balloon exploding in your face or in the face of someone you know represent suppressed anger over a petty matter that may erupt if not deflated.

OUTCOME OF ANASTASIA'S DREAM

There was little information on her ex-boyfriend's social media page, so she decided to contact him to see if he remembered her and maybe still pined for her. He was pleased to hear from her. Once they had exchanged memories, Anastasia knew that the connection was best a happy reminiscence. She declined an invitation to meet. She and her husband went away on a trip. Once a balloon has flown away in a dream, it may be a reminder of what was special but never was meant to last (see "Hot-Air Balloon," p. 248).

Ballroom Dancing

In his dream, Julian, thirty-five, was dancing at his local ballroom. The dancing instructor, wearing a spangled dress, whirled him around, but he kept stepping on her feet. Everyone stopped dancing and started laughing at him. He fled, mockery ringing in his ears.

DREAM BACKGROUND AND MEANING

Throughout his life, Julian had been awkward around people. He had been made to attend dancing classes at the dream ballroom when he was young, his worst nightmare. The only consolation had been Angie, a girl with thick braces but a lovely personality. Everyone laughed at them, as he was short and she was tall. Julian knew Angie was back in the area, very changed, but he was too shy to contact her.

INTERPRETATIONS AND FORTUNE-TELLING MEANINGS

★ If you dream you are dancing gracefully with a partner, known or unknown, love and romance will come or grow.

★ Stepping on your partner's toes means you are overly self-conscious and should not let others deter you from doing what you want for fear of adverse comment.

★ If you are standing on the sidelines, you are missing opportunities to have a relationship, not necessarily one connected with dancing.

★ If you are much younger in the dream scene, there will be an opportunity to rekindle an old love or friendship.

★ If you dream you win a ballroom dancing competition, your talents will gain positive recognition and reward in the public arena.

★ If the dance floor is overcrowded, you may need to actively put yourself forward to gain positive attention in the area of life where you wish to shine.

OUTCOME OF JULIAN'S DREAM

Out of curiosity, Julian went to the local ballroom he had seen in his dream. He met Angie, who worked at the ballroom. Often such dreams are predictive. If you are hesitant about joining communal activities, find one you enjoy, not just one others pressure you to attend.

Bamboo

Naomi, seventy-five, dreamed she was in a forest of thick bamboo. Giant pandas were eating contentedly. She was their guardian, similar to today's Chinese "panda nannies." Chloe, her youngest granddaughter, was with her. One day Chloe would take her place. Naomi often went back to the bamboo forest in her dreams and knew it was where she belonged.

DREAM BACKGROUND AND MEANING

All her life Naomi had been enthralled by giant pandas. But she was worried that after her death her family, who did not share her love of the species, with the exception of eighteen-year-old Chloe, would let her conservation work lapse. Chloe, unlike her siblings, did not want to go to college. Naomi planned to take her to see the remaining pandas in their natural habitat. The family complained that she was rewarding Chloe for her lack of ambition.

INTERPRETATIONS AND FORTUNE-TELLING MEANINGS

* Bamboo dreams say it is important to nourish the heart and soul rather than aim for material gain, and they may be past-world dreams.
* Bamboo growing wild is a sign of lasting prosperity and good fortune.
* Bamboo stakes in a garden tied with red ribbon or cord with nine knots are traditionally a sign of growing good luck.
* A miniature lucky bamboo plant with Chinese coins attached predicts travel with life-enhancing results for others and self.
* Dying bamboo leaves advise paying attention to practical and financial aspects of your life to turn around fortunes.
* Bamboo plants in a garden signal health and long life for those living in the home.
* Making clothes or furniture from bamboo suggests transforming lifetime experiences into worthwhile projects rather than sitting on assets.

OUTCOME OF NAOMI'S DREAM

Naomi took her granddaughter to see the pandas. Chloe was enthralled and joined a volunteer organization, subsidized initially by Naomi, until Chloe was accepted into a training program. Bamboo represents natural resources that can be used in an environmentally friendly way.

Bandages

Jimi, twenty-eight, dreamed he was in an Ancient Egyptian tomb, bandaging and embalming with sacred oils the mummy of a deceased noblewoman with whom he had secretly been having an affair. He was heartbroken but dared not show it as he placed amulets between the layers of bandages. At last, her body was placed in a coffin painted in her image.

DREAM BACKGROUND AND MEANING

Jimi had been having an affair with a beautiful older Egyptian woman, the owner of the restaurant in which he worked. She had been suddenly taken ill and was in intensive care. He couldn't visit to say goodbye. She had always said they were together in Old Egypt and wanted an Ancient Egyptian burial.

INTERPRETATIONS AND FORTUNE-TELLING MEANINGS

* If you are putting a bandage on a lover, family member, friend, or colleague, you will be called to mend a quarrel or dispute.
* If you are being bandaged, you may be accepting a situation you do not really want.
* If blood or pus is seeping under or through the bandage, a matter may be too deep-seated for a quick fix and may take time and patience to heal.
* If you are a nurse, doctor, or paramedic bandaging a wound, you may be called on to fix others' problems, but make sure you ask when you need help.
* If you dream you do not have a bandage to fix your own wound or burn, make sure you care for yourself as well as others.

OUTCOME OF JIMI'S DREAM

Jimi could not attend the funeral but had a private ceremony for his lover in which he made a tiny clay doll, wrapped it in bandages with Egyptian charms, and buried it beneath her favorite lotus plant at the back of the restaurant. He had the dream again in which he saw her flying as a hawk to the stars, a symbol of the freed spirit.

Bank Account Cleaned Out

In his dream, Jim, sixty-eight, was in a gas station, filling up his car. When he went to pay for the gas, his debit card was declined. He phoned the bank and discovered that all his funds had been withdrawn the night before by his son. Jim awoke, relieved that it was only a dream.

DREAM BACKGROUND AND MEANING

For many years Jim had resisted automatic banking. However, his son Todd had talked him into banking online and suggested he become second account holder, as his father had promised to invest in Todd's new business. Because of the dream, Jim was having a change of heart. Banking dreams represent a fear of being taken over and losing control of your independence, finances, or social standing.

INTERPRETATIONS AND FORTUNE-TELLING MEANINGS

★ If you dream of keeping all your money in a home safe, you may worry about others gaining unauthorized knowledge of your private affairs.

★ If you dream of all your money disappearing out of the bank, financial loss may be an old fear, perhaps from earlier setbacks or childhood poverty.

★ If you withdraw all your money from the bank, you may fear that those you help financially only value you for your assets or what you can do for them.

★ If you dream you have spent all your money, you may have been too generous or speculated unwisely in hope of gain, a warning to be cautious with spending or lending on uncertain deals.

★ If your bank refuses to help you if you lose all your money in the dream, an authority figure, whether a parent, boss, or financial organization, may suddenly turn against you.

★ If you dream of someone emptying your bank account to invest in a seemingly foolproof scheme, beware of parting with your money or your account details.

OUTCOME OF JIM'S DREAM

Todd was pressuring his father to fund his new business, using direct access to Jim's bank account. Jim declined. Losing money from your bank in a dream goes beyond surface issues and talks about fears the dreamer has of losing everything financially, emotionally, or career-wise, sometimes justified fears.

Bank Notes, Devaluation

Zelda, eighty-six and a widow, dreamed she heard a news flash on the radio that all bank notes were now worthless. In a panic, she went to her wardrobe, where she kept her life savings, and all it contained was bundles of blank paper. She woke in a panic, checked, and her money was still there.

DREAM BACKGROUND AND MEANING

Zelda did not trust banks and kept her savings at home, since her own mother had lost a huge amount of money owing to the devaluation of bank notes in her homeland years before. Dreaming of keeping bank notes at home indicates a fear of letting go of independence.

INTERPRETATIONS AND FORTUNE-TELLING MEANINGS

★ If you worry about the value of money decreasing, you may have deep-seated fears about poverty, which may or may not be justified.

★ If you dream that your bank notes disappear or become blank if stored at home, you may worry about becoming unable to make your own decisions, especially if family members are controlling.

★ If in the dream you physically put your money in a bank vault, you are taking or taking back your power to control your life by ensuring that you remain financially and emotionally in charge of your own spending.

★ If in the dream there is a worldwide devaluation of the value of money, this reflects deep-seated fears of events over which the dreamer has no control.

★ If in dreams there is a family dispute over cash kept at home by an elderly living relative, family members may have an agenda.

★ If the dreamer needs to see and be responsible for their money as bank notes, others should respect that decision.

OUTCOME OF ZELDA'S DREAM

A kindly bank manager, worried about Zelda's regular cash transactions, offered to show her the vaults where she could physically deposit her bank notes and retrieve them any time. At first she checked weekly, but eventually she learned her money was safe. Dreams about devaluation of bank notes occur especially in older people and can have great emotional significance, which must be recognized.

Bankruptcy

Ivan, fifty-six, dreamed bailiffs were removing all the furniture from his beautiful home and nailing up the windows. He and his wife, Sylvia, were trying to stop them, but the bailiffs said they deserved to lose everything. Finally, Ivan and Sylvia were left in the street with just a small suitcase.

DREAM BACKGROUND AND MEANING

Ivan and Sylvia run a small, very successful business. They never have vacations or weekends off. Since they had a bankruptcy in a former business, caused by an international economic downturn twenty-five years earlier, they constantly worry about finances. Now they are planning on closing the business for a few weeks for an overseas vacation. Sometimes a financial-anxiety dream can reawaken memories of much earlier but not forgotten problems.

INTERPRETATIONS AND FORTUNE-TELLING MEANINGS

★ If you are made bankrupt in a dream, with no danger in real life, moneymaking may be an unacknowledged emotional drain on your personal harmony.

★ If debt is an issue, the dream may be advising you to sort matters out before they spiral out of control.

★ If you are in a courtroom being unfairly harangued by a judge, you may be feeling unnecessarily guilty about spending money on yourself or planning leisure time.

★ Should you witness your relatives turned onto the street, you may have been emotionally blackmailed by family for being ungrateful or undeserving.

★ If you are saved from bankruptcy by a relative or company, you may be offered a loan or financial help by them. Consider on what terms the offer is made.

★ If in the dream you are starting again after bankruptcy, you will find a way out of a restrictive situation, which may be emotional.

OUTCOME OF IVAN'S DREAM

Ivan appointed a manager to work during his vacation. He also took on extra help throughout the year so he and Sylvia could better enjoy life. Warning dreams about finances can refer to neglecting personal quality of life.

Baptism, Naming Ceremony

Nathan, thirty-two, dreamed that his infant son was being renamed by his in-laws, who were barring the church door so Nathan could not enter. Nathan was hammering on the door, saying it was his child too and he would not allow the name to be changed. He woke protesting.

DREAM BACKGROUND AND MEANING

Since Nathan's son had been born, his in-laws had tried to exclude Nathan by influencing their daughter, Tracey, about the baby's name and pressuring her to have the baby baptized in their faith. Nathan tried to be polite but was increasingly frustrated. Baptism and naming-ceremony dreams often have deep meanings, since they are associated with new beginnings.

INTERPRETATIONS AND FORTUNE-TELLING MEANINGS

★ Dreaming of baptizing or officially naming a child is a good omen if you want to conceive.

★ If you dream you are naming a child or older person in a ceremony, this is reassuring if you worry about that child or about an ill or vulnerable adult.

★ If you dream of being baptized as an adult, this represents surrendering to a deep love or a determination to follow a career or course in life that is emotionally fulfilling.

★ If you are changing your name in a ceremony, even if you are not religious, the dream suggests you are seeking a new identity to fit the person you are or wish to become.

★ If you or the infant are given the wrong name at the ceremony, others may be trying to cast you or the child into a particular role.

★ If you dream you are denied access to your child's naming ceremony or baptism, beware of excessive intrusion into the child's upbringing.

OUTCOME OF NATHAN'S DREAM

Nathan applied for a transfer to an interstate office of his firm in another location, and he and his wife moved. Without his in-laws' interference, the family is flourishing. Happy baptism and naming ceremony dreams signify the present and enduring identity of a child. Where a parent's role is denied, the dream can warn that swift, decisive action is needed.

Bar (Saloon)

Bob, forty, dreamed he was in a frontier-town saloon he had just taken over. The bar was crowded, with guys drinking from full bottles of whiskey and scantily dressed women taking gamblers upstairs. Then two rival mobs burst through the swinging doors and a fierce gun battle ensued. Bob hid behind the bar as glasses and bottles were smashed and furniture was destroyed. He watched his business be destroyed in minutes.

DREAM BACKGROUND AND MEANING

Bob was obsessed with spaghetti Western movies of the early pioneers. He had a burning ambition to open a bar based on a reproduction pioneer barroom and hold reenactments of famous gunfights. But he would have to offer his home as security and use all his savings. Barroom dreams are often linked with socializing and socially based business ventures.

INTERPRETATIONS AND FORTUNE-TELLING MEANINGS

★ If you are a bartender in the dream, you may find yourself involved in the problems of people you hardly know.

★ If you are socializing in a bar with strangers, you are seeking acceptance from nonjudgmental people.

★ If you are drinking alone in a bar, you may feel excluded from friends or colleagues because of a difference of opinion.

★ If you are drinking your way through a mini bar in a hotel room, you may be trying to conceal excesses or overspending, not necessarily alcohol-related.

★ If a bar is crowded and you cannot reach the bar to order a drink, there is fierce competition to make yourself noticed.

★ If there is a barroom brawl, you are unwittingly walking into a quarrel or conflict of someone else's making.

OUTCOME OF BOB'S DREAM

After the dream, Bob realized that though his idea was good, it contained risks he could not afford to take. He suggested the idea to a local theme-park organization, which appointed him as manager of the pioneer saloon he set up for them. Bar dreams can be alcohol-related, especially if you are quitting excessive drinking.

Barbecue

Freddie, fifty-five, dreamed he was lighting the barbecue at a family gathering. But the charcoal would not light. When it did, the food did not cook properly. Everyone was becoming impatient. Freddie felt embarrassed at failing at something he had done all his life. His eldest son took over, saying his father was getting too old and should get himself an up-to-date propane barbecue.

DREAM BACKGROUND AND MEANING

Freddie ran the family business, assisted by his two sons. But recently he seemed not to have his former energy, and his sons had been questioning his decisions, introducing innovations, and making him feel old and useless. Barbecuing has traditionally been a way the family alpha male asserts his mighty hunter skills.

INTERPRETATIONS AND FORTUNE-TELLING MEANINGS

★ If you dream a barbecue will not light, it may be time in life to try new methods or make changes in career.

★ If food does not cook properly on a barbecue, you may be losing enthusiasm for parts of your life and need to delegate responsibility.

★ If food burns, there may be undue interference, or you may be trying too hard.

★ If it rains at a dream barbecue, make contingency plans for a coming social event, vacation, or travel that may not work as planned.

★ If there is too much food, you are overestimating your need to nurture others.

★ If you run short of food, you may worry you are not providing sufficient input instead of questioning your need for control.

OUTCOME OF FREDDIE'S DREAM

Freddie realized he was ready to step back in the business. He took a six-month sabbatical and traveled across the States in his camper van. When he returned, the business was running well and so he took more vacations while still maintaining executive control over the company and family barbecues. A barbecue represents family gatherings and can reveal underlying jostling for power between generations.

Bargains

Stan, sixty, dreamed he was walking around a junkyard and saw the antique furniture he had restored through the years in piles of broken pieces. He was on crutches, trying to collect all the parts together, but the stall owner was offering him cheap chipboard furniture in its place. Stan found a wheelbarrow and took his old furniture home and, though he kept falling over, he would not give up.

DREAM BACKGROUND AND MEANING

Stan was injured in a traffic accident and his wife was killed. He was told he would have to move to a smaller house or condo. His sister sold his beautiful antique furniture at a bargain price and replaced it with easy-to-care-for minimalist furniture. He was heartbroken. A true bargain is what is of value to the buyer and no longer of worth to the vendor.

INTERPRETATIONS AND FORTUNE-TELLING MEANINGS

⋆ If you suspect you are being overcharged in an apparently once-in-a-lifetime offer, check around for better offers.

⋆ If you are at a dream car trunk sale, you may be drawn psychically to the place where your bargain awaits.

⋆ If you dream you sell items at a bargain price, you may be undervaluing your own worth.

⋆ If you attend a dream auction and find exactly what you want cheaply, you have a good eye for bargains.

⋆ If you are given an apparently valueless family heirloom, treasure it not just in monetary terms, although it will increase in value.

⋆ If in your dream you go to an antique fair, there is a bargain waiting to be uncovered. Do not be too eager to sell yourself short in any aspect of life.

OUTCOME OF STAN'S DREAM

Stan realized he would never be fit enough to restore antique furniture again. However, as he partially recovered, he started classes teaching enthusiasts how to find bargains at yard sales. A bargain consists of what is of value to the buyer, and its worth may vary according to a person's age and stage of life.

Barrels

Rob, now sixty-five, dreamed he was a young man carrying barrels of contraband spirits onto his small fishing boat from a ship moored at sea. Then, through the fog, lights appeared, and it was the customs officers. Rob threw the barrels overboard and headed out to sea as if he was fishing. But he woke scared.

DREAM BACKGROUND AND MEANING

Rob had a chance to supplement his income by cheaply selling imperfectly sewn reject handbags from the factory where he worked to market stalls. His rationale was that the bags would be thrown away anyway. They were transported from the yard by a regular delivery van. The van driver suggested they sell directly to the market traders and double the profits. Piled-up barrels in a dream suggest accumulating wealth by whatever means, but if the barrels are falling or dumped in the dream, it is a warning.

INTERPRETATIONS AND FORTUNE-TELLING MEANINGS

⋆ A dream of rolling barrels down a hill in a race indicates competition to succeed in business.

⋆ If a barrel is full of beer, wine, or spirits, resources and assets are easily and profitably transferred.

⋆ If a barrel is leaking, it may not be possible to keep a secret or hold on to an advantage.

⋆ If a barrel contains tar, there may be complications releasing resources because of delays in any business venture.

⋆ If a barrel contains contraband goods, risky opportunities will arise.

⋆ If a barrel is empty, a particular source of help or income is drying up and is not worth pursuing.

OUTCOME OF ROB'S DREAM

Rob was caught loading the bags. Because of his good record, he was only demoted. The van driver was dismissed. Barrels have a twofold purpose: to store and to conceal. The nature and outcome of the dream can alert the dreamer to profitability or risk factors involved in any transactions in daily life.

Barriers

Dave, forty-five, dreamed he was late for an important meeting. But the road ahead was blocked and no alternate route marked. He tried another turn that led where he wanted, but again there was a barrier. There was no way through. He phoned to explain he would have to join the meeting by Zoom, but was told someone else had taken his place.

DREAM BACKGROUND AND MEANING

Dave was worried about the security of his position at work. There was a thrusting new management team who regarded him as a dinosaur. But he had doubts about some of their plans; one particular project he knew from experience would be a disaster.

The dream meaning of barriers depends on whether a barrier is temporary or permanent.

INTERPRETATIONS AND FORTUNE-TELLING MEANINGS

* If you dream that barriers are protecting you from a crowd or danger, maintain defenses in your everyday life to avoid being carried along with mistaken opinions.
* Sea or river defenses protect against being overwhelmed by the impulsive actions of others or by excessive emotions.
* A hole or breach in defenses can be positive or negative, according to the purpose of the barrier in the dream.
* If you are held behind barriers from joining in a procession or getting to where you want to go by a police cordon or by closed roads, there may be a problem with officialdom or those undermining your authority.
* If you knock down barriers, you can overcome obstacles with determination and persistence.
* If a barrier has barbed wire or broken glass on top, there may be a high price to overcome it.

OUTCOME OF DAVE'S DREAM

Dave spoke out against the unworkable scheme and was replaced on the project. It failed badly, and the head office appointed Dave as head of planning. The dream barriers were blocking him from making a big mistake. Sometimes barriers warn that this is the wrong time, place, or plan to proceed.

Basement, Cellar

Sandra, seventy-five, dreamed she was in her cobwebby basement, trying to sort the clutter. Suddenly the light went out and she became disoriented. When she eventually found the door, it was jammed. At last, she wrenched it open and woke screaming.

DREAM BACKGROUND AND MEANING

Sandra was moving from her unmanageable old house into a retirement home. She was reluctant to leave furniture and artifacts that were full of memories in the basement, but the task of sorting them seemed impossible. Basements symbolize all we have buried in the unconscious mind, old guilt, regrets, and good and bad memories.

INTERPRETATIONS AND FORTUNE-TELLING MEANINGS

* If you dream you are in a cluttered, dusty, dark basement, known or unknown, you may be overwhelmed by trying to hold on to the past and should let go.
* If a cellar is dark and filled with ghosts or shadows, these represent primal fears or negative feelings you are denying at your own expense to appear Mr. or Ms. Nice Guy or Nice Gal to the world.
* If a basement or cellar has been converted into a den or game room, you have brought together your whole self in harmony and are totally on the right track.
* If you hear a locked basement or cellar door being rattled, someone or something unwelcome from your past may return but, by confronting it, you can remove it once and for all.
* A basement or cellar well-stocked with wine indicates prosperity and celebrations.
* To be clearing out a messy or overfilled basement or cellar says a major move or change will prove successful.

OUTCOME OF SANDRA'S DREAM

Sandra realized she was afraid of letting go of her old life. She booked a reputable antique and clearance company to sort the basement out. Sandra decided to take only her personal effects and buy new things for her new life.

The cellar of a house represents your hidden fears, which, once in the light of day, melt away.

Bat (Mammal)

Marlene, thirty, dreamed she was cowering in the corner of a dark cave with bats swooping all around. She covered her head and face. But when she looked up, the bats were heading toward a point of dim light she had missed in her panic. As she followed and emerged, the bats returned to the cave.

DREAM BACKGROUND AND MEANING

Marlene's fiancé, Doug, wanted her to buy a boat with him so they could travel around the globe. She was not a keen sailor and feared the water. Marlene dreaded the trip, yet refusing seemed disloyal to Doug. Bats signify our inner radar, which we ignore at our peril when someone is taking us on a path that, deep down, we do not want to follow.

INTERPRETATIONS AND FORTUNE-TELLING MEANINGS

★ Bats flying close say, "Trust and be guided by your intuition."
★ Bats sleeping in a dark cave talk of deep repressed fears that need to be brought into the light of day.
★ Being bitten by a vampire bat warns of a powerful psychological or psychic attack in the name of love.
★ Bats tangled in hair say beware of codependency, excessive guilt, or others' manipulation feeding off your energies.
★ Because bats are associated quite unfairly with evil, a bat swooping down upon you in your dream advises you to channel emerging psychic powers into healing or divination to allay uncontrolled fear.
★ A bat transformed into an alluring dark-robed human warns of a tempting lover who may be an unwise choice as a permanent love.

OUTCOME OF MARLENE'S DREAM

Marlene did not want to stand in the way of Doug's happiness but instinctively knew the trip was wrong for her. She suggested Doug crew for a year with a friend. Marlene would meet him in different ports and take sailing and water safety lessons. Bats appear in dreams when unexpressed fears prevent us from dealing with a dilemma rather than feeling at the mercy of fate.

Bear

Olaf, fifteen, frequently dreamed he was a berserker or bear warrior: fearless, leading the battle charge in the name of Odin, the Norse father god. The enemy would retreat in fear. In the dream, Olaf was far taller and stronger than any of the enemy. He woke triumphant, then remembered there was another day of bullying and teasing ahead.

DREAM BACKGROUND AND MEANING

Olaf, though of Viking descent and attracted to tales of the Vikings, was not very strong after a childhood illness. His father insisted he had to deal with the bullying and learn to be a man. Whether a past life, an encounter with a berserker spirit guide, or a spirit bear sustained him, the dreams made Olaf determined to do something about his situation.

INTERPRETATIONS AND FORTUNE-TELLING MEANINGS

★ A bear in sunshine, the symbol of King Arthur, the Sun King, says you will have a chance to assume leadership.
★ A mother bear with cubs is a fertility symbol and reassurance that you are or will be a good parent or involved positively in children's care.
★ A mother bear barring the entrance to her cave warns of overpossessiveness or interference in a maternal relationship.
★ People feeding bears offer caution about becoming too friendly with an authority figure who may suddenly pull rank.
★ A bear eating particular plants reveals that plant medicine may be helpful for your health, since it is said bears know instinctively which plants will cure them.

OUTCOME OF OLAF'S DREAM

Olaf learned martial arts to tackle the almost daily physical attacks. After a successful encounter with a tall, muscly bully, in which Olaf came off best and was suspended for fighting, he found he no longer needed to fight. He just imagined his berserker self and the bullies backed down.

Bear dreams do not mean the dreamer should necessarily physically fight, but they radiate from the dreamer the strength and courage of the bear as energies that bullies sense and back off.

Beard

Sylvia, forty-eight, dreamed she came home early from visiting relatives overseas. Her husband was at the airport and had grown a beard. He walked past her and left with a tall, younger blonde. Sylvia confronted him, and he said he was meeting his boss's fiancée. He told Sylvia to get a taxi home. Sylvia phoned his boss, who had thought her husband was on leave overseas with Sylvia.

DREAM BACKGROUND AND MEANING

Sylvia noticed that before he went overseas her husband was acting suspiciously, buying new clothes, growing a beard, and getting home late. He claimed he was just changing his image. Beards in dreams in a previously clean-shaven person can indicate a more spontaneous side of themselves emerging but can also be linked with secrets.

INTERPRETATIONS AND FORTUNE-TELLING MEANINGS

★ If someone close unexpectedly grows a beard in your dream, he may be hiding something from you.

★ A false beard says you should not take a new acquaintance at face value.

★ If someone you know shaves off their beard in the dream, it warns that they may suffer financial loss.

★ If you dream of an unknown older person with a white beard, it represents a wise influence or traditional knowledge that is proving useful; if misty, it is a spirit guide.

★ If a beard is long, the wearer, if you know them, is or will become a stable influence in your life, even if they do not have a beard in everyday life.

★ A dream of an elaborately trimmed or goatee beard hints at vanity and self-interest in the wearer.

OUTCOME OF SYLVIA'S DREAM

Sylvia confronted her husband about her suspicions. He admitted to having an affair. His beard looked scruffy. Sylvia threw him out. He returned clean-shaven a week later, saying his affair had ended. Sylvia allowed him to stay but no longer feels the same. Beard dreams indicate good fortune but also can conceal more dubious behavior.

Becoming an Author

Henry, seventy-six, regularly dreamed of sitting in a bookstore surrounded by books written by him and a queue of people lining up to have him sign them. He then went to a television studio to talk about the new detective series based on his book and the plans for a second volume. He awoke excited.

DREAM BACKGROUND AND MEANING

Henry, a retired police officer with a serious crime squad, lost his wife soon after retiring and now was lonely and bored. His ambition was to publish a compendium of crime stories based on his experiences in the force. A recurring dream of succeeding as an author is a prompt from our untapped potential to put the process in motion.

INTERPRETATIONS AND FORTUNE-TELLING MEANINGS

★ Should you regularly dream of a specific book based on existing knowledge and experience, the book is already forming and needs to be written.

★ If you are writing your life story in the dream, this refers to life generally, saying you can express your unique talents and personality in the world in any way you choose.

★ If in the dream you hear someone dictating words, this may be your spirit guide, personal muse, or someone from past worlds wanting you to tell their story. Record the words when you wake.

★ If you see yourself writing in a specific location, that place offers inspiration and information for your research.

OUTCOME OF HENRY'S DREAM

Henry joined a creative-writing circle and is being assisted in shaping the book, whether for pleasure, online publishing, or as a bestseller. As a bonus, he met a widow who loves writing and so he is no longer lonely. Dreams inspire many embryonic authors by revealing plots and characters on the dream plane.

Beds

Petronella, thirty-five, dreamed her bed was infested with bugs and she and her husband, Joel, leaped out of bed and rushed to the store to buy a spray. The store was not open and so she sealed up the room and vowed not to reenter until they replaced the bed.

DREAM BACKGROUND AND MEANING

Petronella and Joel were increasingly using the bedroom as a battleground for late-night arguments, and they no longer made love. Joel wanted them to move to his brother's environmentally based logging business. But Petronella was unwilling to leave her city job and lifestyle and move into the middle of nowhere. Bed dreams at their best represent sanctuary from the day and respite from daytime problems, which makes any bedtime dissension seem doubly bad.

A bed in a dream should be a place of positive comfort, restoration, and, if shared, of unity away from the world. However, because of its emotional significance and a sense of vulnerability, it can reveal deep-seated differences that have struck at the heart of a relationship or lifestyle.

INTERPRETATIONS AND FORTUNE-TELLING MEANINGS

⋆ A shared bed is a symbol of a comfortable relationship, of passion, or of dissent and toxicity, depending on the nature of the dream.

⋆ If a bed is uncomfortable or broken, natural peace, especially in a relationship, may have been shattered and needs fixing.

⋆ An infested bed indicates that toxicity has entered a relationship or lifestyle that may need starting over.

⋆ To wake in a dream disoriented in an unfamiliar bed or bedroom suggests you may be unsure where you belong and want to be.

⋆ If in the dream you are buying a new bed, you are entering a new phase in your life or relationship where relaxation, rest, or passion has lost its place.

OUTCOME OF PETRONELLA'S DREAM

Petronella and Joel went for counseling, but neither would compromise. They split amicably but still see each other and are hopeful they will be reunited.

Bee

Talia, twenty-seven, dreamed she was surrounded by flowers, around which bees were swarming and collecting pollen. She wanted to pick the flowers but was afraid to touch them in case she was stung. At last, she reached out toward a flower and all the bees flew upward. The bees returned to the flowers when she had collected her blooms. She woke full of hope.

DREAM BACKGROUND AND MEANING

Talia had been trying without success for a baby as a single parent, using her frozen eggs and donor sperm. There were just enough eggs for one more attempt. She was frightened of trying and failing. Bees have been fertility symbols since Neolithic times, and when they appear in the dreams of anyone trying for a baby they are a very good omen.

INTERPRETATIONS AND FORTUNE-TELLING MEANINGS

⋆ Bees on flowers are a potent sign of imminent conception and a healthy child who will be lucky all their days.

⋆ A single large bee, a queen, buzzing loudly warns of a controlling older woman who can be spiteful if crossed.

⋆ Bees flying in and out of hives are an indication of health, business or career success, and prosperity.

⋆ A bee flying into a room, or seen outside a window trying to enter, heralds good news of friends and family, usually from afar.

⋆ If you dream you are a beekeeper, expect promotion or an increase in status or recognition.

⋆ An empty hive or all the bees flying away warns of empty promises, especially in love, or ventures that will not flourish.

OUTCOME OF TALIA'S DREAM

Talia took a chance and was successful in conceiving, carrying, and delivering a healthy baby. Predictive bee dreams may be picking up the energies around the dreamer that the time is right for fulfilling a desired creative venture.

Beggar, Homeless Person

Phoebe, seventy-two, dreamed she saw a swinging door ahead and opened it. She was in an abandoned, dark street and old women in rags were pushing strollers containing their possessions in garbage bags. She had a stroller, too. Phoebe was  *terrified and tried to get back through the door, but it was one-way. She noticed her stroller was full of old clocks. She woke crying.*

DREAM BACKGROUND AND MEANING

Phoebe's husband had drained their savings and disappeared overseas with a young girlfriend. Phoebe discovered he had been taking out joint loans for years that were in arrears. Now she was threatened with the foreclosure of her home. Homelessness is a primal fear that can go deep in our psyche.

INTERPRETATIONS AND FORTUNE-TELLING MEANINGS

★ If a beggar is menacing, someone close to you is emotionally blackmailing you for money. You should refuse their demands.

★ If you are the beggar, this indicates financial worries with which you need help, and need to economize.

★ To watch yourself begging says that you feel emotionally neglected by those who should care for you.

★ Sitting in a doorway suggests you need to become more emotionally and economically self-sufficient.

★ If you are turned away from a shelter or doorway, it's time to put your own needs first as others are draining your resources and energy.

★ If you dream of an old beggar who resembles you, there may be buried fears about your own future security you need to resolve.

OUTCOME OF PHOEBE'S DREAM

Phoebe was reminded by the contents of her stroller in the dream of the collection of antique clocks she had inherited from her father. Her husband had consigned them to the attic. She had them valued, and they were worth a small fortune. Phoebe paid off her debts. Often a dream will give a clue to some resource or solution we had forgotten or disregarded.

Being Late, Missing Connections

Gabrielle, twenty-three, dreamed she was rushing to the airport to catch a flight with her fiancé, Alan, who was meeting her there. Halfway there in the taxicab, Gabrielle realized she had left her passport at home. She asked the driver to turn around. The traffic to the airport was jammed both ways. Gabrielle reached the gate as it closed. Her fiancé had departed without her. She was strangely relieved.

DREAM BACKGROUND AND MEANING

Alan was driven and made Gabrielle feel that her job was unimportant, though she was in line for a major promotion. After their marriage he wanted her to stay home. Missing a plane or opportunity because you are late questions the advisability of following a particular course of action.

INTERPRETATIONS AND FORTUNE-TELLING MEANINGS

★ If you are not habitually late, missing dream planes or events suggests you may be deliberately putting obstacles in your own way—albeit subconsciously—suggesting that the course of action you are taking may not be what you really want.

★ If you find timekeeping a problem in life, your dream warns you to plan your life better to allow for unforeseen delays.

★ If you dream you are a child late for school, you are being pressured by authority figures in adulthood with impossible demands.

★ If you are constantly running to catch a train or plane in dreams, life is going too fast.

★ If others in the dream cause you to be late or miss transport or a major event, see who is holding you back and question their motives.

★ If a traveling companion does not wait if you are delayed in the dream, do you usually make all the concessions?

★ Regular dreams of missing trains, planes, or appointments indicate mental overload, suggesting you reprioritize what is essential.

OUTCOME OF GABRIELLE'S DREAM

Gabrielle realized she was being swept along by Alan into a role she did not want to take. She broke off the engagement. Lateness in dreams warns us to not let our schedules be dictated by others.

Bells

Tomas, sixty-four, dreamed the doorbell was ringing. He looked through the window and saw it was his next-door neighbor. The bell kept ringing. Finally, he could stand it no more and opened the door furiously. His neighbor was holding Tomas's cat that had been injured and offered to drive Tomas to the vet.

DREAM BACKGROUND AND MEANING

Tomas's doorbell was his defense against the world, especially against his neighbor, who only rang to complain about Tomas's cat going in his garden. Tomas had stopped answering the doorbell, since his only son had moved overseas and people no longer rang to visit. Bells can act as a welcome and invitation to togetherness or as a warning of danger or intrusion and, according to the specific dream, may bring news or attract or repel people.

INTERPRETATIONS AND FORTUNE-TELLING MEANINGS

⋆ If in your dream you hear church bells ringing in celebration, there will be a joyous event for you, a close friend, or a family member.

⋆ If you hear a warning bell, either a church bell or an alarm, travel plans should be checked and domestic security increased, as your radar may have picked up potential problems.

⋆ A single bell tolling heralds an ending, which you should face in order to move to a new beginning.

⋆ If you are ringing an alarm bell in the dream, you may be unconsciously aware of potential pitfalls and hazards that others are ignoring.

⋆ If you hear bells ringing in the distance, continue with plans, as a welcome or advantage will be waiting.

⋆ If you hear legendary bells under the sea or a lake, indicating a buried or drowned city, old sorrows should be released.

OUTCOME OF TOMAS'S DREAM

Tomas's neighbor did ring the bell to say he had heard Tomas's cat meowing in a nearby shed. The cat had been hurt in a fight. Tomas made a higher fence so his cat stayed in his own garden. Bells should not be ignored in dreams, as they are often alerting the dreamer to something they need to know.

Belt

Mike, fifty, had a recurring dream that he was a young teenager. His father was threatening him with his big leather belt. Mike snatched it and started laying into his father until his father begged for mercy. Mike walked out, crying but triumphant.

DREAM BACKGROUND AND MEANING

Mike had been brutally beaten as a child with his father's belt buckle. He ended up in foster care, where he was also brutalized. Since then, he only wore soft fabric belts. Now his father was dying, and Mike's wife said to make peace with the man or Mike might regret it. An ornate leather belt can be a macho sign of physical and sexual control, but also has far less sinister dream meanings for a timid person.

INTERPRETATIONS AND FORTUNE-TELLING MEANINGS

⋆ If you dream that a belt is too tight, you are feeling restricted by the pettiness and narrow-mindedness of someone at work or home.

⋆ If you lose your belt or it breaks and your clothes do not fit, you are worried about keeping up appearances.

⋆ If a belt is too loose and you keep adjusting trousers or skirt in the dream, you may have an image problem.

⋆ Buying a new belt represents acquiring security in the area of life most needed.

⋆ An ornate belt buckle in the dream exposes much of the inner world of the person wearing it.

⋆ A dream of a person not wearing a seat belt in a car or plane during turbulence indicates overreliance on luck.

OUTCOME OF MIKE'S DREAM

Mike, wearing a fearsome leather belt, went to see his father in the hospice. His father was shrunken, broken, and terrified of dying. Mike comforted him and knew it was the last time he would see him. On the way home, he threw the belt in the river, putting the past to rest. Belts represent security and identity as they cover the solar plexus energy center. Where they hold bad memories, a dream can release the dreamer from the past.

Bereavement

Chaoxiang, forty-seven, had regular nightmares that when he went into his parents' bedroom at 6:00 a.m. with their morning cup of tea, neither could be awoken. He dropped the teas on the carpet and lay down with them on their bed, crying.

DREAM BACKGROUND AND MEANING

Chaoxiang moved to the United States with his parents from China when he was twelve years old. Chaoxiang had never married and lived with his parents in their New York home. They were in their mid-seventies and very fit. As a family they were close, and Chaoxiang dreaded the day his parents would no longer be with him.

INTERPRETATIONS AND FORTUNE-TELLING MEANINGS

★ A bereavement dream never predicts someone dying unless they are known to be passing over, when the dream shares a peaceful passing.

★ If you dream of an older relative dying before their time, you are rehearsing feelings at the prospect of their death. This may be more about your own need to make a separate life so you do not die emotionally with them.

★ If you dream about mourning a younger person, this is a natural anxiety dream, unless you are worried about excessive risk-taking, in which case warn them to be careful.

★ If you dream of dying at the same time as a relative, you may need to examine your long-term plans to see if you are overdependent or codependent.

★ If you feel relieved and then guilty in a dream about a particular relative dying, there may be buried justifiable anger that you should resolve during their lifetime.

OUTCOME OF CHAOXIANG'S DREAM

Chaoxiang realized he had based his life solely around his parents. He returned to China, where he still had relatives, got married, and started a business; he often brought his wife to visit his parents. Bereavement dreams can represent separation anxiety at any age, which should be resolved while the family is still alive and well.

Bicycle

Liz, twenty-eight, was a young teenager in her dream, cycling along a flat road with the sun shining. Suddenly it started to rain heavily and Liz stopped to put on her raincoat. At that moment, her father arrived in his car to take her home. Liz thanked him but said she could make her own way. Liz arrived, not at her childhood home, but at the tiny city-center apartment she was renting with her partner—and realized she was an adult again.

DREAM BACKGROUND AND MEANING

Liz's father was pressuring her to move to the house next door to him, which he owned; it would be rent- and expense-free, which was tempting. She knew if she accepted she would be the little girl forever. Defining the adult separate self is a common dilemma when a loving but possessive parent finds it hard to let go.

INTERPRETATIONS AND FORTUNE-TELLING MEANINGS

★ If you dream you are riding a bicycle, you are traveling through life at your own speed and under your own steam.

★ Happiness cycling along a smooth road in good weather indicates a successful outcome to any independent venture.

★ Buying a bicycle presents an opportunity to downsize from a frantic, material-based lifestyle.

★ A flat tire heralds obstacles to business or personal success, which can be fixed with the right strategies and effort.

★ If you refuse a lift and ride your bicycle, this is a reminder of the desirability of freedom without conditions, emotionally as well as physically.

★ Riding downhill too fast or not wearing a helmet reveals taking unnecessary risks, whereas pushing a bicycle up a steep hill shows mounting opposition, requiring perseverance to overcome.

OUTCOME OF LIZ'S DREAM

Liz refused her father's offer of free accommodation next door, and she and her partner scrimped and saved till they bought their own first home. They cycled to work to save money. Cycle dreams suggest it is better to live on your own terms than to accept an easy ride.

Big Break, Scoop

Dora, thirty-four, dreamed the editor said that because everyone else on the journal was covering major stories, she should go to the White House to see what she could uncover about a rumored major scandal. As it was her first real assignment, she was so nervous that she forgot her press pass and was refused entry. Determined not to lose her big chance, she started chatting to an employee, who punched in her own security code, and Dora went through security with the woman seconds before the doors closed. She got her major scoop.

DREAM BACKGROUND AND MEANING

Dora loved working for a major Washington daily newspaper, but she spent her days making coffee for senior journalists. Big-break dreams, while predictive, reveal areas where the dreamer needs to make an extra effort.

INTERPRETATIONS AND FORTUNE-TELLING MEANINGS

⋆ If you dream of a breakthrough in your career, see how by using the ingenuity you showed in the dream you overcame barriers, and apply that to real life.

⋆ If you dream of a break because others are too busy, the dream advises you to be alert to every opportunity.

⋆ If you see a chance slipping away in a dream but retrieve the chance, you will soon get an opportunity. Be prepared.

⋆ If a rival in your dream gets the big break instead of you, watch for underhandedness.

⋆ If areas in the dream indicate where that big break may occur, be alert for them.

⋆ If you are more proactive in the dream than in daily life, imitate the tactics you used in the dream to win.

OUTCOME OF DORA'S DREAM

The dream taught Dora to be prepared and ingenious rather than waiting for fame to come knocking. She was at the office first, left last, and was constantly scanning the wires for big stories not yet broken. Big breaks sometimes come by chance, but dreams generate the necessary impetus and enthusiasm.

Bigfoot

Simon, fifty-five, dreamed he was camping in the wilderness in British Columbia. In the trees he saw a huge, hairy ape-man figure and knew it was Bigfoot. Entranced, Simon stood and watched. Eventually Bigfoot lumbered off into the forest.

DREAM BACKGROUND AND MEANING

Simon had been studying cryptozoology as a hobby for years. He believed Bigfoot did exist in visible spirit form. Simon wanted to take early retirement and travel, collecting data with a view to publishing his theories and hopefully sighting the beast. If you see Bigfoot in a dream, you may be viewing him on the astral or spirit plane and should try to identify the Earth-based location in the dream, hopefully to actually repeat the experience.

INTERPRETATIONS AND FORTUNE-TELLING MEANINGS

⋆ If you are terrified of your dream Bigfoot, you may have unacknowledged fears in your life you need to resolve.

⋆ If you dream you are broadcasting or signing a book you have written about Bigfoot, you are ready to explore the possibilities and wonders of life outside your present lifestyle.

⋆ If you see Bigfoot but no one in the dream believes you when you tell them, you have a huge undertaking where you will need to go it alone.

⋆ If you see Bigfoot in the presence of others but they cannot see him, you have clairvoyant powers you should develop and trust.

⋆ If you follow Bigfoot into another dimension, this is a very special dream and an affirmation that there is more to life than the physically visible.

⋆ If you are trying to save Bigfoot from being caught by hunters, you may need to defend your principles.

OUTCOME OF SIMON'S DREAM

After the dream, Simon resigned and earned a degree in parapsychology with a view to join a US cryptozoology research team.

It is said a Bigfoot has telepathic powers, and in Bigfoot dreams you may be aligning psychically on the dream plane with one of these amazing creatures.

Birth-Family Links

Archie, twenty-six, dreamed he was walking through a blues festival and stopped and stared at an older musician with a clarinet, which Archie also played; the man was an older version of himself. The musician also stopped and said, "My son," and Archie replied, "My father." The crowds separated them. Archie knew it was his birth father. He woke trying to find him again in the crowd.

DREAM BACKGROUND AND MEANING

Archie's mother had died giving birth to him. Archie was happy with his adoptive parents and therefore had never had a desire to find his birth father. However, since the dream Archie had thought a lot about his father. Dreams can awaken birth-family links at a time when one person suddenly thinks of the other.

INTERPRETATIONS AND FORTUNE-TELLING MEANINGS

★ To suddenly dream of a birth parent who resembles you suggests that a telepathic link has been awakened.

★ If you are seeking a birth parent, a dream can offer clues about where the missing parent may be.

★ If you do not wish to make contact, dreaming of the unknown parent is a reminder that seemingly inexplicable interests may have roots in a genetic link.

★ If you dream of unknown relatives, it may be the anniversary of a special time when you are remembered by the missing family.

★ If dreams recur, you may need to make contact, if only once, to fill in a missing part of your life.

★ If you wake feeling angry after a birth-parent dream link, there may be subconscious abandonment issues.

OUTCOME OF ARCHIE'S DREAM

Archie looked through websites for those with an interest in blues. He discovered a photo of a man who at fifty still hoped to turn professional as a clarinetist. Archie read his life story and discovered remarkable similarities. Archie did not contact the man he believed was his father. A dream link may be sufficient to establish birth roots for an adopted child, without opening further doors.

Birthday

Josh, seventeen, dreamed of a special party for his eighteenth birthday. All his friends had been invited, and his parents hired a special venue and his favorite band. He was surrounded by gifts. He woke excited with only two weeks to go.

DREAM BACKGROUND AND MEANING

Josh's parents had not mentioned his party, so he assumed it was a surprise. When on his birthday morning his father said nothing, Josh smiled as he knew this was to put him off the scent. But his parents said they were going away for the weekend. He realized they had forgotten his birthday. After Josh mentioned it, his father gave him fifty dollars to buy his friends a birthday drink. Josh was devastated.

INTERPRETATIONS AND FORTUNE-TELLING MEANINGS

★ If you dream of a birthday celebration and it materializes, this indicates a fortunate year ahead.

★ If you dream of a fabulous celebration and it does not occur, it will be a year when you will have to work hard to fulfill your own expectations.

★ If you dream of receiving a special birthday gift, unexpected good luck in the form of an offer will bring rewards.

★ If your partner forgets your birthday, they may be taking you for granted.

★ If no one remembers your birthday, your expectations of others are too high.

★ If you dream you are organizing a friend's, partner's, or relative's birthday celebration and they are pleased, this is a good sign for mutual give-and-take in the year ahead.

OUTCOME OF JOSH'S DREAM

Josh realized his dream had been a wish-fulfillment dream, since his parents had never celebrated birthdays or Christmases. However, his friends took him out for a good evening on the town. Birthday dreams can have huge hopes attached, not just of the celebration, but for the expression of love in what may be an emotionally constipated family.

Blackbird

Helga, fifty-three, regularly dreamed of a particular blackbird, which perched on her hand to be fed and heralded good fortune the following day. In a very vivid dream, the blackbird dropped a piece of paper on her lap with the name of a hospital in Western Australia. That was the last blackbird dream she had.

DREAM BACKGROUND AND MEANING

Helga was suffering from a progressive disease that was slowly taking away movement and speech. Her Swedish physicians said they could only treat the symptoms but not stop the condition. Helga constantly researched new treatments and had even traveled to the most promising without effect. Why should she take any notice of this dream? Blackbirds, as symbols of mobility and happiness, offer clues to useful information, often involving travel, whether predictive or already on our radar but not consciously followed up.

INTERPRETATIONS AND FORTUNE-TELLING MEANINGS

- ✦ Since blackbirds defend their territory against larger predators, a blackbird indicates you will win a fight against a serious problem or intimidating authority figure if you persist.
- ✦ A blackbird singing says, "Do not be silenced as you have much of worth to say and will be heard."
- ✦ A blackbird flying into your home in a dream says you should be wary of visitors spreading gloom and pessimism.
- ✦ If two blackbirds are fighting over territory, you may need to prevent someone from trying to control you or taking what is rightfully yours.
- ✦ If your blackbird is red-winged or yellow-headed, someone who seems very quiet and reticent should not be underestimated, as they are more switched on than appears.

OUTCOME OF HELGA'S DREAM

Helga recalled that two or three years earlier she had read of the hospital's initial research into her condition, but did not pursue it. Now the hospital was asking for volunteers for new trials. Taking part involved crossing half the world, but initial results are hopeful. Blackbirds were considered healers in Celtic tradition, so a dreamer can have confidence in new healing possibilities.

Blacksmith

Dan, thirty, dreamed he was a Viking blacksmith shoeing the horses of warriors and performing magick around the blazing forge as he turned nails into lucky wolf and bear amulets to protect the warriors. He woke wanting to be part of that world forever.

DREAM BACKGROUND AND MEANING

Dan was a devotee of Viking reenactments and, though he was a welder and could shoe horses, he wanted to go to Scandinavia, where he knew there were blacksmiths following the old ways and recreating Viking grave goods. His family ridiculed him, but he knew the old ways should be kept alive. Blacksmith dreams can be a magical image and may link the dreamer with a particular land and tradition.

INTERPRETATIONS AND FORTUNE-TELLING MEANINGS

- ✦ A blacksmith forming molten objects with fire in a forge may be a past-life dream or memory and promises increased wealth soon.
- ✦ A blacksmith hammering a horseshoe on an anvil says you will achieve your goals if you are prepared to travel.
- ✦ Because the forge and anvil were traditionally associated with marriage and fertility, dreams about you and your partner in a forge heralds a wedding and baby.
- ✦ Dreaming of rituals around a forge promises unexpected magical insights and the manifestation of wishes.
- ✦ The link of creating with fire makes forge dreams a good omen for any craftsperson or creator to find inspiration.
- ✦ If lucky horseshoes are hanging on the forge wall, an approaching time of good fortune will follow.

OUTCOME OF DAN'S DREAM

After the dream, Dan knew what he wanted: to learn the old Viking arts of the forge. He learned Swedish, obtained a job as a welder in Stockholm, and has apprenticed himself in his spare time to a historic guild that is reviving the Viking art of recreating grave goods. Blacksmith dreams often link with old traditions and call those who wish to keep the old ways alive.

Blood

Dan, twenty-five, dreamed he was tied to an altar in Mesoamerica, waiting to be sacrificed so that his blood might be spilled on the ground to bring the rains. As the eldest son of the chief, he was chosen as the sacrifice. Then a huge storm struck and the rains came. He sawed at his bindings with a sharp stone until he was free. He ran, leaving a trail of blood, completing the sacrifice.

DREAM BACKGROUND AND MEANING

Dan's twin sister was very ill with a blood disorder. Since they both had a very rare blood group, Dan promised to donate his blood for the many transfusions she would need. His university was sponsoring a trip to see the Mesoamerican ruins at the time of her treatments, and no one else in the family was a match. She told him he should go, and she would have the treatment when he came back. But he couldn't take the risk. Dreams about blood highlight moral dilemmas.

INTERPRETATIONS AND FORTUNE-TELLING MEANINGS

✷ Blood can be a positive dream symbol indicating energy, action, fertility, a free-flowing life-force, and health.

✷ If in the dream one's own blood is shed on behalf of others, you may fear losing your essential self for a possibly unworthy cause.

✷ If you are bleeding from a wound inflicted by someone you know, you may feel your energy is being drained from you.

✷ If you are trying to stop a wound from bleeding, you may be afraid that something important in your life is slipping away.

✷ Menstrual blood in a dream is a symbol of the strength of the Ancient Egyptian Mother Goddess Isis and support, especially for single parents.

✷ If you dream of a vampire sucking your blood, it may be a complex symbol of codependency or a fatal attraction.

OUTCOME OF DAN'S DREAM

Dan saw his sister through the treatment and never regretted it, as she fully recovered. Dan knew he would not easily be able to go on the trip again. Blood dreams rarely offer easy solutions or quick fixes, but open the way to cosmic exchange.

Body Image

Heidi, fifteen, was a famous model in her dream, incredibly thin, and all her friends watching were envious. But as she reached the end of the catwalk, she fainted. An even thinner friend from the audience took her place.

DREAM BACKGROUND AND MEANING

Heidi and her friends were permanently on strict diets. Heidi was constantly hungry and had lost all her energy. She was on the verge of giving up excess dieting, but her friends said no one would ever date her if she was fat. Dreams, especially among teens and twentysomethings, about being accepted by peers as attractive may act as early warnings that the body is protesting.

INTERPRETATIONS AND FORTUNE-TELLING MEANINGS

✷ If you dream you suddenly go from hugely overweight to thin and back again in the presence of peers, you may be overinfluenced by others' expectations and out of touch with your own needs.

✷ If you are successful in a career depending purely on body image, ask yourself how you can stay healthy and still attain it.

✷ If you dream you are a starving person in a famine, take up a cause to relieve real food poverty.

✷ If you are larger than all your friends in a dream or reality, ask yourself if they are really friends or if you should find a friendship group who like you as you are.

✷ If there is danger in a dream because of excess dieting, what is the payoff of seeking a self-destructive image, and is it worthwhile?

OUTCOME OF HEIDI'S DREAM

After the dream, the friend who took her place on the dream catwalk was rushed to the hospital with the effects of an eating disorder. Heidi realized it could have been her. She started a self-help group for students with body-image issues and plans to study psychology and not become a model. Many younger people have body-image nightmares because of the pressures to conform to celebrity ideals.

Body Piercing

Melvyn, a twenty-five-year-old lawyer, dreamed he had every part of his body pierced, had long hair, and wore brightly colored clothes. He went into the office and everyone stared, but he said he could do his job just as well no matter how he looked. When he reached court to defend his client, the judge threw him out.

DREAM BACKGROUND AND MEANING

Melvyn felt he was a fish out of water. His firm was only interested in wealthy clients and charged high fees when the work could have been completed much faster and cost less. Body piercings represent the desire for individuality and nonconformity that may be at odds with the person's outward appearance.

INTERPRETATIONS AND FORTUNE-TELLING MEANINGS

* If any part of your body is pierced in the dream, even if not in reality, you need to make a statement or take a stand.
* If the piercing is very painful in the dream, are you prepared to make sacrifices to attract the recognition you desire?
* Pierced ears, increasing in meaning according to the number of piercings, represent a need to listen to what is being said and to make your opinions heard.
* A nipple or navel ring talks of matters of the heart and following instincts, often in a relationship where you are unappreciated.
* A nose ring says you should not be limited by others' opinions or approval.
* A tongue ring signifies something you wish to say that may be controversial.

OUTCOME OF MELVYN'S DREAM

After the dream, Melvyn found a legal role in a community charity center advising, defending, and organizing accommodations and educational programs for young people who had left home because of problems. He had a single ear piercing, which made him popular with clients. Body-piercing dreams may cause the dreamer to evaluate what matters to them and reveal their true selves.

Bodyguard

Dylan, twenty-five, dreamed he was a celebrity, surrounded by bodyguards. He saw his family in the crowd and ordered his bodyguards to keep them away from him. However, in the morning he was disappointed to see the only pictures in the newspaper were of his bodyguards shielding him.

DREAM BACKGROUND AND MEANING

Dylan's family was constantly asking when he was going to settle down with a nice girl and give his parents grandchildren. He had told them he was gay, but they insisted it was a passing phase and arranged date after date with girls they considered suitable. Eventually he moved away. Bodyguard dreams often occur when the dreamer feels pressure to become what others want to keep the peace.

INTERPRETATIONS AND FORTUNE-TELLING MEANINGS

* If you dream of being a bodyguard to a close friend or family member, you may be protecting them from their unwise actions, maybe at your own expense.
* If you have a bodyguard in a dream, you may fear acting independently and need the support of others.
* If you realize the bodyguard is yourself, though shown as a separate character, you may be shielding yourself from challenges by others.
* If in the dream you hire a bodyguard, you may be trying to stop someone from becoming too close or intrusive.
* If you are acting as bodyguard to an important politician or celebrity, you may be defending principles that you may not believe to impress someone whose approval you seek.
* If your bodyguard deserts you or fails to protect you, you may be relying on others too much to shield you from matters only you can resolve.

OUTCOME OF DYLAN'S DREAM

Dylan realized that shielding himself from the family was cutting him off from their positive aspects. He went home with his new partner. The family confronted the difficult issues and welcomed his new partner. Bodyguards in dreams offer protection but can isolate the person being protected from meaningful close relationships.

Bomb

Gary, thirty-two, dreamed he was in a bomb disposal unit in wartime London, defusing unexploded bombs. It was essential to have silence as he turned the dial on the bomb. A little boy came from nowhere, calling excitedly. The vibrations could set off the bomb. He beckoned the child and, resting the boy against him, deactivated the bomb. He woke shaking with relief.

DREAM BACKGROUND AND MEANING

Gary was in the middle of a custody battle. His ex-wife was claiming custody of their five-year-old son, but she had serious psychological problems that neither the court nor her physician were aware of. Gary knew there was a risk she would run away with their son. Delicate negotiations were essential so Gary could have custody of his son, who could see his mother under controlled conditions. Exploding bombs in a dream represent lasting destruction, but defusing them will be hazardous (see "Air Raids," p. 25).

INTERPRETATIONS AND FORTUNE-TELLING MEANINGS

★ A dream of a bomb exploding where it can do no harm means pent-up negative energies will be released.

★ If you dream that you or your home is being bombed, you may fear a situation becoming out of control through someone's aggressive attitude toward you.

★ If you dream you find an unexploded bomb, repressed emotions that are hidden even from yourself should be expressed in a controlled way.

★ To safely defuse a bomb says you have the power to reduce an escalating tense situation.

★ A bomb threat signifies trying to keep matters under control.

★ If you dream that a bomb explodes, doing damage, a potentially volatile situation should be avoided.

OUTCOME OF GARY'S DREAM

Before the final hearing, Gary's ex-wife went clubbing, leaving their son alone. Gary got custody and moved close to his ex-wife, who was told she could see the boy if she had treatment. Gary walks a delicate tightrope, but the dream has given him hope that he can keep his son safe. A bomb dream may be a past-life dream, but it always demands action or caution in the waking world.

Bones

Olive, fifty-six, dreamed that her bones were crumbling and she could not move. She called for help but no one heard, and she could not reach the telephone. Realizing she was dreaming, she stood up and telephoned not the ambulance, but the university where she had been considering applying for a senior-citizen grant to take a higher degree in religious studies, her special interest.

DREAM BACKGROUND AND MEANING

Olive's mother had suffered from osteoporosis. Regular checkups showed Olive was clear, but she still worried about future immobility. Now her life was crumbling, as her employer of fifteen years had reassigned her duties, while incentivizing her to take early retirement. But Olive had recently discovered lucid dreaming (the ability to know you are dreaming and change the ending). Lucid dreaming, once learned, can transform a nightmare into a positive solution to be pursued in daily life.

INTERPRETATIONS AND FORTUNE-TELLING MEANINGS

★ To dream of bones after a good dinner says you should seize opportunities to enjoy life to the full.

★ Crumbling bones speak of feeling helpless if change is imminent.

★ If you dream you are burying the bones of a dead bird or animal, it's time to accept what cannot be mended.

★ If you dream of a family member or good friend revealed in a dream as being unduly thin beneath their clothes, they may have an eating disorder and need help.

★ If you fracture a bone in the dream, be careful if you are engaging in extreme activities, but this also can indicate the divulging of a secret.

★ If you dream you are cutting spare meat off a bone and boiling the bones, you may need to find a new source of income.

OUTCOME OF OLIVE'S DREAM

Olive had seen the senior study grant advertised, and she applied following the dream. She used her early retirement as a bonus to restructure her life. Dreams can be a means of overcoming fears, turning them into opportunity within the dream and then into reality.

Books

Jessica, twenty-six, dreamed she was cleaning out the family attic when she came across a book from her childhood that she had loved about a little girl named Maud, who had gone off alone around the world to find the best place to live and had come home because that was best of all. As she turned the pages, Jessica realized she had visited many of the places of which Maud talked. Once she read it, the book crumbled, leaving an empty cover.

DREAM BACKGROUND AND MEANING

Jessica had come home because her grandmother was frail, in palliative care, and not expected to live more than a year. Jessica had volunteered to put her career on hold and live with her grandmother, who had reared her from childhood. But Jessica was having doubts. Books in dreams can be reminders of a less active but more thoughtful approach to life.

INTERPRETATIONS AND FORTUNE-TELLING MEANINGS

* If in a dream you are reading a book, conventional wisdom may be of most use to you now. Study it for answers.
* An open book represents a new opportunity through study of traditional material, or success in legal matters.
* A closed book can indicate that the usual sources of help are unavailable or officialdom is proving obstructive.
* If you are writing a book in your dream, you have much to communicate through the written rather than spoken word.
* If you dream you are seeking the answer to a burning question in a book and drawing a blank, ask an expert for advice.
* Being given a book represents recognition of your achievements and usually a financial reward.

OUTCOME OF JESSICA'S DREAM

As in the Maud book, Jessica realized it was best to remain at home. She tracked down a copy of the book. In times of doubt, she turns the pages, remembering where she has been and will go again. Sometimes coming home is an irreplaceable act of love. A dusty bookshelf is a reminder of wisdom acquired from earlier years, but which may have been forgotten or undeveloped.

Bookstore

Della, thirty-five, dreamed she was running a bookstore when books were first being printed, but some of the manuscripts were considered heretical so she had to keep them hidden. A richly dressed man offered to buy all her special books, but she was afraid it was a trap. She woke feeling she had found her home and returned in many subsequent dreams.

DREAM BACKGROUND AND MEANING

Since reading a historical novel about a young girl taking over her father's bookshop in the times of Mary Tudor in old London, Della knew she had to find a job in an antiquarian bookstore, though she had no training or knowledge of that world. Dreams, especially those triggered by a book, television show, or film, seem sometimes to awaken a deep-rooted passion never felt before and innate knowledge never before recognized.

INTERPRETATIONS AND FORTUNE-TELLING MEANINGS

* Dreaming of buying a particular book in a bookstore indicates by the title an area of knowledge relevant to your future.
* To be working with old or rare books suggests you may be an old soul.
* If you own a bookstore in your dream, you may be a future writer.
* If in your dream a bookstore is empty of books and customers, resources you had hoped to access are not available to you.
* If you are in a huge bookstore and cannot find the section you want, you may be overwhelmed by choices in your life.
* If you dream that a book you buy or sell is on a taboo subject, you are prepared to risk disapproval to break free of prejudice, though you may feel guilty.

OUTCOME OF DELLA'S DREAM

At last Della found a job, running a tea shop attached to an antiquarian bookstore. The owner was constantly surprised by Della's seemingly untaught knowledge of ancient manuscripts, and he made her manager when he retired. Dreams can reveal unusual passions and seemingly inexplicable empathy with a world the dreamer never before considered.

Border

Sylvia, thirty, dreamed she was traveling through Southeast Asia, but had lost her documents as she attempted to cross a major land border to where her fiancé was waiting. The border guards became very angry and waved guns at her. Sylvia ran back, and they started shooting at her. She was wounded and lost her phone as she fell.

DREAM BACKGROUND AND MEANING

Sylvia was planning to join her Indonesian partner, Ajij, to meet his family for the first time. She knew his family had a very traditional lifestyle. After college, Ajij had returned home to help with the family business. Sylvia struggled to obtain the right visas to his country. The dream was an anxiety dream, signifying that a border can mark two very different lifestyles.

INTERPRETATIONS AND FORTUNE-TELLING MEANINGS

★ If you dream you are escaping over the border of a country, you are feeling stifled by your work or home life, but are afraid to say anything.

★ Crossing borders in a dream talks of unexpected travel opportunities and a change in your lifestyle that offers freedom, but also uncertainty over leaving the familiar.

★ Planting a border of flowers around your home or garden, if very orderly, compartmentalizes different areas of your life. An overgrown border suggests that personal and professional boundaries may be blurred.

★ If you dream that a border between countries is closed or you are turned away, it may not be easy for you to be accepted in a new workplace, family, or lifestyle.

★ If you are erecting a new border post, you may be seeking to emotionally distance yourself within a relationship.

OUTCOME OF SYLVIA'S DREAM

Sylvia decided to wait until her fiancé could travel with her from the United Kingdom. She realized that the border dream reflected her unspoken uncertainty about fitting in to a different world. Some borders can be imperceptible, whereas others mark the need to adapt to two different lives to avoid being stuck in no-man's-land between.

Border Control

Evelyn, seventy-one and recently widowed, dreamed she was going through customs. The unfriendly looking customs officer opened her case, pulled out all her clothes and the souvenirs and gifts she'd bought for her family, and threw them on the floor. He told her she had to pay fifty dollars' duty on her purchases. In addition, she owed a fine of a thousand dollars. She was in tears when she woke.

DREAM BACKGROUND AND MEANING

Evelyn was left a large sum of money when her husband passed away and wanted to buy a ticket to fly around the world. As a fan of television shows in which travelers go through customs and get caught with illegal goods for which they are fined or arrested, she was worried she might make a mistake and be arrested in a foreign country. Dreams of customs officers can reflect the fear a law-abiding dreamer has of breaking the rules in an unfamiliar situation.

INTERPRETATIONS AND FORTUNE-TELLING MEANINGS

★ If you dream you are waved through border control on a planned trip, all will go well.

★ To dream of being stopped by customs for carrying illegal goods links with a fear of authority.

★ If you are a fan of border-control programs, worries of being arrested may emerge in dreams, though the fear is unfounded.

★ If you dream of being denied entry to a country by customs officers, you may not really want to go.

★ If you dream customs officers are questioning you, you may have unresolved guilt about leaving your loved ones.

★ If you dream you are a customs officer stopping a friend or relative, you may be worried that they are close to breaking the law, and you may need to speak out.

OUTCOME OF EVELYN'S DREAM

Evelyn initially traveled with a group tour for senior citizens, where everything was taken care of. She had a good trip and now is planning to travel independently. Border-control dreams can be triggered by fear of being alone and unprotected.

Boxing

Brandon, seventeen, dreamed he was walking out of the dressing room as he heard his name called: "Ladies and gentlemen . . . challenging for the title is Brandon." Brandon walked toward the boxing ring with hundreds cheering him on. As he climbed into the ring, the referee approached him. Brandon ran from the ring but then returned and knocked down his opponent. The referee was his father.

DREAM BACKGROUND AND MEANING

Brandon was an avid boxing fan and had told his father he wanted to train as a professional fighter. His father, a domineering character, insisted that Brandon go to college. Brandon had been training at a boxing gym and paying his way with an evening job. He knew his father would continue to harangue him to give up boxing. Should he back down to keep the peace? Boxing dreams reveal the need to fight against someone intimidating.

INTERPRETATIONS AND FORTUNE-TELLING MEANINGS

★ If you dream of boxing, you may have suppressed hostility toward someone appearing in the dream as opponent or referee.

★ If you want to be a boxer, a successful boxing dream indicates you will succeed, but will face opposition.

★ If you are not involved in boxing, a dream victory indicates success in another sport, career, or study where you have fierce competition.

★ If you are refereeing a boxing match, beware of being pressured to support one side over another, especially if the boxers are recognizable in your waking life.

★ If you are in a boxing ring, resting between rounds, you may have a lot of emotions you are keeping inside that need expressing.

OUTCOME OF BRANDON'S DREAM

Brandon discovered boxing scholarships at various colleges where he could get a free college education as well. He stood up to his father, saying that he would go it alone if necessary. Brandon invited his father to see his junior championship match and, to his amazement, his father was proud when he won.

Boxing dreams can give the courage to outface bullies and change the energies around the dreamer, so others respect their opinion.

Bracelet

Lucinda, twenty, dreamed she was on a canoe with her fiancé when her bracelet fell into the water. She tried to retrieve it and tipped the canoe. Her annoyed fiancé swam to shore, leaving her to rescue herself.

DREAM BACKGROUND AND MEANING

Lucinda had a silver charm bracelet, to which her parents added a new charm each birthday. The bracelet was getting tight, and she reluctantly left it with the jeweler, as she was afraid that not wearing it would bring bad luck. When the jeweler could not find it later on, her fiancé told her to demand compensation and forget it, as she could easily buy another. In a dream, bracelets represent protection, especially from emotional hurt.

INTERPRETATIONS AND FORTUNE-TELLING MEANINGS

★ If you dream of being gifted a bracelet, you will have love or the increase of love by the donor.

★ If you dream of wearing a charm bracelet, you will enjoy continuing good fortune. A charm that stands out signifies extra good fortune in the area of life symbolized by the charm.

★ If you lose a charm bracelet in your dream, you may fear that good fortune depends on fate and not on your own efforts.

★ If you dream you are wearing a silver bracelet, this represents new love, trust, and family affection; if gold, lasting love; if copper, health.

★ If you dream that your bracelet breaks or you lose it, you may worry that a relationship is too fragile to last.

★ If you dream of buying yourself a bracelet, especially a charm bracelet, take control of your own destiny rather than relying on others.

OUTCOME OF LUCINDA'S DREAM

The jeweler traced the bracelet, and Lucinda realized that she had not been unlucky when not wearing it. However, she was disappointed in her fiancé's total indifference to her distress at the sentimental value of the missing bracelet. Bracelets are the route to the heart, and their loss can bring to the surface awareness that a lover is less than caring.

Bread

Hannah, thirty-three, a single mother, dreamed she was in an old cottage and her children were crying with hunger. She had no flour to bake bread. She went to the market and stole a loaf from a stall, but was caught and transported to the colonies. Her children were taken from her.

DREAM BACKGROUND AND MEANING

Hannah was in severe financial difficulties. Her husband had recently deserted her and her welfare benefits were slow in arriving. She was missing meals herself to feed the children, but was afraid she might lose them, and she could not get a job to fit in with school hours. Bread features in many past-life dreams, as it is a common staple in many cultures and ages.

INTERPRETATIONS AND FORTUNE-TELLING MEANINGS

★ Dreaming of eating bread says money and good fortune will come into your home.

★ Baking bread indicates happy family gatherings and mutual care.

★ If you dream that you run out of flour or other ingredients, you are being asked to cope with more than you can manage and should seek help.

★ Offering bread around the table indicates you will be rewarded for your generosity.

★ If the bread has gone moldy, sources of finance are not coming through and you may be picking up past-life flashbacks of a time when you were starving.

★ Since bread is sacred in many religions, to offer bread on an altar indicates your prayers will soon be answered in the form of practical help.

OUTCOME OF HANNAH'S DREAM

Hannah fainted at the children's school and admitted she had not been eating so that she could feed the children, but had not revealed the problems for fear the children would be taken from her. She was put in touch with a food bank, and the children were immediately enrolled in breakfast and lunch clubs. The head teacher contacted social welfare and made sure Hannah's payments were processed quickly. Bread dreams often deal with emotional issues and reveal the reasons for buried fears.

Breadcrumbing (Leading a Lover On)

Rachel, twenty-two, dreamed that she received a text from Christopher, her online lover, telling her that he had "strong feelings" for her and he would like to take the relationship to the next level. Then she noticed he had copied six different girls into the same message.

DREAM BACKGROUND AND MEANING

Rachel and Christopher had been speaking online for six months, but at no stage had Christopher offered any indication that he would like to take the relationship further, although he said she was "wonderful and sexy." But every time she responded saying how much she cared, he went silent for days or sent a dismissive reply. *Breadcrumbing* describes the behavior of showing another person occasional signs of romantic interest, offering breadcrumbs, to keep them invested in the relationship. Dreams can pick up true motives via your psychic radar.

INTERPRETATIONS AND FORTUNE-TELLING MEANINGS

★ If you dream that your love, usually an online love, declares and then denies deep feelings and this is actually happening, it is confirmation that the dreamer is being kept dangling.

★ If you dream of a meeting when the love doesn't turn up without reason, this may be mirrored by your love cancelling meetings that were planned in real life.

★ If you dream they are showering you with flowers and jewelry, this is fantasy fulfillment about a love who really offers only intermittent communication to keep the dreamer hopeful.

★ If you dream of your love with another partner, you may be sensing that the online lover is physically unavailable.

★ If you dream of message after message bouncing back and reaching an answering machine, be aware that you are fueling the relationship while receiving crumbs of affection.

OUTCOME OF RACHEL'S DREAM

Tired of dreams that increased doubt, Rachel caught a plane interstate, tracked Christopher down at his work, and was told he was at the hospital with his wife, who was having another baby. Dreams of breadcrumbing, accepting however little love is on offer, can be brutally honest, but may save years of heartbreak and bring the chance of finding committed love.

Breastfeeding

In her recurring dream, Lola, twenty-three, was sitting in a coffee shop breastfeeding her new baby when her partner, Teddy, came rushing in. He threw his coat over her and told her she must leave at once, as people were staring at her breasts. Lola left, embarrassed and annoyed, with her baby screaming loudly.

DREAM BACKGROUND AND MEANING

Lola was six months pregnant and eager to breastfeed her baby when born. Teddy had been the ultimate modern father-to-be. Only on breastfeeding was he strangely silent and, when pressed, he said he did not want other men ogling his wife's breasts. His mother had said breastfeeding in public was positively indecent. Breastfeeding dreams can pick up underlying anxieties and prejudices, difficult to speak of but necessary to express.

INTERPRETATIONS AND FORTUNE-TELLING MEANINGS

* Some partners dream of their own mothers when their wives get pregnant, eliciting primal feelings, especially if the man's mother is possessive or disgusted by sex.
* If a normally placid man becomes angry in the dream, there may be unacknowledged jealousy toward sharing his partner with a baby.
* If a woman who is not pregnant dreams about breastfeeding, babies may be on the agenda.
* If in a dream a pregnant woman cannot feed a baby, this may be anxiety, but the mother-to-be should resist pressures to breastfeed unwillingly.
* If a pregnant woman dreams about breastfeeding a baby in public if everyone is staring and the dreamer is shy or private, she should plan in advance strategies to avoid feeling embarrassed if she wants to breastfeed publicly.

OUTCOME OF LOLA'S DREAM

After the dream, Lola persisted in bringing the real issues she had with her husband into the open. His mother had been stirring up trouble as she had always been jealous of Lola. Lola talked about ways she could feed the baby without embarrassing Teddy when they were together. However, Lola had to work harder to overcome Teddy's fears of it being wrong to have sex with a mother or mother-to-be, which had become an issue. Breastfeeding dreams reveal many layers of anxiety; breastfeeding can be a joyous experience, but only if it is what the mother wants.

Breasts

Kevin, twenty-six, dreamed his wife, Glenda, had grown enormous breasts that in their lovemaking were suffocating him. Then she turned into his mother, who was trying to crush him. He pushed her away, horrified.

DREAM BACKGROUND AND MEANING

Kevin, an only child to an overnurturing and smothering single mom, fell in love with Glenda because she was so independent and never questioned his need for time alone. They had a passionate sex life. However, since marrying she had turned into his mother, constantly fussing around him, incessantly cleaning, and cooking him special meals. It was like having two mothers and was affecting his sex life. Breast dreams can be positive, reassuring the dreamer of their sexuality, or negative if connected with nurturing in the wrong context.

INTERPRETATIONS AND FORTUNE-TELLING MEANINGS

* Having a lover possessing beautiful naked breasts in a sexual dream indicates you are ready for or will continue a passionate relationship.
* Dreaming of breastfeeding, or of your partner breastfeeding a baby, shows you are a loving, nurturing person and may also be a premonition of pregnancy (see "Breastfeeding," opposite).
* Dreaming of being ashamed when your breasts are suddenly exposed talks about fears of letting go sexually.
* If you dream of having breast implants and you have not planned this procedure, you may be worried about your youthfulness and sexuality.
* If you dream of undergoing a breast reduction operation, whether or not you actually need one, it suggests you are tired of being considered purely in terms of your external attractiveness.

OUTCOME OF KEVIN'S DREAM

After a quarrel with Kevin's mother, Glenda declared she was through with the good housewife and nurturing role as she could never compete with his mother. Glenda has reverted to being her passionate, independent self. Kevin is very happy. Breast dreams, because of their dual nurturing vs. sexuality meanings, are complex symbols, especially if the two meanings become entangled in the dreamer's psyche.

Bribery

Cory, fifty-five, dreamed he was appointed to the local council. As he left the hall, a large envelope was placed in his hand, containing a considerable sum of money and the name of a controversial development. Cory was horrified and immediately resigned. The next day he was burgled, and the money taken from his safe, but the police refused to believe him.

DREAM BACKGROUND AND MEANING

Cory had been asked to act as chairman for the local council. There had been considerable rumor over bribes. Cory asked a long-time councilor if this was true. The councilor laughed and said, "It sure is." Cory felt he should try to fight the corruption. Bribery dreams can detect corruption and act as a warning to steer clear of becoming involved.

INTERPRETATIONS AND FORTUNE-TELLING MEANINGS

★ If you dream of being offered a bribe in your workplace to influence a decision, you may be afraid to damage your career by tackling corruption.

★ If in a dream you are offered an inflated price for your home, your house may be worth a great deal more than its market value if it stands in the way of a projected, as yet unknown, development. Should you take advantage?

★ If in a dream you are offering bribes for an advance view of insider information, you may be contemplating taking legal but unethical shortcuts in business or speculation.

★ If you dream you are offered cash with no demands, you may have a chance to borrow easy money, no questions asked. Beware of hidden costs.

★ If you dream you are caught taking a bribe, you may pay a higher price for financial short-term relief than if you face money problems head-on.

★ If you dream of bribing someone to keep quiet over damaging information they have discovered about you, you may never be free of obligation by actually paying.

OUTCOME OF CORY'S DREAM

Cory talked to the police, who dismissed his council corruption fears. His leadership application was mysteriously removed. Bribery dreams often occur at a time of financial crisis where temptation is great, but accepting embroils the dreamer in lasting consequences.

Bridge

Georgina, fifty-five, dreamed she saw a crumbling, rickety bridge. She was frightened to cross, but discovered a boat and rowed across the river. When she reached the other side, she noticed a board in front of her ideal home, saying HALF-PRICE, APPLY TO APPLEYARD'S. Georgina woke puzzled. The name sounded familiar.

DREAM BACKGROUND AND MEANING

Georgina was estranged from her sister Jessie, because of disagreements about the property left to them jointly by their late mother. Georgina lived in the house, as she cared for her mother during a long illness. If the house was sold, as her sister insisted, Georgina's share would not be enough to buy another home. A bridge joins or divides two pieces of land, symbolizing relationships, depending on the state of the bridge. Since a bridge is generally over water, there may be underlying emotions affecting communication.

INTERPRETATIONS AND FORTUNE-TELLING MEANINGS

★ If the dream bridge is traditional and ornate, transition or resolution will be achieved through official negotiations that may take time.

★ If a bridge is old and crumbling, communication involves long-standing grievances needing perseverance to repair.

★ A railway bridge indicates fast, direct negotiations that will be resolved quickly.

★ Building a new bridge takes patience, especially if a relationship is new or occurs after a previous betrayal.

★ A flooded bridge says emotions are running high. Wait for matters to return to normal before tactfully approaching.

★ If a bridge is broken, it may not be possible to repair a relationship or situation unless by a completely new avenue.

OUTCOME OF GEORGINA'S DREAM

Georgina, intrigued, recalled that a friend had mentioned Appleyard's Housing Association, which allowed people to buy a share of a property and live on it. Georgina found a beautiful one-bedroom house by a river through Appleyard's. Her mother's house was sold. Georgina's sister refused to mend relations. Sometimes a predictive dream unconsciously recalls information we processed, so we can cross our dividing river by another route.

Broadcast

Gaston, thirty, dreamed he was appearing on his local radio station to defend his company, which was destroying green land to create a new power station. Before going on the air, he was sharing with the presenter his real feelings about his company's indifference to the environment and the local heritage. Then he realized his microphone was live and every word had been broadcast over the airwaves.

DREAM BACKGROUND AND MEANING

Gaston was publicity manager for a project that would bring great profit to the company but at an environmental cost. He was becoming increasingly uncomfortable about it. After the dream, he realized how careful he had to be about what information became public knowledge. Broadcasting dreams can reveal deception when words are not carefully monitored.

INTERPRETATIONS AND FORTUNE-TELLING MEANINGS

✷ If you are listening to a broadcast in a dream, double-check relevant facts in daily life. Your dream radar may be picking up what is concealed.

✷ If you are making a dream broadcast or being interviewed, be aware of whether what you are saying reflects official policy or facts, which may not be the same things.

✷ If you dream that you speak on air while not realizing you can be heard, this may represent your true opinions.

✷ If you are given a hard time by the presenter, your beliefs may be challenged in daily life.

✷ If you are a broadcaster asking challenging questions, how far are you prepared to go to uncover the truth and maybe face consequences of your own?

✷ If you are broadcasting a dream podcast or communicating with a wider audience online, be prepared to have opinions attacked as well as supported.

OUTCOME OF GASTON'S DREAM

Gaston could no longer continue defending the indefensible and used a broadcast to explain what was really happening. He was instantly dismissed and forced to move away. However, the project did not go ahead. Broadcasts should bring truth into the public domain, but sometimes there is a high cost to broadcaster and interviewee.

Broken Glass

Alison, fifty-five, dreamed she came home to find the glass doors and windows of her home smashed and glass all over the floor. Nothing had been stolen, but she walked out of her house with nothing, apart from what she was wearing, and checked into a hotel.

DREAM BACKGROUND AND MEANING

Alison was intimidated by her ex-husband's unremitting demands that she move out of the marital home so he could move in with his girlfriend, even though the court had given her permission to stay while the house was sold. She saw on the security camera that he was prowling around outside at night and was throwing stones at the windows. If a glass window or door is broken in a dream, it may directly result from fears about your security.

INTERPRETATIONS AND FORTUNE-TELLING MEANINGS

✷ Dreams of breaking through a glass roof or ceiling say that blocks in your career or financial path will soon be lifted.

✷ If you dream you drop a glass dish, you may be contemplating the end of a relationship or friendship. First see if it is retrievable.

✷ If you step on broken glass, you may be taking undue risks in your actions or words.

✷ If your eyeglasses get broken, someone is trying to hide the truth from you.

✷ Breaking a glass window or door in a dream suggests you may need to deal more forcefully with someone with a closed mind or malice toward you, especially if this is smoked or frosted glass.

✷ If you are being attacked by someone holding broken glass, beware of an impulsive act of spite or treachery by someone you thought a friend or ally.

OUTCOME OF ALISON'S DREAM

Alison realized the intimidation was directly creating her bad dreams. She returned to court, obtained a restraining order, and her ex was forced to pay her what he owed in alimony so she could move to where she felt safe. Broken-glass dreams often reflect the fragility of a situation and so can magnify anxieties of what might occur.

Broom

Penelope, twenty-eight, dreamed of marrying her partner, James, in a woodland ceremony with flowers in her hair and jumping hand in hand over a broom covered in ribbons, a traditional sign of lasting commitment. In her dream, they stood the wedding broom outside the honeymoon chalet as a sign none could spoil their happiness. In the morning it was broken.

DREAM BACKGROUND AND MEANING

James was already married, but promised he would leave his wife so he and Penelope could be together. Though they could not marry immediately, he agreed they would have a woodland commitment ceremony. It was planned for six months ahead on the second anniversary of their meeting. Broom dreams talk about determined efforts to clear the way for the future and augur well for new businesses or changing the status quo in relationships.

INTERPRETATIONS AND FORTUNE-TELLING MEANINGS

★ Dreaming of sweeping up while others watch represents doing all the hard work in a particular area of life, especially sorting others' chaos.

★ Riding a broomstick through the sky says you have psychic or healing powers and may indicate a past life as a wise woman or man.

★ Using a new broom talks of new beginnings, successful house moves, or making desired changes in work or domestic arrangements, a sign of good fortune.

★ Using an old broom says you need to make a clean sweep of the past and avoid reviving old resentments and blame issues.

★ A broom standing with bristles upright outside the front door gives assurance that home and family will be safe.

★ A dirty broom is a sign of gossip, false friends, and sweeping away problems rather than tackling them.

★ Broken brooms can be a sign of unfulfilled sexual needs and broken promises.

OUTCOME OF PENELOPE'S DREAM

James had to postpone the woodland ceremony because his wife had been unwell. He has promised Penelope that as soon as things settle down at home, they will have the ceremony and be together. She waits in hope.

Bubbles

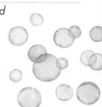

Tricia, forty-five, dreamed she was surrounded by huge rainbow bubbles, trying to catch them, but they were just out of reach. They started to float higher and higher and then disappeared. She saw a bubble machine and blew her own bubbles. She selected a huge iridescent bubble, stepped inside it, flew upward, and discovered that the lost bubbles were still there, waiting.

DREAM BACKGROUND AND MEANING

Tricia had been promised a dream vacation by her boyfriend, but his constant excuses suggested it was not going to happen. In the meantime, he was borrowing money from her until money he said was owed to him by someone else was repaid. He suggested she pay for the vacation so they would not have to wait. Bubbles represent wishes, but by their nature they are insubstantial and cannot be relied upon.

INTERPRETATIONS AND FORTUNE-TELLING MEANINGS

★ If you dream that you are blowing bubbles as a child, this is a revival of earlier dreams and says you can still fulfill them.

★ If you are in a bubble or surrounded by bubbles flying into the air, you have every reason to be optimistic, as happiness is coming into your life.

★ Dreaming you are trapped in a bubble says that you are unable to influence events and feel unable to prevent others from making mistakes that will affect you.

★ A bursting bubble talks about a disappointment with which you have not come to terms.

★ If you are trying to blow bubbles but they do not form or quickly disappear, beware of spending money on a project or situation that may not materialize.

OUTCOME OF TRICIA'S DREAM

After the dream, Tricia realized that the promised vacation was just one of her boyfriend's unfulfilled promises while she subsidized their lifestyle. She booked herself on the vacation alone and met a nice guy. It is important to enjoy the magick of dream bubbles as a means of traveling to where we want to be without losing sight of reality.

Buddha

In her dream, Harriet, sixty-six, heard a huge crash outside. When she went into her garden, she saw that the crane working on the land next door had deposited rubble throughout her meditation garden, smashing her Buddha statues and destroying her plants. She woke feeling totally distraught.

DREAM BACKGROUND AND MEANING

Harriet, recently retired, was looking forward to developing her passion for growing flowers and herbs, whose abundance she credited to her dozens of Buddha statues, collected on her travels. She was planning to open her meditation garden to visitors. But the big house next door was being demolished and replaced with an apartment block. The developers had been intimidating Harriet and pressuring her to sell up.

INTERPRETATIONS AND FORTUNE-TELLING MEANINGS

* If you are making an offering to a Buddha statue in a dream, you are calling abundance, health, and good fortune into your life.
* If you see Siddhartha Gautama, the original Buddha, sitting beneath a tree, his message is to wait and accept destiny, and the spiritual enlightenment you seek will come to you.
* A smiling or laughing seated Buddha statue indicates happiness, luck, and harmony coming or returning to your life.
* A standing smiling Buddha statue heralds prosperity and tells you not to worry about money, as resources will flow to you as needed.
* A Buddha statue with five children in your dream indicates fertility and a happy family, a good omen if you want a baby or want to add to your family.
* If you dream you are meditating in front of a Buddha statue, try to identify the place, as it may become a place of meaning for you.

OUTCOME OF HARRIET'S DREAM

After the dream, Harriet instructed her lawyer to hold out for a good price while she looked for a rural place to establish her new Buddha meditation garden. Buddha statue dreams are a reminder that inner as well as outer harmony are what matters. Rather than resisting, realize that wherever you go, the tranquility in your heart will go with you.

Building Blocks (Children's)

Perry, forty-five, dreamed he was seven years old again, trying to build a tower using a hundred building blocks. He felt that, if he succeeded, his mother, who had left home, would return. His father accidentally knocked over the tower Perry had built. Perry became very distressed, kicking and screaming, and his father smacked him. This was the first time in years that he had had this dream, but it had happened in real life exactly as the dream recalled.

DREAM BACKGROUND AND MEANING

Perry's mother left when he was seven without saying goodbye. He had felt that if he built a tower with a hundred blocks, life could be right again. But he never had succeeded. Recently he had been thinking about his mother, as he was about to marry a woman with two children. He had tracked his mother down, yet hesitated to contact her. Children's blocks in dreams are significant in that, whatever the dreamer's age, there is a degree of uncertainty and vulnerability involved.

INTERPRETATIONS AND FORTUNE-TELLING MEANINGS

* If you dream of being a child building with blocks, you are working up courage to take a risky step.
* If at any age you dream you are building a tower with children's blocks, avoid impatience and carelessness to achieve your ambitions.
* If you are using blocks that slot together, such as Lego, projects and plans are secure but may require cooperation.
* If a block tower falls, the foundations of your plans are insecure.
* If some of the bricks are not the right shape, your support under pressure may not be as reliable as you hoped.
* If you have insufficient blocks to complete your model, you may need extra practical or financial help.

OUTCOME OF PERRY'S DREAM

After the dream, Perry turned up at his mother's door. She refused to let him in, saying her new family knew nothing of him. He gave up trying to reunite. He gave his childhood blocks to his stepchildren. Building-block dreams, like all childhood toy dreams, indicate lingering childhood hopes and disappointments that need resolution or closure.

Building Site

Georgio, thirty-five, dreamed the hotel where he was staying was next to a building site. Work continued late into the night under floodlights and started again early in the morning. He went onto the building site and shouted at the workers, but they could not hear him. Georgio stormed out of the hotel, then realized he had nowhere else to go.

DREAM BACKGROUND AND MEANING

Georgio and his fiancée had moved into an old house that needed total rebuilding. Builders were there from early morning to late at night, and he and his fiancée decorated every evening and all weekend. The place looked like a building site. Building-site dreams can be very exciting, because they reflect a major new project or lifestyle the dreamer is creating.

INTERPRETATIONS AND FORTUNE-TELLING MEANINGS

* If you dream of living or working next to a building site, other people are intruding on your peace and privacy in some area of your life.
* If in your dream your vacation hotel is being rebuilt, your expectations of the vacation may prove disappointing. However, check in advance, as this may be a premonition.
* If you dream of an accident on a building site involving yourself or someone you know, you may be unconsciously aware of a risk or unreliable person.
* If you are renovating your home, even if you dream of an unrecognized building site, look for problems or strategies from the dream to improve your situation.
* If you dream of major demolition work, aspects of your life need to be let go before building new ventures or relationships.

OUTCOME OF GEORGIO'S DREAM

After the dream, Georgio and his fiancée decided to cut down on the speed of the renovations, to take more time for themselves, and to focus on working with the builders to make one area of the home comfortable at a time. Building-site dreams inevitably involve major disruption to lifestyle (see "Renovations," p. 391) and so are asking the dreamer if or to what extent changes are worthwhile.

Bull

Rick, thirty-five, had a dream about the bull running through the streets of Pamplona in Spain he had seen as a child. It both terrified and excited him. In the dream he was riding a bull ahead of all the others. He was certain he could overcome all obstacles to reach his goal.

DREAM BACKGROUND AND MEANING

Rick was training for a major athletics marathon to qualify for the Commonwealth Games, a multi-sport event, after recovering from a serious leg injury. He knew he was risking everything to get back into the sport. But if he did not enter this year, he would lose his chance, as by the next Games he would be too old.

INTERPRETATIONS AND FORTUNE-TELLING MEANINGS

* If you dream of bulls charging or fighting, this is a symbol of power for both men and women succeeding through supreme effort.
* A bull with cows indicates male potency and is an excellent omen for fathering if conception is slow.
* Sitting wrapped in a white bull skin may be an ancestral memory or past-world glimpse of Celtic Druids at Midwinter prophesying the year ahead and may be a sign that your own predictive powers are growing or returning.
* A man wearing bull horns in a dream ritual dates back to the old Minoan bull-worship ceremonies, where the bull priest represented the consort of the Goddess. This is a symbol of fertility, leadership, creative achievement, and twin-soul love.
* A bull pawing the ground represents prosperity, property, and successful business transactions through focusing on your goal.
* An attacking bull speaks of the need to defuse aggression and avoid direct confrontation.
* A bull stopping mid-charge and moving away suggests you should use your power wisely and know when you have reached your limits.

OUTCOME OF RICK'S DREAM

Rick entered the race and qualified for the Games. However, he became aware that the injury was flaring up and accepted that his future lay in preparing other athletes for the Games.

Bungee Jumping, Acrophobia

Mahammad, twenty-eight, dreamed he was with a group of friends, bungee jumping. One by one, his friends jumped. When it came to his turn, he hesitated, but the instructor pushed him. Mahammad, who had always been terrified of heights, screamed with terror, which rapidly changed to excitement. He awoke, feeling free of a fear that had burdened him all his life.

DREAM BACKGROUND AND MEANING

Mahammad had suffered from acrophobia, a fear of heights, since as a small boy he fell off a crumbling cliff edge and was only saved by landing in foliage halfway down. His fear had blighted every area of his life, preventing him from flying, accepting jobs where he needed to use elevators, and climbing ladders. When he was younger, his parents took him to a psychologist, but Mahammad refused to enter the elevator to the psychologist's suite. Dreams provide a safe space for the psyche to naturally overcome a phobia in its own time.

INTERPRETATIONS AND FORTUNE-TELLING MEANINGS

* Dreaming of overcoming a phobia can trigger a cure more effectively than many therapies. The dreamer can wake if things go wrong.
* If you dream of bungee jumping, this is a controlled form of preparing to take a risk in life, knowing you will be supported.
* Bungee jumping is a symbol frequently found in dreams of those who are afraid of heights, as the dreamer is not free-falling.
* Unlike falling dreams, bungee jumping indicates a safe sexual relationship with a caring partner.
* If you succeed in overcoming a fear of heights in a dream, you may not instantly be cured of a phobia, like Mahammad, but may need to experience several confidence-building dreams.

OUTCOME OF MAHAMMAD'S DREAM

Gradually Mahammad tested himself in increasing ways, climbing ladders to fix up his house, which he had long wanted to renovate, and he now has a job on the twentieth floor. However, he is taking it slowly and is not planning on bungee jumping yet. Bungee dreams can encourage a dreamer to widen their comfort zone.

Bureaucracy

In her dream, Wilhelmina, thirty-one, and her husband, Klaus, thirty-five, were standing before a magistrate awaiting his verdict on whether they were suitable adoptive parents for their foster son. The magistrate asked a series of questions that neither she nor Klaus was able to understand, though they had prepared well. The magistrate refused to give a decision. At that moment, their friends and relatives entered the court in support, and their foster son, now a teenager in the dream, arrived to drive them home.

DREAM BACKGROUND AND MEANING

Wilhelmina and her husband were unable to have children of their own and fostered children, usually for short periods of time. However, one boy, at the time of the dream four years old, had been with them all his life and they wanted to permanently adopt him. If the adoption application failed, under new local regulations the boy would be moved to another foster home. A dream can give signs of success, since in this case their foster son had obviously grown up with them.

INTERPRETATIONS AND FORTUNE-TELLING MEANINGS

* If you are waiting for a bureaucratic decision, dreams may offer clues about how to get matters moving.
* If there is no current bureaucratic matter, the dream indicates frustration with a person in authority at work or a stubborn older relative.
* If a bureaucrat in your dream is taking money from someone involved, check what is happening behind the scenes.
* If one person on a panel seems friendly in a dream, they may prove the most helpful.
* If you defeat bureaucracy in a dream, this is a good omen for winning your cause.

OUTCOME OF WILHELMINA'S DREAM

The couple asked respected friends and relations to come to court as witnesses at the next hearing, and the verdict went in their favor. Bureaucracy dreams can sometimes suggest solutions through tactics not previously considered.

Burglar, Intruder

Roxanne, twenty-eight, dreamed she came home to find her apartment totally trashed, but nothing missing except for the engagement ring her boyfriend, Jim, had given her. The burglar had ripped up her clothes. Roxanne was aware Jim and her girlfriend, Tracey, who was staying with them, were sitting on the sofa laughing at her. Roxanne told Tracey to go, but Jim held her protectively. Roxanne found herself in the street outside.

DREAM BACKGROUND AND MEANING

Roxanne had allowed her best friend, Tracey, to move into her apartment temporarily as Tracey had lost her job. Jim, who stayed over most nights, had at first objected, but gradually Jim and Tracey had become such good friends that Roxanne felt the outsider. One day she came home early to find the two of them snuggled on the sofa. Her boyfriend said Roxanne was overreacting when she protested. Burglary reflects lack of security or trust on many levels, often fears of intrusion or betrayal that may be justified.

INTERPRETATIONS AND FORTUNE-TELLING MEANINGS

* Dreaming of a burglar or intruder breaking into your home, your private space, indicates you are being invaded on a personal or even professional level.
* If you find your home trashed, it may be alerting you to actual security risks.
* When personal or precious items are taken or destroyed in a dream, an outsider, usually present in the dream, poses a threat to an important relationship.
* If the intruder attacks you, a rival or false friend may be plotting to destroy your reputation.
* If you overcome the burglar or the police arrive, you will defeat threats to your privacy or physical or emotional security.
* If others in the dream are unmoved or implicated in the burglary, strengthen personal boundaries as they are encroaching on your time, resources, and goodwill.

OUTCOME OF ROXANNE'S DREAM

Roxanne told Tracey to go. Tracey moved in with Jim. He took the engagement ring back. Roxanne is having a vacation from romance.

Bus

Sarah, thirty, dreamed she was waiting to board the school bus with her friends, all still teenagers. She could not find her bus pass, and the driver would not let her on. A Greyhound bus pulled up and the driver asked if she was going to New York. The dream ended with adult Sarah watching the miles speed by on the freeway.

DREAM BACKGROUND AND MEANING

Sarah returned home after a divorce and resumed a social life with friends who had never left the area. Her boss in New York was keeping her job open, but if she returned there it would mean seeing her ex and his new partner every day. The type of bus dream is significant, whether offering adventure and freedom or an easier but maybe dependent way of life.

INTERPRETATIONS AND FORTUNE-TELLING MEANINGS

* Dreaming of waiting for a bus that does not come or is full represents relying on others to fix your life and missing out.
* Being denied entry to the bus or falling off as it departs indicates that a previous option is no longer working.
* Getting on the wrong bus warns against going along with others if it does not feel right, even if easier.
* Two buses arriving for different destinations involves a fast major decision to avoid missing both options.
* Being a passenger involves sharing your life journey. Are you with the right fellow passengers (your current companions in daily life)?
* A bus not stopping when requested or missing your stop symbolizes hesitating at a change that involves going it alone.
* Are you on a shuttle bus when you want to ride long-haul to Samarkand? It may be time to get off at the next stop and find the right bus.

OUTCOME OF SARAH'S DREAM

Sarah realized that retreating to her old lifestyle was not working. She applied for a different job in New York, a place she loved, where she would not see her ex every day.

Bus Does Not Come

Lynette, thirty, dreamed she was waiting for a bus to take her to her new job. Various buses stopped, but none were going to her destination. She worried that she would be late on her first day. She asked other people in the line where they were going, but none were going to her destination. Their buses arrived, and she was left alone. Should she keep waiting, go home, or phone and say she would be late?

DREAM BACKGROUND AND MEANING

Lynette had been offered a job with a group of friends who were eager to start a real estate business. As she had worked in real estate since college, she wondered if her new colleagues wanted her contacts and portfolio. Buses in dreams signify traveling the same route as others. A bus not arriving questions the viability of the destination (see "Bus," p. 76).

INTERPRETATIONS AND FORTUNE-TELLING MEANINGS

* If you dream you are alone, waiting for an overdue bus, you may question if the route is where you should be going.
* If you dream you get on the wrong bus, you may hope that doubts will clear if you persist, which may not be so.
* If you dream the bus has been canceled, new factors may arise to give you second thoughts about your journey.
* If you meet work or business colleagues taking a different bus, they may not be committed to your well-being.
* If the dream bus eventually turns up, there may be delays in plans, whether for a group vacation, a joint venture, or a work relocation.
* If you dream you find yourself at the wrong bus stop, modify your plans to what is available and not what you hope.

OUTCOME OF LYNETTE'S DREAM

Lynette became suspicious when her new colleagues were asking her for advance lists of clients. She decided to stay where she was. Buses not arriving in dreams are very clear pointers telling you to examine if the route is available and still desirable.

Business Icons

Elmore, fifty-five, dreamed he was involved with big business at a major consortium with all the industrial leaders from around the world. They were listening to his plans for his company and agreeing it would become incredibly successful. He woke feeling totally confident about the future.

DREAM BACKGROUND AND MEANING

Elmore had always wanted to start his own business and had original ideas he knew would fill a gap in the market. But he had previously lacked the resources. Now he had a chance to take early retirement and a lump-sum payout, which would see him through the first uncertain months. However, his wife wanted them to enjoy life together. Dreams of business icons demonstrate that an idea is viable by the presence of so many leaders in the dream.

INTERPRETATIONS AND FORTUNE-TELLING MEANINGS

* If you dream of talking with a particular business icon, find out how his success is relevant to your business.
* If you dream of mixing with big business icons, this is an excellent omen for increasing sales and influence in any new business or creative venture.
* If you dream of being turned away or ignored by a big business icon, you may be feeling uncertain about a venture—a lack of confidence rather than a warning.
* If you dream of business leaders arguing, you will need to be very proactive in launching or expanding your business against ruthless competition.
* If you are asked to sign documents by business icons in a dream, it's a warning to be careful to not sign away any rights when launching.

OUTCOME OF ELMORE'S DREAM

Elmore knew that establishing his business was a now-or-never venture. He and his wife went on a long cruise before he began. He agreed to build in vacation time once he was established. Business-icon dreams advise thinking big if contemplating a new stage of life.

Business Partnership Problems

Sarah-Ann, thirty-two, dreamed she was driving with Lucy, her assistant, in the passenger seat. Suddenly the car went out of control. She screamed for Lucy to help, but Lucy was arguing with Simon, her fiancé, on her smartphone. Sarah-Ann awoke just before the crash.

DREAM BACKGROUND AND MEANING

Sarah-Ann ran an alternative therapy business. Lucy wanted to go into partnership with her. But she regularly had dramas with her fiancé, who also worked there. When they were both arguing, the atmosphere was toxic, resulting in clients walking out. Separating business from relationships is a problem highlighted in dream imagery that may not be acknowledged in daily interactions.

INTERPRETATIONS AND FORTUNE-TELLING MEANINGS

★ If you dream you and your business partners are walking or jogging side by side, business connections will continue to thrive.

★ An empty executive desk piled with work indicates it may be time to take on an extra partner.

★ If you are a small child and your business partner is larger than life, you are not getting your fair share of decision-making and perks.

★ If your partner is leading a donkey, you may be doing far more than your share of the workload.

★ If your partner has the face of your love partner or parent who is not part of the business, your business partner may be introducing emotional pressures into the business.

★ If you or your partners are dressed for a vacation, it's time to stop working 24/7.

★ If in your dream you find the safe empty and the accounts files blank, check that all is in order with finances, particularly if you are noting inexplicable losses.

OUTCOME OF SARAH-ANN'S DREAM

The out-of-control car represents business problems spiraling out of control if the partnership goes ahead, as Lucy's mind is on love, not business. Sarah-Ann replaced Simon and told Lucy she had a month to prove she could keep her private issues out of the workplace.

Butterfly

Petra, seventeen, dreamed she was in a garden filled with lavender, her late grandmother's favorite flower. Butterflies of all colors and sizes were flying through the flowers. One brilliantly colored butterfly settled on Petra's hand and remained motionless. Petra woke totally at peace with a sense of her grandmother's presence and the fragrance of lavender, though there was none in her bedroom.

DREAM BACKGROUND AND MEANING

Petra's grandmother died suddenly while Petra was away on a college trip. Petra was grief-stricken and could not sense her grandmother's presence. Throughout history and in many cultures, the appearance of a butterfly in a dream or daily life indicates the presence of a departed loved one.

INTERPRETATIONS AND FORTUNE-TELLING MEANINGS

★ To dream of a butterfly in sunshine among flowers indicates good fortune and news of, or the return of, a friend or family member far away.

★ A particularly beautiful butterfly that settles promises the rebirth of trust and return of happiness after sorrow, loss, or betrayal.

★ A trapped, torn, or dying butterfly signifies fragile hopes and trying to hold on in vain to a rapidly changing situation.

★ Colored butterflies rising in a cloud promise you will make a good impression at a social event or love date.

★ Being surrounded by butterflies represents the need to enjoy the present without worrying about the past or future.

★ A butterfly emerging from a chrysalis advises proceeding cautiously with a new relationship if you have been hurt, rather than rushing straight into new love or ventures.

OUTCOME OF PETRA'S DREAM

After the dream, Petra often saw a brightly colored butterfly, like the dream one, fly indoors or in an unusual place and settle close by. She would also smell lavender and would know her grandmother was near. Butterflies are natural messengers from angels and the afterlife, to reassure that love does not die.

Buttons (on Clothes)

Orla, thirty-five, dreamed she was wearing her smart new button-through dress at her first meeting as senior manager in her new role. As she rose to address the meeting, all the buttons popped and she was left standing with her underwear showing. Though she tried to hold her dress together, the all-male team members were laughing and wolf-whistling. She fled from the room.

DREAM BACKGROUND AND MEANING

Orla was the youngest senior manager ever appointed. The rest of the management team was male, much older, and resented her promotion. There had been sexist comments. Orla felt constantly on trial although she was good at her job and had greatly improved productivity. Should she persevere and hope attitudes would improve? Buttons on clothing in dreams represent holding things together in any context. Coming undone reflects insecurity that the true self, if revealed, would prove inadequate.

INTERPRETATIONS AND FORTUNE-TELLING MEANINGS

- ✶ If you dream that buttons come undone, revealing too much of yourself, you may feel your self-control is slipping and you are in danger of saying or doing the wrong thing.
- ✶ Putting the wrong button in a hole suggests a mismatch between people or talking at cross-purposes. You may be rushing and in danger of making mistakes.
- ✶ Uniform buttons, especially shiny ones, indicate success and prosperity through conformity or traditional methods.
- ✶ Dreaming of sewing on buttons says a relationship or business disagreement can be mended with care.
- ✶ Scattered buttons indicate numerous petty demands and irritations that distract you from what really matters.
- ✶ Too tightly buttoned clothing speaks of inhibitions caused by a restrictive situation or disapproving people.

OUTCOME OF ORLA'S DREAM

Orla checked facts and figures before meetings and refused to respond to inappropriate comments. Her increasing success gave her new authority to outface the schoolboy humor. Matching buttons suggest confidence that will stand scrutiny in any situation. However, Orla no longer wears button-through dresses at meetings.

Buying a Home

Rosalie, twenty-eight, had a recurring dream of herself and her husband, Jake, sitting on the porch of their homestead with their grandchildren. The surrounding acreage was filled with mature tropical fruit trees and, in the distance, sugar cane was growing.

DREAM BACKGROUND AND MEANING

Rosalie and Jake found the home of their dreams in Northern Australia. The house was virtually abandoned. They wanted to buy the land and live in a trailer while they rebuilt the homestead. But both sets of parents, who lived in Sydney, said they could live on the top floor of Rosalie's parents' home, saving for a luxury home while they worked as accountants, their profession.

INTERPRETATIONS AND FORTUNE-TELLING MEANINGS

- ✶ If you find the home of which you have been dreaming, you are drawn there, some say by the spirits of the land.
- ✶ If in the dream you are denied a loan for your chosen home, explore other options of raising money.
- ✶ If you dream of a less-than-ideal home, it may be a good interim purchase.
- ✶ If a house is empty in the dream, it may be waiting for you and could indicate a good bargain.
- ✶ A home in a dream represents your domestic life. Are you alone? Maybe you want or need to be?
- ✶ If there is an unknown partner or children in the new-home dream, that will be an option when the time is right.
- ✶ When we see the same home repeatedly in dreams, especially with the presence of future generations, it is a good omen for settling long-term.

OUTCOME OF ROSALIE'S DREAM

Rosalie and Jake bought their abandoned property. Jake decided to take a course in agriculture while Rosalie does online accountancy to pay the bills. Dreaming of buying a home says we should choose what makes us happy, even if others cannot share the vision.

Cable

Matilda, seventy, dreamed she was worried when workers dug up the underground cables connecting the television, phone, and Internet to her home and then went home as it got dark, leaving no lights or safety barriers. Within minutes, her older sister, who lived many miles away, came visiting unannounced, fell in the hole, and was injured. Matilda was blamed.

DREAM BACKGROUND AND MEANING

Matilda had severed contact with her sister, who was in good health but extremely vindictive and would phone Matilda several times a day to reproach her for her past and present perceived faults. Matilda was frail but felt much better since cutting the connection, despite feeling concerned, as her sister lived on her own in a remote house, was also estranged from her daughter, and refused to move.

INTERPRETATIONS AND FORTUNE-TELLING MEANINGS

★ A big, secure cable holding something safely is reassurance that your life is on track.

★ If the cable is thin or breaking, take care that you are not putting too much faith in a person or situation who appears strong but really is weak.

★ A breaking cable says that you may need to support someone close, as they may be let down by those who should care for them.

★ A cable car suggests you should wait for the whole picture and full facts before responding.

★ If you see a cable running toward your house and entering, you have love or united family relationships.

★ If, however, the cable stops short of the house, there may be a lack of communication that needs fixing.

★ Cable dreams with uncovered wires reveal unfinished business that is consciously or unconsciously worrying the dreamer.

OUTCOME OF MATILDA'S DREAM

After the dream, Matilda contacted her niece and told her she should keep an eye on her mother or arrange for social services to visit, as Matilda lived far away and had her own health issues. Cable dreams can indicate problems with relationships, but also cast questions as to who should be maintaining the cables.

Cactus

Jim, forty-two, dreamed he was trekking over vast desert sandhills. His water bottle was empty. He saw a huge cactus. Knowing there was one kind of cactus whose water was safe to drink, he took a chance. He woke, knowing he was saved.

DREAM BACKGROUND AND MEANING

Jim had been trekking the semiarid regions of Asia after an emotional breakdown. He was robbed by a gang who had stolen his money, identification, and charge cards and was temporarily without funds. He came upon a hostel in the middle of nowhere. The owner said that, to sort out his problems, he could work there in return for his keep, with use of the Internet. Dreams of cactus may appear when the dreamer is in crisis.

INTERPRETATIONS AND FORTUNE-TELLING MEANINGS

★ A cactus in a dream suggests you need more space in your personal and emotional life.

★ A dream cactus in your workspace represents an irritating or irritable colleague at work who constantly invades your space.

★ If you dream you hurt yourself on a cactus, you may need to step back from a potential quarrel between two people you know well.

★ If your cactus is flowering red, white, purple, or pink, happiness and love will come out of past sorrows and hurt.

★ If you are presented with a cactus as a gift, beware of the intentions of the donor, especially if the cactus has yellow flowers (jealousy) or orange (unreliability).

★ If you dream you see cactus growing in a desert, you may find temporary relief in a barren or unprofitable period of your life.

OUTCOME OF JIM'S DREAM

Jim sorted out his finances and was grateful to the hostel owner for taking a chance on him. Jim enjoyed working at the hostel so much that when he got home, he took a job managing a hostel in a similarly remote semiarid area of Spain. Cactus dreams, born out of difficulty, can offer relief from pain and the determination to forge a different life path.

Café

Melody, twenty-four, dreamed she was sitting in the café where she and her friends met every Saturday to talk over the week. She moved to the window table and noticed a new café across the street, where her friends were engrossed in conversation. She felt rejected.

DREAM BACKGROUND AND MEANING

Melody realized she was getting left behind from the friendship group she had known since school. They had joined a gym and an online dating site and were planning an overseas vacation together. Some Saturdays only one or two turned up. Melody feared the friendship group was breaking up. When a café signifies habit rather than anticipation in the dream, it may be time to widen social horizons.

INTERPRETATIONS AND FORTUNE-TELLING MEANINGS

★ If you dream of spending time socializing in a café, you will relax more in the near future or receive an unexpected invitation to a casual fun event.

★ If you pass a café and your friends or family are inside, you should make more time for them.

★ If you dream that your favorite café is unexpectedly closed, consider expanding your social life.

★ If you are working in a tea or coffee shop, your social life may be intruding on work commitments or vice versa.

★ If you dream you are sitting alone at a window table, you should become more socially proactive, rather than being an observer.

★ If you dream you do not have sufficient money to pay your bill and the person with you refuses to pay it, is that person draining your resources or energy?

OUTCOME OF MELODY'S DREAM

After the dream, Melody realized her friends were moving on. She joined the gym, booked the overseas vacation, and joined a dating site, and is enjoying new friendships and, hopefully, romance. She suggested replacing the weekend café meeting with a once-a-month get-together. Happy café dreams signify pleasurable mutual social meetings, but may give the first indication that dynamics are changing, requiring reassessment.

Cage

Ed, twenty-six, dreamed he was trapped in a small cage hung over the walls of a medieval city and left there to die. He fought with the lock. At last, it came undone and the door swung open. But Ed was frightened to leave the cage, as he would have to dive into the deep moat far below and, if seen, would be shot by one of the guards. Ed realized that the alternative was to wait for death. He dived into the moat and reached the bank. The sentries shot at him. He escaped with a minor arrow wound.

DREAM BACKGROUND AND MEANING

This may have been a past-life dream. Ed was slowly dying inside from a loveless marriage. He had worked for his father-in-law since leaving school and the couple lived in a house on the grounds of the family estate. Cage dreams talk about restrictions, whether imposed by fear or by not realizing the consequences of entering the cage.

INTERPRETATIONS AND FORTUNE-TELLING MEANINGS

★ Dreaming of a cage full of birds predicts accumulating wealth or having many children.

★ A bird or small animal in a cage reflects feelings of being trapped by a situation or person.

★ If the cage door is open, but you fear to leave, the price to pay for freedom may be loss of security.

★ Caged wild animals represent suppressing instincts and passions. If the animals escape, they release instincts, whether liberating or destructive.

★ Caging a fierce animal says that with courage you can overcome any opposition or bullying.

★ If you escape from a cage, you can overcome self-imposed restrictions. If recaptured, the price of freedom may seem too high.

OUTCOME OF ED'S DREAM

Ed plucked up the courage to tell his wife he wanted to leave her. To his surprise, she agreed that it would be best if they went their separate ways. Despite this, Ed's father-in-law proved vindictive. Ed left the marriage with very little materially, but with his integrity intact. With cage dreams, ask who is the captor, who the captive?

Caged Bird

Eliza, forty, dreamed she was in Indonesia in a temple, paying for caged birds to be set free. But the freed birds perched in nearby trees and then flew back to their open cages where food was waiting, to be freed by the next set of tourists. Eliza woke disillusioned.

DREAM BACKGROUND AND MEANING

Eliza was working on an Indonesian charity project, rescuing young girls from selling themselves on the streets so they could learn a trade and support their families in the countryside by legitimate means. But she was becoming disillusioned, as many took the training and the grant to start them off in their new trade but sent the money home and returned to the streets.

INTERPRETATIONS AND FORTUNE-TELLING MEANINGS

★ If you dream your freed caged birds fly high and remain in the trees, you are ready to make a bid for freedom in your own life, even at a risk.

★ If you dream the caged birds fly around and return to their cages for food, you or someone close to you may not be ready to leave an unsatisfactory but financially secure situation.

★ If the birds return to their cages, which are then closed, the incentives to remain may be stronger than to go.

★ If the birds will not leave the open cage, major change may take patience.

★ The cage door not closing when the birds return means that sooner or later there will be incentive for change.

★ If you dream there are many birds in a single cage, there may be powerful lifestyle or community pressures on you, or someone close to you, to conform.

OUTCOME OF ELIZA'S DREAM

After the dream, Eliza realized the charity needed to assist rural farmers so that they did not rely on their daughters for support. The girls would then be free to seek a better life for themselves. Birds in cages sometimes represent what may be personally or communally a much more complex issue of freedom versus security.

Cakes

Stephanie, forty-five, dreamed she was in a cake-making contest final against her husband's ex-wife to make a cake for his parents' anniversary. His parents were the judges. She noticed smoke coming from the oven and realized his ex-wife had turned Stephanie's settings to maximum. Her cake was burned and the ex-wife was declared the winner.

DREAM BACKGROUND AND MEANING

Stephanie had been asked to bake a cake for her husband's parents, as it was approaching their anniversary. As she was desperately busy, Stephanie bought an elaborate cake at the bakery. Her in-laws were always very disapproving and still favored their former daughter-in-law, which caused trouble in Stephanie's marriage. Dream cake-baking contests can reveal or confirm favoritism toward or bias against one of the contestants.

INTERPRETATIONS AND FORTUNE-TELLING MEANINGS

★ Eating cakes in a dream is a sign of prosperity, fertility, and a happy family life.

★ Baking cakes heralds unexpected visitors, a party, or a celebration.

★ If you burn a cake in the dream, there will be disagreements in the family and ongoing rivalries testing loyalties.

★ If you are buying cakes, you are eager to gain the approval of the recipient of the cakes.

★ If the cake breaks, those for whom the cake is intended will not be grateful for your efforts to please.

★ When you dream that a cake is unfairly divided or one person eats it all, you need to claim your fair share of credit, payment, or attention.

★ A half-eaten cake indicates someone who is never satisfied and is always seeking something or someone better in their eyes.

OUTCOME OF STEPHANIE'S DREAM

Stephanie's in-laws ate only a small slice of her cake, but praised some inferior cupcakes brought by the ex-wife. Stephanie realized she was wasting her time trying to impress her in-laws and told her husband that in the future, he could see his parents alone. The problem continued until the couple moved away.

Calculator

Patrick, twenty-eight, dreamed he was standing in the center of a giant calculator, but someone else was pressing the buttons. He was trying to calculate how much he owed to credit card companies. Then the calculator became so small that he could not read the figures. Unseen hands held out calculators, each with different answers, until he woke, thoroughly confused.

DREAM BACKGROUND AND MEANING

Through overspending, Patrick had run up big debts on his credit cards. Various loan companies had recalculated his debt and offered consolidation loans at varying rates of interest. This just got him deeper into debt. Calculators operated by others, unless they are reputable sources, represent handing financial responsibility to others, who may have agendas unfavorable to you.

INTERPRETATIONS AND FORTUNE-TELLING MEANINGS

★ If you dream you see a friend or lover using a calculator, they may have a calculating, colder side you may not have acknowledged.

★ If you dream you are using a calculator yourself and your input exceeds output, you will be successful in business or money matters.

★ If in the dream you have lost your calculator or it is broken, this is a time to use your heart and intuition.

★ If a calculator is giving different totals for the same input of numbers, beware of discrepancies in the information you are being given by different sources.

★ If you keep inputting the wrong figures or cannot recall them, you may not want to acknowledge financial problems.

★ If the calculator screen suddenly goes blank, the matter you are calculating has hidden or yet-to-manifest factors.

OUTCOME OF PATRICK'S DREAM

Patrick cut up his credit cards and went to a debt charity that calculated realistic repayments. Patrick has noticed the dream recurs at points when he is about to return to overspending and accepting cheap consolidation loans, dreams he ignores at his peril.

Calculators are impartial and do not lie. Calculator dreams tend to be sometimes unwelcome reality checks.

Calendar

Harold, thirty-four, dreamed of a calendar on which a single date was highlighted in red, a red-letter day. He felt excited, but uncertain. Then all the numbers whirled over his head as if blown by a tornado. Harold ran to catch his red-letter day. He woke as he had it in his grasp.

DREAM BACKGROUND AND MEANING

Harold realized the date on the calendar marked in red was the closing date for an application for a new job in another state. This would give Harold a lot more money and great opportunities. But he had just bought a house with his girlfriend and regularly played on the local soccer team.

When dates fly off the calendar, the temptation is to wait for another chance, which may not come.

INTERPRETATIONS AND FORTUNE-TELLING MEANINGS

★ A dream of a calendar with lots of marks on it says you need to work out your priorities.

★ An empty calendar suggests that you are waiting for something to happen that you need to hasten.

★ A calendar from years back implies that you need to leave some part of the past behind.

★ If a particular date highlighted is not one you recognize, keep the date in mind. Your mood in the dream will tell whether it is to be anticipated or it is a warning.

★ If the date is marked in a different color from the others, you may have forgotten or be suppressing its significance.

★ If the dream calendar is torn or has dates crossed out, you may need to plan the future rather than let others dictate your movements.

OUTCOME OF HAROLD'S DREAM

Harold realized the job was a once-in-a-lifetime chance. He applied and was awarded the job. He and his girlfriend are planning to rent out their house. Harold is looking for a new soccer team. Calendar dreams are reminders of time passing and the need to make each day count.

Camel

Pia, thirty-five, dreamed of wild Australian Outback camels. She was riding on the back of the most magnificent camel as he took leadership of the herd. She knew her future destiny was bound up with the camels and following their trails.

DREAM BACKGROUND AND MEANING

Pia had been on camel treks in Egypt and Australia, her home. She was passionate about the wild camels in Australia, which had been brought over a century or more earlier from Afghanistan and India to help build roads and railways, but now were regarded as pests or exotic food. She planned an overland camel trek through Northern, Central, and Western Australia, following and recording the traditional routes of the cameleers of old. Camels in dreams represent unusual money-making opportunities and a desire to live unfettered by convention, defying even the harshest conditions.

INTERPRETATIONS AND FORTUNE-TELLING MEANINGS

* A dream of a single-humped dromedary camel, found in Egypt and the Middle East, suggests that you need to conserve money and energy.
* A dream of a two-humped Bactrian camel, the only wild creature in inhospitable parts of Eastern Asia, says you will acquire resources to kindle or rekindle your fortunes.
* If you dream of feral camels in a land to which they were imported, such as Australia, you need to transfer and raise resources or finances for a new project.
* A number of trekking camels indicates improved fortunes, through an unexpected windfall, prize, or sponsorship.
* If you dream you are riding or betting on a camel race, you may be asked to take a financial risk with potential rewards.
* Recurring dreams of a camel indicate a journey. You will survive difficulties and uncertainties if you persist.

OUTCOME OF PIA'S DREAM

Pia obtained money for her camel trek by winning major camel races and through sponsorship. She bought four camels and paid for a camera and a sound engineer to record her journey. Pia is convinced she will sell her documentary and book, proving anything is possible if we persevere.

Candles

Nina, thirty, dreamed she was in an old-fashioned cottage, sitting opposite her present husband, with a candle between them. They were hungry. Nina knew they were in Ireland at the time of the potato famine. Their landlord's bailiffs were coming in the morning to evict them, as they could not pay their rent. They were planning to work their passage on the boats to America, but Nina did not want to leave her parents. The candle burned down and they were in darkness.

DREAM BACKGROUND AND MEANING

Nina lived in Boston, and her family had come to America from Ireland, so the dream may have been an ancestral memory. She and her husband had been invited to move to Ireland to manage a family hotel. They were finding Bostonian life too fast. But it was a huge step. Extinguishing a candle marks the end of a phase where you need to close a door. If the candle burns down and goes out, endings occur naturally.

INTERPRETATIONS AND FORTUNE-TELLING MEANINGS

* A solution to a long-standing problem occurs spontaneously if you dream you are lighting candles.
* Birthday candles herald a pregnancy or a family celebration.
* A candle that keeps going out refers to a fear that you are being overlooked at work or in a social group.
* A candle burning with a clear, steady flame indicates financial prosperity and trustworthiness of someone you had been doubting.
* A candle flickering in a draft warns that someone may be wavering in their loyalty to you.
* An unlit candle says you have the potential to create a good impression but must take center stage.
* To see a partner framed in candlelight in a dream suggests a past-life connection.

OUTCOME OF NINA'S DREAM

Nina decided they should go to Ireland for six months and rent out their Boston apartment. She felt it was completing the circle of her ancestral past and the dream was a sign to move on.

Candy

Coral, sixty-six, dreamed she was in a shopping mall with her teenage granddaughter, Sophie, who in the dream was no more than nine or ten. Sophie insisted that they go into a candy store and immediately indicated the candy she wanted. The store assistant handed the candy to Sophie and said to Coral, "Three hundred sixty dollars, please." Coral was horrified at the price. Sophie protested that no other candy would do. To avoid a scene, Coral paid. Sophie ate one piece and threw the remainder in the trash, saying it was disgusting.

DREAM BACKGROUND AND MEANING

Coral enjoyed treating her granddaughter when they went shopping. But Sophie had become increasingly demanding through the years. Coral did not want to disappoint her granddaughter, as she herself often went without as a child. However, now that Coral and her husband were retired, money was more restricted. Candy, being sweet and colorful, represents a desire to please others materially and emotionally.

INTERPRETATIONS AND FORTUNE-TELLING MEANINGS

* A dream where you are enjoying eating candy says you are happy with your body image and sexuality.
* Guilt about eating candy can be a fear of letting go of your feelings and indulging your desires.
* Dreaming of going into a candy store indicates the need for instant gratification.
* If you or someone else eats candy until they feel sick, this is a warning against overindulgence generally.
* If candies are refused or rejected, the dreamer may be trying too hard to please out of misplaced guilt.
* If you dream that candy is too expensive, buying unnecessary luxuries should be reined in.

OUTCOME OF CORAL'S DREAM

Coral and her husband put limits on Sophie's constant demands and were accused of not loving her, the ultimate emotional pressure. However, they stuck to their guns and encouraged Sophie to get a vacation and weekend job to buy her own luxury goods. Because it is hard to separate actual giving from proof of love, candy dreams often have deep meaning for family dynamics.

Cap

Tony, forty-five, dreamed he was climbing a ladder when his cap lifted off. Letting go of the ladder, he pulled it back down, slipped, and badly injured himself. On his way to the hospital, it seemed that no one noticed the bald spots on his head.

DREAM BACKGROUND AND MEANING

Tony was very conscious of the bald patches on his head. As a result, he always wore a baseball cap pulled well down over his face. He worked on a building site, and there were times when he was more concerned about his vanity than safety. His boss warned him that he was an accident waiting to happen. Cap dreams where there is a designer logo are signs of status and street cred, but they can also be a defense against imperfections perceived by the dreamer.

INTERPRETATIONS AND FORTUNE-TELLING MEANINGS

* Dreaming of wearing a baseball cap or a similar one says everything will go well and fun times are ahead.
* A cap pulled over your eyes or worn backward conceals your true feelings.
* A cap pulled over someone else's eyes says they may be hiding resentment toward you.
* A shower cap warns that you are afraid of others' emotions pouring down on you, especially as emotional blackmail or someone excessively seeking sympathy.
* To win a cap in international sport is a high achievement, and in a dream it signifies the opportunity for major successes, though not necessarily linked to sports.
* If the dreamer puts a cap on top of a hat or over a cap they are wearing, the dreamer will make a winning move that cannot easily be beaten.
* Caps in dreams make a positive statement of relaxed confidence if worn to adorn, not conceal.

OUTCOME OF TONY'S DREAM

Tony ignored the dream and had an accident on site in which his cap was destroyed, but he was in too much pain to care. As a result, hard-hat wearing, previously ignored, was strictly enforced, which solved Tony's work problem.

Car

Eleanor, forty-five, dreamed she was driving through empty countryside in the early evening to meet her lover. Suddenly the sky became pitch-black. She realized she was driving without lights and could not find the headlight switch. Eleanor was terrified she would hit another car or be hit, and woke screaming.

DREAM BACKGROUND AND MEANING

Eleanor was contemplating leaving her safe but stagnant marriage for her new love and had an assignation the next day to sign the lease for a new property. A car signifies the self as you go about daily life. The amount of personal control you have depends on how you are driving, or if you are a passenger but want to drive.

INTERPRETATIONS AND FORTUNE-TELLING MEANINGS

* If you dream that the route is smooth and traffic-free, you are in control of your life.
* A broken-down car in a dream advises you to check your actual car, as you may subconsciously have noticed a problem. More generally, consider the viability of options if you are planning a major change and you have doubts.
* Dreaming of a family car is a sign of impending pregnancy if you want children, or an addition to the family in another way.
* Dreaming of receiving a parking ticket or speeding fine shows you are taking one too many chances.
* A vehicle moving too slowly warns that you are holding yourself back. Too fast, you need more excitement in your life.
* If you dream that you keep driving over the same piece of road or are stuck in a never-ending traffic jam, your daily routine may need changing to avoid stagnation.

OUTCOME OF ELEANOR'S DREAM

Eleanor realized she was running from one unsatisfactory situation to another. She did not meet her lover, who turned out to have been convicted for extorting money from lonely women. Headlights not working or a misted or dirty windshield warns that something is being concealed from you. Consider the longer-term consequences of an impulsive action.

Cards

Steve, thirty, dreamed he was playing cards with his new office manager. The manager kept changing the rules while smiling all the time. Then Steve realized the manager had a hidden pack and was substituting cards. Steve did not want to say anything, but had gambled away his wages.

DREAM BACKGROUND AND MEANING

Steve was suspicious of his new manager, although he was very friendly. Amounts of money had been disappearing, which the manager had implied were due to Steve's carelessness. Steve was beginning to doubt himself. However, this had only happened since the change of management. Dream card games can confirm suspicions about concealment in daily life.

INTERPRETATIONS AND FORTUNE-TELLING MEANINGS

* Dreaming you are playing winning hands of cards says you need to take a chance in your life.
* Playing cards for money talks about a potential business or property deal. If you are winning, any risk will pay off. Losing is a warning to be careful.
* If someone you know is cheating at cards in a dream, be cautious of them. If you do not yet know the cheater, beware of trickery from someone entering your life.
* Fortune-telling with tarot or playing cards indicates your psychic abilities emerging. Check the meaning of cards picked in the dream for their message. Remember that the tarot death card never means death, only moving on. Swords in tarot and spades in playing cards can, however, warn of obstacles or double-dealing.
* If you are playing poker or blackjack in the dream, be cautious whom you trust when offered a chance or bargain seemingly too good to be true.

OUTCOME OF STEVE'S DREAM

After the dream, Steve started double-checking and keeping copies of financial transactions. The manager was diverting funds and tried to blame Steve. The manager was merely let go, with no repercussions, as he was the CEO's nephew. Card dreams can be predictive, alerting you to what your conscious mind is doubting.

Castle

Anna, thirty, dreamed she was preparing for her wedding to the lord of the castle and land that adjoined hers. It was said she needed a protector, but she did not want to marry. She closed the drawbridge to his approaching party. The lord laid siege to the castle. Anna would not give in, and eventually he went away.

DREAM BACKGROUND AND MEANING

Anna, a widow, ran a successful engineering company after the death of her husband. Jules, who had a similar though less successful company, wanted to combine his company with hers and become her love partner, too. Anna was being pressured to accept, but she did not want Jules as her business or love partner. Dreams of castles are often past-life dreams. They represent when personal territory needs to be strongly marked out if a person is under threat, which often involves career as well as home.

INTERPRETATIONS AND FORTUNE-TELLING MEANINGS

★ If you dream you own a castle, your financial position and career are safe. Do not be pressured into giving up command.

★ A fairy-tale castle indicates a romantic interlude. Preserve realism until you are sure.

★ A castle under siege reflects others trying to invade your privacy and control your life. What is the price of surrender?

★ If you dream that you close the drawbridge, you may need to withdraw emotionally or physically if you are pressured into a commitment for which you are not ready.

★ A ruined castle stands for a longing for security you had in the past.

★ If you dream you are a child, guest, or servant of the castle owner, you will meet (or already know) a powerful person who will offer you help and protection.

OUTCOME OF ANNA'S DREAM

Anna rejected the offer from Jules. He was very aggressive after her refusal. Her business is flourishing and his is declining. Castle dreams recognize that your home or business is very important to you and worth defending.

Cat

Fatima, thirty-five, was preparing for her forthcoming marriage when she began to have cat dreams. In one, she was walking down the street with her fiancé and a cat pushed against her legs to stop her from walking with him.

In another dream Fatima had been left in the car by her fiancé to sleep there alone overnight. The cat appeared and insisted it was not right for her to be left alone. The cat multiplied into hundreds of tiny cats and then into her fiancé, who was running away.

DREAM BACKGROUND AND MEANING

Fatima was an Egyptologist and dreamed of the cat goddess when she was working in an ancient tomb in Egypt. Cats were sacred to Bast, the cat goddess in Ancient Egypt more than five thousand years ago, and this, along with their association with the Norse goddess of magick, Freya, have made cats a strong image of female magick and intuition.

INTERPRETATIONS AND FORTUNE-TELLING MEANINGS

★ Dreaming of a cat entering your personal space indicates you will become very self-reliant.

★ Meowing, yowling, or talking cats in a dream warn of a false friend who has talked their way into your life.

★ Black cats are considered unlucky in the United States and parts of Europe, but if one comes toward you or crosses your path in a dream, you will gain prosperity and good fortune.

★ Black cats in the United Kingdom and in many Asian countries, such as Japan, foretell that you will be lucky in love.

★ White cats appearing in a dream promise new beginnings and good luck when most needed.

★ If you dream of Ancient Egypt and sacred cats, you are connecting with a very old world and may feel drawn to visit Egypt.

OUTCOME OF FATIMA'S DREAM

Fatima's fiancé deserted her without explanation after the car dream. Cats are very protective of women and were warning Fatima about her boyfriend in the dreams. They remind you to assert your independence.

Cave

Lloyd, thirty-five, dreamed he was exploring a deep cave, accessible only at low tide. He discovered a rusted chest that he was convinced contained treasure. Lloyd decided to drag the box onto a high ledge as the waves were entering, and he waited for the tide to turn. The waves came crashing in, and he clung to the ledge, but the chest was washed away.

DREAM BACKGROUND AND MEANING

Lloyd was an only child and his mother was forty when she gave birth to him. She had treated him as the man of the house after his father left, and Lloyd was content to stay home. He loved caving near his home, but recently he was challenging himself to undertake more and more risky descents. The thrill stopped him from acting on his increasing sense of being trapped by his mother. The cave as womb and tomb can call into question the role of the cave in the dream.

INTERPRETATIONS AND FORTUNE-TELLING MEANINGS

* The cave is an ancient universal symbol of the womb, representing conception, pregnancy, and birth of ideas.
* Since in early times caves were linked with death and rebirth, a cave with increasing light at the end indicates a new beginning.
* If you dream you are trapped in a cave, especially one with rising water, you may be stifled by emotional pressure, especially from an overprotective mother.
* Finding buried treasure in a cave says you have a hidden talent or will receive an unexpected windfall.
* If you are lost in a cave, you may be postponing making a difficult decision.
* If there is a dragon or wicked enchanter or enchantress in the cave guarding gold, beware of anyone offering easy money.

OUTCOME OF LLOYD'S DREAM

After the dream, Lloyd volunteered for the local cave rescue service and was invited to train as a full-time rescuer. With his encouragement, his mother bought a condo in a retirement village. Caves have been sanctuaries throughout the ages, but can also signify traps where past obligations and patterns prevent the light of future possibilities from shining through.

Ceiling Fan

Rosemary, thirty-one, often dreamed she was living in a hut with a straw roof with overhanging trees. There was a huge wind and the roof came crashing in. A tree that fell through the roof crushed her before she could escape.

DREAM BACKGROUND AND MEANING

The dreams began after Rosemary moved to a small rooming house in Lower Manhattan. The only relief from the heat was a ceiling fan directly above the bed. There was no space to move the bed. Rosemary had developed a seemingly irrational terror of the ceiling fan crashing on top of her while she slept. This became muddled with the hut dream. Because their whirring noise can be incorporated into a dream, ceiling fans can evoke buried memories of high winds and danger, sometimes from past worlds.

INTERPRETATIONS AND FORTUNE-TELLING MEANINGS

* A cooling, efficient ceiling fan in a dream indicates the lowering of the temperature of conflicts at work or home.
* If you dream a ceiling fan is broken, you may feel stifled and restricted in your life or in a relationship and need to fix the problem.
* If in the dream a ceiling fan is too loud, you may be absorbing the full force of others' problems. Switch off from trying to resolve matters.
* If a ceiling fan is unstable in a dream, you may fear events crashing down on you if you are in a precarious situation emotionally or financially.
* A ceiling fan can represent paranormal intervention in sleep if you are psychically sensitive, and may translate into disembodied voices or astral travel in a whirlwind.

OUTCOME OF ROSEMARY'S DREAM

Once Rosemary recognized the link between the dream as a past-life memory and the actual fan, the dreams and her fears ceased. However, she bought a silent portable fan for hot weather until she found an air-conditioned apartment. Ceiling fans are by their nature intrusive and, in some dreamers, trigger fears of being spied on from above.

Celebrities

Danielle, twenty-five, dreamed frequently that she had written a screenplay for her favorite film star, Jolene. They were walking up the red carpet together at the premiere with the cameras flashing. Then the lights went out. Danielle was outside and the security guards would not believe she was with Jolene.

DREAM BACKGROUND AND MEANING

Danielle admired the film star in real life and had written a screenplay, which she sent to the star's manager. There had been no response in spite of follow-up emails. Dreaming of being with a celebrity is a wish-fulfillment dream, indicating it is possible that with effort you could attain success.

INTERPRETATIONS AND FORTUNE-TELLING MEANINGS

★ If you dream you are with a celebrity at a star-studded event, you want recognition for what you do and are, whether from your family, friends, or employer.

★ If you dream you are denied access to the celebrity, you feel unworthy, because celebrities seem different from other mortals, and yet you aspire for more in your own life.

★ If you are in a love relationship with the dream celebrity, you feel undervalued in your everyday love life and crave a more glamorous, exciting lifestyle.

★ If you dream that a friend interrupts and takes the celebrity's attention, you resent the fact that they always steal the limelight.

★ If you are working with the celebrity and sharing the limelight, try developing a talent the dream celebrity possesses to bring you money and success.

★ If in your celebrity dream you have a minor role, you should modify your approach to break into the celebrity world.

OUTCOME OF DANIELLE'S DREAM

Danielle sent her screenplay to several minor production companies and has received some interest. Her ambition is to one day write exclusively for Jolene, her dream star. In the meantime, she is studying movie makeup so she can work in a studio and meet the stars. Dreams like Danielle's tell you not to give up hope.

Cell Phone

Judy, forty-eight, dreamed she was late to meet her teenage daughter, Sophie, and was desperately trying to phone her. But she kept misdialing the number, and business calls were intruding every time she heard her daughter's voice. When she finally connected, Sophie could not hear what her mother was saying. Judy woke in a total panic.

DREAM BACKGROUND AND MEANING

Judy is a single parent with a demanding career. Her daughter has taken advantage of her mother's preoccupation and is mixing with the wrong crowd. Dreams of cell phones, like dreams of older-type phones, represent the need to communicate more clearly with loved ones and with the world generally.

INTERPRETATIONS AND FORTUNE-TELLING MEANINGS

★ The success of the dream cell phone call indicates how positive or otherwise emotional interactions are with the person you are phoning.

★ Repeatedly misdialing a number, not getting through in an emergency, and being unable to remember a number are common anxiety dreams about needing help but not receiving it.

★ If a phone keeps ringing but remains unanswered in a dream, or the caller cannot be heard, or you get the busy tone, it suggests frustration and overload in your life and people not taking your worries seriously.

★ If you repeatedly dream that a person who is far away, or one with whom you have lost contact, phones you, but you miss the call, this is a telepathic call to contact the person.

★ If you drop, break, or lose your phone, you may not wish to communicate with the person you intended to phone.

OUTCOME OF JUDY'S DREAM

Judy realized she was trying to be the perfect executive and perfect mother and was wearing herself out. After the dream, Judy switched to a less stressful job, working mainly from home. She was able to talk directly to her daughter and guide her through what proved a difficult time ahead. Problematic phone calls indicate it is time to reprioritize face-to-face connections.

Cemetery

Flouella, sixteen, dreamed she was taking a shortcut home when she found herself in an overgrown cemetery. It was getting dark, and huge trees and tangled branches obscured the path. She stumbled, and a green hand covered in moss reached out of an open grave and seized her leg, while another hand pulled her backward by the hair. She woke screaming.

DREAM BACKGROUND AND MEANING

Flouella dreaded her walk home from school alone as her friends lived in the opposite direction. She had to pass along an overgrown path beside an abandoned cemetery. Flouella was afraid both of spirits and of being accosted, as there had been recent attacks in the area. Cemetery dreams by their nature can evoke supernatural fears, especially if the dreamer has watched scary movies.

INTERPRETATIONS AND FORTUNE-TELLING MEANINGS

★ If you dream of a disused or neglected cemetery, there are many old memories you can now leave behind.

★ If you see an ancestral name on a grave, even if it is an unfamiliar gravestone, that person has a similarity in their life that, if identified, will answer a question you have.

★ If you dream of a scary Gothic cemetery, this is a psychic dream, suggesting spiritual abilities emerging that need channeling to avoid free-floating fear.

★ If you see an open grave, this represents anxieties or negative feelings you have unsuccessfully tried to banish.

★ If you cannot escape or find your way out because of tangled trees, an old problem or person you thought you had left behind may return.

OUTCOME OF FLOUELLA'S DREAM

After the dream, Flouella told her mother how scared she was walking home as the darker winter evenings approached. Because of the attacks, Flouella's mother changed her work hours so she could take Flouella to and from school. Cemetery dreams can trigger deep-seated fears of mortality and evil, especially if there are external factors to add to fears.

Chairs

Steve, thirty-six, dreamed he was setting up a conference, putting notes on all the chairs. But every time he reached the end of a row with the notes, the ones at the beginning of the row disappeared from the chairs. Then he noticed the chairs were also disappearing, leaving an empty hall. The CEO refused to listen to his excuses and told him he was fired.

DREAM BACKGROUND AND MEANING

Steve had been promoted to head of events in his company, but his team resented him as he was not the internal candidate they wanted. He was arranging his first major conference for the different branches of the company, but was worried the team would make him look bad. Chair dreams are based in feeling comfortable and making others feel at ease, so they can be positive or negative, depending on the dream context.

INTERPRETATIONS AND FORTUNE-TELLING MEANINGS

★ If you dream you are enthusiastically setting out chairs for an event, you will have a chance to publicly show your talents.

★ If you are setting out chairs unwillingly, you may be pressured into going along with an unwelcome decision at work or in the community.

★ If you are sitting in a comfortable chair, you may need to take a rest from life or from others' demands.

★ If you are sitting in an uncomfortable chair, you may not want to be in a particular situation or relationship but may feel obliged by duty to stay.

★ If a chair is broken, it may be time to move on, as any welcome will not be genuine.

★ If you are buying new chairs, you may be seeking changes in your family or social life at a price that will be worth it.

OUTCOME OF STEVE'S DREAM

The dream confirmed that Steve could not trust his team, and so he proposed that each branch send members from their own events teams so there would be a good mix. He was praised for making the whole company feel welcome, and the conference went well. Empty chairs represent the potential for acceptance or rejection, depending on who may fill them.

Chameleon

Aaron, twenty-eight, dreamed of seeing a rainbow-colored chameleon sitting on a dark-colored bush, making no attempt to change color or hide. The bush was full of carefully camouflaged chameleons. A gardener started trimming the bush. He did not see the concealed chameleons, and the chameleons could not escape. But he noticed the rainbow chameleon, stopped cutting, and moved away.

DREAM BACKGROUND AND MEANING

Aaron's company had been taken over by a multinational business, which was introducing its own staff. The present workers were trying to avoid being noticed, carefully blending into the background. Aaron felt he needed to make a positive impression. But should he keep his head down like the others and hope for the best? A chameleon that does not change color to blend into the background advocates an independent approach to get positively noticed.

INTERPRETATIONS AND FORTUNE-TELLING MEANINGS

* If the dream chameleon is slowly changing color to blend in with foliage, you may need to temporarily accept the status quo.
* A chameleon sitting on the shoulder of a colleague or friend warns they may be fickle.
* A green chameleon is a sign of good luck, business success, and increasing social opportunities.
* A black chameleon says, "Do not worry about facing change as you will soon fit in."
* A chameleon that changes color rapidly, which is unusual, foretells a sudden advantageous change or chance to travel.
* If a chameleon crosses your path, beware of losing support for a project or scheme that may need to be modified to succeed.

OUTCOME OF AARON'S DREAM

After the dream, Aaron created a new post for himself, liaising with existing customers and suppliers to ease the takeover for them and maintain a familiar face in the months ahead. Unlike most of his colleagues, Aaron was not let go. While chameleons usually represent adapting and fitting in, sometimes standing out can prevent being overlooked.

Chamomile

Poppy, thirty-one, dreamed she was looking out of her window at her chamomile lawn and was pleased that the small yellow, white, and feathery green plants were growing so well. But every flower had the face of a laughing child, and sitting in the middle of the lawn was a little girl, the image of Poppy, who said, "Hurry up, I'm tired of waiting."

DREAM BACKGROUND AND MEANING

Poppy had decided from an early age that she never wanted children, and she and her partner had good careers and traveled frequently. Her mother had been a successful businesswoman who left Poppy to be brought up by nannies. Recently, Poppy had been frequently experiencing the chamomile lawn dream and was thinking more and more about babies. When we see the same child in dreams, it may be a sign that a potential unborn child could be seeking birth.

INTERPRETATIONS AND FORTUNE-TELLING MEANINGS

* If you dream of making or stirring chamomile tea, your life may be too hectic and you need more self-time and relaxation.
* If in a dream your lover offers you chamomile tea, they have a gentle, kind nature and will never let you down.
* If you are planting a chamomile lawn, it is a sign of a happy family with children, whether through birth, remarriage, fostering, or adoption.
* Since chamomile is self-seeding, a flourishing chamomile lawn promises that solo ventures will flourish financially and rapidly expand.
* If the chamomile you planted in a dream is not flourishing, a gentle approach may not work and you should be more assertive.

OUTCOME OF POPPY'S DREAM

Poppy realized she did want a baby. She explored working-from-home options and realized it was possible to be a devoted mother and have a successful career. When Poppy's baby was born, she took a couple of years' leave to enjoy family life. Chamomile is a common symbol of the pleasures of a family, and dreams may recur until a decision about having children is made.

Champagne

Patsy, fifty, dreamed she was at her silver wedding anniversary party. Champagne corks were popping at the huge gathering. But the champagne in her glass was totally flat and tasteless, though of the finest vintage. Her husband toasted her. Everyone clapped, making toasts to the happiest couple they knew. Patsy smashed her champagne glass, walked out, and woke feeling thoroughly disillusioned.

DREAM BACKGROUND AND MEANING

Patsy's family and friends were planning a huge celebration for the couple, but Patsy knew her marriage was a lie. She had discovered her husband had another wife and children in a state he visited every week, supposedly on business. Yet she wondered: How could she hurt everyone by revealing the truth?

INTERPRETATIONS AND FORTUNE-TELLING MEANINGS

★ Dreaming of opening a bottle of champagne indicates you will soon have a reason to celebrate.

★ Champagne exploding in all directions says others will try to claim credit for your achievements or seek a share of a windfall rightfully yours.

★ Flat champagne says you may be expressing pleasure you do not feel.

★ Opening vintage champagne indicates a lasting relationship or long-term success after prolonged effort.

★ Being given a crate of champagne says endeavors will be rewarded by the dream donor, or an unexpected bonus will materialize.

★ Spilling champagne or breaking champagne glasses may represent spoiled pleasure or launching a venture that will bring rich rewards.

OUTCOME OF PATSY'S DREAM

Patsy allowed the party to go ahead and ordered the most expensive champagne on her husband's credit card. Afterward she went away for three months. Though people said she was selfish, she refused to expose her husband to his family and friends, who adored him.

Champagne dreams rightly speak of celebrations or anticipation of great things. But outer celebration should be linked to inner satisfaction.

Changeling

Ben, seventeen, dreamed he was a changeling, but none of his friends knew. However, they suspected one of them was a changeling and were trying to find out who it was. Ben feared if they knew it was him, they would kill him. He was trying hard to mirror the way they spoke, moved, and acted.

DREAM BACKGROUND AND MEANING

Ben had always felt different. He had recently been diagnosed as being on the autism spectrum, but insisted that the diagnosis remain a secret. Changeling dreams are rooted in a sense of being different from family or peers and lacking the confidence to value yourself.

INTERPRETATIONS AND FORTUNE-TELLING MEANINGS

★ If you dream you were exchanged in the cradle for an elven baby, you may feel rejected for misreading the signals of others.

★ If you dream of a changeling being discovered by trickery by a suspicious family, you may be worried others will not accept you because of your challenges.

★ If you find your elven family in a dream but they deny you, you may feel caught between two worlds and should value yourself for the gifts you have.

★ If you dream that you and your family are driven away, you may worry because you are materially less advantaged than your peers.

★ If you dream of having magical powers but are afraid to reveal them, find like-minded spiritual people.

★ If you dream that everyone is staring at you because you have assumed your elven form, you may be afraid of standing out from the crowd. Fitting in will come at a price.

OUTCOME OF BEN'S DREAM

After the dream, Ben confided in his tutor and more sympathetic peers about his condition, and the response was positive. He joined a gifted students' group and an association for others with Asperger's to exchange strategies and to develop talents others did not possess. Changeling dreams may reveal that fears of being perceived as different are worse than the reality, and the fears should be shared.

Chanting

Juliana, fifty-four, regularly dreamed of a ruined abbey and the chanting of monks coming from within, although it was locked. When she peered through the window, she saw the abbey was in darkness, and it became silent. She could not identify the building except that it overlooked the sea. Juliana woke longing to sing again.

DREAM BACKGROUND AND MEANING

Juliana loved the religious choral society of which she was a member. Her lover, her personal physician, also belonged. He promised he would leave his wife when he retired, as he would no longer be breaking ethical rules. But upon retirement he cut off all contact with Juliana. She left the group, heartbroken.

INTERPRETATIONS AND FORTUNE-TELLING MEANINGS

★ If you dream of chanting from a particular culture or age, especially one with which you are unfamiliar, this may be a sign from a past world whose spiritual practices are calling you.

★ If you dream of chanting in an ashram, temple, or abbey from a culture to which you are drawn, explore opportunities to participate.

★ If you can hear chanting only faintly, others are drowning your authentic voice with their demands.

★ If in the dream only you hear the chanting, people around you may be out of step with your needs. Listen to your inner voice.

★ If you are joining in with chants in your sleep, you may have musical or singing abilities as yet undeveloped.

★ Chanting in dreams, whatever the source of the chants, represents a spiritual link in sleep with the sacred.

OUTCOME OF JULIANA'S DREAM

Juliana rejoined the choral group, where she had many friends. Her ex-lover was very embarrassed and left the group. Chanting dreams are profound forms of dreams, since the dream plane links the earth and the heavens through sacred sound. However, the dreams can also represent the pleasure of creative vocal expression, whether publicly or privately.

Chaperone

Annabelle, seventeen, dreamed she was in a Victorian ballroom with her aunt, who was her chaperone. She sat waiting to have her dance card signed by those young beaus her aunt approved of. She suddenly headed for the door, saying, "No more!" and jumped in the coach, instructing her coachman to drive away.

DREAM BACKGROUND AND MEANING

Sometimes Annabelle felt she was living in a Victorian drama with her father and maiden aunt. Her mother had died when she was a child. Annabelle was driven to school and not allowed on dates or to go shopping with her friends. Since her father was not ill-treating her, no one could intervene. Dreams of chaperones occur when the dreamer is feeling restricted and overcontrolled.

INTERPRETATIONS AND FORTUNE-TELLING MEANINGS

★ If you dream of being chaperoned in a historic setting, it may be a past-world dream, and you may be continuing the pattern of allowing someone to overly influence your life.

★ If you are a teen being chaperoned in the dream, whatever your actual age, you may be handing over control to keep the peace or because of self-doubt.

★ If you are chaperoning a well-behaved group of young people, you are confident in your ability to care for loved ones.

★ If you dream you are struggling to keep your charges under control, a rebellious younger person or a partner behaving unwisely could be causing you angst.

★ If you dream you break away from your chaperone, you are ready to live on your own terms.

★ If you are recaptured, you may fear losing the approval of whoever the chaperone represents.

OUTCOME OF ANNABELLE'S DREAM

Annabelle applied to a college at the other end of the country. In the meantime, her tutor arranged field trips connected with her course to give her a taste of freedom. At eighteen she took control of her trust fund and rarely returned home. Chaperone dreams often offer an impetus and means of escape from restrictions.

Chariot

Fiona, twenty-two, dreamed she was being driven in her chariot by her new girlfriend, Sara. They were traveling fast over rough ground. Fiona was afraid of falling. She called for Sara to slow down. Sara went faster and laughed. Fiona seized the reins. Sara tried to push Fiona off before leaping onto a passing chariot. Immediately Fiona was leading a victory parade, wearing a laurel wreath.

DREAM BACKGROUND AND MEANING

Fiona had fallen in love with Sara. Within a week of meeting, Sara had moved into Fiona's apartment. But Sara had taken over Fiona's life and invited people for heavy drinking sessions every evening, although Fiona was studying for her finals. Further, Sara did not contribute to expenses or chores. When Fiona asked for a contribution, Sara accused her of selfishness. Fiona felt her home was no longer hers. Chariot dreams are linked with striving for victory.

INTERPRETATIONS AND FORTUNE-TELLING MEANINGS

* Dreaming of riding a chariot in a victory parade may be a past-life dream. Be confident about future success.
* Riding a chariot into battle advises you to defend yourself against erosion of your personal space.
* To fall or be pulled from a chariot indicates fierce opposition when going for promotion or increased status. Who is pulling you from the chariot?
* Facing a charging chariot on foot suggests you should back off temporarily from confrontation.
* If you are not steering the chariot, are you happy with the direction it is taking?
* Taking over the reins of a chariot going in the wrong direction or too fast may be necessary to reclaim your personal territory.

OUTCOME OF FIONA'S DREAM

Fiona told Sara she could no longer invite people every night and had to pay her share of expenses. Sara became threatening and stormed out to stay with a new girlfriend. Fiona focused on study, qualifying with high honors. Because a chariot represents striving for success, do you want to be victor or prisoner?

Chasing

Tessa, twenty-eight, dreamed she was being chased through the forest by a pack of wolves. She could hear them howling and snapping close by. Tessa could hardly breathe but dared not stop. She tripped in a clearing and was surrounded. But though the wolves encircled her, she realized as she woke that they were protecting her.

DREAM BACKGROUND AND MEANING

Tessa had been physically and emotionally abused in a previous relationship and vowed, "Never again." Now she had met a kind, gentle man, Geoff, who wanted to marry her. But she was afraid and was avoiding him. Being chased by wild animals in a dream is a natural primal flight mechanism in which the animals represent our own fears, which we may erroneously or correctly project onto a new person or situation.

INTERPRETATIONS AND FORTUNE-TELLING MEANINGS

* If you dream you are being chased by someone you fear will kill or kidnap you, you are running from a problem that has become magnified by avoiding tackling it. If there is real danger, seek help.
* Being chased by wild animals says you are trying to suppress strong feelings about love or sexuality.
* If you are chasing someone, you may be trying to overtake them career-wise or attract them if they are a potential lover.
* If you stop to give the pursuer a chance to catch you, you may be running from an opportunity that would benefit you, but would like someone to persuade you.
* Dreaming of playing childhood chase or tag games suggests a competitive streak that you may hide under false modesty.
* If you dream you hide from a pursuer, you will gain breathing space from a problem that may resolve itself.

OUTCOME OF TESSA'S DREAM

Tessa talked to Geoff about her fears. They are taking the relationship slowly and seeing a counselor. With chase dreams, once the fears, which may be real, are faced in daily life, there may not be the need for flight.

Cheerleading

Steph, nineteen, dreamed she was carrying the cheerleader banner onto the playing field and the others were following. Her mother was watching proudly. A huge wind blew and snatched the banner out of her hand. Her mother raced out of the crowd, dressed in full cheerleader regalia, caught the banner, and took Steph's place.

DREAM BACKGROUND AND MEANING

Steph had been prepared from childhood to attend the college attended by her mother and aunts, who had all been part of the cheerleader squad. But Steph did not want to go to her mother's college, and she hated cheerleading. However, Steph felt she had to keep up the family tradition and had been accepted to the college. Cheerleading represents a joyous communal rallying to a cause, but only if it is a cause to which the dreamer subscribes.

INTERPRETATIONS AND FORTUNE-TELLING MEANINGS

★ Dreaming of carrying a cheerleading banner in triumph gives assurance that you will gain recognition and acclaim in your chosen field.

★ Marching in a different direction from the dream squad, whether or not you are actually involved in cheerleading, indicates the need to follow your own path in life.

★ A torn banner or pom-poms flying away suggests you are following a course of action to please others.

★ If you are performing complex synchronized actions, you will find success in your area of expertise through cooperating with others.

★ Leading a cheerleading squad onto the playing field says you will be required to motivate others, whether in the workplace, family, or socially if they are lacking enthusiasm.

OUTCOME OF STEPH'S DREAM

After the dream, Steph realized she was going to her mother's college purely to please her mother. In fact, she wanted to go to a completely different college that specialized in nuclear physics—her real passion. Cheerleading to please others or re-create their triumphs may ultimately prove disappointing for the dreamer and the person she is trying to please.

Cheesemaking

In her dream, Lorraine, thirty-seven, was working as a cheesemaker in a dairy. The family firm switched from cows' milk cheese to goats' milk cheese production overnight. Lorraine was expected to make the change using the same methods and equipment. However, the goats' milk would not set, and time and again she had to throw batches away and start again and was blamed for incompetence.

DREAM BACKGROUND AND MEANING

Lorraine worked as a proofreader of technical magazines for her family's small publishing house. Recently she had been required, as a process of modernization, to edit the material and produce camera-ready copy on her existing computer. Lorraine was finding it hard to adapt to new techniques on the old machines. She could not understand why she was failing when she never had before. Making cheese is a symbol of going through an ordered process from start to finish. Mistakes in the age-old process suggest something is wrong with either the cheesemaker or the equipment.

INTERPRETATIONS AND FORTUNE-TELLING MEANINGS

★ Making cheese involves producing something solid from liquid and so in a dream represents a smooth or problematic transition from start to finish.

★ If cheese curdles or is made into a spread in the dream, this is a poor substitute, whether for goods or in a relationship.

★ Cheesecake dreams involve great riches and profitability from basic beginnings.

★ Eating or selling tasty cheese promises happy gatherings, friendship, and even love.

★ If you are serving or being served moldy cheese, the situation or relationship is past its use-by date, and you should move on.

OUTCOME OF LORRAINE'S DREAM

After the dream, Lorraine realized that, just as in cheesemaking, if her work continued without modification she was doomed to fail. An expert was called in and discovered that the computers were not suitable for the complex editorial work required, as the right software was not installed. Lorraine was vindicated. Cheesemaking dreams can represent all kinds of processes at work or in the home which, if changed, must be modified appropriately.

Cherries

Vanessa, fifty-five, dreamed she was standing on a carpet of cherry blossoms being scattered by the wind. She was sad, because her annual vacation romance would soon end and her lover would return to his wife and family. Then he came across the orchard, carrying a basket of blossoms, and said, "When the cherries are ripe, we will be together."

DREAM BACKGROUND AND MEANING

Every year, Vanessa and Trent went to the cherry blossom festival in Japan. They had met secretly through the years, and each year he sent her a basket of ripe cherries, with his pledge they would one day be together. Her dream promised this was the year. Cherry blossoms symbolize lasting love.

INTERPRETATIONS AND FORTUNE-TELLING MEANINGS

- ★ Cherries, associated with the love goddess Venus, indicate a blossoming love and sexual relationship.
- ★ If you are counting cherrystones in your dream to discover if your love is true, or to find the answer to any other question requiring a positive or negative answer, it is said the dream count will reveal the answer.
- ★ If you dream of being in Japan or China during cherry blossom time, the Chinese goddess Xi Wang Mu, whose sacred cherry trees blossom every three thousand years, promises health and lasting life.
- ★ If you dream of picking cherries, you should reach for what you want.
- ★ If you are taking cherry medicine in the dream, which is good for coughs, express your true feelings to free up your life.
- ★ If you are carving cherry wood in the dream, this predicts good fortune and protection against all harm.

OUTCOME OF VANESSA'S DREAM

As in the dream, Trent arrived with his basket of ripe cherries, saying he would stay with her. But she knew that too many years had passed and said they would meet again in cherry blossom time. Cherry blossom dreams can be sad ones, because the blossoms are so fleeting, and by the time the fruit ripens love may be too late.

Chess

In the dream, Leo, twenty-five, was an amateur chess player, playing against a state champion in a game on which Leo had bet all his money. Leo realized, as the game was turning against him, that it was all or nothing, and made a totally unexpected move. To his amazement, he won the game.

DREAM BACKGROUND AND MEANING

Leo had inherited some money and, against the advice of his family's financial adviser, he was keen to invest in a new company overseas where a small quantity of very valuable diamonds had been found in a newly discovered mine. If there were more, Leo would make a fortune. If that was the extent of the yield, he would lose everything. The opinions of the experts who had initially explored the mine were very divided. Chess relies on strategies, well-practiced moves, and caution, but spectacular wins can occasionally result from taking a sudden chance.

INTERPRETATIONS AND FORTUNE-TELLING MEANINGS

- ★ If you dream you are playing in a grand tournament for a big prize, the stakes are high, whether at work or in your finances. Consider every move carefully.
- ★ If you are in a tournament where you move from player to player, your future depends on different people, each of whom you must convince.
- ★ If you knock over the chessboard, you may be treated unfairly in life and need to stop it.
- ★ If an opponent blatantly cheats and no one notices, beware of dubious dealings in finances by someone who appears plausible.
- ★ If a game goes on too long in the dream, you have already made your decision and further effort is time-wasting.

OUTCOME OF LEO'S DREAM

As a result of the dream, Leo went against the experts who advised caution, invested, and has made sufficient profit to cover his investment with a promise of more. He is learning chess. Chess-game dreams can be slow-moving. The more patience and tactics the dream suggests, the more caution you should exercise in real life.

Childbirth and Labor

Rosa, forty, dreamed that when she went into labor with her first child there was deep snow. The ambulance took her to the local state hospital. She had none of her calming candles and crystals, nor a water birth, because of staff shortages. Only her birthing partner and best friend, Liz, created calm and arranged the pain relief Rosa had sworn she would never have. Rosa resisted a cesarean section, but the harassed obstetrician shouted, "Do you want this damned baby or not?" In the dream Rosa woke shaken, but with a healthy baby.

DREAM BACKGROUND AND MEANING

Rosa loved Liz, but did not trust anyone to share her child, as her own mother had deserted her as a baby. Rosa had arranged for a water birth in an exclusive hospital, and Liz had rehearsed every breath and mantra with her. Childbirth dreams can reflect issues from the dreamer's mother if she was neglectful, and so the birthing mother may struggle for a perfect experience.

INTERPRETATIONS AND FORTUNE-TELLING MEANINGS

★ If your dream is of a relaxed birth with music and candles, this is a reassuring sign your body is moving into alignment.

★ If a dream birth is exceptionally fast, new energies, not necessarily connected with childbirth, are pouring into your life, demanding instant action.

★ If you have a set birth plan and it changes in the dream, this is a sign to remain flexible.

★ If you dream you run away from the hospital while in labor, you may have doubts and worries about pregnancy or a new venture.

★ If you dream of a cesarean section even though you may not want one, you may fear others will take over your child or your love.

★ If you dream of being a birth partner, even if the other person is not pregnant, you will support them in a new venture.

OUTCOME OF ROSA'S DREAM

Rosa relied on Liz during her labor and realized she would be totally trustworthy as a love partner and coparent. The birth was different from Rosa's plan, but that took nothing away from the experience. Birth, whether of an idea, project, relationship, or a child, often involves great effort and trust to flow with feelings.

Childbirth in the Later Years

Maura, sixty-five, dreamed she was in a maternity ward, waiting to give birth. She was her current age in the dream. After her previous traumatic delivery forty years earlier, Maura was warned she could not risk another baby. Everyone was panicking and saying she would not manage. Maura woke, knowing she would survive.

DREAM BACKGROUND AND MEANING

Maura's daughter, Rosemary, was very ill and would be hospitalized for several weeks after an operation, followed by several weeks' total rest. Rosemary had a very lively two-year-old daughter, Ruth, but was a single parent, and Maura was her only help. Maura's friends were saying that Maura could not possibly look after Ruth, as Maura had a heart condition, and the little girl would have to go into foster care. But Maura knew Ruth would not cope away from the family. Childbirth dreams in an older mother often herald a renewal of enthusiasm, health, and impetus for new things.

INTERPRETATIONS AND FORTUNE-TELLING MEANINGS

★ If you dream you are trying for a baby in your middle years or beyond, this later childbirth dream is a good omen, especially if you are having fertility treatment.

★ If you are in your middle years and do not want a baby, expect opportunities for a major career change or creative venture.

★ If you are undertaking extra responsibility for children in your middle or later years, this dream assures you that you will cope and gain pleasure.

★ If in the dream you leave the baby in the hospital or refuse to care for the infant, you are being asked to take on more than your fair share of responsibility for grandchildren or adult children relying on you.

★ If you are reliving in dreams giving birth to your own child, your teen or adult children may be manipulating you over imagined shortcomings.

OUTCOME OF MAURA'S DREAM

Maura welcomed her granddaughter, who settled in well, and this was a great relief to Rosemary, who focused on getting well. Late-baby dreams can also foretell the birth of a beloved grandchild with whom the dreamer will develop a special bond.

Childhood Home

Lesley, sixty, dreamed she was in the backyard of her childhood home, long demolished. She was planting flowers and bushes where nothing had grown. There was a rusty garbage can in the corner of the yard. Inside were beautiful plates in perfect condition and immaculate embroidered linen, never used. Lesley was very happy that her old home now had a lovely garden, and she vowed to use the forgotten treasures she thought she had given away.

DREAM BACKGROUND AND MEANING

Lesley had left her childhood home at twenty after her mother's sudden death, and all the contents had been cleared by an auction house. Lesley thought she had put her past out of her mind. Dreams of a former childhood home can lead a trail back to severed links with former happiness or sadness consciously buried and not resolved.

INTERPRETATIONS AND FORTUNE-TELLING MEANINGS

* To dream of being back in a childhood home indicates unfinished business, perhaps after a bad experience or a sudden breaking of links.
* To dream of fixing or cleaning the childhood home or garden years later shows the resurfacing of something missing from the present that existed in childhood.
* To discover unexpected treasures in a former childhood home revives forgotten happy memories and values.
* To rebuild or fix a childhood home opens the way to making positive changes in the future.
* If a childhood home cannot be put right in the dream, it is time to grieve for what was lost and move on.
* If in your dreams you make a childhood home beautiful, you are creating inner harmony by incorporating your earlier life into the person you are now.

OUTCOME OF LESLEY'S DREAM

Lesley had deliberately never collected beautiful things as her mother had done, as she regretted giving them away after her mother's death. After the dream, she decided, in memory of her mother, to create a beautiful garden in her present home for the grandchildren to play in, and to acquire new treasures. In dreams much can be repaired and renewed on the thought plane and can positively affect the way we take our lives forward.

Children

Daisy, forty, dreamed she was in a store filled with children— some cuddly babies, some cute toddlers. She realized she was there to choose the child she was expected to have with her partner, Jimmy. Daisy's and Jimmy's mothers were peering through the window excitedly, and Jimmy was kicking a ball around with a group of children, dressed in full soccer uniform. The sales staff warned Daisy that the store would soon be closing. Daisy walked out the door.

DREAM BACKGROUND AND MEANING

Daisy was being pressured to have a baby by her partner, both sets of prospective grandparents, and friends who had children. She felt railroaded into a role for which she was not ready. Unknown children in dreams can occur at times when the dreamer is considering or being persuaded to start a family.

INTERPRETATIONS AND FORTUNE-TELLING MEANINGS

* To regularly dream of a particular infant suggests that, if you are eager to start a family, a baby may be waiting to enter your life.
* If an older dream child joins you, this may be a reassurance that, even if you have suffered miscarriages, you can have a healthy child.
* If you dream of many children playing, the idea of your having a child may appeal to others more than to you.
* If you are aware that time is running out in the dream, the dream may alert you to the crucial question of whether you want a child or not.
* If in the dream you are happily playing with children and do not want any of your own yet or maybe ever, this may be your inner child, seeking fun and adventure rather than responsibilities.
* If you walk away from a child or children, and if potential grandparents and an eager partner are present in the dream, you have uncertainties about becoming a parent.

OUTCOME OF DAISY'S DREAM

Daisy realized she might never want a child and explained this to her partner and their parents. The potential grandparents were devastated. Eventually, Jimmy went off with another woman. Dreams can allow the dreamer to explore her true feelings about children, rather than blindly following others' wishes.

Children's Past-Life Homes

James, five, often dreamed of a white house with a black horse and carriage outside, in which he was taken for rides. When awake, he would ask his mother to take him back to his other family, which was waiting for him. Sometimes he woke distressed, but he could offer no details about the place or his other family.

DREAM BACKGROUND AND MEANING

James had talked of the dreams since he could speak clearly. His mother, Tricia, promised she would take him there, as she hoped that would stop him from being so distressed. But being unable to fulfill the promise made matters worse. Young children frequently dream and talk of earlier lives, though memories fade around age seven, so this should be accepted as part of life and not unduly emphasized or tested for accuracy.

INTERPRETATIONS AND FORTUNE-TELLING MEANINGS

★ If a child talks about an earlier life, seen in dreams, to the child it is very real, so the child should be allowed to freely talk of them.

★ If a child recognizes a place or old furniture or artifacts in a museum that were seen in a dream, this helps the child to gradually understand that change occurs over time.

★ These dreams are quite common in children. The child is not psychologically disturbed, just psychically sensitive.

★ If past-life dreams frighten the child, bedtime rituals can be devised to keep away the fears, as the child will not believe they are just from their imagination.

★ If other parents laugh or professionals become alarmed, encourage the child to talk about these dream worlds within the privacy of the family.

★ If the dream worlds become too dominant, make sure the child has plenty of physical exercise and a calm bedtime.

OUTCOME OF JAMES'S DREAM

In time the dreams became fewer as school, new friends, and sports were predominant in James's world, and eventually they faded from memory. Childhood past lives are a precious reminder that we may experience more than one lifetime.

Christmas (Yule)

Alicia, thirty-one, dreamed it was Christmas and her children were unwrapping their presents, scattering paper everywhere. She was very happy, as it was her first Christmas as a single parent. They cooked the Christmas meal together, then sang carols. She then woke, realizing there was no money for presents.

DREAM BACKGROUND AND MEANING

Alicia's ex-partner had gone overseas with his new girlfriend with vague promises to the children of presents upon his return. He paid no alimony, and Alicia was struggling financially. She didn't want to disappoint the children. Dreams of Christmas are often of an ideal, but if the family is happy in the dream it promises a joyous time ahead.

INTERPRETATIONS AND FORTUNE-TELLING MEANINGS

★ If you dream of Christmas and it is the middle of the year, you may need fun and a family get-together if life has been challenging.

★ If you dream of struggling to get everything done for Christmas, take a step back and downsize the celebrations.

★ If you dream of a nightmare Christmas with family disputes, modify your plans and reduce invitations to troublemakers.

★ If you dream of childhood Christmases and Santa Claus, focus on the magick of Christmas and not material goodies.

★ If you dream of going home for Christmas and it is disappointing in the dream, make an excuse and celebrate Christmas your own way.

★ If you dream of walking away from a celebration you have laboriously prepared for ungrateful relatives, ask what would make you happy at Christmas and make everyone else fit in.

OUTCOME OF ALICIA'S DREAM

The dream seemed real, but Alicia wondered how she could buy the presents. The answer came when a pop-up bargain store opened in the mall, selling nothing for more than two dollars. She was able to fill the children's Christmas stockings. Christmas dreams can involve wish-fulfillment of perfection but can also revive enthusiasm for making, not buying, happiness, the true spirit of Christmas.

Christmas Tree

Andrea, seventy, dreamed that she and the family were dragging home a gigantic Christmas tree with roots, which after Christmas would be planted in the garden. They decorated it with family baubles collected through the years, each with a story. But everyone disappeared, and she was left alone with a battered artificial tree and broken decorations.

DREAM BACKGROUND AND MEANING

Andrea, a widow, was aware that this would probably be the last family Christmas, as two of her children were moving overseas with her grandchildren. But everyone had reasons not to come. Dreams of Christmas trees for some families represent coming together on festive occasions as a sign of love, but for others they can be a sad reminder of happy times past.

INTERPRETATIONS AND FORTUNE-TELLING MEANINGS

* If in the dream you are buying a tree with roots, this represents deep underlying family unity.
* If you are buying a Christmas tree without roots, enjoy the occasion without expectations of others.
* If you are decorating a shiny artificial tree you do not like, consider what would make you happy, not just at Christmas but generally.
* If you are struggling to mend a shabby artificial tree, it's time to move on to creating a new future.
* If you dream you are at a community event, watching the Christmas tree lights turned on, you are ready to step back from the responsibility of trying to make everyone happy.
* If you dream that all the Christmas trees are sold, you have given too much and should now be giving to yourself.

OUTCOME OF ANDREA'S DREAM

Andrea bought a tree with roots. Through a local charity she invited young teens in foster care to spend the festive season with her. Her family unexpectedly arrived and were indignant that their mother had seemingly replaced them. Christmas tree dreams reveal how we may impose our personal brand of happiness on celebrations, but may not realize that it is no longer what others wanted, or never was.

Church

Peter, forty-one, regularly dreamed that he was in church on a Sunday morning with his wife, Jill, next to him, praying. He was incredibly happy, as she was not religious. She disappeared, and the priest announced that Peter would be banned from services because he had allowed her to leave.

DREAM BACKGROUND AND MEANING

Peter, son of a Presbyterian minister, was an avid churchgoer. Jill increasingly resented his time-consuming commitment to the church, especially all day on Sunday, her only day of leisure. When couples from different cultures and religions marry, or couples where one member has no religion marry, and when there are family cultural differences, dreams about church, mosque, temple, or synagogue can reveal deep divisions.

INTERPRETATIONS AND FORTUNE-TELLING MEANINGS

* A church building or service represents structured spirituality and living, which, depending on the dream, may be either secure or limiting.
* If one of a couple attends church and their partner or child is absent or leaves, one or both need to compromise if the relationship is to thrive.
* If you dream you are preaching in the pulpit, your values are important and you want others to see life your way.
* If you are harangued from the pulpit, you are suffering control issues if you or a family member go against convention or family traditions.
* The dream of a formal religious wedding, christening, or naming predicts a marriage or birth in the family, even if you are not religious.
* A dream of an abandoned or converted church suggests that the dreamer wants to break with tradition, probably left over from childhood.

OUTCOME OF PETER'S DREAM

Jill wanted to spend her Sundays kayaking and had joined a club. Peter realized he was going to lose Jill, as they were developing different lifestyles. He compromised and went along to the water sports every second Sunday. She helped organize water-sports activities for young churchgoers on the other weekends. No one commented adversely.

Church dreams can offer structure and purpose as long as life does not become rigid.

Cigarettes

Gaston, thirty-five, dreamed that he ran out of cigarettes and all the shops were closed. His live-in partner, Stu, said this was a good time to quit. Gaston was desperate and broke the window of the local corner store to steal cigarettes. He seized several packs and ran, deciding that he would deal with any consequences later.

DREAM BACKGROUND AND MEANING

Gaston smoked sixty cigarettes a day, having started smoking at age fourteen. Though he had a chronic cough and his physician warned him that he had the lungs of a fifty-year-old, Gaston still believed he could give up smoking any time. He rejected the idea of e-cigarettes. Stu hated the smell of cigarettes and said Gaston should quit or the relationship was over. Addiction to cigarettes can be revealed in a dream if the dreamer is denying the problem.

INTERPRETATIONS AND FORTUNE-TELLING MEANINGS

* If you dream that you light a cigarette in a location where they are not permitted, you are ready to challenge the status quo.
* If you inhale deeply and blow smoke rings, you embrace life—good and bad—on your own terms.
* If you blow smoke into someone's face in the dream, you may resent them.
* If a cigarette will not light or goes out, you need extra effort in generating a project or financial deal.
* If you give up smoking in your dream, you have the willpower to quit in daily life.
* If you are using an e-cigarette in the dream, you may feel slightly disappointed that you are settling for second best.

OUTCOME OF GASTON'S DREAM

After the dream, Gaston accepted that he was addicted to cigarettes and that giving up was incredibly difficult. He is now looking for a fellow smoker as a partner. Smoking dreams spell out to the dreamer the advisability of taking action, but only the dreamer can decide if the social and emotional cost of giving up cigarettes is greater than the benefits.

Circles

Petra, fifty-five, dreamed that she was going around in circles trying to find her way to a hotel in an unfamiliar city. There were no cabs, her smartphone battery was dead, and everyone she asked directed her back to the same place, the railway station. Frustrated, she caught the train home.

DREAM BACKGROUND AND MEANING

Via social media, Petra had restored contact with a group of school friends. Petra was aware that she had always been the scapegoat, neither as rich, clever, or attractive as the others. Now she was extremely successful, with a lovely family, but had noticed that on social media the girls treated her the same way as they had in school. Should she attend the upcoming reunion? Going around in circles in a dream suggests that the answer to a question will always be the same.

INTERPRETATIONS AND FORTUNE-TELLING MEANINGS

* Circles, large or small in a dream, symbolize love and unity with no vying for superiority, especially if family, friends, or colleagues gather around a circular table.
* If you dream that two circles are interlocked as gold or silver jewelry, this indicates a forthcoming marriage or love union.
* If smaller circles are part of the design, that suggests the number of children or grandchildren there may be.
* A broken circle predicts new people coming into your family or social circle or, if you are divorced, that you may remarry. However, you may need to move on from a relationship or activity that is no longer working.
* If you dream of an ancient stone circle or a circle of robed people, you may be linking into a past world.
* If you dream of crop circles spontaneously appearing, you may encounter cynicism toward spiritual beliefs or practices.

OUTCOME OF PETRA'S DREAM

Petra realized that if she met her old circle of friends, she would still be cast as the scapegoat. She did not attend the reunion and instead withdrew contact. Circles can be symbols of strength and hold friends or family together, but they will break if members vie for superiority.

Circus

Marlene, forty-six, dreamed she was riding a white horse at great speed around a circus ring. She leaped onto the tightrope and swung high above the big top on the trapeze. She woke disappointed and discontented.

DREAM BACKGROUND AND MEANING

Marlene never had a job, as she married very young and had five children in quick succession. Her husband had a high-paying position but had his own life. The children were now independent. Marlene had circus blood generations back and longed to join a traveling circus. Her family laughed and said she should grow up and settle down. She traced her circus relations. Should she contact them or dismiss the fantasy? While dreams of circuses can be illusion dreams, they also represent the inner child, too often buried under convention.

INTERPRETATIONS AND FORTUNE-TELLING MEANINGS

* If you dream you are enjoying watching a circus, it's a good time for family matters and reunions with someone from your childhood.
* If you dream you are performing in the circus, you need a more fulfilling role in life to express your talents.
* Circus dreams can indicate a future love interest outside marriage, which you can choose whether or not to develop.
* If you are performing daring feats in the circus ring, you may be stifled by those around you in order to fulfill their needs.
* If the audience is caught up in the excitement, a seemingly impossible dream can be achieved, at least partly.
* If the circus ring is empty, you may feel you have missed out on life but can discover your true purpose.

OUTCOME OF MARLENE'S DREAM

Marlene contacted her circus family, which was looking for someone to organize circus-skills classes in the winter when the circus did not travel. Twice a year she would travel with the circus to give the students practical experience. Circus dreams are a reminder that it is never too late to make dreams come true, even if it means risking disapproval or ridicule.

City

In his dream, Luigi, twenty-five, wandered aimlessly around the city before phoning his folks back home in Italy and pretending he was having a great time. He climbed steps and found himself in an area that could have been his home village, with lanterns that lit the tavernas, people chatting in the street in Italian, and even olive trees. He was so happy.

DREAM BACKGROUND AND MEANING

Luigi had an internship in architecture but was homesick. At night the area where he worked emptied of people, who dashed home on the subway to their families. Luigi was contemplating returning to Italy, but his job was an opportunity of a lifetime. Impersonal cities in dreams represent a sense of isolation in a fast-moving world.

INTERPRETATIONS AND FORTUNE-TELLING MEANINGS

* If you dream of moving to a big city, opportunities are coming your way, maybe a promotion or the chance to join a big organization.
* Dreaming you are lost in a city suggests you are worried about working or socializing in an impersonal environment or being overlooked by an official organization you are trying to deal with.
* Dreaming you are enjoying the fast pace of city life offers a stimulating new environment through joining collective ventures or business with others.
* Dreaming of walking through a neglected area can represent fears of a strange and potentially hostile environment.
* If you dream of a city where you previously lived, you are longing for some aspect of the past.
* If you are wandering aimlessly around a city, you may not yet be ready to make a major decision.

OUTCOME OF LUIGI'S DREAM

After the dream, Luigi changed his walking route and eventually found steps leading to what he later discovered was the Italian quarter. He instantly felt at home and moved there. Being drawn telepathically through a dream can reveal a city made up of hidden villages, which are the true heart of a city beyond its impersonal facade.

City Walls

Reuben, thirty-one, dreamed he was living within the walls of an ancient city, with the sea on one side and fortified gates on the other. He wanted to leave but needed a special permit to pass through the gates. His only alternative was seaward, but the descent down the sea wall was dangerous. He woke secure, knowing he was trapped by the very security that protected him.

DREAM BACKGROUND AND MEANING

Reuben had a safe job in which he could steadily progress. He had no money worries. But the thought of being trapped in the same boring career filled him with dread. City walls represent a sheltered lifestyle, but living by the restrictions of your chosen life, career, or relationship may be the trade-off.

INTERPRETATIONS AND FORTUNE-TELLING MEANINGS

✴ If you dream of living within the walls of an ancient city, this may be a past-life dream. The degree of freedom you have to come and go will determine whether this is security or restriction.

✴ If in the dream you lack a permit to pass beyond guarded gates, the dream is pointing out the high price you pay for limiting yourself to material advantage.

✴ If you are trying to escape in the dream, you may need to pay a high price for changing your lifestyle and career.

✴ If you escape by water, you are acknowledging a dissatisfaction with a desired emotion or relationship.

✴ If you escape through a gate by negotiating with the guards, you may be able to follow opportunities through official channels.

✴ If you dream that you try to slip through the walls and are injured, you need to accept that you must stay put for now.

OUTCOME OF REUBEN'S DREAM

After the dream, Reuben acknowledged that his current profession enabled him to educate his children, give the family a good lifestyle, and save for the future. City-walls dreams represent security, unless they are stormed in the dream, in which case safety may be only illusory.

Clay

Peg, forty-five, dreamed she was making clay pots, statues, and animals in her pottery studio. Before she could fire them, they came to life and marched into the spare studio she no longer used. Waiting were rows of children and adults sitting on the benches and holding lumps of clay expectantly.

DREAM BACKGROUND AND MEANING

Together Peg and her husband owned and operated a successful pottery manufacturing and retail outlet for many years. But since his death six months earlier, the business was looking rundown and neglected. Clay dreams are a sign that you can reshape your life.

INTERPRETATIONS AND FORTUNE-TELLING MEANINGS

✴ If you dream you are making a clay pot or statue, create the future you want from your present expertise and talents.

✴ If someone else is making the pot or statue, do not let others shape your destiny.

✴ If you are stuck walking through clay, you may have to work harder than expected to break the influence of a destructive person or habit.

✴ If you are using clay in your dream as a beauty treatment or health remedy, it may benefit you in everyday life, so note the color and kind of treatment.

✴ If you break a clay pot or one breaks in the kiln, your endeavor may need rethinking and greater care in creation to avoid mistakes caused through haste.

✴ If you dream you are making models with children's colored play clay, it is a good omen for having a baby. The number of children playing with you, if you do not have any, may indicate the size of your family.

OUTCOME OF PEG'S DREAM

After the dream, a customer came into the pottery and asked if Peg gave lessons. On impulse Peg said yes. She converted her husband's old studio and now runs classes for adults and children. As a result, Peg's sales are also flourishing. Because clay is so malleable, you already have the gifts for success if you use them in a new way.

Cleaning

Layla, fifty-two, dreamed she was desperately trying to clear up her son's mess. His bedroom was covered in potato-chip packets and soda cans, but the more she cleaned, the more the garbage piled high. Her former mother-in-law appeared, saying Layla was a neglectful mother, living in a pigsty; no wonder her husband had left her.

DREAM BACKGROUND AND MEANING

Layla's husband had moved out after an affair with a younger woman who became pregnant. Layla's former mother-in-law came regularly to blame Layla for the marriage breakup. When Layla's son got into minor trouble with the law, because he was bullied and tried to please the bullies, her former mother-in-law said it was because Layla was such a bad mother. Dreams like this are exaggerations of an actual situation and seem to confirm negative comments. Clean houses are regarded as symbols of a worthy person.

INTERPRETATIONS AND FORTUNE-TELLING MEANINGS

* If you dream you are cleaning a mess created by others, you may be taking on too much responsibility for other people.
* If you are cleaning a stain that will not come out, others are off-loading guilt or unfair blame not rightly yours.
* If you are cleaning a kitchen, you will have domestic happiness and family celebrations.
* If you are cleaning a childhood home, you may be seeking approval from employers or older family members.
* If you clear away all the clutter and garbage, you are ready for a fresh start.
* If you are cleaning before the arrival of an important visitor, refuse to be intimidated by others' unreasonable standards in any area of life.

OUTCOME OF LAYLA'S DREAM

Layla barred her former mother-in-law from her home and supported her youngest son. Her husband did not attend the court proceedings. The magistrate gave her son a caution and praised her as a caring mother. Cleaning dreams represent an attempt to control a situation outside of your power to fix.

Cliff Edge

Mel, twenty-eight, had a recurring dream that she was too near the edge of a crumbling cliff. She was drawn against her will to stand on the edge. Her foot slipped and she was falling fast. She always woke before hitting the rocky shore, totally disoriented.

DREAM BACKGROUND AND MEANING

Mel was in love with Ed, a charismatic, passionate, unemployed guy. He had moved in with her and was, unknown to her, selling drugs while she was at work. The police were called by neighbors, and her lease and career were in danger, as her boyfriend insisted the drugs were Mel's.

Falling-off-cliff dreams, like other falling dreams (see "Bungee Jumping, Acrophobia," p. 75), indicate letting go of sexual inhibitions, and sometimes overriding normal caution.

INTERPRETATIONS AND FORTUNE-TELLING MEANINGS

* If you dream that you climb a cliff easily, take a chance on reaching for success or promotion.
* Dreams of rappelling or hang-gliding from a cliff, or turning falling into flying, talk of unexpected help or luck widening your horizons.
* If the cliff edge is crumbling or you nearly lose your foothold, be careful of financial, love, or career risks.
* Getting too near the edge of crumbling cliffs warns against being seduced into unwise behavior.
* Descending a cliff to rescue someone trapped by the tide or stuck halfway indicates that your help will be needed. Don't fall for a hard-luck story and jeopardize yourself.
* Dreaming of a car or person falling over a cliff represents an area of life out of synch, especially if someone else is controlling your life.

OUTCOME OF MEL'S DREAM

Mel realized Ed was using her as a safe haven for his drug dealing while she took all the risks and paid the expenses. He disappeared after the police visit. Cliffs mark the limits of the land and suggest a degree of uncertainty, which must be evaluated according to their stability in the dream.

Climate Change

Emma, thirteen, had recurring nightmares that the North Pole had melted and there was a huge flood that affected many parts of the world. She woke trying to stay afloat and save the family as the water rose and the home was submerged. But no one was listening to her warning.

DREAM BACKGROUND AND MEANING

Emma attended an alternative school in Detroit, Michigan. The curriculum included lessons on climate change and saving the environment. Emma talked of little else at home and was constantly lecturing the family about wasting resources. She had applied to represent the school at a junior conference in Washington, DC, and sent letters to world leaders on behalf of the school group she had organized. Her parents were extremely concerned that climate change was becoming an obsession.

INTERPRETATIONS AND FORTUNE-TELLING MEANINGS

★ Dreams about climate change are common among committed young people and, if talked about, will lose their fear.

★ Climate-change dreams can be predictive, especially among teenagers whose psychic powers are evolving.

★ A climate-change dream in adults can offer an incentive to become more environmentally aware and make even a small difference.

★ Climate-change dreams can also reflect general fears about being overwhelmed by situations at work or financially that are beyond our control.

★ If in the dream you are drowning because of floods or affected by hostile weather patterns, you need to acknowledge deep emotions in a relationship that need talking through to lose their power.

★ If you dream of forest fires or extreme heat and drought, you should not be swept up by others' anger or fan the flames of gossip and jealousy.

OUTCOME OF EMMA'S DREAM

Emma was chosen as the junior school representative at the conference because of her knowledge and commitment. Several government departments she contacted replied. The head teacher told Emma's parents that they should be proud of her. The nightmares stopped.

Clocks

Nigel, twenty-five, dreamed he was with his late grandfather, who was young and dressed in a servant's uniform. His grandfather was winding up a grandfather clock in a stately home. His grandfather said, "It is my lifetime ambition to own a grandfather clock like the rich folk. Now all must share it." Nigel woke confused.

DREAM BACKGROUND AND MEANING

There were major family disputes over Nigel's late grandfather's valuable antique grandfather clock. The old man had bought it when he established his own business as a reminder of the one he had wound daily when he worked as a servant. Nigel told the family of the dream, which he took to be a message.

Machines that measure time, whether they are watches or smartphones, have the same dream meaning as clocks. Clocks are, however, still the main dream symbol for time.

INTERPRETATIONS AND FORTUNE-TELLING MEANINGS

★ If you dream you hear a clock chiming, the time is coming when you can fulfill an important need or wish.

★ A clock whose battery has died or is unwound warns of minor delays to plans.

★ If you dream that an alarm clock fails to ring, you may be ignoring signs to seize an opportunity or avert a potential disaster.

★ If time is moving extra fast or you keep checking the time in your dream, you may be overwhelmed by too many tasks and should slow down.

★ Clock hands or numbers going backward suggest that a former relationship or unresolved issue may be reemerging.

★ A broken clock indicates that the time has passed to revive a relationship, unless the clock is mended in the dream.

OUTCOME OF NIGEL'S DREAM

Nigel investigated and discovered that the stately home where his grandfather once worked was now a museum. The family agreed that the clock should be donated to the museum so many could enjoy it. Grandfather and grandmother clocks represent family respect, and Nigel's grandfather did not want the family divided over the clock.

Clothes

Nan, thirty, dreamed she was getting ready for an important party where she would meet people who could advance her career. Everything she tried on was stained or far too large or small. She rushed to the department store and chose an outfit that fit perfectly, but she realized she had left her purse at home. Nan ran out of the store wearing the outfit and arrived at the party out of breath and disheveled, pursued by security guards. They made her take it off, leaving her wearing nothing but her underwear.

DREAM BACKGROUND AND MEANING

Nan was trying for a top job in an all-female firm of lawyers. Her colleagues were always immaculately groomed. Although Nan knew she was a good lawyer, she was a single parent and could not keep up with the morning grooming regimen. Clothes represent the outer image we present to the world, and if they are dirty or creased in the dream, this reflects our fears that we are somehow inferior.

INTERPRETATIONS AND FORTUNE-TELLING MEANINGS

*   Buying new clothes in your dream implies a desire to create a good impression. Be guided by your choice.
*   Wearing the wrong clothes at a party or for work can mean that you are afraid of the disapproval of those around you.
*   Torn clothes say petty spite is worrying you more than you acknowledge.
*   If you buy piles of clothes and leave them in their bags in the dream, you have an inner dissatisfaction with who you are and try to compensate by continually reinventing the outer form.
*   If you dream that you are stealing clothes, you want to be like someone you admire or envy.

OUTCOME OF NAN'S DREAM

After the dream, Nan focused on her cases, not her appearance. To her surprise, she was offered the job she wanted. The CEO said clients felt safe with her because she looked approachable and genuine, not like a clotheshorse. How we dress can mistakenly be based on the superficial criteria imposed by others and not on a reflection of our true selves.

Clothespins

In her dream, Angela, fifty, was a little girl, and some traveling women came to the door selling wooden clothespins. Angela was excited, because her mother made her dolls from individual clothespins, dressing them with scraps of material. Angela woke feeling the old happiness at her homemade toys.

DREAM BACKGROUND AND MEANING

Angela's three young grandchildren were constantly wanting expensive gifts and, with Christmas coming, Angela was worried about how she was going to buy anything from the list their mother had supplied. She felt her grandchildren were growing up to be very materialistic. Dreaming of clothespin dolls is a reminder that the best toys do not have to cost a fortune.

INTERPRETATIONS AND FORTUNE-TELLING MEANINGS

*   If you dream of seeing washing on a clothesline in the breeze, home life will go smoothly and, for the person to whom the garments belong, there will be special happiness through simple pleasures.
*   If you dream you are using clothespins to hang your outer garments on a clothesline, you are concerned how others see you.
*   If you dream you use clothespins to hang your under-clothes, you are willing to express your true self without worrying what others think.
*   If clothespins break or come unfastened, scattering the washing, a close friendship or love affair may seem to be unraveling and need extra care.
*   If you dream of old-fashioned wooden clothespins, this may be nostalgia for an older, simpler lifestyle.
*   If you dream you run out of clothespins before hanging out all the washing, you may feel that demands are making you spread your attention too thin.

OUTCOME OF ANGELA'S DREAM

Angela borrowed old-fashioned clothespins from her own mother and made a whole village of dolls, even painting their faces. The children were entranced, and on Christmas morning they played with the dolls more than the expensive toys for which they had asked. Since clothespins signify unity, a clothespin dream represents holding a family securely in love and not through material offerings.

Clouds

Pete, forty-five, dreamed he was holding a barbecue for his boss, work colleagues, and families in the yard. There was not a cloud in the sky. Suddenly, fast-moving black clouds appeared, so dense that it was almost like night. Pete was holding a bag of gold, his savings. The dark clouds continued to descend and blotted out the garden. By the time the clouds cleared, his boss had disappeared with the gold. Pete woke confused.

DREAM BACKGROUND AND MEANING

Pete's boss had invited Pete to become a partner in the company. Pete's late grandfather had recently left him a sizable sum, but Pete had hesitated about investing, though the company figures look promising.

INTERPRETATIONS AND FORTUNE-TELLING MEANINGS

★ Gold-edged clouds or the sun breaking through indicate dreams coming true, ambitions fulfilled, and favorable resolution if there has been doubt or despondency.

★ White fluffy clouds promise a happy, long-overdue outing or vacation with friends, partner, or family.

★ Storm clouds or fast-moving clouds say that a confrontation or change you have been dreading will clear the atmosphere at home or work.

★ Increasing gray or black clouds advise caution in any projected undertaking. If blanketing the dream scene, beware of hidden motives.

★ A cloudless sky promises contentment and a problem-free period ahead.

★ If clouds are moving to the right, this is a good omen. If to the left, prepare yourself against opposition to plans from others.

★ Check for images in the dream clouds, as these will hold further information.

OUTCOME OF PETE'S DREAM

Pete refused the offer. His boss persuaded another employee to invest, but soon afterward he disappeared with the money. Pete's boss had been diverting company funds into an overseas account for months. Where clouds play a significant part or backdrop to a dream, their color and density advise whether this is a good time to proceed with plans or an offer, and suggest that matters are not as clear as anticipated.

Clown

Theodore, thirty-three, dreamed he was watching clowns in a circus ring when he was dragged into the ring, dressed as a clown, and chased around the circus ring by clowns blowing old-fashioned car horns. Theodore tried to pull the mask off, but it was stuck. Terrified, he looked for the exit, but the clowns jumped on top of him so he could not breathe. With a huge effort he pushed them off, ripped off the costume, and pursued them out of the ring, to the cheers of the crowd.

DREAM BACKGROUND AND MEANING

Theodore has a clown phobia, so the dream was doubly frightening. He was in the armed services and suffered covert bullying because he is gay. He responded with humor because he was afraid the bullying would escalate. Depending on whether you like or fear clowns, dream clowns can have a sinister side, linked with the archetypal trickster.

INTERPRETATIONS AND FORTUNE-TELLING MEANINGS

★ If you dream you are dressed as a clown, making others laugh, are you hiding fears and trying to please others too much?

★ Being chased by a malevolent clown warns that there is someone concealing cruelty behind humor.

★ If a clown plays a joke on you that you do not find funny, beware of a trickster in your life or someone trying to secretly undermine you.

★ Watching clowns in a circus indicates that you need more fun, rather than watching from the sidelines.

★ Dreaming you are wearing clown makeup or a costume you cannot remove says you find it hard to reveal your true self.

★ If a clown appears at work or at home in a dream, be careful you do not sacrifice common sense for popularity.

OUTCOME OF THEODORE'S DREAM

Theodore made an official complaint against the worst bullies, who were persecuting other gay soldiers as well. He was asked to help organize a new department for LGBT soldiers. The risk of being mocked may be outweighed by the need to reveal your true self.

Cobra

Phoebe, seven, dreamed she saw a huge cobra climbing the staircase with its hood extended toward the top-floor classroom where her mother was a teacher. The cobra entered her mother's classroom and bit Phoebe's mother on the neck. Her mother died instantly. Phoebe rushed into her mother's bedroom, crying, "Mom, are you all right?"

DREAM BACKGROUND AND MEANING

Phoebe had been worried after her mother's twin brother had been killed in a traffic accident. Since then, her mother had been very impatient with Phoebe. Phoebe told her mother she hated her. Phoebe had a fascination with the cobra in the local zoo, but since the accident had become afraid it might escape and kill them. The cobra goddess in both Ancient Egypt and India was a destroyer but also a Mother Goddess, seen protecting children.

INTERPRETATIONS AND FORTUNE-TELLING MEANINGS

★ If you dream of a cobra coiled protectively around a child, you have more power than you realize, but take care not to retaliate in anger against rivals.

★ If you dream of a cobra rearing up ready to strike, beware of a maternal figure or controlling female who can become vicious if wishes are ignored.

★ If you dream of a cobra spiraling upward out of the basket of a snake charmer, someone charismatic may try to charm you.

★ If a cobra kills a mother figure in a dream, you have maternal anger issues.

★ If you kill a cobra, you can defeat opposition, but be sure your actions are justified.

OUTCOME OF PHOEBE'S DREAM

Phoebe described the dream to her mother, who realized she had been so consumed in her grief that she had been impatient with Phoebe. They visited the zoo and Phoebe saw that the cobra could not escape. Dreaming of cobras, one of the most powerful venomous snakes, is linked with primitive fears of death, birth, and fertility embedded in the human psyche, which can be released when you experience personal tragedy, especially when young.

Coffee

Maeve, thirty, dreamed she was making coffee at the stall where she worked and the line was stretching around the corner. The boss was getting angry because she was too slow, and she was muddling up orders in her haste. Finally, Maeve spilled coffee, burned herself, and ran off.

DREAM BACKGROUND AND MEANING

Maeve worked at a high-pressure call center. She was expected to be always cheerful, keep calls to a maximum of three minutes, and never offer a refund, however justified. Maeve was not sleeping at night and was aware that she was making mistakes.

INTERPRETATIONS AND FORTUNE-TELLING MEANINGS

★ To dream of sharing coffee is a good sign of amicable cooperative dealings at work, or a flourishing friendship or family gathering.

★ If the dream coffee is bitter, be prepared to deal with someone who is sharp-tongued and overcritical.

★ If coffee is weak, promised support may not be forthcoming, or enthusiasm may be halfhearted.

★ To spill coffee indicates wasted energy on a cause that was not worthwhile.

★ To be reading fortunes with coffee grounds says the future will be unexpectedly revealed.

★ To be making or buying coffee for others says you will be called on to offer support or revive enthusiasm in a project or situation.

★ The kind of coffee affects the meaning of the dream: latte means lighthearted, but not necessarily trustworthy; filtered means getting half the story or truth; espresso or black means to the point; and cappuccino suggests not to be taken seriously.

OUTCOME OF MAEVE'S DREAM

Though Maeve needed the money, she realized the job was making her ill and stressed. She resigned and after a week or so found she felt full of energy and enthusiasm again. She has started a delivery service of coffee to offices from the coffee shops in the area where she worked. Coffee dreams talk about stimulation, but can warn of stress overload building up.

Coins

Eddie, thirty-five, dreamed he was dressed in pirate attire, loading a box of pieces of eight coins into his small boat. He knew he could live comfortably all his life on the proceeds. But, feeling himself being watched and afraid, he left the box on the shore.

DREAM BACKGROUND AND MEANING

Eddie lived close to the edge of the law. After a gang fight, he had picked up a wallet from the floor that contained many thousands of dollars. He knew it was illegal money, but it would enable him to start a new life with his girlfriend. But had he been seen? Pieces of eight are valuable silver Spanish dollar coins that were used as currency throughout the Americas and worldwide between the fifteenth and nineteenth centuries.

INTERPRETATIONS AND FORTUNE-TELLING MEANINGS

★ If you dream that coins shower from the sky, especially gold ones, this is a sign your finances will improve greatly from an unexpected or unexplored source.

★ If the coins are running through your fingers and you cannot catch them, you may be regularly wasting small amounts that are leading to debt.

★ Finding ancient coins says a previous investment or moneymaking scheme will bear fruit.

★ If you dream you are counting coins for a purchase in a store rather than using a credit card or dollar bills, you may be contemplating a purchase you cannot afford.

★ Dreaming of picking up coins dropped on the sidewalk is traditionally a sign of good luck, especially the day after the dream.

★ If you dream the coins are fake gold or silver, beware of scams or a bargain too good to be true.

OUTCOME OF EDDIE'S DREAM

A gang member asked Eddie if he had seen the wallet, and Eddie handed it over. He decided he and his girlfriend should go away immediately so they could live without fear. Dreaming of being given silver coins represents financial wishes coming true, but there may be an emotional price.

Comedy, Comedian

In her recurring dream, Jenny, twenty-six, was on stage at the famous Comedy Cellar in New York City. Midway through her act, she was interrupted when another comedian appeared from backstage; at the same time, Jenny disappeared into a sinking floor. All the while, she heard the audience hysterically laughing at the other comedian. She woke in tears.

DREAM BACKGROUND AND MEANING

From a very early age, Jenny had wanted to be a comedian. She did stand-up at as many open-mic nights as possible to perfect her craft and was gaining a reputation as an accomplished comedian, destined for bigger things. But, despite this, she had strong self-doubts about her ability. Comedy by its nature is risky if it fails to entertain, and comedians are especially sensitive to not raising a laugh, a fear that reflected in Jenny's anxiety dreams.

INTERPRETATIONS AND FORTUNE-TELLING MEANINGS

★ If you dream you are on stage as a professional comedian and people are laughing and applauding, you have the confidence as well as the talent to perform in your chosen communication field.

★ If no one laughs at your jokes, you have very high standards and can spoil your own performance through anxiety.

★ If you dream you are making colleagues, friends, or family laugh, this may be an effective way you gain approval for your aims.

★ If someone is making you laugh, you may rightly wonder what they are concealing.

★ If you end comedy dreams in tears, you may be using humor to hide sorrow.

OUTCOME OF JENNY'S DREAM

The dream told Jenny that the only way to overcome doubts was to keep performing. She decided to audition for theater, radio, and television sitcoms where she is one of a team, until she builds up her confidence for solo work. The best comedians are naturally insecure, as that gives them rapport with the audience. True comedy involves pathos, but the anxiety of failure dreams is a price comedians pay.

Comet

Mandy, thirty-seven, dreamed she was sewing the Bayeux Tapestry to commemorate the Battle of Hastings in 1066, when William the Conqueror had invaded England. She was sewing an image of Halley's Comet in the sky, which had appeared in the months before the battle, the Normans claimed, heralding victory. She looked out of the window and there was a comet blazing across the sky. But none of the other women would believe she had really seen one.

DREAM BACKGROUND AND MEANING

Mandy loved history and wanted to write historical novels. She was especially fascinated by the feisty women who had come to England with the invaders. She had been born when Halley's Comet appeared in 1986, and everyone said that made her very lucky. Comets were often regarded as portents of great good fortune, though in some cultures they were considered warnings of regicide (the action of killing a king), as happened in 1066 to the opposing King Harold.

INTERPRETATIONS AND FORTUNE-TELLING MEANINGS

* A comet in a dream heralds a sudden, unexpected opportunity to shine that may be short-lived and should be seized.
* If a comet appears momentarily and disappears, do not rely on lavish promises of wealth or success.
* A comet hitting Earth brings a radical shake-up of ideas that demands instant response.
* Because Halley's Comet is the only comet visible to the naked eye that appears more than once in a lifetime, if it manifests in a dream it means you may have a second chance to attain what is desired.
* A comet moving around the sun says you need to travel to gain what you want, as opportunity will not come to you.
* A comet with an exceptionally long tail warns that the effects of an impulsive action may be a long time clearing.

OUTCOME OF MANDY'S DREAM

After her dream of seeing Halley's Comet in the sky through the dream window, Mandy applied for and obtained a loan to study early history at a university. She is writing a trilogy of the Norman invasion, including the second appearance of Halley's Comet seventy-six years later. A comet in a dream can be considered heralding new energies.

Coming First

Ray, twenty-five, dreamed he was for the first time sitting in first class, sipping champagne on a transatlantic flight. Then, just after takeoff, an apologetic flight attendant told him that a very important guest was on board and needed Ray's seat, so Ray would have to move into economy. Ray protested but did not feel sufficiently confident to stand his ground.

DREAM BACKGROUND AND MEANING

After years of hard work, Ray had been promoted and was entitled to travel first-class when on a business trip. Traveling first-class represents the impetus to strive for the best in a chosen area of life.

INTERPRETATIONS AND FORTUNE-TELLING MEANINGS

* If you dream you get first place in a race or an examination, acknowledge your ambitions and do not stand aside for others less deserving.
* If you are first to arrive at a celebration or meeting in your dream, you may be overly eager to make a good impression.
* If you are beaten to first place by someone who is cheating, you may need to assert your rights if the odds are stacked against you.
* If you dream of your first love many years later, you may be disenchanted with an existing relationship and need to recapture your earlier enthusiasm.
* If you dream of love at first sight, this can be a premonition that you will meet the right person and know instantly.
* If you win first prize in a competition or raffle, luck is on your side for a once-in-a-lifetime opportunity.

OUTCOME OF RAY'S DREAM

Ray boarded the first-class section of the plane, but he was concerned about a distressed elderly woman who could not find her seat in economy. Ray offered her his seat, but instead the flight attendant had her upgraded to first class near Ray. Coming first in any area of life may be more important to the dreamer than the tangible reward.

Commitment

In his dream, Terrance, thirty-one, purchased a property with his boyfriend, Scott, and discovered that Scott was extremely untidy, drank excessively, and was prone to temper fits. Upon awakening, Terrance wondered if this could be the real Scott or if he was seeking a reason to avoid commitment.

DREAM BACKGROUND AND MEANING

Terrance had been dating twenty-four-year-old Scott for a few weeks. Scott had suggested they purchase an apartment together and, in the meantime, he moved into Terrance's rented apartment. Terrance was feeling pressured. Scott accused Terrance of having a commitment phobia. Commitment dreams often pick up issues beneath the surface, to be acknowledged and hopefully resolved.

INTERPRETATIONS AND FORTUNE-TELLING MEANINGS

* If you meet someone for the first time and see yourselves married in a dream, this could be love at first sight but may be falling in love with love.
* If you dream of you and a prospective partner together happily in old age, your subconscious is picking up deep compatibility.
* If your partner is pushing for commitment and you are uncertain, a dream in which they show a very different side of their character may advise caution.
* If you want commitment but you dream of your partner alone or with someone else, this may reflect uncertainty by your partner about settling down.
* If you dream of your lover still committed to an ex, this may be an anxiety dream, but do not ignore doubts that your hidden radar may have picked up.
* If you dream of being committed to someone who isn't your current partner, it's time for a relationship check to see what can be mended.

OUTCOME OF TERRANCE'S DREAM

Terrance realized he did not know that much about Scott, who had been involved in other fast-igniting commitments that had ended acrimoniously. Terrance invited Scott to stay most weekends, but has noticed one or two aspects of Scott with which he is not comfortable. Scott is threatening to move on. Commitment dreams can offer a prediction of future bliss or otherwise.

Compass

Etta, twenty-three, dreamed she was totally lost in a dense forest and walking in circles. It was getting dark and she was scared. Suddenly she found she was holding her late grandfather's compass, which he had used in the navy and which had always fascinated her. The compass needle swung and stayed in one direction. She followed it and found her car.

DREAM BACKGROUND AND MEANING

Etta felt directionless and had tried various college courses but given up on them all. She had come home but knew she was drifting. The only career that interested her was the navy. Compass dreams center around issues of direction or lack of direction and may involve choosing a path and following it all the way.

INTERPRETATIONS AND FORTUNE-TELLING MEANINGS

* If you dream you are holding a compass and it points unwaveringly ahead, you can be sure you are taking the right direction in life.
* If you find a compass, you need to discover the right way ahead, which may involve following different directions until one feels right.
* If you are buying a compass in the dream, you will have the opportunity for travel, whether for a vacation or for relocation.
* If you are given a compass by an older friend or family member in a dream, living or deceased, their life direction may be of direct relevance to your future.
* A compass needle wildly spinning says you are being pulled in too many directions to fulfill others' demands.

OUTCOME OF ETTA'S DREAM

Etta had been entranced by her grandfather's adventures in the navy. After the dream, she realized she had to stop drifting in circles, choose a direction in life, and stick to it. She applied to the navy and loved the fact that her future was mapped out. Her grandma gave her the old compass that had belonged to her late grandfather when Etta obtained her first permanent posting, and she often felt him guiding her. Compass dreams may occur at a time of indecision in the dreamer's life and help the dreamer become aware that following a straight course is not boring but secure and ultimately rewarding.

Competition

Meg, twenty-one, dreamed she was in a relay race competing with her three older sisters, but no one else was taking over the baton. When she won single-handed, her sisters came to claim the trophy and pushed her to the back.

DREAM BACKGROUND AND MEANING

Meg was always competing for attention in the family. Her sisters were attractive and successful with busy social lives while she stayed home, and guys barely noticed her, compared to her sisters. She was musically gifted but never pushed herself forward, as her achievements paled beside theirs. Competition dreams represent striving to win or be noticed, whether a game of chance or one where skills are involved, and the dreams may occur where you feel rated second-best.

INTERPRETATIONS AND FORTUNE-TELLING MEANINGS

★ If you dream you are competing in a game of skill and win, you will succeed if you put yourself forward for promotion or reward.

★ If you win a competition where chance features, this is a lucky time for you.

★ To dream about competing in sports has to do with the rivals against whom you are competing and how you can defeat them.

★ If you are watching others win a competition or someone wrongly collects your prize, you need to be more assertive.

★ If you dream you are disqualified from a competition, you are seeking recognition in the wrong way or place and are being unfairly judged by the wrong criteria.

★ If you are involved in a team and go solo in the dream, it may be time to stop hiding in the shadows and take center stage.

OUTCOME OF MEG'S DREAM

Meg realized that she needed to compete in an environment where she did not suffer from comparison with her sisters. She won a music scholarship overseas. Now she no longer sees her sisters as competition. Competition dreams refer to the way the dreamer sees themselves, which can cause self-defeat by trying to win on other people's terms.

Complaining

Oliver, fifty-five, dreamed he was shut in a booth and complaints were flying simultaneously by email, phone, and face to face. Every three minutes a bell rang, and a disembodied voice told him to move on to the next. People were getting very angry as the queue grew longer and the calls and emails more strident. Finally, he put down the shutters and unplugged the phone and computer.

DREAM BACKGROUND AND MEANING

Oliver's extended family was constantly complaining about other family members. He was becoming exhausted. Since his father had died, Oliver had become everyone's first port of call.

INTERPRETATIONS AND FORTUNE-TELLING MEANINGS

★ If in your dream you are complaining about bad service or faulty goods, it may be a rehearsal for a real-life complaint you have about a person selling you short with their negative, whining attitude.

★ If someone says you are making an unnecessary fuss, the person may be using emotional blackmail to keep you compliant.

★ If others are complaining to you about your children or a family member, refuse to act as peacemaker, as you will be unfairly blamed in the middle.

★ If you dream a neighbor or manager at work complains because you will not dance to their tune, do not accept responsibility.

★ If in your dream you are listening to complaints by others about their problematic life, be careful you do not assume responsibility for fixing that life.

★ If you dream you are answering an official or legal complaint against you, you may be intimidated by their calling an authority as a power play.

OUTCOME OF OLIVER'S DREAM

After the dream, Oliver realized he was on overload. He decided that in the future he would listen without comment and end the conversation with "I hope you solve it." Gradually they all stopped asking Oliver to fix their complaints. Complaint dreams are common to family or workplace peacemakers, but once they remove themselves from the firing line, the problems usually dramatically improve.

Computer

Sally, forty-five, dreamed she was working on her laptop early in the morning, preparing for an important Zoom presentation with the new CEO. But her keyboard was sticking. The Internet went down and her screen went blank. Her little daughter was crying. Sally yelled at her; then, feeling guilty, she went to pick her up. By the time Sally had comforted her, she had missed the meeting.

DREAM BACKGROUND AND MEANING

Sally was a single parent with a high-powered job. Though she had the latest equipment for working from home, she was aware that she was at the mercy of her machines and always had half an eye on them when caring for her daughter. Computers represent organizing our lives efficiently and adding to our information base, which can make life easier or cause overload.

INTERPRETATIONS AND FORTUNE-TELLING MEANINGS

★ If you dream you are working on your computer, you have all the knowledge and expertise to succeed, but must retain your work-life balance.

★ If you are reprogramming your computer, you may need to change the status quo and impose your own ideas.

★ If your computer breaks down, you may be relying on modern technology too much to make life work and may be ignoring personal needs.

★ If you dream that your computer has a virus or infects other computers, beware of interference or misleading information from rivals who would delight in your failing.

★ If your keyboard is jammed, communicate more directly your ideas and feelings.

★ If you dream you are in a room filled with computers and operators, your unique gifts may be lost in the crowd.

OUTCOME OF SALLY'S DREAM

Sally realized she was glad she had missed the dream meeting, as she would have been given extra responsibility. She questioned whether she should temporarily cut back on her race for the top, as she was missing out on motherhood through work overload. Computers are an incredibly useful part of life but can become the ruler and not the servant.

Conference

Louette, forty, dreamed she was the headline speaker at an international conference, representing her company. She stood at the podium, gazing at the hundreds of assembled delegates, and realized to her horror that she had forgotten her speech notes, and her PowerPoint presentation was malfunctioning. She stumbled through the speech, but much of the audience walked out.

DREAM BACKGROUND AND MEANING

Louette had been invited to speak in the small auditorium before the main speech of a major conference. She was very nervous, as to succeed would open the way for more important slots.

INTERPRETATIONS AND FORTUNE-TELLING MEANINGS

★ If you are speaking at a conference in the dream amid rapturous applause, you will succeed in any leadership bid.

★ If in a dream you are organizing a face-to-face or Zoom conference, note who is helpful and who less so, as the dream is a rehearsal for any seminar, workshop, or conference.

★ If you are in a Zoom conference and the sound fails, you are not being heard in your career or in any community ventures. Express yourself more powerfully.

★ If you dream your computer loses its Internet connection during a Zoom conference, be careful you are not being left out of major decision-making and information in your workplace.

★ If you get lost on the way to a conference or conference room and miss your slot, now may not be the right time to step into the limelight.

★ If you lose your notes in the dream, be sure in advance that you have memorized relevant facts and figures, so you can put forward a case with confidence in any situation.

OUTCOME OF LOUETTE'S DREAM

Forewarned by the dream, Louette double-checked every detail and the technology. A main speaker did not turn up, so Louette appeared on the main stage and was well received. Whatever the size or importance of a gathering, conference dreams offer clues as to the way a forthcoming event will unfold.

Confidence

Perry, fifty-two, dreamed he was addressing the annual meeting of his company, putting forward major new ideas for streamlining inefficiencies and doubling profits. When he had finished, he was given a standing ovation, and the CEO came onstage and named Perry employee of the year. Perry woke with applause ringing in his ears.

DREAM BACKGROUND AND MEANING

Perry's wife laughed at his grandiose ideas, because he was as timid as a mouse. As Perry got older, he became increasingly frustrated at younger, less-experienced employees being promoted, but his lack of confidence had always held him back. His wife said it was too late to change. Confidence dreams, however, are an excellent dress rehearsal for acting more assertively in life.

INTERPRETATIONS AND FORTUNE-TELLING MEANINGS

★ If you display the confidence in a dream that you lack in daily life, use the dream impetus to bring out that confidence.

★ If you express ideas in the dream that you know are winners, present them in writing if you lack the confidence to speak out about them.

★ If in your dream you encounter an overconfident colleague, do not be afraid of challenging them.

★ If someone knocks your confidence in a dream but you bounce back, you should persist in expressing your feelings and ideas.

★ If you are a child in the dream, laughed at in class for getting an answer wrong, do not allow old setbacks to cloud your present competence and expertise.

★ If in the dream you are speaking or broadcasting on an area of expertise, that is the area in which to begin to speak or act confidently.

OUTCOME OF PERRY'S DREAM

Perry was asked to speak at a conference and, after the dream, instead of refusing as usual, he agreed. Once he started speaking, he became confident and did receive that standing ovation. Confidence dreams can reverse a cycle where an early setback amplified fears of failing.

Continuing Link of Love After Death

Dorothy, sixty, dreamed she had the sensation of being awake in her sleep. Out of a mist, she saw her mother, looking about ten years younger than when she had died. Dorothy said, "Oh, Mom, is it really you?" Her mother replied, "Yes, darling, of course it's me." Dorothy then said, "I love you, Mom," and her mother answered, "I love you too."

DREAM BACKGROUND AND MEANING

About four months after her mother's death, Dorothy and her sister had a private sitting with a medium, which proved disappointing. That night, Dorothy told her late mother before she went to sleep how much she missed her. The dream followed. Vivid dreams of a deceased loved one are a common way a loved one will contact a grieving relative.

INTERPRETATIONS AND FORTUNE-TELLING MEANINGS

★ If seeing a deceased loved one seems more vivid than in an ordinary dream, you are meeting with your loved one on the dream plane.

★ If a mediumship session is disappointing, your deceased relative may be a private person who prefers to talk directly through dreams.

★ If you dream of a deceased relative rather than seeing their ghost, it may be they would not wish to frighten you.

★ If you dream regularly of an older wise relative who in life offered advice, they may appear in dreams at times when you have a dilemma.

★ If dreaming of a deceased relative frightens you, before sleep ask them to not appear in a dream but give you a sign while you are awake.

★ If a deceased relative gives bad advice in a dream, they may be no wiser in the afterlife than when alive.

OUTCOME OF DOROTHY'S DREAM

Since the dream, Dorothy has never again felt sad about her mother's death, as she knows her mother is well and happy. A common sign that a dream is connected with the Other Side is when the deceased person looks well and much younger, having shed pain and sickness, even just weeks after the death.

Cooking

Ava, fifty, dreamed she cooked a huge feast in the local hall for everyone she knew. But no one came, and she was struggling to keep the food hot. Eventually Ava accepted that no one was coming and took the feast to the local food kitchen for the homeless.

DREAM BACKGROUND AND MEANING

Ava was the matriarch of an extended family and was famed for her banquets, to which she regularly invited the whole family. Recently the family had been coming less and she was feeling unwanted. Cooking dreams are rooted in nurturing and providing food for others but may be a sign not only of caring but also of being needed.

INTERPRETATIONS AND FORTUNE-TELLING MEANINGS

* Dreaming of enjoying cooking is a creative dream about fertility, family gatherings, and happiness.
* If you dream the kitchen is messy and everything is burning, someone interfering in your domestic life should be told to back off.
* If you dream you are cooking for others but resent it or have too many meals to prepare, reduce overnurturing others.
* If you are preparing a banquet, a major idea or plan will materialize and bring rewards.
* If you dream you are happy microwaving or cooking for yourself, you will benefit from focusing more on your own needs.
* If you dream you are unhappy cooking for yourself, or that others turn down invitations to eat with you, find new outlets for your nurturing.

OUTCOME OF AVA'S DREAM

After the dream, Ava asked the family why they rarely came for meals. They explained that their lives had become so much busier. Ava volunteered at the food kitchen and discovered they were short of cooks and food. She now cooks for thirty or more every day and loves it. Cooking dreams can redirect nurturing energies to where they are most needed if the original recipients have moved on with their lives.

Copper

Katarina, forty, dreamed she was standing beneath a tree of real copper leaves that were shaking in the breeze and whispering, "Trust us." A huge wind blew the copper leaves into a pile, now whispering, "Use us." Katarina picked up as many as she could and went to a mineral store, where she was offered a lot of money for the beautiful specimens. Katarina kept one to make into a pendant. She gave the profits to her parents and caught the train to the city.

DREAM BACKGROUND AND MEANING

Katarina's parents had built up business debts during the recession. Katarina gave up a chance to join a jewelry-design consortium. She fitted her personal work around keeping her parents' business afloat. Copper combines love and abundance, rather than material advantage.

INTERPRETATIONS AND FORTUNE-TELLING MEANINGS

* Dendritic copper (copper in branched shapes) is a traditional good-fortune charm, predicting a lucky financial break.
* If in a dream you are wearing a copper bracelet, your health will improve and chronic conditions stabilize.
* Though copper is not as valuable as silver or gold, if you dream of a pile of copper coins or nuggets, earnings will exceed expenditures.
* If in your dream you are dowsing with copper rods, you will find something precious that you have mislaid.
* Sacred to the Ancient Greek and Roman love goddesses Venus and Aphrodite, a copper ring on your wedding-ring finger in a dream brings or increases love. On the corresponding finger of the opposite hand, it heralds a new friend coming into your life.
* Because copper is a natural fertility symbol, if you dream of making love spontaneously in a beautiful place, you can call in powerful sensuality when modern contrivances like ovulation charts have taken away the magick.

OUTCOME OF KATARINA'S DREAM

After the dream, Katarina created the dream copper pendant and won a competition. She made a successful range of dendritic copper jewelry. She paid off her parents' debts and they retired. She started her own consortium, based around copper creations.

Corners

Humphrey, sixty-five, dreamed he was at school and was made to stand facing the corner because he could not answer a question. He hated the corner of the classroom, because he was not allowed to move or speak. At going-home time, the teacher forgot to tell him he could go, and he remained there for a few minutes crying.

DREAM BACKGROUND AND MEANING

Humphrey's desk had been moved to a corner of the office, and it brought back memories of an actual childhood experience in the classroom. He now feared he was being forgotten, as his long-dreaded retirement was imminent. A corner can represent excitement at the next chapter of life or uncertainty and fear.

INTERPRETATIONS AND FORTUNE-TELLING MEANINGS

★ Dreaming of turning from a dingy corner onto a bright path ahead represents having turned the corner, and life will start to get easier.

★ If in the dream you cannot see around a corner, you may fear what lies ahead.

★ If you believe someone is hiding around a corner, check details of any plans for hidden costs or problems.

★ A dark corner in a dream can offer either refuge from the demands of others or an unknown future, depending on the mood of the dream.

★ If you are forced into a corner in the dream by an adversary, beware of letting your guard down with someone who may seek to deny your options.

★ If in the dream you are living at the corner of a street, you may be faced with two choices, though you may choose a completely different one.

OUTCOME OF HUMPHREY'S DREAM

When a young colleague stopped at his desk and said, "Oh, I thought you had retired," Humphrey knew it was time to turn that corner. He took his retirement almost instantly and went on an extended trip around America. Corner dreams can be liberating if the dreamer uses them as a stepping-stone to a new path.

Cosmetic Surgery

Magda, fifty-five, had a dream set in Elizabethan times that her face was covered with smallpox scars and her lover had left her for a beautiful young woman. She was offered a concealing makeup made of white lead and vinegar to bring him back, but knew it was dangerous.

DREAM BACKGROUND AND MEANING

Magda was considering cosmetic surgery, as her husband had left her for a younger woman. She knew deep down the surgery would not bring Lenny back and was risky as she had health issues. If you are contemplating cosmetic surgery in a dream, it often signals underlying dissatisfaction with your physical appearance and lack of self-image.

INTERPRETATIONS AND FORTUNE-TELLING MEANINGS

★ If you are having cosmetic surgery in your dream, ask yourself if changing your appearance will improve your life.

★ If you see yourself young and beautiful again after your dream surgery, is there something you need to recapture from your youth?

★ If cosmetic surgery goes wrong in the dream, you may be focusing on changes to yourself when the problems lie in others.

★ If you look entirely different after your dream cosmetic surgery, are you concealing your authentic self to make a better impression?

★ If you dream you are having successful reconstructive surgery for an actual scar or disfigurement, your intuition will guide you to the right clinic you saw in the dream.

★ If you are having dream surgery, are you seeking to erase part of your personality or memories?

OUTCOME OF MAGDA'S DREAM

Magda realized that the surgery would be for Lenny, not for herself, and she did not want him back anyway. Instead, she worked with natural remedies and vitamins, fitness, and diet and is very happy with the result. While cosmetic surgery can enhance confidence, the dream may reveal that your real desire is to be attractive to someone else, not yourself.

Cotton Candy

Alyse, twenty-eight, dreamed she was a small girl walking along the beachfront with her mother. Upon seeing a cotton candy vendor, she asked her mom if she could have some. Her mom refused. Alyse let go of her mom's hand, ran to the cotton candy stall, and bought the biggest bag available. Her mom snatched the cotton candy away and threw it in the trash can.

DREAM BACKGROUND AND MEANING

Alyse was brought up by foster parents, as her mother was found to be an unsuitable parent. Her foster parents were very strict and told Alyse she was a child of sin that they had saved. Her childhood was one with few treats. Now Alyse would like to meet her mom, despite her foster parents having always insisted that her mother is a wicked woman. Cotton candy represents all that is fun, as opposed to living by the rules of self-denial.

INTERPRETATIONS AND FORTUNE-TELLING MEANINGS

★ If in a dream you are enjoying cotton candy as an adult, you are ready for lighthearted fun if life has become too serious.

★ If in the dream you are made to feel guilty as a child for wanting treats, you may find it difficult to overcome unwarranted guilt at pleasure as an adult.

★ If your cotton candy is thrown away in the dream at any age, but especially as a helpless child, you may as an adult need to overcompensate but often feel guilty.

★ If you eat too much cotton candy in your dream and feel sick, you may indulge in unhealthy or unwise habits to defy the status quo.

★ If you dream you are making or selling cotton candy, there may be an unexpected chance for an impromptu vacation or spontaneous adventure.

OUTCOME OF ALYSE'S DREAM

After insisting that she be given the relevant information, Alyse finally met her birth mother, who was fun-loving and incredibly kind. Alyse moved in with her. Dreams can reveal that forbidden fruit can be harmless and fun once the moral judgment is removed.

Counselor

Sue, fifty, dreamed she was with her former English teacher, pouring out her fears and unhappiness. She could not stop crying. Her teacher held her and let years of injustice at last be released. Sue tried to hold on to her teacher, but her teacher said, "You have decided what to do and can carry it through." The dream ended.

DREAM BACKGROUND AND MEANING

Sue's teacher had died years before, but she had supported Sue through her school days. She knew Sue had a hard time after her mother died and her new stepmother moved in with three teenage boys; they all made Sue's life a misery. Now Sue's stepmother was very ill, and it was expected that Sue would nurse her, though the stepmother and her sons had continued to exclude Sue from the family. Whether a returning spirit or a memory of a wise counselor, activated when needed, a former mentor can return in dreams to offer support.

INTERPRETATIONS AND FORTUNE-TELLING MEANINGS

★ If you are receiving wise advice in your dream from an unknown misty figure, it may be your spirit guide, an angel, or your wise higher self.

★ If your counselor is a teacher or mentor from your childhood, you may be needing extra reassurance about unresolved childhood sorrows.

★ If you dream you are giving the advice, there is something you need to say but have been holding back because of fear of interfering.

★ If you dream you are listening to a stranger's troubles, you are a natural counselor and should consider taking training.

★ If you dream you are sitting between two counselors, you are being given conflicting advice about a decision and should trust your own intuition.

OUTCOME OF SUE'S DREAM

Sue told her stepmother's sons that they must look after their own mother, and when she died Sue cut off communication. Counseling dreams offer courage to overcome unwarranted guilt or obligation, and they provide the strength to finally rid yourself of burdens.

Counting Money

Pieter, fifty-seven, dreamed he owned a moneylender's office. His customers were his adult children, each with a hard-luck story. He was counting out for each a pile of gold coins from his own money. He then realized he had no money left in his pile. But it was too late—his children had gone.

DREAM BACKGROUND AND MEANING

Pieter was anxious. Much of his money was tied up in his children's houses and in the loans he had willingly made through the years. Though his children were now established, they still regularly sought money from him. He was starting to worry about his own future.

INTERPRETATIONS AND FORTUNE-TELLING MEANINGS

★ If in your dream you are counting a huge pile of your own money, financial matters will improve and extra resources will come.

★ If you are counting money into piles, take time to consider options and affordability before making a financial decision.

★ If when counting money you drop it, beware of finances draining away on hidden persistent outgoings.

★ If you are counting your money in the dream and there is less than you thought, you may have been denying the extent of money disappearing.

★ If you have only a few coins left in your own pile after giving to others, are you being too generous?

★ If you are counting stolen money, is there a risk that your source of income may be taken from you, or is this dream due to fear because finances are becoming stressful?

OUTCOME OF PIETER'S DREAM

Pieter realized that if he continued to hand money to his children he would have little left for his own old age. Now that they were financially comfortable, he suggested to them that they could stand on their own two feet. They conceded that their father was right. Counting money into two piles in a dream, one for giving and one for receiving, may show the dreamer that their own finances should be rebalanced.

Country Music

Jodie, twenty-five, dreamed she was singing with Dolly Parton and other famous Country stars in a grand finale in Nashville. At the after-show party, Dolly said Jodie showed great talent and offered her a supporting-act role in her show. Jodie woke, wondering if this was the day to head for Nashville.

DREAM BACKGROUND AND MEANING

Jodie took waitressing jobs so she could play in clubs if an artist did not turn up. But she wanted the big time and believed she might launch her career as a singer-songwriter if she lived in Nashville. If you regularly dream about becoming a well-known Country singer-songwriter, your dreams are telling you to take a chance.

INTERPRETATIONS AND FORTUNE-TELLING MEANINGS

★ If you dream about Country music, the dream may represent a nostalgic desire for a slower way of life, centered around the home and family.

★ If you regularly dream of a particular Country song, the words will hold a message for you.

★ If in your dream you create an original Country song, remember that many musicians create in their sleep.

★ If you dream you are performing with a successful Country artist, living or deceased, consider what they can teach you from their lives.

★ If you are asked to understudy for a famous singer in your dream, you may be able to launch a career as a tribute act.

★ If you dream you fail an audition, you may need to develop more confidence before testing yourself against competition.

OUTCOME OF JODIE'S DREAM

After the dream, Jodie applied for a job at Dolly Parton's theme park and met the star. Gradually, Jodie was offered small roles within the park and has sold one of her original songs. Despite huge competition, she believes her dream will come true. Dreams of fame and fortune act as an incentive.

Coyote

Lou, thirty-three, dreamed he saw a family of coyotes in scrubland at the back of his house. Though they were regarded as scavengers, he thought they were beautiful and brought life to his staid neighborhood. But his neighbors got a posse together to shoot them. Lou defended the coyotes, and the neighbors said he didn't belong in their neighborhood. Lou woke feeling angry.

DREAM BACKGROUND AND MEANING

Lou did not fit into his very conventional neighborhood and encouraged wildlife in his garden and on the land at the back of his home. He had always wanted to be a park ranger but had a very good job fixing alarms. A coyote in a dream as a scavenger as well as a hunter will transform a discarded ambition dismissed as impractical.

INTERPRETATIONS AND FORTUNE-TELLING MEANINGS

* If a coyote appears in a dream, it is telling you that you may need to free yourself from the status quo and live your own way.
* Since Coyote in Navajo myth created the Milky Way by throwing a bag of stars into the sky, his regular appearance in dreams is leading you to express your creative spirit, which may presently be stifled.
* Since Coyote is also the trickster in myth, beware of a charismatic humorous person in your life who may have questionable values and could mislead you.
* If you dream a coyote attacks, which is quite rare unless it is defending its young, you may be considering an unwise action that could have self-destructive consequences.
* If you dream you are part of a coyote family or pack, coyotes may be your spirit animal.
* A coyote appearing, if they are not native to your land, is a very special creature heralding the incentive for major change.

OUTCOME OF LOU'S DREAM

Lou joined a volunteer park ranger organization during his vacations. When he was sure it was the life for him, he sold his suburban house and trained in wildlife conservation.

Coyote is not an easy dream companion, as he always questions motives and purposes and points over the horizon to a wider world.

Crab

Ferdy, twenty, dreamed he was on an uninhabited tropical island in Southeast Asia during World War II. The island was plagued by giant crabs at low tide, which could give a nasty bite. Ferdy was afraid to go to sleep in case one attacked during the night. Another soldier, knowing his fear, dropped one in his tent as a joke. Ferdy smashed the shell with his rifle butt and lost his fear.

DREAM BACKGROUND AND MEANING

It was Ferdy's late grandfather who had been on the island with his platoon and who had told Ferdy stories of the fearsome crabs when he was a boy. Now Ferdy was in college but was reluctant to go out except for classes because everyone else seemed so confident and he stuttered when he became self-conscious. Sometimes we can inherit a dream from an ancestral family member that holds an answer to a present-day dilemma.

INTERPRETATIONS AND FORTUNE-TELLING MEANINGS

* If you dream of seeing a hermit crab, someone may be trying to take over your life or love, or to copy your style.
* If you dream you are pinched by a crab on the shore, burrowing in the sand, be careful of a hidden enemy who may suddenly strike. If more than one crab, other rivals may be jealous of you.
* To find an empty crab shell or claw says you will overcome all opposition and spite.
* If you see crabs being carried on the tide, you may be afraid to challenge the opinions of others you consider intolerant or overcritical.
* If you are catching crabs but putting them back in rock pools, a rival will acknowledge your power, but you will tolerate their behavior within limits.
* If you dream you are catching crabs to cook, after overcoming a rival you will absorb their status or power.

OUTCOME OF FERDY'S DREAM

After the dream, Ferdy saw a counselor, who offered him much-overdue speech therapy. Within six months the stutter was gone. Giant crabs in dreams can represent a potential attack, which leaves the dreamer hiding from real or imagined threats instead of tackling the fear the crab signifies.

Crane (Bird)

Jessica, forty-five, dreamed she was watching a beautiful crane wading through the shallow water. Suddenly men arrived with hounds that were splashing through the reeds, baying and snarling. Jessica called out to warn the bird, which extended its wings and soared upward. The hunters turned their hounds on Jessica. She woke screaming.

DREAM BACKGROUND AND MEANING

Jessica is under contract to a high-paying advertising agency. However, she has serious doubts about the agency's vaunted environmental ethics. She has been warned that, should she rock the boat, she will never again work in New York. Jessica has a comfortable lifestyle, but every day compromises her integrity.

A crane is a symbol of wisdom, immortality, and truth in cultures from Japan and China to Ancient Greece. Aoibh, wife of Manannán mac Lir, Celtic God of the Sea, was turned into a crane by her husband to stop her sharing knowledge with humanity. But in crane form she could fly and teach the whole world.

INTERPRETATIONS AND FORTUNE-TELLING MEANINGS

★ A dream of a crane soaring into the sky indicates fulfilling ambitions and traveling extensively.

★ A nesting crane talks of health, long life, and joy from younger generations.

★ A flock of cranes promises meeting like-minded people as friends and in the workplace, but you need to seek them.

★ A pair of cranes symbolizes lasting commitment with your twin soul, known or unknown.

★ Cranes being shot or attacked says others will try to bring you down but will spur you on to make even greater impact.

★ Seeing cranes when you are studying or about to take an examination assures that your knowledge will carry you to success.

OUTCOME OF JESSICA'S DREAM

Jessica applied for a job with an international charity at a lower salary but a place where she would be free to follow her principles. Her former company was later revealed to be exploiting environmentalism for profit.

Cranes appear when truth and knowledge come at a price but ensure lasting results.

Credit/Debit Cards

Kamellia, seventy, dreamed she entered a store to buy an outfit. She handed over her debit card, but it was declined due to insufficient funds, despite her being certain that she had enough money on the card. She then handed the cashier a second card with the same result. She left the store embarrassed and feeling personally inadequate.

DREAM BACKGROUND AND MEANING

Kamellia recently retired, having been self-employed for most of her life. She had accumulated sufficient savings, enabling her to enjoy a comfortable retirement. Since her husband, Don, had also retired, however, they wondered what would happen when their savings dwindled. Credit cards and credit ratings in dreams can reflect our own sense of self-worth and self-esteem.

INTERPRETATIONS AND FORTUNE-TELLING MEANINGS

★ If you regularly dream of your credit card being maxed out, you may be secretly worried about overspending and maybe need to think about wise budgeting.

★ If you dream your card is declined and you know there is money in it, this may be a long-term warning that you should be thinking about getting money from a new source.

★ If your card has no upper limit, you may find new income unexpectedly coming your way.

★ If your card is lost or stolen, you have drains on your time and emotions as well as finances that you should resist.

★ If in a dream you hand your card to someone else to use, you may be blurring your identity in order to win their approval.

★ If you dream you apply for a credit card and are refused, you may doubt your ability to succeed because of a temporary setback.

OUTCOME OF KAMELLIA'S DREAM

Kamellia realized she was not prepared to retire and economize, and so she started a successful part-time business using former contacts who had missed her, which still allowed her time for leisure without worrying about the cost.

In your eyes, credit and debit cards may symbolize your outward value based on what you can borrow, rather than your true worth.

Creeping

Troy, thirty-six, dreamed of someone creeping after him down a dark alleyway. Unable to bear it any longer, Troy turned and rushed to where he thought the figure was hiding, but there was no one. He continued down the alley, and so did the creeping figure. He woke feeling threatened.

DREAM BACKGROUND AND MEANING

Troy's company had installed security cameras at their workplace. Troy was uncomfortable being constantly under surveillance. He was contemplating leaving his much-loved job because of this. Being pursued by a creeping figure in a dream taps into deep fears of being watched.

INTERPRETATIONS AND FORTUNE-TELLING MEANINGS

★ If you dream of someone creeping after you, this indicates eavesdropping or spying on your life, whether by someone known or by official surveillance.

★ If you dream you are creeping to not be heard, you may be trying to avoid an argument where you know the other person will be angry, though you are in the right.

★ If you dream you hear someone creeping toward you, you are worried about being caught unprepared.

★ If someone in your dream is creeping, in the flattery sense, to win your favor, beware as to their true motives.

★ If you are caught creeping away from a troublesome situation, you may have no choice but to directly confront the person or problem.

★ If the entire dream is spent creeping and hiding to avoid attention, you are feeling intimidated and should decide whether to leave, protest, or ignore it.

★ If you dream you see a mouse or other rodent or a spider creeping toward you and you are afraid, you underestimate your power to deal with petty intrusions.

OUTCOME OF TROY'S DREAM

After unsuccessfully complaining, Troy found another job where his privacy was not compromised. Creeping dreams are more common in modern times when closed circuit television (CCTV) is increasingly used in homes, workplaces, and public areas. In spite of its advantages for security, technological creeping taps into primitive fears of constantly being observed.

Creepy Crawlies

Ronald, twenty-eight, had a recurring dream that he was a small boy sent to a newly colonized faraway land. He worked all day on the farm and at night was shut in a filthy hut filled with spiders and biting, crawling bugs. Local indigenous people attacked the farm because the farmer had killed one of their hunters. They heard Ronald's cries and rescued him.

DREAM BACKGROUND AND MEANING

Ronald was a tough baseball player terrified of creepy crawlies and worried that his teammates might find out his fears. He and the rest of the team had been asked to take part in a televised charity event in which they were to crawl through a narrow glass tunnel filled with spiders and creepy crawlies. Dreams of confronting our greatest fears can help the dreamer overcome them.

INTERPRETATIONS AND FORTUNE-TELLING MEANINGS

★ If the dreamer has a past-life dream that explains a phobia, reliving and overcoming the experience usually relieves the dreamer of the fear.

★ If you dream of bugs or spiders (see "Spiderwebs," p. 441) crawling all over you, you feel invaded by countless endless demands on your time.

★ If in your dream you kill the bugs, you are taking control of your fears.

★ If the creepy crawlies multiply or are instantly replaced, you are not facing the real problem behind the persistent fears.

★ If you dream you are shut in a confined space with creepy crawlies, you need to find an escape from invasion by others of your personal space and privacy.

★ If you face your fears in the dream and overcome them, you can achieve this in daily life using the same energies.

OUTCOME OF RONALD'S DREAM

After the dream, Ronald publicly admitted his fear of creepy crawlies, and many others shared their phobias. He entered the event and was highly sponsored because everyone knew it would be hard for him. Following the task, his fears diminished. Dreams of creepy crawlies can encourage the dreamer to share their fears, and in doing so the fears lose much of their power.

Crossroads

Chas, forty-eight, dreamed he was standing in front of the judge in a bankruptcy court. His wife, Carol, was in the judge's chair, listing his failings in their shared business and their marriage. She insisted it was time for him to go his way and she, hers. She pointed to a door in the courtroom and instructed him to go through it. As he did, there was a crossroads. He tried to go back, but the door was barred. He sat at the crossroads, not knowing what to do.

DREAM BACKGROUND AND MEANING

Chas and Carol had been having marital problems since their small manufacturing business was closed due to bad investments. Carol wanted to start the business again, alone, but Chas insisted that together they could save the business and their marriage. Crossroads dreams come at crunch points in relationships, careers, or businesses.

INTERPRETATIONS AND FORTUNE-TELLING MEANINGS

✴ Dream crossroads always represent a turning point in your life.

✴ If the directions are clear, make a fast decision. If signs are obscured, proceed slowly until you are more certain.

✴ The roads marked may represent the past, present, and future or a true crossroads where, if two or more people are involved, there may be conflict or compromise by choosing a joint route.

✴ Since crossroads are traditionally associated with the supernatural, places of offerings, and burial sites of bad witches and suicides, crossroads dreams have many layers of meaning.

✴ As a crossroads is traditionally where ley energy lines cross (see p. 284), resting at a crossroads holds a great deal of potential power.

✴ If a dream ends at a crossroads, it may offer clues as to the best way forward (see "Pathways," p. 355).

OUTCOME OF CHAS'S DREAM

Chas was not prepared to let go of the business or the marriage without a fight. He gave his wife the option of rebuilding the business or pursuing a new path together for one more year. They started an Internet café near a major college, offering a home away from home for homesick students. The worst thing in crossroads dreams is to remain too long at the center, going neither forward nor backward.

Crow

Titania, sixty, had recurring dreams of an old woman in Scotland walking with a crow on her shoulder, breaking the ice for the moorland animals. Titania tried to follow her, but the mists came down.

DREAM BACKGROUND AND MEANING

Titania had always been drawn to the ancient Scottish world but had never visited. She was planning to retire to Florida and write her first novel, but totally lacked inspiration and felt a compulsion to visit old Scotland. Her friends said she was crazy. Dreams can draw us to our spiritual home, and crows are powerful messengers.

INTERPRETATIONS AND FORTUNE-TELLING MEANINGS

✴ In spite of superstitions, crows in dreams never herald death; rather, they point to challenges that, if met, bring opportunity.

✴ In Amerindian lore, dream crows are associated with wisdom, magick, and intelligence and act as spirit guides, transmitting wisdom through signs and omens.

✴ If you dream you hear crows cawing, beware of bad advice connected with property.

✴ Dreams of crows stealing jewelry warn you to take care whom you trust with your finances or reputation.

✴ Since in myths the crow was burned black and lost her singing voice because she pulled down the sun to warm the earth, crows shrieking before returning to their trees at night indicate that a short-term sacrifice will have positive long-term results.

✴ Crows circling over your home suggest that a source of income or money that you have given up pursuing will suddenly materialize.

OUTCOME OF TITANIA'S DREAM

Titania discovered crows were sacred birds of the Celtic Scottish Crone goddess Cailleach Bheur, the Blue Hag, described with a crow on her shoulder and a holly staff. Titania felt the dream was calling her and used her lump-sum retirement payment to visit Scotland, where she knew she had distant ancestry. Titania was inspired to write a whole series of ancient Celtic magical books. Crows as birds of wisdom and magick offer inspiration, maybe involving a life change and travel.

Crown

Bill, twenty-five, dreamed he was sitting on a throne at his coronation. When the crown was placed on his head, lords and ladies in velvet robes started trying to seize the crown, shouting he had no right to it. Bill realized jewels were falling out of the crown. He walked out of the ceremony wearing it and woke knowing the crown was his.

DREAM BACKGROUND AND MEANING

Bill left school without qualifications. However, he wanted to become a lawyer. Bill was working his way through law school, doing shifts in the evenings to support himself. His fellow students, most from wealthy families, told him he was wasting his time. He had just one more year to go but wondered if he should continue in the face of such discouragement.

A wish-fulfillment dream tells you to aim for the top in your career or money-making ventures.

INTERPRETATIONS AND FORTUNE-TELLING MEANINGS

* A dream of a crown, especially a gold one being carried toward you, promises you will achieve recognition or financial gain within the year.
* Being crowned indicates increased status, leadership, or authority in your career.
* Someone else being crowned says you may be asked to support a friend or colleague in a bid for success, but it may not be in your interest.
* Missing gems represent partial achievement of ambitions. Watch out for others trying to steal your glory.
* A crown of flowers represents increasing popularity and romance. If of fading flowers, this may be only temporary.
* A dream of a broken crown, or one other people try to steal, warns that you have jealous rivals who would dethrone and replace you.

OUTCOME OF BILL'S DREAM

Bill continued with his study, came out top of the year, and was offered a prestigious post with a group of civil rights lawyers. Reach for the success that is rightfully yours, accepting that there will be those who will resent you.

Cruise

Ray, sixty-four, had a recurring dream in which he was on a world cruise. He was given a noisy cabin with no windows, no air-conditioning, and a television that didn't work. He complained to his cabin steward, who told him that he had to put up with it or he could leave the ship at the next port and lose his money.

DREAM BACKGROUND AND MEANING

This dream worried Ray because he had been saving for the vacation of a lifetime when he retired. He was uncertain whether to abandon the idea in case the dream was a warning.

Cruise dreams, if positive, advise going away for a while if you are tired or feeling jaded with life, as cruises represent adventure with minimum effort.

INTERPRETATIONS AND FORTUNE-TELLING MEANINGS

* If you dream your cruise ship sails through calm waters toward a desired destination, that is a good omen for any vacation or venture where you entrust arrangements to others.
* If your cabin and the ship are luxurious and comfortable, time to step back and let others take responsibility on your behalf for a time in life generally.
* A stormy sea or a shipwreck suggests hidden worries and guilt about spending money indulgently if you are normally cautious over finances.
* If the dream cruise or indeed any organized vacation or venture goes wrong in a dream, it reveals doubts about allowing anyone to take over or ease your role at work in case you are found replaceable.
* If you dream of a shipboard romance, you are unconsciously seeking excitement and variety in your love life, especially if the person in the dream is not your real-life traveling companion.

OUTCOME OF RAY'S DREAM

Ray joined an online club for experienced cruise passengers and booked a short cruise, which he thoroughly enjoyed. Find out in advance what is on offer so there are no nasty surprises.

Crumbling, Collapsing

Rocky, forty-four, dreamed he was climbing steep steps carved in the mountainside to reach a ruined shrine where it was said beautiful and rare sacred crystals could be collected. But as he climbed higher, the steps below were crumbling. He realized that he could not come down the same way, but decided he would worry about the descent once he reached his destination.

DREAM BACKGROUND AND MEANING

Though Rocky was married with three children, he was living a lie and had fallen in love with a much younger man. They were planning to buy a share in a mine in the mountains. Rocky was planning to tell his wife and move out immediately afterward. He feared his children would be devastated. Collapsing structures, whether natural or human-made, can sometimes temporarily be shored up, but ultimately offer no return.

INTERPRETATIONS AND FORTUNE-TELLING MEANINGS

★ A crumbling or collapsing bridge in a dream warns that a relationship or family is in danger of splitting apart.

★ Crumbling steps indicate walking away from an unsatisfactory situation but with consequences.

★ A collapsing building says that a relationship or domestic or business venture has been neglected or others have worked to undermine it.

★ Repairing a collapsing or crumbling structure in a dream says it may be possible to restore or mend a relationship or financial matters.

★ If you collapse in a dream, it is not necessarily a physical warning; rather, you have been overloading your life with worry and responsibility.

★ A collapsing wall may actually break down unnecessary barriers or divisions.

OUTCOME OF ROCKY'S DREAM

After the dream, Rocky decided he should leave home, but still see the children and set up an independent life before moving in with a male partner. His new partner would not wait. Rocky is considering living alone till the children are old enough to fully understand. Collapsing or crumbling dreams inevitably involve destruction of what is no longer sound, but, where others will be affected by the collapse, may need careful consideration.

Crutches

Barrington, fifty-four, dreamed he had broken his leg and was walking with crutches. But his friends and family were all trying to support him, and he was slipping on his crutches as the unasked-for helpers unbalanced him. When he protested, they insisted that without them he might seriously injure himself, and what would they do without him?

DREAM BACKGROUND AND MEANING

Barrington, who had always organized the lives of friends and family, had suffered a minor heart attack. But his friends and family would not leave him alone. If he did not make contact, they dashed around to check on him. Crutch dreams represent temporary dependency but can too often reveal unasked-for help from those who need to be needed.

INTERPRETATIONS AND FORTUNE-TELLING MEANINGS

★ If in the dream you are on crutches, you may worry about depending on someone who may not be reliable.

★ If a family member is on crutches or is using yours in the dream, are you taking too much responsibility for their happiness?

★ If you dream you are giving a person a single crutch, explain that financial or emotional help is temporary until they get back on their feet.

★ If you are refusing others' help in your dream, you are more than ready to cope single-handedly and should say so.

★ Using a makeshift crutch says you will come up with an ingenious solution to a setback.

★ If someone at work offers you crutches, you will be given help toward advancement. Beware, nothing is free.

OUTCOME OF BARRINGTON'S DREAM

Barrington knew everyone was terrified of losing him, as he was the hub of everyone's world, and they were overcompensating. He sent an email to everyone, explaining that he appreciated their concern but would let them know if he needed anything. When he recovered, Barrington withdrew from making himself overly responsible for others' lives. Crutches dreams have complicated hidden implications over who is dependent, and a strong figure temporarily incapacitated can send family and friends into panic mode.

Crying

Maria, thirty-three, dreamed she heard a child crying for her mother in a house she recognized as her childhood home. A little girl was sitting in the middle of an empty floor, and all the furniture had gone. The child said, "I knew you'd come back for me," and would not let Maria go. Maria wondered who she could phone to rescue the child, but the child still clung and seemed strangely familiar to her.

DREAM BACKGROUND AND MEANING

Maria was very wealthy and had a jet-setting partner, and there was no room for children in their full lives. But when Maria was young, the bailiffs had come, and her mother handed Maria and her little sister over to the welfare department. A cry from the heart in childhood can become suppressed and leave an insecurity hard to erase.

INTERPRETATIONS AND FORTUNE-TELLING MEANINGS

* To cry in a dream may reflect a disappointment or sorrow you have not acknowledged but need to express.
* If someone you trust comforts you in the dream, talk through your worries and fears with them.
* If in the dream a friend or family member is crying, even if they seem happy superficially, this is a telepathic cry for help.
* If in the dream you are crying with happiness at a wedding or another joyous celebration, this predicts a forthcoming event.
* If you see a drama king or queen crying in the dream, be wary of wasting sympathy.
* If you hear crying in the dream but can see no one, it may be a spirit who wants to share their sorrows and has contacted you on the dream plane.

OUTCOME OF MARIA'S DREAM

After the dream, Maria recalled what she had suppressed for years: her little sister crying for Maria to come back when the welfare department took them to separate homes. Maria had tried to trace her sister when she was old enough and is persisting in her search, as she thinks her sister was taken overseas by a service family. Once crying in a dream can be understood, the old pain loses its power.

Crystal Ball

Christabel, thirty, dreamed she was gazing into a clear crystal ball in which she could see constantly changing images, her white wedding, two beautiful children, a house by a stream, and herself surrounded by copies of a novel she had published. Then the visions disappeared. All that remained was her own reflection, alone in her small apartment. She woke disappointed.

DREAM BACKGROUND AND MEANING

Christabel was psychic though she did not possess a crystal ball. For some time she had been wanting to have a relationship with the boy next door, but as she had not let him know she was interested, he had married someone else. Her freelance editing work was drying up. Her own ambitions to write had never materialized. Was her dream crystal projecting only wish-fulfillment? Crystal ball dream images can mask our true destiny, if we fix on unrealistic expectations.

INTERPRETATIONS AND FORTUNE-TELLING MEANINGS

* A dream crystal ball with clear images that do not fade suggests a future you can attain.
* A cracked crystal ball implies focusing on a future you want but are not making happen by your lack of action.
* A crystal ball without images or where images fade indicates that you may have become disillusioned because your desires did not materialize as quickly as hoped.
* Reading a crystal ball for others says you have emerging clairvoyant powers you could develop professionally.
* Dropping or smashing a crystal ball warns you to rethink your future rather than allowing fate or chance to dictate it.
* Dreaming of seeing a lover, creative success, or travel emerging from mists in a crystal ball foretells happiness or success, whether expected or not, sooner rather than later.

OUTCOME OF CHRISTABEL'S DREAM

Christabel realized she was waiting for her ideal life to manifest rather than working toward what she wanted. She applied to a publisher for a job as a junior editor/proofreader, took a creative writing course, rented an apartment by the river, and joined a dating site. Crystal balls can delay fulfillment by implying that the ideal future can happen without effort.

Crystals

Beverley, thirty-two, dreamed she was in a huge cave with crystals of many colors shimmering from the roof and walls. As she touched the walls, single crystals came out easily. She sat down and held them one at a time, knowing instinctively where she should place each against her body. The soft brown crystals with inner lights took away pain, pink gave her peace, gentle purple brought her body into balance, and clear shining white and sparkling yellow filled her with energy. As she left the cave they were gone. Beverley woke feeling well and happy.

DREAM BACKGROUND AND MEANING

Beverley was suffering from an illness that left her constantly exhausted and often unable to move. Physicians could not offer a diagnosis or remedy, and she despaired of ever being cured. Crystal dreams invariably involve healing and are a subconscious way of linking with their timeless power.

INTERPRETATIONS AND FORTUNE-TELLING MEANINGS

★ If you dream of particular crystals, even if you know nothing of crystal lore, try to identify them, as they will offer healing.

★ If you discover a crystal cave, your crystal gifts may come from past worlds, indicating you are connecting with ancient wisdom.

★ If you break or lose a crystal, you have lost touch with your spiritual side and need to reconnect with nature.

★ If you dream you are healing someone you know with a crystal, they may be secretly worried about their health and glad to talk about it.

★ If you dream you are healing someone you do not know, your natural healing gifts are emerging with crystals or earth remedies such as herbs.

★ If you discover a special unpolished crystal in your dream, it may come into your life spontaneously and be powerful for healing and meditation.

OUTCOME OF BEVERLEY'S DREAM

After the dream, Beverley visited a crystal store and purchased a brown smoky quartz, pink rose quartz, purple amethyst, clear quartz, and yellow citrine and slept with them around the base of her bed. Her health and energy levels gradually improved. She has started to study crystal healing.

Crystals provide noninvasive healing, and their spiritual energies heal the body on the astral level we visit in dreams.

Cuckoo

Beth, forty-one, dreamed of an old woman releasing a cuckoo from her basket. Beth asked why, and the woman said she was releasing the first cuckoo of spring and with it the springtime. The old woman told Beth to wish for anything she wanted. Beth asked to go home. The old woman said cuckoo dreams come true in strange ways and told her to follow the cuckoo call.

DREAM BACKGROUND AND MEANING

Beth was homesick for Australia but did not have the fare home. Beth had linked into a legend in which an old woman traditionally lets a cuckoo out of her basket at Heathfield Spring Fayre in Sussex, United Kingdom, in mid-April to mark the beginning of spring. Cuckoos often appear in dreams when the dreamer fears being in the wrong place.

INTERPRETATIONS AND FORTUNE-TELLING MEANINGS

★ If your dream cuckoo lays its eggs in another bird's nest, beware of assuming others' responsibilities.

★ Your dream of cuckoos heralds new beginnings, new opportunities, and attempting what seems impossible.

★ If you are following the cuckoo call, you will need to seek success, as it will not come to you.

★ If your cuckoo is leading you into a thicket with its call, beware illusionists, con artists, and those misleading people for their own gain.

★ The cuckoo call is a natural money-bringer. If money features in your dream, it is said you will have prosperity for the twelve months ahead.

OUTCOME OF BETH'S DREAM

After the dream, Beth applied for a job for which she had not felt sufficiently qualified, and she was appointed. She met an Australian guy at the new workplace. They fell in love and are living together. Their parents sent them the fare home for Christmas, but they are planning to return to the United Kingdom and to visit the Cuckoo Spring Fayre in April.

Curses

Ross, forty, dreamed he was in a museum where a shipment of Egyptian mummies had arrived from an obscure and, he suspected, illegal source. Smoke surrounded the mummies and he heard a low-pitched wailing sound, and Ross knew they were cursed. He studied the hieroglyphs and matched them to ones in Egyptian spell books to summon ancient deities to remove the curses. He cleared the artifacts, but no one believed that the curses had existed.

DREAM BACKGROUND AND MEANING

Ross worked for a dealer of ancient artifacts who often acquired artifacts illegally. Ross worried because he knew plundered items often were protected by curses. The owner told him to keep quiet or he would lose his job. Curses can be attached to artifacts as well as to people, but may simply reflect the negative energies of the original owner or plunderer.

INTERPRETATIONS AND FORTUNE-TELLING MEANINGS

* If you dream of someone you know cursing or ill-wishing you, counteract their negativity in the real world by watching for any underhanded actions.
* If you dream of a family curse dating back generations, send blessings after the dream ends and the curse will remain in the ether as a past life.
* If you dream that an artifact you have been given or sent by an unfriendly relative is bringing you bad luck, you are picking up negative vibes from the donor. Cleanse the item with incense.
* If you buy a strange item from an indigenous culture and dream of it coming to life, rid yourself of it, as curse ceremonies may be attached.
* If you curse someone in a dream, deal with justifiable anger toward them in a controlled way in daily life. Cursing always rebounds on the sender.

OUTCOME OF ROSS'S DREAM

Ross took a new job working to prevent the illegal importing of ancient artifacts. He subtly cleared of negative energies those artifacts that could not be returned. Dreams open us to awareness of ill-wishing and cursing in our everyday world. In acknowledging and rejecting the negative vibes, whether curses or hostility, the dreamer automatically neutralizes them.

Cuteness

Flora, sixteen, who was tall, well-built, and athletic, dreamed she was going to a party with her best friend, Tamsin, who was doll-like, with fluffy blonde hair, a soft voice, and cute clothes. Tamsin insisted she dress Flora, who Tamsin said always looked awful. Tamsin brought a short baby-doll pink frilly dress, and pink ribbons for Flora's hair. When they arrived, everyone laughed at Flora and all the boys flocked around cute Tamsin. Flora left, humiliated.

DREAM BACKGROUND AND MEANING

Flora and Tamsin had been friends since kindergarten. Flora was the foil for Tamsin, who acted sugar-sweet in public but could be very spiteful. Flora felt huge and ungainly compared with her cute friend. Cuteness in dreams can reveal a soft side to the dreamer, but cuteness is a double-edged sword for those who are its victims.

INTERPRETATIONS AND FORTUNE-TELLING MEANINGS

* If you dream of cute, fluffy baby animals, this may reveal the need for you to acknowledge and express your more vulnerable side.
* If you dream of cuddly babies and adorable toddlers, even if you do not consciously want a baby, these may be unconscious instincts expressing themselves in dreams.
* If someone acts like a cute teddy bear in life but like a marauding tiger in your dreams, you should be wary of manipulation.
* If you try to be cute or are persuaded to dress in an inappropriately cute way in a dream, the person persuading you is deliberately eroding your confidence and identity.
* If someone tells you that you are cute in a dream and you take this as patronizing, you may need to express yourself more assertively so people take you seriously.
* If you dream you see a guy or gal you consider cute, you may enjoy romance and flattery but want greater depth in the long term.

OUTCOME OF FLORA'S DREAM

The dream confirmed for Flora how manipulative her friend was and that Tamsin had played on her cuteness. Flora started to dress and act as she wished and joined a sports gym. Cuteness can be a desirable quality in baby animals and human infants, but when older men and women play on their charm and vulnerability, it can become destructive.

Cyclone, Hurricane, Tornado

Paul, sixty, dreamed he was standing outside his house, watching a tornado blowing pieces of his beloved home everywhere. He frantically tried to catch parts of the house as they swirled into the air. Paul was becoming ever more frantic. Finally, he sought shelter. Once the fierce winds ceased, nothing remained. He woke with a strange sense of shedding a liability.

DREAM BACKGROUND AND MEANING

Paul's business had failed. He was struggling to keep his home from foreclosure but was relentlessly pursued by creditors. Paul could not bear to lose all he had worked so hard for over the past thirty years.

Cyclones, hurricanes, and tornadoes can represent life spinning out of control and the need to accept what must be lost in order to start anew.

INTERPRETATIONS AND FORTUNE-TELLING MEANINGS

★ Dreaming of chaotic weather approaching indicates that unavoidable arguments and feuds are about to break out. Time to take precautions.

★ Sheltering from a cyclone says avoiding direct confrontation is better than hitting trouble head-on.

★ Recurring high-wind dreams represent excessive passion or extravagance that needs to be kept within limits.

★ Cyclones can represent a lack of excitement or adventure that can lead you to unconsciously destabilize a secure, predictable relationship out of boredom.

★ Frequent cyclones can also represent a chaotic person who rushes through your life creating mayhem, whose effects should be limited or banished.

★ A cyclone warning that does not materialize indicates an unnecessary stress buildup, when problems could be peacefully resolved.

OUTCOME OF PAUL'S DREAM

Paul's brother offered Paul work at his mountain center in Scotland. Paul was an expert rock climber. He handed the keys of his home to the real estate company and went to work with his brother, initially for six months. They were so successful that he moved there permanently. A dream cyclone, hurricane, or tornado advises waiting for a storm to pass before making major decisions.

Daisies

Davinia, sixteen, dreamed she was a medieval maiden and her true love, her present boyfriend, was going to war. She gave him a pressed daisy as a symbol that he would remain faithful and she plucked petals off the daisy chain she had made as she said, "He loves me, he loves me not." When she ended the chant, it said, "He loves me not." Davinia ran to the gates, but the knights had gone. Her precious daisy charm of fidelity was crushed in the mud.

DREAM BACKGROUND AND MEANING

Davinia was very insecure about love because her father had left her mother for a younger woman. Now Davinia was having doubts about her new boyfriend, who was moving with his family to another state soon. He promised to keep in touch, but she was constantly torturing herself with thoughts that he would forget her. The result of playing the game with daisy petals is largely random and can cause unnecessary anxiety in a relationship.

INTERPRETATIONS AND FORTUNE-TELLING MEANINGS

★ If you dream of making daisy chains, whatever your age, a dearly desired wish will come true.

★ If you dream of a field of open daisies and want a child, this is an excellent fertility symbol.

★ Dreaming of closed daisies is a symbol of protection from unwanted love. According to Roman myth, the forest nymph Belides transformed herself into a daisy to escape from the amorous Vertumnus, god of seasons, change, gardens, and fruit trees.

★ Dreaming of walking through endless fields of daisies warns against becoming entrapped by illusions of perfect love, traditionally being enchanted by the fey.

★ Dreaming of being given daisies by someone you like a lot suggests romance may grow, though not necessarily forever.

★ Crushed daisies may indicate the desire to escape from possessiveness.

OUTCOME OF DAVINIA'S DREAM

Davinia interpreted her dream as a sign of her boyfriend's infidelity rather than of her own fears of his being unfaithful. When he caught her going through his texts, he said they should split.

Dam

Finbarr, forty-two, dreamed he was gazing over the edge of an almost dried-out dam. He examined the inlet pipes and found one completely blocked. An engineer told Finbarr he was wasting his time. Finbarr persisted, removing the dead vegetation from the inlet. He found a switch at the top of the dam that would restore the water flow. Soon the reservoir was filling again and Finbarr was a local hero.

DREAM BACKGROUND AND MEANING

Finbarr's PVC manufacturing business was slowly declining, as he had lost a major international customer. His bank refused to lend him money. But Finbarr knew that there was life in the company and was determined to not give up. Dams represent the accumulation of resources. Because they contain water, there is invariably an emotional connection with making business work.

INTERPRETATIONS AND FORTUNE-TELLING MEANINGS

* A dream of a reservoir filled with water says your financial resources will be strong as long as you do not act extravagantly or wastefully.
* An overflowing or fractured dam wall reveals you have been keeping quiet about matters that make you angry. You need to express yourself calmly but firmly to avoid sudden inappropriate outbursts.
* Building a dam and flooding land represent building up long-term security and accepting temporary sacrifices.
* A dried-up or empty reservoir talks about the draining of resources that may need a new source for replacement.
* A polluted reservoir warns against letting problems and toxicity build up in a relationship, home, or workplace that will seep into every aspect if not tackled early.
* A dream of a beaver building a dam recommends hard work and adaptability if you are to create firm foundations for any venture.

OUTCOME OF FINBARR'S DREAM

Finbarr used the last of his money to travel overseas to find new customers in person. He also contacted many financial institutions, not just his usual sources, and obtained backing from an enterprise fund. Dam dreams may contain built-in solutions.

Damage

Maureen, forty, dreamed she was pouring tea from a valuable family teapot belonging to a set bequeathed by her late maternal grandmother. Her maternal aunt Beatrice had come to tea. Beatrice was complaining as usual about Maureen's shabby home and comparing Maureen unfavorably with Maureen's sister, the family favorite. Maureen snapped and hurled the teapot full of tea against the white wall. Her aunt was furious and vowed never to return. Maureen woke, guilty but relieved.

DREAM BACKGROUND AND MEANING

Maureen hated the tea set and used it only when her aunt came to tea. The tea set was all Maureen had been bequeathed on the old lady's demise, though Maureen's sister had received a large sum of money and jewelry. Damage dreams may hold suppressed anger, often released in the dream.

INTERPRETATIONS AND FORTUNE-TELLING MEANINGS

* If you dream that someone gives or sells you a damaged item, you may be secretly resentful that that person is not giving you their full attention or devotion.
* The area of damage and its cause in the dream—accident, vandalism, or weather damage such as a storm—indicates a vulnerable area of life, such as structural instability in a property that needs checking.
* Dreaming of damaging the body may warn of an undetected vulnerability—for example, damaging a limb if not taking care at a sport or if that is naturally a weak body area.
* If you dream that you damage a family heirloom, ask yourself if it holds bad or sad associations that make you unconsciously want to destroy it.
* If the damage can be repaired, the situation is retrievable.
* If the item is permanently destroyed in the dream, the question is: Has a damaged area of life outworn its use?

OUTCOME OF MAUREEN'S DREAM

Maureen put the tea set in a glass cabinet and met her aunt in a tea shop. She also started to stand up to her aunt. Damage in dreams holds suppressed emotions linked with the giver's relationship to the recipient.

Danger

Melinda, nineteen, had a recurring dream that it was pitch-black and she was walking along a path with high bushes on either side. She could hear footsteps and whispering but could see no one. She stopped, and the footsteps and whispering also ceased, but they continued as she went forward. Suddenly a huge shadow enveloped her, and she knew there was no escaping the danger.

DREAM BACKGROUND AND MEANING

Melinda was a nurse who often worked late shifts. The dreams began after late-night buses were out of service so she had a long walk home, as she could not afford a taxi. There had been attacks in the area and the dreams directly mirrored her justifiable fears. Often danger dreams do reflect a real-life danger. While they are not predicting that danger *will* materialize, they alert the dreamer to take avoidance steps.

INTERPRETATIONS AND FORTUNE-TELLING MEANINGS

★ If a dream of danger recurs without an obvious everyday trigger, the dreamer may have unconsciously noticed a problem with wiring, a worn stair, or unresponsive brakes that could develop into a dangerous situation.

★ If the dreamer is rescued from danger by an invisible force, they are protected by a spirit guide, guardian angel, or deceased relative.

★ If a dreamer sees an attack by a particular person who seems friendly, this may be a subconscious warning of their unreliability.

★ If you dream about being in danger from malevolent spirits, your psychic powers may be picking up vibes from a distressed spirit or a place where a historic tragedy occurred.

★ If a family member is in danger in your dream, warn them against bad habits or unnecessary risk-taking.

★ While danger dreams are often anxiety caused by stress overload, this overload may lead to extra risk-taking and so fulfill the fear of the danger.

OUTCOME OF MELINDA'S DREAM

Melinda mentioned her dream at work and discovered other nurses were worried because of the lack of late-night buses. They approached the management, who reluctantly agreed to pay for minibuses to take the nurses working late shifts home.

Dangerous Dog

Daphne, forty-six, dreamed she was taking two wolves she had found in the woods for a walk on a leash. All other dogs backed away and people stopped to admire the gray, glossy creatures. When they reached home, she let them free, but instantly they backed her young teenage daughter against a wall and attacked. Daphne was trying to fend the wolves off, but she and her daughter were both covered in blood and she woke screaming.

DREAM BACKGROUND AND MEANING

Daphne loved dogs and willingly took a pair of German shepherds from a friend who was worried because they were snappy with the children. The dogs were very protective of their new family, though aggressive toward visitors and other dogs. Dangerous-dog dreams are rooted in a natural fear we have of being attacked by wild animals, but usually they have some validity.

INTERPRETATIONS AND FORTUNE-TELLING MEANINGS

★ If you dream of domestic dogs turning into wild animals, you may be picking up underlying unpredictability that should be noted.

★ If in a dream domestic dogs attack a family member, especially a child, there may be issues over the dog's possessiveness toward the owner.

★ If you are controlling a pack of dream wolves or wild dogs, your own dogs accept you as the alpha of the pack.

★ If you continually dream of a particularly large dog, it will come into your life as a gentle giant, for it has made a telepathic link with you.

★ If you see your dogs in a dream worrying sheep, this may alert you to be especially careful near livestock.

OUTCOME OF DAPHNE'S DREAM

In spite of recurring dreams, Daphne was totally confident in the docility of the dogs until her daughter tripped while carrying food and the dogs came snarling around her as she lay on the ground. Daphne realized she could not keep the dogs. Even seemingly docile animals can be unpredictable, and dreams can pick up advance energies of possible danger.

Dangerous Jobs

Angus, twenty-three, dreamed he came across a police raid on a major drug bust while he was on patrol. He realized it had gone horribly wrong, and many police officers were wounded. He tackled a man with a machine gun, disarmed him, and cuffed him. Angus was commended for bravery, but his family was filled with anger.

DREAM BACKGROUND AND MEANING

Angus was a police officer in charge of the local station in the small town where he grew up. He was becoming increasingly frustrated with routine work. He had seen an advertisement to train for the special Violent Crimes Unit in the city a hundred miles away. His family begged him not to apply. Exciting, dangerous jobs in dreams represent actual or desired opportunities to push life to the limits.

INTERPRETATIONS AND FORTUNE-TELLING MEANINGS

* If you dream you are fighting dangerous criminals and winning, you are ready to tackle a major injustice.
* If you dream of having a dangerous, exciting job but yours is safe and routine, you may need more challenge in your working life.
* If you dream of being in the rescue services but are being held back from entering a burning building to save lives, you are frustrated that you cannot take decisive action.
* If you dream you are facing danger on a battlefield with the armed forces, you are ready to take a major risk to succeed.
* If you are a racing driver in the dream and your car crashes, going all out for a desired result will require caution.
* If you dream you run from a risky situation for safety but return to the danger zone, you may have to choose between security and adventure.

OUTCOME OF ANGUS'S DREAM

Despite his family's protestations, Angus decided to join the Violent Crimes Unit. Sometimes accepting a dangerous job in a dream reflects the conflict between personal desires for fulfillment and the wishes of others to keep us safe but restricted.

Date (Fruit)

Sir Christopher Wren, the seventeenth-century architect who rebuilt much of London after the Great Fire in 1666, dreamed he was in a place where date palm trees grew. A beautiful woman gave him dates from a tree. He ate them and felt well and strong.

DREAM BACKGROUND AND MEANING

The morning after the dream, Sir Christopher, who was having serious problems with his kidneys but did not want the physicians to treat him with blood-letting, the brutal treatment popular at the time, sent for some dates and ate them. Through dreams we can tap into the ancient subconscious power some humans and animals such as monkeys and bears retain to know instinctively the plants and fruits that will bring a cure for specific ills.

INTERPRETATIONS AND FORTUNE-TELLING MEANINGS

* Seeing dates growing on a tree indicates resources and talents that will bear fruit in the months ahead.
* Dreaming of eating dates anticipates a pregnancy or a chance to launch a new project.
* Buying dried dates warns against waiting too long before speaking or acting.
* Fresh dates in a dish being offered to you by a lover, known or unknown, suggests a new beginning that will bring passion and gratification of sexual desires.
* A date tree that produces no fruit says a relationship may be short-lived and superficial if based only on outward attraction and desire.
* If you refuse dates offered to you in a dream, consider whether you should accept rather than reject a job offer or love proposal out of fear of committing yourself and waiting for a better offer that may not come.

OUTCOME OF SIR CHRISTOPHER'S DREAM

Sir Christopher Wren recovered by trusting the healing remedy shown to him in the dream. The Ancient Greeks and Romans had dream temples where Asclepius and his daughters Hygeia and Panacea brought dream remedies and curative rituals to those who slept in the temple.

Dawn

Susanne, sixty, dreamed it was the first day of spring and dawn was breaking. She had waited so long for the change of the year. Where she lived in Sweden, it was dark until midmorning. She was young again and gathered the first flowers that had pushed their way through the melted snow. She looked along the forest track and saw her son, Christoffer, returning after many years' absence.

DREAM BACKGROUND AND MEANING

Susanne lived alone in a wooden house on the edge of the forest. Her son had left home after a bitter fight with his stepfather, Stefan, and he vowed never to return if Stefan was in the home. Stefan left soon after to live with a much younger woman, taking all Susanne's money. But she had not been able to tell Christoffer he was right. Every spring at dawn she picked the first flowers and believed she would see her son on the track. The spring equinox, like dawn, signifies new beginnings, reconciliation, and love restored.

INTERPRETATIONS AND FORTUNE-TELLING MEANINGS

* If you dream you are running toward the dawn, you will experience a big surge of health and enthusiasm.
* A dream of the slowly breaking dawn promises everything will be better than the previous day.
* A soft pink dawn dream indicates the conception or birth of a baby, or new love based on trust.
* A bright-red dawn heralds rain, symbolizing washing away worries and stagnant energies.
* A dream of a gray or stormy dawn says you may need to overcome opposition or your own doubts, but that better times are coming.

OUTCOME OF SUSANNE'S DREAM

The dream occurred on the spring equinox, which Susanne took to be a very hopeful sign, and she wrote one last time to the old email address she had for her son, telling him she was living alone and would welcome him. For the first time, he replied. Since it is said the darkest hour is before the dawn, dawn breaking in a dream is always a good omen, even if the dreamer has almost given up believing in better times.

Debts

Carrie, twenty-five, dreamed she was in a dungeon in old London. She had been thrown into prison with her parents because they could not pay their debts. A wealthy man she had encountered came, promising he would pay all their debts if Carrie married him. He was a lot older and often drunk. Carrie could not leave her family in prison. The dream ended with Carrie getting into his carriage with a sinking heart.

DREAM BACKGROUND AND MEANING

It was probably a past-life dream. Carrie had in this life accumulated loans to pay for college, living beyond her means and mixing with a wealthy crowd. In her first job as a trainee lawyer, she found she was defaulting on loan repayments. The senior partner in the firm had promised to pay off her debts and advance her career if she became his mistress. She was tempted but did not trust him. Debts, whether emotional or monetary, can offer quick-fix solutions that rarely work.

INTERPRETATIONS AND FORTUNE-TELLING MEANINGS

* Dreaming of paying off debts indicates recovery from an illness or crisis.
* If you dream about mounting bills, family, a love partner, or friends may be emotionally blackmailing you.
* If you have actual debts and dream about being rescued by a wealthy lover, beware of instant repayment schemes, as offers may be too good to be true.
* If you have debts and dream of being interviewed by a stern bank manager, it's time to seek a realistic repayment program.
* If you dream of gold coins showering down, there may be a money-spinning idea, so brainstorm.
* If you dream of your partner or adult child loaded with luxuries, this may be a subconscious warning to check their spending habits.

OUTCOME OF CARRIE'S DREAM

Carrie realized the price was too high. She found another job and entered an official debt management program. She also now chooses friends on budgets. Often debt dreams are not about money, but about people who make us feel obliged to them emotionally.

Decapitation

Alison, thirty-three, had a recurring dream that she was at the Tower of London as one of the ladies-in-waiting who accompanied Queen Anne Boleyn, wife of Henry VIII in 1536, to be beheaded by a French swordsman. Then she fled to take care of Anne's infant daughter, Elizabeth, whom she knew she must guard till Elizabeth became head of state as queen and avenged her mother.

DREAM BACKGROUND AND MEANING

Alison started having the dreams after visiting the Tower and witnessing where Anne Boleyn died. She felt connected and thought that the dream was from a past life. Alison was in line for promotion to head of radiology at her hospital. However, she feared the appointment was rigged in favor of the head manager's daughter. To lose your head suggests that a bid for the top to become head of an organization or society is not going to happen because of others' malice and double-dealing.

INTERPRETATIONS AND FORTUNE-TELLING MEANINGS

★ To dream of your body without a head seems horrifying, but it simply means your head and heart are moving in different directions than your logic and feelings, and the heart has won.

★ If you dream you witness a head rolling after an execution, be careful that you do not lose your head in love or illusion.

★ If you are the executioner, you may need to silence someone verbally or legally, as unfair talk is damaging your reputation.

★ If you dream you find a headless body and you recognize an enemy or rival, past or present, they no longer have power over your thoughts.

★ If you regularly dream of headless bodies, watch fewer scary movies or use your dreams as a basis for writing horror and fantasy fiction.

OUTCOME OF ALISON'S DREAM

Alison did not get the job and realized she had to move on, as promotion at her current hospital would always be used as a reward by the top. She studied Anne Boleyn and is writing a novel to vindicate her. Decapitation dreams, once they're understood, lose power to terrify, instead offering stored power to restore logic if the heart is unwise.

Decay

Charles, thirty-five, dreamed his teeth were decaying and turning black. The dentist said Charles had to wait until they eventually fell out or became so painful they needed removing. Charles was horrified, as his career depended on speaking to large groups. He woke and dashed to the mirror, relieved that his teeth still looked in good condition.

DREAM BACKGROUND AND MEANING

Charles had been getting fewer speaking and conference engagements than usual. He was increasingly finding it difficult to deliver incisive, original words on talk shows and conferences. Was this the beginning of the end of his career? Decay dreams, especially of teeth, if the dreamer relies on appearance professionally and socially, reflect the dreamer's fears of a career decline.

INTERPRETATIONS AND FORTUNE-TELLING MEANINGS

★ Decaying buildings suggest that the dreamer is clinging to the past and passing by fresh opportunities.

★ Dreaming of decaying fruit or vegetables promises a natural ending, the way to new growth in health or finances.

★ If in your dream you detect hidden decay in your home, there may be structural repairs not obvious externally.

★ If you find a decaying animal or bird in your dream, a relationship or situation is too far gone to be revived.

★ If you dream you can fix the places where decay caused by physical, emotional, business, or financial neglect can be replaced, do not give up without trying one more time.

★ If you dream everything you touch crumbles with decay, rebuild your life rather than ignoring or covering over what is rotting.

OUTCOME OF CHARLES'S DREAM

Charles accepted that it was time to restructure rather than ignore the inevitable decline of his speaking career, symbolized by the decaying teeth. He started an agency training new, younger speakers and finding them outlets, using his experience and contacts. Decay dreams seem by their nature to be gloomy, but the process of decay is necessary in the cycle of change, leading to new beginnings.

Deceased Grandparents

Caitlin, nineteen, dreamed she was walking toward her grandfather's house next door when she saw her deceased grandmother in the yard. She hugged her grandmother and asked why she was there. Her grandmother smiled, and Caitlin realized this was the last time she was going to see her. Caitlin knew her grandmother was going to pass over, and suddenly her grandmother was gone.

DREAM BACKGROUND AND MEANING

Caitlin had been devastated when her grandmother died unexpectedly and found it hard to grieve openly. She had been very close to her grandmother and still often felt her presence. The bond between grandparents and grandchildren is very strong. Deceased grandparents may make contact with grandchildren through dreams, to let them know love goes on.

INTERPRETATIONS AND FORTUNE-TELLING MEANINGS

★ Grandparents' connection with grandchildren through dreams at any age allows a nonfrightening way to reach them if an actual manifestation would be unsettling.

★ If you dream of a deceased grandparent, they may have advice for you as they would have in life.

★ You may dream of a deceased grandparent's comforting presence at a time when you feel alone or insecure.

★ If you were not present when a grandparent died, or if they died before you were born, a single dream may establish or reestablish the connection of love or heal a quarrel.

★ Even if you do not believe in spirits, a deceased-grandparent dream will strengthen the sense of family connection, especially if existing parental connections are tense.

★ If you dream of a grandparent from generations back, you may, on investigation, find that a particular great-grandparent has life path similarities to yourself.

OUTCOME OF CAITLIN'S DREAM

Caitlin realized her grandmother was now her spirit guardian and that dreams might become the way her grandmother communicated. Spirits, especially deceased grandparents, may remain around for days, weeks, or even months after their death, in order to remain with their grandchildren when grief is most acute.

Delivery (Packages)

Penelope, nineteen, dreamed she was in her student apartment, but there was no room to move because queues of delivery people were carrying box after box of bedding, food, clothes, and even furniture from her mother. Then the delivery people checked the orders, picked up the boxes, and took them back outside where people—old, young, and families—were happily carrying the boxes away.

DREAM BACKGROUND AND MEANING

Penelope's mother was suffering from empty-nest syndrome and every week would send items she had found for Penelope's apartment and food parcels enough to feed twenty. Penelope was grateful but she did not need them, and the apartment was becoming cluttered. But when she mentioned this to her mother, her mother became upset.

INTERPRETATIONS AND FORTUNE-TELLING MEANINGS

★ A dream of a surprise delivery promises unexpected good news or the arrival of a beloved friend or relative.

★ If an expected delivery is delayed in a dream, you may have to wait longer than anticipated for positive results of an action or transaction.

★ If a delivery does not arrive or the contents are broken, you may experience a broken promise.

★ If you are delivering a gift to a friend or family member far away or estranged, the dream expresses telepathic communication between you both that should be followed up.

★ If you dream your delivery is made to the wrong house, ensure that you are not overlooked at work or socially, with someone else getting the praise or credit.

★ If you dream of receiving or sending a food delivery, someone close needs extra nurturing, but avoid creating overdependency.

OUTCOME OF PENELOPE'S DREAM

The next time Penelope went home, she and her mother walked past a newly established food bank and on impulse went in. Penelope's mother, while chatting with the organizer, discovered that they were desperately short of volunteers. Penelope's mother is now a coordinator, and Penelope has her apartment back. Delivery dreams can reveal the true destination of a delivery, where it is intended and where most needed.

Dementia, Alzheimer's Disease

In his dream, Adam, thirty-four, went to his parents' home for his dad's birthday. Adam gave his dad a present. As his father removed the wrapping, he said to Adam, "That's very kind of you. Do I know you?" It was then that Adam woke, sure that something was wrong.

DREAM BACKGROUND AND MEANING

Adam had suspected for some time that his father's memory was failing. Adam's mother, along with other family members, refused to accept that anything was wrong. Adam knew he would upset the family if he sought medical advice without their agreeing to it. A dream of someone close losing their memory may be an early warning sign that only you have picked up or others are denying.

INTERPRETATIONS AND FORTUNE-TELLING MEANINGS

*   If you dream of a relative with mist around their head or white cotton wool like wisps, there may be some question of memory that needs investigating.
*   If you dream of an older relative getting confused even if they are not displaying signs of it in daily life, your automatic radar may be detecting early confusion.
*   If you dream of yourself or a relative dashing around dropping and losing things, this may be a sign of stress overload and suggests slowing down.
*   If a relative with early dementia lives alone and you dream of a fire or accident, it could be a signal that supervision should be increased.
*   If you dream of yourself and your partner or parents being much older but fit and alert, this is a good omen, especially if dementia is in the family.

OUTCOME OF ADAM'S DREAM

Adam told his parents his company was subsidizing general health checks for immediate family. They all went along. Adam's father's condition was picked up. His father admitted he had been worried but had not wanted to make a fuss. Dreams can alert the dreamer to potential health issues to enable early intervention.

Demons

Gareth, seventeen, dreamed nightly of hideous demonic figures trying to drag him to hell to rip out his soul. He tried to resist them, but they were stronger. He could see fires through a gateway and smell sulfur. He woke screaming.

DREAM BACKGROUND AND MEANING

Gareth has experimented with summoning demons using incantations from the Internet with his now ex-girlfriend. When they broke up, she and her girlfriends threatened to send demons to plague him, and the dreams began. Gareth dreads going to sleep but is too embarrassed to confide in his family.

Demons and the Devil, even if you are not religious, appear, especially in dreams of people from their teens to thirties, representing the struggle to accept and reconcile negative emotions within the self.

INTERPRETATIONS AND FORTUNE-TELLING MEANINGS

*   Demons poking and prodding you warn against overindulgence.
*   Small black demons represent irritating factors in your life that you are avoiding tackling.
*   A demon appearing in your bedroom when you are half awake, especially if resembling the archetypal Devil with forked tail and horns, talks of conflicts about your own sexuality if you feel inhibited.
*   A demon trying to possess you may be the result of dabbling with the negative aspects of magick or a ouija board. Consult a healer, priest, or priestess.
*   A dream of demonic possession can also reveal suppressed anger or resentment that you should express calmly but firmly.
*   Dreaming of defeating a demon through prayer, using a cross or spiritual chants, says you will overcome temptation or major fear.

OUTCOME OF GARETH'S DREAM

Gareth admitted to his mother that he had been dabbling in the occult. His mother confided in a healer, who taught Gareth protective prayers to recite before bed. The dreams stopped. His mother complained to the school about bullying by the girls. Demonic dreams have been experienced for thousands of years in conventional and indigenous spirituality. They can be positive in acknowledging deep-seated fears and inner conflicts.

Dentist

Philippa, twenty-five, dreamed she was inside a huge mouth filled with decaying teeth. At the end was a door, and through it an office where a fearsome dentist with gigantic pliers waited. Philippa turned to run but the door slammed behind her. Then she was surrounded by rainbow mists and drifted away, totally relaxed. When she woke, a voice said the session was over and everything was fixed.

DREAM BACKGROUND AND MEANING

Philippa had a dentist phobia because when she was a child a dentist had drilled her teeth without anesthetic. As an adult she avoided going to the dentist, but her teeth were decaying and causing pain. Dentist dreams are often to do with childhood trauma.

INTERPRETATIONS AND FORTUNE-TELLING MEANINGS

★ If you dream of a dentist looming over your face, you may have a natural aversion to people you do not know intruding on your personal space.

★ If you dream of a malevolent dentist with torturous instruments, this is an anxiety dream, based on primal fears of being taken over and controlled by others.

★ If in your dream you feel pain in your teeth, this may be a reminder that you need a checkup.

★ If you dream that you can't find a dentist when you urgently need one, you are unconsciously reminded that you need to take more care of personal health and well-being.

★ If you dream you have missed or are late for an appointment, this represents a missed chance to impress others, since teeth are concerned with communication and looking good.

★ If a dream dentist extracts your teeth, you may fear loss of power and not being able to express yourself assertively.

OUTCOME OF PHILIPPA'S DREAM

Philippa told her friend Liz about the dream and the rainbow mist that made the experience bearable. Liz found a dentist who practiced hypnosis. The experience removed her fears. Dentistry dreams are among the most common anxiety dreams, whether or not people have had bad experiences in the past.

Department Store

Josephine, fifty-five, dreamed she was in her favorite department store, which was full of beautiful clothes that matched or coordinated with hers, and there was a huge selection in every size. Josephine could buy whatever she wanted, but she always walked out with nothing, knowing she could go back anytime. She woke incredibly happy after her virtual shopping trip.

DREAM BACKGROUND AND MEANING

Josephine generally bought her favorite brands online, as there never seemed time for window-shopping in her packed schedule. Dream shopping trips at their best offer the pleasure of a wide selection and plenty of time and represent pure wish-fulfillment.

INTERPRETATIONS AND FORTUNE-TELLING MEANINGS

★ A fun shopping trip in dreams can be even more relaxing than a real-life one, has no agenda or stress, and allows the dreamer to wake happy and refreshed.

★ If you dream you are being pressured by family or buying far too much, which you will never use, you may be trying to gain approval from others to fill an insecurity about being loved and lovable.

★ If you dream a department store is closed, you may be feeling deprived and restricted by the demands of others from fulfilling your own needs.

★ If you go for coffee or to the juice bar with a person you meet in the department store, this may be someone you need to meet more often.

★ If you dream that someone is criticizing everything you buy or says you are wasting your money, beware of people who put a damper on your enthusiasm or are mean-spirited.

OUTCOME OF JOSEPHINE'S DREAM

Josephine's shopping dreams remained pure pleasure, and she always woke happy and stress-free. Dream shopping in a department store represents a way we can reward our personal self-worth. Only when credit cards are declined or cash runs out in the dream is it a warning to the dreamer to look realistically at their actual budget.

Deputy

Conrad, fifty, dreamed he was deputy sheriff in an old Western town, running the jail, arresting outlaws, and keeping order while the sheriff drank the day away. Outlaws broke into the office. Conrad shot them and realized he had the chance to shoot the sheriff and blame the dead outlaws. However, one of the outlaws still alive shot the sheriff before collapsing.

DREAM BACKGROUND AND MEANING

Conrad had been deputy headmaster of a challenging inner-city school. The headmaster did virtually nothing. The annual inspection was coming up, and Conrad felt it was time to consider his own career. Deputy dreams may bring to the surface resentments when a deputy gets no credit for hiding a chief's inadequacies.

INTERPRETATIONS AND FORTUNE-TELLING MEANINGS

* Depending on how you feel about being a deputy in a dream, the dream may reflect disappointment at being second best.
* If you are appointed deputy and the chief is absent in your dream, you will soon get a chance to show your competence.
* Becoming a deputy is traditionally associated with a rise in politics, whether in government or community.
* Being asked in your dream to be deputized at the last minute indicates that you should be ready for a leading role at short notice.
* If in your dream you are a deputy in the military or security services, you may find yourself taking a risk to back up an unpopular decision that will prove to be the right one.
* If you usurp the position you are serving as deputy in the dream, you have a choice between opportunity and ethics.
* If you dream that a rigged election made you deputy when you should have been leader, be warned of favoritism and nepotism.

OUTCOME OF CONRAD'S DREAM

After the dream, Conrad realized that if he ran the school single-handedly as usual during the inspection, the headmaster would show his incompetence. The headmaster took early retirement. Conrad got his position. Deputy dreams reveal opportunities to rise high by showing others your ability to assume leadership, not ruthlessness.

Desert

Aisha, fifty-six, dreamed she was Queen of the Bedouin and was given whatever she asked for. Then there was a sandstorm, and the encampment was gone. Aisha was alone in the middle of the parched desert. Then it rained and the desert was filled with flowers.

DREAM BACKGROUND AND MEANING

Aisha had worked for twenty years in a relatively liberal state in the Middle East. She loved living in a luxury compound with its built-in social life and being driven where she wanted. But her contract was ending and she could not find another job at her level. She did not want to go home to windy Seattle, where she had lost touch with everyone. Whether or not you are familiar with deserts in real life, a dream of a desert extending in all directions indicates a relationship or career that needs major input to restore life.

INTERPRETATIONS AND FORTUNE-TELLING MEANINGS

* Dreaming of a sandstorm or being alone in the desert says you have lost your support network and should seek another.
* A dream of flowers blooming in the desert indicates a revival in fortunes and enthusiasm.
* Desert extending across the horizon reveals that a particular lifestyle has run its course.
* A mirage of an oasis (see p. 333) warns against relying on others and fate to fix any losses.
* If you dream you are a roaming Bedouin, you will gain freedom to live in your own way where you most want.
* If you dream it suddenly rains in the desert, an unexpected source of inspiration or opportunity brings replacement for what you most need.

OUTCOME OF AISHA'S DREAM

The wife of Aisha's CEO suggested Aisha should start a business under the umbrella of her present sponsors, recruiting suitable female employees both within and beyond the Middle East and traveling to other cities in the United Arab Emirates to interview academics keen to work in schools and companies where families would know they were safe. Flowers do bloom in deserts, and what appears dead may have new life.

Deserter

Jack, twenty-one, often dreamed he was running away from the trenches where all his friends and officers had been killed. He kept running and reached a village across the border in Holland, where a young woman whose husband had been killed hid him in her cellar. After the war, using her husband's papers, he ran the local bar with her.

DREAM BACKGROUND AND MEANING

Jack had been dreaming his uncle's story. No one knew what had happened, and his uncle was treated as a war hero. Jack thought his uncle might have deserted and started a new life in the confusion after the war, as no body was found, but he did not investigate for fear he would upset the family. Jack was considering quitting the army, but his family said it was his duty to continue the family tradition in honor of his uncle. Deserter dreams are often complex; duty set by others may conflict with the dreamer's authentic self.

INTERPRETATIONS AND FORTUNE-TELLING MEANINGS

★ If you dream you are deserting a security service in your dream, a big organization or strong family is pressuring you to conform to their ideas.

★ If you dream you help a deserter escape, your commitment to your workplace or family may be tested.

★ If you succeed in escaping, you will be able to extricate yourself from an unfair obligation.

★ If you dream you are caught after deserting, emotional pressures run deep. You may need to wait for the right time to leave.

★ If you capture a deserter, you may go along with the status quo but have unacknowledged doubts about its rightness.

★ If you wound or kill a deserter in your dream, you are denying part of yourself that wants freedom.

OUTCOME OF JACK'S DREAM

The dreams continued, and one night he heard a voice saying, "Being true to yourself prevents unnecessary sacrifice." Jack quit the force as soon as he was able to, for a job clearing the names of World War I soldiers shot for desertion who had suffered a mental breakdown. Dreamers can assume the lives of relations where there is a mystery. The dream life can answer a current dilemma and sometimes clear up the mystery.

Designer Goods

Tilly, twenty-five, dreamed she was walking down Rodeo Drive in Los Angeles, looking to buy a pair of red designer high-heeled shoes with ruby studs. Though they were uncomfortable, she walked out of the store wearing them with the $3000 label still attached, and dropped her old shoes in the trash. While looking at her reflection in windows, she did not notice a hole in the sidewalk. Her heel caught and was totally ripped off. Tilly went back to the store, but they said the shoe was not repairable.

DREAM BACKGROUND AND MEANING

Tilly was obsessed with designer goods and saved all her wages to buy them. A friend invited Tilly on a major overseas trip, but Tilly did not want to waste her savings. She had seen a pair of designer shoes costing the same as the trip. She kept her designer goods in a special cupboard, but never used them.

INTERPRETATIONS AND FORTUNE-TELLING MEANINGS

★ If you dream of buying unlimited designer goods, you may be compensating when life is mundane, especially if money is short.

★ If in your dream you keep designer goods in unopened boxes, the fantasy outweighs the reality.

★ If you buy fake designer goods in your dream and are happy with them, you may be content with superficial forms of happiness, rather than substance.

★ If you dream you cannot afford designer goods and are window-shopping, you feel outside the action, watching others' happiness or true love.

★ If you dream your designer goods are faulty or break, you may feel cheated by efforts you have put into a particular project that did not materialize.

OUTCOME OF TILLY'S DREAM

Following the dream, Tilly wondered if her designer-goods spending was worthwhile. She decided to travel around Indonesia, Thailand, and Vietnam with her friend. On the trip Tilly was offered fake designer goods and could not tell the difference. Unless you are wealthy, designer-goods dreams tend to elevate possessions over experiences until something goes wrong.

Designer Luggage

Tanya, forty, dreamed she and her girlfriend, Lois, were staying at the Ritz in Paris. The porter placed Tanya's designer luggage on the trolley but abandoned Lois's well-worn backpack on the sidewalk. Lois was furious, but the porter said clearly the owner of such luggage was not a Ritz person. Tanya went into the hotel alone.

DREAM BACKGROUND AND MEANING

Tanya had matching designer luggage. Lois, however, insisted on using an old backpack. Tanya found this embarrassing. It was becoming an issue for Tanya. Differences in luggage in dreams can reveal or confirm significant differences in priorities and attitudes to life to the dreamer.

INTERPRETATIONS AND FORTUNE-TELLING MEANINGS

★ If you dream of having battered luggage while those around you have designer luggage, you may worry you have something to prove.

★ If the person in the dream with the battered luggage is a partner or close friend and refuses to upgrade, you can either accept their values or decide not to.

★ If you dream you take the wrong luggage from an airport carousel and it is superior to your own, you aspire for higher status.

★ If you dream that someone takes your luggage and leaves you with inferior suitcases, you may worry your image is letting you down.

★ If you are buying matching luggage in the dream, this says you will rise in status and prosperity, but maybe at a price emotionally.

★ If you abandon a partner or friend if they are excluded in your dream world because of their poor image, there is serious talking to be done.

OUTCOME OF TANYA'S DREAM

Lois told Tanya she was shallow. Tanya has tried to change but still struggles with her girlfriend's lack of care regarding her image. Designer bags in a dream can represent a bid to seek acceptance by the world, which may involve leaving behind those who do not share that desire.

Desk

Dulcie, fifty, dreamed she was back at school on the first day of the term, fighting for the best desk in the classroom, at the back, near the window and radiator. She placed her satchel on the chosen desk, but the contents were emptied onto the floor by the class bully's clique. When she had retrieved them, there was only the desk right under the teacher's eye remaining.

DREAM BACKGROUND AND MEANING

Dulcie's office layout had been changed from small private cubicles to open-plan. Everyone sat wherever there was spare desk space. She hated not having her own permanent space. Desk dreams reflect the sense of claiming a space that the dreamer regards as their own.

INTERPRETATIONS AND FORTUNE-TELLING MEANINGS

★ Dreaming of sitting at a school desk as an adult says you are not being taken seriously in your career.

★ A dream of a tidy workplace or business desk promises financial and business affairs that prosper.

★ If a desk is piled high with unsorted papers and chaos and it is your mess, it is time to deal with outstanding matters.

★ If you dream that someone else is creating the chaos on your desk, refuse to take responsibility for burdens offloaded on you.

★ If in your dream an authority figure is sitting behind a huge, polished desk, you may feel intimidated about asking for your rights to be respected.

★ If you dream you are sitting behind a big desk but your feet do not reach the floor, you may fear having your authority questioned.

OUTCOME OF DULCIE'S DREAM

After the dream, Dulcie got permission to work mainly from home. She created a home office on which she stamped her personality. On the one day a week she went into the office, colleagues saved her the same working space, which in time became known as hers. Desk dreams can be remarkably territorial and reflect the need of the dreamer to have a den, often forgotten in modern office arrangements.

Dessert

Maia, thirty, dreamed she was sitting at the kitchen table enjoying a rich fruit, chocolate, and cream dessert piled high in the dish. Suddenly the table was illuminated by spotlights in the middle of a stage. The audience were the members of her weight-loss club, booing and hissing at her for breaking her diet.

DREAM BACKGROUND AND MEANING

Though Maia had joined a weight-loss club, her heart was not in it. She frequently secretly cheated. She was dieting to fit into the family heirloom wedding dress. Maia was marrying her childhood sweetheart and moving into a house on the road where both families lived. But she kept postponing the wedding until she could fit into the dress. Dessert dreams may represent a conflict between what you really want and what others say you should want.

INTERPRETATIONS AND FORTUNE-TELLING MEANINGS

★ If you dream you are enjoying a delicious dessert, indulge your sensual nature; the dream may be a symbol of uninhibited sexual pleasure.

★ If you dream you feel guilty enjoying a dessert, you may be suppressing your true feelings and desires.

★ If you dream you are caught eating a rich dessert while you are on a diet, you may be subconsciously seeking discovery.

★ If a dessert tastes sour or rancid, then forbidden pleasures may be less satisfying than anticipated.

★ If you drop a dessert intended for a special occasion, you may not, deep down, want to take part in the occasion.

★ If you dream you are making a dessert, ask for whom you are making it—or do you want it for yourself?

OUTCOME OF MAIA'S DREAM

Maia realized she was sabotaging her diet because she did not want to slot into the life her parents had planned for her since her childhood. She and her fiancé went traveling for a year to see what they wanted for their future, together or apart. Dessert dreams can be very deep where issues of guilt, obligation, and personal desires become entangled in the interference of others.

Detour

Donna, thirty-eight, dreamed she was driving to the airport with her daughter Felicity, ten, as Felicity was going on vacation with her father and his new girlfriend. The road to the freeway was blocked by an accident. Donna detoured along back roads, but traffic was at a standstill, and she was rerouted back onto the original road, which was still blocked. Donna phoned her ex-husband, who accused her of sabotaging the holiday and said that they would go without Felicity. Donna woke relieved.

DREAM BACKGROUND AND MEANING

Felicity's father and his new partner were heavy drinkers and were staying in Berlin, the clubbing capital of Europe. How could Donna spare Felicity from a vacation on which she did not want to go without breaching custody? Detour dreams are useful when a problem cannot be tackled head-on in any area of life.

INTERPRETATIONS AND FORTUNE-TELLING MEANINGS

★ If a road is blocked in your dream and the detour takes you miles out of your way, you may not want to go on the journey.

★ If in the dream you hit numerous detours that send you in the wrong direction, you may be subconsciously putting obstacles in the way of a plan not of your choosing.

★ If you dream that a crash causes a detour, are you taking too many risks to avoid hitting trouble head-on?

★ Setting up diversionary tactics to avoid a confrontation will bring temporary relief, but you will eventually have to deal with the situation.

★ If your detour takes you to an unexpected location, the place will be of positive significance to you.

★ A detour dream the night before a major trip warns of potential danger unless you change your timings or route.

OUTCOME OF DONNA'S DREAM

Owing to passport-renewal delays, Felicity's passport arrived the day before the trip, but Donna told her ex it had not arrived. He was happy for an excuse to leave Felicity behind. Detour dreams can be your psychic radar, anticipating delays on a planned journey or more complex issues fraught with emotion.

Diamonds

Jethro, twenty-three, dreamed he discovered a mine with many diamonds piled at the entrance and no one guarding them. He filled his pockets and hands with them and walked away fast. But as he crossed a river on a high, rickety bridge, the bridge began to sway and crack. He realized the diamonds were weighing him down. Jethro could choose to hold on to the diamonds and maybe get across, but he would be taking the risk that the bridge would collapse when he was halfway across if he did not throw them into the water.

DREAM BACKGROUND AND MEANING

Jethro was preparing for his final exams. His gaining a prestigious job depended on the test results. Jethro had been offered an advance look at the exam papers. However, he knew if he was caught cheating it would ruin his chances of having a good career. Diamonds, more than any other gem, represent temptation, and dreams can express ethical versus profit issues.

INTERPRETATIONS AND FORTUNE-TELLING MEANINGS

* ★ A dream of a brilliant diamond ring assures love will be true and eternal.
* ★ Dreaming of owning a diamond mine or prospecting for diamonds promises good long-term rather than instant returns in speculation or investment.
* ★ A stolen diamond is a sign of underhanded dealings and advises the dreamer to consider the consequences if the dealings are detected.
* ★ A fake diamond says you should not be fooled by offers that seem too good to be true in any area of life.
* ★ Dreaming of a tray of diamonds in a jewelry store advises you to make choices carefully in love or business and to not be misled by superficial appearances.
* ★ Dreams of antique or secondhand diamond jewelry warn of inheritance disputes or family quarrels about the fair distribution of joint resources.

OUTCOME OF JETHRO'S DREAM

Jethro decided to decline the opportunity of an advanced peek at the exam papers. However, while waiting for his results he still wondered if he should have taken the risk. Diamonds, because of their beauty and value, are often implicated in dishonest dealings in dreams and reality.

Dice

Louis, twenty-six, dreamed he was a monk in a Tibetan Buddhist monastery, using a dice oracle, based on a mantra system. People were lining up to consult him, but when his eyes were gazing upward, supposedly seeking inspiration from the saint of the oracle, he was really planning his escape from the tedium of the monastery, where his parents had enrolled him as a monk. He wanted to tell dice fortunes throughout the world.

DREAM BACKGROUND AND MEANING

Louis was a lucky dice gambler. His parents were paying for a course in systems analysis and had bought him a small apartment. The question in dice dreams is who is rolling the dice of the dreamer's destiny.

INTERPRETATIONS AND FORTUNE-TELLING MEANINGS

* ★ If you are playing dice in your dream, you are taking a chance on fate to offer a profitable future.
* ★ If you are consistently winning in your dice dream, you should not worry about the viability of leaving security, as luck is on your side.
* ★ If the dice go blank, you may be taking one too many chances. Put practical backup plans in place.
* ★ If you dream that someone in your life is playing dice, they may be uncertain about a decision regarding you or your relationship.
* ★ If you dream you throw all sixes, it's a good time for speculation or launching an uncertain business venture.
* ★ If you dream someone is playing with weighted dice, they will be very convincing but not reliable.
* ★ Dreaming of rolling the dice without gambling suggests you should test the viability of a situation.

OUTCOME OF LOUIS'S DREAM

Louis decided to take six months off to test his luck. He was not successful. However, he intends to visit Tibet, where Buddhist monks still use a dice oracle, to see if his future lies in clairvoyance or if he should focus on his potentially lucrative business career.

Dinghy

Jordan, thirty, dreamed he had bought a top-class racing dinghy with an inheritance from his late uncle. He took it out to sea alone, as he did not want to share it with his best friend, Ed. He had quarreled with Ed, who told him if they wanted a better dinghy they could save up the money and buy one together. Jordan's new dinghy was washed onto some rocks. Ed rowed out in Jordan's old dinghy and saved his friend, but the new boat was lost.

DREAM BACKGROUND AND MEANING

Jordan and Ed wanted a racing dinghy, and Ed suggested they share one by upgrading Jordan's existing boat. But Jordan was convinced that his late uncle, whose will was being disputed, had left him enough money to buy his own luxury racing model. Dreams where something anticipated by the dreamer is wrecked may warn the dreamer that they may not acquire it in the first place.

INTERPRETATIONS AND FORTUNE-TELLING MEANINGS

* If you dream you are floating out to sea alone in a dinghy, you may be turning your back on friends and leaving yourself vulnerable.
* If you are using a dinghy to row out to a larger boat, your ambitions will be fulfilled.
* If you are being towed in a dinghy by a larger boat and enjoying the experience, independence is important to you, but you need support.
* If you are rescued from a sinking dinghy (see "Lifeboat," p. 286), you should not waste time craving for what is lost.
* If you dream of dinghy racing in a basic boat, you will achieve tangible results rather than superficial acclaim.

OUTCOME OF JORDAN'S DREAM

After the dream, Jordan realized that Ed was taking the right approach in more modest aims and willingness to earn the money. After the will was resolved, Jordan had just enough with what he and Ed had earned to buy an outboard motor and racing sail to modernize his dinghy.

Dinosaur

Conan, six, dreamed regularly of a huge, bright green dinosaur outside his bedroom window and was terrified to go to bed. His mother could not convince Conan that there was no dinosaur, and in his sleep he would be pointing at the window, clinging to her.

DREAM BACKGROUND AND MEANING

Conan had loved playing with his model dinosaurs. He had developed his dream terror after seeing a roaring full-sized model dinosaur in a museum. Children have the ability of eidetic imaging where they can take an image from a book or their imagination and project it as three-dimensional and real. Dinosaur night terrors are common among children, as there are ever more realistic representations in the waking world.

INTERPRETATIONS AND FORTUNE-TELLING MEANINGS

* If you dream you see dinosaurs roaming across a plain, an idea of yours may be outdated and need rethinking.
* If dinosaurs are fighting one another, someone's narrow-minded attitudes may be affecting your home life or work.
* If you dream you find dinosaur bones, you need to fit together different talents or factors to take a huge step forward.
* If a dinosaur attacks you, a rival in your workplace may bring up old grievances or mistakes. If you defeat the dinosaur, you will triumph.
* If you dream you see dinosaurs moving away into the distance, some regret or attempt to recreate the past should be let go.
* If there are dinosaur footprints in your dream, you will have the chance to take a major step forward by reviving an old project or venture.

OUTCOME OF CONAN'S DREAM

Conan's mother realized it was pointless denying to Conan the existence of the dinosaur. She bought Conan a soft toy green dinosaur and said it was the dinosaur's baby, explaining the green dinosaur was just checking through the window that her baby was being looked after. The dreams ceased. Dinosaur dreams, like other monster dreams in adults and children, are real on the dream plane. In adults their purpose is to acknowledge a seemingly insoluble problem that, once faced, will cut the dream dinosaur down to size.

Disappearing

Jocasta, fifty-eight, dreamed she was in the same office in which she had worked since leaving school, but no one could see her. Colleagues were passing their hands through the space where she was sitting and totally ignoring what she was saying. One of the new staff said that with the advent of technology she could not see the point of Jocasta's job and that she would soon be laid off.

DREAM BACKGROUND AND MEANING

Jocasta was responsible for making sure all the office work was coordinated. She was also the go-to person for queries. But recently staff members were bypassing her and sending email messages to one another. Jocasta was feeling irrelevant. Disappearing dreams can reflect a sense of being taken for granted, whether by family, a partner, or work colleagues.

INTERPRETATIONS AND FORTUNE-TELLING MEANINGS

★ Significant people who disappear in your dream may reflect your fears that a relationship may not last.

★ If your children disappear in a dream and cannot be found, this is a common anxiety dream in an increasingly dangerous world.

★ More generally, children disappearing in dreams indicates feelings of being overburdened by the welfare of others.

★ If you disappear and no one notices, you may be insecure about your own value in the setting shown in the dream.

★ If you dream a magician makes your wallet or credit cards disappear, identify the magician, as they may be less than open in their dealings.

★ If you dream a magician makes a rabbit disappear and it does not come back, someone you trust in everyday life may be promising what they cannot deliver.

OUTCOME OF JOCASTA'S DREAM

Jocasta applied for and was given early retirement and started a quilt-making business from her home. The office was far less efficient without her, and management asked her to return, which she refused to do. Sometimes it is not until we disappear from a familiar role that we are appreciated.

Disconnection

Gary, a forty-year-old Englishman, called the cell phone of his girlfriend, Sukie, and received the message from his own phone: "This phone has been disconnected." Upon reaching home, he discovered all his utilities had also been disconnected, as had his Internet. He sat in the gloom, unable to fathom what had happened or why.

DREAM BACKGROUND AND MEANING

Gary had been feeling totally disconnected at work, from his family, and even from his girlfriend, as he had recently discovered that his much older sister was really his mother, and his mother was really his grandmother. His birth father had been an American serviceman. Gary felt that his whole life had been a lie. He no longer wished to connect with his family in their newly discovered roles. Disconnection dreams can occur when a major lie or false identity is revealed.

INTERPRETATIONS AND FORTUNE-TELLING MEANINGS

★ If you dream of having basic services disconnected without warning, you may not feel connected to everyday life and need to reconnect in a new way.

★ If in a dream utilities and basic services are disconnected because of nonpayment, address financial problems.

★ If you are disconnected from means of communication such as phone or Internet in a dream, sort out your thoughts and feelings before reconnecting with anyone who misled you.

★ If you dream that someone you love has been disconnected from communication devices, they may be struggling to express their fears and feelings.

★ If in the dream you are excluded in the workplace from decision-making, this may be due to a colleague who is cutting you out of the communication loop.

OUTCOME OF GARY'S DREAM

After the dream, Gary told Sukie of his discoveries, and she was amazingly supportive. They went to the United States to try to trace his birth father before deciding how or if Gary wanted to reconnect with his family. Disconnection dreams are rarely trivial but result from a shock or major rejection.

Discouragement

Evan, thirty-eight, was putting the finishing touches to a portrait when his model stood up and looked at the work. She took a knife from the table and sliced the painting into pieces. Evan woke, realizing that the model was his wife, Catherine.

DREAM BACKGROUND AND MEANING

Evan was a talented artist. However, though he had displayed work in small galleries throughout the United States, he had remained relatively unknown. He brought in an income as a part-time art teacher, but his wife said he did not have the necessary dedication to succeed as an artist. Evan was starting to wonder if he should get a job as a full-time teacher. This dream can apply to any creative or passionate interest where there is a conflict over priorities.

INTERPRETATIONS AND FORTUNE-TELLING MEANINGS

★ Dreams can often reveal a degree of hostility by someone close.

★ If a dream reveals opposition to the dreamer professionally following a creative path, the person raising objections may have hidden motives.

★ If such dreams recur, there may be escalating issues between the dreamer and opposer, due to jealousy, financial worries, or a power play.

★ If discouraging dreams involve aggression, ask how important the creative craft is to you and if part of your essential self is under attack.

★ If the dream discouragement is ongoing in life, it cannot be ignored, but consider compromise.

★ If the dream opposer is generally loving except in this area, question the real problem: creativity may be a focus but not the cause.

OUTCOME OF EVAN'S DREAM

After a vicious argument in which Catherine did damage a painting, Evan probed as to the real problem. Catherine had given up a promising career as an artist to enable Evan to pursue his art. But she felt that he was wasting time instead of accepting definite commissions. Evan took on more teaching hours, so Catherine could express *her* creativity. They are currently working on a husband-and-wife exhibition. Dreams can reveal that the person appearing to be the villain may in fact be at least partly the victim.

Dishes

Philippa, thirty, dreamed that her boyfriend came home and asked, "Mother, when will supper be ready?" She snarled that she was not his mother, but he persisted in calling her "Mother." When he had finished eating, he left the dirty dishes on the table. She hurled them at him. They shattered on the floor. She stormed out, leaving him to clean up the mess.

DREAM BACKGROUND AND MEANING

Philippa had been living with her boyfriend for five years, but recently had become increasingly resentful because he would eat and, when finished, walk away. She made jokes that she felt she was becoming more his mother than his lover. Dishes center around nourishing and nurturing, and in dreams they can ideally represent unity and contentment in the home.

INTERPRETATIONS AND FORTUNE-TELLING MEANINGS

★ Dreaming you are given a full dish of food is a prosperity dream.

★ Cooking a special dish for a partner or family who is appreciative speaks of growing closeness and mutual give-and-take.

★ Being given an empty dish suggests you cannot expect generosity from others but will need to provide for yourself.

★ Serving people from a dish so there is none left for you says you are giving too much of yourself.

★ Breaking a dish indicates that you are contemplating a major domestic life change and, if breaking it is deliberate in the dream, resentment is building up.

★ Dreaming of a pile of dirty dishes left for you to wash suggests that you are taken for granted.

OUTCOME OF PHILIPPA'S DREAM

Philippa explained to her boyfriend just how demeaning it was being treated like his mother and that in the future he must share the cooking and cleaning up or she would walk. They had been saving money by eating at home but decided they would inject fun and excitement back into the relationship by spending time together away from home. While dishes represent domestic bliss at their best, they can indicate a stifling domestic regime where people fall into stereotyped roles.

Disinfectant, Antiseptic

Virginia, sixty, dreamed she was hiding her many bottles of disinfectant around the house, but she could not conceal them all. She had been stockpiling it because there was a major epidemic and a shortage of disinfectant in the stores. She heard that the police were in her street, arresting hoarders of disinfectant. In panic, she poured the contents of all the bottles down the drain and placed the bottles in the communal garbage bin.

DREAM BACKGROUND AND MEANING

Virginia, an ex-nurse, was frantically disinfecting surfaces, as she knew how easily viruses spread. She purchased an excess amount of disinfectant, as there were panic shortages. After the dream she felt guilty.

INTERPRETATIONS AND FORTUNE-TELLING MEANINGS

★ Disinfecting your home in a dream represents the desire to rid your home of critical relations or neighbors who are invading your personal and family space.

★ If you are using antiseptic on a cut or wound on yourself or a loved one, you are trying to remove a bad influence or atmosphere that is affecting your family.

★ If you are disinfecting places where water enters and leaves your home, you are trying to cleanse yourself from feelings of guilt over bad habits that may affect others.

★ If you dream you drop and break a bottle of antiseptic or disinfectant, you are finding it hard to maintain your high standards and may be overly concerned about germs and dirt.

★ If you are using a disinfectant spray in your dream, you may be seeking to prevent spite, gossip, and unkind words at a future gathering.

OUTCOME OF VIRGINIA'S DREAM

After the dream, Virginia realized that she was becoming obsessed, and she volunteered at the local immunization clinic to help prevent the spread of the disease. She took along her spare disinfectant to give away at the clinic to those who did not have any. Disinfectant dreams alert the dreamer to anxiety overload, where sensible precautions move close to obsession.

Disinformation, Fake News

Trevor, a fifty-six-year-old reporter, dreamed he met a former member of the British royal household who told him scandalous information about a member of the royal family. Trevor was worried that this was untrue but knew it would be hard to disprove. He assured his editor that the source was 100 percent genuine, and the story was featured on the front page of the newspaper and picked up by other journals. He heard that the person slandered was devastated, but it considerably advanced Trevor's career.

DREAM BACKGROUND AND MEANING

Trevor refused to use news that was obviously totally fake, but was instructed to come up with something spectacular. After the dream, Trevor was introduced to a member of the royal household staff who had been dismissed, who promised Trevor gossip that would give him headline coverage. Disinformation dreams may reflect a dilemma between choosing fame and fortune and facing a loss of integrity or remaining silent.

INTERPRETATIONS AND FORTUNE-TELLING MEANINGS

★ If in your dream you are suspicious about what you are reading or being told, your unconscious radar is warning you to check facts before acting.

★ If you dream someone is spreading untruths or rumors about you on social media or as gossip, beware of the information you offer about private matters.

★ If you are told information in a dream that is contrary to what is being spread, trust your instincts.

★ If you are offered money in a dream for information of uncertain origin, you may be tempted to damage the reputation of someone for financial advantage. Consider the consequences of being wrong.

★ If you are supporting a conspiracy theory in your dream, do the people persuading you have their own agenda for misleading?

★ If you are denying disinformation in your dream, you may be called on to take a stand in your daily life to prevent an injustice.

OUTCOME OF TREVOR'S DREAM

Trevor's first major royal scandal was rapidly discredited. Trevor took a job at a local journal that paid considerably less money, but did it so he could sleep at night.

Disjointed Dreams

Petronella, thirty, dreamed she walked into a market that sold old clothes. She emptied the contents of her suitcase onto one of the tables. Petronella then asked a stranger where she should go, and he told her to follow the bridges and the flooded pathways where people were wading through. She was afraid the water might be too deep, as the river seemed to extend everywhere. Petronella then waded through the river and saw a signpost, half submerged, pointing to London.

DREAM BACKGROUND AND MEANING

Petronella was confused by her dream, as it was one continuous dream but was disjointed. She had resisted leaving her abusive relationship and going far away. Disjointed dreams take much unraveling but may point to a sequence of events where each part in real life depends on following the previous one.

INTERPRETATIONS AND FORTUNE-TELLING MEANINGS

* If the first part of a disjointed dream involves traveling, you need to urgently put a plan into action if you are currently in danger or distress.
* If the next part sees you shedding unnecessary possessions, you may need to travel light.
* If the subsequent part of the dream involves open spaces, you will win freedom.
* Water or rivers emphasize the emotional cost, especially if there is danger of drowning in the dream.
* If you see a signpost, whether obscured or half submerged, it may give you a clue about a place you may find help.
* If the dream seems unfinished, picture the last part of the dream and in your mind walk back into it, and you may be able to put all the parts together.

OUTCOME OF PETRONELLA'S DREAM

Petronella left, telling her husband she was going on vacation. Since she had relatives living just outside London in a riverside town, she stayed with them while she put her life together. Disjointed dreams are like puzzles. If each step is followed, all will turn out well.

Dismissal (Firing)

Joe, thirty-three, dreamed he was at the small accounting firm where he worked. He asked his boss for paternity leave after the birth of his first child. His boss told Joe to clear his desk and leave instantly, accusing Joe of incompetence and laziness.

DREAM BACKGROUND AND MEANING

Joe had been worried about his boss's attitude toward paternity leave, despite being entitled to it under the law. Whenever Joe mentioned dates, the boss hinted that Joe's position might not be secure if he took time away. The boss had already moved his nephew Scott, a trainee accountant, into Joe's office, though there was not enough work for two. Dreams can pick up trends that have been building awhile.

INTERPRETATIONS AND FORTUNE-TELLING MEANINGS

* If you dream of a dismissal situation that mirrors a potential scenario, have your defense ready.
* If the dream dismissal is not expected, you may be feeling unnecessarily guilty that you are not giving your best at work or home.
* If you do not work or are not worried about dismissal, the dream reflects uncertainty about a relationship or property tenure.
* Fighting an unfair dismissal claim in a tribunal or court suggests unfairness in your life or work that needs resolving before it escalates.
* If you dream you are blamed for someone else's incompetence, be alert in the days ahead for possible treachery.
* If you dream you are dismissed after an angry confrontation at work, deal with problems through official channels rather than being provoked to overreact.

OUTCOME OF JOE'S DREAM

As expected, Joe's boss was looking for an excuse to give his nephew Joe's job, though Scott was incompetent. Joe had facts, figures, and legal contacts prepared when he asked for paternity leave. By the time Joe was legally obliged to return to the office, he had another job offer. His boss asked him to stay, as his nephew had caused chaos, but Joe refused. Dismissal dreams can differentiate between fears and likelihood.

Distress Flares

Jake, twenty-five, dreamed he was on a small boat that hit rocks and started to leak water. He tried to send up a distress flare, which would not ignite, and then another, which exploded in the water. He realized he was on his own and started to bail so he could paddle the boat to shore. Bruised and battered, Jake reached land but knew he should have checked his own safety equipment in case rescue did not come.

DREAM BACKGROUND AND MEANING

Jake was an adventurer traveling the world. He often encountered difficulties, mainly when his money ran out, but his long-suffering parents always bailed him out financially. However, after the last mini-crisis they said "no more" until he could show he was trying to help himself.

INTERPRETATIONS AND FORTUNE-TELLING MEANINGS

★ Dreaming of sending up a distress flare indicates you are feeling isolated and need to talk over your worries.

★ If you dream you see a distress flare and go to the rescue, a family member or friend may ask for your help soon.

★ If you dream a distress flare fails to ignite, you may have to deal with your own problems, as anticipated relief is not coming.

★ If there is no response to your flare, someone you thought would support you may disappoint you by their lack of response.

★ If you realize in the dream that you have left your flares behind, you may need to adapt your plans and rescue yourself by other means.

★ If someone close to you frequently sends up unnecessary flares, they may have demanded your help or sympathy one too many times.

OUTCOME OF JAKE'S DREAM

Jake ran out of money in New Zealand and could not pay his hostel fees. He contacted his parents to bail him out, but they told him to sort it out himself. He had to work at the hostel to pay off his accommodation. He decided he would have to think seriously about his future, since his parents no longer answered his distress calls. Distress-flare dreams where the dreamer is not rescued can cause a radical rethink about what constitutes a real emergency.

Divorce

Ricky, thirty-six, dreamed he came home to find his partner, Allen, gone and their daughter, Lily, missing, He found a note saying Allen wanted a divorce, no reason. Allen would not answer his phone. Ricky frantically searched for them, as he did not want the relationship to end.

DREAM BACKGROUND AND MEANING

Allen usually stays home with two-year-old Lily as Ricky has a high-flying career. Recently Ricky has been coming home late and they have quarreled. Allen resents the fact that he stays home 24/7. Ricky says he never sees Lily except when she is going to bed and has to work overtime to support the family. Generally, divorce dreams are an all-or-nothing statement of an unsatisfactory situation to be tackled if the relationship is to survive.

INTERPRETATIONS AND FORTUNE-TELLING MEANINGS

★ If a relationship is not making you happy, the dream alerts you to the need for a drastic, make-or-break change.

★ If you are happy, divorce dreams indicate necessary change within the relationship, perhaps because of a new baby, children from a previous relationship, or worries over finances.

★ If there is a third party in the dream, known or unknown, examine whether fears of infidelity are justified or are just insecurity.

★ If in the dream your partner has left, look for dream clues as to what in their life is wrong, not necessarily in the relationship, but circumstances.

★ If you are actually divorcing and your partner has emptied the marital home in the dream, secure your rights. Your unconscious may be picking up on potentially unfair dealings.

★ If you dream you are justifying the divorce in front of a judge, there may be unacknowledged resentments requiring compromise that need expressing and resolving.

OUTCOME OF RICKY'S DREAM

Allen and Ricky decided to both work from home so they could share chores and the joy of parenting. The relationship improved dramatically. Generally, divorce dreams do not foretell trouble, but point to existing problems being ignored.

Dog

Jacob, fifteen, had a recurring dream that his dog, Shep, who had recently died, was playing ball in the garden. Jacob was called inside by his mother. Shep followed, but his paws were muddy, so Jacob's mother chased Shep outside. Jacob could not find Shep and blamed his mother. She replied that Shep had gone forever and Jacob should accept it.

DREAM BACKGROUND AND MEANING

Jacob had a special German shepherd who had been with him all his life. Jacob is incredibly shy. Jacob's mother reluctantly decided to have Shep euthanized, as the dog was very ill and in constant pain. Jacob blamed his mother and could not get over his loss. For some owners, the death of a pet is no different from losing a family member, and grieving can go on for many months. Dreams are a common way of maintaining the connection during the mourning period.

INTERPRETATIONS AND FORTUNE-TELLING MEANINGS

* Dreaming about your dog, or a friendly dog if you do not have one, represents the need for a supportive loyal friend, especially if you lack human companionship.
* A dog running toward you in a dream indicates a reunion with an old friend, or a new one coming into your life.
* A ferocious dog represents feared hostility, whether your own suppressed anger or that of an unpredictable acquaintance.
* If you dream of a dog that has died, this may be direct contact or a reminder of the undying love between you.
* If you dream a dog slips the leash and runs away, you are unconsciously worried about losing a friendship or control of a situation.
* Dreaming of a constantly barking dog indicates you have something important to say. Choose the right time and do not overstate your case.
* If you are afraid of your dream dog, examine fears of being let down.

OUTCOME OF JACOB'S DREAM

Jacob adopted a rescue animal and is joining activities to make new friends. He made a special shrine for Shep.

Dog Poop

Meghan, thirty-five, dreamed she was late for the office Christmas dinner and took a shortcut across the park. She slipped in her new silver high-heeled shoes but thought nothing of it. However, when she sat down to dinner, she could smell dog poop and noticed she had left a trail of brown stains all the way from the door. She ran to the bathroom and tried to clean the bottoms of her shoes, but her hands became covered. She could not face going back.

DREAM BACKGROUND AND MEANING

The neighbor's dog often defecated on Meghan's lawn and on occasion she had trodden in it. Meghan had tried reasoning and complaining to the town council, but nothing had worked. Dog poop in a dream often reflects mounting frustration with the problem in everyday life.

INTERPRETATIONS AND FORTUNE-TELLING MEANINGS

* Like all feces dreams, dog poop represents prosperity through breaking free of restrictions.
* If you dream you get covered in dog poop, you have a desire to act or speak spontaneously, regardless of consequences.
* If you dream you are cleaning up the mess from someone else's dog, you may feel resentful of being expected to fix others' problems.
* If the owner of the dog denies liability, someone around you is refusing to accept responsibility for causing chaos in your life.
* If you are taking drastic action against the owner, you may be losing patience with others who are making your life difficult.
* If in the dream you have created a mess through stepping in dog poop in a setting where you were trying to make an impression, you may fear that others are standing in judgment.
* Becoming obsessed with dog feces appearing everywhere in a dream suggests that fears of intimacy in your life are isolating you from expressing your desires.

OUTCOME OF MEGHAN'S DREAM

To her neighbor's annoyance, Meghan used a legal spray to protect her property, and after that the problem ceased.

Dollar

Jed, twenty, dreamed he found a rare silver dollar on the sidewalk. He thought of his grandma's words, "Find a silver dollar, pick it up, and all year you'll have good luck." Straightaway he was sent a text offering him a job interview, as someone had left suddenly, his grandma gave him a birthday check early, and a friend paid him money he owed without being asked. Jed woke feeling lucky.

DREAM BACKGROUND AND MEANING

Jed had no job, no money, and only his grandmother's couch to sleep on. But after the dream he felt much more hopeful and asked around local restaurants for waiting jobs. Dollar dreams, especially featuring silver or gold ones, mark a regeneration of good fortune that changes the energies around the dreamer for the better, because they feel lucky.

INTERPRETATIONS AND FORTUNE-TELLING MEANINGS

* To dream of a silver dollar brings good luck, especially in speculation and new enterprises.
* To dream of gold dollars predicts a lucky win and building up long-term prosperity.
* If you empty your purse, pocket, or wallet of your last dollar bill in a dream, the day ahead will not be good for moneymaking.
* A silver dollar in a mojo bag you are making says you can create your own good luck.
* To find a dollar heads-up on the ground indicates more will follow. Facedown warns you to avoid easy money.
* To drop a purse or wallet containing dollar coins says you can overcome a potential financial setback.

OUTCOME OF JED'S DREAM

Jed found a restaurant where the only waiter had recently left without giving notice. Jed was given a job helping the elderly woman who owned the place, and built up skills as he progressed. He saved his money and, when she retired, he took over the restaurant, renaming it "The Silver Dollar." Dollar dreams can trigger initiative that has been lost and, in many cases, seem to attract opportunity.

Dolls

Pippa, thirty-five, dreamed she was trapped inside a porcelain doll in a toy store. She called out, but no one heard. She was bought by a collector and placed in a glass cabinet to be admired. The dream ended as she was struggling to get free.

DREAM BACKGROUND AND MEANING

Pippa was incredibly intelligent but, because she was beautiful, was treated like a trophy by her older, wealthy partner. He would not allow her to work, but she was given a high-limit credit card and membership to a fitness studio to fill her days. When they were entertaining, she was not expected to express an opinion. Dolls being dressed or put in display cases in dreams represent the dreamer feeling valued only for their appearance.

INTERPRETATIONS AND FORTUNE-TELLING MEANINGS

* If you are a child in the dream, playing with a much-loved doll, you are looking back to an actual or imagined past when you were loved and cherished.
* If in a dream you are hitting or hurting a doll, you may be remembering your own bad experiences as a child.
* Playing with dolls or pushing one in a stroller may express desire for a child of your own.
* If you dream of someone sticking pins in a wax doll and melting it, this may signify a past world where you witnessed bad magick or a psychic attack against you in your waking life.
* If you are the doll being held by a child, you may as an adult accept being controlled or manipulated.

OUTCOME OF PIPPA'S DREAM

Pippa got a job in her former profession of accountancy. Her lover was not happy with her newfound independence, and they separated. Dolls in dreams can be complex symbols, and the relationship between doll and dreamer can reveal unrealized emotions regarding dependency.

Dolphin

Adam, twenty-five, dreamed he was walking out to sea, letting the current carry him away. He was not sad, as he had no family to grieve for him. Suddenly he was surrounded by a family of dolphins. One pushed Adam from underneath and two more supported him, gently nudging him back to the shallows. He woke at peace.

DREAM BACKGROUND AND MEANING

Adam's soulmate had died of leukemia, and Adam's life had fallen apart. He had taken a beach shack far from anywhere. He knew he could not go back to his old life and had lost the will to live. Dolphins throughout history and in myth have rescued drowning sailors and swimmers in trouble, so this was a special dream, showing Adam he had much to live for.

INTERPRETATIONS AND FORTUNE-TELLING MEANINGS

* To dream of swimming with dolphins in the ocean indicates that emotional or physical healing on a very deep level is occurring for the dreamer.
* To see a dolphin approaching you says you have natural healing powers that can be developed, especially with water-based therapies.
* If you are naturally logical, a dolphin leaping high from the water advises you to trust your intuition and take a leap of faith.
* A dolphin who rescues you in a dream if you are in trouble promises that emotional turmoil will cease, but you must use your life well.
* Dreaming of a mother and baby dolphin is a good omen for first-time mothers who may be struggling, telling them not to doubt themselves nor aim for perfection.
* Hearing a dolphin song in a dream says you are connecting in sleep with spiritual dimensions and the dolphin is your special power totem.

OUTCOME OF ADAM'S DREAM

After the dream, Adam realized he had to go back into the world. As an experienced diver midway through medical school, Adam decided to specialize in dolphin therapy after qualifying. On his last night at his shack, he heard the dolphins singing out at sea. Dolphin dreams are keynote dreams with an important message to replace despair with hope.

Donkey

Laura, forty-five, dreamed she was on holiday in Sicily and saw a donkey lying on its side, unable to go any farther under a heavy burden. The owner was beating it. She shouted for him to stop, but he ignored her. At last, she gave the owner all the money she had and led the donkey away.

DREAM BACKGROUND AND MEANING

Laura was overburdened with two demanding teenagers, a labor-intensive and challenging job, and a partner who refused to help around the house. She was constantly exhausted, but her family did not take her seriously.

INTERPRETATIONS AND FORTUNE-TELLING MEANINGS

* A dream of a heavily loaded donkey says you should not take on burdens for those who can care for themselves.
* Leading an unwilling donkey indicates you may have to be patient to persuade someone stubborn to see your point of view.
* If you are rescuing a donkey, you may need to rescue yourself and insist on help to fulfill all your commitments.
* A seaside donkey giving rides says you should value a patient and helpful, even if unexciting, friend or partner.
* A braying donkey is a call to action, heralding a period of hard work leading to worthwhile long-term results.
* A donkey with a clear cross on its back predicts you may have to make a sacrifice to help someone in need.
* The donkey's treatment in a dream reveals whether you are appreciated or are wearing yourself out for ungrateful people in your life. The question after the dream is: What will you do to improve the donkey's lot?

OUTCOME OF LAURA'S DREAM

Following the dream, Laura realized she had to rescue herself, and so she went on vacation alone to Sicily for two weeks. While there, she adopted an abused donkey at a local sanctuary. Shocked by having to fend for themselves, Laura's family, while not becoming angels, is making much more effort.

Doormat

Lottie, fifty-five, found the doormat jammed firmly under the door, denying entry to the house when she put her key in the door. She banged on the door, rang the bell, even phoned the family inside, but everyone ignored her. She found a side door that was open but, when she explained her difficulties, the family laughed and asked when dinner would be ready. She left and drove away.

DREAM BACKGROUND AND MEANING

Lottie had become an unpaid servant, and her family only spoke to her when they wanted something. Appreciation was nonexistent. A widower she had met asked her to move in with him. She sensed he was looking for a cheap maid and, in all likelihood, an intimate relationship. Often a person referred to as a doormat has created and perpetuates the role. A dream can act as an awakener.

INTERPRETATIONS AND FORTUNE-TELLING MEANINGS

⋆ A festive doormat in the dream is a sign of family unity and a forthcoming celebration.

⋆ If you dream you are buying a new doormat, you are unconsciously changing the rules by which you conduct your domestic life.

⋆ If a doormat is tattered in the dream, a frequent visitor may have outworn their welcome.

⋆ If you dream you are hiding the key under the doormat, it is a warning to be more careful with domestic security and who you let into your heart.

⋆ If a doormat becomes jammed in the door, barring entry, you may no longer feel happy in your own home.

⋆ If your face is printed on a doormat in the dream, this may be a message that you are not respected.

OUTCOME OF LOTTIE'S DREAM

Lottie realized she was being treated as a doormat. She took a job as a live-in housekeeper for a wealthy man, reasoning she might as well be paid for what she did. She lives in luxury and has help with the chores. Dreaming of doormats is a clear indication that the dreamer is being trodden underfoot and needs to act before becoming worn out.

Double, Doppelgänger

Des, thirty-five, saw his double in different dreams and knew it was his spirit self. The doppelgänger was having an amazing time, flirting with beautiful women, making controversial suggestions at office meetings, taking part in extreme sports, and in each dream inviting Des to join him. Which was the real Des?

DREAM BACKGROUND AND MEANING

Des knew his anxieties were holding him back. As a child he had been incredibly adventurous, but his twin brother had died in a cliff-climbing accident when they were twelve. Des had always blamed himself for not saving him. Doppelgänger dreams may occur at times when we feel we are living a half-life.

INTERPRETATIONS AND FORTUNE-TELLING MEANINGS

⋆ Seeing a double in a dream or receiving double the money you asked for means rewards will be greater than expected.

⋆ If in your dream you see two identical versions of a person you know in daily life and they are not twins, beware that the person may be two-faced or deceiving you.

⋆ If in your dream friends or family say they have seen you in places you never go, you may be projecting a different image to them to win approval or impress.

⋆ If you are upset by seeing your spirit double, you may have an identity crisis about who you really are.

⋆ If another person's doppelgänger attacks you in a dream, make sure, however beloved the person, you resist attempted mind control.

OUTCOME OF DES'S DREAM

Des realized that both personas were the two aspects of himself, if only he could combine them in everyday life. If the dream shows your doppelgänger taking part in daring activities or being a social success and that is what you want, they are telling you that you have all those abilities within you.

Dove

Raphaël, fifty, dreamed that he and his wife, May, were standing on an unknown seashore when twenty-five doves, one for each year of their marriage, circled around. The birds flew back and forth until Raphaël and May followed. The doves entered a dovecote in the garden of a neglected oceanside café. There were olive trees in the garden and multicolored birds flying free. Raphaël woke, sad that the dream had ended.

DREAM BACKGROUND AND MEANING

Raphaël was aware that since the children had left home, he and May had been rattling around the empty house. The magick between them was rapidly disappearing. Raphaël had been offered early retirement. They had talked about sinking their capital into an oceanside café in Spain with a bird garden, birds being their hobby. But they hesitated to leave their established urban life. Doves symbolize peace, and, since a dove found the new land after the biblical Flood receded, the beginning of new life.

INTERPRETATIONS AND FORTUNE-TELLING MEANINGS

* A single dove indicates a quarrel will soon be mended.
* A flock of doves is a sign of family happiness and lasting love with a special person.
* A dovecote, with doves flying in and out, heralds a profitable move to a permanent home or business.
* Homing doves entering a dovecote for the night confirm the viability of a settled future at a time of restlessness.
* If doves fly away and do not return, you need to actively strive for a desired lifestyle rather than waiting for opportunity to appear.
* If the doves are driven off by predatory birds, beware of those who would stand in the way of happiness.

OUTCOME OF RAPHAËL'S DREAM

Raphaël and May went to Spain for a month and found an oceanside café for sale in a tourist resort that they could renovate. They bought it and are negotiating to purchase the land next door for a bird sanctuary, olive grove, and dovecote.

Dragonfly

Anita, twenty-four, dreamed she was walking through water meadows surrounded by fields of flowers. Dragonflies of all colors were flying overhead. She saw a dragonfly tangled in bushes and knew it would tear its wings if it kept struggling. Her boyfriend, Troy, who was striding ahead, called for her to hurry; he wanted to get back to the hotel for drinks with his business associates. Anita stopped and freed the dragonfly. When she returned to the hotel, Troy was the center of an animated circle and did not notice her.

DREAM BACKGROUND AND MEANING

Anita was engaged to a highflier, but realized they had little in common. However, her parents said she would be a fool to give Troy up, as he offered her admission to the jet-set world. Dragonfly dreams are positive dreams, a reminder it is time to enjoy leisure, nature, and beauty and consider your priorities, which may not be achievement-focused.

INTERPRETATIONS AND FORTUNE-TELLING MEANINGS

* A dream of a dragonfly hovering over water promises good news from overseas.
* A dragonfly settling on you says fulfillment may be within you, not with others, right now.
* A dragonfly in your home indicates that family or friends may outstay their welcome.
* A shower of dragonflies offers choices and different directions you had not considered or had dismissed as not possible.
* A crushed or trapped dragonfly warns that your feelings will be disregarded by someone you expected to be more understanding.
* Dragonflies flying free in gardens are symbols of happiness and wishes fulfilled. The larger the dragonfly, the greater the good fortune.

OUTCOME OF ANITA'S DREAM

Troy told Anita his friends were starting to find her boring and so was he. She quit her job in Troy's company and returned to her original plan of studying wildlife habitats.

Dragonflies can bring messages from deceased relatives and distant ancestors. Any advice or warnings within a dragonfly dream should therefore always be taken seriously.

Drawing

Hermione, forty, dreamed she was in a convent, drawing and coloring medicinal flowers from the herb garden. She was a novitiate, and an older nun was teaching her the meanings of the flowers. Hermione was totally at peace, though she knew her husband had put her aside and shut her in the convent so he could marry a younger girl to give him children.

DREAM BACKGROUND AND MEANING

Hermione's husband blamed her for their inability to have a son to inherit the family estates. He told her if he was free he could marry a woman who would give him children. He had treated her badly, and Hermione wanted to leave him. However, she knew he would leave her penniless. Her only joy was her love of drawing. This may have been a past-life dream and, as with many such dreams, a guide will remain as a spirit guardian through the ages.

INTERPRETATIONS AND FORTUNE-TELLING MEANINGS

★ If you dream that you create beautiful drawings, you can take control of your life, for your perspective is the correct one.

★ A drawing that does not resemble the subject says you are concentrating too much on setbacks and not solutions.

★ If you draw a picture and rub it out, you may need to undo words or actions spoken in haste.

★ A child's dream drawing reveals what is in the child's mind.

★ If you dream you are drawing a self-portrait, you may be trying to project a new image to gain approval.

OUTCOME OF HERMIONE'S DREAM

The local natural history museum was looking for an artist to work in the medicinal herbs section. Hermione started work and soon had enough money to leave her husband. She also sold wildflower drawings through the museum. With what her husband was forced to give her, Hermione purchased a small home with an herb garden. Drawing dreams represent modest but attainable goals and remind the dreamer that with patience they have the power to create their own destiny.

Dreamcatcher

Zara, thirty-five, dreamed she was sitting in a tepee with an old Native North American woman who was making a dreamcatcher. It was very unusual, a silky web with gray feathers and a single turquoise crystal. She handed it to Zara and said, "Grandmother Spider taught mothers and grandmothers to make dreamcatchers to keep away infants' nightmares." The woman's face changed into that of Zara's grandmother, who had brought her up and had recently died.

DREAM BACKGROUND AND MEANING

Zara had suffered bad dreams since childhood, and her grandmother would sit with her until she went back to sleep. Since her grandmother's death, the nightmares had returned. The dreamcatcher is regarded as offering protection from bad dreams at any age.

INTERPRETATIONS AND FORTUNE-TELLING MEANINGS

★ If you dream of an old Native American woman weaving dreamcatchers, you are connecting with Ojibway dreamcatcher legend and are protected from paranormal and earthly harm while you sleep.

★ Since the Lakota people believe the dreamcatcher links with the realms of unborn children, a dreamcatcher dream is a good omen when trying for a baby.

★ A symbol among the Cree nation for protection of warriors, a small dreamcatcher worn in your hair indicates the overcoming of fears and dangers.

★ A torn dreamcatcher warns against being deceived by those who appear protective but will betray you.

★ Since among the Ojibway people a child is given their dreamcatcher once the assigned dreamer has dreamed their name, seeing a swaying dreamcatcher says you will discover your life purpose.

OUTCOME OF ZARA'S DREAM

While traveling near the Great Lakes where the Ojibway live, Zara saw the dreamcatcher from her dream at a roadside market, bought it, and her nightmares stopped. Sometimes she feels her own grandmother near when she wakes in the night. A dreamcatcher with a single crystal, especially turquoise, represents emerging power to create beauty.

Drones (Aircraft)

Matt, fifty-five, dreamed he was flying his drone in the early morning when it was surrounded by other drones, dive-bombing and attacking it and him. He ran for shelter, leaving his wrecked drone behind. The drones then returned to an alien mother craft.

DREAM BACKGROUND AND MEANING

Matt had joined a local drone club but found the members very unwelcoming. There was an annual competition involving drone control and maneuvers, but already minor damage had been done to his drone during practice and his signal had been blocked. Drone dreams are often symbols of vying for control that may have nothing to do with the actual drone but its potential as a weapon in the wrong hands.

INTERPRETATIONS AND FORTUNE-TELLING MEANINGS

★ If you are flying a drone in a dream, you may be keeping your emotional distance from someone whose intentions you are unsure of.

★ If you are operating a spy drone, you may be suspicious of someone's intentions toward you.

★ If a dream drone is causing disruption to your life, whether shutting air space, being used for attack, or causing an accident, beware of interference in your life by someone with a hidden agenda.

★ If you lose control of your drone, your power to affect a situation may be less than you hoped.

★ If your drone becomes stuck in a tree or breaks, circumstances may prevent your having all the facts you need for a decision.

★ If you are receiving or using drones for deliveries, someone you doubted may prove useful.

OUTCOME OF MATT'S DREAM

Matt discovered from a former member that few new members ever stayed in the club. Most members were ex-army, who used the drone club for private military exercises and disruption of air space. Matt moved to another club and is making new friends. Drone dreams, usually experienced by those involved in the drone world, can reveal potential problems with other drone users if the drones become an instrument of power and competition.

Drowning

Philip, eighty, dreamed he was walking along the canal bank in the fog as a small boy going to see his grandfather in the lockkeeper's cottage. A bigger boy was holding his hand. The bigger boy missed the bank's edge and instantly disappeared under the water. The dream ended with Philip having a strong desire to walk into the canal after the boy.

DREAM BACKGROUND AND MEANING

As Philip got older, he would often have the same dream, and he asked his mother, a widow, and his much older sisters, who the boy was. They said it was just a dream, but Philip retained the illogical desire to walk into deep water and drown, combined with a terror of drowning. Drowning is a common dream, representing a sense of feeling overwhelmed.

INTERPRETATIONS AND FORTUNE-TELLING MEANINGS

★ If you have an illogical fear of water, yet dream of drowning, this may be a past-life dream that, once acknowledged, removes the fear.

★ If you dream of drowning but are rescued, you will receive help if you seek it in overcoming a major problem or worry.

★ If you dream of falling into water and starting to swim, there is a way out of difficulties if you take swift, decisive action.

★ Dreaming of one of your children drowning represents fear that you cannot protect them as they become more independent.

★ Dreams of a drowning family member can be a warning to take extra precautions.

OUTCOME OF PHILIP'S DREAM

Philip confronted his surviving older sister, and she related an actual drowning that had happened when Philip and his brothers had set off in the fog to visit their grandfather, after they had been left on their own when she was supposed to be caring for them. The drowned boy had been wiped out of memory as a family secret. Philip's vague recall surfaced only in dreams. If you regularly dream of someone unknown drowning, this could be an early suppressed memory of a family secret, not necessarily water-related, that has been drowned out of consciousness to avoid blame.

Drunkenness

Cindy, thirty-eight, dreamed she was sixteen again. Her mother, Sue, arrived late at the high school concert, in which Cindy had a starring part, swaying and carrying an open bottle of whiskey. She saw Cindy on stage, shouted, and then wove her way onto the stage. The other parents laughed. Cindy ran offstage in tears.

DREAM BACKGROUND AND MEANING

Since giving birth to her daughter, Cindy had been haunted in dreams by her past, when her mother was constantly drunk. Sue had refused all help, so Cindy had cut off contact, but felt guilty that Sue did not know about her granddaughter. Cindy was reluctant for her daughter to spend time with her alcoholic grandmother. Frequently, dreams about an alcoholic in the family may carry warnings to not get involved (see "Wine," p. 512).

INTERPRETATIONS AND FORTUNE-TELLING MEANINGS

★ To dream of being drunk, if you do not drink excessively, talks about fear of losing control.

★ If in a dream you are drinking to excess, you may be tempted to abandon common sense and give way to temptation.

★ If you are craving a drink in a dream and this is out of character, you may want to shed your inhibitions but fear the consequences.

★ If in a dream someone you care for is very drunk, you may worry about their reliability in a crisis.

★ If someone is deliberately trying to get you drunk in a dream, question their motives for controlling you in everyday life.

★ If there is only alcohol to drink in a dream and you are very thirsty, are you prepared to take the consequences of satisfying a desire?

OUTCOME OF CINDY'S DREAM

Cindy contacted her mother and agreed she could see her granddaughter if she did not drink in her presence. But when they met, Sue was already drunk, and Cindy knew her daughter must come first. Dreams of being inebriated can refer to any excess where the results can negatively affect others. If referring to an actual excessive drinker, they will detect the likelihood of the inebriated person changing.

Duck

Beverley, fifty, dreamed she found a wild rainbow duck with a broken wing and made a nest for it in the shed. The duck's wing mended, but she realized the duck had lost all its rainbow feathers. Though there was a pond in the garden, it never swam. She tried to persuade it to fly as its feathers were falling off through lack of use.

DREAM BACKGROUND AND MEANING

Beverley's daughter, Ellen, returned home after her relationship broke up, she lost her job, and she developed glandular fever. Beverley enjoyed having her daughter home, as she lived alone and worked part-time. But the months passed and Ellen showed no signs of getting a job or moving back to her old life. Beverley worried that Ellen had slipped back into the dependent-child role. Duck dreams reflect the domestic scene and family relationships.

INTERPRETATIONS AND FORTUNE-TELLING MEANINGS

★ Migrating ducks flying in a dream indicate it is time to move on or return home, depending on the nature of the dream.

★ A flock of ducks on a pond signifies domestic happiness.

★ Two ducks swimming side by side indicate a settled relationship.

★ Two ducks swimming one toward the other marks courtship and mutual attraction.

★ Two ducks followed by ducklings signifies imminent pregnancy, especially adding to existing children.

★ Drakes fighting over a duck warn of relationship rivalries and jealousy, regardless of the sex.

OUTCOME OF BEVERLEY'S DREAM

Beverley asked her daughter what she wanted to do. Ellen said she did not want to go back to her old life, but wanted to train as a nurse. They found her a place at the local hospital, and she came home some weekends. Gradually she has increased her social life and is dating a radiologist. When a dream duck loses its feathers and its desire to swim back into life, it is time to gently encourage it to leave the nest.

Dust

Adriana, forty, dreamed that she was companion to a cantankerous old lady who hated anyone touching her late husband's possessions. Every time Adriana dusted, the old lady complained. Adriana went upstairs to her own quarters and dusted and cleaned them thoroughly, deciding to forget the rest of the house.

DREAM BACKGROUND AND MEANING

Adriana was living with her mother in a huge, cluttered house. She had moved there after her father died. Her mother refused to move to somewhere smaller or employ a cleaner. Despite Adriana working hard to keep the house clean, her mother complained that she wanted everything left as when Adriana's father was alive. Dust that settles can make an unsatisfactory situation seem immovable and represents a desire to preserve everything as it was.

INTERPRETATIONS AND FORTUNE-TELLING MEANINGS

★ Dusting furniture and ornaments in a dream represents clearing out memories of unhappy times.

★ If your present or former home in your dream is covered with thick dust, unfinished business needs resolving.

★ Magick dust, whether fairy dust or stardust covering you, is a wish-fulfillment dream where life is instantly transformed, but nevertheless it heralds good luck.

★ Dust covering a specific object from your childhood or earlier life reveals opportunities that were never followed up but could still be rekindled.

★ An approaching cloud made of dust, or dreams of the great Dust Bowl in Texas and Oklahoma in the 1930s that made the land arid, suggests the need to move on from what cannot be prevented.

★ If you dream you successfully clear dust from your home and sweep it out the front door, you will rid yourself of a troublesome domestic matter.

OUTCOME OF ADRIANA'S DREAM

Adriana used her savings to convert the top of the house into a self-contained modern-fitted apartment for herself that would be easy to keep clean. She allowed her mother to keep the remainder of the house as dusty as she wished. Eventually, her mother employed a cleaner. Dust dreams may occur when an actual clutter or cleaning issue is becoming unmanageable, and they often suggest a solution.

Dyeing

Adam, fifty, dreamed he dyed his hair brown to hide the gray, which he feared revealed his age. But every time he rinsed his hair after applying the dye, it reverted to gray and indeed became grayer. Then his hair started coming out, and he was too embarrassed to go to work.

DREAM BACKGROUND AND MEANING

Adam was jokingly being called "the old man of the office" by his much younger colleagues, as his hair was rapidly turning gray. Dyeing hair can represent worry about the way others perceive the dreamer, which may signify the dreamer's own negative view of themselves.

INTERPRETATIONS AND FORTUNE-TELLING MEANINGS

★ If you dye your hair in a dream, you are ready to update your image and try a new approach to life.

★ If you choose a drastic change of hair color, consider what lies behind your desire for change and if it will be of benefit.

★ If you dye your hair to hide gray or white, you may be concerned about aging issues and about becoming irrelevant in a work or social situation.

★ If you dream that hair dye goes wrong and you are left with a garish or inappropriate shade, disguising your real self may not make you happy.

★ If you dream that someone else dyes your hair and it goes wrong, beware of jealousy by the person coloring it.

★ If a hairdresser is dyeing your hair, you may be doubting your own experience and expertise.

★ If in your dream the dye runs onto a garment, a change considered permanent may be short-lived.

OUTCOME OF ADAM'S DREAM

The day before he was going to dye his hair, there was a major crisis at work, and none of his coworkers knew how to solve the problem. Adam quickly fixed the blip and realized that experience was to be valued and not hidden. Dyeing can enhance the dreamer's confidence but equally may hide their true, valuable self.

Dying

Poppy, twenty-eight, dreamed she was in a hut in what seemed to be a prison camp. A soldier came outside and aimed his gun straight at Poppy through the window, killing her. Poppy realized that as a spirit she could walk through the wall. She went to a building where emaciated people lay in hospital beds and opened all the doors to try to let them escape. But there was nowhere they could go. Poppy woke feeling deeply moved.

DREAM BACKGROUND AND MEANING

Poppy had been very concerned about death, suffering, and dying since she had recently discovered when an elderly relative died that some of their overseas family had perished in the Auschwitz concentration camp. Her immediate family would never speak of it.

INTERPRETATIONS AND FORTUNE-TELLING MEANINGS

* If there has been a recent death in the family, dreams of dying or being killed are one way the mind tries to process mortality, especially if never before encountered.
* Dreams of being a spirit may relate to the astral form of the dreamer traveling to a world connected with a family death, which may be unresolved.
* Dreaming of dying never means that the dreamer or a close relative is going to die, but refers to endings of a particular phase, which can liberate the dreamer where an ending is necessary.
* If the dreamer has experienced a health scare or near-fatal accident, a dream can work through the what-if process and bring peace.
* If in the dream the dreamer is aware of being a spirit able to leave the body and travel, this can allay deep unacknowledged fears of death and dying.

OUTCOME OF POPPY'S DREAM

After the dream, Poppy found pictures of the concentration-camp hospital where experiments were carried out on prisoners and realized that in the dream she was trying to free them. She is planning to visit the place where some of her relatives died. Dying dreams, whether dramatic or gentle, may occur when the dreamer is trying to make sense of their life purpose.

Dying Happy

Caroline, fifty, dreamed that her father, James, was mowing his expansive lawn on his tractor. He stopped the tractor, sat at the table in the sunshine, poured a glass of his favorite wine, washed his glass, and said, "I'll be off, then." He walked away down the lane where his late wife was waiting. Caroline went to his room. He had died in the night.

DREAM BACKGROUND AND MEANING

James, a retired farmer, had moved to France after the death of his wife, to the place they both loved, where he had single-handedly converted a barn into a comfortable dwelling. Through the years he had slowed down, but sat happily in the sun drinking wine. Seeing a deceased relative in their natural setting and leaving it happily confirms that their life cycle was complete.

INTERPRETATIONS AND FORTUNE-TELLING MEANINGS

* If you dream of an elderly relative who died contentedly in their sleep, they were ready to move on and wanted no fuss.
* If you dream of a relative moving toward the light, the sunset, or over the horizon, they are telling you they passed in their own way and time.
* If you dream of a deceased relative carrying out work they had not done for years, that offers reassurance that they have shed physical limitations.
* If they are not aware of you in the dream, they have started their next journey.
* If you see another deceased relative waiting for them in the dream, this says they are not alone.

OUTCOME OF CAROLINE'S DREAM

Caroline's father asked her to cut the lawn, so it would be tidy when people came, which made no sense to her. After a good meal, he went to bed. The morning following the dream, she found him, still seemingly asleep. They held the wake in the gardens. Dreams of the newly deceased can, if the person was not demonstrative, allow them to happily slip away.

Eagle

Thomasina, sixty, dreamed she was riding high in the sky on the back of a golden eagle toward the noonday sun. She remembered that the eagle was the bird that could fly closest to the sun, and when they landed high in the mountains she knew there was nothing and no one to stand in the way of happiness.

DREAM BACKGROUND AND MEANING

Thomasina and her husband, Julian, had planned to travel the whole of the American continent in their newly acquired Winnebago. But Julian had died suddenly, and her friends and family said she should sell the vehicle and move into a retirement village. However, she was determined to go and had the route planned. The eagle is the most fortunate of omens for making the seemingly impossible a reality.

INTERPRETATIONS AND FORTUNE-TELLING MEANINGS

*   Dreaming of an eagle flying high says your ambitions will be realized and travel especially favored.
*   Flying on the back of an eagle is a sign of emerging shamanic abilities, especially connected with the Americas, where the eagle represents the Great Spirit.
*   The eagle represents the ability to reach out for major ventures and adventures.
*   Being carried off against your will by an eagle signifies official or family attempts to restrict freedom.
*   The appearance of an eagle indicates a legal matter against corrupt authority settled in your favor.
*   A nesting eagle represents the need to withdraw from daily noise and chaos.

OUTCOME OF THOMASINA'S DREAM

Thomasina set off on her trip. She was not alone, because her nieces and nephews joined her on different parts of the journey and she made many friends along the way. Eagle dreams say, "Why not?" They infuse enthusiasm and confidence to experience special moments and fly high.

Ear

Gerry, fifty-four, had a recurring dream of being in an old town square and having his ears cut off and his tongue split because as a novice monk he had unmasked a senior monk boasting about how he and the other monks used money from the charity box to buy rich food for the monastery. Gerry was thrown out of the monastery but was taken in by an old man who taught him how to read people's lips.

DREAM BACKGROUND AND MEANING

Gerry was gradually losing his hearing but was too proud to admit it and wear hearing aids. It was affecting his job, and he was managing mainly on lip reading. Sometimes a dream will reveal a past-life connection or a distant memory of hearing loss in an earlier world. Hearing-loss dreams can be a warning sign that action may be needed.

INTERPRETATIONS AND FORTUNE-TELLING MEANINGS

*   If a benign figure is whispering in your ear or you hear a disembodied voice, this is your spirit guide bringing wise advice.
*   If you see an ear next to a keyhole, beware of eaves-droppers spreading gossip.
*   If in your dreams you hear words in your ear, this is your clairaudient or psychic hearing power emerging.
*   If you see a disembodied ear in your dream, news is coming that you can turn to your advantage.
*   If you have an earache in your dream, you have been bombarded too much by other people's demands and complaints.
*   If in your dream you cannot hear what someone is saying, the person is obscuring the facts or maybe you are not listening.

OUTCOME OF GERRY'S DREAM

The dream prompted Gerry to see an audiologist, who recommended a small operation and was able to provide discreet hearing aids that brought Gerry back into the hearing world. His own developing lip-reading abilities prompted him to take a sign-language course and start an evening class for people with hearing impairment. Ear dreams are above all a reminder to listen to what is actually being said and not how we interpret it.

Earrings

Jane, thirty-five, dreamed she had broken one of the gold earrings that her fiancé, Rick, had given her. She went into a jewelry store with her best friend, Jenny, to see if it could be mended. Jenny offered to swap earrings and take the broken one, but hers were not real gold. Rick came in and gave Jane a box with gold earrings with tiny diamonds. She woke happy and reassured.

DREAM BACKGROUND AND MEANING

Jenny told Jane that Rick was being unfaithful, as she had seen him lunching with another woman. Jane accused Rick, and he became angry at her lack of trust, which Jenny said proved his guilt. Losing or breaking an earring suggests someone is deliberately deceiving you. Check before acting on this information.

INTERPRETATIONS AND FORTUNE-TELLING MEANINGS

★ Dreaming of being given earrings is a sign of devotion and trustworthiness. It also says that you will soon hear good news about or from the giver.

★ If you dream that you exchange earrings with someone else, beware of listening to false information, especially if the earrings you are offered are of inferior quality.

★ Gold earrings indicate lasting prosperity and faithful love; silver, a mystery, which will be cleared up once you know the facts.

★ Earrings with precious stones promise happy marriage and fidelity.

★ Pearl earrings are a sign of fertility and pregnancy.

★ Dreaming of having your ears pierced suggests you will be told information that is painful but necessary to hear.

OUTCOME OF JANE'S DREAM

Jane knew her friend was jealous, as she had once dated Rick. Rick explained he had been lunching with Jane's sister, planning Jane's birthday gift. On her birthday, Rick gave Jane earrings to match her engagement ring to wear on their wedding day, real gold with diamonds.

Earring dreams advise you to discover the motives of a person giving you bad news or gossip.

Earth

Pablo, eighteen, dreamed he was hiding in a spacecraft heading away from Earth. He was afraid because he did not have a spacesuit or safety equipment, but if he revealed himself the mission would be abandoned. He woke, his head spinning, scared he would not survive.

DREAM BACKGROUND AND MEANING

Pablo had a secure family life and had qualified for college. His friends were taking a gap year and going backpacking around the world. Pablo intended to go in defiance of his parents, who said he could not use the college fund they had saved. Earth dreams can represent a safe if dull option, rather than living on dreams.

INTERPRETATIONS AND FORTUNE-TELLING MEANINGS

★ Looking down on planet Earth from space may be an out-of-body dream or mind travel and represents emerging psychic abilities.

★ If you are traveling away from Earth toward the Moon or toward another planet, ensure that you are prepared to leave security and certainty behind.

★ If you dream of planet Earth spinning far above you as you travel through space, it may be time to deal with everyday issues before or rather than opting out.

★ Walking on earth or soil says that you should seek a practical solution to difficulties, rather than hoping for a miracle.

★ If you are making footprints in earth, time to assert your rights and wishes or express your feelings to the person you love.

★ If you are digging in the earth, something from your past will be helpful to recall, but not at the expense of reviving old grievances.

OUTCOME OF PABLO'S DREAM

After the dream, Pablo realized he had never been away without his parents and had no idea how he would manage financially or practically. Pablo decided to spend the vacation volunteering with inner-city schoolchildren on a wilderness trip. Dreams of seeing planet Earth revolving around the sun are a reminder that there is a time and place for everything, and we are not the center of the universe.

Earthquake

Louisa, twenty-five, dreamed she was at her wedding reception, and the two families were arguing and fighting. Then there was a huge rumbling. The floor shook and cracked, and food, glasses, the wedding cake, tables, and chairs were flung everywhere. Louisa's new husband, Grant, caught her hand and they escaped through an emergency exit. Suddenly they were at the airport, boarding a plane in their wedding finery. Louisa woke feeling happy for the first time in weeks.

DREAM BACKGROUND AND MEANING

Louisa's wedding plans had been hijacked by both families, who disliked each other intensely and were arguing over every detail, even before the venue had been booked. Louisa was afraid the day would be an expensive disaster, as neither family would back down. An earthquake highlights potential emotional disruption in any area of life, which, if ignored, will escalate into a disaster.

INTERPRETATIONS AND FORTUNE-TELLING MEANINGS

★ Dreaming of an earthquake is an indication of insecurity in a relationship, family, or work situation based on warning signs that you may have been ignoring on a conscious level.

★ Collapsing buildings indicate that there may be a financial, domestic, or career problem you need to tackle head-on.

★ Escaping an earthquake assures you of reclaiming personal power through taking avoidance tactics.

★ Depending upon the dream location, being caught in an earthquake warns of underlying insecurity about a coming event in that area.

★ If you are watching the earthquake from afar, this shows a shaky situation from which you should detach yourself before it affects you personally.

★ If you feel the ground shaking and ornaments start to fall, change is inevitable but will bring freedom to build life your own way.

OUTCOME OF LOUISA'S DREAM

Louisa and her fiancé told their families they were having a quiet wedding on a remote tropical beach, and organizing separate parties for both families on returning. You should accept that you need to take the first rumblings of trouble seriously and act decisively.

Easter Eggs

Lucy, eighteen, dreamed she was taking part in an Easter egg hunt. A good-looking boy she knew from college was also running, looking for chocolate eggs. The two of them ended up alone, smashing the eggs together into one large egg and were eating chunks out of it. Lucy woke feeling excited.

DREAM BACKGROUND AND MEANING

Lucy wanted a new boyfriend after the breakup of her first serious romance. She was attracted to the boy in the dream but was afraid, as her previous boyfriend had pressured her into sex and had been very demanding. She was confused, as she felt half child, half woman. Easter eggs, as a symbol of spring, new beginnings, and romance, indicate a transition between innocence and readiness for sexual love.

INTERPRETATIONS AND FORTUNE-TELLING MEANINGS

★ If you are a child in the dream, Easter-egg hunts represent a desire for more fun and adventure in adult life.

★ Easter eggs symbolize fertility and so are a good omen if you want to conceive a child.

★ Sharing Easter eggs with a partner indicates a positive sexual encounter based on mutual trust.

★ To be hunting for Easter eggs with a rival in love or work says much is hidden under the surface of friendly words.

★ If you find a well-hidden Easter egg in a hunt, you will meet a new romantic love or be given a romantic surprise by an existing partner.

★ If you find yourself eating Easter eggs alone, this marks a new beginning in life. Let love find you when the time is right.

OUTCOME OF LUCY'S DREAM

Lucy is taking the new romance slowly and does not feel pressured. They are enjoying just spending time together for now. They both love chocolate. Easter-egg dreams contain a degree of embryo sensuality if an unknown partner appears in the dream, and indicate that the person will soon appear, if they are not already around.

Echo

John, thirty-five, dreamed he was in a deep cave, calling for help, but all he could hear was his own echo. He discovered that the entrance to the cave had been sealed. At last, light appeared. Soldiers came rushing through a newly opened passageway and dragged John to a dungeon, though he protested his innocence.

DREAM BACKGROUND AND MEANING

John, new to his accountancy post, was a lone voice in his company, warning them that their financial position was in a terrible state and the IRS was about to initiate an investigation. John's predecessor, Mack, the owner's brother, had not completed tax returns for years or kept accurate records. Everyone said John was exaggerating. John feared he would be implicated when trouble hit. This may have been a past-life dream triggered by the financial chaos.

INTERPRETATIONS AND FORTUNE-TELLING MEANINGS

★ Dreaming of your own voice echoing means you may have to keep repeating yourself before you are heard.

★ An echo recognized as someone significant from your past reminds you that a previous situation is being repeated, but you should handle it differently.

★ If another's words are echoed in your voice, you may be trying to fit in with the opinions of others.

★ If it is your words echoed in another person's voice, beware of someone trying to blame you or take what is yours.

★ If your echoed words are continuously repeated, you may be stuck in a routine or impasse and need a new approach or tactic.

★ If an echo is heard from a distant mountain, you have a long way ahead to attain your goal.

OUTCOME OF JOHN'S DREAM

John filed recent accounts with the IRS, explaining he had only recently taken over, and he resigned. The company was heavily fined, but John was cleared by the IRS of wrongdoing. An echo in a cave reminds you of what has been buried but needs bringing into the open.

Eclipse

Karen, fifty-nine, dreamed she was sitting on a hilltop in bright sunlight when the sun darkened until the sky was totally black. She was too afraid to move. Then the sun became gradually brighter than before, spinning in the darkness, with fire shooting from it in all directions. Karen woke, filled with joy and inspiration. She took out her notepad and started scribbling design after design, based around spinning suns and fiery sunbeams set against a dark sky.

DREAM BACKGROUND AND MEANING

Karen's design business had not been doing well recently, as she had been lacking inspiration. Her main customer was threatening to replace her unless she came up with a dynamic design for a new solar product by the end of the week.

In ancient times, eclipses in dreams were believed to be a dragon swallowing the sun or moon. However, more positively, they trigger dynamic rapid transition during the dream state to inspire a revival of creativity in the days following the dream.

INTERPRETATIONS AND FORTUNE-TELLING MEANINGS

★ A solar eclipse in a man's dream indicates the presence or approach of a dominant woman.

★ A lunar eclipse heralds a controlling man in or coming into a woman's life.

★ A solar eclipse dream reflects temporary setbacks or lack of inspiration in business, resolved better than before, perhaps in another direction.

★ A lunar eclipse dream warns of family disagreements because of jealousy, especially with a maternal figure.

★ If it is a total eclipse, part of your personality is being overshadowed or belittled by friends or family.

★ A partial lunar eclipse says you should declare love, and a solar eclipse is saying that you should step center stage, testing your talents.

OUTCOME OF KAREN'S DREAM

Karen created a new design portfolio, *Eclipse,* based on her dream. Three companies are bidding for the rights. Eclipse dreams often trigger new ideas by clearing blocks and redundant mindsets.

Eel

Renalda, twenty-six, dreamed she was snorkeling in the sea, surrounded by giant multicolored eels, which were trying to entangle her. She tried to lose them in the reef, but they followed her and held on tighter. They were beautiful, but she realized they would crush her. She grabbed her knife and slashed at them. As each died, it became a rainbow fish.

DREAM BACKGROUND AND MEANING

Renalda was involved in a steamy love affair with a man who denied her nothing. She was finding it hard to remain detached and wanted her lover to leave his wife, but he had insisted there be no strings attached. Killing eels entangling you represents seeking freedom from emotional ties going nowhere.

INTERPRETATIONS AND FORTUNE-TELLING MEANINGS

* A wriggling eel indicates someone who is trying to get out of a promise they have made.
* If you have caught an eel on a fishing hook, beware of a charismatic but unreliable person in your life who you may find hard to let go.
* Holding an eel that is trying to slip away suggests the need to hold on to advantage or sudden good fortune.
* If you are repelled by being given an eel, this may represent sexual passion without commitment, or fear of your own unrequited sexual feelings.
* If you catch a huge electric eel or sea snake, your certainties may be suddenly shaken, but this could lead to new energies and opportunities.
* If you see eels swimming through murky water, there are deep feelings you find hard to express or reveal that, if left unspoken, will prevent a relationship from going forward or end a relationship that seems to be going nowhere.

OUTCOME OF RENALDA'S DREAM

Renalda realized her love was causing her pain. She broke off the relationship and went on vacation to swim among rainbow fish and heal. Eels, by their nature elusive, can represent immediate gratification but rarely offer lasting happiness, love, or good fortune.

Efficiency

Katie, thirty-two, dreamed she was being incredibly efficient, preparing all the files for the day, as well as getting the coffee brewing, to impress her new manager, who would be starting the following day. But the new boss breezed straight by without a word, knocking coffee all over Katie's carefully arranged files. She demanded that Katie clean up the mess, warning her that if she made one more mistake, she would be out. The dream forewarned Katie that trouble lay ahead.

DREAM BACKGROUND AND MEANING

True to the dream, nothing Katie did could please the new manager, who blamed Katie for every mistake, even though it was the manager who was inefficient. Katie collected evidence against her manager. Dreams of efficiency and inefficiency can be predictive if the dreamer picks up chaotic energies around a person even before knowing them.

INTERPRETATIONS AND FORTUNE-TELLING MEANINGS

* If in a dream you are efficient and appreciated, you will be offered career advancement.
* If you are organizing a celebration for family and it runs smoothly, life in general will be problem-free.
* If you dream of disorder no matter how efficient you are, you will struggle in a situation reflected in the dream.
* If you constantly dream that you are frantically putting right domestic disorder, but it is never clean enough, this may be causing stress overload.
* If someone in your dream blames you for their inefficiency, be warned that they are looking for a scapegoat.
* If you have discovered a more efficient way of organizing the workplace or finances but encounter resistance, remember that some people prefer an existing system, however chaotic.

OUTCOME OF KATIE'S DREAM

After a mistake even the manager could not blame on Katie's inefficiency, Katie presented her carefully collected evidence to the CEO, who dismissed the manger and offered Katie her job. Eventually, chaos cannot be ignored, but Katie's dream alerted her to the need to prove her efficiency if under attack.

Efforts

Ferdy, forty-five, dreamed he was pushing his car while steering it. His next-door neighbor said he could not help as he had hurt his back. His best friend in the street said he could not help because he was late for work. Ferdy felt resentful, as he had always helped them. Then Bert, the scruffily dressed neighbor who lived at the end of the street, without a word pushed the car till it started.

DREAM BACKGROUND AND MEANING

Ferdy was organizing a street party to celebrate the seventieth anniversary of the rebuilding of the street after it was razed during World War II. But everyone was too busy to help. Bert, the neighbor ostracized by everyone because of the state of his house and garden, volunteered to provide furniture and donated a substantial sum toward the catering. Dreams can distinguish between those who are all talk and real helpers.

INTERPRETATIONS AND FORTUNE-TELLING MEANINGS

★ If you dream of making an effort to complete a project or study for an examination, it is a good sign that you will succeed.

★ If in the dream your extra efforts are appreciated at work, by your family, or by the neighborhood, all will prove worthwhile.

★ If you are unappreciated in the dream, you are wasting your time making an effort with that person.

★ If you are making a huge effort in your dream for a cause close to your heart, you will make progress.

★ If you are making a physical effort in your dream and cannot go on, you may need to ask for help.

★ If you dream you are trying to fix a relationship or get on better with difficult relatives, the dream energies will bring positive results.

OUTCOME OF FERDY'S DREAM

The scruffy neighbor worked really hard fixing decorations and music and arranging for the local press to attend. A journalist recognized him as a very wealthy philanthropist whose family had lived on the original street. Often dreams reveal that those who make the most noise about making an effort do the least.

Electric Cars

Lavinia, fifty-eight, dreamed she was driving a brand-new electric Tesla Roadster car, having traded in her beloved Dodge, which she had driven happily for twenty years. The new car ran out of power in the middle of nowhere. When she was finally rescued, Lavinia abandoned the electric car on the side of the road.

DREAM BACKGROUND AND MEANING

Lavinia's friends have insisted she should buy an environmentally friendly electric car. But she is resisting and is also struggling with the new technology at work. Since cars represent the way you travel through life, breaking down in the middle of nowhere suggests that she was insecure with the modern world, symbolized by the electric car failing.

INTERPRETATIONS AND FORTUNE-TELLING MEANINGS

★ If you dream that an innovative product or method feels wrong, you may not be ready to update your lifestyle.

★ If a modern environmentally friendly product or method fails in your dream, your heart and the changing world may be in opposition.

★ If you dream you cannot find a charging station for your electric car, you may not be prepared to leave your comfort zone, whether a house move, career, or lifestyle change.

★ If you dream you are benefiting from an electric car or modern technology, this may be a good time to upgrade your life.

★ If you are the one seeking innovation, you may need to press ahead and adapt to technological teething troubles.

★ Dreams of breaking down or of a modern device malfunctioning reveal fears of asking for help if technology is moving too fast.

OUTCOME OF LAVINIA'S DREAM

Lavinia bought an updated lower-emission Dodge. She enrolled in a course to deal with the new technology at work. She has fitted solar panels on her house. Dreams can reflect what we really want rather than what friends and family think we should have or do, and suggest we take life at the pace that is right for us in balancing innovation and tradition.

Electric Shock

Max, forty-two, dreamed he realized he was full of static electricity when everything metal he touched, from door handles to supermarket carts, gave him a mild but painful electric shock. He felt totally helpless and woke up, wondering if the sensation would ever end.

DREAM BACKGROUND AND MEANING

Max worked very long hours, going into the office on weekends and staying most nights till midnight. His manager suggested he slow down or he would end up with burnout. Max had split with his partner of ten years, who became tired of his long working hours and bringing work home. Dreams of static electricity warn of overload in the dreamer that is building to crisis point.

INTERPRETATIONS AND FORTUNE-TELLING MEANINGS

★ If you repeatedly dream about yourself or a family member receiving an electric shock, check appliances, especially those seen in the dream.

★ An electric shock where you are not hurt in the dream suggests an unexpected if unwelcome jolt to set you on a new path after a period of inactivity.

★ An electric shock where you are hurt suggests a sudden betrayal from someone you trusted.

★ If you dream you get a sudden mild shock from an appliance, this is a sign of repressed anger or resentment. Resolve it.

★ A dream of an appliance sparking from the plug or adapter is a warning to not make a hasty decision, however great the apparent rewards.

★ A short circuit disabling lights and appliances in the dream is a sign you need more action to prevent a project or relationship from fizzling out through lack of attention.

OUTCOME OF MAX'S DREAM

Exhausted one morning, Max plugged in a kettle that had been sparking for some time and gave himself a bad electric shock. He was hospitalized with burns for weeks. His ex-partner came to visit, so he has not given up hope. Electric shocks in dreams are often warning dreams.

Electronic Publishing

Ellie, twenty-eight, dreamed she was at an awards ceremony with the biggest online publisher, being given an award for bestselling fiction series of the year. Best of all, the publisher who had rejected her several times was lining up to offer her a contract. Upon awakening, Ellie wished the dream had lasted much longer.

DREAM BACKGROUND AND MEANING

Ellie had been trying to get her teen-psychic series published without success. She was considering self-publishing, but the publisher wanted a lot of money up front. Sometimes wish-fulfillment dreams can offer the incentive to try a new outlet or resource.

INTERPRETATIONS AND FORTUNE-TELLING MEANINGS

★ If in a dream you see your work high in online publishing charts, this suggests you will find a way to get your literary efforts noticed.

★ If in your dream you are uploading your autobiography, you have something important to communicate to the world, even if you are not writing a book.

★ If you become famous through your dream online book, social media generally may be the way to raise your profile in any area of life.

★ If your online book crashes or refuses to upload in your dream, it may not be ready for publication yet.

★ If your dream book disappears from the online publishing site, you have allowed fear of competition to negatively impact upon your efforts.

★ If you see your online book being contracted by a conventional publisher, online publication is the major first step to literary success online or traditionally.

OUTCOME OF ELLIE'S DREAM

Ellie had dismissed electronic publishing as too complicated. After the dream, she asked a friend with computer know-how to put her works online. They sold reasonably well, and a publisher who had originally rejected her first book expressed an interest in seeing the series. Electronic publishing dreams confirm that you have something to say, whether in the form of an online book, blog, or podcast, and energetically raise your sphere of influence on and offline.

Elephant

Graham, twenty-eight, dreamed he was riding on an elephant, leading a herd through open grassland. He was happy and confident. Then shots were fired. The elephants stampeded, and Graham could hardly hold on. Poachers were following, but Graham persuaded his elephant to turn. The herd followed and crushed the poachers' trucks. The elephants continued to a shrine where Graham made offerings to a golden statue of Ganesha, the elephant-headed Hindu god.

DREAM BACKGROUND AND MEANING

Graham was planning on quitting his city life and high-powered career and spending a year in an ashram in the remote Indian countryside. His friends and family were worried that he was exposing himself to unknown dangers. Elephant dreams represent huge undertakings involving life changes to attain wisdom or fulfill a worthwhile goal.

INTERPRETATIONS AND FORTUNE-TELLING MEANINGS

★ Seeing Ganesha in a dream, who is invoked before any great undertaking or journey and as the overcomer of obstacles, indicates successful ventures and travel beyond the normal comfort zone.

★ Riding an elephant foretells riding high in a career and long-term prosperity, but, equally importantly, alternatively acquiring great wisdom and knowledge through study.

★ If you see an elephant performing in a circus or confined in a dream, beware of someone in authority abusing power or restricting your progress.

★ A stampeding herd of elephants represents situations spiraling out of control. But if the stampede is controlled, powerful advances follow in any area.

★ A white elephant traditionally represents being given unsought responsibilities, which should be shed as soon as possible.

★ An elephant in an unusual place (the proverbial elephant in the room) says that an important but uncomfortable matter should be confronted that will not go away.

OUTCOME OF GRAHAM'S DREAM

The dream gave Graham confidence to overcome any difficulties on his trip. However, it also aroused his interest in elephant conservation. Dreams about elephants also represent family love, and Graham was able to reassure his family by promising them regular updates and safeguards.

Elevator

Lorna, thirty-five, dreamed she was traveling alone in the elevator from her thirtieth-story office when the elevator stopped between floors. The lights went out and the emergency alarm failed to respond. Her smartphone was out of range. She started to scream and bang on the door but realized the building was empty. She heard a voice saying words last quoted at school, "All shall be well." The lights came on, the elevator moved upward to the floor above, and the doors opened. Lorna laughed with relief.

DREAM BACKGROUND AND MEANING

Lorna had recently been let go at work. Because she had been with the company only a short time, there was little compensation. She had been on several interviews without success and was worried about paying the rent when her money ran out. Being trapped in the dream elevator reflects the hopelessness she felt about the future. Elevators mirror the way life is moving, upward, downward, or stuck going nowhere.

INTERPRETATIONS AND FORTUNE-TELLING MEANINGS

★ Dreams of ascending elevators herald a rise in status and wealth career-wise; descending elevators, discouragement or reduction in opportunity.

★ Being stuck in an elevator between floors indicates feeling trapped by a situation.

★ The elevator rising through the roof and flying offers opportunities to soar, but with the risk of going farther or faster than wanted.

★ If others press the button and take you in the reverse direction you wish to go, your life is being controlled.

★ Being rescued from a stuck elevator, or the elevator suddenly starting, says help will come from a reliable source to resolve a dilemma.

★ A free-falling or crashing elevator warns against impulsive decisions and overambition.

OUTCOME OF LORNA'S DREAM

Lorna received a job offer from her former company. If negative, elevator dreams refer to short-term restrictions; if positive, an approaching time of new opportunity.

Elocution

Peter, thirty-two, dreamed he was eight years old and telling his mother about school that day. He was speaking with the natural London regional accent he had adopted from his father, who had left home. Without warning, his mother, who had aspirations of grandeur, slapped him on the back of his head and told him to talk properly.

DREAM BACKGROUND AND MEANING

The dream was based on recurring experiences in his childhood that he thought he had forgotten. His mother paid for elocution lessons so he would learn to speak without an accent. Now, as the father of a nine-year-old boy, Peter was concerned that his son spoke in the same regional accent as Peter did. Should he send his son to speech lessons? Dreams can, years later, highlight long-buried traumas from childhood.

INTERPRETATIONS AND FORTUNE-TELLING MEANINGS

★ If others cannot understand you in the dream, even if in real life you have no accent, what you are saying is being deliberately misinterpreted.

★ If you are mocked or bullied in the dream because your accent does not match those around you, you are being unfairly pressured to fit in with the status quo.

★ If in your dream you are taking lessons to iron out your accent, are you compromising to be accepted or to express yourself more clearly?

★ If you dream about having what was considered an inferior accent in childhood, your deep-seated insecurity is still something you subconsciously fight against.

★ If in a dream you are teaching elocution, you are trying to get others to accept your life view.

OUTCOME OF PETER'S DREAM

After the dream, Peter realized how bad he had been made to feel by his mother, because his accent reminded her of his father. Peter's wife pointed out that celebrities, television personalities, media presenters, and even royalty adopted regional accents, sometimes deliberately. Peter allowed his son to talk however he wanted and healed a lot of his own childhood embarrassment at sounding different. Elocution dreams are about image and creating impressions rather than valuing the authentic speaking self.

Emails

Francisco, thirty-five, dreamed he was hurrying to send his emails so he could meet his new girlfriend. He pressed SEND and immediately realized he had accidentally sent an email complaining about his boss's incompetence and laziness to his boss, rather than to the intended recipient, a colleague. Francisco awoke panicked.

DREAM BACKGROUND AND MEANING

Francisco had been regularly using work time to send emails connected with his own online business. A colleague threatened to report him unless Francisco mailed him confidential information on changing share prices. Francisco did not want to get into trouble for working on his website, but knew sending the confidential information would be damaging to the company. If you send the wrong email in a dream, you may be wanting to speak your mind to a particular person.

INTERPRETATIONS AND FORTUNE-TELLING MEANINGS

★ If you dream you receive information in an email of which you were not aware, your predictive mind is processing knowledge not in conscious awareness.

★ If you are writing an email in your sleep, record the contents when you wake, as it is one you may not have realized you needed to send.

★ If your email server gets a virus in a dream, beware of others reading your private emails and using them against you.

★ If all your emails disappear along with the backup, you are ready to start again, in either your work or love life.

★ If an email you have worked on in your dream disappears off the server without a trace, it is information best kept to yourself.

OUTCOME OF FRANCISCO'S DREAM

Francisco forwarded to the CEO emails from the blackmailer, who had been so confident of Francisco's cooperation that he had mailed Francisco precisely what he wanted to know. The blackmailer was dismissed without a reference and Francisco set up his own business full-time. Emails can be double-edged swords, as they can transmit important information or be used by the unscrupulous against the sender.

Embalming

Lotta, thirty-five, dreamed that she was one of the Chinchorro people who lived around northern Chile and southern Peru from about 7000 BC. They were fisherfolk who embalmed their dead and buried them in the desert sands. Her little girl had died and she believed, like many bereaved mothers, that mummification could cheat death.

DREAM BACKGROUND AND MEANING

Lotta was a successful archaeologist, and her partner was an esteemed professor. She had accidentally become pregnant and was delighted, but miscarried. Her partner had a vasectomy so there would be no more. But Lotta believed her baby would come back and contemplated getting pregnant alone, though it would damage her career.

INTERPRETATIONS AND FORTUNE-TELLING MEANINGS

★ If you dream of an embalming in an ancient culture such as Old Egypt, you may be connecting with a past life or ancient memory relevant to your present life.

★ If you dream you are an embalmer, there may be something in your past you wish to preserve.

★ If someone is no longer in your life, even if living, the Ancient Egyptian process was said to enable the spirit to return to the body, and so it may be possible to rekindle a connection.

★ If in the dream you are being forced to watch an embalming, you may be reluctant to move on from a certain phase in your life.

★ If you are refusing in the dream to have a departed animal embalmed in the modern world, you may want to move on to a new pet but feel guilty about doing so.

OUTCOME OF LOTTA'S DREAM

Lotta realized a baby was important. She had her eggs frozen and told her partner she would have a child alone. They parted, and she is dating a young archaeologist who one day would like a family. Embalming dreams reflect issues of preserving what is of worth but not being trapped in a past from which it is necessary to move on.

Embarrassment

Flo, thirty-six, dreamed she forgot the name of the visiting celebrity she was introducing at the annual company dinner. In her embarrassment, she tipped her glass of champagne over on the celebrity's dress. She saw her parents standing at the back and her mother mouthed gloatingly, "You are such an embarrassment." Flo burst into tears and ran.

DREAM BACKGROUND AND MEANING

Flo had been easily embarrassed in childhood. Her parents were quick to point out her mistakes. At work, Flo was confident except when her parents were with her. She had been asked by her aunt to organize her parents' ruby wedding anniversary celebration. She knew she would ruin everything. Childhood embarrassment can reappear when the people who made you feel bad still trigger feelings of inadequacy.

INTERPRETATIONS AND FORTUNE-TELLING MEANINGS

★ If in the dream you enter a spiral of embarrassing behavior, however competent you are normally, you are allowing outgrown voices that make you feel bad to enter your head.

★ If the people embarrassing you in the dream are authority figures from your childhood, or if you are a child in the dream, deep down you may still believe you are inadequate.

★ If you are trying to spare others' embarrassment, you may be putting yourself down and others may not appreciate it.

★ If someone is deliberately embarrassing you in a dream, question their intentions toward you, and their own agenda.

★ If you worry about a specific occasion, your dream will confirm the cause of your embarrassment.

★ If you overcome your embarrassment or confront the perpetrators in the dream, you can start to banish your fears.

OUTCOME OF FLO'S DREAM

Flo realized her parents were responsible for her lack of confidence. She arranged for a company to organize the celebration. It is harder to resolve things if the root cause of your embarrassment is deceased. But accept that the inadequacy was or is theirs, and avoid contact with them or thinking of them whenever you feel on trial.

Emigration

Dorothy, eighteen, dreamed she was near a beach in Southern England and saw thousands of swallows migrating south for the winter. But five remained sitting in a tree on the shoreline. Dorothy worried that they had been left behind, but then she realized they were perfectly content, knowing the others would return.

DREAM BACKGROUND AND MEANING

Dorothy was planning to emigrate with her mother and stepfather to Australia. But she was having doubts, as all her friends and relatives were in the United Kingdom and she had been offered the chance to study for a nursing degree at a medical facility there, as well. Emigration dreams can highlight the dilemma between the desire to widen horizons versus leaving what is familiar and loved.

INTERPRETATIONS AND FORTUNE-TELLING MEANINGS

★ If in the dream you see birds remaining behind despite a mass migration, you may have more reasons to keep life as it is than to initiate change.

★ If you see yourself moving to a different land, this does not necessarily mean you will or need to emigrate, but that you are ready for changes in your life.

★ If you dream you are packing to emigrate, you may be seeking an escape from current problems that need to be tackled first.

★ If you dream of returning to your homeland after emigrating, you may be making changes for the wrong reasons.

★ If in your dream there are delays or major obstacles in the way of emigrating, you may want a more exciting lifestyle rather than a location change.

★ If you dream of emigrating alone, you may have outgrown a relationship or lifestyle and need new experiences.

OUTCOME OF DOROTHY'S DREAM

After the dream, Dorothy realized she was moving to make her mother happy, but her life lay in the United Kingdom. She moved in with her grandparents and promised to visit her mother. If the emigration dream involves reluctance, any major change, especially one involving permanent relocation, may be just to please others.

Emptiness

Antonia, twenty-one, dreamed she returned home from college to find the family home empty, no people, no furniture, not even a note or text message. She sat on the stairs and saw her phone was empty of credit. She tried knocking on neighbors' doors, but there was no answer. When she peered through their windows, their houses were also empty of furniture and, strangest of all, there were no parked cars or traffic on what was usually a busy street. Antonia felt completely empty.

DREAM BACKGROUND AND MEANING

Antonia was reluctantly planning to go home at the end of college because she had nowhere else to go. She knew her parents had never wanted a child. She had split with her girlfriend and for the first time she had no plans. Empty dreams reveal a gap in the dreamer's life that they need to decide how to fill or allow fate to carry them, which may not be where they want to be.

INTERPRETATIONS AND FORTUNE-TELLING MEANINGS

★ If you dream your home is empty, it may be time to consider moving on to a more fulfilling lifestyle or location.

★ If a refrigerator or freezer is empty, you have given away all your energies to others.

★ If you dream a bottle of wine is empty, you can either find more wine to prop up a temporary situation or relationship or face reality head-on.

★ If a gift box is empty, you may need to create your own happiness.

★ Dreaming of standing in a beautiful place with space all around and no people represents the Taoist sense of peace and stillness, a sign you may have filled your life with too much activity.

OUTCOME OF ANTONIA'S DREAM

Antonia's parents emailed her to say they were moving overseas. The dream had forewarned her, and she volunteered for a residential program to help homeless families with a view to getting a permanent post using her social science degree. Empty dreams can be positive. By knowing what we cannot have, we can make active decisions about the direction we want to go or accept a period of reflection until the answer comes.

Emu

Robbie, seventy, dreamed he was a pioneer in old Australia, traveling from place to place, helping cut the first highways through the Outback. As he watched the emus running across the horizon in his dream, he was totally content and knew that, like them, he would never settle down. Night after night he dreamed of his emus and wanted to follow them.

DREAM BACKGROUND AND MEANING

Robbie had brought up his children alone after his wife left him when they were young. Now they had their own families, and he sold his home for a big motor home to live in on the road, making friends wherever he went. But his children were worried about him and wanted him to live close to care for him. The nomadic Australian emu, smaller than its African ostrich relative (see "Ostrich," p. 342), represents sociability and the need to travel with its own kind, always free.

INTERPRETATIONS AND FORTUNE-TELLING MEANINGS

★ If you dream you see emus on the move, you may be restless for change.

★ When you hear the female emus' drumlike mating call and see their dance, love is in the air.

★ If a male emu is making the nest, you have or will find a devoted partner and parent for your children.

★ Emus running fast indicate overseas travel or useful business contacts from the Southern Hemisphere.

★ Since an emu is credited with creating the sun from the yolk of her egg in Australian aboriginal lore, an emu egg signifies joy, fertility, and original ideas.

★ A dream of an emu on a nest is especially good for single fathers or those of either sex whose female partner has moved on, leaving them with children, as typically emu females leave males to incubate the eggs and rear chicks.

OUTCOME OF ROBBIE'S DREAM

Robbie knew it was now or never. He set off in his motor home, promising to keep in touch. The first night camping in the bush, he saw his emus on the horizon and knew it was his sign. Emus are a wonderful totem for all, wherever they live in the world, for releasing the spirit of adventure and the road that will never run out.

End of the World, Apocalypse

Annette, thirty-five, dreamed she belonged to a cult that was on top of a mountain waiting for celestial fire to wipe out the earth. The leader promised that if they threw themselves off the mountain, they would be instantly transported to paradise. Annette decided she did not want to die and ran down the mountain, pursued by cult followers.

DREAM BACKGROUND AND MEANING

Annette was overwhelmed by debt and could see no way out of her troubles. A cult dream predicting the end of the world reflects major insecurity in your life.

INTERPRETATIONS AND FORTUNE-TELLING MEANINGS

★ Dreams of the end of the world can be a way your mind seeks escape from overwhelming life pressures.

★ If the world is being taken over by aliens, too many scary movies may be reflected in dreams, indicating isolation or alienation from family, friends, or colleagues.

★ If you dream you are being judged for sins at the end of the world, you may have unresolved and perhaps unfounded guilt.

★ If you have experienced a major setback that feels like the end of the world, the dream may be processing overwhelming feelings to bring solutions in the morning.

★ If you dream you survive the end of the world, your fears will not materialize.

★ If there is a nuclear attack or asteroids colliding with the earth, the dream images express fears of matters outside your control to which free-floating anxiety becomes attached.

OUTCOME OF ANNETTE'S DREAM

After the dream, in which Annette rejected the option to accelerate the end of her world, she went to a debt charity, which stopped a threatened repossession order and ruthless debt collectors. It was not easy, but with emergency welfare grants Annette was able to get her life back on track and start studying. An end-of-the-world dream can mark a psychological watershed, after which the will to survive kicks in.

Entitlement

Becky, twenty-five, dreamed she waved her pass at the steward to admit her to the royal enclosure, but he said the card had been canceled as the fees were unpaid. When she reached home, she raged at her parents, who had never denied her anything. They told her their business and home were being foreclosed on, and Becky would need to get a job.

DREAM BACKGROUND AND MEANING

As a child, Becky had been given everything she wanted: a pony, designer clothes, and the latest technology. Her parents often overstretched themselves, as their daughter threw a tantrum if denied. Now her parents had serious financial problems and insisted that Becky work in the family business.

INTERPRETATIONS AND FORTUNE-TELLING MEANINGS

* If you dream of being entitled to the finest of everything, this may be a wish-fulfillment dream you have when life gets hard or mundane.
* If someone in your dream is boasting of their luxurious lifestyle, you may realize they are shallow and not worth emulating.
* If you dream of losing everything, you may be buying one too many indulgence.
* If you are wealthy and dream of a display of designer goods collapsing on top of you, you may wonder if there is more to life than acquisitions.
* If someone steals your dream luxuries, you may be afraid of people only liking you for what you have.
* If in your dream you are in a competition with close friends who have the best luxury items, you may question if they will be true friends through good times and bad.

OUTCOME OF BECKY'S DREAM

Becky joined the family firm and enjoyed it greatly, working hard and succeeding in restoring solvency. She found her old friends boring and is dating an apprentice with whom one day she will open a business. Entitlement dreams question values but foster a love of beauty without materialism.

Erectile Dysfunction (ED) Pills

Constantine, sixty-five, dreamed his wife was young again and they were making passionate love. Then suddenly she aged and, though he had taken his erectile dysfunction pill, he felt no desire. For sex, he went to a bar frequented by beautiful women.

DREAM BACKGROUND AND MEANING

Constantine and his wife no longer had sex. Since she had gone through menopause, his wife had become eager for lovemaking. Constantine was unable to become aroused and started taking erectile dysfunction pills. He no longer desired his wife and instead began flirting with younger women. Dreams of taking ED pills refer not only to increased libido but also to necessary emotional adjustments in lovemaking.

INTERPRETATIONS AND FORTUNE-TELLING MEANINGS

* If a man dreams of taking ED pills, he is seeking to restore or maintain joy and passion in his life, not necessarily sexual passion.
* If a woman dreams of giving her partner ED pills, she is most probably experiencing a surge of sexual desire.
* If in a dream a man hides his ED pills, he may feel guilty about seeking pleasure rather than focusing on duty and obligation.
* If a woman in her dream finds concealed ED pills, her partner may be contemplating straying.
* If a man loses his ED pills and cannot obtain more in his dream, he may be insecure about his potency in career or socially.
* If in his dream a man drops his ED pills in public, he may fear others will discover the insecure guy behind the mask.

OUTCOME OF CONSTANTINE'S DREAM

Constantine discovered the girls in the bar were only after his money. He realized he was no longer the virile stud his pills had promised. He and his wife are now working on their sexual relationship. Erectile-dysfunction-pills dreams, with their promises of restored virility, can raise questions about the deeper aspects of a relationship, which may need redeveloping, revising, and reviving.

Escaping

Aster, fifteen, regularly dreamed she was in a dark street with what she thought were gas lamps, being followed by a man wearing a long overcoat and hat. She sped up, and so did he. She knew he had a knife. She disappeared through an open doorway into a yard and bolted the gate. She heard him rattling the bolt and woke screaming.

DREAM BACKGROUND AND MEANING

Aster lived in a very understaffed orphanage. The other girls would climb out of the window to meet older men who bought them drinks, gave them cigarettes, and promised them jewelry. Aster was reluctant to go, but the others said it was quite harmless. Escaping dreams vary in meaning according to whether you are the captor or captive and escaping from danger or running toward it.

INTERPRETATIONS AND FORTUNE-TELLING MEANINGS

⋆ Dreaming of escaping from danger is a sign that you will overcome restrictions.

⋆ A pet escaping is an anxiety dream that warns that you have too much to do to be able to properly take care of everybody.

⋆ Escaping from jail says you will be able to extricate yourself from trouble of your own making.

⋆ Escaping from a war zone talks about problems outside your control, where you may find moving away is better than staying and fighting.

⋆ Escaping from a wild animal highlights primitive fears and self-destructive feelings.

⋆ If you dream you are escaping from an assassin, someone in your life is lying about you or spreading rumors.

OUTCOME OF ASTER'S DREAM

Aster realized the dream was warning her of danger on the streets at night. Despite this, she ignored the dream and went along. The men forced themselves on the girls and they ran away, but then were scared because the men knew where they lived. Ignoring dream warnings sometimes can have dire consequences.

Escapologist

Donna, twenty-five, dreamed she was watching an escapology show with her partner, Jodie, when she noticed that Jodie was absent from her seat. Jodie was in a huge tank of water, tied with chains and padlocks. Then she was gone.

DREAM BACKGROUND AND MEANING

Jodie was vague about what her life was like before meeting Donna. They rapidly fell in love, but Jodie said she worked up north. She would stay with Donna for weekends, but said she could not take calls during the week because of her work. Donna wondered if Jodie was in another relationship or was a con woman, but she really loved her. Jodie promised they could soon be together permanently. Escapology dreams can express doubts about someone who is evasive about their life while away from a lover.

INTERPRETATIONS AND FORTUNE-TELLING MEANINGS

⋆ If your love or business partner is an escapologist in a dream, ask questions about their past and present.

⋆ If you dream you are breaking free from chains and a sealed box, you are fighting against a dependency situation where you feel confined.

⋆ If you are in deep water, you may find it hard to express or understand your emotions and so run from them.

⋆ If you dream you are an escapologist imprisoned high in the air, you may be using travel as a way of avoiding commitment.

⋆ If you cannot free yourself from the escapology confinement, you may need time to break away from a stifling situation.

⋆ If you dream the escapologist is using illusion to appear to be trapped, you may have reason to distrust someone.

OUTCOME OF DONNA'S DREAM

Donna demanded an explanation for Jodie's mysterious behavior. Jodie explained she was on early release from jail. Jodie's former partner had framed her for fraud and was herself acquitted. Jodie was due for permanent release in the next month. While escapologist dreams can indicate dubious dealings and a double life, there may be a more innocent explanation.

Ethereal Beings

Natalie, forty-five, dreamed she was surrounded by misty floating nature spirits, the colors of the flowers in her garden. They brushed her with their wings, scattering fragrance. Though a cynic, she found their presence immensely comforting. They transformed into laughing children. One of them was her daughter.

DREAM BACKGROUND AND MEANING

Natalie had lost her belief in magick when her young daughter had died a few years earlier due to a medical mistake. With the compensation, Natalie purchased her house and invested the rest. The dream shocked her because her daughter had often talked of her special magickal friends. Natalie believed her daughter had sent them. Ethereal being dreams can remind a dreamer that life must go on, though in a different way.

INTERPRETATIONS AND FORTUNE-TELLING MEANINGS

★ A dream of insubstantial, misty floaty beings, whether angels, fairies, or nature spirits, brings a message from the spirit world for you.

★ If you are naturally skeptical, an ethereal-being dream suggests that you follow your intuition and heart.

★ If your children experience ethereal-being dreams, the world of magick is protecting them.

★ If an ethereal being opens a doorway in your dream, through it you may see or sense those you have loved and lost.

★ If you are traveling with an ethereal being through mists, this is an out-of-body experience and, if you are troubled, shows that life beyond this one exists.

★ If you see the same ethereal being in many dreams, this is your special guardian, guiding you toward an important decision.

OUTCOME OF NATALIE'S DREAM

Natalie heard that the local kindergarten her daughter had attended was in danger of closing through lack of funds, which would leave local parents unable to work. She donated a substantial amount of money and subsidies for parents who could not afford the fees. Ethereal-being dreams appear as a reminder that, however dark life may be, it is possible to reach out to a magical world and restore light.

Evergreen Trees

Stu, sixty, dreamed it was Christmas and he brought home a big evergreen tree. But once it was indoors, all the greenery fell off and his wife brought down the old artificial evergreen tree from the attic. Stu was so disappointed, he left the family celebrations.

DREAM BACKGROUND AND MEANING

Stu was dreading the family Christmas, as Thanksgiving had been a disaster with family arguments and a burned meal. He told his wife he wanted to go away for the festival, but she said no as it was a family tradition. Stu threatened to go away alone. An artificial decorative evergreen says that you may be in denial of reparable cracks in a relationship or situation.

INTERPRETATIONS AND FORTUNE-TELLING MEANINGS

★ If you dream that you and a lover, known or as yet unknown, are walking beneath evergreen trees, it is a good omen that love will last forever.

★ If an evergreen tree is covered in snow, you will in time survive present difficulties.

★ Flourishing evergreens in a forest are a sign of good or improving health and long life.

★ A decorated living evergreen Thanksgiving or Christmas tree heralds happy family gatherings, the mending of petty quarrels, and the return of absent or estranged family members.

★ Evergreen trees covered with berries or cones indicate an ongoing steady source of prosperity.

OUTCOME OF STU'S DREAM

After the dream, Stu realized that going away would solve nothing, and so he compromised with a modified celebration, seeing family members on different days and organizing a Secret Santa, where everyone contributed a gift for a chosen person. He bought a real evergreen tree with roots in a pot, which flourished when he planted it in the garden afterward. Evergreens in dreams represent enduring qualities of family life that, if nourished, overcome inevitable familial problems.

Evil Eye

Polly, forty, often dreamed of a huge blue eye staring at her in her dreams, and she heard strange whisperings. The next morning, her blood pressure soared. The dreams had happened only since she had been in Sicily.

DREAM BACKGROUND AND MEANING

Polly was pregnant for the first time and staying with her husband and his family in Sicily. The family was pleased she was having a boy to carry on the family name. Her fifty-year-old sister-in-law, who had never conceived, said how lucky Polly was, but added that pregnancies could easily go wrong, while she stared hard at Polly's stomach. The evil-eye superstition, which still exists in many lands, especially in the Mediterranean area and Eastern Europe, can appear in dreams at a time someone is sending envious thoughts.

INTERPRETATIONS AND FORTUNE-TELLING MEANINGS

★ If you dream of a huge blue eye, you may be aware of someone feeling jealous, though not necessarily sending bad wishes.

★ If you dream of olive oil in an eye shape with a wise old woman pouring it, you are tapping into a traditional evil-eye remedy.

★ If you dream of being given a blue glass bead amulet, you should buy one if you are feeling spooked by others' jealousy.

★ If in your dream someone you know speaks envious words, avoid staring into their eyes, as this increases the power of the envy.

★ If you are encircled by staring eyes in your dream, you may be subject to intrusion by colleagues or by a controlling family.

★ If you are spooked by your evil-eye dreams, buy yourself an Egyptian Eye of Horus charm to return ill-wishing.

OUTCOME OF POLLY'S DREAM

Polly and her husband went home and broke contact with the sister-in-law until the baby was born, safe and healthy. Whether evil-eye dreams are caused by anxiety, especially when a person is vulnerable, or by someone actually wishing ill, fears of being too happy can be resolved psychically or psychologically by wearing a blue glass eye bead.

Examinations

Nathan, fifty, had a recurring dream that he was back at school, taking an examination in a huge hall filled with other students. He had not prepared for the examination. Everyone else was writing, but the questions swam in front of his eyes. Nathan's mind went blank. He woke in a total panic, running from the examination hall, pursued by the examiner, a former critical teacher, shouting that Nathan had failed, as always.

DREAM BACKGROUND AND MEANING

Nathan's workplace was being taken over and, because of his age, he was afraid he would be let go. Nathan was due to be interviewed by the new CEO, who was rumored to want major changes to personnel. Examination dreams may recur at times where our expertise or performance is called into question, because examination pressure is imprinted on our minds from an early age.

INTERPRETATIONS AND FORTUNE-TELLING MEANINGS

★ If in your dream you are taking a school examination, you may be afraid that you know far less than other people you are competing against at work.

★ If you are successful in the dream exam, be reassured in testing times.

★ If failing, this is an anxiety dream reflecting buried feelings of inadequacy, rooted perhaps in discouragement by a teacher or overstrict parent.

★ An oral crucial interview or practical test reveals a need to be recognized by those in authority for your achievements.

★ If you dream of a medical examination, you may be unconsciously worried about your health, or a checkup may be overdue.

★ If you are late for the exam or cannot find the venue, you are postponing facing your own usually unfounded fears of failing.

OUTCOME OF NATHAN'S DREAM

Nathan's interview went well, as his expertise and experience were seen as an asset by the CEO in maintaining stability after the takeover.

Consider whether extra preparations are needed for any forthcoming challenge, or if you are aiming too high too soon.

Exit

Romany, twenty-nine, dreamed she was visiting an exhibition of ancient artifacts, but she could not find the way out. Romany walked around several times, but the entrance had a one-way turnstile. She tried following other people. They disappeared, and those she asked the way out could not hear her. The lights went off. Romany was alone in the darkness. At last, she touched a handle in the wall and was free.

DREAM BACKGROUND AND MEANING

Romany was in an increasingly abusive relationship. Everyone said her partner, Josie, was a wonderful person, and they could not understand the problem. She and Josie had a joint business, organizing events. Romany could not afford to buy her partner out. Romany was desperately unhappy. Exits are often harder to find than entrances.

INTERPRETATIONS AND FORTUNE-TELLING MEANINGS

* ★ If you dream there are no exits, you may have unfinished business or need to decide if you do want to escape regardless of consequences.
* ★ If the only exit is barred, you must take drastic action involving loss, if necessary.
* ★ Should there be a number of different exits, you should try several approaches to discover the best way out.
* ★ If an exit leads into darkness, take a step into the unknown.
* ★ If you are trying to find the exit in a maze (see p. 303), others are misleading or disbelieving you. Trust your own instincts and logic.
* ★ If you reach an exit that turns into an entrance, by leaving a situation you will find a new beginning that may not be easy but worthwhile.

OUTCOME OF ROMANY'S DREAM

Romany realized she was giving mixed messages, including to herself. If she left the abusive relationship, she would lose the business and with it the home above it. But she knew that for her safety she had to go, and she has started working for a big events company. Once a decision to leave is made, a previously unseen exit may appear.

Exotic Dancer

Lily, twenty-one, dreamed she was onstage at one of New York's top nightclubs. She was dancing slowly and seductively to the cheers of the audience. To her horror, her father entered the club, dragged her offstage, and insisted she come home at once. The manager told her to get back onstage. She woke not knowing what to do.

DREAM BACKGROUND AND MEANING

Lily wanted to be a professional dancer on Broadway, but found it difficult to fund herself through stage school as her family refused to help. She had been offered a job at a high-class nightclub in New York as an exotic dancer, where she could earn her fees quickly, as it was so well paid. She knew her parents would be shocked. If you face disapproval from a partner or parents in your dream, they may be limiting your free spirit.

INTERPRETATIONS AND FORTUNE-TELLING MEANINGS

* ★ If you dream you enjoy performing, you crave more excitement in your life.
* ★ If you are watching your partner perform for you, it's a good time to up your sex-life tempo.
* ★ If your partner is performing for others and you are jealous, your partner needs more appreciation.
* ★ If you are happy they are performing in public, do you regard your partner as a trophy to be envied?
* ★ If you are the center of a chorus of exotic dancers, you seek a high-profile performing career.
* ★ If you are self-conscious about your body, exotic-dancer dreams say to value yourself as you are.

OUTCOME OF LILY'S DREAM

Lily accepted the job and told her family. The family said that if she went ahead they would cut her off. Before long she was offered a place at the Folies Bergères in Paris by a talent scout at the club and did not need to go to stage school to achieve success. Dreams can show possibilities of shaping the future in unexpected ways.

Ex-Partner

Lois, thirty-eight, dreamed that her first love, Lizzie, arrived at her wedding ceremony and walked down the aisle. As in the movies, Lizzie told Lois the wedding could not go ahead. Lois and Lizzie ran out of the chapel to where Lizzie had left the car engine running. They drove off laughing, with everyone chasing after them.

DREAM BACKGROUND AND MEANING

Lois had broken up with Lizzie, whom she had met at college, and shortly afterward she met and became engaged to Sophie. They had decided to marry as soon as possible. Recently, Lizzie had contacted Lois and suggested they should meet. Ex-partner dreams may go back to a first love. However, if an ex is still part of the dreamer's or their partner's life because of business or children, dreams may reflect conflicting feelings.

INTERPRETATIONS AND FORTUNE-TELLING MEANINGS

★ If in your dream you are making love to an ex-partner, make your present love and relationship more exciting.

★ If your ex-partner contacts you on social media, you may be tempted to reconnect. Be cautious, as old problems may still exist.

★ If you have found love on the rebound but dream of your ex, you may need a period of independence to regain your separate identity.

★ If you dream of a bad ex relationship, acknowledge unfinished pain so you do not transfer the trauma to your new relationship.

★ If you dream of remarrying an ex, examine which aspects of the relationship you miss and whether reconciling is desirable or viable.

OUTCOME OF LOIS'S DREAM

Lois realized she was rushing into marriage as an antidote to her confused feelings about her ex. She postponed the wedding and is spending time finding herself as a single person. If an ex-partner causes problems or tries to split a new relationship, examine their motives and see if your loyalties lie in the past or present, or even future love.

Expatriate

Barry, sixty-five, had a recurring dream that he was living on a beautiful island in Thailand with a gorgeous young Thai girl tending his every need. In the dream he was an expatriate living on his pension, which went a long way as living was so cheap. His days were spent at the beach bar, and when he staggered back to the beach bungalow, his woman was waiting with a meal.

DREAM BACKGROUND AND MEANING

Barry was a retiree living in a small mid-Australian town. It was his dream to live in Thailand and get a devoted young wife. But Barry was still married, and his wife was planning that they travel around Australia. An expatriate dream often occurs when the dreamer is bored with their current life and believes living in an exotic location will be a panacea for the boredom.

INTERPRETATIONS AND FORTUNE-TELLING MEANINGS

★ If you dream of a new, younger, exotic partner as part of the expatriate lifestyle, are you also younger and more adventurous in the dream or seeking a return to youth?

★ Is this fantasy scenario connected with personal or current relationship problems and, if so, can they be resolved?

★ If you dream of an expatriate future, can you fit into a new culture, new laws, and maybe a less-developed infrastructure?

★ Could or would a present partner adapt to an expatriate lifestyle, or is it the exciting new dream partner that is the real attraction?

★ If the dream is recurring, can you make corresponding plans to further the dream? Should you?

OUTCOME OF BARRY'S DREAM

Barry talked in his sleep and his current wife wanted to know if his fantasy dreams involved her. He lied, and she agreed to go on an extended vacation to Thailand. Barry hated the heat, the mosquitoes, young girls pestering him for money, and exotic food. They came home and traveled in Australia. Expatriate dreams can be the ultimate fantasy, but if the dreamer does not change, then they may not enjoy the reality.

Extramarital Affair, Infidelity

Cody, thirty-three, regularly dreams of his wife, Helena, leaving the marital home in the middle of the night, without warning. He runs after the car, calling to her to come back. When he returns indoors, his ex-lover, Penelope, is waiting in bed. In everyday life, Helena reassures Cody everything is good, but the dreams persist.

DREAM BACKGROUND AND MEANING

Cody had an extramarital affair with Penelope, a work colleague, three years ago. Penelope pressured him to leave his wife, threatening to tell Helena. Cody confessed to his wife, who forgave him, vowing never to speak of the affair again. Now Penelope has returned to the office after a long absence overseas and is flirting with Cody. An infidelity dream can reveal unresolved issues in a committed relationship.

INTERPRETATIONS AND FORTUNE-TELLING MEANINGS

* If you dream of beginning or renewing an affair, temptation may be growing or returning and needs acknowledging and resolving one way or the other.
* If your lover replaces your partner in bed, or you are caught cheating, you seek the thrill of the chase.
* If your lover, known or unknown, seduces you in the dream, are you seeking to offload responsibility for straying?
* If your lover and partner appear in the same dream, do you want both or either? Would you prefer to be or should you be alone?
* If your partner leaves you in the dream though an affair has ended, deep down they have not forgotten or fully forgiven. Extra attention is needed in the relationship.
* Should you be having a dream affair with a celebrity, you need more excitement in your present relationship.

OUTCOME OF CODY'S DREAM

Cody applied for and was offered a transfer to another branch of the company in a different state. He and Helena made a fresh start, away from old memories. Extramarital dreams are good barometers for avoiding or tackling lingering or new-love temptation.

Eyeglasses

Grainne, thirty-three, dreamed she was wearing an enormous pair of eyeglasses that enabled her to see through walls, over immense distances, and into others' innermost secrets. But the eyeglasses were incredibly heavy and she could not move in them. Yet she was reluctant to lose their power. Unable to withstand their weight any longer, she took them off and was relieved.

DREAM BACKGROUND AND MEANING

Grainne discovered by chance that her manager was having an affair with her greatest rival, who was competing with Grainne for a promotion. The company had a strict policy against workplace relationships, and so her knowledge gave Grainne power over them. Through careful observation she had built up plenty of evidence. But should she use this unfair advantage to gain a promotion? Eyeglasses dreams talk about what is a clear vision of a situation or what is distorted or underestimated for personal advantage.

INTERPRETATIONS AND FORTUNE-TELLING MEANINGS

* If you are wearing eyeglasses in a dream, even if you do not in daily life, your subconscious may be suggesting it is time for a vision test.
* If dream eyeglasses are too strong, others may be giving you a distorted view of the world or exaggerating problems.
* If dream eyeglasses are too weak, focus on the main priority rather than spreading your attention.
* If you break or crack your eyeglasses, beware of deception and hidden agendas.
* If you lose your eyeglasses, you may be under an illusion or delusion, so check your facts.
* If you cannot see clearly, even wearing dream eyeglasses, a matter may not yet be clear. It is better to wait than surmise the truth.

OUTCOME OF GRAINNE'S DREAM

Grainne decided the burden of ruining her colleague's career was too heavy. She kept quiet about what she had seen and gained her promotion anyway. Eyeglasses can sometimes occur in a predictive dream in which seeing ahead can be either an advantage or a warning.

Eyes

Trina, twenty-one, dreamed she was in a room with open eyes staring from every wall. Each time Trina shut an eye, another opened. The walls were closing in. She covered her own eyes, but every time she peeped, the eyes were still staring. The dream continued all night.

DREAM BACKGROUND AND MEANING

Trina had created some unique designs at her fashion college and believed she might win an internship to a major fashion house. She had been careful to not show her designs to anyone, but she had an uneasy feeling that someone had been spying on her. Our psychic radar can warn us in eye dreams that we are being secretly observed.

INTERPRETATIONS AND FORTUNE-TELLING MEANINGS

⋆ If you see an eye peeping through a keyhole, be careful what you say or do, as someone is trying to catch you out.

⋆ A huge blue staring eye represents the evil eye of envy and warns of a jealous person pretending to be a friend.

⋆ If you are wearing a blindfold over your eyes, you are avoiding a painful issue.

⋆ If you can see a long distance, look for an opportunity further afield in travel or career.

⋆ If you see yourself in a mirror with very large eyes, you will be viewed with favor.

⋆ If in your dream you are having an eye test, you need expert advice and help to discover the solution to a confusing dilemma.

OUTCOME OF TRINA'S DREAM

Trina, on investigation, discovered that her best friend, Jackie, was planning to enter remarkably similar designs to her own in the competition. Trina remembered she had given Jackie her computer password when Jackie had offered to make some printouts for Trina. Trina told her friend she had dates for the original designs and insisted Jackie withdraw her entry. Trina did not win, but was highly commended and was offered an internship with another prestigious fashion house. Eye dreams can open our eyes to both possibility and deception.

Facelessness

Konrad, twenty-one, dreamed he was locked in a nightmare where no one, including himself, had a face, just a blank where it should have been. Konrad walked away, but the faceless people followed him. He started running and so did they. When he stopped he could no longer distinguish himself from the faceless crowd.

DREAM BACKGROUND AND MEANING

Konrad's first job after college was in a huge, impersonal organization where social interaction was discouraged. After work he would go home to his television. He had been popular at college but had lost contact with his friends. He felt he had lost his identity. Dreams of facelessness occur when we are not connecting with people around us.

INTERPRETATIONS AND FORTUNE-TELLING MEANINGS

⋆ If you are the only person in the dream without a face, you may feel you are not noticed or appreciated and should consider moving.

⋆ If no one has a face except you, you can make your own mark on a project or enterprise.

⋆ If in a dream you and a love partner lack faces when together, you need to build up new shared memories.

⋆ If your partner or family have faces and you do not, your confidence has been eroded by them.

⋆ If someone close to you changes their face or hides their features, there is another side to their personality.

⋆ If you are faceless in a mirror, you may be hiding your true self from the world.

OUTCOME OF KONRAD'S DREAM

After the dream, Konrad attended a college reunion and found he was still popular with his friends. He took a job nearer home in a smaller, friendly establishment, kept in touch with old friends, and went to family events. Facelessness dreams often reveal that we are in the wrong environment, and our identity will reassert itself, given the right input.

Faces

Zeta, eighteen, dreamed that Chloe, her new best friend at college, kept changing her expression, from guarded to welcoming, while she was talking to Zeta. When her face was reflected in a mirror, Chloe looked conniving, though when she turned she was smiling again. Zeta woke thoroughly confused.

DREAM BACKGROUND AND MEANING

Zeta had been pleased when Chloe had singled her out to share a room and said how much she admired Zeta for winning a scholarship. Chloe smiled enthusiastically as she said what great fun they would have together. But when one of the college in-crowd approached, Chloe gave Zeta a blank stare, broke off their conversation, and walked away mid-sentence. Dreams often reveal a person's true nature by the face shown in the dream. Changeability of expression, according to who is present, indicates a two-faced attitude toward people who are considered useful.

INTERPRETATIONS AND FORTUNE-TELLING MEANINGS

* Dreaming of being surrounded by happy faces indicates fortunate times ahead.
* If known faces are harmonious, this indicates unity with family and informal celebrations.
* An angry face on someone who normally is smiling may be a warning that he or she may be hiding negative feelings.
* If you dream of friendly faces before starting at a new workplace or activity, your radar is picking up that you will be welcome.
* If someone you know puts their face very close to yours in the dream and you feel uncomfortable, they may invade your privacy.
* If someone is concealing their face or avoids meeting your eyes, they probably have a hidden agenda.

OUTCOME OF ZETA'S DREAM

Zeta realized Chloe only made an effort to charm her at times when she needed Zeta's help with an assignment or wanted to borrow money. Eventually, when Zeta refused help, Chloe could not hide her resentment and the contempt on her face, and Zeta dumped her. Faces, unlike body language, can conceal feelings, but a dream will reveal the truth.

Factory

Dawn, twenty-two, had a recurring dream that she was working in a wartime munitions factory. She had a letter in her pocket from her love on the battlefront but had not yet read it. There was a huge explosion and, staggering out of the melting metal building, she realized she had lost her letter.

DREAM BACKGROUND AND MEANING

Dawn believed she knew her soldier boyfriend from her previous life and that they had both perished in the war. She had a boring job and could not wait to travel with him. He had not proposed, but said he loved her. Each time she had the dream, it ended without her reading the letter. A factory represents how you organize your working life; the type and state of the factory will express your feelings and needs. A toy factory represents happiness at work; a furniture factory, the desire to settle down.

INTERPRETATIONS AND FORTUNE-TELLING MEANINGS

* If you dream of an efficient factory with happy workers, your life will run smoothly.
* If you are stuck on a production line, your present life is going nowhere.
* If you dream of a Victorian factory with oppressed workers, an injustice concerning your current workplace status quo needs to be put right.
* If you dream you build or own a new factory, you can make your own fortune and go as far as you want.
* If a factory is abandoned or run down, you are working too hard at a thankless task.
* If factory workers, including you, are on strike, you will be seeking major changes in your current workplace.

OUTCOME OF DAWN'S DREAM

Dawn told her boyfriend about her dream. He laughed, but to her amazement sent her an old-fashioned letter saying he was too shy to ask, but would she marry him? She knew that had been the contents of the letter in her factory dream.

Failure

Bethany, forty-five, dreamed she had failed to meet her sales target though she had done everything she could. Orders she had won disappeared from her computer screen, and her manager would not believe she made them. Her friend Doreen sympathized. Doreen's orders had doubled, and she was made sales employee of the month, a position Bethany usually held. Bethany was demoted.

DREAM BACKGROUND AND MEANING

Bethany had been the star of the sales department, in line for promotion. Her friend Doreen's job was in jeopardy. Bethany had transferred a few smaller sales to Doreen to boost her figures. Now the tables were turned, and Bethany seemed to be losing sales without reason, but Doreen was unstoppable. If failure is unexpected, your dream radar may alert you to underhanded dealings or adverse factors causing your failure.

INTERPRETATIONS AND FORTUNE-TELLING MEANINGS

⋆ Failure dreams can indicate areas where the dreamer is aware on a deep level that success might not bring happiness.

⋆ Failure in a dream examination, test, or interview can symbolize fears of not living up to the unrealistic expectations of others.

⋆ Failing-health dreams indicate stress, doing too much, or awareness of a health issue before it manifests in the body.

⋆ Dreaming of a relationship failing may reflect a past betrayal, projected on the present situation, making the dreamer more likely to fail.

⋆ If in a dream you experience a business or financial failure, check the reliability of others involved and proceed with caution, as relevant factors may yet be revealed.

⋆ If you dream you fail to be included in a team, whether in sports or in the workplace, your lack of confidence may be causing you to make mistakes.

OUTCOME OF BETHANY'S DREAM

Bethany found the dream was coming true and checked Doreen's sales figures. She discovered her missing sales were swelling Doreen's success rate. Bethany's transferring a few sales earlier had allowed Doreen to open a channel between the two accounts. Bethany confronted her friend, who soon afterward left the company. If failure is inconsistent and inexplicable, the cause of the trend should be examined.

Fairies

Fenella, twenty-five, often dreamed she was by the stream near her great-aunt's home, watching the fairies dart in and out of the water or fly with their gossamer wings into their floral dwellings. Then noisy machinery came, the water was churned into mud, and the fairies were crushed.

DREAM BACKGROUND AND MEANING

Fenella had always been fascinated by fairies and recalled seeing them as a child. She wrote children's fairy books and was currently working on a fairy oracle. Her boyfriend, Neville, a surveyor, was skeptical and said it was about time she grew up. She had inherited her great-aunt's cottage and land near the stream, and Neville wanted to bulldoze the area and build houses, which he said would make them a fortune. Whether or not fairies are real or exist on the astral plane, the realm parallel to the dream world, they reinforce a belief in magick and goodness.

INTERPRETATIONS AND FORTUNE-TELLING MEANINGS

⋆ A magical dream that says your secret wishes will soon come true, whatever your age.

⋆ If a fairy has a message for you, this will help answer a long-standing problem.

⋆ If the fey are hostile, beware trickery by someone you believe in.

⋆ If the fairies take you to their magical land to dance and feast, you may be under illusions about a love promise based on material advantage.

⋆ Flying fairies with delicate wings speak of romance in its early stages or where previous betrayal makes one or both lovers hesitate.

⋆ A fairy godmother signifies a nurturing female who will help you to achieve your desires.

OUTCOME OF FENELLA'S DREAM

Fenella realized that Neville was interested in her for her property. They separated and she created a fairy grotto by the stream so that visitors' children could share the magick of her own childhood. Fairies do not need to be objectively verifiable to create a sense of beauty and wonder in the most mundane places and situations.

Fairy Tales

Greta, twenty-six, dreamed she was a princess, locked in a tower by an evil sorceress. She called in vain for help, but no handsome prince came. Outside the window was a hydraulic lift, and the builder fixing the tower gave her a lift to the ground. She felt cheated.

DREAM BACKGROUND AND MEANING

Greta loved fairy stories and frequently read them to her preschool class at the village day-care center where she worked. She dreamed of romance and her handsome prince claiming her, but she lived at home and the years were passing. She considered online dating unromantic. Fairy-tale dreams reveal symbolic ways of changing our life path from victim to hero or heroine.

INTERPRETATIONS AND FORTUNE-TELLING MEANINGS

★ The happy-ever-after aspect of fairy-tale dreams reflects a happy ending in love or making your fortune by creating opportunities rather than waiting for life to come to you.

★ A fairy-tale dream is a good dream if you want to become pregnant or are expecting a baby, if you are reading fairy tales to children, who may be your as-yet-unborn or unconceived children.

★ If you are the hero or heroine of your dream, you will win through any difficulties if you take control rather than waiting for rescue.

★ If you are under threat from a wicked magician or sorceress in dreams and life, you will overcome someone who restricts your progress, maybe a reluctant part of yourself.

★ If you are writing a fairy story in the dream, it will chart the progress of your life and suggest strategies and solutions.

★ If the ending of the fairy story in the dream is not happy, ask who is standing in the way of the happy ending and why.

OUTCOME OF GRETA'S DREAM

After the dream, Greta realized she had been waiting for rescue too long. She took a job in a city day-care facility, started online dating, met not the rich handsome prince but a nice ordinary guy. Fairy-tale dreams occur when the dreamer is holding themselves back by unrealistic expectations.

Fairground

Peggy, fifty, dreamed she was a young woman in a Victorian fairground, riding on the carousel with her lover, who worked for the fair. She was happy and wanted the ride to never end. Her father arrived, stopped the carousel, and dragged her away. She escaped, and the dream ended with Peggy joining the fair.

DREAM BACKGROUND AND MEANING

Peggy's dream mirrored what should have been a happy real-life ending but was not. Peggy's father had broken up her relationship with the man she loved, who worked in a re-created Victorian fairground. Peggy never married but did not have the courage to give up her comfortable lifestyle and follow her love. Her father, now dead, had left her a lot of money. She was determined to find her first love, whose father had owned the real-life Victorian fairground she had seen in dreams. Finally, she discovered the fairground he was now running at a local state fair. Would she dare approach him? The revolving carousel in dreams and reality needs to complete its cycle before the next ride can begin.

INTERPRETATIONS AND FORTUNE-TELLING MEANINGS

★ If you dream you are enjoying fairground rides, you will have greater pleasure in your social life if you relax more.

★ If you win a prize at a fair, you will be lucky in love and money by taking a chance.

★ An accident on a fairground ride says other people are taking over your life. Stop before you get hurt.

★ If the fairground is closed or empty, you may be denying your own instinctive nature.

★ If you are in charge of a fairground ride, you may feel responsible for too many people's happiness.

OUTCOME OF PEGGY'S DREAM

After the dream, Peggy visited her lover's fairground but realized it was too late for love. She rode the carousel and completed the ride. Sometimes we must complete a significant dream scenario that mirrors real life, even years later, to fully let it go.

Falling Trees

Veronica, thirty-five, dreamed she heard a strong wind outside and cracking tree branches. She saw the huge fir tree outside the window swaying and tried to persuade her mother to leave the house. Instead, her mother dashed upstairs to get her jewelry box before Veronica could stop her. The fir crashed through the roof and Veronica realized her mother was trapped. Veronica tried to reach her mother, but there was another crash and darkness, and Veronica realized she had sacrificed her life in vain.

DREAM BACKGROUND AND MEANING

Veronica was emigrating to Australia to be with her fiancé and suggested that her mother come for a three-month vacation when Veronica was settled. Veronica was worried about leaving her mother alone in a tumbledown house in the middle of nowhere. Her mother had asked her not to go. But this was Veronica's chance for happiness. Falling trees represent the breaking up of what seemed security when necessary change must occur.

INTERPRETATIONS AND FORTUNE-TELLING MEANINGS

★ If trees come crashing down on a house in a dream, there may be worries about the general well-being of a family member living there.

★ If in the dream a tree does a lot of damage as it falls, there are potential hazards in a plan that need resolving before proceeding.

★ If you are cutting down trees but facing opposition, you should persist to let light and new energies into your life.

★ If a tree falls on a house, it foretells domestic disruption but may set you free.

★ A falling tree crushing you says someone may be sabotaging your chance of happiness, unconsciously or otherwise.

OUTCOME OF VERONICA'S DREAM

After the dream, Veronica realized the house was no longer habitable. Veronica went to Australia and invited her mother for a three-month vacation while the house was sold. Veronica returned temporarily to settle her mother in a small, comfortable apartment in a retirement village. Sometimes falling-tree dreams are a drastic but necessary sign that change must occur for new growth.

False Economy

Angus, sixty-five, dreamed he was at the top of a ladder, painting the gutters, when a pain in his injured arm made him lose his grip. He fell several feet, injuring himself badly. He woke to the sound of an ambulance siren, but knew he would not be covered by his medical insurance, as he had recently cut his coverage to save money.

DREAM BACKGROUND AND MEANING

Angus lived alone and was financially secure. However, the house was badly in need of painting, but Angus thought it a waste of money to pay a professional. As a result of an injury ten years earlier, he had a damaged right arm, which made climbing ladders and do-it-yourself projects hazardous. If in your dream you foresee an accident due to skimping on essentials, your subconscious is warning you of potential dangers in false economy.

INTERPRETATIONS AND FORTUNE-TELLING MEANINGS

★ If you dream of debt collectors banging at the door, though you have sufficient funds, ask yourself what you fear: old age, dependence, loneliness?

★ If you are cutting corners on insurance and security and dangerous scenarios recur in dreams, your dreams are alerting you to remedy the loopholes.

★ If you see yourself starving and in rags, this may be a past-life dream where old memories make you afraid of having nothing.

★ If you dream of being constantly harangued by your parents for wasting money, these are redundant voices that make you feel unnecessarily guilty for spending your own money.

★ If you dream of robbing someone or turning them out of their home, there may be some justifiable guilt you carry concerning money dealings. If it can't be put right, let it go.

OUTCOME OF ANGUS'S DREAM

Angus paid to have his house painted and made sensible plans for his old age. False economies may be based on a sense of lack of entitlement, but we can end up spending twice as much to remedy unnecessary skimping.

Fangs

Jodie, twenty-eight, dreamed she had grown Dracula-like fangs overnight. She was due to have her perfect white wedding and move into their perfect new home, filled with the generous wedding presents the couple had been given. But now she looked hideous. She woke screaming and rushed to the mirror.

DREAM BACKGROUND AND MEANING

Jodie felt like a fraud playing a part in the two families' stage production, and she had even had white veneers on her teeth for the perfect smile in the photos. It was too late to pull out of the wedding, but she feared she could not continue the act and was angry with herself for being swept along by other people's fairy tales. Fangs can represent the eruption of negative feelings if you are going along with others. The mouth represents communicating our true self, and fangs say something that should not be ignored.

INTERPRETATIONS AND FORTUNE-TELLING MEANINGS

★ If you dream of growing fangs, you may be afraid of revealing your negative feelings.

★ If in the dream someone emotionally close has fangs, they may be inadvertently draining your energies.

★ If all the people in your dream have fangs and are biting people Dracula-style (see "Werewolf," p. 505), identify them, as you may be being controlled or manipulated by being made to feel different in the workplace, by family, or among neighbors.

★ If you dream you are having your fangs removed, you may be trading approval for your own power of expression.

★ If you dream you feel powerful with fangs, you should act decisively to change a status quo that is stifling you.

★ Fangs in dreams signify a power conflict. Are you the perpetrator or victim? If the victim, can you or do you want to take back control, maybe at the price of others' disillusionment?

OUTCOME OF JODIE'S DREAM

Jodie did not have the courage to cancel the wedding. She hopes she can keep smiling and make everyone happy (except maybe herself), and that the fairy tale might come true.

Fantasy Fulfillment

Prudence, fifty-five, often dreamed she had a string of young lovers. She would choose one to wine and dine her and return with her to her penthouse, where they would make riotous love till the morning. After the dream she always woke contented.

DREAM BACKGROUND AND MEANING

Prudence worked for the Internal Revenue Service (IRS), and her younger work colleagues laughed at her because she lived alone with her cats. They offered to take her out on the town but she politely refused. A colleague left a pornographic magazine as a joke on her desk, which she put in her bag. Fantasy-fulfillment dreams do not have to indicate a desire for a love affair, but for some people can provide the fulfillment needed, which remains a fantasy.

INTERPRETATIONS AND FORTUNE-TELLING MEANINGS

★ If you have exotic dreams and your life is sedate, these may come from a past world where you experienced a life of passion.

★ If you are not interested in pursuing sexual fulfillment, the dream may indicate you should use your fantasies in art, writing, or music to experience waking ecstasy.

★ If you are in a relationship, fantasy-fulfillment dreams can be incorporated into a richer sexual life or compensate for an unenthusiastic partner without straying.

★ If you have exotic dreams that bring you pleasure, allow them to secretly enrich your waking life.

★ If in your sleep you are witnessing others' sexual exploits, record your dreams, as you may be developing your first novel or erotic journal column.

★ Whatever your age, your fantasy-fulfillment dream may be opening the way to a new relationship where passion awaits.

OUTCOME OF PRUDENCE'S DREAM

Prudence read the pornographic magazine while eating her supper and realized she could write a far better sexual-problems column than it had, based on her dreams. Under an assumed name, she sent samples to the magazine and was offered a trial column. She was delighted when she heard her colleagues discussing it. Fantasy-fulfillment dreams can be developed, used commercially, or just enjoyed.

Fantasy Writing

Callie, nineteen, an artist and aspiring author, dreamed an unfolding story every night of a teenager lost between worlds, trying to get back to the present where his family believed he was missing and probably dead. She followed him as he went through often-terrifying fantasy worlds.

DREAM BACKGROUND AND MEANING

Callie faithfully recorded the accounts she had dreamed, but after sending her manuscript to a lot of publishers had received no response. She wanted to be a published author but was on the verge of giving up.

INTERPRETATIONS AND FORTUNE-TELLING MEANINGS

- ✷ In the modern world, an ongoing dream can be from a past life when someone tells us their story.
- ✷ If you dream of a famous fantasy writer like C. S. Lewis, who wrote the Narnia tales, or of J. R. R. Tolkien's sagas, you are attending a master class on the astral plane.
- ✷ If you dream of your book becoming a series, ask your dream figure to show you more of the story and other characters who may presently be on the sidelines.
- ✷ If you create a total fantasy, this may be coming from your own inner psyche and says you are a natural writer.
- ✷ If your fantasy dreams cease, you have sufficient material and should focus on readying them for publishing.
- ✷ A book the dreamer is given in sleep, if not related to an existing film or book, comes from the astral plane and should be pursued.

OUTCOME OF CALLIE'S DREAM

Callie explored the world of fanzines and fantasy sites. A lot of customers were eager for the next installment of her writing. She built up a fan base via a website she created, but still applied to every publisher, large and small. Eventually a publisher noticed her success and gave her a modest commission. Fantasy-inspired dreams will find expression sooner or later but require huge dedication and maybe an inroad through social media.

Fasting

Eileen, twenty-one, dreamed she was sitting in a temple on top of a high mountain, fasting to cleanse herself of her sins. She felt good for the first few hours, then started to feel hungry. After twenty-four hours with only sips of water, she was weak and light-headed. She started to eat the food in the pack she had brought for after the fast. The others turned on her, and told her she was weak and wicked. She woke feeling she was a failure.

DREAM BACKGROUND AND MEANING

Eileen belonged to a super-slim, super-fit family. Although she was not overweight, they were always criticizing her for not taking care of herself. They all fasted for forty-eight hours every weekend, but Eileen found it incredibly hard. In fact, it made her eat far more on the days she did not fast. Her family said she was weak-willed and she should increase fasting to three days. Fasting can, in moderation and without pressure, be spiritually and physically cleansing. Dreams about coercion suggest its purpose is being distorted.

INTERPRETATIONS AND FORTUNE-TELLING MEANINGS

- ✷ If you are dreaming of fasting as part of a vision quest, religious festival, or other experience, you may gain insights in the dream or a new level of awareness.
- ✷ Dreaming of obsessive fasting suggests a poor self-image, often created by others.
- ✷ If you are fasting in the dream and angry, you may be resenting denying yourself food.
- ✷ If others are preventing your fasting, they may be unwilling to witness positive changes in you that threaten their own life view.
- ✷ If you are fasting in the dream as a protest for a cause, you need to be careful to not damage your own well-being.

OUTCOME OF EILEEN'S DREAM

Eileen gave up fasting, ignored her family's jibes, and her weight and fitness stabilized. Encouraging fasting can become a form of pressure as a means of control.

Father's Day

Hugh, thirty-six, dreamed that his two small boys were running toward him, arms outstretched. He took them to an ice cream parlor and back to his house, where he had bought them both the latest gaming devices as his Father's Day present to them. Then he woke, feeling his stomach sinking at the missing years, for they were now in their teens.

DREAM BACKGROUND AND MEANING

Hugh had not seen his boys since they were small. His ex-wife had done everything to keep them apart. He had stayed out of the way, as they had a new dad. But this year, Hugh was determined to see his sons on Father's Day. His ex-wife had, amazingly, raised no objections. Father's Day dreams can be bittersweet, anticipating family unity or a reminder of what has been lost.

INTERPRETATIONS AND FORTUNE-TELLING MEANINGS

★ If you dream of happy Father's Days when you were a child or had young children, there is nostalgia for the family togetherness rather than for its commercialized aspects.

★ If you are estranged from your own father or children, to dream of happier Father's Days is a good sign that the energies are right for reconciliation.

★ If your father is deceased and you miss him or have regrets about your parting, you may see him in Father's Day dreams and feel closer on waking.

★ If you dream of an unhappy Father's Day experience, there may be underlying resentments or highly unrealistic expectations to be resolved.

★ If you dream of Father's Day and you and your father or children cannot be together, the dream reveals there is still a telepathic paternal link.

★ If you do not know the location of your birth father or children, a dream may give you a clue.

OUTCOME OF HUGH'S DREAM

Father and sons were initially shy and tense, but by not overemphasizing the father connection they started to relax. Father's Day energies are a good impetus for building or rebuilding if years have passed.

Fear of the Dark

Vera, fifty-eight, dreamed she was walking home through the streets in pitch blackness during the London blitz. There was total silence. So much of the street had been destroyed that she could not recognize any landmarks. She called her husband, who was home on leave and promised to meet her. There was an explosion.

DREAM BACKGROUND AND MEANING

Vera, recently widowed, was trying to adjust to living alone after having been married to her husband for many years. From a very early age she had been scared of being alone in the dark. This feeling was worse than ever now that she lived alone. Vera's dream may have been a past-life wartime experience when she and her husband were killed in a bombing raid. The darkness signifies the reemergence of a suppressed memory, amplified by his death.

INTERPRETATIONS AND FORTUNE-TELLING MEANINGS

★ If you dream you are lost in total darkness, there may be an incident from childhood or a past world you should share.

★ If you dream of ghosts in the dark and wake up terrified, your psychic powers are emerging unchecked. Channel them into healing.

★ If you dream you are attacked in the darkness, you may have fears for your physical safety. Ensure that your home is safe at night.

★ If you are lost in a totally unfamiliar, dark place, you fear change imposed by others.

★ If you are blind in the dream, you may be worried about your eyesight or about generally losing your faculties as you get older. Have a checkup to reassure yourself and to pick up any issues.

OUTCOME OF VERA'S DREAM

Vera put ornamental lampposts in her front and back gardens that shone all night. She also rented a room to a local student so she would not be alone after dark. Darkness is a primal fear of being vulnerable, representing fears hard to bring to the surface, which hide unresolved in the shadows of our mind.

Feast

Becky, fifty-five, dreamed she had organized a surprise family feast to celebrate the return of her son, Jed, who had been serving overseas. She had invited family and friends and prepared every food imaginable plus a welcome-home cake. Jed took one look at the feast and walked out. Though everyone at the feast complimented Becky on her catering, she was heartbroken.

DREAM BACKGROUND AND MEANING

Becky noticed that Jed had been very withdrawn since returning from military service overseas, spending most of the time in his room. She wanted to hold a feast so that everyone could welcome him home as a hero. Feasts are a way of showing appreciation to an individual, but dreams can reveal whether such a gesture would be appropriate.

INTERPRETATIONS AND FORTUNE-TELLING MEANINGS

★ If you dream a feast is held in your honor, you will attain the recognition, acknowledgment, and reward you deserve, whether at work, socially, or in the family.

★ If you are organizing a feast in a dream, extra work may fall on you regarding a family celebration, work, or business event, but you should not do more than your share.

★ If the dream is of an engagement, wedding, christening, or naming feast, a forthcoming marriage or pregnancy will enter your life or that of a close friend or family member.

★ If no one comes to a dream feast you prepare, you may be giving something to the wrong people, offering what is not needed, or not offering something at the right time.

★ If a dream feast degenerates into a quarrel or fight, beware of trying to unite people who are set on dissension.

OUTCOME OF BECKY'S DREAM

After the dream, Becky phoned her son's best friend, who told her that her son was suffering from posttraumatic stress disorder (PTSD) and needed quiet time and space. She canceled the feast and made sure he was not disturbed. Feasts mark festivals and personal celebrations, whether for a small family or for community. Dreams often reveal the energies that will determine the best form of celebration.

Feathers

Chloe, forty-two, dreamed she was wearing a cloak of different feathers, standing with a very ancient woman who was performing a feather ritual. Chloe rose on the back of a huge black swan, flying high above forests and bubbling hot springs. She woke feeling better than she had for years.

DREAM BACKGROUND AND MEANING

Chloe was a busy advertising executive in Dublin, Ireland, but for years had suffered from chronic pain and exhaustion. She had New Zealand ancestry, but since she had no living relatives in Ireland to tell her about them, knew little of them. Was this the time to find out about her heritage? Feathers and feather cloaks are associated with magical flight in cultures as far apart as Norse traditions and Australian aboriginals, and are a special sign of healing and blessings.

INTERPRETATIONS AND FORTUNE-TELLING MEANINGS

★ Finding a white feather or seeing it floating down in your dream indicates the presence of your guardian angel.

★ A peacock feather warns of the presence of envy and jealousy.

★ A feather from a bird of prey says you may need to fight for what you want but will succeed.

★ Feathers carried upward by the wind foretell a rise in good fortune and desired travel.

★ A shower of feathers smothering you says you may feel overwhelmed, but the responsibilities will prove lighter than expected.

★ Meeting someone wearing or carrying a feather warns against inconsistency and unpredictability.

OUTCOME OF CHLOE'S DREAM

Chloe went to New Zealand after the dream and, on a trip to a traditional Maori village, discovered that the chief female tohunga, the magic healer, wore a feather cloak. Chloe discovered she came from a long line of indigenous people, who welcomed her. The old grandmother tohunga was the woman in the dream. Chloe's condition dramatically improved as she worked with indigenous plant medicines and black swan feathers.

Feather healing and magick are practiced in many indigenous cultures such as native North American tribes.

Feet

Toby, twenty-two, dreamed he could hear footsteps ahead but there was no one in sight and, whenever he stopped, the footsteps ceased, beginning again when he moved forward. Then there were several pairs of unseen feet, forcing him into a marching rhythm. He was swept along until he reached the recruiting office of the military. But then he walked in the opposite direction.

DREAM BACKGROUND AND MEANING

From childhood on, Toby had been expected to follow in his family's footsteps and join the military. He resisted, despite intense pressure, and agreed to an interview with the military, which he passed. Yet he still hesitated. Unseen footsteps in a dream can guide the dreamer in a set direction but may emanate from the past and may no longer have validity.

INTERPRETATIONS AND FORTUNE-TELLING MEANINGS

★ Stamping your feet in a dream suggests you feel strongly about an issue and will not be deterred.

★ If you dream of marching feet, especially if you are one of the marchers, it signifies moving in a direction shared by others, where you seem to have less choice than you imagined.

★ If you are standing or walking alone, you are asserting independence and desire to walk your own path.

★ If you dream you trip and miss your footing, you may be on uncertain ground and should check your facts before speaking or acting.

★ If your feet are tied together, you may find it hard to continue with a project without first freeing yourself from others' obstacles and objections.

★ If your feet are hurting, seemingly from walking back and forth between two people who are calling you, cut back on trying to be everything to everybody everywhere.

OUTCOME OF TOBY'S DREAM

Toby sensed they were his father's and grandfather's footsteps, leading him along a career path that had been right for them but was not right for him. He refused to join the military. Feet and footstep dreams often occur when the dreamer needs to follow their own direction.

Fertility

Jeanette, thirty-nine, dreamed she found a jeweled egg in the grass. When she held it, the egg opened. Two identical rainbow birds flew out and sat singing side by side on a high branch. She was filled with joy and woke her partner, Gillian, to share the dream.

DREAM BACKGROUND AND MEANING

Jeanette and Gillian had been using donor sperm and in vitro fertilization (IVF) to try to conceive their first child, without success. Jeanette was worried she was unconsciously blocking conception, because her mother lost three children at birth, and Jeanette was anxious she might have the same experience. Fertility dreams usually express their meaning in symbols that have been used for thousands of years and relate to the natural world.

INTERPRETATIONS AND FORTUNE-TELLING MEANINGS

★ Dreams that are indications of potential conception include a pomegranate bursting open and its seeds scattering in the air; sharing a coconut with a partner; a hatching egg; and rabbits running in an open field.

★ Apples falling from a tree suggest the baby will be a boy, and pears falling from a tree signify the baby will be a girl.

★ Being given red roses by your partner in the dream predicts a boy, and white roses, a girl.

★ Sharing a bag of hazelnuts with a partner suggests early conception and a second and even third or fourth birth, closely following the previous ones.

★ Matching lotus flowers indicate twins; three lotus, triplets; and a whole bunch, a large family.

★ Seeing a baby in a dream reassures you that you can have a child or children, especially if you see the birth in the dream or regularly dream of the same baby or child. This may be the soul of your yet-to-be-conceived child waiting to take birth.

OUTCOME OF JEANETTE'S DREAM

Jeanette gave birth to healthy identical twins, and this relieved her fears. Gillian is trying for their third child to complete the family. Fertility dreams are reassuring where one or both members of a couple are fearful.

Feuding Family

Sue, sixty-three, dreamed she was in a shopping mall, pushing a trolley full of groceries. As she was about to leave the mall, she noticed her elder sister, Jane, pushing a trolley that suddenly overturned, spilling all her groceries on the floor. Jane got down on her knees to pick up the groceries, but was having great difficulty due to having rheumatoid arthritis. Sue left the mall and didn't look back.

DREAM BACKGROUND AND MEANING

Sue and Jane had not spoken for years, due to a disagreement over money they received upon their mother's death. Although Sue came off worse, she wanted to reconcile with her sister, as she believed the longer the estrangement, the less chance of burying the hatchet. Feuding family dreams are often deep-seated, although their effects may be repressed in daily life.

INTERPRETATIONS AND FORTUNE-TELLING MEANINGS

★ If in a dream you act vengefully and uncaringly toward a friend or relative, even if there is no outer sign of a feud, underlying resentment may grow if not resolved.

★ If you dream of reconciling a feud, the other person or people involved may be having regrets and connecting in sleep.

★ If you are involved in family litigation and dream of winning, there may be a way you can obtain satisfaction out of court.

★ If you dream of deceased relatives trying to bring reconciliation to the family, factors you do not know of may clear up a misunderstanding or impasse.

★ If you dream of feuding members of the family as children, that may be where resentments began.

OUTCOME OF SUE'S DREAM

After the dream, Sue still felt very bitter, but realized that years were passing and Jane was in need. She contacted Jane and started helping her with her shopping. They realized that their mother had deliberately caused rivalry between them right up to when she had made her will, to continue the trouble after her death. Family feud dreams can reflect quarrels beginning years or generations earlier and retain unnecessary anger that should have been left behind.

Finding Freedom

Eric, twenty-five, dreamed he was at a rock festival, helping roadies to set up the stage. The roadies asked Eric to travel with them, setting up festivals and living in the vans. He agreed. He phoned his parents and, ignoring their protests, told them he was not coming home.

DREAM BACKGROUND AND MEANING

Eric had recently discovered that he was adopted and came from traveling folk, which explained why he was always happiest at festivals with his guitar and tent. His adoptive parents had spent a fortune on his education and believed that once he settled down he would lose his obsession with freedom. Dreams of becoming free can refer to a specific restrictive situation or to a more general desire to live your own way, which may come from past generations (see "Escaping," p. 171).

INTERPRETATIONS AND FORTUNE-TELLING MEANINGS

★ Any dream where you find freedom from a difficult or unwelcome situation is an omen of good luck.

★ To dream that you free yourself or are freed from a jail or locked room foretells the end of living by others' rules.

★ Breaking away from a boring lifestyle in a dream indicates a new, freer beginning.

★ If in your dream you resign from a sedentary job to live and work on the road, be sure you are not running from yourself and taking your problems with you.

★ By confronting rumor, lies, and malicious actions in a dream, you set yourself free from the power of others to hurt you.

★ If you dream of setting a bird free from a cage, that may reflect your own desire for a less limiting life. However, captive birds may find it hard to adjust to living wild.

OUTCOME OF ERIC'S DREAM

After the dream, Eric joined a company setting up entertainment events interstate and eventually started his own festival business. Despite loving his newfound freedom, Eric regularly returned home to visit his adoptive parents, who eventually came to accept that he had found his wings.

Fingers and Thumbs

Peggy, forty, dreamed she had long, slender fingers, all beautifully manicured and polished, and her new husband was putting a beautiful sapphire ring on her heart or wedding finger. Then her hand became rough-skinned and calloused and the ring looked so out of place she took it off and handed it back.

DREAM BACKGROUND AND MEANING

Peggy ran a successful market gardening business. She was very self-conscious and hated wearing her engagement ring, because it was far too dainty for her hands. Finger-and-thumb dreams represent how we see ourselves and accordingly present strength and beauty, or present inadequacy if we are self-conscious of our appearance.

INTERPRETATIONS AND FORTUNE-TELLING MEANINGS

★ If you dream you are pointing the index finger of your writing hand at someone in your dream, you blame them for a mistake, even if you do not say so.

★ If someone is pointing a finger at you in a dream, you may be surprised at their identity, if they are supportive in life.

★ An engagement ring, wedding ring, or eternity ring on your marriage finger indicates a long-lasting, faithful love who you will soon meet if you do not already know them.

★ If you dream you are crossing your fingers or holding your thumbs, in some cultures it means good fortune will soon enter your life.

★ If someone crosses their fingers while making a promise in the dream, do not trust them.

★ If you continually drop precious objects in your dream, called being all fingers and thumbs, someone has undermined your confidence.

OUTCOME OF PEGGY'S DREAM

Peggy described her dream to her fiancé. They exchanged the ring for a ring of jade mounted in silver, jade being the stone of the land as well as of faithful love. He said he loved her hands, as they showed her love of the earth (see "Hands," p. 234). Our fingers and thumbs express who we really are, and dreams can confirm that the true self is worth more than superficial grooming.

Financial Abuse in the Golden Years

Gloria, ninety-one, dreamed that an officer from the bank asked her about money that William, her only son, was withdrawing from her account. She wouldn't comment, since William had threatened that if she complained he would have her committed to a nursing home as incompetent. She woke, terrified of his power.

DREAM BACKGROUND AND MEANING

Gloria had been left a large sum of money after her late husband's business was sold, after which William persuaded her to give him full control over her finances. Since signing, he was keeping her short of money. Financial and mental abuse that can tip over into physical abuse confirms for the dreamer that they are not losing their faculties.

INTERPRETATIONS AND FORTUNE-TELLING MEANINGS

★ If you dream of hiding or denying abuse by a family member, you may be wrongly blaming yourself for the situation.

★ If in a dream you are being abused by a relative or carer, this can be an alert that you are losing control by way of veiled threats.

★ If you are in your golden years and dream someone close is stealing your money, seek legal advice before handing over control.

★ If the dream reflects what is happening and you feel helpless, it's time to seek official or charitable help, when the abuser is not around.

★ If your dream leaves you feeling uneasy, this is more than an anxiety dream. Act before the situation escalates.

★ If you are happy yet dream of a carer or relative financially abusing you, this may reflect fear of loss of control.

OUTCOME OF GLORIA'S DREAM

While her son was absent for two weeks on a vacation, paid for with her money, she contacted the original lawyer, who reversed the power of attorney, which had been obtained under coercion. An aid charity helped her move into a sheltered facility. Family financial-abuse dreams may predict the need to have safeguards in place before threats are carried out.

Financial Control Between Couples

John, thirty-seven, dreamed he went to his bank to withdraw a thousand dollars to pay for car repairs. He handed the bank clerk his debit card and was informed that the money had been transferred to his wife's sole account. Furious, he confronted his wife, June, who informed him that he could no longer withdraw money from the account without her authorization.

DREAM BACKGROUND AND MEANING

John and June had been married for fifteen years. When the children were young, they shared everything. This changed three years earlier when John lost his job. Even though John was now working again, June had retained full control of household finances and gave him a small daily allowance. Dreams about joint financial matters can reveal underlying power struggles in a relationship.

INTERPRETATIONS AND FORTUNE-TELLING MEANINGS

* If money is used as a weapon of control, dreams over joint finances can expose wider resentments between parties.
* If dreams reflect the control of one partner financially, look at the deeper issues causing this.
* If you are embroiled in a divorce settlement and dream of your ex-partner hiding money, your dream may be showing matters that need closer scrutiny to ensure an equitable split.
* If a financial arrangement between partners has changed, the dream highlights the need for renegotiation.
* If you are a child in the dream and your partner is a parent, accepting unequal financial arrangements may be irking you.
* If money is the elephant in the room, examine dependency or codependency issues within the relationship.

OUTCOME OF JOHN'S DREAM

John had gone along with financial arrangements to keep the peace. In the past he had wasted money gambling online, so June had imposed spending restrictions. They have now agreed to have a joint account to which each contributes for expenses, and separate accounts in which surplus can be spent as the individual wishes. Financial dreams reflect the delicate balance between joint solvency and individual financial autonomy.

Fire

Pam, fifteen, dreamed she was playing truant with her boyfriend, Tom. They had taken his father's pickup truck for a barbecue in the forest. The weather had been dry and there were warnings not to light fires. Tom laughed and said he knew what he was doing. But the barbecue got out of control and a tree caught fire. They fled after causing a major forest fire. Pam woke, scared someone had seen the truck.

DREAM BACKGROUND AND MEANING

Pam knew she was playing with fire as her boyfriend, who was older, had been banned from driving but still drove his father's pickup truck, as his father was in jail. She skipped school to be with Tom and enjoyed the thrill of starting minor fires with him. Fire by its nature is unpredictable, as a human quality and in its natural element. Fire dreams are sometimes a warning that luck may be running out.

INTERPRETATIONS AND FORTUNE-TELLING MEANINGS

* Dreams of hearth fires or log burners are symbols of a happy, settled domestic period and a sign of committed lovers settling together in the near future.
* A dream of a house on fire, if the fire is accidental, signifies a major domestic change but also suggests checking wiring and possible fire hazards.
* Dreams of an arsonist warn of someone reckless around you at work, or a friend or family member who may cause destruction to others.
* A forest fire warns that gossip and rumor may spread rapidly and should be quelled at its source.
* Fire used in magick ritual in dreams suggests sudden inspiration and manifestation of desires in daily life, but advises care in what the dreamer asks for.

OUTCOME OF PAM'S DREAM

The dream scared Pam. Her school told her parents of Pam's truanting, and she was no longer able to see Tom. Before long he was arrested, when one of his arson attempts escalated out of control. Fire dreams are inevitably active and can indicate a more exciting period ahead. But handle with caution.

Fire Escape

Boris, thirty-nine, dreamed he was attending an incredibly boring meeting. He was due to make his presentation after the break but knew any decisions had already been made. During the break he descended a fire escape and drove away, with no idea where he was going.

DREAM BACKGROUND AND MEANING

Boris was a senior manager in a large organization, employed solely as the mouthpiece for the head office, implementing decisions that were often against the interests of his workers. Now he was being asked to introduce a series of layoffs among the older workers, and he doubted they would get another job. Fire-escape dreams represent a potential way out of a difficult situation when fighting on is useless.

INTERPRETATIONS AND FORTUNE-TELLING MEANINGS

★ If there is a fire in the dream and you are using the fire escape, it may be time to bail out of an ethos with which you disagree.

★ If you dream you are using an external fire escape at home or work, you may want to leave rather than confront the problems.

★ If you dream there is a fire you are trying to extinguish while others are fleeing down the fire escape, you may be showing loyalty to those who do not merit it.

★ If there is a fire and you are not sure whether to fight it or use the fire escape, there may be a sudden moral decision thrust on you at work.

★ If there is a blocked fire escape in your workplace, your unconscious radar may have picked up a security risk. Check.

★ If someone is deliberately blocking a fire escape in an emergency, anticipate alternatives in your work or home life if you feel trapped.

OUTCOME OF BORIS'S DREAM

Boris decided to warn the union of the proposed layoffs, and he resigned before he was forced to implement them. If you descend a fire escape in a dream, it may be hard to climb back up, but escape may be the best option if you suspect a simmering situation will erupt.

Fireworks

Bonnie, thirty-eight, dreamed she had taken her children to a fireworks display. But she knew something was wrong. The bonfire was flaming dangerously near the pile of fireworks, and people were lighting fireworks without supervision. There was a huge explosion. Bonnie seized her children's hands and ran away.

DREAM BACKGROUND AND MEANING

Bonnie's ex-husband and his new young girlfriend were taking the children to a festival that ended with a huge fireworks display where there had been accidents in the past. Under custody arrangements, Bonnie was obliged to let the children attend, though her younger daughter was worried about going with her father, whose sudden explosions of bad temper she feared.

INTERPRETATIONS AND FORTUNE-TELLING MEANINGS

★ Dreams of a spectacular fireworks display promise a celebration, good fortune, or victory.

★ Being invited to an elaborate fireworks display suggests the organizer in the dream may be trying to make a big impression.

★ If smoke obscures the fireworks or they fail to ignite, an effort to make an impression may prove disappointing.

★ Rockets shooting directly upward, lighting the sky, herald the fulfillment of a short-term ambition, especially in the performing or creative arts.

★ If fireworks explode, causing a fire, the dream advises taking care if you are organizing or attending a display in the daily world. More usually it refers to anger that has been building up in someone volatile.

★ If a fireworks display ends in a final burst of cascading lights, this is a symbol of passionate sex, sometimes involving giving way to temptation.

OUTCOME OF BONNIE'S DREAM

Bonnie talked to her ex's girlfriend, who had never met the children, and explained how having to watch two lively children could spoil her fun. As a result, the girlfriend chose to not take the children to the fireworks. There was a fireworks explosion at the festival, which confirmed Bonnie's predictive fears. Fireworks dreams can herald celebrations but also, depending on the nature of the dream, actual or emotional danger, sometimes both.

First Impressions

*Redmond, twenty-five, dreamed he was
sitting alone in a waiting room before
an interview. A scruffy older man
joined him. When the man asked him
why he wanted the job, Redmond said
it was just a stepping-stone. Then the
older man was gone. When Redmond
entered the interview room, the man was in the CEO chair.*

DREAM BACKGROUND AND MEANING

Redmond had rehearsed his introduction to the interviewing
board, as he knew the importance of first impressions. In the
elevator Redmond met an older man, also apparently going
to the interview, which reminded him of the dream. When the
man tried to be friendly, Redmond was dismissive of him. First
impressions are important in every aspect of life and hard
to correct.

INTERPRETATIONS AND FORTUNE-TELLING MEANINGS

★ If you dream about unexpected circumstances surrounding
an interview, your radar may be picking up factors of which
you may be unaware.

★ If you dream of meeting a distinctive person in the dream,
they may be involved in the interview process or in future
business connections, however unlikely that may seem.

★ If you are aware that you did not make a good first
impression in the dream, be alert to the problem issue to
create a better second impression.

★ If you meet someone you want to impress in love, and first
impressions are good in the dream, there is a psychic spark
between you.

★ If you dream of making a bad first impression on someone
you instantly dislike, this person may be a reflection of
negative characteristics within yourself.

★ If you meet someone for the first time and they do not make
a good impression, give it a second chance, as they may
have hidden their true self.

OUTCOME OF REDMOND'S DREAM

Redmond ignored his dream and did not get the job. The
man in the elevator was on the interviewing panel. First-
impressions dreams are important, as the least likely people
may turn out to be influential in a career or as a future love.

Fishing

*Bartolo, sixty-five, had a recurring dream that he threw a line
into the water. As he reeled in his catch with great difficulty, he
landed a shark. Bartolo tried to release the shark, but it seized
his arm and violently flipped back into the water, holding on to
Bartolo. Bartolo woke, knowing resistance was useless.*

DREAM BACKGROUND AND MEANING

Bartolo, though retired and now living in the United States,
had retained part ownership of the family fishing business
back in Italy. He still ocean-fished regularly from his motor
launch in Rockport, Massachusetts. Now the family fishing
business, along with others in the fishing village back home,
was being sold to a Far Eastern consortium. This he opposed,
as the business had been in the family for generations. Fishing
dreams involving a predator fish indicate powerful opposition
beneath the surface, which can threaten the person fishing.

INTERPRETATIONS AND FORTUNE-TELLING MEANINGS

★ Dreaming of catching fish swimming in clear waters
indicates a secure venture where prosperity will come
through perseverance.

★ If you are wading into deep water, you will succeed through
your enterprise, but should take care.

★ Muddy or cloudy waters warn of hidden dangers but also
possible hidden rewards.

★ If you dream you catch nothing, you are wasting your time
pursuing a venture and should move on.

★ Since the ichthys (or ichthus) fish symbol was displayed by
early Christians to mark a secure house, dreaming about
a model of a fish indicates the trustworthiness in other
fisherfolk in the dream.

★ A dream of a fishing trip on a stormy sea or one where you
encounter dangerous catches says the odds against you
are too great.

OUTCOME OF BARTOLO'S DREAM

Bartolo accepted that he was outnumbered. He discovered
that the community was planning a court case to compel him
to agree. However, he realized he was not ready to retire,
and still takes tourists fishing on his boat in Massachusetts.
With fishing dreams, look for the meaning hidden below
the surface of any situation, especially if there is
potential opposition.

Fitness Classes

Andrea, thirty-five, dreamed she was in an aerobics class for the first time, standing at the back, where she hoped she would not be noticed. She could not follow the instructions or work out what the others were doing, as they seemed so fast and competent. Then she tripped and split her leotard right up the back, and everyone laughed. She got changed and, as she left the gym, saw some women outside, walking into the woods. They asked her to join them.

DREAM BACKGROUND AND MEANING

Andrea had joined a gym and started attending fitness classes because she believed it would be a good way to make new friends in addition to getting healthier. But she felt inadequate and everyone ignored her. Sometimes a fitness dream shows whether we should persevere or seek an alternative.

INTERPRETATIONS AND FORTUNE-TELLING MEANINGS

* Dreams of moving in harmony suggest you are in tune with others socially and will soon make new friends.
* If you keep getting the movements wrong in fitness-class dreams, others may be giving you conflicting messages in life generally.
* If in your dream everyone in your fitness class laughs at you, you may be feeling unnecessarily inadequate in the workplace, socially, or within a relationship.
* If you dream you hurt yourself on equipment or fall, you may be trying too hard to fit into an environment that may not be for you.
* If you are practicing alone rather than in a class and enjoying it, you may be happier working on individual exercise or sports.
* If you are excluded or the doors are barred, there is almost always a happier alternative shown in your dream.

OUTCOME OF ANDREA'S DREAM

Andrea realized that she did not enjoy the regimented activities and was not getting to know people. Inspired by the dream, she found a walking club that organized social events as well as fitness activities. Activities can be a way to make friends; your dreams will guide you to what is right for you.

Flags

Oswald, thirty, dreamed he was a standard-bearer in a battle against the Danes and carried a special raven banner, woven magically by Viking women so the raven would appear to move during the battle and frighten the enemy. He could hear the raven rallying the army above the battle cries. Suddenly the raven was gone and the flag empty. Oswald knew the battle was lost.

DREAM BACKGROUND AND MEANING

Oswald, who was of Swedish origin, had joined a radical peace group and had taken part in several high-profile protests, one of which had ended in a violent clash between protesters and the law. His employers were very conventional. They told Oswald that unless he left the radical group, he would not go far in his career. Oswald had been asked to carry the peace flag in the next rally. Marching behind or carrying a flag indicates loyalty to the cause represented by the flag, but open support may come at a cost.

INTERPRETATIONS AND FORTUNE-TELLING MEANINGS

* Dreaming of hoisting or holding a flag high shows a need for courage and rallying support for your cause.
* A ripped flag says you are backing the losing side in an argument.
* A red flag is a warning to not press ahead with a plan or confrontation.
* A white or empty flag suggests you may have to give way on a principle or decision to keep the peace and for your self-preservation.
* Waving flags as royalty or a sporting victory parade goes by indicates a desire to be seen as belonging to the majority view.
* Waving flags in a carnival represents spontaneous joy and participating wholeheartedly in fun.

OUTCOME OF OSWALD'S DREAM

Oswald realized from the dream that he was losing faith in the organization, as there were many radicals. The disappearing raven suggested the movement might lose its legitimacy. He resigned and joined a peace organization, working through petitions rather than by direct action. Flags are rallying points for action. Many standard-bearers traditionally fall with their flag if the cause is just.

Flash Mob, Spontaneous Gathering

Katriona, seventy, dreamed she was sitting alone in the hotel foyer in Thailand, wondering if she should go back to Australia or stay. Without warning, the room came alive with singing and dancing by a flash mob. Leading the flash mob was a rabbi she knew, singing her favorite song, "Hava Nagila," accompanied by about fifty colorfully dressed people of all nationalities, snaking in and out among the sofas. They pulled her to join them, and she started laughing. Then, suddenly, they were gone. Katriona woke, believing this signaled happy times ahead.

DREAM BACKGROUND AND MEANING

Katriona was on an extended vacation in Thailand with her husband, with a view to settling there for at least part of the year. However, since their arrival, they had experienced a flood, caught food poisoning, and her husband had developed a lung infection. Finally, Katriona was bitten by a temple dog and had to undergo treatment for rabies. Should they abandon the dream and go home? Mysterious spontaneous gatherings often appear in dreams when the dreamer is feeling low, as a reminder that life can be good.

INTERPRETATIONS AND FORTUNE-TELLING MEANINGS

* Having a flash mob appear in a dream is an excellent omen for future happiness in a planned endeavor.
* A flash mob appearing in your dream heralds unexpected good fortune and future celebrations.
* If you are pleased to see the flash mob enter your dream, you are ready for a positive change in lifestyle, especially concerning travel and relocation.
* If you are organizing a flash mob via social media, you may be called on to inject fun and spontaneity into an unpromising planned social event.
* If you are leading the flash mob in a spiraling dance or initiating the singing, you will be given a chance to shine.
* If your flash mob does not disappear as fast as it appears in the dream, friends, neighbors, and family may outstay their welcome unless you impose limits.

OUTCOME OF KATRIONA'S DREAM

After the dream, life seemed to improve. Katriona and her husband extended their stay to take advantage of forthcoming major local festivals. Flash-mob dreams can stir positive energies and attract good luck.

Flat Tire

Ariane, seventeen, dreamed she was on her first solo road trip when her car swerved, narrowly missing a truck, and she realized she had a flat tire. She attempted to put the spare tire on but was unable to undo the wheel nuts. She tried hailing passing vehicles for assistance, but no one stopped. When she phoned her father, he said that if she was old enough to have a car, she was old enough to change a tire.

DREAM BACKGROUND AND MEANING

Ariane recently passed her driving test, and her father gave her a car. She ignored her father's warning to regularly check the oil levels and tires. She told him he was just fussing. A flat-tire dream, especially among under-thirties, says that to gain independence, it is necessary also to assume the responsibilities that go with it.

INTERPRETATIONS AND FORTUNE-TELLING MEANINGS

* If you dream of having a flat tire, check your car before a journey, as your subconscious may have noticed something amiss.
* If you dream you are confidently fixing your own tire, hazards on your life journey will be easily overcome by your own efforts.
* If someone offers to help you change a tire in your dream, note if you know the person, as they or someone coming into your life soon will be extra-cooperative.
* Since cars refer to the way we go through life (see "Car," p. 86), they are a wake-up call to not rely on others to resolve our problems.
* Motoring hazards caused by carelessness about car safety warn us that we are relying on Lady Luck or our guardian angel to bail us out.

OUTCOME OF ARIANE'S DREAM

After the dream, Ariane realized she could not call her father every time she had a problem in her life or with her car. She took a car-maintenance course and went on a cheaper vacation so she could afford to join a roadside-assistance service. Dreams do not predict motoring hazards but possible pitfalls that should be anticipated.

Flatulence

Morgan, thirty-five, dreamed he was receiving a top award for which he had worked for years. But as he made his acceptance speech, he broke wind loudly. Everyone laughed, but the award was taken from him for showing disrespect for the organization.

DREAM BACKGROUND AND MEANING

Morgan had worked hard for years and believed he was finally in line for the employee-of-the-year award. But some jealous colleagues were probing into his background when, as a youth, he had been in trouble with the law. Flatulence dreams can reveal fears of being found unworthy in a professional or social situation.

INTERPRETATIONS AND FORTUNE-TELLING MEANINGS

★ If you dream of being flatulent at an important business meeting or social occasion, you may secretly disapprove of the agenda.

★ If you dream of being flatulent in a public place, you have aggressive, angry feelings about the unfairness of your life.

★ If you dream your partner is flatulent when you had hoped they would impress, you may be imposing unrealistic expectations on them.

★ If you are flatulent in recurring dreams, you may have a minor digestive condition.

★ If you manage to refrain from releasing wind in a dream despite an overwhelming desire to do so, you are maintaining a necessary polite calm exterior, but need to address your inner turmoil.

★ If you dream of an important figure you admire releasing wind in public, you may have doubts about an authority figure in your life who may not be all they seem.

OUTCOME OF MORGAN'S DREAM

Morgan decided to admit his past to his senior executive, even at the risk of losing the award. The director said the company was aware of his past, as they had investigated his background when he started working there, and he had proven himself in every way. He received his award. Flatulence dreams can reveal a need to bring to the surface what may be hidden worries and insecurities.

Flea

Sylvia, thirty, dreamed that her mother-in-law moved into Sylvia's home with her huge, unruly dog. Almost immediately Sylvia noticed her carpets and sofas were hopping with fleas, and she realized they were coming from the dog. Her mother-in-law denied her dog had fleas. She packed her things and her son's things and left, and all the fleas jumped back on the dog.

DREAM BACKGROUND AND MEANING

Sylvia had only been married a couple of months, and her mother-in-law was used to having the run of the house where her son Greg had lived alone. She constantly criticized Sylvia's housekeeping. Sylvia hated the dog which, despite her mother-in-law's obsession with cleanliness, had fleas. Flea dreams can represent minor injustices and irritations, especially from unwanted visitors or those who outstay their welcome.

INTERPRETATIONS AND FORTUNE-TELLING MEANINGS

★ If you dream that a flea is sucking your blood, you are being invaded by parasitic people and those who drain your energy and self-confidence.

★ If you dream that your home or workplace is infested with fleas, gossip and rumors are spreading that need handling firmly.

★ If you dream you are covered in flea bites, minor worries are preventing you from relaxing and need resolution to stop them from getting worse.

★ If you dream that your dog has fleas, a friend you thought was loyal may betray you.

★ If you dream that you kill the fleas or remove the source, it is in your power to clear what or whoever is troubling you.

OUTCOME OF SYLVIA'S DREAM

After the dream, Sylvia confronted her mother-in-law and insisted she come when invited as a visitor and not interfere with Sylvia's quite adequate domestic arrangements. To Sylvia's and her mother-in-law's amazement, Sylvia's husband backed her, as he was tired of being treated like a helpless little boy now that he was married, but had been too intimidated by his mother to say anything. Flea dreams can warn of your or others' bad habits that are affecting your harmony and well-being. Of course, dreams about fleas can also indicate dry or irritated skin disturbing your sleep.

Flock of Birds

Sonia, forty-four, dreamed she was watching the sky turn dark as hundreds of egrets flew south for the winter over the small vacation house her parents had given her in rural central France. She was sitting outside in her motor home,  *which was packed with her belongings, as she had decided her attempt to earn her living as an astrologer in the local town had failed. But the birds were going south, and she was heading back north to rainy London.*

DREAM BACKGROUND AND MEANING

Sonia had given herself six months to make a living in France with her unique form of astrology. But she had not sold a single birth chart, and her savings were low. When migrating birds appear in a dream, they are calling the dreamer to follow.

INTERPRETATIONS AND FORTUNE-TELLING MEANINGS

- ★ If you dream that the birds in the flock are all taking the same direction, you will become in harmony with others if you do not lose sight of your objective.
- ★ If the flock is settled on a tree, you will meet like-minded people from whom you may benefit.
- ★ If birds in the flock are fighting, beware quarrels over family or workplace rivalries.
- ★ Birds flying straight toward the dreamer or overhead indicate that happier times are coming.
- ★ If the flock suddenly changes direction, there may be sudden changes of heart, resolving doubts or inconsistency from those close.

OUTCOME OF SONIA'S DREAM

After the dream, Sonia rented out the vacation home for the whole of the spring and summer. She moved into her motor home and followed the egrets south to the tourist areas for the fall and winter and sold many charts, returning temporarily with the egrets to set up the home for herself for the summer. Flocks of birds represent movement and following unwaveringly the path of the sun to success.

Floods

Penny, seventy-two, dreamed she and her husband, Jim, were watching the waters rise outside their home, though in reality there was no river near. Jim insisted the waters would not reach them; Penny begged him to collect what they could and leave. He refused to take her fears seriously. The waters continued to rise, and a rescuer in a boat came. Penny took what she could carry, but Jim remained, telling her she was stupid to panic. Penny watched the house submerging, but could do nothing except save herself.

DREAM BACKGROUND AND MEANING

Jim wanted to invest their savings and remaining pension fund in his best friend's get-rich-quick scheme. Penny was worried, as the friend had failed financially before. Jim insisted he was going ahead, and she had no choice. Flood dreams warn of impending disaster and the need to take rapid action to survive.

INTERPRETATIONS AND FORTUNE-TELLING MEANINGS

- ★ If you dream that a flood traps you, you are being swamped by others' emotions or demands and repressing feelings of anger or helplessness.
- ★ If a bridge is flooded and the floods extend beyond it, a normal source of help or reasoned action will be blocked.
- ★ If you are drowning in a flood, you are becoming overwhelmed by a situation or relationship in your life and should back off fast.
- ★ If you have a boat, or someone rescues you in one, the obstacles are surmountable with help.
- ★ A flooded house warns of potentially perilous home finances or risky investments that can threaten domestic resources.
- ★ A dream of rising floods, especially if the person you are with refuses to recognize the danger, is a warning that a situation is growing out of control. Reclaim your power by insisting on evasive action.

OUTCOME OF PENNY'S DREAM

Penny saw a lawyer to safeguard her half of the assets. Jim went ahead and lost everything. Flood dreams are "act now" warnings of the possibility that there may be partial losses.

Floor

Stephen, fifty, dreamed he was checking the function room being used for a major company event when he noticed that the elaborately patterned carpet was crawling with spiders. The cleaning staff had gone home, so he found a broom and swept them out the door, as he heard the first guests arriving; he knew he would be blamed.

DREAM BACKGROUND AND MEANING

Stephen had ambitions to rise high in his company. Recently there had been complaints about events organized by his department, and he was held responsible. A major interstate awards ceremony was due to take place, and Stephen warned his staff that if anything went wrong, they would be in trouble. Floor dreams warn of basic details being missed that adversely affect the bigger picture.

INTERPRETATIONS AND FORTUNE-TELLING MEANINGS

★ Because floors represent basic aspects of life—food, shelter, comfort, etc.—if you dream you are cleaning or mending a floor, your money situation will improve and ventures will be successful.

★ A dirty or cluttered floor says you may have forgotten priorities.

★ If a floor is solid and well cared for, you have a good support system of friends, family, and colleagues.

★ If a floor is luxuriously carpeted, you are in a secure position career-wise and have established credibility.

★ If a floor has broken boards or feels unsafe, be certain that the support you are being offered is reliable.

★ If you dream you take the floor in a meeting or social event and people focus on you, this is a good chance to advance your career.

OUTCOME OF STEPHEN'S DREAM

Recalling the dream, Stephen went to the venue in advance of the awards ceremony. The floor had not been cleaned since the previous event. He cleaned it himself, realizing he had been too busy focusing on promotion to check vital details. When a floor is prominent in a dream, it alerts the dreamer to become more aware of checking that the groundwork is sound.

Flowers

Zara, thirty-five, dreamed she was disappointed when her husband, Jimmy, presented her with a bouquet of dried flowers on her birthday. She discovered a receipt for an enormous bouquet of cut flowers sent by her husband to his personal assistant. On the doorstep was a pot of growing hydrangeas someone had sent, which she planted in the garden. When she telephoned the florist, she was told she had ordered the hydrangeas as a birthday gift to herself.

DREAM BACKGROUND AND MEANING

Zara knew that her husband was having an affair with his personal assistant, the latest of many extramarital affairs he had had. But she also realized he would not leave her because she had major shares in the company and knew that his latest conquest would soon be replaced. Zara felt she was too young to stay in a loveless marriage in the vain hope that Jimmy might turn to her again. Dried flowers should be replaced by growing ones to restore self-love and move forward to a new life.

INTERPRETATIONS AND FORTUNE-TELLING MEANINGS

★ Flowers, especially roses (see p. 402), are the ultimate symbol of love and romance.

★ Dreaming of walking through a garden of colorful flowers says you will soon find romance or rekindle passion.

★ Receiving a dream bouquet from someone you do not know suggests that you may have a hidden admirer.

★ Dying flowers warn about a relationship or friendship that has run its course.

★ Artificial flowers advise against insincerity and those who flatter for personal advantage.

★ Flowers growing in pots predict slow-growing, lasting happiness, whereas cut flowers represent a show of affection lacking depth that will soon wilt.

OUTCOME OF ZARA'S DREAM

The dried flowers told Zara love was gone. In the dream she had replaced them with growing flowers ordered for herself. She bought Jimmy out of the company and transformed a lackluster business that had been allowed to drift by her Lothario husband. She is not looking for love. We should not rely on others to supply growing energies in our lives.

Flower Show

Pauline, sixty-four, dreamed she won first prize every year at the village floral display. But when she went into the greenhouse the day before the show, all the flowers had wilted. She could not bear the shame and so she traveled to a distant garden center and spent a fortune on their finest potted blooms. But as she was wheeling her cart, she met the village gossip, her major rival, who asked Pauline why she was buying flowers. Pauline abandoned her cart and fled.

DREAM BACKGROUND AND MEANING

Pauline was especially anxious because the annual flower show was approaching, and her flowers had not thrived. She was contemplating substituting ones from a well-known garden center twenty miles away. Flower-show dreams, whether or not the dreamer is interested in flowers, represent a chance to show talents and receive acclaim, but they can reflect an actual problem where the dreamer is focused on winning to the exclusion of everything else.

INTERPRETATIONS AND FORTUNE-TELLING MEANINGS

* If you dream that your entry wins in a flower show, you will be recognized for your efforts and achievements as a result of patience and effort.
* If you dream you are growing flowers for a show, accept that there may be no easy shortcuts to success.
* If you dream your flowers wilt and you cannot enter them in the show, your efforts may not have materialized as you hoped, but you should value what you did achieve for its own sake.
* If you are judging a flower show, people may seek to influence you for their own gain, as the symbol represents hidden pressure.
* If you dream the flower show is canceled, you may have been focusing on appearances rather than substance.

OUTCOME OF PAULINE'S DREAM

Pauline realized she had been concentrating on winning the annual flower show to the exclusion of enjoying her garden throughout the year. She started taking flowers to the local nursing home and teaching flower arranging. Flower shows, whatever they signify socially, at work, or in the community, often focus on impressing others, rather than enjoying beauty for its own sake.

Fly (Insect)

Bettina, twenty-five, dreamed she had prepared a buffet for her parents-in-law's anniversary, but someone had removed the lids too early. As it was a hot day, flies were swarming all over the food. She could not spray without tainting the food, and there was no time to prepare more. Bettina saw her sister-in-law, Gracey, laughing and realized Gracey had removed the covers.

DREAM BACKGROUND AND MEANING

Gracey had been the only younger-generation woman in the family before Bettina came along. Gracey resented Bettina, as Bettina had developed a close relationship with her new mother-in-law. As a professional chef, Bettina was asked to cater for family events, which Gracey used to do. A dream invasion of flies can be a warning of a malicious attack to spoil your efforts, usually due to jealousy.

INTERPRETATIONS AND FORTUNE-TELLING MEANINGS

* If you dream that flies are crawling on food, it's a forewarning that spiteful people will try to spoil a relationship, or difficult relations will sour a celebration.
* If you are surrounded by a swarm of flies, you have too many problems and irritations to deal with.
* A buzzing fly you cannot catch warns against open-ended invitations to relations, friends, or neighbors, who may be hard to persuade to leave.
* Dreaming of killing flies says you can and should remove persistent threats to your health and well-being.
* A fly disturbing you while you are driving says a journey may be disrupted by minor irritations.
* If you dream you find maggots and flies in a cupboard where you keep food, you may be feeling guilty about neglecting others. Accept that you cannot be everything to everyone.

OUTCOME OF BETTINA'S DREAM

Bettina understood Gracey's resentment. As there was a big celebration soon, Bettina asked Gracey to help her and made sure Gracey was given the credit. Slowly she brought Gracey around by making sure she never felt unappreciated. Letting a fly out through an open door or window in a dream can allow it to join the chain of nature, rather than being killed.

Flying

Debi, now forty-two, dreamed that she was a teenager flying straight upward, through the roof, into space among the stars, and she saw Earth far below. The dreams progressed to being chased by pursuers each night and escaping by launching herself into the air, flying wherever she wanted, and sometimes diving underwater, finding secret caverns.

DREAM BACKGROUND AND MEANING

Debi, a web designer living in central France, experienced regular flying dreams between ages eleven and eighteen that would take her wherever she wanted through a technique called "lucid dreaming," where the dreamer is aware of being in a dream (see "Lucid Dreaming: Awareness That You Are Dreaming," p. 12). Flying dreams are often linked with falling dreams, where the dreamer is able to save themselves by floating or flying.

INTERPRETATIONS AND FORTUNE-TELLING MEANINGS

* If you fly out of trouble in a dream, this gives you power in daily life to overcome fears and attacks.
* Flying dreams are associated with out-of-body experiences, in which the spirit or mind is able to leave the body in the dream state and travel to a chosen destination.
* Flying dreams are associated with freeing oneself from restrictions, a major step forward in connecting with spiritual realms.
* Children's flying dreams occur because the child has not developed the concept of what is logically possible and so can fly anywhere in dreams and, when they awaken, can describe with accuracy what they saw.
* With adolescents, teens, and twentysomethings, flying experiences may be linked with emerging sexual powers.
* The emergence or reemergence of flying dreams in adults reflects growing psychic powers, especially for extraterrestrial experiences.

OUTCOME OF DEBI'S DREAM

Debi's final flying dream came after a gap of many years, when she flew over the Acropolis in Athens. She saw the sun rising over the distant ruins. When the alarm clock went off, she was so disappointed to awake.

Since many flying dreams are triggered by escaping from danger, astral dreams are no longer so necessary and therefore rarely occur once earlier fears are overcome.

Fog, Mist

Tom, twenty-three, dreamed he was on an unfamiliar beach when suddenly thick sea fog came down. He could not stay on the beach, as the tide was coming in. Slowly, he found his way to the rope marking the steps to the top of the cliff. He cautiously climbed the steps, because on the other side of the steps was a steep drop. As Tom got nearer the top of the steps, the sun broke through and the last few steps were bathed in brilliant light.

DREAM BACKGROUND AND MEANING

Tom was an athlete who had experienced a serious leg injury. He had been offered a major operation with a 50 percent chance of success. If it went wrong, it would leave his leg immobilized. Without the operation, he could work as a coach but not return to competing, his childhood ambition.

Mist and fog dreams occur when the way ahead is not clear. All factors should be considered before proceeding.

INTERPRETATIONS AND FORTUNE-TELLING MEANINGS

* A dream of sudden or dense fog indicates conflicting emotions or information.
* If there are figures concealed in the mist, beware of deception and hidden rivals.
* If fog suddenly clears, go ahead with a planned seemingly risky choice.
* Fog that does not disperse indicates the need to check every stage in advance, as there are factors you do not yet know.
* If the fog is obscuring potential hazards, like a cliff edge, wait until you can see options clearly rather than rushing blindly ahead.
* If you dream you are driving through fog, collect all the available information, use your instincts, and, if necessary, ask for help in seeing the right way forward.

OUTCOME OF TOM'S DREAM

Before proceeding with the operation, Tom decided to seek a second opinion about a new technique. This technique proved a success, as indicated by the dream fog clearing, and by the fact that Tom was climbing the dream steps without difficulty.

Food Bank

Susan, thirty, dreamed she was selling ribbons in the streets with her small children, but no one was buying. She saw a charity soup kitchen. She was too proud to accept charity, as she had been a longshoreman's wife until her husband had been injured and dismissed. She saw a rich woman stepping out of her carriage who dropped her purse. Susan handed it back, and the woman bought all her ribbons.

DREAM BACKGROUND AND MEANING

Susan, a single mother, had been hit by hard economic times. She had gone for the first time to a food bank. But pride stopped her from entering. Food-bank dreams are common in difficult times, raising unconscious issues about accepting charity for people who had until then been independent.

INTERPRETATIONS AND FORTUNE-TELLING MEANINGS

★ Obtaining resources from a food bank can evoke feelings of shame or relief, to be considered logically upon waking.

★ Dreaming of you or your children being hungry reveals fears of not being able to provide for loved ones.

★ If you dream of stealing food, you may be seeking a quick fix that involves risk when normal avenues are closed.

★ If you dream of working in a food bank, you may be asked to assume responsibility for family members or friends fallen on hard times.

★ If you dream of walking past a food-bank box without donating, you should resolve personal worries before expending spare energy and resources to help others.

★ If you are struggling financially and dream of food banks, your unconscious radar may alert you to other sources of help in the dream, which you had not noticed before.

OUTCOME OF SUSAN'S DREAM

Susan swallowed her pride and received a warm welcome. The organization was advertising for a paid worker to negotiate with supermarkets for surplus food. Susan got the job. Food-bank dreams represent the need to seek practical as well as economic aid beyond the usual resources.

Fool's Gold

Jim, thirty-eight, dreamed he was in a cave whose black walls were glistening with what he believed were pure gold flakes. He purchased the rights at an incredibly low price to take whatever he could carry. Jim knew he would never need to work again. He was puzzled because flakes of gold were cascading off the crumbling black rock, but he put them in his sack, sure he could separate them later.

DREAM BACKGROUND AND MEANING

Jim's investments in gold, recommended by his father, were not making spectacular gains. A friend suggested that he invest in cryptocurrencies. His father advised caution, but Jim went ahead anyway. Pyrite, also called iron sulfide, resembles gold but has far less value, and so dreams of this "fool's gold" warn to exercise caution.

INTERPRETATIONS AND FORTUNE-TELLING MEANINGS

★ Pyrite was regarded as a magick fire stone from Paleolithic times on, because it emitted sparks and was found near real gold. It suggests that the dreamer is being dazzled by untried and untested promises of instant wealth.

★ If in a dream you are sold a bag of what you are told is pure gold, ensure that the seller in your waking life does not prove unreliable or dishonest.

★ If you are holding fool's gold and it crumbles or flakes, you may be seduced into temptation in love for instant thrills.

★ If you dream you can afford only fool's gold, make the most of the positive aspects of what you can manage, rather than overextending yourself financially.

★ If in your dream you have doubts about whether you are being given fool's gold or real gold, do nothing until you are certain.

★ If you dream you are certain you have real gold, you have made an investment or business decision that will prove profitable.

OUTCOME OF JIM'S DREAM

After his initial euphoria, Jim discovered hazards with cryptocurrencies. A small quantity of what is genuine may prove to be of greater value than false excess, whether in a relationship, finance, or business.

Forgery

Josie, fifty-five, dreamed that she was making a perfect copy of an old original painting when the angry original artist stormed in, demanding to know why she was stealing his work. She tried to explain that she had to earn her living and her own paintings were not good enough to sell. The painter said she was a disgrace to the profession and put a palette knife through the picture she was forging.

DREAM BACKGROUND AND MEANING

Josie was very good at copying less-well-known paintings and had found an agency that specialized in selling them. But she was always worried that she would be exposed as a forger. Forgery dreams are fraught with doubt, whether fear of being tricked or of deceiving others by presenting a false persona to the world.

INTERPRETATIONS AND FORTUNE-TELLING MEANINGS

* If in your dream you are sold a forgery, someone close to you is deceiving you.
* If you are forging money, you may feel unable to ask for your true value for fear of rejection.
* If you dream that you recognize a painting or antique as forged but no one will believe you, trust your own judgment and do not fall for others' illusions.
* If you dream a new friend or colleague has an obviously forged document or check written out to themselves and signed by you, do not trust them with your money or your heart.
* If you dream you are creating fake qualifications in your career, you may be worried about being inadequate at your job or not as good as others.
* If you dream you are trying to pass a forgery off as the genuine article, you may doubt your abilities to succeed in your own right.

OUTCOME OF JOSIE'S DREAM

After the dream, Josie felt guilty, as she feared that the spirit of the artist had really visited her. Her forgeries were not as good as usual, and the agency told her they had found an advanced technological method of creating forgeries. Forgeries in any area of life always fall short of the original and can leave the forger feeling they have sacrificed their unique identity.

Former Home

Gwen, forty-five, constantly dreamed she was in the house she had left ten years ago. Everything was exactly as it had been. She was painting the house from top to bottom with her best friend as a surprise for her husband. But he walked in and told her they were moving. She woke protesting that this was her home.

DREAM BACKGROUND AND MEANING

Gwen was living in a modern luxury home, which her husband had chosen after his promotion, across the country from her former home. Even after ten years she hated the new neighborhood. She had brought her family up in an old, rambling, shabby house she still called home. Dreams often take us back to the place we consider home.

INTERPRETATIONS AND FORTUNE-TELLING MEANINGS

* If your dreams are set in a former home, your unconscious is detecting a lack in your present domestic circumstances, whether it is rooted in the actual home, a relationship, or an inner discontentment.
* If you never dream about your present home, you may not harmonize with its energies.
* If you dream you are sitting among packing cases in your former home and refuse to move, you may not have mentally unpacked in your new home.
* If you dream of your children being young and happy in a former home, you may be feeling that your present life is passing you by.
* If you dream of your happy former home when it was not happy, the restlessness may need resolving elsewhere in your life.

OUTCOME OF GWEN'S DREAM

Gwen decided that now that the children were older and her husband was away traveling most of the year, it was time she created a life of her own. She realized she and her husband had outgrown each other, and she returned to the area she considered home. Dreams are a good way of alerting us to our inner feelings and where we really feel at home.

Fortune-Teller

Lorraine, forty-six, was sitting in a darkened fortune-teller's booth at the end of the pier. The fortune-teller was pulling out tarot cards at great speed. She told Lorraine she was going to leave her husband for a man in the office and that they would start a business together. Lorraine was astounded. It was as if the fortune-teller was seeing into her mind.

DREAM BACKGROUND AND MEANING

Lorraine was unhappily married. The man in the office had not asked her out, but she felt he would once she left her husband. Lorraine had tried different fortune-tellers, and all said she should leave her husband. Now she planned on consulting the fortune-teller on the pier. Fortune-telling dreams often tell the dreamer what they want to hear, and it becomes a self-fulfilling prophecy, giving the dreamer permission to take the desired action.

INTERPRETATIONS AND FORTUNE-TELLING MEANINGS

★ If the fortune-teller seems familiar in the dream, your own wise unconscious mind may be advising you in the guise of a fortune-teller.

★ If the fortune-teller reveals images in a crystal ball, the messages will help you to see the best future path ahead if you note what they mean to you.

★ If the fortune-teller in the dream picks only bad cards, this is not an omen of disaster, rather a reflection of your own buried fears.

★ If the fortune-teller predicts major changes, these are options you are considering for which you are seeking permission.

★ If you dream you are telling fortunes for someone you know, beware of making decisions for them and being blamed if they go wrong.

OUTCOME OF LORRAINE'S DREAM

The fortune-teller on the pier was closed. Lorraine's sister said Lorraine should try to fix her marriage because the great love and future business partner might in fact be her present husband. If not, only she could decide whether to leave him. Even the best fortune-teller, in dreams or in actuality, ultimately offers an opt-out clause of matters only the dreamer should solve.

Fostering Children

Celeste, fifty, dreamed her big house was filled with laughing children, sitting around the table with freshly baked bread and homemade lemonade. Then the children started arguing and fighting and there was broken crockery and glass all over the floor. Celeste wished they would go away. She woke to the peace of a silent house.

DREAM BACKGROUND AND MEANING

Celeste's children had left home and were not in any hurry to have children themselves. Bringing them up had been the happiest years of her life. Recently, she had seen an appeal for fostering children. Her friends said she should enjoy her child-free years. Fostering dreams rehearse challenges and doubts we may have if we are viewing the experience through rose-tinted glasses or as an antidote to an empty nest.

INTERPRETATIONS AND FORTUNE-TELLING MEANINGS

★ If you dream you are playing with a child belonging to one of your own children, this is a happy omen for future grandchildren.

★ If you see a relative's or friend's child staying with you in a dream, you may be asked to help if there are imminent problems or illness in their home.

★ If you see in the dream foster children being defiant as well as appreciative, be realistic about your own stores of patience and compassion for helping sometimes-distressed children to settle.

★ If you dream you are crying when a child leaves, you may get very attached and consider long-term fostering or adoption rather than short-term care.

★ If you keep seeing the same child in a dream and you have applied to foster someone, this child may in time become part of your family (see "Bureaucracy," p. 75).

OUTCOME OF CELESTE'S DREAM

Despite the dream, Celeste went on a course for prospective foster parents and welcomed three siblings for six months. Though the experience was rewarding, she realized that she and her husband were not ready to plunge back into 24/7 care. Celeste is taking a teacher's assistant course at the local school. Fostering dreams can link to unfulfilled personal needs, but if they have a feel-good factor they may offer reassurance that the welcome you provide will more than be repaid.

Fountain

Rani, twenty-two, dreamed she was standing by a public fountain, throwing coins and making wishes, with her parents and sister there with her. She saw Paul, the man she loved, approaching. She took his hands and they danced in the fountain. Soaked through, Rani threw off her sari. Her mother shouted that her daughter was dishonoring the family and they must leave at once. But Rani continued to dance in the fountain with her love, and the family left angrily without her.

DREAM BACKGROUND AND MEANING

Rani was in love, but her new partner belonged to a different religion and culture than hers. Only recently had her secret been discovered by her sister, who told their very traditional family, which was arranging a marriage for her back in India. Rani had been forbidden to see Paul. Rani knew that the consequences of being with Paul meant exclusion from her family and community. Splashing in a fountain heralds the removal of inhibitions, especially regarding love.

INTERPRETATIONS AND FORTUNE-TELLING MEANINGS

* Dreaming of a clear fountain denotes growing or continuing good health, happiness, and prosperity.
* A cloudy or neglected fountain says you need to pay attention to your own needs, especially physical ones, and acknowledge, not repress, your true emotions.
* A dried-up fountain warns that a relationship or situation has run its course and will require huge effort to revive it.
* A fountain filled with coins represents success in creative ventures and the fulfillment of wishes.
* A dream of an overflowing fountain in a public place represents the consequences of revealing true feelings as the price to be paid for living authentically.
* A dream of a large ornamental fountain with fish indicates fertility and happy marriage.

OUTCOME OF RANI'S DREAM

Rani realized she had to risk the disapproval of her family if she was to find happiness in love, and she chose the relationship. Powerful love and sexual attraction underpin many fountain dreams and, if these feelings are secret, they will soon be revealed.

Fox

Tessa, forty-five, dreamed of a beautiful silver fox being chased by a pack of dogs. She opened the door, let it in, and the dogs howled and scratched outside but eventually went away. Then the room was filled with wild animals of rainbow colors that swirled around and then disappeared with her silver fox.

DREAM BACKGROUND AND MEANING

Tessa had taken a year's sabbatical to concentrate on her artwork. But she had lost all the inspiration she had had as a hungry young student. Now she at last had the desired time to concentrate on her art but had nothing she wanted to paint. In some Indian creation stories, Silver Fox made the universe out of clay and danced and sang the world into being, helped by Coyote. Silver Fox awakens creativity if life has become too predictable.

INTERPRETATIONS AND FORTUNE-TELLING MEANINGS

* If a fox appears in your dreams, you need to question the status quo and discover viable alternatives if your thinking is becoming circular.
* If you are the fox, you will survive a present crisis but may need to be more single-minded and self-focused.
* If you dream of a vixen with her cubs, family matters will take center stage, and it is important to stay united.
* If you dream a fox is slaughtering chickens, beware of someone who is a ruthless influence in your life who gains access to your heart through flattery. Use subtlety and tact to persuade others to your point of view rather than direct confrontation.

OUTCOME OF TESSA'S DREAM

After the dream, Tessa got out her old acrylic paints and created beautiful dancing animals in rainbow colors creating the world and rediscovered her enthusiasm and originality.

Fox in Celtic mythology showed the way into the Otherworld of light and beauty, and fox dreams can likewise restore magick where comfort has taken away the edge of possibility.

Fracture

Paolo, twenty-eight, dreamed he was on the ski slopes before anyone, practicing his jumps. He laughed at his instructor, who told him to wait until the slopes had been assessed. Paolo decided to go off first and challenge himself. He set off confidently, but there was an unusual amount of sheer ice. As he landed, his leg cracked and he felt a terrible pain. He knew it was the end of his chances, maybe forever.

DREAM BACKGROUND AND MEANING

Paolo was planning to gain a place on the Olympic ski team. He knew that he was taking risks, but by the next Olympics he feared younger, fitter guys would be competing against him. Fracture dreams represent interruptions to plans, not necessarily through actual injuries. However, if the dreamer is knowingly taking physical risks, damaging himself is a possibility.

INTERPRETATIONS AND FORTUNE-TELLING MEANINGS

- ✶ To dream of a fractured leg or ankle talks about a setback in plans to move forward actually or in business and finance.
- ✶ To dream of a fractured arm or wrist warns of a mis-understanding in a relationship or communication unless care is taken.
- ✶ A dream of a partial or hairline fracture says it is not too late to pull back if you or a partner is taking undue financial risks or neglecting your safety and well-being, though the dream is not directly predictive.
- ✶ If a relationship is fractured, it may need patience and dedication to mend, depending on the degree of the dream fracture.
- ✶ If you are dreaming of a fractured skull, it may be necessary for a major rethink of your life direction, especially if others have been unwisely influential.

OUTCOME OF PAOLO'S DREAM

The dream was so vivid that it remained with Paolo all morning, which made him take his coach seriously. The area he skied in the dream had suffered a rockfall overnight, covered by fresh snow, and would have been hazardous. Fracture dreams can pick up unconscious dangers around the dreamer. If you dream of your child suffering a fracture, take extra precautions the following day.

Framed Photos

Edwina, fifty-six, had recurring dreams in which, as she looked at a photo of herself and her husband, Geoff, on their wedding day, which was set in an ornamental gold frame, the picture changed to Geoff and his first wife at their wedding. This lasted just a few seconds before her own wedding photo reappeared.

DREAM BACKGROUND AND MEANING

Edwina had been happily married to Geoff for three years. He had been widowed five years earlier. She had never been married before, and she knew that he and his first wife had not been happy. Yet even today there were photos of his first wife all around the home, and Geoff spoke of her as if she had been a saint. Picture frames can hold a person frozen perpetually in an idealized form, and changing images can represent sometimes-justifiable resentment.

INTERPRETATIONS AND FORTUNE-TELLING MEANINGS

- ✶ If you dream that the image within a photo frame changes to someone from the past, there may be unresolved issues where the person's memory intrudes on a present relationship.
- ✶ If a picture frame is surrounded by roses and hearts in the dream, the person connected to the picture may be overidealizing the character in the picture.
- ✶ If you dream of a picture frame containing the photo of a deceased relative you were estranged from, express regret and move on.
- ✶ If a picture frame contains a misty moving picture, a new love or friend is coming soon.
- ✶ If you see a future event framed, such as your wedding or the birth of a baby, this predicts a happy situation before too long.

OUTCOME OF EDWINA'S DREAM

After the dream, Edwina told Geoff how she sometimes felt second best to his first wife. He admitted he felt guilty that he had not done more to make their relationship work. He kept just one picture on display and put the rest away. Picture frames mark a point in time that sometimes needs to be replaced with present images, marking a new phase of life.

Fraud, Scam

Gerry, seventy-four, dreamed he was opening his safe and giving a smartly dressed man all the money inside along with his wife's jewelry, because the man said that kind of safe was being targeted for thefts in the area. When the man drove off, Gerry worried that he should not have handed everything over, as he did not even have a receipt. He woke panicking but, upon checking, the contents of the safe were untouched.

DREAM BACKGROUND AND MEANING

Gerry had been anxious that his pension fund was not performing well, and he had seen an advertisement online with promising returns. A reassuring financial adviser had been to visit, and Gerry was impressed with how much money he would gain. But after the dream, Gerry started to have doubts that it might be too good to be true. Fraud dreams act as an automatic radar to alert us when we should check before acting.

INTERPRETATIONS AND FORTUNE-TELLING MEANINGS

★ If a fraud dream seems urgent and stays with you after waking, this is a psychic dream and should be taken seriously.

★ If someone you do not know well is stealing money in your dream, beware of sharing financial information.

★ If you dream of being given a pile of money and you have been offered a get-rich-quick scheme, check the details before committing.

★ If you dream you are cheated in a workplace sweepstakes or lottery, you may be feeling victimized and passed over for a raise or promotion.

★ If you are planning a major scam in the dream, you may have a chance to make a lot of money quickly, but it may involve risks of being caught.

OUTCOME OF GERRY'S DREAM

Gerry phoned his bank and discovered he was about to hand all his money over to a con man. Scam dreams can pick up doubts in our subconscious about the validity of a financial transaction.

Freeway, Highway

Christopher, thirty-five, dreamed he was commuting down a crowded freeway and saw the exit to Happy Valley, which he had driven past a hundred times. On impulse he followed the small road to a deep green valley with a river running through it. Removing his socks and shoes, he paddled in the shallows as he had as a child and decided this was where he was meant to be. Christopher woke sensing imminent change.

DREAM BACKGROUND AND MEANING

Christopher traveled along the freeway so frequently he only saw the road ahead. He had been offered a promotion and a higher salary but would be away from his family more than he'd like. He increasingly felt like a stranger to his wife and children. If you turn off the freeway to take a quieter route, you may need to slow your life down so that you do not miss what is worthwhile.

INTERPRETATIONS AND FORTUNE-TELLING MEANINGS

★ If a dream freeway journey is swift and uneventful, the path through life will be unimpeded, but maybe unfulfilling.

★ If the freeway is blocked by an accident, the dreamer's travel plans or progress in a venture will be temporarily delayed by unpredicted circumstances.

★ If you dream you are being consistently overtaken by others going faster, you may be frustrated by a lack of progress due to others' unhelpfulness.

★ If you dream you are being forced to drive faster than you want by a truck close behind, you may feel pressured into decisions or actions before you are ready.

★ If you miss the freeway entrance or exit, deep down you may be unsure that the way through life you are taking is correct.

OUTCOME OF CHRISTOPHER'S DREAM

Christopher was no longer enjoying traveling the narrow corridor that took him away from the people he wanted to spend his time with. He took his family to Happy Valley, saw a leisure business for sale, and moved, accepting a huge salary cut but a far richer quality of life. Freeways are valuable for reaching from A to B quickly, but become restrictive if B is not the right destination for happiness.

Freezer

Zachary, forty-five, dreamed he was trapped in a walk-in freezer in his restaurant at closing time. The chef had turned the lights and alarm system off, thinking she was the last to leave. Zachary's smartphone would not work inside the freezer. He was panicking. Suddenly he heard the outside door of the restaurant opening and he shouted as loud as he could. The chef had returned because she had forgotten her purse and so released him.

DREAM BACKGROUND AND MEANING

Zachary, who owned the restaurant, had been warned by staff several times that the freezer lock and alarm were malfunctioning. Because he had been very busy as the restaurant was packed after a review in a national foodie journal, he had delayed fixing it. Freezer dreams can represent delaying things that should be dealt with urgently, and they can act as a reminder of possible dire consequences if ignored.

INTERPRETATIONS AND FORTUNE-TELLING MEANINGS

★ A dream of a full freezer suggests you have considerable stored potential to be used when the time is right.

★ A freezer filled with party food says you will be asked to organize a celebration or receive an anticipated invitation to one.

★ An empty freezer reveals that you have no more to offer to an overdemanding person emotionally, or indicates a situation that has taken all your reserves.

★ A freezer that has defrosted or is defrosting speaks of a potentially wasted journey or enterprise that is not worth repeating.

★ An overheating freezer expresses attempts to revive or generate enthusiasm or love where feelings have cooled.

OUTCOME OF ZACHARY'S DREAM

As a result of the dream, Zachary had the freezer alarm and lock fixed the next day. Our subconscious can predict a likely outcome of inaction in a freezer dream. This may have been a premonitory dream, as Zachary found himself shut in the freezer late at night a few days after the repair, but was able to use the fixed emergency release button.

Freight, Cargo

Duncan, forty-five, dreamed he and his new wife, Penny, were moving and shipping their possessions to a new location thousands of miles away. His father insisted on arranging it for a cheap price, but the container ship was not seaworthy. The containers with all their possessions were washed up on a remote beach after the ship hit rocks and broke up.

DREAM BACKGROUND AND MEANING

Prior to Duncan's recent marriage, his father had run Duncan's life. Penny was highly independent, and when Duncan was offered a job overseas she was very unhappy that his father was coming to choose a house for them. She insisted that his father could come for vacations, but that was all. Transporting-freight dreams can have deep-seated significance of what is of emotional value for the future and what should be consigned to the past.

INTERPRETATIONS AND FORTUNE-TELLING MEANINGS

★ To dream you are responsible for transporting unwanted freight suggests carrying heavy burdens from the past.

★ If you dream the cargo is successfully delivered and sold, you have valuable experiences and assets that will bring financial gain.

★ Riding or driving a freight train suggests temporarily assuming extra responsibilities to bring about a positive life change.

★ Carrying freight by water talks about emotional burdens to be lifted.

★ Carrying freight by air suggests expansion and profit through international and/or online transactions.

★ If freight is spilled or broken in transit, there may be casualties because of carelessness. Only involve yourself in business or financial transactions with those who are 100 percent reliable.

OUTCOME OF DUNCAN'S DREAM

Duncan decided to sell their present home fully furnished and travel light. Penny told her father-in-law they were taking virtually nothing and for a time would move around until they found the right home. Annoyed, he said that in that case he would not come at all. Freight can represent assets and what has been accumulated. However, if in the dream it represents a millstone, the dream may be advocating leaving the past behind.

Future

Philippa, forty, dreamed she was at her birthday party with banners with her name and "Congratulations for being seventy-five years young" written on them. She was surrounded by her siblings, her children, who in the dream were adults, her grandchildren, and an as-yet-unborn great-grandchild. Philippa was crying with happiness.

DREAM BACKGROUND AND MEANING

Philippa constantly worried about her health since she was a single parent with five young children. There were no relatives to care for them if anything happened to her. Dreams of the future can be reassuring if we are worried about our mortality.

INTERPRETATIONS AND FORTUNE-TELLING MEANINGS

★ If you see yourself in the future achieving in a particular profession, becoming famous, or having a successful business, this reveals what is possible if you persist now.

★ If you dream of yourself well and healthy as a much older person or with grandchildren and great-grandchildren, this can allay fears of dying young.

★ If you see yourself incapacitated in the future, this is not a definite prediction but suggests you should take care of yourself and stay fit to avoid future problems.

★ If you dream of your wedding and your partner is hazy, this is because you have not yet met them.

★ If you see your future children in the dream, this can be immensely reassuring if you are trying for a baby.

★ If you see a future you do not like, the future is not fixed and you can start making changes, whether in career or relationships, to alter that future.

OUTCOME OF PHILIPPA'S DREAM

Philippa was immensely reassured to see herself at seventy-five, as by then her children would all be adults. While seeing ourselves at a certain age does not predict that that is when we will die, it shows we have the potential to reach that age and beyond. Dreams of the future show what is possible but not certain and can offer reassurance if we are constantly worrying.

Future Lives

Dave, seventy, dreamed of sitting on a slow-moving train, seeing snapshots of his next lifetime passing by. In this future world he progressed from a small child into an old man. He married his twin soul, who he could not be with in this lifetime.

DREAM BACKGROUND AND MEANING

Dave had been feeling insecure, as several of his contemporaries had recently died. He did not believe in an afterlife, but found it hard to accept that he would just cease to be. Dreaming of a future lifetime can reassure the dreamer that life does go on.

INTERPRETATIONS AND FORTUNE-TELLING MEANINGS

★ If you glimpse a remarkably ordinary, contented future life in a dream, there is hope that in that life there will be no major dramas but a gradual evolution through wisdom acquired in the present life.

★ If you dream of someone who died young in this lifetime growing fit and healthy in the next lifetime, this offers consolation for a seemingly senseless loss.

★ If you dream of reconciliation in the next life with someone from whom you are estranged, there may be hope in this life for building bridges.

★ If you dream of being with your true twin soul in the next lifetime, try bringing the opportunity forward into this life.

★ If you dream of a useful invention in the next life, the foreknowledge can perhaps be helpful for humanity.

OUTCOME OF DAVE'S DREAM

Because the dream was remarkably ordinary in its glimpses of future worlds, it gave Dave reassurance that he could transfer his essential self to the next life, sharing his acquired wisdom with descendants yet unborn. Future-life dreams, especially where they show the development of a talent or being with someone you truly love, can kick-start a new determination to make the most of this lifetime, especially if you do not believe in heaven (see "Future," opposite).

Gallery

Martin, twenty-five, dreamed he was in a medieval world, playing the lute in the minstrels' gallery above the big hall where a family was dining. He knew he was where he belonged.

DREAM BACKGROUND AND MEANING

Martin had applied for a job in a city art gallery but had not told his parents, as they expected him to work on the family horse-breeding ranch. Martin had studied art at college, which the family saw as just a phase, although he had already sold several horse-themed pictures. Both art galleries and minstrels' galleries (balconies for musicians) represent an alternative perspective on life.

INTERPRETATIONS AND FORTUNE-TELLING MEANINGS

★ If you dream others are admiring your paintings in a gallery, even if you are not an artist in everyday life, your creative and communicative abilities will gain recognition or bring profit.

★ If you dream you are viewing famous old paintings, you may regret a lost opportunity, but it is still not too late.

★ If you are bored walking around an art gallery, you are not in tune with your current lifestyle but for now should go along with the status quo.

★ If you are looking down from a minstrels' gallery, this may be a past-life memory and suggests you are detached from the mainstream of events.

★ If you are hiding in a minstrels' gallery, you may feel unwilling or unable to express your opinion or true feelings.

★ If you fall or are pushed from a gallery, beware of those who resent your rise to success.

OUTCOME OF MARTIN'S DREAM

Martin told his parents of his plans to leave. They were devastated. They offered to convert the top of the house so he could have his own studio. He agreed to stay if he could spend part of his day painting. His horse pictures became well known in the locality. To dream of any gallery indicates the widening and raising of the dreamer's perspectives: if an art gallery, different life views; if a minstrels' gallery in a home or public building, stepping outside the box.

Galley Slave

Drew, forty-five, often dreamed he was a galley slave, captured by the Romans on the south coast of England. He was bitter because he had been a farmer and knew he could die, from either exhaustion or floggings, without ever walking his land again. He was unchained for a few minutes when they arrived on English soil and he ran. He was free.

DREAM BACKGROUND AND MEANING

Drew was trapped by his loveless marriage; his mortgage on a home he detested, far away from his childhood home on his grandfather's farm; and a data-processing job where he worked from morning till night. His grandfather had died and Drew wanted to revive the dilapidated farm. But his wife insisted they sell the land to move to a big house in a prestigious suburb. Maybe a past-life dream or memory, a galley-slave dream expresses the frustration of being trapped.

INTERPRETATIONS AND FORTUNE-TELLING MEANINGS

★ Dreaming of being a galley slave reflects being unwillingly committed to an unsatisfactory lifestyle.

★ If you are captured in the dream, you may have been led by love or guilt to make long-term sacrifices.

★ If you escape from the galleys in your dream, look for an opportunity to free yourself from what is stifling you.

★ If you are a galley master in the dream, you may be pressured to increase production by unethical means to satisfy the demands of a ruthless organization.

★ If you are rowing in harmony with others, pressures will ease until you can change things or complete your obligations.

★ If you are being punished in the dream for not rowing fast enough, others are unfairly driving you to the point of burnout.

OUTCOME OF DREW'S DREAM

Drew's wife refused to move to the farm. He went anyway, and now the farm is flourishing through his hard work. Galley-slave dreams often reflect that the dreamer has arrived at a breaking point and is prepared to risk all to escape an unsatisfactory lifestyle.

Gambling

Maureen, fifty-four, dreamed she was greeted like royalty as she entered an exotic casino with wild animals in gilded cages high above the gaming floor. She was given a pile of gambling chips for free. Time after time she won. Suddenly the wild animals escaped and the gamblers and croupiers ran screaming to the exits. Maureen carried what she could of her winnings, but tripped and saw a leopard standing over her, snarling.

DREAM BACKGROUND AND MEANING

Maureen was a compulsive online gambler. Unknown to her husband, she had borrowed against the house to pay her debts and was missing loan payments. Maureen believed a jackpot win would put everything right. Gambling dreams are about assessing the wisdom of taking risks in finances, relationships, or speculation.

INTERPRETATIONS AND FORTUNE-TELLING MEANINGS

* Dreaming of an exotic casino suggests you are craving more excitement and glamor in your life.
* A seedy gambling den, playing with menacing gamblers, or the presence of wild animals in cages warns that you may lose a great deal through trusting unreliable sources.
* A dream of betting on horses or dogs or on a baseball or soccer team and winning says following your hunches in your daily life may bring advantage.
* If winning numbers are given in a dream by a deceased relative, use those numbers when you feel lucky.
* If you dream you are presented with a huge check at a lottery awards ceremony, good luck is coming your way, maybe through a moneymaking idea.
* If a croupier or well-dressed gamblers in a card game are encouraging you to vastly up your stakes, beware of a get-rich-quick scheme you may be offered.

OUTCOME OF MAUREEN'S DREAM

Maureen realized she was risking the family home with her addiction, confided in her husband, and has joined Gamblers Anonymous. Most gambling dreams are very glamorous but may have a frightening ending, casting doubts on your own perhaps excessive reliance on lucky breaks in life.

Games

In his dream, Troy, eighteen, was in the batter's box with everyone watching, and his father, dressed in a full college baseball uniform, was pitching the baseball hard at him. Troy missed, but his father kept hurtling balls toward him, becoming angry when Troy failed to hit a single one. Humiliated by the laughter and jeers, Troy ran off the field, pursued by his furious father.

DREAM BACKGROUND AND MEANING

Troy was going to attend his father's old college but felt under pressure because his father had won a baseball scholarship, whereas Troy had little interest in sports. People still talked about his father's sporting achievements. Troy feared he would be judged against his father's sporting abilities. Though he had been offered a prestigious literature scholarship, he was contemplating pulling out. Games in dreams where you are on trial to succeed can reflect valid fears, especially for someone who is not naturally competitive.

INTERPRETATIONS AND FORTUNE-TELLING MEANINGS

* Dreams of playing ball or team games of any kind suggest a harmony in your dealings with others.
* If you dream that physically active games are giving you pleasure, it is an indication of good or rapidly improving health.
* Dreaming of unduly competitive games, or ones where you are losing badly or keep forgetting the rules, reveals pressures to conform or to succeed.
* Playing board games can indicate that there will be a settled period in your life if there has been chaos.
* Dreaming of playing alone says you need more personal space if you are happy in the dream.
* If you dream you are excluded from the games of others or never picked for teams, it suggests that someone is making you feel unwanted or inferior.

OUTCOME OF TROY'S DREAM

Troy decided to go to another college, rather than live in his father's shadow or try to be what he was not. His father was disappointed, but Troy flourished and even occasionally played baseball for fun.

Gaming Characters

Benjamin, twenty-two, dreamed he was the Avenger character in his favorite video game, holding the Sword of Destiny. He was facing his new, bullying manager, who appeared in the game as a hideous little troll, slashing at everyone's legs with his Dagger of Doom. Benjamin stood firm and with his sword drove the troll into the deepest, darkest forest, never to be seen again.

DREAM BACKGROUND AND MEANING

Benjamin's former supportive manager had recently retired, and the new manager, who everyone thought resembled a malevolent troll, was controlling and extremely lazy. He bullied Benjamin, who was a gentle giant and towered over his boss. Though Benjamin loved his job, he was contemplating quitting. Benjamin was an avid gamer. Gaming dreams, which recur in frequent game players, encourage the dreaming mind to cast up strategies for dealing with everyday opportunities and challenges.

INTERPRETATIONS AND FORTUNE-TELLING MEANINGS

★ If you dream of being a character in a game, note which strengths the character possesses that would be helpful in daily life.

★ If the character you represent is one of the superheroes or superheroines, see how adopting their name mentally would increase your power and confidence.

★ If you defeat a real-life rival or bully, who is also a character in the game, the dream suggests ways of overcoming negativity in the waking world.

★ If you are controlling the game in the dream but are not part of it, you have more power over an ongoing situation than you realize.

★ If you lose the dream game, you may need to build up more confidence and expertise to fulfill an ambition in the daily world. For now, use delaying tactics.

OUTCOME OF BENJAMIN'S DREAM

At work the next day, Benjamin imagined he was an Avenger with his Sword of Destiny. He felt much more confident dealing with the manager, who sensed a change in Benjamin and backed off. Gaming dreams are an excellent way of rehearsing how to overcome problems. Only when almost all dreams are about gaming should the dreamer spend more time in the everyday world.

Gardens

Christian, thirty-seven, was dreaming of his garden high up on the Tablelands near Cairns in the northeast tropics of Australia. His cart was ready, loaded with the produce he had grown for the daily markets. But his wife, Steph, was not there, and without her the garden seemed empty. He noticed herbs, Steph's special interest, sprouting up among his vegetables. Instead of digging them up as weeds, he transferred them to an area he had not yet planted and they instantly grew.

DREAM BACKGROUND AND MEANING

Christian wanted to transform the large overgrown garden of their new home into vegetable patches and tropical fruit trees and gradually buy up the land around to become totally self-sufficient. But his wife wanted to grow beautiful flowers and indigenous herbs to start a healing business, and neither would give way. A garden marks your personal expression of your boundaries with others, and its size and wildness or orderly nature represent growing your life plans, which may need compromise.

INTERPRETATIONS AND FORTUNE-TELLING MEANINGS

★ If you dream that a garden is full of vegetables and fruit, you will become prosperous through practical endeavors in any area of life.

★ A well-tended formal flower or herb garden suggests fulfillment within a structured environment and the blossoming of creative or spiritual ventures.

★ A dream of a neglected garden says you should care for yourself more and ask the help of a loved one to restore order in your world.

★ A barren garden advises escape from negative influences that constrain your growth and happiness in whatever area of life.

★ Walking in a walled garden suggests romance growing into passion if one partner is hesitant to express themself sexually.

OUTCOME OF CHRISTIAN'S DREAM

Christian realized that both he and his wife could have their own businesses by sharing the land. His wife grew her herbs and flowers, and they had the pleasure of working together and setting up their own stalls in the markets. A garden in a dream can show ways that, given flexibility, two people can grow their dreams and lifestyles side by side.

Gargoyles

Christopher, twenty-one, studying in Oxford, United Kingdom, frequently dreamed that one of the hideous winged stone gargoyles set on the roof of the Gothic church right opposite his window waited until he left for lectures and flew after him. Blackness would whirl, and Christopher would fight to wake up, only to find that the gargoyle had driven him inside the church where, long ago, he was a priest.

DREAM BACKGROUND AND MEANING

Christopher had always been fascinated by gargoyles. He was studying architecture but hated his course, as his real interest was the philosophy of mortality and the battle between good and evil. He often found himself in the gargoyle church, trying to make sense of his life. Gargoyles, though appearing malevolent, were intended to protect buildings from demons and evil spirits as well as, more practically, to act as waterspouts. Gargoyle dreams occur to spiritual people at times when life lacks meaning or is superficial.

INTERPRETATIONS AND FORTUNE-TELLING MEANINGS

★ If you dream of gargoyles, you may have strong, deep spiritual or religious connections with earlier centuries. Gargoyles date back to Greco-Roman times.

★ If you dream you are being chased by a flying gargoyle, you may be running away from making significant choices.

★ If in your dream a gargoyle guides you into a religious or spiritual building, you may be attracted to the occult or to a traditional religion.

★ If rain is pouring from the mouths of a row of gargoyles, you have deep unacknowledged needs for a life with meaning and will not be happy till you recognize this.

★ If you dream you are carving gargoyles on an old building, you are ready to move toward taking tangible steps to follow your true destiny.

OUTCOME OF CHRISTOPHER'S DREAM

Christopher realized that his gargoyle dreams were guiding him to a life in the church, and he has started training as a priest. Gargoyle dreams occur in sensitive people who may confront the big issues of life at a relatively early age.

Garlands

Theo, twenty-one, dreamed he was riding in a chariot, covered with garlands and wearing a laurel leaf victory garland. He had been promised a place in the Senate, but the victory was hollow as Theo had not been allowed to bring his Celtic wife to Rome, and instead was pledged to a senator's daughter he did not love. He took off the garlands and said he would live on his own terms.

DREAM BACKGROUND AND MEANING

Theo had been offered a prestigious position with a top law firm a thousand miles away, thereby fulfilling his parents' ambitions for him. He was in love with a local girl, but his parents insisted he marry a woman whose wealthy family he had known from childhood and whose family owned the law firm that offered him the job. Garland dreams may herald a major victory, but the price may seem too high if the victory is the fulfillment of others' ambitions.

INTERPRETATIONS AND FORTUNE-TELLING MEANINGS

★ If you dream of wearing a garland of flowers given by someone you love, happy vacations and a love celebration can be anticipated.

★ If you dream you are weaving garlands, you may be asked to make a short-term sacrifice of your time, effort, or possibly finances for a long-term gain.

★ If you dream you are given a bay laurel garland of victory, a venture will be rewarded.

★ If you dream you are smothered by garlands thrown by well-wishers, you will receive the support of others but maybe not personal fulfillment.

★ If you dream flower garlands die or fade, a success may be short-lived.

★ If paper garlands appear in the dream, others may try to dictate your path.

OUTCOME OF THEO'S DREAM

Theo told his family he would not take the job, nor would he go along with his parents' marriage plans, and he was going to marry the woman he loved. Garlands indicate celebrations that may not offer the victory the dreamer was wanting.

Garlic

Dustin, sixteen, dreamed he was running through fields of wild garlic, putting as much distance as possible between himself and the shapeless black form pursuing him. He knew evil creatures were repelled by garlic and thought if he left the fields the creature would devour him. Dustin knew no one else could see the creature and that eventually he would have to stop running and be swallowed up.

DREAM BACKGROUND AND MEANING

Dustin's mother had a new boyfriend who was a brute but a pillar of the small local community. Several times Dustin had run away but was returned by the police, who believed his stepfather's lies as he was on the police board and explained away Dustin's cuts and bruises as self-harm. His mother was too scared to expose her boyfriend's lies. His teachers would not listen, as his stepfather was also one of the school governors. Garlic dreams may occur when a dreamer feels helpless and needs protection.

INTERPRETATIONS AND FORTUNE-TELLING MEANINGS

* If you dream of garlic cloves hanging in your kitchen, you will become or remain financially secure, and good luck and good health will enter or reenter the home.
* If you dream you are eating garlic and you are worried that your breath smells, you may need to conceal future plans from someone disapproving.
* If you are wearing a garlic clove around your neck, you may be under attack but being blamed or disbelieved. Persist, for you will be vindicated.
* Wild flowering garlic represents protection, in the form of unexpected help or intervention against evil.
* If you see a clove of garlic on a window ledge, especially west-facing, one of your ancestors has a message for you that will appear as a sign in your daily life.
* If you are cooking with garlic, this is a powerful fertility symbol and also a sign of a good life together if you are preparing a meal for a lover.

OUTCOME OF DUSTIN'S DREAM

A new police officer replaced the retiring one, befriended Dustin, and warned off his stepfather, risking his own career prospects. He sent Dustin on weekend courses and, as soon as Dustin was old enough, enrolled him as a full-time cadet, so he could leave home. The garlic-field dreams ended.

Garnet

Beth, thirty, dreamed that her antique garnet ring, inherited from her late grandmother, turned almost black and left soot-like marks on her finger that would not wash off. The black was spreading to her other fingers. Beth tried to remove the ring, but the ring became tighter. The black was spreading up her arms. At last, she cut off the ring and threw it in the river.

DREAM BACKGROUND AND MEANING

Beth's ring seemed to bring her nothing but bad luck. Her grandmother had caused great family divisions in her lifetime. Now there were disputes over her inheritances so none of the family was speaking. Garnet heirlooms are not unlucky, but can transmit the negative vibes of the donor, unless disputes are amicably settled.

INTERPRETATIONS AND FORTUNE-TELLING MEANINGS

* Traditionally protective against vampires, a glowing red garnet warns against someone close draining your resources or energy in the name of love.
* A dream of a garnet ring promises love in later life or the revival of passion in a relationship grown stagnant.
* Since a red garnet was said to light Noah's Ark, garnet jewelry dreams predict a fortunate house move or relocation.
* Dark garnets say that focusing on past injustices or betrayal in a relationship prevents going forward, either together or separately.
* Dreams of garnets falling out of jewelry warn of quarrels with a partner in love or business, preventable by raising problems before they escalate.
* Dreams of being offered garnets at a cheap price advise caution in taking the easy route or choosing bargains with strings attached.

OUTCOME OF BETH'S DREAM

Beth called the family together and all agreed the inheritances had brought them misfortune. They decided to sell the grand-mother's artifacts, give the money to charity, and split cash inheritances evenly. The bad luck stopped.

Garnet dreams can reflect underlying disharmony, as garnets possess heavy energies. Once that is resolved, garnets restore in dreams and life their glowing beauty and capacity to transmit love.

Gaslighting, Mind Manipulation

Laura, thirty-one, dreamed that her baby was missing; she was frantic because she had seen her husband leave and return without the baby. The police arrived, carrying her little son, to arrest her for abandoning him in the local park. They refused to believe in her innocence.

DREAM BACKGROUND AND MEANING

Before Laura had a baby, she was a successful business-woman. Her husband, Paul, insisted she stay at home with the baby, isolated her from her family, and constantly told her what a bad mother she was. Laura would find the baby left on high surfaces or the feeding bottle heated to boiling. Paul said she was losing her mind and was a danger to the child. Was she going mad? Gaslighting or mind manipulation is a cruel form of psychological control, but dreams will often reveal the true situation.

INTERPRETATIONS AND FORTUNE-TELLING MEANINGS

★ If you dream of being unjustifiably blamed for mistakes at home or work and are starting to doubt yourself, a dream will reveal the culprit.

★ If in your dream you are trying in vain to convince authorities of your competence, someone may be deliberately gaslighting you as a form of control.

★ If you wake from a dream confused about what is a dream and what is reality, collect evidence if you feel you are being manipulated.

★ If in your dream you are in the hospital when you are not ill, you are being stripped of your power, whether at work or home. Trust your own judgment.

★ If a controlling partner is being unusually helpful in a dream, this may be a forewarning of an ulterior motive.

★ If you are being recorded on a camera or audio device in your dream, someone may be trying to incriminate you into saying or doing something you will regret.

OUTCOME OF LAURA'S DREAM

After the dream, Laura started to secretly record video of her husband and collected evidence of him trying to harm the baby. Laura confronted Paul and suggested he leave home before she called Social Services. Gaslighting is a much-underrated problem in today's society, and dreams can offer the impetus for the dreamer to initiate defensive action.

Gasoline

Derek, fifty-eight, dreamed he left home late, intending to pick up gas en route to meet his wife at the airport as she returned from her overseas trip. He passed two gas stations on the freeway, then realized the tank was getting low. Before he reached another, his car ran out of fuel. By the time the roadside assistance service arrived, his wife had caught a taxi and was waiting at home, fuming.

DREAM BACKGROUND AND MEANING

As far as his wife was concerned, Derek could do nothing right. He had met his wife while on vacation in the Philippines; then she returned to Texas with him and obtained a permanent resident card. Now she was spending increasing time with new friends in the local town. If the dreamer ignores an opportunity to fill the vehicle with gasoline, they may subconsciously not want to reach their destination.

INTERPRETATIONS AND FORTUNE-TELLING MEANINGS

★ If you dream your vehicle is filled with gasoline and heading for the open road, life ahead will expand, in both work and pleasure.

★ If your gas tank is empty and you reach the gas station just in time, you may have felt drained by life, but life will improve.

★ If in your dream you run out of gas in the middle of nowhere, check your vehicle for roadworthiness.

★ If the gas station is out of fuel, you should not rely on the usual resources or support networks.

★ If by mistake you fill your car with diesel instead of gasoline, plans may have to be revised.

★ If you are driving an electric car, you may have to or may need to move on from what is outworn or outmoded.

OUTCOME OF DEREK'S DREAM

Derek's wife said the marriage was over and she was returning to the Philippines for three months, after which they would sell the house. He heard she was dating a guy from the Philippines who ran a bar in town. Gasoline dreams can mark the end of the road in a life stage or relationship.

Gates

Francis, twenty-six, dreamed he was strolling along an open road when suddenly the way was barred by high iron gates with wire on top and no means of communicating with anyone inside to open them. He could not climb over them or go around and was about to turn back the way he had come. He noticed a heavy iron bar halfway up, pushed until he thought he would collapse, and the gates swung open.

DREAM BACKGROUND AND MEANING

Francis worked hard at his career as an attorney and had passed every stage with honors. But his path to obtaining a practicing certificate was suddenly blocked because, where his contemporaries had sponsors connected with their families, Francis had paid his own way. Gates that block the way ahead in a dream represent obstacles that others or circumstances have imposed that must be overcome to progress.

INTERPRETATIONS AND FORTUNE-TELLING MEANINGS

★ A dream of open gates heralds a welcome result to a social situation, a new stage in a career, or joining a family through marriage or remarriage.

★ A locked gate, especially a high one, warns that a particular venture or relationship can be fulfilled only with compromise and determination.

★ Rusted gates represent a past relationship best let go.

★ Broken gates say you are not creating sufficient barriers against intrusion.

★ Golden gates, if open, lead the way to a happy situation or prosperous result to a venture.

★ If gates are guarded or with wire on top or there are gates that unexpectedly appear, the dream says "push hard," especially if you are seeking fame or fortune.

OUTCOME OF FRANCIS'S DREAM

Determined, Francis applied to a less prestigious legal practice, which would finish his training in return for a lower salary and his taking on the routine or difficult cases no one else wanted. He qualified, joined the company as partner, and raised its profile so it became recognized for handling difficult cases. Gates dreams are connected with accessing necessary resources or opportunities that may offer the impetus to push through obstacles.

Gateway

John, forty-six, had a recurring dream of walking through a French town, wearing eighteenth-century clothes. He was always with the same beautiful woman with a hat decorated with plumed feathers. He loved the woman, but when they reached the gateway leading through the town gate out of town, he always stopped, afraid. She walked through without him.

DREAM BACKGROUND AND MEANING

Though John, who lived in Scotland, had a good job in engineering, he wanted to start his own business. But he feared he might fail. He did not experience the depth of feeling for his wife as he did for his dream twin soul and hoped she would find him.

When we dream of the perfect partner, they may be a love from a past life, but can also reflect a dissatisfaction with life generally that holds us inactive, waiting to be rescued.

INTERPRETATIONS AND FORTUNE-TELLING MEANINGS

★ Gateways in dreams represent a transition involving taking a chance.

★ A past-world love scenario can indicate hesitation and opportunities missed that we need to fulfill, not necessarily in love.

★ If you dream of the same gateway in subsequent dreams, try to locate it. Walking through it may lead to resolution.

★ Seeing your twin soul walking through a gateway you did not follow suggests that maybe you do not really want to risk what you have.

★ If a gateway has crumbled, you cannot go back to the past but must go forward by another route.

★ If an assailant bars the gateway, is that your fears or actual opposition?

OUTCOME OF JOHN'S DREAM

After much research, John identified his gateway in central France. John and his wife went on vacation and he walked through the gateway with her. They found a small holiday complex not far away, bought it, and settled in France. Walking through gateways may bring a different but equally satisfying destiny from what you have idealized.

Generation Gap

Iris, seventy-five, frequently dreamed of her teenage grand-daughters going out in the evening and being kidnapped. In her dream, three men seized them and forced them into cars, and they were never seen again.

DREAM BACKGROUND AND MEANING

Iris, a widow, recently moved in with her only daughter, Gina, her husband, and their three teenage daughters. Her grandchildren wore clothes Iris considers indecent and she was always criticizing them and their loud music. The girls resented the fact they now shared a bedroom. Iris told her daughter and granddaughters of her dreams, but they laughed and wore even more revealing clothes to annoy her.

INTERPRETATIONS AND FORTUNE-TELLING MEANINGS

★ If dreams of a younger generation's potential danger are regular, they do not indicate immediate peril but general anxiety about their safety.

★ If, however, there is one dream that is urgent, specific, and lingers all day, it should be taken more seriously.

★ If people in a multigenerational family are quarreling in a dream, the dream may go deeper than surface issues and may hide space and privacy needs of all the generations.

★ If the younger generation dreams about an older family member suddenly disappearing or being put into a nursing home, this reflects escalating resentments that need resolving before harsh words are spoken.

★ If there are dreams of totally happy family occasions, with tolerance by each generation, there is sufficient underlying goodwill for at least partial compromise.

★ If different family members dream of building works, moving furniture, or the older generation leaving peacefully, alternative practical solutions should be considered to avoid emotional flashpoints.

OUTCOME OF IRIS'S DREAM

Gina found photos of Iris as a teenager wearing incredibly short miniskirts and riding on the back of a motorbike with a hippie. The girls explained the tracking devices on their phones and promised to check in regularly. The family built an extension so the older and younger generations could have their space. Generation-gap dreams are often based on different viewpoints that, with compromise on all sides, can increase love, not interference.

Genie

Bart, twenty-five, dreamed he found an Aladdin-style oil lamp in a yard sale and took it home. A genie appeared out of the lamp, promising three wishes. But if Bart made the wrong wishes, he would be trapped inside the lamp. Bart was terrified. The genie became enormous and menacing. Bart ran downstairs onto the sidewalk and was too scared to go home.

DREAM BACKGROUND AND MEANING

Bart had been sorting through his late grandfather's attic. He felt bitter because his share of the inheritance was small, compared with that of his cousins. At the bottom of a dusty trunk, he found a small bag of diamonds. His grandfather had mined in South Africa and in his last days had rambled on about his hidden treasure. Bart wondered if he should sell the diamonds on the black market, or if it was too risky—and was it wrong?

Genies in dreams represent an instant shortcut to money or fame in a situation where you should weigh the pros and cons before acting.

INTERPRETATIONS AND FORTUNE-TELLING MEANINGS

★ A dream of a genie appearing from a lamp or bottle in a puff of smoke promises major wishes coming true.

★ Dreams where genies offer wishes with conditions attached warn of trickery.

★ Dreams of jinn, Middle Eastern genies appearing from a fire, reveal you have rapidly evolving psychic powers you should channel to avoid their getting out of control.

★ If you dream you let a genie out of a bottle, you may be tempted to reveal secrets. Consider consequences first.

★ If you dream your genie is benign, unexpected help from a mentor will aid success and prosperity in your career.

★ If your genie is menacing, beware offers that seem too good to be true.

OUTCOME OF BART'S DREAM

Bart reluctantly handed over the diamonds to his grand-father's estate, and they proved to be imitations. However, the older family members, impressed by his honesty, shared part of their inheritance. Genie dreams are exciting ones at times of major change and risk.

Ghost

Fiona, forty, dreamed she was in her childhood home, which was abandoned. She tried to escape, but the door had banged shut. She could not open it. In the corners were hissing, menacing shadows curling toward her. Fiona struggled with the door and at last it opened. She ran up the dark street, not looking back, and woke sobbing.

DREAM BACKGROUND AND MEANING

Fiona left home when she was eighteen after the sudden death of her mother. Her father had treated her mother badly, so there had been no contact between them since she left, but she had recently heard through a cousin that her father was dying in the hospital. Dreaming of trying to escape from a familiar haunted house indicates that someone from the past, living or deceased, who you do not wish to think of, is returning to your life.

INTERPRETATIONS AND FORTUNE-TELLING MEANINGS

* If the ghost is a benign family member or a deceased friend, they may have a message for you.
* If you regularly dream of spirits, your mediumship gifts are developing. Once channeled, scary ghost dreams will stop.
* Dreaming of being chased by spirits reveals that you may have unsuccessfully tried to bury grief or an unresolved family issue after the death of that family member.
* Ghosts of old teachers and mentors appearing in dreams offering advice suggest that you may need support from a wise living source. They may also be spirit guardians who still watch over you.
* Shadow spirits are a reminder to acknowledge and let go of hidden unresolved generational traumas to take away their present power to haunt.
* A spirit who in their lifetime wronged you may return in dreams to try to put the relationship right.

OUTCOME OF FIONA'S DREAM

Fiona visited her father in the hospital and made her peace with him. After his death, she had no more frightening paranormal dreams. Troublesome ghost dreams may recur until the source of the dilemma is resolved.

Ghosting (Sudden Breaking of Communication)

Ruth, fifty-one, dreamed she telephoned Charles, her long-standing friend. Instead of ringing, she heard a voice saying, "This phone is disconnected." Concerned, she went online and tried to reach Charles by FaceTime. Although she called six times, there was no answer. She was now frantic and sent an email—which bounced back. Upon awakening, she wondered if Charles intended to cut her out of his life.

DREAM BACKGROUND AND MEANING

Ruth had enjoyed a friendship with Charles for over two years. They would speak each day, either on FaceTime or on the telephone. The friendship suited them both, as neither wanted to commit and they lived in different states. But recently contact had been initiated by her, and Charles had sounded hesitant. Being gradually ghosted or suddenly blocked by a friend or lover may be first picked up in dreams if energies between you are changing.

INTERPRETATIONS AND FORTUNE-TELLING MEANINGS

* If you dream of someone who you regularly contact suddenly ghosting you from their life and actual communication is dwindling, there may be a genuine reason. Give them the benefit of the doubt.
* If you can no longer see the person in your dream but a white shimmer, like a ghost, they may be deliberately cutting off or planning to cease connection. Ask why.
* If communications constantly get blocked in your dreams, mirroring the real-life lack of contact, the connection may have become too intense. Back off for a while.
* If a connection is going well in everyday life but you dream of being ghosted, this may be an anxiety dream on your part, maybe due to rejection in an earlier relationship.
* If in the dream the person is uncommunicative, you may be picking up their unrelated hidden worries, rather than rejection.

OUTCOME OF RUTH'S DREAM

Charles did suddenly stop all contact days after the dream. Ruth persisted, and Charles admitted he had met a woman who was extremely possessive. Ruth was upset, but realized the friendship was holding her back from finding face-to-face companionship. The severing of a dream connection may provide warning weeks before the actual ghosting.

Giant

Bruce, nineteen, dreamed he was trying to enter the law school gates but a giant was blocking the way. No matter how hard Bruce tried to get around the giant, the giant became larger and wider. Bruce decided to give up, but realized the giant had the face of his father. Bruce charged at the giant, and the giant dissolved.

DREAM BACKGROUND AND MEANING

Bruce's father had bullied Bruce and mocked him because Bruce was an academic and not good at sports. Although Bruce's mother had left her abusive husband and Bruce had not seen his father for a year, he still heard his father's denigrating voice in his head. He had been offered a scholarship to law school. Should he take the scholarship, or was he useless, as his father had told him all his life?

INTERPRETATIONS AND FORTUNE-TELLING MEANINGS

* A giant in a dream can represent great power or a huge ambition or undertaking.
* A friendly giant offers help from powerful sources in overcoming opposition or in advancing causes.
* A terrifying giant signifies hostility from an intimidating person or a sense of being overwhelmed by life.
* If you are a small child in the dream, the giant may represent an authority figure from when you were young or someone in your present world whose criticisms make you feel inadequate.
* Fighting a giant and winning, David-and-Goliath style, says you will succeed even if the odds against you seem gigantic.
* Giant dreams can be fears magnified out of proportion by repressing them, so they appear as terrifying giants.

OUTCOME OF BRUCE'S DREAM

Since he had confronted and overcome his father in the dream, Bruce realized he did not need to accept his father's flawed assessment of his worth, and he took his place in law school. The identity of the giant and the power they have over our lives, actual or past, determines how we can overcome them or shows that, if confronted, they will disappear.

Gift

Maisie, thirty-eight, dreamed she was on the way to her local Florida mall to buy Christmas presents. She saw a cab, hailed it to the airport, and bought a ticket for a Christmas vacation alone in a snowy paradise. She woke feeling excited as she made snow angels in real snow.

DREAM BACKGROUND AND MEANING

Maisie was dreading buying the annual Christmas gifts from a huge list, some for relatives she hardly knew, who never said thank you. Her husband always gave her something for the kitchen and her teenage children presented a huge list of excessive demands. The spirit of Christmas giving had disappeared. Gifts should be an outward sign of appreciation but may become a substitute for real thought and care.

INTERPRETATIONS AND FORTUNE-TELLING MEANINGS

* Dreaming of receiving a thoughtful gift is a sign of caring in love or friendship from whoever is making the gift.
* Dreaming of buying yourself a gift says that you should be more generous to yourself if you are always the giver to others.
* To be disappointed by a gift you receive in a dream or to not receive one when you are expecting it means you are not expressing your own needs in life generally.
* If a carefully wrapped gift is empty, you may find that a new love or friend is shallow and superficial.
* Dreaming of returning an unwanted gift to a store says that what you want from life and what you are being offered are different.

OUTCOME OF MAISIE'S DREAM

After the dream, Maisie contacted her relatives and told them she was making a donation to charity instead of buying them gifts. She told the immediate family they were going away to a snowy cabin in the woods for Christmas as the family gift, and gave the teens a modest limit to choose one gift each. They all had a real Christmas. When the material value of gifts outweighs intentions, they become a burden, not a blessing.

Ginger

Phoebe, fifty-three, dreamed she was making gingerbread men for her young grandchildren, who were coming for a visit, and she set the gingerbread men in the oven to bake. When they were ready, she took them out of the oven but, as in the fairy tale, they began escaping in all directions. Phoebe pursued them, dusted them off, put them on the table, and the grandchildren loved them.

DREAM BACKGROUND AND MEANING

Phoebe's children reared their children to be logical and discouraged belief in fairies and Santa. Phoebe wanted to take her grandchildren to Disneyland before they were too old. But their parents wanted the money to be spent on an educational trip, supervised by them, so there would be none of Grandma's nonsense.

INTERPRETATIONS AND FORTUNE-TELLING MEANINGS

★ If you dream you are adding ginger to a savory dish, you seek to up the tempo of your daily life.

★ If you are adding ginger to a dessert, you need more passion and excitement in a relationship.

★ To dream you will be growing ginger and selling ginger roots says you have ambitions you may not have expressed that will bring money in your chosen field.

★ Drinking ginger tea or eating ginger cookies in a dream is a good sign if you are trying to become pregnant or are in the early stages of pregnancy and worry.

★ If you add too much ginger to a mix in your dream, you have strong feelings for someone, or about a family matter you may be concealing.

OUTCOME OF PHOEBE'S DREAM

Phoebe's dream convinced her that her grandchildren needed to experience fantasy as well as logic. However, she booked a shorter trip than she originally planned, so there would be money to spare for the educational visit as well. The children were enchanted by Disneyland, and the youngest told Phoebe she had once seen a gingerbread man running across her grandma's kitchen floor. Ginger is a natural symbol for pushing the boundaries of possibility between logic and fantasy and embracing both.

Giraffe

Angus, twenty-eight, dreamed he saw a young giraffe, separated from the herd, being attacked by a pack of hyenas. He fired his gun high in the air to frighten them away. The giraffe came to him and lowered its head. Angus felt the giraffe was marking him as a leader.

DREAM BACKGROUND AND MEANING

Angus knew he had leadership qualities. The others in his air force squadron, who had at first been hostile to him, turned their attention to bullying a new recruit. The new guy was very tall, and they complained he was a liability on patrol. Angus knew he had to either join in the bullying or defend the recruit, which he chose to do. Helping a giraffe in a dream says you have the courage to accept that you will need to stand out if you are going far in life.

INTERPRETATIONS AND FORTUNE-TELLING MEANINGS

★ Dreaming of giraffes racing across the savannah says that by acting swiftly you can avoid difficult situations.

★ Giraffes extending their necks over an enclosure warn against becoming too closely involved in other people's problems.

★ When you dream you see a giraffe eating the tops of trees, someone close may be exaggerating the truth.

★ A giraffe in the distance indicates foresight and says you should trust intuition or dream predictions.

★ If you dream a herd of giraffes is running away, you may find that colleagues or friends are unwilling to confront injustice and will deny that problems existed.

OUTCOME OF ANGUS'S DREAM

After the dream, Angus stopped a particularly vicious attack on the recruit and, as expected, he became the subject of bullying. But he refused to back down, and eventually the others left the recruit alone. Angus was promoted and stamped out bullying. Angus knew that his dream giraffe was a special spirit animal that assisted him to rise high.

Gladiator

Andy, twenty-four, dreamed he was a captive Celt, fighting against Rome's best gladiator. Andy was armed with only a short sword and small shield. The battle was fierce. The gladiator was overconfident, believing he could easily finish off the poorly armed Celt. He attacked but was badly injured by Andy. Andy, offered the chance to become a gladiator, went home.

DREAM BACKGROUND AND MEANING

Andy was competing for a place at a college. But competition was fierce, and Andy was afraid that his lack of family connections with the college would work against him. His main rival came from a wealthy family who were donors to the college, but Andy was determined to win a place on his own merit. In his interview, he stated that because he had to make his own way in the world he would work twice as hard.

INTERPRETATIONS AND FORTUNE-TELLING MEANINGS

* If you dream you are a gladiator fighting someone you know, they may be an adversary from a past life.
* If you dream you are a gladiator and defeat your enemy, you will win when standing up to a bully in your daily life.
* If you dream you are fighting a wild animal, you may be relying on your confidence and not on instincts.
* If you dream you are defeated in the arena by trickery, rethink tactics to overcome deception in daily life.
* If you dream you are crowned champion against all comers, you will succeed in the way most desired.
* If in the dream you are aware you are fighting purely for the entertainment of others, someone in your present world is not giving you the respect and consideration you deserve.

OUTCOME OF ANDY'S DREAM

Andy impressed the interview board when he said he would rely on himself and not on his family to succeed. He was awarded a place. However, he decided to attend a college where learning took precedence over prestige. Gladiator dreams often reflect the gladiator's opponent as the underdog who wins through courage and determination.

Glass

Coral, twenty-eight, dreamed she was wearing glass slippers and a gorgeous dress, and her prince was dancing with her. It struck midnight and, as Coral ran downstairs to her glass coach, she lost one of her glass slippers. Another princess kicked it out of the way and, being delicate, the slipper shattered as the other princess rushed to claim the prince.

DREAM BACKGROUND AND MEANING

Coral was in love with Gus, a coworker who everyone said was a playboy. He treated her as if she were made of glass, and told her that he was in love with her. Another woman in the office was making a play for Gus. He assured Coral the other woman meant nothing, but said care was needed as she was the CEO's niece. Dreams of glass, especially of fairy-tale glass slippers, can warn that a situation is fragile and may not last.

INTERPRETATIONS AND FORTUNE-TELLING MEANINGS

* If you are enclosed in glass in a dream, you may feel that no one is listening to you.
* To see a full glass or one that is being filled for you indicates your wishes will be fulfilled.
* To see a half-empty glass questions whether you should view it as half full and change your perspective.
* If you dream your house or workplace is made of glass, you may be under constant scrutiny.
* A glass ceiling above you traditionally limits your progress but can be penetrated.
* If you are drinking from a delicate glass, wealth and status will increase, but exercise great care to make it last.

OUTCOME OF CORAL'S DREAM

Coral saw her prince leaving work with the CEO's niece. When she rang his phone during the evening, as they had a date, he did not answer. Gradually, Coral realized that he was performing a delicate balancing act between them, but if any heart was going to shatter it was hers. Glass slippers are the stuff of fantasy and romance but, in dreams and in reality, glass may be too delicate to survive daily living (see "Broken Glass," p. 71).

Gloves

Louette, seventy-five, dreamed of being young, presented at court wearing a white crinoline dress and white silk gloves. To her surprise, her granddaughter Caitlin appeared, heavily pregnant in a revealing red dress. The courtiers tried to usher Caitlin out. But Louette was not having her granddaughter sidelined, gave Caitlin her own gloves, and presented her to the king and queen with great pride.

DREAM BACKGROUND AND MEANING

Louette had a pair of heirloom elbow-length white silk gloves she had worn in England as a debutante and at her own wedding. Now that Caitlin, the only girl in the family, was getting married, Louette offered them. But her grand-daughter refused because she wanted a simple wedding. Giving gloves symbolizes an offering made in love.

INTERPRETATIONS AND FORTUNE-TELLING MEANINGS

★ A pair of white gloves in a dream is a sign of a betrothal or a wedding in the family, or an invitation to a formal occasion.

★ Boxing gloves suggest a formal challenge to your authority where there are underlying strong feelings; a baseball glove suggests friendly rivalry.

★ Wearing gloves on a cold day indicates you should be prepared for an unenthusiastic response to a request or an overture of friendship.

★ To drop a glove is considered unlucky unless someone else picks it up; it warns against being too trusting with people you do not know well.

★ A lost glove says a petty quarrel with a lover or partner can be avoided with tact.

★ If you dream gloves are too small or large, a friend may not be sincere, or you are disguising your true self.

OUTCOME OF LOUETTE'S DREAM

Louette realized that the most important gift to her grand-daughter was her blessing. Caitlin asked if she could carry the gloves instead of a bouquet as a token of the continuing family love and said she would keep them safe for her yet-unborn daughter on her wedding day. The kind of gloves, whether the latex dishwashing kind, driving gloves, or winter woollies, and their condition in the dream, indicates their meaning and usefulness to the dreamer.

Glowworm

Leticia, forty-eight, dreamed of being in a boat floating in glowworm caves, looking up at the thousands of fabulous tiny lights, at Waitomo on New Zealand's North Island. Then someone on the boat trip started exclaiming loudly about the wonderful creatures, and instantly every glowworm light went out. Leticia woke angry and disappointed.

DREAM BACKGROUND AND MEANING

Leticia had always been attracted to the Waitomo glowworm caves, though they were on the other side of the world, where she had distant family she had never met. Not long after the dream, a chance came to visit Waitomo, as her extended family was having a reunion for family members from all over the world. Family legend said the glowworm was their special creature. But Leticia was afraid that if she went, the reality might spoil the fantasy. Dreams of glowworms are a profound symbol of the wonders of life, nature, and spiritual encounters and should be treasured.

INTERPRETATIONS AND FORTUNE-TELLING MEANINGS

★ If you see glowworms in a dream but have never encountered them, you may be ready to expand your personal horizons of possibility and to shine creatively, particularly in the performing arts.

★ If you often dream of glowworms, you need to find new meaning and adventures in your life.

★ If you are following a trail of glowworms in the dark, the way ahead is very different from what was expected, but potentially far brighter.

★ If you dream that noise makes glowworms put out their lights, others may be discouraging or cynical about your new path.

★ Seeing glowworms on a path represents upcoming good fortune and spiritual riches.

OUTCOME OF LETICIA'S DREAM

Leticia went to New Zealand, traveled through the glowworm caves on a family boat, and witnessed an amazing display. She decided to stay in New Zealand to learn more about her family's connection with glowworms. Dreaming of glowworms is not common, but it always marks out the dreamer as unique, if they follow their own light.

Glue

Pete, thirty-five, dreamed he was gluing together a model plane with his seven-year-old son, Jacques. Jacques was getting impatient because he wanted to play with the plane, but the glue was not working. Pete knew it needed to be left to dry. Jacques threw a tantrum and Pete, who hated constructing models, hurled the plane on the floor and stepped on it. Jacques cried for his mother.

DREAM BACKGROUND AND MEANING

Pete was finding weekly access visits with his son hard, as Jacques only wanted to play soccer on weekends. The only time they connected was when Jacques was talking about the soccer club he had joined. Pete was interested, as he had been a professional soccer player before an injury. Glue dreams occur when a relationship is in danger of coming apart.

INTERPRETATIONS AND FORTUNE-TELLING MEANINGS

★ If you dream you are gluing a broken item together, there is a chance a broken relationship or quarrel can be fixed.

★ If you and a business partner, love partner, or family member are gluing something you are making together, the partnership will be strong and enduring.

★ If a tube of glue dries up in the dream, you may need a new approach to bring or restore unity.

★ If your eyelids are glued together in the dream, someone is trying to stop you from seeing the truth or the reality of a situation.

★ If your lips are glued together, attempts are being made to silence you by those who disagree with your opinions.

★ If you dream that a glued item comes apart, you need to question the lasting quality of the relationship or business deal and if you want it to continue.

OUTCOME OF PETE'S DREAM

Jacques's mother was glad to be free of being involved in his soccer and suggested Pete take Jacques to club practice and games. Pete became involved and was asked to help coach the team. Glue needs compatible surfaces to bind things successfully; once they are found, the bond is unbreakable.

Gnome

Bettina, twenty-five, dreamed she was in a garden full of brightly painted gnome statues. She was putting coins under each one for prosperity and good luck. But, to her amazement, the gnomes all marched out of the garden, saying, "Earn your own passage." She could not stop laughing and woke up hopeful for the first time in ages.

DREAM BACKGROUND AND MEANING

Bettina wanted to go backpacking around the United States from the United Kingdom after completing college. She could not raise enough money from her vacation job, and her parents could not help. She had been buying lottery tickets and casting money spells from her magick book, but nothing worked. Gnomes, as the archetypal Earth spirit, point to practical solutions, requiring effort, rather than to money wishes coming true by magick or luck.

INTERPRETATIONS AND FORTUNE-TELLING MEANINGS

★ Dreaming of a garden gnome indicates gaining the resources you need, if you are prepared to work for them.

★ A malevolent gnome refers to a bad-tempered older male relative who is stingy with money and praise.

★ Forest gnomes digging for gold suggest a solution to your financial problems is very near. Explore options, as riches will not come looking for you.

★ Gnomes encountered in the forest indicate good fortune from an unexpected opportunity, or information that will set you on the right track.

★ A broken gnome statue talks of a wasted chance that could still be retrieved with work.

★ Gnomes in a garden are symbols of a happy home, protected from harm, where prosperity, once earned, remains.

OUTCOME OF BETTINA'S DREAM

After the dream, Bettina explored possibilities of working in the United States. She discovered a Camp America scheme where she could work at summer camp and then have a month's travel afterward. Gnome dreams reveal unconsidered financial solutions where the dreamer makes their own wishes come true.

Goat

Geoff, seventy, dreamed he was herding sheep and goats. He reached a gully where a huge angel stood, barring the way ahead. The angel told Geoff he had fallen off the steep mountain path with the goats, but all the sheep could come to heaven. Geoff left the goats and stepped confidently forward. The angel said, "You must go with your own kind," and would not allow Geoff to enter heaven. Geoff woke protesting.

DREAM BACKGROUND AND MEANING

Geoff considered himself a friendly guy and was most offended when one of the women at work called him a dirty old goat when he hugged her. The human resources officer told Geoff that another woman had also complained that he was overfamiliar. Geoff had been brought up in a Bible-reading household and so knew that people were divided into sheep and goats in a parable. Goats were deemed unworthy of paradise.

INTERPRETATIONS AND FORTUNE-TELLING MEANINGS

* A charging buck is a symbol of power and assertiveness, which can tip over into aggression; a good omen for a man seeking to father a child.
* A nanny goat in a dream is an indication of fertility and, if the goat is with kids, the dreamer will be a good mother.
* A buck high on a rock represents sexual passion, which, if misused, suggests the dreamer is showing sexual overtones in inappropriate situations.
* Seeing a buck with a nanny goat for women dreamers indicates an exciting new flirtation and, for men, a love rival.
* The buck's association with the Egyptian creator Amun-Ra can represent the energy necessary for achieving ambitions, if the goat is climbing mountains.
* Dreaming of a herd of goats suggests that like-minded people may become inclined to overly boisterous behavior when together.

OUTCOME OF GEOFF'S DREAM

Geoff realized he had lost sight of other people's personal boundaries since the death of his wife, and that he needed to find a new partner to channel his free-flowing affections. In a dream, the goat can be a warning that some may mistake overfriendliness for predatory intentions.

Goblins

Eugenie, fifteen, dreamed she was surrounded by small black hairy goblins with eyes glowing like coals. When she was walking home in the dark, they would jump out from behind trees, snatch at her clothes, and scratch and poke her. Terrified, she ran, but they just ran faster. Finally, she stopped, turned around, made the sign of the cross, and said, "Begone, foul fiends." They changed into bats and flew away.

DREAM BACKGROUND AND MEANING

Eugenie was being teased mercilessly at school by a gang of girls because she was very clever but did not have designer clothes or the latest technology. Eugenie was psychic and often saw the spirit world and nature spirits, both benign and malevolent. Goblin dreams are most common in adolescence; they express fears of being helpless toward both paranormal influences and earthly attacks.

INTERPRETATIONS AND FORTUNE-TELLING MEANINGS

* If you dream of a plague of goblins, you have a lot of distractions that you need to remove to become powerful.
* If in the dream goblins are poking and prodding you, there are irritating petty minor bullies who prey on your fears but, once confronted, will back away.
* If a goblin follows you, you have things in your past to be resolved.
* If you encounter goblins in a dark place, your fears of your own inadequacy are manifesting as threatening goblins.
* If you defeat or drive off the goblins in the dream, you are releasing justifiable anger you have suppressed.

OUTCOME OF EUGENIE'S DREAM

After the dream, Eugenie realized she did not have to accept the unfair teasing. Other students who were different were also being intimidated by the same girls, and Eugenie befriended them. The gang then found it harder to intimidate a group who together would stand up to them. Overcoming the goblins is a rehearsal for fighting back in the everyday world.

God

Liane, sixty-two, dreamed of God expressing anger because she did not attend church and instead followed alternative spiritual practices. Liane told God her reiki and crystal healing did more good than going through the motions of conventional religion. Her elder sister, appearing in the dream dressed as a nun, insisted that Liane give up her wicked ways or she would burn in hell. Liane woke distressed.

DREAM BACKGROUND AND MEANING

Since retirement, Liane had discovered healing gifts and had joined a Wiccan circle based in nature spirituality. Liane felt guilty, as her unmarried older sister, who she lived with, said she was dabbling with the Devil. Dreaming of a judgmental God reflects underlying guilt about not fulfilling the expectations of others to conform to a worldview often imposed from childhood.

INTERPRETATIONS AND FORTUNE-TELLING MEANINGS

* God dreams represent, even for nonreligious people, the need for approval by those using conventional rules as a smoke screen for control.
* If you dream that a white-bearded God reproaches you for abandoning a traditional rigid lifestyle, not necessarily religion, others may be off-loading their own prejudices.
* If you encounter a loving god or goddess figure in a dream, your psychic powers are emerging.
* If you recognize a specific god or goddess, this represents happiness and good fortune.
* If you are threatened with risking hell by family or religious figures, they are projecting their own doubts.
* If someone close to you hides behind rules and prohibitions, they need your supposed inferiority to affirm their superiority.
* If you dream an unseen God is watching you, examine what you feel you need to hide about your lifestyle or beliefs.

OUTCOME OF LIANE'S DREAM

Liane invited her sister to a healing session, but she refused. Liane realized it was time to move out of the family home they had shared since her divorce so she could live her life her own way. God dreams can represent judgment. Do not accept judgment if others use manipulation to limit your freedom.

Goddess

In her dream, Katalina, forty, was crying while sitting under a palm tree on a tiny Pacific island. A voice spoke to her: "Katalina, please don't worry. I have fixed everything. All will now be well." Katalina knew this was Kali, the Hindu goddess, who appears fearsome but is compassionate to those in need who do not give up in the face of adversity.

DREAM BACKGROUND AND MEANING

Katalina was running a business selling new-age books, crystals, tarot cards, and statuettes of goddesses from different ages and religions. Though she was European, she felt great affinity with the Hindu goddesses. Business was slow, and Katalina wondered how long the business could survive. Goddesses from different cultures will manifest in the dreams of those who can transform spiritual help into action.

INTERPRETATIONS AND FORTUNE-TELLING MEANINGS

* If you see a goddess you relate to, hers is the particular strength you need right now to resolve a problem.
* If a goddess from a particular culture appears regularly in your dreams, you may have been a devotee in a past life and will still find wisdom in her teachings.
* If you are visited by a fierce goddess such as Kali, if you fight on, you will win.
* If you hear the voice of a goddess but do not see her, you will know who is speaking, and you need to put her words into action.
* If you do not recognize the goddess in your dream, explore dream clues afterward, as a sign relating to her in the everyday world will provide an answer.
* Even if you are a logical person, whether male or female, the presence of a goddess in your dream is a sign of great blessing on your endeavors.

OUTCOME OF KATALINA'S DREAM

After the dream, Katalina used every means possible to make her business work. The right people and the right opportunities appeared, and she turned the business around. A goddess in a dream is usually followed by the opening of the right doors to make your efforts effective.

Gold

In his dream, Ronaldo, forty-four, was working in an underground gold mine in Western Australia. He saw a small nugget on the ground and put it in his pocket. Worried that he had been seen, he handed the gold to security, saying he had found it as he was leaving. His dream ended instantly, with Ronaldo regretting his honesty.

DREAM BACKGROUND AND MEANING

Ronaldo had worked for a large mining company for fifteen years. Because of bad investments and a recent divorce, he was in financial trouble. Ronaldo had overheard a conversation between two mine employees in which they discussed regularly stealing small pieces of gold. Upon hearing this, he reported it to management.

INTERPRETATIONS AND FORTUNE-TELLING MEANINGS

★ To dream of piles of gold, there for the taking, says you have the power to make serious money within a few years.

★ To dream of a gold mine offers a chance to discover a new source of riches.

★ If you dream gold slips through your hands and disappears, be wary of get-rich-quick schemes.

★ To dream you are given gold jewelry says your love will be true and will cherish you forever.

★ If in the dream you steal gold, you may regret attempting a less-than-honest solution to your financial woes.

★ If you dream of panning for gold, be discriminating about what is of worth in any area of your life. Beware of settling for fool's gold, worthless glittering iron sulfide.

OUTCOME OF RONALDO'S DREAM

Ronaldo's workmates involved in the thefts were caught and prosecuted. Ronaldo, having proved such an honest employee, was invited to work in security within the mine, where employees were allowed to go panning for gold in the nearby river when off duty. He made a modest fortune honestly. Of all metals, gold attracts the strongest desires and emotions. To dream of it opens the way to making money by legitimate means, but integrity may prove the true riches.

Gold Digger

Zola, twenty-eight, dreamed she was seated at the bar of a Los Angeles nightclub famous for its wealthy clientele. She was approached by a sophisticated middle-aged man, who offered to buy her a drink. Zola was very impressed, knowing he could give her the lifestyle she craved. They went home to his luxury apartment. She woke depressed at the stark reality of her life.

DREAM BACKGROUND AND MEANING

Zola, beautiful and talented, was struggling to find work in the film industry. Her friend, who lived in the same rooming house, said they should go to an upmarket bar where they would meet wealthy guys in town for a good time, and maybe some film producers. The alternative was to go home to her parents, as she was running out of money.

INTERPRETATIONS AND FORTUNE-TELLING MEANINGS

★ If you dream of an easy route to a good lifestyle, you need to accept the price as well as the rewards.

★ If you dream of meeting and marrying a wealthy partner, you may be guided to the place in your dream where entry to a more upmarket lifestyle awaits.

★ If you dream of being wealthy in your own right, you should develop your talents as well as finding the right contacts.

★ If you end up in a dangerous situation in your dream, heed specific warnings, as your unconscious radar is picking up signals.

★ If you dream your family is angry with you if they discover your new lifestyle, you may have unacknowledged doubts about the advisability of focusing on finding a wealthy escort.

★ If you see yourself happy back home with the guy next door, you may need to reassess whether you want wealth at any cost.

OUTCOME OF ZOLA'S DREAM

Zola and her friend met some wealthy guys in the bar who showed them a good time. Zola is enjoying the luxury lifestyle and hopes her part-time boyfriend will one day marry her, or she will meet a producer to open the route to the silver screen. Becoming a trophy escort can give a good-looking person, male or female, the benefits of wishes fulfilled as long as their glamor lasts.

Goldfish

Eli, thirty-six, dreamed he discovered a tank of goldfish in his shed he had totally forgotten. The water was green. Most of the fish were dying. Eli tried to clean out the tank, but even in the now-clear water all but three floated on their sides. He carried the tank with the remaining fish into the sunlight.

DREAM BACKGROUND AND MEANING

Eli had been given extra responsibility at work, and he worked evenings and weekends to gain a promotion. Suddenly he remembered he had promised to care for his children the coming week, as his ex-partner, the custodial parent, was having an operation. Eli had failed to hire a sitter, and knew his employer would not understand if he took last-minute leave. But the children needed him.

Goldfish represent prosperity but, as living symbols, ask whether that is monetary or emotional.

INTERPRETATIONS AND FORTUNE-TELLING MEANINGS

* Eight dream goldfish and one black one in a tank represent good luck and abundance in feng shui.
* Dream goldfish swimming in a pond or large aerated aquarium indicate security without losing freedom, the dream dilemma.
* A dream of fish dying reveals guilt at lack of care for those represented by the dream goldfish.
* Well-cared-for fish in a tank represent domestic happiness.
* Fish confined in a bowl warn of restrictions. Whose?
* One larger goldfish attacking others indicates problems with control at home or work.

OUTCOME OF ELI'S DREAM

Eli knew he was losing the love of his three children because he often canceled visits due to work. Now he insisted on emergency leave, though his boss hinted it might cost Eli his promotion. Eli realized from the dream and the three surviving dream fish that he needed to change priorities. Goldfish, as creatures of water, refer to deep emotional issues. The state of the dream goldfish may indicate whether you have switched love off because it is too painful.

Good Manners, Politeness

Stan, sixty-one, dreamed he was sitting on a bus when he noticed a pregnant woman standing in the aisle. He immediately stood up and offered her his seat. Instead of thanking Stan, she abused him, accusing him of being a chauvinist and misogynist. He tried explaining that he was just trying to be polite, but she continued with the abuse. The driver, becoming aware of the argument, stopped the bus and insisted that Stan get off immediately.

DREAM BACKGROUND AND MEANING

Stan was born in an era when opening a car door or offering a woman your seat on public transport was acceptable polite behavior. After this dream, he wondered if perhaps his conventions were outmoded. Dreams about good manners reinforce the dreamer's ethics in a world where others may have different values.

INTERPRETATIONS AND FORTUNE-TELLING MEANINGS

* If someone in a dream is excessively polite, they may simply be seeking admiration.
* If in the dream you are being considerate to others, do not let anyone influence you toward selfishness because of their poor standards.
* If you dream of being in a royal court or in the Victorian era, you may need to sometimes adapt gestures of old-fashioned courtesy without sacrificing consideration.
* If you are abused in a dream for being excessively courteous, selfish people in your life are seeking to divert attention from their own grasping ways.
* If you are behaving rudely in a dream, you may have wrongly been made to feel inferior or out of touch by others.

OUTCOME OF STAN'S DREAM

Stan realized many people did appreciate his good manners and that by abandoning the standards of a lifetime for popular opinion, he would be denying his authentic self. He noticed that his taciturn teens, who privately mocked his politeness, displayed consideration to others in public. Politeness dreams can reflect any area, principle, or issue of life where the dreamer is pressured to abandon what they know to be right.

Grain Crop

Jonquil, thirty-five, dreamed she was in a flour mill where grain was being ground into flour. She was trying to lift the heavy sacks to pour down the grain chute, because her brother had disabled the mechanical hoist. But they were too heavy. Her brother told her to leave it to him, as she was too weak, but he dropped the sacks and the grain spilled everywhere. She restored the hoist and the mill ran smoothly, but her brother left in a temper.

DREAM BACKGROUND AND MEANING

After her father died, Jonquil wanted to join the family business, as she was a fully qualified lawyer, specializing in mediation. But her brother, who had run the company single-handed since her father retired, said there was no place for her in their aggressive no-win, no-fee culture that had had spectacular successes but also spectacular losses. She knew he was struggling and knew many of the cases could be settled without major litigation. Storage bags filled with grain represent the accumulation of prosperity, but wealth is to be shared so it is not squandered.

INTERPRETATIONS AND FORTUNE-TELLING MEANINGS

* If you dream of a grain crop that is not growing, a project, venture, or relationship needs more effort and input.
* A trampled grain crop or rotting grain warns of opposition to a venture because of resentment or jealousy.
* Gathering a grain crop represents the successful completion of any endeavor when the right factors have come together.
* A harvest festival grain sheaf indicates the celebration of a birth, marriage, or anniversary in the family or your own life.
* Eating cereal or bread made from grain indicates long-term benefits from cooperation.

OUTCOME OF JONQUIL'S DREAM

Jonquil insisted that she join the practice despite her brother's objections, and as a result the firm became much more stable with far fewer losses. Grain crops and grain dreams represent how what is created can most usefully be processed, using the most effective means.

Grandchildren

Vera, sixty-five, dreamed she opened the door and there were her two grandchildren, now teenagers, who had come to stay. She had not seen them for years and was very excited. They said their mother had gone away. Vera was very happy, as she had thought she would not see them again.

DREAM BACKGROUND AND MEANING

Vera had been banned from seeing her grandchildren after her son, their father, had divorced their mother when the children were three and five. All Vera's gifts and cards had been returned unopened by the mother, who had taken the children to the other side of the States. She had not allowed Vera even to mail or phone them. Dreams of grandchildren confirm the telepathic link of love, even if actual access is limited.

INTERPRETATIONS AND FORTUNE-TELLING MEANINGS

* If you dream of grandchildren living far away, they may be thinking of you and missing you.
* If you dream of a grandchild in danger, especially if you know they take risks, there is no harm in sending them extra love and, if you are really worried, tactfully checking on them.
* If you see a grandchild crying in a dream, even if they say they are fine, there may be a secret worry you are picking up.
* If you dream about your grandchildren when they were much younger, they may need extra reassurance if they are feeling insecure.
* If you see your young grandchildren as adults, this provides reassurance you will have a long, healthy life if you have been worried about your health.

OUTCOME OF VERA'S DREAM

This dream was so real, Vera thought it might be worth another try at being allowed to see her grandchildren. Her ex-daughter-in-law had been dumped by the partner who had prevented contact, and was struggling to cope with two rebellious teenagers. Vera's grandchildren were permitted to regularly visit Vera. A grandparent link is free from many of the conflicts of parenthood, so grandparents can more easily communicate in dreams and in actuality with grandchildren.

Grapes

Andy, thirty-five, dreamed he was standing in his vineyard in France with his wife, contemplating their rich harvest of grapes. The local pickers expertly picked the grapes and exclaimed on the rich harvest, but to his horror drove off with the grapes.

DREAM BACKGROUND AND MEANING

Andy and his wife had purchased a vineyard in France, but he had hit official licensing problems, not helped by his poor knowledge of French. He had signed away his grapes to his uncle's winery, as suggested by an official at the Town Hall, which offered virtually no profit. Grapes represent potential wealth, but a dream can reveal who will benefit from that wealth.

INTERPRETATIONS AND FORTUNE-TELLING MEANINGS

* Successfully growing grapes in a dream is a sign of coming prosperity, but only through wise commercial enterprises.
* If you dream of being given a bunch of grapes, your health will improve; if you are well, you will enjoy good health in the months ahead.
* Picking grapes to make wine in the dream is a fertility symbol, whether for a baby or launching a project.
* In a dream, treading grapes indicates your enemies will be overthrown, but only if you take and maintain control of the process.
* If you are eating grapes, you will enjoy luxury, sexual pleasure, and an appreciative lover, especially if you are being fed the grapes.
* A ruined grape harvest indicates your investments may not pay off because of outside factors or personal carelessness.
* If you dream that the grapes are sour, beware of a friend or colleague who will resent your success and speak ill of you.

OUTCOME OF ANDY'S DREAM

Andy's brother, who spoke fluent French, went to help and discovered that the official in the local Town Hall had taken advantage of Andy's lack of French to legally but unjustly tie them into a poor deal. This was reversed, and Andy was able to sell his grapes at a good profit. Grape dreams can reveal how to avoid financial pitfalls and reap profit through this potentially wealth-bringing symbol.

Grasshopper

Penny, forty-five, dreamed she had finished her chores. Everything was in its place, and she was enjoying coffee by the open garden door. Suddenly, hundreds of grasshoppers were leaping on every surface of her kitchen and even on her hands and clothes. She screamed and tried to squash as many as she could. Then they were gone, as swiftly as they had come.

DREAM BACKGROUND AND MEANING

Penny's fourteen-year-old daughter had been asked to join an educational trip to Vietnam. But Penny was worried. Penny had never traveled because she was too nervous, but her daughter was confident and eager to see the world. Penny had refused to let her go but was aware she was allowing her own fears to affect her daughter's spirit of adventure. Grasshopper dreams speak of change, travel, and not worrying about *what-ifs* and *maybes*. Killing grasshoppers in a dream means rejecting those adventures.

INTERPRETATIONS AND FORTUNE-TELLING MEANINGS

* If you dream of a grasshopper hopping, beware of a lover or friend who constantly changes their mind and arrangements at the last minute.
* If in a dream you hear grasshoppers chirping but do not see them, this warns against hidden gossip.
* The grasshopper in a dream represents enjoying life in the present and not unduly worrying about the past or future.
* If a grasshopper appears and disappears in the dream, unexpected travel will occur, a vacation rather than relocation.
* A plague of grasshoppers warns of unwanted visitors with annoying habits who outstay their welcome.
* A dream of a giant grasshopper represents a big leap forward in career or finances.

OUTCOME OF PENNY'S DREAM

Penny took the dream as a sign that she should allow her daughter to go on the trip. She was starting to regret that she had never traveled, so she booked a vacation for herself and her husband to Paris. Grasshopper dreams are filled with take-a-chance energies that do not promise security but invite taking leaps of faith.

Greeting Cards

Hattie, thirty-five, dreamed she sent her mother-in-law a very elaborate hand-printed birthday card, with a dutifully loving message. But when she saw the card on her mother-in-law's shelf, the card was blank inside. She rewrote the message, but no matter how many times she tried, the loving message disappeared. Then, to her horror, abusive words appeared in the card in bright red ink. She was condemned for ruining the birthday and fled.

DREAM BACKGROUND AND MEANING

Hattie discovered that no matter how hard she tried, nothing was good enough for her husband Harry's family, who constantly compared her unfavorably with Harry's first wife. Her carefully worded cards and presents were ignored, and they never remembered her special occasions. Their inhospitality was bringing her to a breaking point. Dream birthday messages in cards reflect our true feelings and release pent-up resentment in a safe way.

INTERPRETATIONS AND FORTUNE-TELLING MEANINGS

* To send a card for any occasion in a dream to someone you know well reflects your attitude toward the person and event, according to the card and the message.
* If you receive a dream card from someone you know, their message will express their true feelings about the occasion, whether love or resentment.
* If you receive an anonymous card, like a valentine or one left blank, the sender has hidden feelings for you and will soon make these known.
* If you post or send an electronic card that does not arrive in the dream, this is a communication best let go.
* If a card you receive is torn or dirty, the sender is not sincere and should be watched for underhanded dealings.

OUTCOME OF HATTIE'S DREAM

Hattie realized that sooner or later she would snap and say something inappropriate, as she would never be accepted. She insisted that in the future her husband deal with his own relatives, and she took a step back. Greeting cards in dreams are very significant, because they reveal what we cannot say directly.

Grim Reaper

Debi, fifty, recalled clearly when she was twenty and having a flying dream. She flew into a town with a street made of earth. Standing on top of a flat-roofed single-story building was the Grim Reaper. She was not afraid, but hugged him, saying, "Hi, Dave." His hood was thrown off and his scythe disappeared. She took him by the hand and off they flew. He was so heavy that she couldn't keep him high off the ground and they crash-landed, laughing, in a very muddy, flooded field.

DREAM BACKGROUND AND MEANING

Debi, who was young and healthy and, having grown up on a farm where her father humanely slaughtered his own animals, had a respect for but no fear of death. For her the Grim Reaper was a symbol of enjoying every moment of life, and in the dream was seen as a vibrant, sexual male. The concept of the Death Angel has, however, become an object of terror through the centuries.

INTERPRETATIONS AND FORTUNE-TELLING MEANINGS

* Scary dreams of the Grim Reaper may occur when the dreamer suddenly encounters the concept of death for the first time.
* If you dream that the Grim Reaper knocks on the door, no one in the house is going to die, but perhaps there are threats of divorce, bankruptcy, or repossession that need confronting.
* If the dreamer escapes or hides from the Grim Reaper, there may be a temporary respite from problems.
* If the Grim Reaper turns away, then difficulties will likewise be averted.
* To see the Grim Reaper in the distance suggests the ending of a phase involving relocation or travel, which will bring new beginnings.
* If the Grim Reaper carries a covered box away from your home, a hidden bad habit or addiction may be threatening your health or that of a loved one.

OUTCOME OF DEBI'S DREAM

Debi had a pragmatic attitude to loss and betrayal and, as a result, had survived a challenging life without fear or self-pity. Grim Reaper dreams can reflect the process of incorporating mortality into life without becoming obsessed about death.

Groundhog Day

Celine, twenty-nine, dreamed on the evening of Groundhog Day (February 2) that she saw a groundhog come out of his burrow, see his shadow because the sun was shining, and return to his burrow. This predicted six more weeks of wintry weather. Celine woke frustrated.

DREAM BACKGROUND AND MEANING

Celine was an avid fan of the film *Groundhog Day*, in which the weatherman was forced to relive February 2 over and over. She wanted to go trekking from England to New Zealand with her boyfriend, Joel, but he was getting tired of her delays and said he was setting off in six weeks' time, with or without her. Sometimes a predictive dream can mark a deadline if fears hold us back.

INTERPRETATIONS AND FORTUNE-TELLING MEANINGS

★ If you dream of the groundhog not seeing his shadow because of cloudy weather and staying out on February 2, it is a good omen for an early spring and putting plans in motion at once.

★ If you dream of the groundhog seeing his shadow and returning to the burrow, wait a little longer, but start now getting plans in place.

★ If you dream of repeating the same groundhog dream cycle all night, you are stuck in a routine.

★ If you dream of the older festivals, the Celtic celebration of Imbolc, the first day of spring, or the Germanic Christian celebration of Candlemas, doubts and self-imposed delays may be rooted in past-world or childhood insecurity.

★ If you dream of being at the famous Groundhog Day festival in Punxsutawney, Pennsylvania, responsibilities and obligations to others may be holding you back.

★ If you dream of the groundhog on February 1 or the evening of February 2, the dream is of special significance.

OUTCOME OF CELINE'S DREAM

Celine knew in her heart she wanted to go to New Zealand, and six weeks' time would give her time to quit her job and get ready. A delay in your dream groundhog's movements may offer you breathing space to come out of your personal hibernation.

Guilt from Beyond the Grave

Mario, sixty-seven, dreamed he was sweeping outside his house when he felt very tired. He went inside for a rest and could hear his late wife's voice berating him for being lazy. He carried on, but every time he took a rest from the chore, her voice nagged him to not be so idle. He awoke from the dream feeling guilty, haunted by his wife's final reproach that his neglect had made her ill.

DREAM BACKGROUND AND MEANING

Mario had worked hard all his life. When he retired, his wife was continually finding him jobs and making him feel guilty when he rested. She became ill and blamed him for the illness that ultimately caused her death. Now he was driving himself to the point of exhaustion. Dreams can rerun old scenarios where the dreamer unfairly relives the guilt and blame that was heaped on them by the dying.

INTERPRETATIONS AND FORTUNE-TELLING MEANINGS

★ While departed loved ones can talk to us in dreams, if the relationship was not harmonious, the dreamer hears the dying person's reproaches without any chance to resolve them.

★ If a deceased relative blames you in a dream for their illness or unhappiness, it is important to not accept their distorted view of reality.

★ If in the dream the deceased points out your faults, remember the deceased also had flaws.

★ If a dream drives the dreamer into needless activity, consider whether this serves any purpose.

★ If the dreamer awakes angry, it indicates that there might have been confrontation or parting, had the deceased lived.

★ Since emotional blackmail can continue from the afterlife, refuse to let your future end with the bereavement.

OUTCOME OF MARIO'S DREAM

Mario realized his wife should not be able to harangue him from beyond the grave, so he moved to a new home, free of memories. Dreams where the deceased is unkind can lead to the realization that it is acceptable to dislike the person's behavior without guilt, and without demonizing or overidealizing them.

Guilt Trip

Stephanie, forty-five, dreamed she was on a singles cruise, sipping champagne, when an officer told her that her mother back home had fallen and badly injured herself. Stephanie was overcome with guilt for leaving her and had to be hoisted up by helicopter and flown to shore. When she arrived home, her mother had only sprained an ankle.

DREAM BACKGROUND AND MEANING

Stephanie was planning her first holiday overseas without her mother. As the unmarried child, she had been expected to stay home with her widowed mother. Her mother, even though she was very fit, made Stephanie feel selfish for going on vacation, although Stephanie had arranged for her twenty-one-year-old niece to move in while she was away. Her mother warned that she might not still be alive when Stephanie got back.

INTERPRETATIONS AND FORTUNE-TELLING MEANINGS

★ If you dream that someone who makes you feel guilty had a dreadful accident when you are not around, it is pure anxiety holding you captive.

★ If in the dream you are dragging a ball and chain or tied with cords to the person making you feel guilty, it is time to break free from false obligations.

★ If in the dream you speak harshly toward the guilt-inducing perpetrator, there is mounting suppressed resentment at being denied your own life.

★ If you dream you are accused of murdering an ungrateful person you care for, you are killing your own freedom.

★ If you escape from the dependent person and do not fall for emotional blackmail in the dream, you can free yourself in daily life to live your own way.

OUTCOME OF STEPHANIE'S DREAM

After the dream, Stephanie had a fabulous incident-free cruise without guilt. Stephanie's niece asked to stay permanently, lured by free accommodation, and she ignored her great-aunt's power games. Stephanie moved out. Guilt-trip dreams can express the dreamer's worst fears, but when they do not materialize, the guilt trip begins to lose its power.

Hacking

Glenn, twenty-eight, dreamed his best friend, Zak, was sitting at Glenn's home computer, logging in while Tricia, Glenn's girlfriend, was leaning over his shoulder, reading Glenn's emails, which clearly showed that Glenn was cheating. Zak was comforting her. Glenn knew he was innocent.

DREAM BACKGROUND AND MEANING

Glenn realized his home computer was being hacked when his girlfriend became convinced that Glenn was cheating. Computer expert and best friend Zak had helped Glenn set up a new security system on his computer. But things got worse, and the emails from the fictitious girlfriend increased. Zak was secretly showing them to Tricia. Hacking dreams can pick up information about the hacker that the conscious mind and even cybersecurity miss.

INTERPRETATIONS AND FORTUNE-TELLING MEANINGS

★ If you dream your phone is being hacked, beware of gossip behind your back.

★ If you dream of your passwords being stolen, be careful who you trust.

★ If the hacker in the dream has infected your computer with a virus or Trojan horse, beware that you are not blamed for spreading misinformation about others.

★ If in the dream you discover your virus protection is out of date and warnings appear, you may need to take greater care with personal, work, and domestic security.

★ If your dream hacker communicates with you via your computer, you may be suffering interference or emotional blackmail from a family member.

★ If in a dream someone is hacking into your bank account, you may have been too generous or may have been overspending to impress.

OUTCOME OF GLENN'S DREAM

The hacking spread to Glenn's work computer. Since Zak worked for the same company, Glenn realized the dream was pointing to Zak trying to take over his girlfriend and job. He blocked Zak and changed passwords. This solved the work problem, but too much damage had been done with his girlfriend. If you dream someone is controlling your computer, you may be especially vulnerable to external intrusion, whether personal or professional. The hacker may be close to home.

Hair

Hilary, eighteen, dreamed she was having her hair cut by her best friend, Cilla, in a beauty salon. To her horror, her friend took a pair of garden shears and hacked into the middle section. Hilary ran from the salon, sobbing, as she knew she could not now go to the prom, to which her new boyfriend was partnering her.

DREAM BACKGROUND AND MEANING

Cilla was jealous of Hilary's relationship. A dominant person, she had persuaded Hilary to spend her money on an expensive, hideous dress. Now she had offered to do Hilary's hair and makeup. Hilary did not want to offend her friend by refusing, but was suspicious, as she knew Cilla also liked her boyfriend. Having your hair cut badly in a dream warns that someone is draining your energy or dominating you.

INTERPRETATIONS AND FORTUNE-TELLING MEANINGS

* Shining long hair symbolizes strength, sexual attraction, and good health.
* Hair falling out in a dream indicates fears of loss of power and charisma.
* If you dream your hair is tangled, you may have tied yourself up with too many responsibilities at the expense of your own harmony.
* If your hair is blowing free in the wind and you are happy, break free of others' restrictions.
* If you are brushing your hair while gazing in a mirror, you may see your true love, present or future, behind you in the dream mirror.
* Washing your hair in a dream signifies clearing unresolved issues that are causing uncertainty in your actions and reactions.

OUTCOME OF HILARY'S DREAM

Hilary returned the dress to the store and bought the one she liked. She had her hair and makeup done at another salon. Her new boyfriend loved the look. Hilary and Cilla are no longer friends.

Hair represents the image we present to the world. If you dream that your hair is blowing everywhere after being fixed, you may be worried about the impression you are making on the world.

Hair Loss

Wyatt, twenty-eight, had a recurring dream that he was about to take part in a photo shoot when he was told that, because he was going bald, he was no longer able to feature in the commercials. Wyatt was devastated and felt that his modeling days were over.

DREAM BACKGROUND AND MEANING

Wyatt had been aware for several months that he was starting to lose his hair. In addition to designing and writing television commercials, he often featured in advertisements, and he hoped to increase the modeling side of his job. Hair loss in a dream, whether actually occurring or not, casts up issues of holding on to your youth in a world where retaining young looks is highly valued.

INTERPRETATIONS AND FORTUNE-TELLING MEANINGS

* If in a dream your hair suddenly falls out, you are afraid of losing your power and charisma, perhaps because of a relationship or career setback.
* If you are a woman losing hair in your dream, you have rivals in love or career who undermine your confidence.
* If you are a man losing your hair in your dream, you may have come up against competition in your career from younger people and may fear being overlooked.
* If you actually suffer hair loss and it grows back in a dream, you will find a new strength and talent to empower you in a field that values experience over youth.
* If you deliberately have all your hair cut off, you are feeling confident in your sensuality.
* If in a dream you try to hide your baldness with a wig, you may be accepting others' assessment of your own worth.

OUTCOME OF WYATT'S DREAM

Wyatt took a chance and launched a freelance agency promoting younger guys in various stages of baldness and did the photo shoots himself. Hair-loss dreams are very emotional at times when others or society are making us feel insecure about our true worth.

Halloween

Felicia, fifteen, dreamed she was in a ruined house alone. Lighted skulls were appearing out of the darkness, and invisible cobweb hands were touching her. She thought it must be someone playing a Halloween trick, but then she was surrounded by tiny black demons with red eyes, prodding her with needles and chanting curses. She woke screaming.

DREAM BACKGROUND AND MEANING

Felicia had been dared by her friends to spend Halloween alone in a local abandoned house. They had all been playing with a ouija board during sleepovers, and Felicia had been chosen by the spirits to pass on messages. Many of them were accurate, but they became increasingly bizarre and dangerous. She wanted out, but feared being called a coward. Halloween, traditionally the time of remembering deceased family members, has become a fun festival, but occult energies are especially strong at that time and may threaten those who dabble unwisely.

INTERPRETATIONS AND FORTUNE-TELLING MEANINGS

- ✶ If you are standing at a windy crossroads in your Halloween dream, listen to hear what you need to know for the next twelve months.
- ✶ If you dream of a dark house with strange noises and ghostly figures, even if it is not Halloween, an unwelcome person from your past may suddenly reappear.
- ✶ If you are trick-or-treating in a Halloween dream, someone close is flattering or flirting to gain monetary or sexual advantage over you.
- ✶ If someone you know is dressed in a strange costume, there may be undesirable hidden aspects of their personality.
- ✶ If you dream your Halloween pumpkin will not light, you are being told to take the initiative in love at this traditional time of discovering a twin soul.

OUTCOME OF FELICIA'S DREAM

Felicia confessed to her mother what they had been doing. Her mother knew a healer, who talked to all the girls and gave them holy water to take away any bad energies they had picked up. Felicia still had bad dreams for several weeks. Frightening Halloween dreams are a warning not to dabble with unknown powers at any time of the year.

Hammer

Charlie, forty-five, dreamed he was in a blacksmith's forge, watching the blacksmith hammer a horseshoe into shape. The blacksmith handed him the hammer and told him to finish the job himself, but the hammer broke as Charlie hit the anvil. The blacksmith said if he could not shoe his own horse he would not be going anywhere. Defiantly, Charlie fixed the hammer and shoed his own horse.

DREAM BACKGROUND AND MEANING

Charlie, a builder, was planning to travel the day after the dream to borrow money from his wealthy father. Charlie's business had been hit hard by the recession. Charlie's father had always said Charlie had to stand on his own two feet and had not even helped him with college fees. Hammer dreams can represent vital communications, but it may be that the dreamer has to use the hammer himself if others will not help him.

INTERPRETATIONS AND FORTUNE-TELLING MEANINGS

- ✶ To dream you are making or mending something with a hammer promises success if you are strong and determined.
- ✶ If you are hammering a nail in a wall while speaking determinedly, you are emphasizing how important your words are.
- ✶ If in your dream a judge or another senior official bangs the wooden gavel on the desk, you are likely to learn the results of a long-running dispute, successful or otherwise.
- ✶ If you dream you drop a hammer, you may be considering giving way to emotional pressure.
- ✶ If a hammer breaks, be prepared for powerful opposition to a plan; but if you mend it, you can regain control.
- ✶ If you dream you are attacked with a hammer, beware of coercion to make you change your mind.

OUTCOME OF CHARLIE'S DREAM

Charlie realized that he would be wasting his time asking his father for money, as his attitude had never softened. He took on extra work and pulled his company out of debt. A dream may reveal that only the dreamer's own determination and perseverance will fulfill the purpose for which the hammer is or should be used.

Hammock

Alexander, forty-two, dreamed he was lying contentedly in a hammock under a mosquito net in a rain forest. He was alone and at ease. As he dozed, he noticed a huge python encircling the hammock and realized he had left his knife on the ground. He struggled to escape as the creature crushed him.

DREAM BACKGROUND AND MEANING

Alexander had left his home after he discovered his wife was having an affair with a neighbor. He had taken leave from work and gone on a long vacation to the mountains. A hammock represents freedom from responsibility but is not permanent protection against harsh reality.

INTERPRETATIONS AND FORTUNE-TELLING MEANINGS

⋆ If you dream you are sleeping comfortably in a hammock, you may need more leisure time in the natural world to let problems take care of themselves for a while.

⋆ To relax in a hammock says you should step back from a situation or confrontation and let others sort out their own problems.

⋆ To swing in a hammock suggests postponing a decision, perhaps because the situation is unstable, which will eventually need resolving.

⋆ If a hammock is swaying in the wind, gently go with the flow of life; if the hammock is out of control, others may try to disturb your tranquility with their demands.

⋆ A dream of falling out of a hammock, or of a breaking hammock, warns that you need to take more precautions in business or finances, rather than leaving things to chance.

⋆ If you dream you are sleeping in a hammock in your bedroom, you may feel unsettled and need to resolve domestic issues or free yourself.

OUTCOME OF ALEXANDER'S DREAM

The dream made Alexander realize that, with a family and home, he could not just walk away, however hurt he was. He had to either fix the relationship or make an amicable split for the sake of the children, as otherwise he would never be free. He contacted his wife to talk over the future with her. Hammock dreams symbolize freedom only if the dreamer first resolves underlying issues.

Hamster, Gerbil (Pet Rodent)

Mary, thirty-five, dreamed her husband, Allan, brought home a hamster and put it in a glass tank without a lid. Mary was concerned that the cat might kill it if there was no cover. Her husband insisted she was fussing unnecessarily. When she looked, the cat was in the tank, with the hamster in its mouth. Allan blamed Mary for not taking better care of the hamster.

DREAM BACKGROUND AND MEANING

Mary and her husband, Allan, were considering having a baby, but she worried he would opt out of practical support, leaving everything to her. Dreaming of caring for a small animal reveals how much responsibility a partner would assume toward a baby, helpless child, or pet.

INTERPRETATIONS AND FORTUNE-TELLING MEANINGS

⋆ If you dream of happily caring for a small pet, you have a natural gift with children and small animals.

⋆ If you do not like small pets but are responsible for one in the dream and it does not thrive, you may not feel ready to have a child.

⋆ If you are expected to care for a pet in the dream but your partner offers no assistance, you may be concerned about whether they would be a good parent or stepparent.

⋆ If you dream that the creature is injured or killed in your care although it was not your fault, you may habitually assume unnecessary guilt when things go wrong.

⋆ If you dream that you give back a small pet to the original owner, you should cease accepting responsibility for others' burdens.

⋆ If you dream that you find a small lost pet and no one claims it, others may too often impose guilt on you so you will sort out their problems.

OUTCOME OF MARY'S DREAM

Mary realized from the dream that Allan expected her to take responsibility in their relationship but contributed little himself. She decided to delay trying for a baby. A small helpless creature is a dream symbol when you are questioning who you can call for support when needed.

Handbag, Man Bag

Esther, thirty-three, dreamed she was using her new handbag, which she hated. It was deep, with lots of inner pockets. Every time she wanted to find something, she had to empty the bag. She bought an identical bag to her old one, transferred everything, and cast the offending bag into the garbage can.

DREAM BACKGROUND AND MEANING

Esther's sister-in-law, Flo, had moved in with Esther and her husband, Hugo, while waiting for her new house to be completed. Instantly, she rearranged the whole house and replaced Esther's handbag with an organizer, saying Esther could not find anything in her old one. Hugo did not protest at his sister's behavior, as she dominated his life. Handbags are very personal items, reflecting what is of value to us.

INTERPRETATIONS AND FORTUNE-TELLING MEANINGS

* If you dream that you keep leaving your handbag in public places and it is still intact when you return, you are open and confident about revealing your inner self.
* If you leave your handbag in public places and it is missing when you return, you are too trusting.
* Since a handbag contains all your essential items away from home, if you cannot find what you need in your bag, you may have too much clutter in your life generally.
* If you dream your handbag is stolen, someone around you is overly curious about your private life.
* If you dream your handbag strap breaks, you may be overloading your days with too much activity.
* If you dream your bag is empty, be cautious about revealing too much about yourself to acquaintances.

OUTCOME OF ESTHER'S DREAM

After the dream, Esther restored her home to the way that worked for her. She retrieved her handbag and refilled it. When Flo caused a scene, Esther arranged accommodations for Flo in a local motel. She told Hugo that if he objected, he could move out with his sister. Handbags reflect our life priorities, and to have someone rearrange our bag in a dream or in real life should be resisted.

Hand-Me-Downs, Secondhand Goods

Stephanie, thirty-eight, dreamed she was young again, forced to wear her cousin's hand-me-downs, which were always too big and frilly. Her friends teased her and refused to be seen with her. She woke embarrassed but relieved that she need no longer go back to those days.

DREAM BACKGROUND AND MEANING

Stephanie was engaged to a man who had been married before. Though he never talked about his first wife and they were moving to a new house together, Stephanie always felt she was second-best. She insisted on replacing everything from his old life. But whatever he said, it did not reassure her, and the feeling was causing problems in the relationship. Brand-new does not always imply superiority over secondhand if what is secondhand—whether a relationship, situation, or item—is valued and given in love.

INTERPRETATIONS AND FORTUNE-TELLING MEANINGS

* If in the dream you are wearing ill-fitting, unattractive hand-me-downs and cannot afford anything else, you may still be reacting to past humiliation where you felt second-best.
* If you dream you are in a thrift shop, choosing an outfit for a special occasion, you may feel undervalued by whoever is going with you to the event.
* If you see exactly what you want but it is secondhand, you may be underrating a situation or offer because of its lack of status.
* If you are handing on clothes to someone you care for, you are giving them part of yourself, and this expresses mutual trust, unless they are refused.
* If you are giving unwanted items to a thrift store, see what of yourself you are rejecting or giving away.

OUTCOME OF STEPHANIE'S DREAM

The dream reminded Stephanie that feeling second-best was a childhood memory and should not apply to the present situation. She opened a business selling barely worn, trendy clothes for teenagers who could not afford new, and it became a cult place to shop. Dreams about secondhand goods and rejection usually are rooted in actual incidents that, though buried, can cloud judgment even after the hurt has faded.

Hands

Steve, forty-eight, dreamed he was shaking hands with his best friend, Porter, and handing him a large amount of cash to invest on his behalf. Steve noticed Porter's wife had the car engine running. Porter snatched the money and ran to the car, making a rude hand gesture as they sped off. Steve woke up full of doubt.

DREAM BACKGROUND AND MEANING

Steve had been awarded a big bonus, and Porter suggested he invest it in an overseas bank, saying it could be done with no paperwork. Steve hesitated. Hands are very significant in their dream meaning, from the acknowledging wave of royalty to a subject, to a comforting hug. The dream content will reveal the nature and sincerity of the hand contact.

INTERPRETATIONS AND FORTUNE-TELLING MEANINGS

★ If a dream hand is outstretched in friendship, it indicates a positive connection, perhaps from someone previously considered indifferent or hostile.

★ A closed hand warns of meanness from a close friend or family member.

★ Seeing praying hands covering yours is a spiritual dream revealing that your guardian angel or spirit guide is present.

★ A dream of hands being bound or handcuffed indicates a sense of being restricted, unless it is a sexual fantasy dream.

★ A fist, especially waved in the face, can reveal escalating anger that needs to be deflected.

★ Holding hands with someone you desire as a lover or within a relationship following coldness or estrangement is a good omen of coming together physically and emotionally.

OUTCOME OF STEVE'S DREAM

Steve found out more about offshore investments. He concluded that signing formal paperwork was the only way to gain any security. Steve withdrew from the deal and is no longer friends with Porter. Undisguised body language in dreams is clear, and hand movements in particular reveal true intentions when words deceive.

Handwriting

John, forty-four, dreamed he was a trusted monk preparing an illuminated manuscript for a gift to a ruling monarch. But the words would not quite fit on the vellum. He left a word out at random and finished the manuscript. However, he had omitted a crucial word, which gave the message the opposite meaning and advised the king to be warlike, regardless of the consequences. To his relief, no one detected the mistake.

DREAM BACKGROUND AND MEANING

John had sent a hastily scribbled message at work, as the email system was down and the recipient was not answering their phone. Later he realized he had left out a vital word and had advised the company to resist a takeover, not to accept it, which was the safe option. John dared not admit his mistake, as it could be worth millions of dollars. Dream handwriting can sometimes reveal what is the correct advice, not what is consciously expected.

INTERPRETATIONS AND FORTUNE-TELLING MEANINGS

★ Written communications in dreams, especially when handwritten, have even deeper significance than spoken or printed messages.

★ If in the dream your hand is guided by an unseen force, this is automatic writing, containing information from deep within the psyche or from your guardian angel or spirit guide.

★ If in a dream you are handwriting, you may have something very important to communicate that you have not consciously acknowledged.

★ Indistinct or unintelligible writing can indicate you are uncertain of your own feelings and desires.

★ Writing crossed out, torn, or smudged can reveal that there is conflict or that what someone is communicating is not their genuine feelings.

OUTCOME OF JOHN'S DREAM

Share prices increased dramatically, and the takeover was not necessary. John was credited for keeping his nerve. Had he sent an email, he might have retracted the error, with disastrous consequences. Handwritten messages are rare, but can be guided by our wise self or even by a spirit guardian and in crucial matters can cut through logic to as yet unknown information.

Hare

Molly, thirty-eight, dreamed she saw a hare released from a trap, followed by chariots with knives on the wheels. She realized she was witnessing a battle between Celts and Romans. Two chariots drew alongside her, one Roman, one Celt. She was told she must choose sides or be crushed. The hare reappeared and guided Molly safely to where it was nesting. The moon was shining brightly.

DREAM BACKGROUND AND MEANING

Thanksgiving was approaching, and both sets of parents were pressuring Molly and her husband to visit. Their parents lived in different states. Molly was having a difficult pregnancy and wanted to spend Thanksgiving at home. Molly's husband opted out of the decision. In Celtic battles, a hare was released to gain the favor of Andraste, the Moon goddess. The hare was her sacred creature.

INTERPRETATIONS AND FORTUNE-TELLING MEANINGS

★ To dream you see a hare running states you should shed an obligation or demand.

★ A hare being chased by dogs suggests arguments among friends or family. Beware of attempting to make peace.

★ Associated with Ostara, Norse goddess of spring, a dream hare sitting on its hind legs represents new beginnings and directions.

★ Hares are linked with the moon in Indian, Buddhist, and Celtic traditions. Surrounded by moonlight, they indicate you should not make unreasonable sacrifices for the sake of pleasing others.

★ Two hares fighting says there may be rival opinions or bids for your favor. Find an alternative.

★ Dreaming of a nesting hare signifies fertility and is a good omen for busy working parents.

OUTCOME OF MOLLY'S DREAM

Molly chose to follow her dream hare to its nest and make her pregnancy the priority. Molly told both sets of parents they were welcome to visit. Once the baby was born, Molly and her husband would spend Thanksgiving with one set of grandparents and Christmas with the other. The hare, unlike the more sociable rabbit, ultimately is a creature that chooses its path.

Harp

Linda, forty-five, dreamed she was watching a medieval battle. In the center was a young harpist. None of the arrows were reaching him. Gradually the battle nearest to the harpist stopped and the warring soldiers sat together close to him. Slowly the battle ceased until all the combatants were sitting and listening. Then the harpist became Linda.

DREAM BACKGROUND AND MEANING

Linda often felt she was living in the middle of a war zone when her teenage stepchildren came and clashed with her own teens. Her husband left Linda to keep the peace. Often associated with past worlds, harp dreams refer to stable periods or gentle transitions, rather than dramatic changes.

INTERPRETATIONS AND FORTUNE-TELLING MEANINGS

★ If you dream you are playing a harp or listening to one, you will experience a period of peace and harmony with others.

★ Melodious harp music is a sign of betrothals, weddings, and reconciliation.

★ A broken harp indicates a troublesome relation playing favorites or setting one family member against another.

★ An out-of-tune harp says there is underlying discord, better brought to the surface than left to simmer.

★ If you hear invisible celestial harps playing, it's time to get in touch or reconnect with your spiritual nature.

★ Continuing harp music throughout the dream warns us to persist, to harp on about a matter of importance or a request that others are ignoring.

OUTCOME OF LINDA'S DREAM

Linda decided to make a sanctuary for herself with candles, crystals, and gentle background music, and insisted that anyone entering the room had to be totally quiet. Linda retreated there from the children's squabbles. Increasingly, one or more teens joined her. This eventually improved the atmosphere. Linda made time for creating personal harmony and tranquility, rather than trying to solve others' squabbles.

Hat

Pru, forty-five, dreamed she was wearing an old hat with a wide brim and veil so that no one would recognize her. She was heading for an interview at a new company. She suddenly realized she had nothing to hide, as she deserved recognition. She took off the hat, dumped it in a garbage can, and returned to her own organization, where she demanded an interview with the CEO to ask for a promotion.

DREAM BACKGROUND AND MEANING

Pru was planning to apply for a new job with a rival company because she felt undervalued at her current workplace. However, she was worried that if she did not get the job and her present company found out, she might be demoted or even fired. Hats can act as a statement of worth or as protection to prevent detection. A dream can reveal which kind of hat we need.

INTERPRETATIONS AND FORTUNE-TELLING MEANINGS

★ If you dream you are wearing a fancy hat, a wedding or family gathering is likely.

★ A hat that does not fit in a dream indicates you are trying too hard to impress others.

★ If you are wearing a hat as part of a uniform, others are trying to make you fit into their life view.

★ If the wind blows your hat off, unexpected changes are due that may involve an advantageous career change if you follow the hat.

★ If you do not normally wear a hat but dream you are buying one, your status or promotion prospects will soon be raised.

★ If you are wearing an old or battered hat, you may be fearful of losing a familiar if unfulfilling lifestyle.

OUTCOME OF PRU'S DREAM

Pru's hat dream made her realize her own value in her role. She approached her CEO and said she was thinking of applying for a new job elsewhere. The CEO said she did not want to lose Pru and gave her an instant salary increase and promotion. Hat dreams reveal how we perceive ourselves, and that can reflect the image we project to the world.

Hatching

Nathan, thirty-eight, dreamed he found a huge egg that was starting to crack. Eventually a small dinosaur emerged. Nathan was excited because this was almost a miracle, but he also felt very burdened. He felt responsible for its well-being. He loaded the dinosaur in his jeep but did not know what to do with it, so he took it home to his wife, Sue.

DREAM BACKGROUND AND MEANING

Nathan and Sue were expecting a baby, which had completely derailed their plans to travel the world, working from their computers. They had assumed they would never have children and believed that parents should build their lives around their children. Hatching dreams occur at change points, where options must be rethought to make room for the hatchlings.

INTERPRETATIONS AND FORTUNE-TELLING MEANINGS

★ If you dream you see eggs hatching, this is a good omen for conception and healthy pregnancy.

★ If you dream that you or someone is hatching a plot, it can be good or malicious, depending on its purpose.

★ Eggs being incubated represent ideas or projects that need time and care to come to fruition.

★ The size and type of the hatching egg affect the meaning. A bird's egg represents the potential to get ideas off the ground; a chick's, domestic bliss; a water bird's, love; and a crocodile's, wariness of someone you help.

★ Empty shells suggest hurrying to take advantage of a new beginning that is available.

★ If the eggs are smashed or the chicks are eaten by predators, accept that matters did not work out and realize that you may need to take more precautions next time (see "Nest," p. 327).

OUTCOME OF NATHAN'S DREAM

Sue pointed out that this was an ideal time to travel, as babies were very portable, and in the early years they would enjoy the freedom of nature while they took turns to work. Hatching always has an element of the unknown, but brings a new creation to add a different but exciting dimension to a well-planned life.

Hatred Beyond the Grave

The night before a serious operation, Helena, forty-five, dreamed of her red-haired stepmother standing in front of a house in Australia, telling her, "You'll never set foot in my house." In her dream, Helena insisted, "Yes, I will." There followed a battle of wills in which Helena mobilized her strength for the operation, to defy her stepmother and go to her father's house.

DREAM BACKGROUND AND MEANING

Helena recalled that when she was a child, her stepmother had entered the family home as her father's mistress and ordered Helena and her mother into the street. After her operation, Helena wrote quite spontaneously to the father she hadn't seen for thirty years, telling him she forgave him. Through a dream, unresolved hatred can sometimes be a powerful catalyst for the dreamer to transform earlier negativity into personal power to fight back.

INTERPRETATIONS AND FORTUNE-TELLING MEANINGS

★ If you dream of hatred against you from a deceased relative, it has no power to harm.

★ If in a dream the person who died with bad feelings toward you seeks reconciliation, this can close a family feud.

★ If you dream of an angry ghost you do not know, it may just need to have an injustice acknowledged.

★ When you wake, see if you can forgive the person or, if not, let the wrong go in the way that feels best for you.

★ Check the date you had the dream, as it may be the anniversary of their death or of a tragedy in their life that no one living remembers.

OUTCOME OF HELENA'S DREAM

A return letter told Helena that her stepmother had died about the time of her dream. Helena's father offered to pay her return airfare if she would stay with him in Australia. Helena had the satisfaction of stepping inside her stepmother's house, and helped her father take all the stepmother's belongings to the garbage dump. Hatred can survive death and may manifest in dreams until one of the parties lets go, even if forgiveness is not possible.

Hawk

Felicity, twenty-eight, dreamed she saw many large birds squawking and circling over a field, ignoring mice scurrying on the ground, as they wanted better prey. A magnificent hawk sat on a fence, occasionally swooping for a mouse, but waiting silently. A cottontail rabbit appeared. The other birds were too busy fighting among themselves, and the hawk claimed the prey.

DREAM BACKGROUND AND MEANING

Felicity was a production assistant in a provincial theater. She learned all the parts so she could fill in if there was an emergency. The actors laughed at her, saying she was wasting her time.

A universal symbol of the sun and the ability to soar high, the hawk appears in the lore of many lands, including native North America, Celtic Britain, Aboriginal Australia, India, and Ancient Egypt, where it was associated with Horus, the sky god, and with the freed human spirit.

INTERPRETATIONS AND FORTUNE-TELLING MEANINGS

★ A dream of a hawk swooping indicates the need to be more focused and ruthless to gain advantage.

★ A hawk soaring says, "Aim high and go it alone."

★ A hawk catching prey promises success by waiting for the right moment to act.

★ If you dream that a hawk is watching you, keep a close eye on rivals, who may be planning an attack when least expected.

★ As the hawk, like the eagle, is said to fly closest to the sun without being burned or blinded, be courageous in pursuing a major ambition.

★ As the hawk is sometimes associated with the magician Merlin, if you dream of one, an unexpected opportunity may arise that must be instantly seized.

OUTCOME OF FELICITY'S DREAM

Felicity persevered, taking any part available in the production when someone was absent. During a virus pandemic, both the star and the understudy were taken ill, and Felicity was the only one who knew the part. She was a great success and now has been offered a permanent minor acting role. A hawk is a positive sign to remain alert to opportunities and challenges.

Hazelnuts

Corinne, twenty-eight, dreamed she was standing beneath a hazel tree, sheltering from the rain, when the wind blew and nuts came tumbling down all around her. She filled her shopping bag with the nuts, and there was no room for the purchases she had intended to make. But her partner, Jess, did not mind, as the results of their latest pregnancy test had come back positive.

DREAM BACKGROUND AND MEANING

Corinne and Jess were trying for a baby with a sperm donor who was a good friend, but had had no luck in twelve months. Private treatment was prohibitively expensive. Corinne felt the dream was a good omen saying they should keep trying. Hazelnuts hanging on a tree represent the potential for the fulfillment of wishes through persistence.

INTERPRETATIONS AND FORTUNE-TELLING MEANINGS

* Hazelnuts cascading down are a powerful fertility symbol, often signifying twins.
* If you are given a bag of hazelnuts when dreaming of your wedding, betrothal, or commitment ceremony, this promises a long-lasting, happy relationship.
* If you dream of nine hazelnuts floating in a well, an ancient Celtic sign of wisdom, it is an encouraging sign for study, creative ventures, tests, and examinations. The nut kernels symbolized the nine poetic nuts of inspiration hanging on the tree over Connla's Well in Tipperary, Ireland.
* If you are dowsing in your dream with a traditional hazel rod with hazelnuts attached, you will find the answer or resource you are seeking.
* Hazel staves decorated with nuts symbolize justice and success in a legal or compensation case.
* Dreaming of making hazelnut butter is an excellent sign for making money through your own talents, and especially for starting a business.

OUTCOME OF CORINNE'S DREAM

Corinne and her partner agreed to continue trying before seeking expensive private treatment, and she became pregnant a month later. Hazelnut dreams always signify good news and the resolution of worries in the best possible way.

Healing

Sebastian, twenty-eight, dreamed he was at the healing grotto at Lourdes with his friend Jeremy, who was very ill. A woman gave Sebastian and his friend a yellow rose, symbol of Our Lady of Lourdes. Sebastian felt tingling in his hands and a light coursing through his body. He put his hands on his friend, who was instantly healed.

DREAM BACKGROUND AND MEANING

Sebastian had recently noticed tingling in his hands, and when he touched Jeremy, his friend seemed calmer. But Sebastian was frustrated that he could not cure his friend as he had in the dream. Healing powers may be revealed in dreams but may, in the waking world, offer relief rather than miracles.

INTERPRETATIONS AND FORTUNE-TELLING MEANINGS

* If you dream of healing others but have no knowledge of this world, it is a sign you have healing gifts.
* If you dream of being visited by an angel or spirit guide in your dreams who passes healing powers through your head or hands, this is a spiritual experience.
* If in your dream you visit a particular healing shrine, it may hold special significance for you spiritually.
* If you are learning healing and have dreams of performing healing miracles, keep trying, even if frustrated by slow progress.
* If you fail to cure someone in a dream, this can mean bringing peace and may be the best outcome if a cure is not possible.
* If you are being healed in a dream by an earthly healer, angel, or guide, it is a sign that your health will improve.

OUTCOME OF SEBASTIAN'S DREAM

After the dream, Sebastian accompanied Jeremy to Lourdes, and Jeremy found great consolation in the experience. Sebastian did not receive any dramatic powers, but the strong presence of faith there persuaded him to learn healing through a local church group circle. Healing dreams can awaken the dreamer to explore the world of healing.

Hearth

Hilda, seventy-five, often dreamed of sitting by the open fire at the hearth as a child, making toast on a fork and telling stories by firelight or listening to the radio. She did not want to go to bed, as she was snug in her checkered dressing gown and slippers, listening to the adults talking.

DREAM BACKGROUND AND MEANING

Hilda lived in a nursing home. She was well cared for by the staff, who would watch her draw her armchair close to the radiator, imagining it was her childhood fireplace. Her daughter worked long hours and her grandchildren rarely visited. The staff of the place feared she was not thriving. The hearth is an old-fashioned symbol, which, for some dreamers, recalls childhood security, real or imagined, or expresses an archetypal longing to find a welcoming sanctuary.

INTERPRETATIONS AND FORTUNE-TELLING MEANINGS

* A traditional focal point of the home and the original place of worship of household gods, the hearth speaks of the need for domestic security.
* To see a family gathered around a hearth in your dreams, even though you may not have one, predicts welcoming an addition to the family.
* If the dream hearth is empty or dusty, there may be unacknowledged fears about home circumstances or an unwanted upheaval.
* If the fire is burning too fiercely in the hearth, the dreamer may be overwhelmed by domestic concerns.
* Dreaming of lighting a hearth fire is a wish-fulfillment dream indicating a desire to create or restore a happy domestic scene and unite family.
* An outdoor or ritual hearth represents the sacred nature of the family and community and may signify an inner spiritual loneliness.

OUTCOME OF HILDA'S DREAM

Hilda's daughter explained that her mother had previously possessed an old-fashioned hearth and missed it. The nursing home created an artificial hearth in her room with an electric fireplace that had realistic-looking coals, and they made sure Hilda had her tea in her dressing gown by the hearth. Hilda's well-being greatly improved. Dreams can reveal what symbolizes feeling at home for a person, especially at times of insecurity or loneliness.

Heaven

George, eighty-one, often dreamed he heard his late wife, Violet, calling to him: "George, I'm all right. It's beautiful here." On hearing Violet, George flew through the air, landing at the gates of heaven, where Violet was waiting. They held hands through the gate, but George could not enter. Violet told him it was not his time. He must fulfill their earthly plans. When George awakened, he was sad that Violet was not next to him, yet happy that she was at peace.

DREAM BACKGROUND AND MEANING

George had been married to Violet for fifty-seven years, and they had been childhood sweethearts. Violet had passed away one year earlier. Dreams of seeing a loved one in heaven may involve astral travel, because it is said love survives death. Other people dream of heaven when they momentarily die during an accident or operation but are sent back by an angel or deceased relative to complete their earthly purpose.

INTERPRETATIONS AND FORTUNE-TELLING MEANINGS

* If you dream of heaven, great happiness is coming your way soon.
* If you dream a deceased relative is waiting, they may have a message or warning for you.
* If you dream of a judgment throne or angels holding the book of life, you have unresolved guilt to put right or let go.
* When life is going badly, dreams of heaven reassure you that life will get better. It never means you are soon going to die.
* If you see a single angel, your guardian angel is near, offering protection and reassurance.
* Dreaming of heaven as an empty garden says you should reconnect with your spiritual nature.

OUTCOME OF GEORGE'S DREAM

George realized that he had to go on with life. He accepted an offer to visit his daughter and grandchildren on the other side of the world, which he had been planning with Violet. Heaven dreams can be a reminder to find happiness in the here and now.

Helicopter

Alison, fifty-five, dreamed she was booked on a world cruise with close friend Maria. However, three months before they were due to sail, Alison had a dream in which her friend was being winched off the ship on a rescue helicopter because she was very ill.

DREAM BACKGROUND AND MEANING

It was a warning dream, so vivid that on Alison's insistence Maria went to the doctor and found a heart problem that was deteriorating and needed an urgent operation. Since helicopters are used as emergency rescue vehicles, the dream helicopter was picking up the energies of a potential hazard that might have demanded urgent intervention while they were at sea.

INTERPRETATIONS AND FORTUNE-TELLING MEANINGS

* Dreaming of piloting or flying in an executive helicopter indicates unexpected abundance, promotion, and increased status.
* A short helicopter pleasure trip says you should seek more leisure and pleasure if you are feeling weighed down by life.
* A crash you witness or experience in a dream warns that care is needed with finances and impulsive behavior, especially if someone else is piloting, as they may be taking a risk with your resources.
* If you dream you are piloting a rescue helicopter, you may be called upon to help or advise in an emergency at work or to assist a family member who has gotten themselves into trouble.
* If you are being winched up on a helicopter, you may have subconscious fears about the advisability or safety of a course of action. Check your health, any travel arrangements, and your insurance if you have a major trip planned.
* Military helicopters suggest conflict in your personal or professional life, or possible security problems in your home.

OUTCOME OF ALISON'S DREAM

Alison and Maria postponed their trip for a year until Maria was fully fit. If a helicopter dream is very vivid and remains all day, it may be predictive. Beware of helicopter dreams where the helicopter flies overhead and does not land, as your fears may be causing you to miss an opportunity.

Hen

Louisa, fifty, dreamed she found black feathers and a dead black hen on her doorstep, often considered a sign that someone has placed a hex or negative spell. While burying them away from the house, she saw black feathers falling from the sky. She ran inside.

DREAM BACKGROUND AND MEANING

Louisa had always been happy at work, where she was a supervisor, but recently a new worker, Rebecca, approximately Louisa's own age, had joined the company. Rebecca started spreading rumors and gossip about Louisa, whose coworkers then started ignoring her. Black hen feathers in a dream indicate ill-wishing, whether earthly or paranormal, but if malice is confronted it loses any power.

INTERPRETATIONS AND FORTUNE-TELLING MEANINGS

* A hen in a dream indicates the arrival or increasing influence of a nurturing, motherly presence in your life.
* If your hen is making a loud clucking sound, you may encounter a fussy person at work or a neighbor who interferes and annoys you but means no harm.
* If your dream hen is overprotective of her chicks, you should be very tactful, as a family member may be unnecessarily defensive of her offspring.
* If there are many hens in the dream laying eggs, you will benefit financially from your efforts; it is also a fertility symbol.
* If hens in the dream are laying no eggs, you may need to look for other sources of income than your usual one.
* If the hens are attacked or killed by a fox, you should protect older vulnerable friends or family members from being conned financially.

OUTCOME OF LOUISA'S DREAM

After the dream, Louisa told Rebecca that if she continued causing trouble she would report her to management for bullying. Louisa then confronted the other women, explaining that the gossip had to stop instantly or she would recommend that the troublemakers be dismissed. Hens in dreams, though often unifiers, can peck one another when in a flock for the best place in the coop.

Herbs

Molly, thirty-eight, dreamed she was a wise woman in late medieval times with a beautiful herb garden from which she made healing remedies. Her husband wanted her gone because she could not have children, and he reported her to the church as a witch. She fled to a convent where the nuns worked with herbs, tending the herb garden and recording herbs in paintings.

DREAM BACKGROUND AND MEANING

Molly was training to become a holistic practitioner. But her husband, a doctor in a small town, objected, saying she would ruin his reputation, and he threatened to divorce her.

INTERPRETATIONS AND FORTUNE-TELLING MEANINGS

★ To dream of making herbal remedies may be a past-life dream, especially if you have innate knowledge of unusual herbs.

★ If you are taking a particular accepted herbal remedy in your dream, though you know nothing of herbal medicine, check, as the natural product may be helpful if conventional medicine is not working.

★ If you are consulting an herbalist in your dream, you or someone close will soon be healed naturally of a health worry.

★ If you dream that certain herbs are dangerous, this is a warning, so investigate before touching or using.

★ If you dream of adding culinary herbs to a meal, you will soon be welcoming unexpected visitors.

★ If in your dream you are planting an herb garden, this is telling you to adopt a more natural way of living.

OUTCOME OF MOLLY'S DREAM

After the dream, her husband became ill. Conventional pain relief remedies did not work. Reluctantly, he took an herbal remedy, which worked, but he insisted it was coincidence. To save her marriage, Molly reluctantly gave up studying herbalism. Instead, she painted cameos of the herbs she saw in the hedgerows. Dreaming of herbs can suggest a natural gift for herbalism, but sometimes the price of following an age-old tradition can be too high when a person is threatened by immovable prejudice that exists even in modern times.

Herd

Florian, thirty-four, was crossing a field where a herd of cows was grazing. The quickest way was through the herd, and he was totally confident that they would back away. But he noticed that some of the cows had calves and were circling him menacingly. He started to run, tripped, and feared he was going to be trampled.

DREAM BACKGROUND AND MEANING

Florian had always gotten along with the all-female workers in his office and, since he was spoiled at home by his mother and sisters, he took his colleagues for granted, expecting them to wait on him. A new female manager joined the company and accused him of being sexist, insisting that he take his turn with chores like making coffee. When surrounded or threatened by a herd, human or animal, beware of taking others for granted.

INTERPRETATIONS AND FORTUNE-TELLING MEANINGS

★ If you dream of herding peaceful animals such as sheep or cows, beware that you do not assume others will automatically follow you.

★ If you dream of wild herds, you may need to go along with the majority view.

★ If you are riding on the back of a wild horse galloping with a herd, you crave freedom.

★ If you are following a herd at a distance, you are not ready to take the lead or not even sure you want to.

★ A herd of cows or goats being milked is a sign of growing prosperity.

★ If you dream that a herd will not go in the direction you want, you may need to be more assertive or accept a nonleadership position.

OUTCOME OF FLORIAN'S DREAM

Florian talked over the situation with his mother, who agreed that he did behave like the leader of the herd. Florian made a real effort to fit in at home and work. Herd dreams are linked with issues of leading and following and say, "There is a time to lead and a time to follow."

Hero, Heroine, Heroism

Joe, thirty-one, had a recurring dream that an armed burglar broke into the house while his wife, Lisa, was in the bath. Joe rushed downstairs. He fearlessly disarmed the burglar and held him until the police arrived. He was Lisa's hero. Next morning, Joe was on the front page of the local paper.

DREAM BACKGROUND AND MEANING

Joe had been married two years. Their home was robbed while Lisa was asleep. Joe was out with his friends. Since then, he had felt guilty for not protecting her. Heroic dreams are wish-fulfillment dreams where we show others our true worth, an archetypal characteristic in mythology.

INTERPRETATIONS AND FORTUNE-TELLING MEANINGS

* If you are a hero or heroine in your dream, you may feel you need to prove yourself to a loved one or someone at work.
* If someone else is a hero or heroine in your dream, you may have doubts about coping in a crisis and rely on others too much.
* If you are a superhero or superheroine in your dream, there is a major social or legal injustice happening, and you need to stand out from the majority view.
* If you dream you are defeating many foes, stick by your principles, even against seemingly impossible odds.
* If you are helping save others with a living or a historical hero or heroine, you have an unexpressed desire to make the world a better place. You should further this ambition within your life and work.
* If you are facing and overcoming your greatest fear in the dream, you will defeat it in real life.

OUTCOME OF JOE'S DREAM

Joe was quite small and had always been timid. He took self-defense classes and is now confident that he can protect his wife and home. If you fear you have failed in real life as a superhero or superheroine, you may need to redefine what courage is.

Hiding

Morag, thirty, dreamed she was playing paper chase with her long-term boyfriend, Mark, who was leaving a trail of shredded checks and credit card statements. She was trying to collect them, but the wind was blowing them away, and Mark kept changing direction. Eventually, she became annoyed at the pointless game and went home.

DREAM BACKGROUND AND MEANING

Morag had become worried because Mark had stopped using online banking, as he said there were too many fraudsters. He told her he was dealing with the check and credit card statements, as she traveled a lot. Several times their joint credit card had been declined. The dream alerted her that something was not right. Dreams can suggest that one person is withholding information from another, if games in the dream involve creating diversions.

INTERPRETATIONS AND FORTUNE-TELLING MEANINGS

* If you are hiding from someone close to you, you may be unwilling to commit yourself in a relationship.
* If you are hiding money or valuables in the dream, an acquaintance or work colleague may be trying to steal your ideas or credit.
* If you dream you are playing hide-and-seek, you may be leading someone on romantically, then pushing them away, or vice versa.
* If you hide from unseen danger you feel in the dream, this could be your own fears, from which you are escaping.
* If you are hiding to secretly observe someone or are aware that someone is hiding and watching you, there is a lack of trust.
* If you suspect that someone with whom you are communicating online is concealing their identity, the dream may reveal the reason for hiding.

OUTCOME OF MORAG'S DREAM

Morag restored their online finances and discovered that she and Mark were heavily overdrawn. When she confronted Mark, he admitted that he had been hiding debts because he had gambled all their money away. Morag took over the finances, which are slowly getting straight. Hiding dreams often confirm the dreamer's unacknowledged suspicions about concealed information.

Hippopotamus

Esme, thirty-five, dreamed she was inside a mud-brick home beside the Nile, alone with her three children. Near the door was a large statue of an upright pregnant hippopotamus. All who entered to do harm turned away, afraid. In the river were half-submerged hippos and their calves.

DREAM BACKGROUND AND MEANING

Esme was in substandard accommodations with her children, persecuted by the landlord's henchmen, who wanted to evict her although she paid her rent. None of the social agencies would rehouse her. Esme researched the dream hippopotamus statue and discovered it was Taweret, the hippopotamus goddess of Egypt, who protected women and children from all harm. A hippopotamus, especially one in goddess form, can appear in a dream to mothers and other women who are being intimidated as a sign that help will come from an unexpected source.

INTERPRETATIONS AND FORTUNE-TELLING MEANINGS

★ The Egyptian hippopotamus goddess is a symbol of fertility and safe childbirth, and an excellent omen for conception and a healthy pregnancy.

★ If you dream that the hippopotamuses, semiaquatic creatures, are partly submerged in water, you have strong feelings you are suppressing. Express them, as you have more power than you think.

★ If you dream a hippopotamus attacks you, stand your ground against it and other bullies, rather than backing away, since they can outrun people.

★ If you dream you see a hippopotamus confined in a small enclosure with no water, someone may be trying to make you feel inferior, overweight, or ugly to boost their own ego.

★ If a benign hippopotamus comes toward you, a kind, reassuring woman will offer you support.

OUTCOME OF ESME'S DREAM

After the dream, Esme saw a charity store for new mothers and children in the mall. An older woman running the shop put Esme in contact with the organizer who could offer clean, safe accommodations to women and children in danger. Soon after a hippopotamus dream, a welcome source of help invariably appears.

Hoarding

Elenie, fifty-six, started dreaming about her home being filled with hundreds of rolls of toilet paper, packets of pasta, and far too many loaves of bread to fit in the freezer. Only she and her husband lived at home, and he discouraged visitors. She woke, panicking that there would not be enough to eat.

DREAM BACKGROUND AND MEANING

Elenie feared a food shortage because of recent delivery-driver strikes. She was a natural hoarder and often threw away excess food that was beyond its sell-by date. As a child, her family had been very poor, and she had often gone to bed hungry. However, she had been married for thirty-five years and her husband had always earned a good wage. Hoarding can often be traced back to early deprivation or past lives, expressed in dreams in exaggerated form to alert the dreamer that hoarding is not necessary.

INTERPRETATIONS AND FORTUNE-TELLING MEANINGS

★ Hoarding dreams represent a lack of love and security or fear of their loss.

★ Unnecessarily hoarding food supplies suggests inner emptiness in a relationship.

★ Dreaming of hoarding money, whether by the dreamer or by a close relative, warns against possessiveness and a dislike of spontaneous pleasure.

★ Keeping prized possessions hidden and making do with what is old or worn suggests holding back from sexual pleasure and passion for fear of becoming vulnerable.

★ If in the dream others ask to share what you have hoarded and you refuse, you may find it hard to be generous to others, perhaps because of earlier betrayal.

★ If you dream that what you are hoarding is stolen from you, you may not be able to remain insulated from the world and from your own negative feelings.

OUTCOME OF ELENIE'S DREAM

After the dream, Elenie realized she was wasting money by overbuying and then throwing away the excess. She also realized that her husband had always withheld affection from her as a form of control and had isolated her from her family. They are going to marriage counseling and this is relieving her hoarding. Hoarding dreams reflect distress in the dreamer, who is constantly afraid of losing everything.

Hobbies

Vince, sixty-eight, dreamed he was with his beloved model train set, but it started to malfunction and then stopped. He phoned the store that usually obtained parts for his collectors' items, and was told they were closing down. He woke, worried it would mean the end of his hobby.

DREAM BACKGROUND AND MEANING

Vince was an avid collector of model trains and had a huge and very valuable layout in his attic. As he had grown older, he spent less time with it, but could not bear to sell it. When he passed on, it would most likely be thrown away as junk. A hobby can be personal, but if it totally excludes others, it may represent your avoiding the world.

INTERPRETATIONS AND FORTUNE-TELLING MEANINGS

* If you dream you are relaxing by enjoying a solitary hobby, you may need more self-time away from others and work.
* If you dream you have a pile of discarded hobbies, you are seeking to find meaning in your life and may need to persevere with one, rather than giving up at the first obstacle.
* If you dream you are sharing a hobby with friends or family you have not seen for a while, contact the people in the dream to breathe new life into the hobby.
* If you are no longer enjoying a hobby in your dream, you may have outgrown a phase in your life.
* If you are practicing a hobby because you always have, be sure it is not holding you back from a more people-centered life.
* If you dream that your collection is broken or faded, there may be aspects of your life where you are holding on to what no longer exists.

OUTCOME OF VINCE'S DREAM

After the dream, Vince contacted the local model-railway society, which was organizing an exhibition for the public and fundraising for a building for a permanent collection. Vince, his expertise, and his collection were welcomed. Hobbies represent the part of the dreamer that expresses and enriches their life.

Homecoming

Lottie, thirty-six, dreamed she arrived on a remote Scottish island. She went to the local post office, which doubled as a kindergarten. Children were playing on the floor as customers came and went, and Lottie stayed to help. She went to a song-and-dance evening and knew she had come home. The dream unfolded all night with mundane happy scenes. When she woke, she tried to return to the dream and felt a sense of loss when she could not.

DREAM BACKGROUND AND MEANING

Lottie was a journalist who traveled the world. She had recently been searching for a place where she could settle down and start her own small production company. However, except in her dream, she had not felt that sense of homecoming anywhere. Dreaming of settling in a dream location can guide the dreamer psychically to a place with similar energies to the dream setting or occasionally to the actual place.

INTERPRETATIONS AND FORTUNE-TELLING MEANINGS

* If you do not want to leave the location of which you are dreaming, there is a special quality of life that would make you happy there.
* If in the dream you enter the life of the community, it may relate to an old world you once knew.
* If the location has identifiable features, try to trace it, as there may be someone or something waiting.
* If you return time and again to the same dream community, you are ready to put down roots, and the right place will be revealed in actuality, maybe even the dream location.
* If there is a special house where you always live in the dream, that or a similar house may be where you belong.

OUTCOME OF LOTTIE'S DREAM

Lottie often returned to the place in her dreams. While making a program in London on forgotten ancestry, she discovered that *her* family had lived on a Scottish island, generations earlier. She has applied for a job running television programs for a group on the islands and plans to visit her ancestral heritage.

There may be a historical connection with the place in the dream, and your ancestors may be calling you home.

Homesickness

Jacqui, thirty-nine, had a recurring dream she was in her childhood village, packing to go to school camp. Though Jacqui wanted to go on the trip, she was afraid her mother would die before she returned. Jacqui knew she would be homesick the whole time and ran home, sobbing.

DREAM BACKGROUND AND MEANING

Jacqui had migrated from the United Kingdom to Western Australia with her husband and child and loved their new life. However, as the only child of a possessive, hypochondriac single mother, Jacqui constantly worried that something would happen to her mother, twelve thousand miles away. Dreaming of being homesick for our childhood home, or one where we have spent many years, may highlight present worries we need to fix.

INTERPRETATIONS AND FORTUNE-TELLING MEANINGS

★ If you dream that your former or childhood home is either occupied by strangers or abandoned, there are unresolved issues from childhood.

★ If you dream that you cannot find your way to your former home, it is time to focus on the future.

★ If you dream of moving to or living in a previous home, you may not feel at home in your current location.

★ If in the dream you are a child, you want to be cared for and cherished more in your adult life.

★ If you have a past-life dream of a home to which you long to return after the dream, you may need a slower pace of life and more time with those you care about.

★ If you are homesick when you see the stars, you may be a star soul and should develop your psyche.

OUTCOME OF JACQUI'S DREAM

Because these dreams made Jacqui homesick, her husband said they could move back to the United Kingdom. But when Jacqui went home, the area had changed drastically and she knew no one. Australia is now her home and she is very happy. Homesickness can represent restlessness linked to relationship, work, or lack of fulfillment.

Honey

Amber, eighteen, dreamed she was cooking a honey cake to impress her new boyfriend, but she had run out of honey. Taking a risk, she went to where she knew there was a wild beehive in a tree in the next field. Seeing no bees, Amber clambered up and put her hand inside the hive to take some honeycomb. Immediately, the bees were swarming around and she was badly stung.

DREAM BACKGROUND AND MEANING

Amber was recently able to access her late aunt's inheritance, which was intended to form part of her college fund. Amber's boyfriend wanted to spend the whole summer vacation trekking overseas. He suggested that Amber dip into the fund to pay for the trip, as both sets of parents disapproved and would not help. Honey stolen in a dream warns that instant prosperity may come at a price.

INTERPRETATIONS AND FORTUNE-TELLING MEANINGS

★ To dream of being given honey is a sign of money coming your way.

★ Eating honey, especially with a partner, is a fertility symbol and a sign of happy honeymoons and love trysts.

★ Dreaming of taking some honeycomb from a hive using proper equipment indicates that you will receive a message from a distant friend or family member that will lead to a trip to see them or to their returning.

★ Sharing honey at a meal with friends or family promises harmonious times and prosperity in the home.

★ Using honey-based healing or beauty products is a sign of good or improving health.

★ Jars of honey in a storage cupboard promise continuing prosperity and abundance and building up resources if they are unopened.

OUTCOME OF AMBER'S DREAM

Amber realized she was risking her future, though she very much wanted to go with her boyfriend. When she suggested a vacation camping in the wilderness, he lost interest and is now dating a girl from a wealthy family. Because honey represents abundance and spiritual wealth, money issues can be linked with moral dilemmas.

Hoodie, Hooded Jacket

Nancy, sixty-five, dreamed she was surrounded on the staircase leading from her apartment by young people wearing hoodies. She was terrified, as she associated hoodies with criminals. She tried to go back upstairs but slipped. They carried her upstairs, made her tea, and called the ambulance. Two of the girls went with her to the hospital.

DREAM BACKGROUND AND MEANING

Nancy had always been afraid of the hooded youths who hung around her complex. Security guards would chase them off, though they never did any harm. Her dream made her wonder if her judgment had been prejudiced. Young people wearing sweatshirts or jackets with hoods covering their faces represent fears of attack by unknown forces and can be seen as a threat.

INTERPRETATIONS AND FORTUNE-TELLING MEANINGS

★ If you dream about young people wearing sweatshirts with hoods pulled over their faces, you may feel insecure about potential hidden danger in your life generally, allowing imagination to fill in the gaps.

★ If you are wearing a coat with the hood pulled over your face in the dream, there are private aspects of yourself you wish to conceal.

★ If you are attacked in your dream by young people wearing hoods, this may express fears fueled by popular media imagery.

★ If you see sports players wearing hoods while training, you have hidden talents and should take up a new form of outdoor exercise.

★ If you dream you pull the hood off a caller at your door, you may find your own face staring back, representing hidden issues you are not yet ready to confront.

★ If you are part of a gang wearing hoodies, whatever your age, you should find like-minded people to develop a talent as yet untried.

OUTCOME OF NANCY'S DREAM

After the dream, Nancy started talking to the youths outside her apartment and organized the neighbors to campaign for a youth community center. Hoodie dreams remove stereotypes and help the dreamer to develop hidden aspects of themselves.

Horse

Siobhan, thirty, since seeing the white chalk horses on the hills in southern England, had had dreams of being a priestess of the Celtic horse goddess Epona. She dreamed she was riding bareback on a huge white stallion across the hills, the wind streaming in her hair. She woke excited.

DREAM BACKGROUND AND MEANING

Siobhan, once a skilled passionate horsewoman, had given up riding after a bad accident with her beloved white horse. She paid a local stable to care for her horse and had not even visited it. But in her dreams, her joy had returned. She knew she must return to riding or sell the horse. The horse, an animal first domesticated in about 1750 BC, is a magical symbol of swiftness, loyalty, and power that depends on mutual trust between horse and rider, and trust between them or between two people is a central feature of horse dreams.

INTERPRETATIONS AND FORTUNE-TELLING MEANINGS

★ If you dream that you put a saddle or halter on a horse and it is cooperative, you will persuade someone significant to accept your point of view.

★ If the horse is restless or shies away, it may be harder than you think to persuade others to compromise. Persist, for you will win.

★ If you are riding a winged horse through the skies, opportunities are limitless, but do not become careless, as there is a long way to fall.

★ If you are galloping on a horse, travel is favored, especially long-distance.

★ If you dream that you win a horse show or race, you will gain recognition at work or business through combining your skills with a like-minded colleague or partner.

OUTCOME OF SIOBHAN'S DREAM

Siobhan visited the stables and fell in love with her horse again. At first she went on short rides, but she gradually built up her confidence. She has resumed her original plans to buy into the stables to organize riding holidays, especially for novice or nervous riders. Horse dreams can create or restore a love of horses, especially if the dreams link to old worlds.

Horseshoe

Hermione, twenty-one, dreamed a shaft of moonlight illuminated the drawer in which she kept a silver horseshoe charm. Her luck could not be worse in every aspect of her life. In the dream she slipped the horseshoe on a chain around her neck and it sparkled. When she woke, she felt confident that all would be well.

DREAM BACKGROUND AND MEANING

Hermione received the horseshoe charm for her twenty-first birthday and had placed it in a drawer. After the dream, since she was going through a run of bad luck, she retrieved it and started wearing it. Instantly, her luck changed. Could the horseshoe really have magical powers, or was it coincidence? Horseshoes are traditionally considered both luck bringers and protective. A dream can remind the dreamer that they may possess the initiative to put life right, triggered by the horseshoe.

INTERPRETATIONS AND FORTUNE-TELLING MEANINGS

✴ Dreaming of finding a full-size horseshoe heralds an imminent wedding or major love commitment.

✴ To be given and wear or carry a horseshoe charm facing upward attracts the protection of the moon, or if facing downward drains away bad luck.

✴ Because of its links with St. Dunstan, the blacksmith saint who nailed the Devil to the wall of his forge, horseshoes represent prosperity through the removal of obstacles.

✴ If you dream that a horse loses a shoe, there may be temporary delays in travel plans.

✴ To see a horseshoe hanging on a fence in a dream indicates a significant rise in financial or business fortunes.

✴ To be shoeing a horse in the dream says, "Reach for a profitable change by taking the initiative."

OUTCOME OF HERMIONE'S DREAM

Life continued to go well for Hermione. She decided to share her luck by giving the charm to a friend going through a bad time, and her luck also changed without affecting Hermione's. Dreams can link into an ancient symbol that may have accumulated power, whether psychically or psychologically.

Hospital

Yvonne, forty-four, dreamed she was in the hospital with her now-deceased mother, waiting for an operation to remove a malignant growth from her mother's leg. But the operation went horribly wrong, and her mother died. The surgeon came in and said that Yvonne needed a similar operation or there was real danger she would share her mother's fate. Yvonne ran.

DREAM BACKGROUND AND MEANING

The dream was a repeat of what had actually happened to her mother years before and was responsible for Yvonne's fear of hospitals. Yvonne now had a small benign lump on her leg, which the surgeon said she could remove during day surgery under local anesthetic. Often fears of hospitals have their root in actual trauma, and dreams can rerun the trauma until eventually it is resolved or accepted.

INTERPRETATIONS AND FORTUNE-TELLING MEANINGS

✴ If you frequently dream of an earlier negative hospital experience, it is not resolved and you may need expert reassurance.

✴ If in your dream you have a successful operation, a problem will be removed or fixed in your daily life.

✴ If you dream you do not want an operation that you need, it may be because of health or financial problems.

✴ If you dream the physician or surgeon is incompetent and suggests remedies you know are wrong, you may doubt an expert in other areas of your life.

✴ If you see yourself leaving the hospital fit and well, this is a good omen for any intervention in any area of your life.

✴ If you dream that you leave a hospital without having the treatment, you may not be ready to hand over control to others.

OUTCOME OF YVONNE'S DREAM

Yvonne discovered that at another hospital it was possible to undergo minor surgery using hypnosis, which was successful. A hospital dream, whether it describes healing and recovery or deterioration and death, reflects the dreamer's attitude toward intervention in their life.

Hostage

Poppy, twelve, dreamed she was in a bank in London with her mother when masked raiders ran in. One of them seized Poppy's mother, Suky, and backed out of the bank with a gun to her head. Poppy woke, terrified that she would never see her mother again.

DREAM BACKGROUND AND MEANING

Poppy's father had told Poppy that he would be claiming full custody of her and taking her to the other end of the country to live with her stepmother, who she hated, unless Suky signed the house over to him and his new wife (who was expecting a baby) and Suky withdrew all claims for child support. Poppy was terrified of being taken from her mother, though her mother said she would fight for Poppy and their home. Hostage dreams, unlike kidnapper dreams (see p. 268), speak about situations where the hostage taker has a purpose in using the hostage as a bargaining chip.

INTERPRETATIONS AND FORTUNE-TELLING MEANINGS

* Seeing oneself as a hostage with an unknown captor in a dream can indicate that a bad habit or addiction is preventing your living freely.
* If you dream a child or parent is taken hostage, an ex-partner is using emotional blackmail, usually for financial advantage.
* If you are a hostage taker, you may risk losing everything you would have gotten by negotiating what you want at work or in a relationship. Is it worth it?
* If you dream that the ransom you are demanding is too high, whether financially or plea bargaining, you may have to compromise or walk away with nothing.
* If you dream you are negotiating for the release of a hostage, you may find that you are torn between both parties in a family, friendship, or workplace feud.

OUTCOME OF POPPY'S DREAM

After the dream, Poppy's mother agreed to give her husband the house, so as not to distress her daughter, and agreed to give up child support. In return, her ex gave her full custody of Poppy, which he never wanted anyway. Hostage dreams are usually very complex and indicate a need to establish what the hostage taker really wants and how far the hostage will compromise and pay out, whether financially or in concessions, in return for freedom.

Hot-Air Balloon

Simon, thirty, dreamed he and his partner, Shelley, dressed in Victorian clothes, were in a hot-air balloon passing over the English Channel between England and France. They dreamed they were apothecaries and the balloon was filled with remedies. It became windy, and the balloon was blown off course. Simon landed it on Jersey, the biggest Channel Island. They saw the beautiful green island and the deep blue sea, and Simon declared this was home.

DREAM BACKGROUND AND MEANING

Simon and Shelley had been studying herbal medicine and acupuncture and were considering moving to rural France, though they needed to improve their French to practice professionally. A dream of a hot-air balloon, especially if you are in historic clothes, can be a past-life dream with relevance to a decision in the present world.

INTERPRETATIONS AND FORTUNE-TELLING MEANINGS

* Dreaming of embarking on a balloon journey offers a long-term perspective of the future, which may reveal factors to change your plans.
* If the balloon floats gently across the sky, let destiny take control for a while.
* If you are watching others flying in a hot-air balloon, you may regret a missed opportunity.
* A smooth flight and landing promises that you can rise above restrictions and achieve freedom.
* Flying high indicates long-distance travel or permanent relocation. If you want to change locations, but do not know where, the balloon's ultimate destination will guide you.
* If you dream that your balloon suddenly loses height, gets tangled in trees, or crashes, check your plans before embarking on any change. It can also mean that this may be the wrong time to try for what you want.

OUTCOME OF SIMON'S DREAM

After Simon's dream, he and Shelley settled initially in Jersey, where both English and French were spoken, with the option of going to France when they had become bilingual. Hot-air balloons may, if caught by wind, blow you off course to what may be the right place for you.

Hotel

Linda, thirty-five, dreamed she was staying in a huge, modern hotel with many floors. The elevators were not working and she had to carry her bags up seven floors. The room direction signs were missing, and she wandered seemingly endless corridors to locate her room, which was dirty, and the bed was broken. She vowed never to travel from home again.

DREAM BACKGROUND AND MEANING

Linda was in the security services, so was used to frequent location changes, but she desperately wanted her own home. She had been offered a promotion, but it meant she would be constantly moving bases, sometimes staying for weeks on end in hotels. Linda wanted a settled life where she could make friends and find a partner who worked regular hours. Hotels in dreams represent temporary resting places, and their comfort or otherwise reflects how secure the dreamer feels in their current lifestyle (see "Motel," p. 320).

INTERPRETATIONS AND FORTUNE-TELLING MEANINGS

* Dreaming about a luxurious vacation hotel in an exotic location expresses a desire to temporarily leave domestic and work responsibilities behind.
* A hotel with a broken elevator signifies temporary blocks in career or finances due to others' incompetence.
* A broken bed or dirty room says changes in life will not be as advantageous as expected.
* Poor service in a hotel represents a lack of nurturing in the dreamer's life by those who should care.
* Getting lost in a huge, impersonal hotel or one where floor and room signs are missing indicates an urgent need to resolve future plans to avoid drifting.

OUTCOME OF LINDA'S DREAM

After the dream, Linda put a deposit on an apartment where she could spend her leave, even if she could not have much time there initially. She took the promotion but after three years planned to quit the services and make a secure life. Hotel dreams signify either a desire for reduced responsibility for others or for stability, according to the nature of the dream hotel.

Household Guardian

Flo, thirty-five, dreamed of a wooden house with a veranda and a very old lady sitting in a rocking chair and knitting. She was welcoming and said, "I've been waiting for you." Flo went inside and the old lady poured tea from a pot shaped like a house. Flo felt totally at home and was sorry to wake.

DREAM BACKGROUND AND MEANING

Flo, who was pregnant, and her husband, Mark, despaired of quickly finding a house they could afford. Flo's aunt mentioned a house being auctioned. No one would buy it because it was said to be haunted by the old lady who had lived there all her life. Household guardians, unlike conventional ghosts, are attached to a property rather than to their own family and invariably make their presence known through dreams.

INTERPRETATIONS AND FORTUNE-TELLING MEANINGS

* If you regularly dream of a shadowy presence in your home but do not feel spooked, this is the household guardian who was so happy there and after death never moved on.
* If you dream of the house as it was years before, research the previous owners, as one may be identified as the guardian of your dreams.
* If your children dream of an old man or woman in their bedroom at night, it may be a household guardian who loved children, checking that they are safe.
* If you regularly dream of your pet being stroked or petted by the same person in your home, the household guardian may have been an animal lover.
* If you dream of being warned of danger by a benign presence seen ever more clearly, check areas that the presence indicates that could allow intruders in or are fire hazards.

OUTCOME OF FLO'S DREAM

Flo and her husband bought the house at a very low price and have felt protected ever since. Flo has seen pictures in the local library of the old lady and her unusual teapots. A household guardian may deter other prospective buyers of their home until the right family comes along.

Hypnosis

Lucille, sixty-five, dreamed her new partner, John, was a hypnotist in a stage show and she was his assistant. She walked among the audience, selecting those wanting to join John onstage. Under hypnosis each handed her their wallets. Lucille counted the contents and put the wallets in a chest. John told each hypnotized participant to say, "I will double my money." John clapped and Lucille handed each wallet back to its owner. Each contained double the amount of money previously in them.

DREAM BACKGROUND AND MEANING

Lucille, a widow, had met John at her art class and had fallen instantly under his spell. He wanted them to buy an art gallery together on the coast of New England. He promised to double her contribution once his late mother's will cleared probate. Her friends and children warned her that he was using his charm to con her out of her money. Yet the dream assured her that he was honest. The integrity or otherwise of the hypnotist is revealed in these deep psychic dreams.

INTERPRETATIONS AND FORTUNE-TELLING MEANINGS

* If you dream you are being hypnotized, a work colleague or family member may be deceiving you about their intentions.
* To hypnotize people in a dream says you can influence others positively to see things your way and discover unconsidered solutions.
* Should you dream you deliberately resist hypnosis, all is not as it seems. Hidden agendas are at work.
* If you dream you volunteer to be hypnotized at a stage show, someone wiser will help resolve your problems.
* If you cannot be hypnotized, though you want to be, you have valid doubts about allowing someone close to take control of your life.
* If you dream that the hypnotist programs you to do foolish things, beware of being led into temptation by a charismatic friend.

OUTCOME OF LUCILLE'S DREAM

Lucille went ahead with the gallery purchase. Soon afterward, John's mother's will cleared and he paid a substantial amount toward the gallery. Dreams of hypnosis occur somewhere between the dream and psychic planes and reveal unconscious truth.

Hypochondria

Marcel, thirty-seven, dreamed he was in a hospital waiting room. He entered a small room where a doctor informed Marcel that he had a serious respiratory condition and his heart was in the state of a person twice his age. His mother, now deceased, turned up and said, "I knew you were delicate and that wife of yours should take better care of you." Marcel woke, relieved that at last his health fears had been confirmed.

DREAM BACKGROUND AND MEANING

Marcel had complained for years of being ill with the latest health scare in the media and believed his heart and lungs were not working properly and that he might have an underlying incurable blood disease. Tests had found nothing wrong. His wife was tired of caring for a semipermanent invalid and was threatening to leave him. What could he do, he asked, when he was so ill? If you often dream of your own funeral, you may be overly concerned with your health or seeking a reason to opt out of an active life.

INTERPRETATIONS AND FORTUNE-TELLING MEANINGS

* If you dream of being seriously ill and have symptoms, there's no harm in having a checkup.
* If, however, you regularly have such dreams but don't have any symptoms, the cause may be anxiety, or because you feel neglected and crave sympathy.
* If you constantly dream of a partner or children becoming ill and dying, you may be afraid of being abandoned.
* If your dream confirms your illness but tests do not, it may be that as a child you got attention only when you were ill and the habit has become attached to adulthood.
* If a physician in a dream says you are a hypochondriac, this may be your inner voice reassuring you that you are not ill.

OUTCOME OF MARCEL'S DREAM

Marcel realized after the dream that he was unconsciously using illness to hold on to his wife, though this was having the opposite effect. The appearance of his mother telling him that he was delicate reminded him that his mother encouraged him to be sick, a role he transferred unconsciously to his wife. Hypochondria dreams can reveal the true reason for hypochondria, which is usually buried in the past.

Ice

Ed, fifty-one, dreamed he was skating on a frozen lake toward the center where a fairy-tale ice princess with a headdress of icicles was holding out her hand. His family and friends were on the edge, warning him to stop, as all around him the ice was cracking. He laughed. Then, as he reached the ice maiden, the ice collapsed. She was gone and he plunged into the black waters. He woke shaking.

DREAM BACKGROUND AND MEANING

Ed was having an affair with his young personal assistant, Sue. But Sue kept withdrawing emotionally and told Ed he had to leave his wife and children before she would commit to him. Ice dreams advise proceeding cautiously in less-than-ideal circumstances, and show that ice is generally a temporary surface and not to be relied upon long-term.

INTERPRETATIONS AND FORTUNE-TELLING MEANINGS

★ Dreaming of cracking ice on a lake or river represents an insecure situation.

★ Icebergs say that what is known is only a small part of the story, and the hidden factors should be explored as to reliability in any situation.

★ An icy road or sidewalk is an advance warning of hazards ahead.

★ Falling on ice, or skidding or crashing a car on an icy road, says a situation is spiraling out of control because of increasing recklessness.

★ A glacier indicates inevitable slow progress that must be accepted.

★ Ice skating represents unbridled pleasure, though with risks of falling and getting hurt.

★ Melting ice is a good omen if there has been an estrangement or coldness in a relationship, but warns you to not trust promises made to you in the heat of passion.

OUTCOME OF ED'S DREAM

Ed knew Sue had previously initiated office affairs with other married men and had lost interest once they had broken up their families for her. Ed resigned from his job, set up his own business, and is trying to repair his marriage.

Identity Theft

Thomas, sixty-seven, who had been debt-free all his life, dreamed he had debt collectors banging on the door and constant phone calls and mail demanding repayment of huge loans. He woke hiding from the persistently ringing telephone.

DREAM BACKGROUND AND MEANING

The dream frightened Thomas, as he had recently lost his passport after returning through an airport but, because of a bout of influenza, had not reported it missing. He had received a letter from a credit company he did not know about a late payment on a card he did not have. He was worried that he had become a victim of identity theft. A dream may give the first hint of someone stealing the dreamer's identity.

INTERPRETATIONS AND FORTUNE-TELLING MEANINGS

★ If you dream of identity theft, someone you know is seeking to override your confidence and opinions.

★ If you dream of numerous false demands in your name, you may fear losing your identity in a soulless organization.

★ If you dream of seeing someone living in your home with your family, those emotionally close may not be allowing you to be yourself.

★ If in your dream someone at work is presenting your ideas as their own, you may be feeling insecure and need to establish whether this is an inner fear of being replaced or an actual attempt to undermine you.

★ If you dream of someone dressed in your clothes with your partner, you may have doubts about your relationship.

★ If you are stealing someone's identity to make money or gain status, what is lacking in your life that you need to imitate someone else?

OUTCOME OF THOMAS'S DREAM

Thomas immediately informed the police and his bank and changed all his passwords. He is still being bothered about the false debt. Dreaming of identity theft can be a straightforward warning by your unconscious to be careful to not reveal personal details.

Illicit Drugs

Bruno, twenty, dreamed he was walking through fields of poppies in Asia. A man in sunglasses offered to buy the crop, as they were of great value to him. Bruno knew about their use in producing illicit drugs. He burned down the fields and woke fleeing in his car as far as possible from danger.

DREAM BACKGROUND AND MEANING

Bruno was employed in the nuclear industry, a source of power that, like drugs, could be used for good or ill. He was invited to join a Middle Eastern company, secretly working on the production of nuclear weapons. Bruno was offered a huge salary. But was there a way out afterward, knowing so many secrets? While some poppies are grown for pain relief, others are sources of heroin and so represent getting sucked into a world where involvement is dangerous.

INTERPRETATIONS AND FORTUNE-TELLING MEANINGS

★ If you crave illicit drugs in the dream, you may be seeking a quick fix to lessen painful feelings.

★ If you see family members or partners taking drugs in your dream, it may be an early warning of unacknowledged addictive behavior.

★ If in your dream you are threatened by a drug baron, you may be pressured to act against your principles by a powerful figure.

★ If an addicted family member is undergoing detox in the dream, this is a good omen for successful treatment.

★ If you or a family member is buying or selling drugs in the dream, you or they may be seeking thrills regardless of consequences.

★ If you dream that you find a cache of illicit drugs, you may be faced with a dilemma about making money by dishonest means.

OUTCOME OF BRUNO'S DREAM

Bruno turned down the job in the Middle Eastern company, as the more he looked into it, the more he disliked the situation. He took a new job in nuclear power, researching medical imaging on a remote Scottish island. Dreams about illicit drugs warn against getting into anything where it may be hard to pull out.

Illusion

Tony, fifty-five, dreamed that a beautiful young girl dressed in flowing white robes beckoned him. He followed her through a flower-filled forest to a deep pool where they swam together. She took him back to her village where the elders were waiting to marry them. But everything disappeared.

DREAM BACKGROUND AND MEANING

Tony was separated from his wife. His friend Kim had returned home from a holiday in Thailand with a beautiful young bride. Tony had been dating a widow his own age. Kim made him question his choice. Illusion dreams are wish-fulfillment, but if the images fade before the end of the dream, they may not translate into reality.

INTERPRETATIONS AND FORTUNE-TELLING MEANINGS

★ If you dream of a solution, such as walking toward an oasis, that suddenly disappears, this is telling you to strive for a more realistic relationship or opportunity.

★ If the magick remains to the end of the dream, it may be attainable.

★ If you dream that a stage magician doubles your money and then disappears in a puff of smoke, beware of a charismatic figure.

★ If your dream is surrounded by mist or you are floating on clouds, this is an escapist dream to be enjoyed but not taken seriously.

★ If an attractive partner comes close and then fades and you cannot touch them, you may have a wonderful romance rather than a permanent future.

★ If you see yourself as a celebrity, you may have incredibly good luck, but more likely you will experience a gradual but lasting improvement in your circumstances.

OUTCOME OF TONY'S DREAM

Tony took his friend's advice, but he found that many of the young girls only wanted a rich boyfriend. He came home disillusioned and proposed to his older woman friend, who turned him down after learning of his overseas escapades. If we settle for illusion as seen in a dream, we may lose out on happiness waiting in the real world.

Immigration

Imran, thirty-two, dreamed he was a child in a small boat carrying immigrants from a war zone. The dinghy hit the rocks. He was washed onto the shore, the only survivor, and was adopted by a family whose language he could not understand. He was afraid the police would arrest him, as he had lost all his papers.

DREAM BACKGROUND AND MEANING

Imran, who lived in the United States, belonged to a tight-knit second-generation immigrant community where older folk still spoke their own language and followed the festivals of their homeland. He had many American friends but felt he was trapped between two worlds. His parents had found him a bride from the community, but he had an American girlfriend he wanted to marry, whose parents were also opposed to the match. Immigration dreams reflect a sense of not belonging and alienation from family and community, which can have many causes.

INTERPRETATIONS AND FORTUNE-TELLING MEANINGS

★ If you dream of being a child alone in a different community, you may be aware that your ideals and ideas are different from those of your family or work colleagues.

★ If in your dream you are an illegal immigrant or asylum seeker, you may have been made to feel insecure and need to find people who share your life view.

★ If you cannot speak the language of your new dreamland, you may be feeling that people are not listening to you. You may need to communicate in a different way.

★ If you dream your family exists entirely separately from your new homeland, you may have a very controlling family or a relationship you have outgrown.

★ If in a dream you are helping immigrants or asylum seekers to settle in your land, you may act as peacemaker at work or in the family or community.

OUTCOME OF IMRAN'S DREAM

Imran and his girlfriend decided to move to New York together to establish their own identities. Immigration dreams, unlike emigration dreams, often reflect issues of fitting into families, workplaces, and communities, even if legal immigration issues are not involved.

Immobility, Paralysis

Paul, forty-four, dreamed he was totally paralyzed from the neck down and was abandoned in a wheelchair in the corner of the sports stadium, watching the other athletes competing as he used to. He tried in vain to move but gave up, tears streaming down his face, and knew his life was over.

DREAM BACKGROUND AND MEANING

Paul had discovered he had a slow wasting disease, though he was still able to walk and use his hands with difficulty. He felt useless going to the stadium each day, watching athletes do what he could no longer do. Dreams of sleep paralysis, where the sleeper cannot move or speak immediately before going to sleep or waking, while not uncommon, can escalate into a full-blown nightmare if the dreamer is worried about being helpless.

INTERPRETATIONS AND FORTUNE-TELLING MEANINGS

★ If you are immobile in a dream, this reflects an inability to influence events in life.

★ If you are abandoned in a wheelchair in a dream, you may feel life is passing you by and no one is listening to you.

★ If you are being pushed in a wheelchair by a partner, relative, or workmate who is taking you where you do not want to go, you may need to assert yourself.

★ If you dream your hands and arms are paralyzed, you may be finding it hard to reach out to others and express love.

★ If you dream your legs are paralyzed, you may be stuck in a situation that right now you cannot leave.

★ If you dream you are being pursued and attacked, you are suffering from buried anxieties that you should confront.

OUTCOME OF PAUL'S DREAM

Paul realized he was understandably accepting defeat, rather than focusing on his remaining physical powers and alert mind to still make a difference. He joined a society for those with his condition and started raising money for research, by having fun events. Immobility dreams in any context represent fears of being dependent on others, which need to be faced in order to maximize the dreamer's strengths in any situation.

Incense

Polly, thirty-five, dreamed she was mixing flowers and spices to make incense, sitting beneath a palm tree in a Middle Eastern market. She was surrounded by tubs of flowers, herbs, leaves, and spices. As people approached, Polly instinctively knew the right blend for the wishes they wanted to be fulfilled. This was what she was meant to be doing.

DREAM BACKGROUND AND MEANING

Polly had a small market stall in Boston where she sold everything magical—tools, books, crystals, and statues. However, she was not making much profit, as she had to buy small quantities of stock from a warehouse and therefore was paying high prices. Incense dreams awaken the deeper parts of the mind, which can manifest spiritual powers in the daily world.

INTERPRETATIONS AND FORTUNE-TELLING MEANINGS

- ★ If you dream you are making incense, you are bringing together different aspects of your life and talents in profitable but harmonious ways.
- ★ Offering lighted incense at an altar says you will encounter a mentor or authority figure who will help fulfill your ambitions.
- ★ If you dream that the incense will not light, you have to make your own way to success.
- ★ If you are buying incense, you will need to invest in your future success financially, or with greater effort.
- ★ If you are a priest or priestess at an altar, making incense offerings, this may be a past-life dream and reflects emerging spiritual and psychic powers.
- ★ If you are choking on incense smoke or the incense smells foul, someone in your life is trying to stop you from speaking out.

OUTCOME OF POLLY'S DREAM

After the dream, Polly made a trip to Morocco to learn from different incense stalls and stores. When she returned, she concentrated on making incense to order for passing customers, plus ready-made incense for different purposes. She was able to expand to online sales and eventually opened a small shop where customers could select and mix their own ingredients.

Incompetence

Imogen, twenty, dreamed she was working at her new job in a small café and the customers, her old teachers, complained she was too slow. She had dropped all the cookies on the floor, incorrectly calculated the checks, and overcharged them. The owner became angry and told Imogen to get out because she was incompetent.

DREAM BACKGROUND AND MEANING

Imogen had left school without a certificate, as her teachers told her she was useless and slow, but later it was discovered she was dyslexic. Her mother's friend offered her a job in her café. Imogen was fearful of being incompetent. Dreams of incompetence can surface even in the most competent person if they are met with an unfamiliar situation that rekindles old fears.

INTERPRETATIONS AND FORTUNE-TELLING MEANINGS

- ★ If you are always failing in a dream and getting simple tasks wrong, you may have been made to feel like a failure in the past by parents, teachers, or peers.
- ★ If you are normally competent in life but fail in a dream, this is a pure anxiety dream you may have when encountering a new situation.
- ★ If you dream of being socially incompetent, you may be afraid of revealing your true self, especially sexually.
- ★ If you dream that you cannot use equipment or techniques at work that you operate easily in daily life, you may fear you are not worthy of your present position, especially if someone is undermining you.
- ★ If you regularly dream of being reproached by family or a boss, you should consider if it is the situation or people that are wrong and not you.
- ★ If you dream of being criticized by people from your past in current settings, you are defeating yourself in advance by listening to old voices and put-downs.

OUTCOME OF IMOGEN'S DREAM

Imogen worked in the café unpaid for a few days to learn all the basic tasks. This made her very confident. Dreaming of being incompetent can act as a spur and incentive for becoming extra-competent.

Incubus, Succubus

As Astrid, seventeen, lay in bed she was aware of a heavy weight pressing down on her and a shadowy form crushing her. She screamed, but no sound came out. Astrid started praying silently though she was not religious, and the weight disappeared.

DREAM BACKGROUND AND MEANING

Astrid experienced what may be a paranormal sexual attack involving a form of sleep paralysis. Incubi may appear to young women as demonic figures or shadows at night, and succubi appear to young men as predatory hags. This kind of dream assault was first described by St. Augustine in the sixth century. They are usually experienced by both sexes from adolescence up to the age of about thirty. Astrid was being pressured by her much-older partner, Alex, to go to sex parties and participate in threesomes. She did not want to lose him, but what he proposed distressed her.

INTERPRETATIONS AND FORTUNE-TELLING MEANINGS

★ If you have recurring dreams, you may be under pressure to have sex before you are ready.

★ If you are spiritual, especially in your teens or early twenties, you may be experiencing a surge of psychic power and should talk to a medium, healer, or counselor.

★ If dreams involve sexual abuse, they often reveal earlier suppressed sexual trauma that needs resolving.

★ If the figure is demonic, you may be suffering from sexual intimidation by an older person at work and need support.

★ If the figure is shadowy, there may be unresolved fears centered around sexuality, especially if sex is a taboo subject within the family.

★ If you dream you fail to fight off the incubus or succubus, you may feel secretly guilty about enjoying sex.

OUTCOME OF ASTRID'S DREAM

Astrid dumped her much-older partner and found a new partner closer to her age who respects her. Often linked with sexual control of a partner in the everyday world, these dreams can reflect deep-seated doubts.

Indifference

Paula, thirty, dreamed she had her purse and phone stolen in an overseas market and was pushed to the ground, cutting her knees and hands. Her friends laughed and walked on, telling her to catch up. She was stranded alone, miles from the hotel, with no money for a cab. At last, a market stall trader came to her aid, bathed her knees, and asked her husband to drive Paula home.

DREAM BACKGROUND AND MEANING

Paula had been invited on vacation with some new friends from work. They promised her an amazing time clubbing in the love capital of Europe. She knew it was not for her, but they said she was being prudish. Indifference dreams expose those people around you who may not stick around if you're in trouble.

INTERPRETATIONS AND FORTUNE-TELLING MEANINGS

★ If friends treat you with indifference in dreams, see who helps, accepting that you may sometimes need to find kindness beyond your apparent friendship group.

★ If you are in trouble in a dream, note who you do know who comes to your aid.

★ If you dream you drop your money and those around you help to pick it up, you can rely on them to stick by you in a crisis.

★ If friends or family take the money and leave you stranded, you may be too trusting of them.

★ If you feel indifferent toward a friend in a dream, you may sense they are showing you surface affection.

★ If you are dressed in your best and get an indifferent response, there may be underlying jealousy, masked as not caring.

OUTCOME OF PAULA'S DREAM

After the dream, Paula realized that her friends only wanted to know her because her father was the boss at work. She canceled the vacation with them but went with an old friend she had known since childhood. Indifference dreams can mask a deeper hostility, so examine the motives of those who may be using you while secretly resenting your appearance, status, imagined wealth, or success.

Indigenous People and Cultures

Pauline, forty, dreamed she was visited by the Australian Aboriginal Dreamtime, the ever-present first world of the Aboriginal creator spirits. An Aboriginal man and, behind him, women and children emerged from a wall. They seemed to be protectors.

DREAM BACKGROUND AND MEANING

Pauline had recently arrived in Australia from Scotland. The area of the dream was once the homeland to Aboriginal people. Pauline had come to Australia to get a good education for her autistic son and was worried about whether she had done the right thing. Indigenous dreams from various cultures can welcome settlers from other lands who need support.

INTERPRETATIONS AND FORTUNE-TELLING MEANINGS

★ If you dream of indigenous people while staying near one of their sacred places, it may be the anniversary of a tragedy or celebration and you may be connecting with the energies in the land.

★ If you dream that the way is barred when visiting a place sacred to indigenous people, it may be a time private to the guardians connected with the site. Try later.

★ If you dream of belonging to an indigenous people, you may have a distant connection with the bloodline, or the culture may hold wisdom for you.

★ If you frequently dream of indigenous spirits in your home, wherever you live in the world, your home may be built close to a site or energy line along which ancient peoples passed for their ceremonies. They will be protectors of your home.

★ If in your dream you are house-hunting near an indigenous site, ask the blessings of the land guardians as, if withheld, that will not be a lucky home for you.

OUTCOME OF PAULINE'S DREAM

Pauline found a job as a nurse in an Aboriginal health setting, and their healing ways greatly helped her son. In the modern world we have lost touch with the rich world of dreams as a source of psychic wisdom, which can come through access to ancient cultures.

Infection, Pandemic

Audrey, twenty, dreamed she was listening to her favorite band. She started coughing and continued to cough and choke. People were trying to move away from her. The coughing became so loud that she was escorted out. She was told she could be arrested for infecting the audience.

DREAM BACKGROUND AND MEANING

Audrey was due to attend a concert, twice postponed because of a pandemic. Then she was due to fly overseas on vacation. She knew there was a risk of catching an illness by going to a crowded concert. Current worries can be played out in dreams and realistic risks can be highlighted.

INTERPRETATIONS AND FORTUNE-TELLING MEANINGS

★ If in the dream a family member suffers from an infectious disease, it reflects fears that they are being badly influenced by someone outside the family.

★ Pandemic dreams are more likely if there is a real danger, though they can occur anytime the dreamer fears events beyond their control are preventing a much-desired plan from materializing.

★ Dreaming of a cut or wound becoming infected may be a warning of an actual injury, or it can reflect an escalating quarrel.

★ Dreams of the plague or Black Death may be past-life memories triggered by worries about vulnerable family members becoming sick. However, such dreams are not predictive.

★ If everyone is unfairly blaming you for spreading a disease, you may be accepting the role of victim or scapegoat.

★ If you are physically deteriorating in your dream, you are overworked or overstressed by others' demands.

OUTCOME OF AUDREY'S DREAM

While Audrey's dream was triggered by anxiety, it was also a warning that she might have to choose between events, as she would not be allowed on the plane if she was sick. Audrey reluctantly gave her concert tickets to a friend and went on vacation, being extra careful to avoid crowded places. Dreams can expose fears from childhood of being left vulnerable and alone when a parent becomes ill.

Inflation

Jeremy, sixty-five, dreamed he was in the supermarket, buying a loaf of bread. He put down a bill and the teller shook her head. He added more bills until he had emptied his pockets. Gnomes came from all directions, snatching at the money and taking the bread. When he tried to stop them, they pushed him out of the way and said his money was worthless because of inflation, and he would have to starve.

DREAM BACKGROUND AND MEANING

Jeremy was worried about the rate of inflation, which made his pension worth so much less. If you dream of inflation at a time when inflation is rising steeply, it is an anxiety dream, warning you to take greater care of personal resources and to economize.

INTERPRETATIONS AND FORTUNE-TELLING MEANINGS

★ If you dream of inflation spiraling out of control, you may have actual money worries, whether due to excessive regular expenses or to overspending.

★ If you dream of not being able to buy basics because inflation is so high, and there is no major inflation, you may have too many demands on your time and resources.

★ If you dream of inflation spiraling and it is not high at the time of the dream, this may forewarn you to save more, in case personal or global demands increase.

★ If you dream of inflating a life raft or lifejacket before you are traveling, you are suffering from anxiety, but there is no harm in checking travel arrangements for potential problems.

★ If you dream of inflation dropping rapidly, your own finances are safe and will remain so.

OUTCOME OF JEREMY'S DREAM

Jeremy sold his house and had plenty left over to be able to go on vacations, which he had not done for years. He also revived his old hobby of repairing antiques, now that he no longer had to repair his house, and supplemented his income. Dreaming of rising inflation often is a warning that you fear something in your life, maybe an emotion, getting out of control.

Injustice

Trent, forty-two, dreamed he was riding out as a crusader against injustice. But he was captured by a man with the face of his present-life brother, who said Trent must hand over a huge sum of gold as a ransom. Trent woke feeling angry because the man had emptied the gold into the sea, laughing.

DREAM BACKGROUND AND MEANING

Trent was in a dispute with his brother over his late father's farm, which Trent had run during his father's long illness. Now his brother demanded that Trent pay him a disproportionate amount of money to buy him out. Trent could not face a court case, but could not afford to pay, either. Dreams of injustices can symbolize a situation that is too painful to confront directly.

INTERPRETATIONS AND FORTUNE-TELLING MEANINGS

★ If you dream of a childhood injustice, there may be a current injustice that is triggering the memory.

★ If you dream of an unjust decision in a legal matter, avoid becoming embroiled in disputes with officialdom right now, though right is on your side.

★ If you know the unjust person in the dream, the injustice may be rooted in old resentments not of your making that cannot be put right.

★ If you dream of righting an injustice or fighting for a just cause and winning, this is a good omen for getting justice in a matter troubling you.

★ If you dream of an unjust deed escalating out of control, however morally right you are, it may not be worth pursuing, to keep your peace of mind.

OUTCOME OF TRENT'S DREAM

Trent knew his brother was angry because he believed Trent had always been his father's favorite. He wanted revenge against Trent for what he considered his father's indifference. Trent decided not to fight legally, but to sell the farm and, with his rightful half, start again. His brother, a dedicated gambler, soon lost the money. Injustice dreams can be deep-seated and can suggest whether it's best to fight or walk away.

Interview

Connor, thirty-two, dreamed he woke up late for his interview because his alarm did not go off; then he spilled coffee on his shirt and had to iron another one, and he got stuck on the freeway in heavy traffic. He arrived at the correct building, but could not locate the interview room. By the time he reached the interview, his mind went totally blank in front of the panel, and he knew he had not gotten the job.

DREAM BACKGROUND AND MEANING

Connor had been seeking another job, since the company he worked for had folded after a major economic crash. When Connor was finally offered an interview, he was incredibly nervous. He was having nightmares about everything that could go wrong. Interview dreams, especially when linked to an actual job interview, reflect anxiety and tend to highlight potential hazards.

INTERPRETATIONS AND FORTUNE-TELLING MEANINGS

★ If you dream of being late for an interview, you may feel you are not where you should be in your career and are striving to catch up.

★ If you cannot find the dream interview location, you may not be in the right place or be prepared for any promotion or opportunity you are seeking.

★ If you do a brilliant interview in the dream and are offered the job, you can be confident you have the right energies to succeed.

★ If you cannot hear the questions or stumble over the answers, you may worry about coming across well on a date or impressing someone new in your life.

★ If you are being interviewed by the media, you may be worried about the image you are projecting.

★ If you are interviewing others, you may need to be more selective about those you choose as friends or business colleagues.

OUTCOME OF CONNOR'S DREAM

As a result of the dream, Connor double-checked everything in advance. He left extra time and just missed a pileup on the freeway that would have made him late. He was offered the post. Interview dreams can, if positive, give out extra confidence vibes to help you succeed in any area of advancement.

Inventions

Jack, fifty-five, dreamed that his friend Thomas, wearing a mask, was breaking into his shed at midnight and filling a bag with Jack's inventions. When Jack approached Thomas, he ran off into the night.

DREAM BACKGROUND AND MEANING

Jack regularly adapted household items for his physically challenged wife, and some adaptations were so ingenious that his friend Thomas said they would make a fortune. Jack had offered to cut Thomas in if he did the marketing. Recently, however, Jack noticed that some inventions remarkably like his own were being sold. Dreams can warn of the theft of ideas and can reveal the identity of the person responsible.

INTERPRETATIONS AND FORTUNE-TELLING MEANINGS

★ If you invent something in a dream, note all that you can remember when you wake, as the creative part of the brain works overtime at night.

★ If you are puzzling over a missing link that is preventing your invention from working, a dream may reveal the answer.

★ If an invention in a dream makes a lot of money or wins acclaim, it is worth marketing, even for moderate success.

★ If you dream you are seeking to make your living through your inventions, this is a good time to seek outlets.

★ If in the dream your invention is rejected, remember that the rejection may be due to problems with the company you approached, or the invention may simply be ahead of its time. Keep trying.

★ If you are inventing ideas for a book, play, music, or a creative venture, you may see the complete production in the dream.

OUTCOME OF JACK'S DREAM

Jack made inquiries of the manufacturer selling the inventions and found out that Thomas had been presenting the ideas as his own. Jack made sure he kept future creations secret. After he made a few profitable inventions, the company offered Jack a contract. Thomas quickly left the scene after transferring the patents to Jack. Inventions in dreams, even if you have never patented anything, indicate you should market your ingenuity as you have a creative lateral mind.

Island

Millie, twenty-four, dreamed that she was on an island, but when the tide came in, she had to retreat to the top of the hill in the center. The space was crowded with people who knew one another but ignored Millie. Millie was lonely in her dream and yet lacked the freedom to make friends. Millie looked out to sea for a rescue boat, but it never came.

DREAM BACKGROUND AND MEANING

Millie was working at what should have been her ideal job, an au pair in a remote luxury villa on a beautiful island connected to the mainland only by boat or helicopter. The other staff had their own quarters and spoke mainly Spanish. When visitors came, Millie was expected to stay in her room, and she became increasingly isolated, having only the children for company. In dreams, islands can be sanctuaries, but they can become prisons if they isolate the dreamer from life and from other people.

INTERPRETATIONS AND FORTUNE-TELLING MEANINGS

★ If in your dream you are happy on a desert island or with someone special, it may be time to take more leisure or private space for you and your partner.

★ If you dream the island is overgrown and you are stranded, you may feel life is closing in on you.

★ If you dream you are on vacation on a tropical or well-loved island, an unexpected vacation or adventure is soon coming your way.

★ If the island is being engulfed by the sea, your privacy or personal space is being gradually encroached upon.

★ If you are happy to be leaving an island, you are ready to widen your horizons.

OUTCOME OF MILLIE'S DREAM

After the dream, Millie realized that the luxury and high wages did not compensate for the isolation. She applied for a position working in a summer camp where there was a good social life among the camp counselors. An island, however luxurious, must offer not only a refuge from hectic life but also suitable company to share the tranquility.

Ivy, Clinging Plants

Gareth, forty, dreamed he was struggling through ivy-choked trees and bushes, trying to find his way to his mother's house in the dark. But when he reached the house, ivy had grown over the front door and windows. The harder he pulled it away, the thicker it grew back, until he was totally entangled. His mother was calling his name.

DREAM BACKGROUND AND MEANING

Gareth dreaded telling his widowed mother he was relocating to another state for his job, as she depended on his twice-weekly visits, which would no longer be possible. But he wanted the promotion and above all, independence. Ivy especially refers to excesses of maternal and overnurturing love.

INTERPRETATIONS AND FORTUNE-TELLING MEANINGS

★ Ivy clinging to and choking another plant warns of possessiveness and control in the name of love.

★ To dream of admission to an Ivy League educational establishment indicates high scholarly ambition for oneself or a loved one and can be predictive.

★ Decorating the home with holly and ivy at Christmas promises happy family gatherings, especially if you have been apart or estranged.

★ Ivy growing up the side of a house says the home will be protected and emphasizes the nurturing role of a maternal figure.

★ However, ivy damaging the brickwork warns that the atmosphere is stifling and is based in guilt.

★ Ivy growing near water heralds a beloved family member or lover returning home from another state or from overseas.

OUTCOME OF GARETH'S DREAM

Gareth knew it was now or never. He visited every six weeks and kept in touch via social media. To his amazement, his mother created a social life in the local community. Gareth realized he had been holding her back by giving in to her possessive demands. Ivy is beautiful. However, if it is allowed to cling too closely it becomes destructive and sometimes fosters an unconscious codependency between the ivy and what it clings to.

Jaguar (Animal)

Martin, sixty-five, dreamed he was riding on the back of a jaguar through the skies. He knew he was an Aztec shaman, on his way to fight the nightly battle so that the sun might be reborn the next day. He knew he must recall the right words or the sun would not rise. He woke at dawn, knowing he had shared a sacred rite.

DREAM BACKGROUND AND MEANING

Martin had joined a London shamanic group, but the teacher constantly criticized him. His teacher claimed Aztec ancestry and told Martin he could not have a jaguar as his shamanic steed, as they belonged only to powerful shamans like himself. If you are riding a jaguar in a dream, you have a great deal more power than you realize or are told.

INTERPRETATIONS AND FORTUNE-TELLING MEANINGS

★ If you dream you are flying through the sky with your jaguar, you need to take what seems a risky step, which will pay off.

★ If you are running from a jaguar, you may be ignoring powerful emotions and sexual passion toward someone who has recently come into your life.

★ If you see a jaguar alone in the forest, rely on your own wisdom and do not seek the approval of or emulate others.

★ If you see your dream jaguar climbing a high rock, believe in your ability to rise high in your chosen field.

★ If you dream that a jaguar attacks, you may be defeating yourself by not confronting fears and injustices.

OUTCOME OF MARTIN'S DREAM

Martin went to South America and traveled with indigenous shamans. He found a translation of his dream sun rite and was told his totem was the jaguar. Upon returning home, Martin started his own shamanic group.

Many jaguar dreams link with past-world memories of the Mayans and Aztecs, acting as a reminder that personal intuition in any spiritual art is more important than ego.

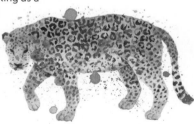

Jam, Jelly

Dennis, fifty-two, dreamed he was a child alone in his mother's kitchen. She had spent the day making different jams for a family party and had told him not to touch them. But taking a spoon, he dug deep into a pot to taste some. Since the jam was still hot, he burned his mouth and dropped the jar, spreading the sticky, partly set liquid all over the table and the floor. His mouth was so painful that he had to tell his mother and was sent to bed without supper.

DREAM BACKGROUND AND MEANING

Dennis had discovered his late mother's most recent will, which was less favorable to him than the official one with the solicitor. He was considering destroying it. But would he be discovered? Jam or jelly dreams promise togetherness, but warn of divisions if the jam is not shared around.

INTERPRETATIONS AND FORTUNE-TELLING MEANINGS

★ Dreams of making jam or jelly promise a happy home life and family celebrations.

★ If you are picking fruit to make jam or jelly, it may take time to build up or restore a relationship but will be worth the effort.

★ To dream that you are eating jam or jelly not intended for you means that a thoughtless or unethical dealing may lead to discovery.

★ If jam or jelly is too sweet, beware of excessive flattery or praise, as you may find the speaker two-faced.

★ If you dream you are sticky after eating jam or jelly or get it on your clothes, it will be hard to keep a secret or deny involvement in taking more than your share.

OUTCOME OF DENNIS'S DREAM

After the dream, Dennis was nervous that somehow his late mother was watching him. He handed over the will to the attorney, who agreed it was legal. Dennis was less wealthy as a result but had a clear conscience and continued to enjoy good relations with the family. Jam or jelly dreams often hark back to childhood happiness but also to misdeeds that can reflect present dilemmas of conscience.

Jar

Sylvia, fifty, dreamed she was twenty years younger and bottling jam from fruit she had collected. Her children, who in the dream were very young, were eager to sample the finished product. The jam was still hot, but the youngest child, Barry, took a huge spoonful and screamed, as he had burned his mouth badly. In the ensuing chaos, the jars were tipped over and spoiled.

DREAM BACKGROUND AND MEANING

Barry, now twenty-seven, was still a problem for Sylvia since he had recently returned home after another failed relationship and a job loss. He was a huge drain on Sylvia's and her husband's resources at a time when they wanted to cut back. Because of Barry's drinking and drug-taking, the grandchildren no longer came to visit their grandparents at their home. Jars represent family harmony in dreams and are a barometer of domestic happiness or otherwise.

INTERPRETATIONS AND FORTUNE-TELLING MEANINGS

* ★ Dreaming of full jars of honey, jam, or preserved fruits says you will have sufficient resources for your needs.
* ★ Empty jars or ones that are broken foretell that a planned bonus or windfall may be delayed or unwisely spent.
* ★ A hard-to-open jar is a warning to not reveal secrets except to those you know you can trust.
* ★ An open jar with contents spilled suggests that someone close has betrayed a confidence.
* ★ If you are filling jars with jam or fruit, you need to prepare for the future, as there may be demands for your money and resources.
* ★ If you dream the contents of a jar have gone moldy, you or someone close has been holding back from seizing opportunity, and the moment may have passed.

OUTCOME OF SYLVIA'S DREAM

Sylvia knew she had to take a stand. She paid for yet another detox clinic and told Barry it was his last chance—after that, if he did not show progress, he was on his own. Barry realized she meant it. Jar dreams are at the heart of the family but can highlight when one person is disrupting that harmony.

Jazz

Paul, thirty, regularly dreamed he was playing jazz and blues on paddleboats with the late Louis Armstrong and hoped to make a career with Louis, who was obviously going places. But the dream always ended with Louis going his own way. Paul was offered a job as a jazz pianist in a bar in New Orleans by a paddleboat customer. However, he declined as he was worried he would not make enough money to live.

DREAM BACKGROUND AND MEANING

Paul was a piano teacher in a small Southern town but would frequently haunt the jazz and blues bars of New Orleans. He had entered a talent show in a New Orleans bar, and when he won he was offered a job playing every night. He knew this was his chance to enter the world he loved, but he was worried about financial security.

INTERPRETATIONS AND FORTUNE-TELLING MEANINGS

* ★ If you dream of a world where you feel you belong or belonged, this can be a sign to take a new life direction.
* ★ If you dream of playing jazz or blues, especially with a famous musician, you have unfulfilled creative gifts.
* ★ If you dream of jazz, your life right now may lack spontaneity and joy, which could be incorporated with courage into your present world.
* ★ If you dream of improvising as a member of a jazz band, you may find that the need for security increasingly presents restrictions.
* ★ If you dream you are listening to jazz, you may benefit from letting the flow of life take you where it will.
* ★ If your present life has parallels with a dream world, especially if the dream is recurring, you may be able to apply the lessons of the dream to your current situation.

OUTCOME OF PAUL'S DREAM

Paul resigned from his job and took the job playing in the bar. He gave piano lessons in his spare time for extra money. Jazz dreams can generate ingenuity so you can achieve both the spontaneity and the structure that lie behind the jazz genre.

Jealousy

Since her remarriage following her first husband's death, Dianne, fifty-six, had frequently dreamed that her new husband, Richie, was cheating on her. In her dream, she saw him in a diner late at night, holding hands with a waitress in her twenties.

DREAM BACKGROUND AND MEANING

Dianne met Richie shortly after her husband's death. They married within three months. Richie had proved a wonderful, loving husband who had shown no sign of straying. Her friends and family, however, said it was too soon to remarry, as she could not really know Richie. When Richie was traveling for work, he often stayed at a particular motel with a diner. They had started to quarrel when Dianne voiced her suspicions.

Dreaming of your partner being unfaithful may be a guilt dream saying that you should not be together if others disapprove or you feel disloyal to a former partner.

INTERPRETATIONS AND FORTUNE-TELLING MEANINGS

★ If you are jealous because of a past betrayal, the dream jealousy may be pure anxiety.

★ If you know the identity of the dream tempter, there may have been inappropriate flirting and you may need to intervene.

★ If you catch your partner with someone younger, more beautiful, or more dynamic in a dream, your poor self-image may be manifesting as jealousy.

★ If your partner is displaying jealousy in the dream, are you restricted in the actual relationship?

★ If a friend or child is jealous of your relationship, are you denying them attention, or are they being overpossessive?

OUTCOME OF DIANNE'S DREAM

Dianne felt disloyal to her deceased husband by being happy with Richie, and she was self-sabotaging the new relationship. Richie suggested Dianne travel with him sometimes. The diner waiting staff were an older husband-and-wife team.

Hidden insecurity or personal fears of either partner can be projected as infidelity.

Jeans

Juliet, seventeen, dreamed she was wearing the latest fashion in jeans and everyone was admiring and envying her. Then she realized she had turned into her grandmother, who was wearing the jeans, and she woke confused.

DREAM BACKGROUND AND MEANING

Juliet was having a hard time with her friends, as they all had the latest fashion jeans, but Juliet's parents could not afford to buy them. Her friends often ridiculed her cheap jeans. Jeans in dreams may reflect the unhappiness of the dreamer because a cheap label made them feel socially inferior.

INTERPRETATIONS AND FORTUNE-TELLING MEANINGS

★ To wear designer jeans in a dream indicates a desire to show the world you are at ease with yourself.

★ If you dream you are trying on jeans, whatever your age, you may be attempting to adopt a more relaxed, casual approach to life.

★ If jeans are too small or too tight, you are feeling restricted by the demands of others to conform to their rules. If too large, you are trying to please everyone.

★ If you are dreaming of wearing jeans in a formal setting and are comfortable, you are ready to make your mark on the world.

★ If you dream you are receiving disapproval for wearing jeans in the wrong setting, you may have doubts about challenging accepted practices.

★ If, in the dream, jeans are deliberately ripped as a fashion statement, you are expressing that material advantages do not matter as much as being free.

OUTCOME OF JULIET'S DREAM

Juliet was looking at photos of when her grandmother was a teenager and realized that her grandmother was wearing what were now vintage fashion-label jeans. Her grandmother said she still had them and was going to throw them out. Juliet rescued them and is now the envy of everyone, thanks to her special jeans. Dreams may often offer a clue to resolving a problem where the solution is present but not noticed.

Jellyfish

Mira, thirty-eight, dreamed she was swimming, pulling a lifeboat filled with people she had rescued from the sea. The sea suddenly filled with jellyfish, which started stinging her. She tried to get the boat to shore in spite of the stings, but realized the rescued passengers were the jellyfish.

DREAM BACKGROUND AND MEANING

Mira was a training officer with a state department. She had recently been promoted as head of the team. Because the other members were older, though less competent, they resented her promotion and were making it hard for her, hoping she would resign. Mira was covering up their incompetence and laziness, as she did not want to get them in trouble with senior management. But she dreaded the spiteful remarks from those she was helping. Jellyfish represent unpredictability in others.

INTERPRETATIONS AND FORTUNE-TELLING MEANINGS

★ If you dream you are swimming with jellyfish but do not get stung, you will survive attacks or spite against you.

★ If jellyfish attack in the dream, beware of work colleagues or a social group joining forces to undermine you.

★ If jellyfish seem menacing but do not attack, the people represented by the jellyfish are spineless and so may use passive resistance.

★ Jellyfish drifting with the tide warn against letting problematic matters remain unaddressed.

★ If you are watching jellyfish floating away from you on the outgoing tide, a threat or a malicious person or people are moving out, or will soon move out, of your life.

★ Should you dream the jellyfish are floating on the incoming tide, be careful of the intentions of new people coming into your life.

OUTCOME OF MIRA'S DREAM

After the dream, Mira astounded herself and her team by reporting the ringleader to her boss after a major error, as the ringleader was both incompetent and causing trouble. He was removed from the team. The others fell into line. Jellyfish dreams are generally warnings of ongoing situations involving kindness to those you should distrust.

Jinx

Josie, twenty-eight, dreamed she was entering a show-jumping event and was upset to see Crystal, a relatively new competitor, in the stables. Crystal smiled and attached a little doll, supposedly for luck, to Josie's horse's bridle and said, "No hard feelings, win or lose." Josie knew Crystal had jinxed Josie's horse before. Josie rode into the ring, panicked, and stumbled at the first hurdle.

DREAM BACKGROUND AND MEANING

Josie was entering a major show-jumping competition to qualify at the national level but feared that if Crystal was there she would say something strange that unnerved or unsettled her horse. This was an anxiety dream, mirroring life and warning of a self-fulfilling prophecy of failure.

INTERPRETATIONS AND FORTUNE-TELLING MEANINGS

★ If you suffer bad luck in a dream, you may worry that present good fortune, love, or happiness may not last.

★ If in the jinxing dream you regularly see the same person, they may be deliberately ill-wishing you.

★ If in the dream you overcome the jinx using a lucky charm or ritual, this method will overcome jinxes in everyday life.

★ If you dream you are jinxed at every turn, you may be suffering stress overload.

★ If you are jinxing yourself in a dream through over-confidence, it's time to check whether you are relying on luck too much.

★ If you dream you are crossing and uncrossing sticks or carrying out an unjinxing ritual, this may refer to a past life in which you were a wise man or woman.

OUTCOME OF JOSIE'S DREAM

Josie knew she was allowing herself to be spooked. She bought a tiny lucky horseshoe charm for her horse's bridle and took her boyfriend along to care for the horse before the show, so she did not need to go into the stables and see Crystal. Josie won, and once the cycle was broken there were no more problems. It is possible to jinx ourselves through anxiety that makes us panic and encourages mistakes.

Jockey

Harper, seventeen, dreamed she was riding a horse in a major race and was leading the field as she rounded the final corner into the home stretch. She could hear other horses catching up with her. She didn't panic but gave the horse a pat on the neck and whispered, "Good boy." Her horse won easily.

DREAM BACKGROUND AND MEANING

Harper had always wanted to be a jockey. But she grew too tall and heavy, and so took up athletics. She was offered a scholarship to a college where she could further her sporting ambitions. But increasingly she had been dreaming of the horse-racing world again and had become convinced that racehorses should be encouraged to win with horse whispering and not with a whip. Jockey dreams suggest success in whatever way you choose if you go all out for it.

INTERPRETATIONS AND FORTUNE-TELLING MEANINGS

* If you always back the same jockey in a dream, you may be on a winning streak in speculation where skill and luck combine.
* If you dream you are a jockey and consistently come in first, it's time to test your skills against others, whether in business or in competition.
* If you dream you lose a race as a jockey, you may lack confidence in your own abilities, or may have been told you cannot succeed in your chosen field.
* If you are leading a horse and a jockey into the race arena, your gifts may lie in training others to compete or perform.
* If you are replaced as a jockey before a race, explore alternative approaches or roles.
* If you are watching someone else riding a horse in a race, you may have unfulfilled wishes and desires.
* If you fall off the horse during a race, or if the horse falls, beware of those who try to prevent you from fulfilling an ambition.

OUTCOME OF HARPER'S DREAM

Harper diverted her studies to learning about the welfare of horses and training them, and she joined a large racing stable as a groom. Harper found she had a gift for encouraging and calming horses through talking to them, and she was able to teach this technique to jockeys and race trainers. Jockey dreams represent going all out for ventures, if necessary, by adapting a new approach to your chosen field.

Judge

Ben, forty-five, dreamed he was in a glass dock and the judge was in a glass box. Ben's ex-wife was in a third glass box. They were supposed to communicate through microphones and headphones, but Ben's microphone and headphones were broken. Increasingly desperate, Ben banged on the glass but could not get attention. The court emptied. Ben broke through the glass to see his ex-partner taking their children away in an airport taxi.

DREAM BACKGROUND AND MEANING

Ben was trying to prevent his ex from taking their children to live overseas with her new partner. Preliminary hearings had been judged in her favor. The judge had accepted her family's untrue statements that Ben was an alcoholic and a danger to the children. A final hearing had been set. A judge can represent condemnatory people or voices in your head from the past.

INTERPRETATIONS AND FORTUNE-TELLING MEANINGS

* If in the dream you are awaiting a verdict from a judge, you may be feeling guilty about a step you want to take.
* If a jury is listening to evidence, other people will try to influence you to change your mind.
* If you are judging a competition, you will be asked to choose between two people. If neither is right, do not be pressured into deciding.
* If you are awaiting the results of a real-life settlement, court case, or tribunal, a successful dream outcome is a good omen.
* If you lose in the dream, note any dishonest witnesses or indifferent representation and make real-life changes, or investigate further.
* If you dream that the judge will not listen, avoid being silenced by an authority or official figure who pulls rank.

OUTCOME OF BEN'S DREAM

Ben obtained reliable medical and social witnesses to counteract the lies. The judge refused permission to remove the children from the country except for vacations. Judge dreams warn that others may not approve of your decisions or actions. Trust your own judgment.

Juggler

Clive, forty-two, dreamed he was in a talent contest, juggling balls at great speed. The audience and judges were cheering. Suddenly a stray ball came flying from the wings, causing Clive to drop the lot. His best friend, Tim, who was in the front row of the audience, jumped on stage, picked up the balls, handed them to Clive, and turned the incident into a comedy routine that won the competition.

DREAM BACKGROUND AND MEANING

Clive was worried, as his old company insisted that he give a month's notice before leaving his job. But he needed to attend a three-week trade fair with the new business he was starting with Tim. He could not be in two places at once, but didn't wish to let either Tim or his old company down.

INTERPRETATIONS AND FORTUNE-TELLING MEANINGS

* Dreaming of juggling indicates a time of trying to balance different priorities and meeting conflicting demands.
* If you are keeping all the balls in the air, you will succeed in combining multitasking demands.
* Should you drop a single ball, check your priorities to see which commitment or activity can be dropped to give you more time.
* If you drop all or most of the balls, you are trying to do too much at once and should delegate.
* If you find yourself juggling in synch with a known or unknown person, you will receive an advantageous business offer or solution.
* If your partner drops or throws the balls wide or too far, your partner may be putting their own interests first.

OUTCOME OF CLIVE'S DREAM

Tim said he could easily set up and run the business during the week with the help of the competent apprentice they had employed. Clive could commute to attend when it was most busy, on the weekends. Sometimes teamwork in juggling can enable all the balls to stay in the air once we accept that we are not indispensable and that we can't do everything ourselves.

Jumping

Jack, seventeen, dreamed he was with Spring-heeled Jack, the United Kingdom's semi-mythical Victorian spirit who could jump higher than any human, over trees, hedges, and even houses. Jack took his hand and together they leaped skyward. Spring-heeled Jack told Jack he should enter a local junior athletic competition, held in four weeks' time, as a sports coach from a well-known university would be present, offering a scholarship to the most promising athlete.

DREAM BACKGROUND AND MEANING

Jack was high-jump champion in high school, but he was aware that most of the other prospective athletes had extra private coaching. He knew his family could not afford to pay for him to go to college. No one else, it seemed, knew about the sports coach, and many of his rivals were not bothering to enter the competition, as there was a major soccer game that weekend. This was a psychic dream, alerting Jack to possible success. Jumping dreams can bring a swift route to the top, given determination, however unpromising that route may initially seem.

INTERPRETATIONS AND FORTUNE-TELLING MEANINGS

* If you dream of jumping high in a dream, you will be able to defeat any obstacles on the road to personal fulfillment.
* If you jump sufficiently high in your dream, you may find you are flying (see p. 198), as this is a natural progression.
* If you are successful in a dream jumping competition, you will succeed in any ambitious venture.
* If you fall while jumping or are pushed out of the way, you should be more assertive.
* If you are jumping from a height or into water, leaving your comfort zone is the price for rising high.

OUTCOME OF JACK'S DREAM

When the coach talked to Jack after the competition, he told Jack he was looking for natural talent, and Jack had won the scholarship. Jumping dreams offer the dreamer the courage to go for what is wanted, and to not focus on the doubts, but on every opportunity.

Jury

Norris, twenty-five, dreamed he was sitting in the center of a circle of the extended family and community of his future wife, Nala. Each gave an opinion on Norris's moral fitness and beliefs. Norris was not allowed to speak. They then voted by a show of hands whether Norris was worthy of marrying Nala, and the majority were against him.

DREAM BACKGROUND AND MEANING

Norris had fallen in love with Nala, who belonged to a very strict, closed religious community. He was given the chance to convert to her faith, but he refused. Her family was adamant that she either give him up or leave the community. Jury dreams are concerned with collective decisions and opinions where the dreamer is defending what they believe is right.

INTERPRETATIONS AND FORTUNE-TELLING MEANINGS

* If you dream you are cleared of a charge by a jury, your good reputation will be restored or vindicated.
* If a group of people is listening to a case against you, you may be seeking to gain recognition for your beliefs or point of view and win others over.
* If you are being misrepresented to the jury, you may be unfairly judged because your worldview is at odds with the status quo.
* If you are a member of a jury, you may feel pressured to go along with popular opinion.
* If a dream jury is made up of people who are biased against you, you are wasting your time arguing your cause.
* If you dream you are trying to avoid jury service, you may be unwilling to express an opinion on a subject but are being pressured to do so.

OUTCOME OF NORRIS'S DREAM

Norris realized that Nala would not go against her family and community. After the dream, he heard she had been sent overseas to marry. Juries do not always mean justice, though they should. Where the majority view is weighted against the dreamer, the dream can warn of this and allow a new approach or support to get a fairer hearing.

Kaleidoscope

Beryl, thirty-two, dreamed she saw a silver kaleidoscope in a yard sale and realized it was very old and delicate. When she shook it gently, all the small colored pieces of glass enclosed her and took her to an old-fashioned nursery where a little girl with a smocked dress was playing with a doll's house. The little girl smiled and said, "I knew you would come back for me." The scene swirled and the dream ended.

DREAM BACKGROUND AND MEANING

Beryl desperately wanted a baby but was afraid to have one because her family had a hereditary condition that could be passed on. Though Beryl knew she did not have the condition, she was afraid she might be a carrier. Kaleidoscope dreams are very special because kaleidoscopes create seemingly random images that can translate as actual pictures in the dreamer's mind.

INTERPRETATIONS AND FORTUNE-TELLING MEANINGS

* To dream of the swiftly changing designs indicates you will be made several offers, but it may be hard to choose, so wait.
* If the image settles into a harmonious design, there will be happiness in existing love, or a new love will enter your life.
* If you do not like the image and turn the kaleidoscope again in the dream, you may need to be patient for a troublesome matter to clear.
* If someone else changes your kaleidoscope picture, they are trying to get you to see the world from their point of view.
* If you try to hold an image static too long, you may be blocking your own opportunities through fear of change.
* If you are turning the image clockwise, creative ventures are coming together; if counterclockwise, there will be unavoidable delays in business plans.

OUTCOME OF BERYL'S DREAM

The dream showed Beryl a healthy little girl and suggested they had been together in a past life. Beryl went for tests and found she was not a carrier of the hereditary condition. She became pregnant and had a beautiful daughter. Kaleidoscope dreams can show a picture of what has been and can be again.

Kayak

Maisie, thirty, dreamed she was an Inuit girl living in the north of Canada. An older man in a kayak came paddling upstream. She fell instantly in love and set off with him. But he proved cruel to her once her settlement was out of sight. She demanded he take her back. He refused. She stole his kayak and bravely set off for home.

DREAM BACKGROUND AND MEANING

Maisie's dream is an archetypal legend set around kayaks and cruel men turning into evil sea birds, which she might have heard as a child. Maisie was in love with her college professor. Though he had said they would live together, he was already flirting with other students and lowering the grades on her work. Kayaks moving fast through water represent surface charisma that can be misleading.

INTERPRETATIONS AND FORTUNE-TELLING MEANINGS

* If you are kayaking alone, the dream advises reliance on your own resources.
* If you are kayaking in harmony with someone else, this promises happiness with the person sharing the kayak.
* If you and someone else are paddling the same kayak in different directions, negotiate with the other person on a joint strategy.
* If the kayak capsizes and you are clinging to the side, you may rely too much on an unreliable person or an unstable situation.
* If you abandon the kayak and swim for shore, there may be a venture, a person, or an activity you should drop that is weighing you down.
* If your kayak is leaking, temporary measures will hold matters stable.

OUTCOME OF MAISIE'S DREAM

Maisie confronted the professor publicly and made him apologize and buy her a ticket home. She is now studying at a local university. Dreams can cause relevant legends to resurface at key moments. Kayaks, by representing swift emotional as well as actual movement, may appear at a transition time when sometimes one can only try to steer to the right destination, which may be home.

Kettle

Greta, seventy-four, dreamed she was lifting a heavy iron kettle onto a gas stove and making tea for visitor after visitor from her extended family. They were pouring out their troubles, taking food from her shelves, and leaving without a word of thanks. Though normally upbeat, Greta woke feeling resentful that she had become just an ATM for her family.

DREAM BACKGROUND AND MEANING

Greta had come into a modest inheritance. Since she had told her family, they came to see her only to ask for financial help and never showed appreciation for her hospitality. If she protested, they said, "You can afford it." A kettle can appear as a past-life symbol and, if you are a natural giver, this may have been the pattern in earlier worlds. Few kettles appear as electric kettles or boiling water taps in dreams, though this may change in the future.

INTERPRETATIONS AND FORTUNE-TELLING MEANINGS

* A dream of a kettle on a stove is a timeless symbol of domestic unity with family members, but it must be reciprocal.
* A kettle burned dry indicates that all has been said on a certain topic and it has run out of steam.
* Pouring boiling water onto tea or coffee points to the desire to nurture others. If used in tea or coffee divination, this heralds great foresight.
* A rusty kettle says emotional and family life have been neglected but can be restored.
* Spilling the contents of a kettle, if it is cold, indicates a wasted effort or a relationship gone cold.
* If you burn yourself on a hot kettle, domestic problems are escalating and you should stand back from acting as peacemaker.

OUTCOME OF GRETA'S DREAM

After the dream, Greta made herself less available to her family and put limits on her generosity so they realized that a bottomless bank should not be the condition for togetherness. Kettles, like kitchens (see p. 270), represent hospitality, not exploitation.

Key

Tricia, fifty, dreamed she was in her late great-grandmother's house, though it had been sold. At the top of the stairs was an unfamiliar door with a key in the lock. It opened on a room filled with rows of old-fashioned ball gowns. Her great-grandmother, now young, was dancing in a bright red dress. She smiled at Tricia, indicated the rows of dresses, and disappeared. Tricia woke trying to get back into the dream.

DREAM BACKGROUND AND MEANING

Tricia's great-grandmother had bequeathed Tricia a box of her vintage dresses in perfect condition, including a red ball gown. Tricia loved the dresses and longed to re-create similar garments. Her time was her own, but she lacked the necessary skill. Dream keys may open doors to a lucrative future with unused resources.

INTERPRETATIONS AND FORTUNE-TELLING MEANINGS

* A key in a door represents an answer to a problem revealed in the dream or soon after.
* The key to a new house says you will soon be able to move into the house of your dreams.
* A key to a tumbledown house warns of expensive bills connected with your current dwelling. You may have to compromise on a move.
* Keys appear when you are contemplating a new sexual relationship, and they counsel waiting if you are uncertain.
* Losing your keys reveals worries about the stability or emotional security of your home or workplace, depending on what the missing keys should open. Watch for treachery or someone trying to take your place.
* If a key does not fit, accept that a desired avenue may be impractical or ultimately unfulfilling.

OUTCOME OF TRICIA'S DREAM

Tricia decided to go to design college and learn to make vintage-style clothes with a view to opening a rental shop for media companies and individuals wanting to rent period-inspired clothes for special occasions. Her logo was the red ball gown. Locked rooms and boxes reveal hidden talents and opportunities waiting to be discovered.

Kidnapper

Alison, thirty-five, had a recurring dream that her ex-husband came in the night and stole their son away, taking him on a plane to the other side of the world, where her ex had family. He refused to communicate or return her son.

DREAM BACKGROUND AND MEANING

Alison's ex-husband belonged to a different culture. Though Alison trusted him to not take their son out of the country without her permission, she was disturbed that his family was immersing their son in their religion and culture on access weekends. She feared she might lose him in the future if he came to prefer his other family. Kidnapping dreams can occur where there is basic insecurity about a child being unduly influenced by family members, especially if the members have very different beliefs.

INTERPRETATIONS AND FORTUNE-TELLING MEANINGS

* A kidnapping dream is a normal anxiety dream, as a child becomes more independent or frequently wanders off in public. Such dreams may be relieved by having agreed-on safety rules on outings.
* If you dream you are being kidnapped, this may express fears of an ex-partner harming you, or fears of losing your home or children through divorce proceedings.
* If you are the kidnapper, you may have feelings for someone that you cannot reveal.
* If you dream you know the kidnapper, they may have control over you in your everyday world. Can you break free?
* If you dream that your love partner is kidnapped, you may fear someone is trying to lure them away.

OUTCOME OF ALISON'S DREAM

Alison realized that her son belonged to two different cultures and she could help him to reconcile them and value both. However, she obtained a court order with her ex-husband's agreement that her son would not be taken out of the country until he was older and able to decide for himself. Kidnapping dreams are rooted in the fear of losing someone or something precious and need resolving or an increase in basic security to take away their power to terrify.

Kindergarten, Day-Care Center

Bethany, thirty-five, dreamed she was in a huge day-care center, trying to collect her son. There were crowds of parents. The center cleared and a member of staff told Bethany her son had been taken to the facility across the road. Bethany rushed across to find it in darkness and her son crying alone. She woke sobbing.

DREAM BACKGROUND AND MEANING

Bethany was due to return to work after maternity leave but could not find the right day care, as the one she favored had a huge waiting list. A single mother, she needed to work to support herself and her son. The exaggerated starkness of a dream may reassure the dreamer that their concerns are genuine and not just anxiety.

INTERPRETATIONS AND FORTUNE-TELLING MEANINGS

* A dream of a children's day-care center full of babies is a good omen if you want to start or add to your family.
* If you are pregnant, a day-care center is a sign that all will go well with the birth and after the birth.
* If the dream day-care experience is bad, you may worry about leaving children or a sick family member in such a place.
* For those who love fur babies, day care is a sign you will be offered a young animal that will bring great happiness.
* If you dream you are working in a childcare center where too many children are demanding attention, you may be taking care of the needs of too many people, adults as well as children.
* If you dream that day care is a happy experience, you may decide to take up a career involving children.

OUTCOME OF BETHANY'S DREAM

Bethany was talking about her dream to another mother, Louise, who was going back to work at a similar time. Louise was also worried about the quality of day care on offer. They agreed to share the cost of a private, qualified nanny. As the result of a bad dream, there was extra incentive to resolve a problem in a new way.

King

Thomas, sixty-six, dreamed he was standing on the battlements of his castle, but he had not seen invaders for many years. He returned to his throne room, but no one came with petitions. He called for the queen, his wife, and the princes and princesses, his children, but the palace was silent. He had a kingdom with no subjects.

DREAM BACKGROUND AND MEANING

Thomas was the patriarch of the family, fixing problems for his adult children, subsidizing them, and repairing their homes. But Thomas knew he was no longer needed. Kings represent benign fathers, grandfathers, or authority figures. However, there comes a point when a king should allow younger royalty to assume responsibility.

INTERPRETATIONS AND FORTUNE-TELLING MEANINGS

* If you dream you are the king surveying your kingdom, you will have major opportunity for a promotion, business success, or making money.
* If you dream that a wise older man or someone in authority will help you with a problem with officialdom, it is a good omen for dealing with the court or financial institutions.
* If a king is hostile, whether or not it is someone you know or from a past-life scenario, you may assume the role of victim through lack of confidence or intimidation.
* If you dream your king has always protected you, you may be paying with overdependency.
* If your dream king features as an idealized authority figure, bank manager, physician, or college professor in your dream, separate your professional from personal feelings unless you are encouraged to think otherwise.

OUTCOME OF THOMAS'S DREAM

Thomas's wife threatened to leave him, as she said she had married a father, not a husband. He was shocked and realized that, having never had a father in his own life, he may have overcompensated. The family admitted they sometimes took his help to avoid offending him, and suggested he and their mother make plans for their future as both were approaching retirement. Thomas hoped it was not too late. Sometimes a king develops fears of no longer being wanted or needed.

Kitchen

Mona Lena, fifty, dreamed she was cooking in her childhood kitchen. She was very young and could not reach the work counters. Her family, including her husband, who were their present ages, were banging on the table with their silverware, demanding dinner. Then her mother, who had died years earlier, brought in a tray of food and said, "You should take care of your family." Her mother then disappeared. Mona Lena was adult again and continued serving the family.

DREAM BACKGROUND AND MEANING

Mona Lena's mother had brought her up to believe a mother should always put her family first. But none of the family, including Mona Lena's husband, helped around the house. Mona Lena was the main wage earner since her husband had lost his job, but she felt guilty when she was too tired to cook. Kitchens are emotional places, representing contentment or guilt.

INTERPRETATIONS AND FORTUNE-TELLING MEANINGS

★ If the dream kitchen is warm and orderly, you will find happiness in the home and in family celebrations.

★ If the kitchen is messy, you need to tidy financial and emotional clutter.

★ If you dream that the kitchen is never clean, no matter how hard you try to keep it that way, you may have taken on too many emotional problems belonging to others.

★ The kitchen represents the nourishing, nurturing part of the self and past or present maternal influences.

★ Someone cooking, past or present, signifies the need of the dreamer for emotional nourishment and nurturing. Listen to your heart.

★ A very old-fashioned kitchen may be a past-life dream. Look for repetition of present situations.

OUTCOME OF MONA LENA'S DREAM

After the dream, Mona Lena told her husband she was exhausted from working long hours and running the house. He had not thought she might need help. He organized the teens with a chore schedule. But it took a while for Mona Lena to overcome her built-in guilt about letting others clean the kitchen. Mona Lena had become young in the dream because she needed nurturing.

Kite (Toy)

Sunita, eighteen, dreamed she was flying a bright red kite in the Sankranti festival in Mumbai with her family. She ran fast until it reached high in the sky. But the wind tugged hard and the kite disappeared from sight. She ran after it and discovered it was tangled in a tree, which she considered a bad omen for the achievement of the great family ambitions for her.

DREAM BACKGROUND AND MEANING

Sunita's parents wanted her to go to medical school in England, where they had relatives. But she had to pass her exams with high marks. She was worried she was aiming too high and would be content with local training, to which it was not so difficult to gain entry. Flying a kite promises that your ambitions will come true as long as the kite does not escape, which means you may have to chase fulfillment.

INTERPRETATIONS AND FORTUNE-TELLING MEANINGS

★ Dreams of kites flying high, especially over water, foretell a vacation, study, or opportunities overseas.

★ If the kite string snaps or the kite disappears, consider modifying your ambitions, not abandoning them.

★ Making a kite suggests that plans need to be carefully formulated for a forthcoming venture.

★ Dreams of mending a kite that is grounded say to relaunch a venture, learning from what previously went wrong.

OUTCOME OF SUNITA'S DREAM

When she went to the annual kite-flying festival, Sunita met an engineering student from the same campus as the local medical school, and she later married him. He rescued her kite when it became stuck in a tree. She studied at the local medical school to be near him, and they both flew matching kites at their wedding. Although the height of a kite can indicate the achievement of lofty ambitions, sometimes happiness can be found at less elevated heights.

Knight

Joanne, eighteen, dreamed she was following Joan of Arc into battle and, like her, was wearing full armor. When they reached the city gates, Joanne's current boyfriend, who was a knight, bundled her onto his horse, saying war was no place for a woman and he was taking her home. She woke fighting him off.

DREAM BACKGROUND AND MEANING

Joan of Arc was Joanne's heroine. Joanne wanted to become a frontline soldier and already was one of the star cadets. But her boyfriend, also a soldier, said battle was no place for women, as they were a liability to the guys. She should find a role to accommodate his traveling lifestyle, he said.

Knights and rescued maidens reflect stereotypes that still exist, even in modern society.

INTERPRETATIONS AND FORTUNE-TELLING MEANINGS

★ Dreaming of a knight in shining armor suggests you are looking for a magical solution or ideal person to transform your life.

★ If you rescue yourself or the knight in the dream, you will succeed by acting on your own initiative.

★ If you wait for your knight, who does not arrive, you may be postponing opportunities to resolve your own difficulties or to succeed through your own efforts.

★ If you dream you are the knight or assisting him or her, then there is a matter of justice about which you need to take a stand.

★ If you are always rescuing people from their difficulties, are you ignoring your own needs and rejecting help?

★ If there is a wicked knight in your dream, identify who in everyday life is masquerading as a hero or heroine.

OUTCOME OF JOANNE'S DREAM

Joanne joined the army and proved herself equally as competent as any man in her platoon, if not more so. She and her boyfriend split up as she was promoted over him. Knight dreams may reverse who is the rescuer and who is the rescued.

Knitting

Trudy, forty-nine, dreamed she was an expert knitter. But every time she started knitting a shawl for her eagerly awaited grandchild, the stitches came undone, and she despaired of finishing it before the birth. Trudy phoned her pregnant daughter, Liz, who laughed and said no one had shawls these days and why didn't her mother buy something useful, like diapers? Trudy woke feeling hurt and rejected.

DREAM BACKGROUND AND MEANING

This is an old-fashioned dream but still common, as grandmothers through the generations of Trudy's family had presented the new parents with a hand-knitted lace shawl. Irrationally, Trudy feared that something bad might happen if she broke the tradition.

INTERPRETATIONS AND FORTUNE-TELLING MEANINGS

★ To be knitting is a sign of a happy home and family, betrothals, and births, a wonderful dream.

★ Tangled or dropped knitting warns of misunderstandings in communication and advises you to get agreements in writing as well as verbally.

★ To be winding wool suggests the need to prepare for any future venture or event and not leave anything to chance.

★ If you dream of an older relative knitting, whether living or deceased, they are saying it is important to bring the family together, as someone may be hiding anxieties and fears.

★ If you are knitting in the dream and you do not knit in everyday life, you will find yourself closely involved in office or family politics and maybe acting as peacemaker.

★ If you are knitting baby clothes, this is a good sign for an imminent pregnancy for you or for a close family member.

OUTCOME OF TRUDY'S DREAM

Liz admitted to her mother that she was terrified of having a baby, as her mother had been so competent. Trudy shared the uncertainties she herself had experienced as a young mother and offered to help Liz in any way, but promised to not interfere. Trudy explained about the family tradition of making a shawl, and Liz said she would like one after all. Knitting symbolizes nurturing, especially concerning mothers and babies, but there may be other equally loving ways of expressing care once misunderstandings are untangled.

Knots

Penny, thirty, dreamed she was trying to untangle her hair, which had become badly knotted. She could not cut out the knots as there were too many. The comb broke, and the pain made her cry. Her best friend, Norine, who she had known since childhood, appeared. Norine gently removed the knots and disappeared without saying a word.

DREAM BACKGROUND AND MEANING

Penny was having problems keeping up with her new high life in the city. She was struggling financially, socializing and vacationing with her recently acquired wealthy friends, as she had lied and said that she too came from a monied background. Knots have dual purposes; they may bind together in friendship or love or make complicated tangles where an initial untruth can become ever more binding.

INTERPRETATIONS AND FORTUNE-TELLING MEANINGS

* Dreaming of having knots in shoelaces or tangled clothing suggests checking your schedule for an important date or a meeting you have forgotten.
* Tying knots while chanting magical words links to a past world where you were a wise man or woman.
* Tying rows of knots says, "Build up your resources before acting or speaking."
* Dreaming of a lover binding you against your will is a warning to listen to underlying fears about the relationship.
* An impossibly knotted computer or charger cable warns that you may be overloading your life with conflicting demands. If knotted wool, beware of crossed communications.
* Jewelry tangled together in a box, or knots in necklaces, advise you to solve love complications before committing.

OUTCOME OF PENNY'S DREAM

Penny went home for a few weeks. Norine was still there for Penny, and Penny talked over her problems as she always had. As a result, Penny was honest with her new friends, and the worthwhile ones did not care whether she had money or not. Unraveling tight knots with or without help may be painful but is ultimately liberating.

Kwan Yin

Waylen, thirty-six, dreamed he was in a temple in Thailand, making an offering to a huge golden statue of Kwan Yin, his ideal of the perfect woman he wanted to find. But the gold started to flake off, continuing until she was just brown clay. He took his offerings away, angry that even the perfect Mother Goddess was flawed.

DREAM BACKGROUND AND MEANING

Waylen had had many relationships. In every case the partner, who he had rapidly become besotted with, had revealed failings. His mother, who had died when he was young, was the only perfect woman he had known. Now he had met a feisty woman, Edwina, who was not interested in living up to his ideals. Yet he could not get her out of his mind. When we set a partner on a pedestal, they inevitably fall short of the ideal.

INTERPRETATIONS AND FORTUNE-TELLING MEANINGS

* Women, whether religious or not, dream of Kwan Yin, the Mother of Compassion, and Christians dream of the Virgin Mary, when they are about to become pregnant.
* This is a very special dream, saying that blessings will fall on your home and your life.
* Kwan Yin is a good omen for mothers, grandmothers, and would-be mothers.
* If Kwan Yin appears forbidding or indifferent, you are trying too hard to please a controlling mother or to live up to the standards of one who is deceased.
* Dream goddesses represent looking for an ever-smiling, nurturing partner, rather than an equal.
* Seeing a statue of Kwan Yin is an omen of good luck and prosperity.

OUTCOME OF WAYLEN'S DREAM

Edwina pointed out he had been too young to know what his deceased mother was really like. Waylen was furious, but realized the idealized memories of his mother were condemning him to a life of loneliness. With Edwina's help, Waylen is learning to love people as they really are. Goddesses are perfect but should not be substituted for human love.

Labels

Lottie, twenty-two, dreamed she was working in a restaurant sorting bottles of wine for a special event, but all the labels had fallen off and she did not know which was of which vintage and intended for the top tables. She knew nothing about wine and so took a chance. All the guests were happily drinking the wine. However, she was scared that someone might identify a cheaper bottle and complain.

DREAM BACKGROUND AND MEANING

Lottie had applied for a job with a luxury jewelry store despite being just out of art college. She was worried that her lack of experience and knowledge would be exposed. Label dreams indicate the importance of a guide but are not the sole criteria for what is of worth.

INTERPRETATIONS AND FORTUNE-TELLING MEANINGS

★ If you dream you are labeling objects, clothes, or piles of paper, you are trying to bring order and organization to an area of disorganization in your life.

★ If you dream the labels come off goods, you may need to assess for yourself the relative merits of an offer or situation.

★ If items are wrongly labeled, you may doubt the true nature of a person or situation.

★ If you dream you are wearing a label to identify yourself or your role at a meeting or conference, you may feel prejudged or undervalued.

★ A designer label in a dream suggests that you may be being judged on superficial criteria.

★ If an item has a REDUCED label, you may fear that your own welcome or usefulness is waning.

OUTCOME OF LOTTIE'S DREAM

When Lottie went for the interview, there was a fairly easy test, which she passed. The owner had guessed from her profile that she did not know a lot about gems but liked her enthusiasm and desire to succeed, and she was taken on as an apprentice. Label dreams, where the criteria depend solely on price or external assessment of worth, can sometimes mislead about what will be of value to the future owner.

Lace

Robyn, fifty-six, dreamed she was helping a wealthy bride put on one of Robyn's exclusive lace bridal gowns before the wedding. The lace started to unravel. Every time Robyn sewed it, the same thing happened, until the entire front was tattered. The bride became hysterical and threw Robyn out of the hotel bedroom, vowing that Robyn would never work in New York again.

DREAM BACKGROUND AND MEANING

Robyn was very successful and could not keep up with the demand for her custom-designed lace wedding dresses. She had been asked by a large New York company to allow them to make up Robyn's designs. Though this would bring great profit, Robyn was worried about their quality, as she sewed every dress herself. Lace, by its nature, represents intricate, painstaking work that needs care.

INTERPRETATIONS AND FORTUNE-TELLING MEANINGS

★ If you dream you are making lace or sewing lace items, the dream promises you will never be short of life's necessities, but you will work hard to succeed.

★ If you dream you are buying or wearing lace, you will have happiness and enough money all your days.

★ Wearing a lace wedding dress promises lifelong fidelity.

★ Lace becoming unraveled or ripping suggests you are not taking enough care in the area indicated by the dream. Overhastiness may damage your reputation.

★ Mass-producing lace items in a factory or warehouse says you are being asked to compromise your authentic self for profit or for a quick fix.

★ Selling lace suggests you may be envying others' happiness or love rather than seeking your own.

OUTCOME OF ROBYN'S DREAM

Robyn turned down the offer to allow the company to make her bridal wear. She realized success lay in her reputation for individual, personalized creations. She was asked to make a dress for an A-list celebrity. Demand increased even more, and Robyn took on a talented apprentice who she trained for routine tasks. Lace says, "Quality outweighs quantity every time."

Ladder

Josie, twenty-two, dreamed she was at the top of an aerial ladder, rescuing people from a burning apartment. None of the male firefighters could squeeze through the only accessible window. She emerged triumphant, was awarded a medal for her courage, and woke happy.

DREAM BACKGROUND AND MEANING

Josie was the first woman to join the fire rescue service in her small, conservative hometown. The guys were overprotective and sent her on fire prevention work at schools and on jobs rescuing cats from trees. Josie was increasingly frustrated, as she was trained for major incidents. A ladder connects you with an area of your life that needs mending or building but is presently out of reach, to be gained through step-by-step advancement.

INTERPRETATIONS AND FORTUNE-TELLING MEANINGS

* Climbing a ladder symbolizes steps toward achieving ambitions and so is a powerful sign of imminent success; the higher the ladder, the greater the success.
* Fear at climbing a high ladder or clinging to one swaying in the wind indicates anxiety about aiming high and failing.
* A ladder with broken rungs reveals that there are obstacles to success that you can overcome with patience and perseverance.
* To descend a dream ladder suggests disappointment with desired results that may have not been as long-lasting as hoped.
* Falling or being pushed from a ladder warns you to beware of rivals who may seek to exploit hesitation.
* If the dream ladder is held as you climb, you will receive support in gaining success or promotion. Climbing an unsupported ladder indicates that you need to make your way by your own means.

OUTCOME OF JOSIE'S DREAM

Josie started an interstate online female firefighting group that met regularly and produced a video showing women in action in major incidents. As a result, Josie is slowly being accepted as a full member of her team. Ladders in dreams give rapid access to fulfillment but may involve uncertainty, as ladders are by their nature unstable.

Lamp

Rosemary, forty-five, dreamed she was standing outside her former family house, which was in darkness. Suddenly, lamps came on at every window in what her mother used to call the nightly lighting of lamps on winter evenings. Rosemary knocked on the door and was greeted by all her family, including her grandmother, who looked well and young again. Rosemary knew she had come home.

DREAM BACKGROUND AND MEANING

Rosemary had won a scholarship to an American university years before and, though she lived in England, had made her life in Pennsylvania. She had been home only two or three times. Each time, the return was harder, since she had grown away from her folks. Now her grandmother, in a care facility with dementia, was dying. But should Rosemary go home, although her grandmother might not recognize her? In dreams, especially ones about light, we may see a deceased or dying relative well and strong again.

INTERPRETATIONS AND FORTUNE-TELLING MEANINGS

* Dreaming of finding a magic lamp means your dearest wishes will come true (see "Genie," p. 214).
* Switching on a lamp indicates that you will recover a lost possession or money you are owed.
* Seeing a lamp shining in a window reminds you to contact absent friends or family members, especially if you parted under difficult circumstances.
* A bright lamp suggests that you should concentrate on a particular area of your life, rather than trying to do everything.
* A full oil lamp, which may be a memory from a former life, promises financial and business success.
* An oil lamp that is empty or goes out warns that resources or partners for an anticipated business investment are not reliable.

OUTCOME OF ROSEMARY'S DREAM

Rosemary went home and was welcomed by the family. She went to the care facility to see her grandmother, who had a brief lucid moment and recognized Rosemary. She died soon afterward. Lamps can represent coming home and say that the relighting of family love may be possible.

Lamppost

Pearl, twenty-seven, dreamed she saw a lighted old-fashioned lamppost in the distance. As in the Narnia children's stories, the lamppost marked a completely different world. It led to a battlefield with Scottish clans and soldiers in red livery, many lying wounded or dead. Pearl was carrying herbal potions and bandages and helping both sides. She knew her husband had died and that this was the Culloden battlefield.

DREAM BACKGROUND AND MEANING

Though Pearl had lived all her life in the United States, she had been attracted to Scotland and its history since childhood. Pearl knew very little about her ancestry, as her adoptive parents had discouraged her from tracing it. But she always felt the United States was not her home. Lamppost dreams often have a psychic component, marking boundaries between dimensions and time frames.

INTERPRETATIONS AND FORTUNE-TELLING MEANINGS

* Old-fashioned lampposts in dreams invariably point to a relevant past world of significance for the present.
* If you are lighting a row of gas lamps on an old-fashioned street, or modern lampposts, illuminating them one by one, step-by-step insights will explain a mystery.
* If it is dark and there are no streetlights, secrets may be hidden from you that concern you. Ask.
* Neon city lights suggest that you should take care to not shatter the fragile illusions of someone close.
* An ornamental lamppost outside the front door reassures you that home and family will be safe from danger, if you are worried.

OUTCOME OF PEARL'S DREAM

After the dream, Pearl booked a trip to Scotland. At Culloden she was drawn to a plaque for the McGregor clan and started to cry. She discovered that many clans went to America after the defeat of Bonnie Prince Charlie in 1746 at Culloden. Once home, Pearl started tracking her birth family. She is convinced that her ancestors were talking through the dream. Some seemingly past-life dreams may be ancestral memories.

Lance, Spear

Philip, thirty, dreamed he was carrying a golden lance, riding toward a knight in black who was surrounded by henchmen all wearing black. Philip was afraid but lifted his lance straight in front of him and charged. To his amazement, the knight swerved out of the way and everyone cheered. Philip woke as flowers cascaded down.

DREAM BACKGROUND AND MEANING

Philip had started a new job. Though he was very competent, the leader of the office clique constantly mocked him because Philip had a slight stammer. This ridicule made the stammer worse. Philip planned to leave, although he loved his job.

Often a past-life dream, a lance or spear dream can be associated with the Holy Grail chalice and the sacred sexual rite, and so appear as if love has a spiritual aspect.

INTERPRETATIONS AND FORTUNE-TELLING MEANINGS

* Dreaming of aiming a lance straight ahead assures you have clear direction. Do not hesitate to act decisively.
* To throw a lance or gallop with a lance upright toward an opponent indicates fighting for justice or a principle.
* If you are wounded in the back by a spear, beware of betrayal by a hidden enemy.
* A broken or captured lance advises you to avoid an argument or confrontation you cannot win.
* Carrying your lance in a victory parade says you will come out on top against bullying, sarcasm, or criticism.
* To be given a ribbon by a fair man or woman to tie to the lance indicates that you will find a supportive love, or an existing lover will back you in a family quarrel.

OUTCOME OF PHILIP'S DREAM

Philip confronted the office bully and told him to back off or he would make an official complaint. Philip spoke clearly and, to his amazement, the bully and his henchmen left him alone thereafter. Philip went to speech therapy and has been promoted over the bully. Courage in adversity is the message of lance and spear dreams.

Languages

Sacha, fifty-eight, dreamed she was in a marketplace selling spices. But she could not understand what was being said, though some of the words sounded familiar. She started to cry, and a young girl standing near the stall offered to interpret. Suddenly, understanding came flooding through, and Sacha could speak fluently. Sacha woke feeling confident.

DREAM BACKGROUND AND MEANING

Sacha's company had recently introduced complex time-saving technology, but Sacha could not understand it. Her employer was becoming impatient. A new technical adviser had been appointed to aid the transition, but she was young enough to be Sacha's granddaughter, which Sacha found humiliating.

INTERPRETATIONS AND FORTUNE-TELLING MEANINGS

★ If you dream you are talking in an unknown language, a family member or work colleague is unwilling to listen to sense.

★ If you cannot understand people talking in a different language, you may need to change your line of argument, if trying to persuade older relations to change.

★ If some words seem familiar, the language dream may be past-life recall from another culture.

★ Someone deliberately not understanding your language may be missing the point through fixed attitudes.

★ If all the people around are speaking an unfamiliar language, it's time to widen your horizons, vacation somewhere exotic and take on new challenges, or move on.

★ If you are using an interpreter in your dream, you may need a mediator with someone who refuses to see your point of view.

★ If you are interpreting in the dream, the person you are interpreting for may be relying on you too much.

★ Hearing people speaking a variety of languages in your dream says you will have opportunities to travel or encounter new people and ideas.

OUTCOME OF SACHA'S DREAM

Since Sacha needed her job, she reluctantly overcame her humiliation and asked the young adviser for help. In a short time, the new processes made total sense. Unfamiliar ways of communicating, once interpreted, will open new channels of understanding.

Lantern

Jude, nineteen, dreamed he was trying to stop smugglers who were using a lantern to guide ships onto rocks. He knew they suspected him, and he was in danger. Jude was given the lantern to hold so the ship's captain would mistake the beam in the fog for a lighthouse and be steered onto the rocky coast. At the last minute, Jude dimmed the lantern, jumped into the water, and, against all odds, was picked up by the ship and warned them of the dangers.

DREAM BACKGROUND AND MEANING

This was perhaps a past-life dream. Jude had been swept up into a gang in his housing development, which was breaking into the houses of older people and threatening them with knives. Jude hated what they were doing. The gang warned Jude that if he told anyone, he would be knifed. Lanterns can illuminate the right pathway but mislead those who follow what seems the only path.

INTERPRETATIONS AND FORTUNE-TELLING MEANINGS

★ An old-fashioned lantern suggests a past-life dream to clarify a current dilemma.

★ A dim lantern suddenly brightening heralds an improvement in health for you or a close family member.

★ Following a guide with a lantern through darkness says you should trust the advice of a wise mentor when you are not certain how to act.

★ Striking out alone with a lantern indicates you should pursue your own path.

★ A lantern going out says you maybe need to move on in a particular situation that is making you unhappy.

★ To be given a lantern in a dream says you will be offered opportunities to make money. A lantern taken from you warns that rivals will try to overshadow you.

OUTCOME OF JUDE'S DREAM

Jude called the police before the next raid and left the area fast. He had a few hard years but eventually joined the police. Lantern dreams often highlight a situation where drastic action and courage are needed to turn life around.

Lasers

Felix, twenty-six, dreamed he was undergoing laser eye surgery, as his vision had become blurred. The surgeon asked if he really wanted to see, and Felix said of course he did. Once the blurring was gone, he saw he had signed a contract giving his business partner full control over the business and 75 percent of the profits.

DREAM BACKGROUND AND MEANING

Felix, whose eyesight was perfect, suspected his business partner was dealing behind his back to sell medical laser equipment that the company was patenting to a regime where it would benefit only the wealthy. Felix had promised it to the public health system at a discount. There seemed no way of deviating from the course now set by his partner. Laser dreams can refer to any matter involving precision and can reveal unvarnished truth.

INTERPRETATIONS AND FORTUNE-TELLING MEANINGS

★ If you are wavering over a decision, dreaming of a laser beam says, "Go ahead without hesitation."

★ If you are undergoing laser surgery in the dream, you will see clearly when and how to end an obligation.

★ If a solution is elusive, seeing a laser beam shining in the sky says you will receive sudden information pinpointing an answer.

★ A laser light show in your dream warns that a seemingly perfect offer or relationship may be temporary or illusory.

★ If in the dream you are undergoing laser eye treatment, misunderstandings or false impressions will be cleared up, but may bring disillusionment.

★ If you can see a laser beam shining directly ahead, it's time to prioritize and focus on the most pressing problem or ethically lucrative project.

OUTCOME OF FELIX'S DREAM

Felix had suspected for some time that his business partner was double-dealing. He went to the Patent and Trademark Office and was able to put a block on the unethical deal. His partner insisted that Felix buy him out. Since integrity mattered to Felix, he obtained a bank loan, and the business now focuses on working to benefit the public health system directly. Lasers cut through deception and remove what is morally diseased and so are a powerful if sometimes challenging dream symbol.

Last Day of Vacation

Drusilla, seventy, had a recurring dream of being in the same cottage on top of a steep hill with her ex-husband and her now-adult children young again, reluctantly packing to go home. There was confusion over what belonged to the family and what belonged to the cottage. The dream ended with Drusilla planning to stay longer.

DREAM BACKGROUND AND MEANING

Drusilla's ex-husband had remarried and their children, now in their forties, were scattered around the world. She had a good career and friends, but these dreams left her with a longing for idyllic past vacations that had been nowhere near as perfect in reality. The last-day-of-vacation dreams represent an unacknowledged dissatisfaction with the daily world and a desire for a life with more meaning.

INTERPRETATIONS AND FORTUNE-TELLING MEANINGS

★ If you dream that you postpone packing in favor of one last outing, there are aspects of the past you desire to recapture.

★ If you are reluctant to leave the same unfamiliar place in recurring dreams, it may be an actual location that, when discovered, will bring happiness.

★ If you dream you are on the last day of vacation with people who now are older or not part of your life, you may have unfinished business concerning ways you feel you failed.

★ If you are packing and are not sure what belongs to you and what is from the location, part of your spontaneous self is missing.

★ If in the dream you extend your stay, try to reconnect with the people in the dream at their present age or stage in order to strengthen or form new bonds.

★ If you dream you leave the vacation location, it is too late to recapture the past.

OUTCOME OF DRUSILLA'S DREAM

Drusilla scheduled a long vacation to visit her children, which she had been postponing, and increased online communication. She finally acknowledged her regrets for a marriage she had let go without trying to save it, and sent her ex the family photos she had been withholding. Last-day-of-vacation dreams can alert us to the need to make daily life more fulfilling and to plan future vacations to make new memories.

Laundry

Lottie, sixty-five, dreamed she was an orphan in a Victorian workhouse and was working in the laundry. She had to wash the heavy sheets. Because she was a good worker, the overseer told Lottie she could learn sewing instead. But she refused, because her little sister still wet the bed, and if the staff had known, they would beat her. Lottie replaced the sheets without anyone knowing. But she hated the laundry, and her hands were red and raw.

DREAM BACKGROUND AND MEANING

Lottie was living with her ninety-year-old mother, who had dementia and was incontinent. She had promised to care for her mother at home as long as possible. Laundry dreams may be past-world memories or may question the burden of caring for others.

INTERPRETATIONS AND FORTUNE-TELLING MEANINGS

* Dreaming of scrubbing clothes by hand indicates mistakes you want to put behind you.
* Using a laundromat says you may see or hear from someone from your past you would prefer to forget.
* Should you dream that you have piles of washing, you are taking on too many worries and burdens of others.
* Drying laundry in the open air says you should ignore others' negativity and restrictions.
* If you dream that, after washing, clothes are still dirty or stained, it is not as easy as you hoped to walk away from burdens.
* A broken washing machine says you need to rely on yourself rather than on others to move forward.
* Since laundry involves clothes, you may be worried about the image you create in the world and so keep reinventing yourself.

OUTCOME OF LOTTIE'S DREAM

Lottie in the dream knew her sister would grow out of bed-wetting. Her mother, at the other end of the spectrum, will inevitably need full-time care and will not recognize Lottie. Laundry involves ongoing cleansing and advocates patience, perseverance, and hard work as long as necessary until a new beginning is possible.

Lavender

Catherine, twenty-eight, was much older in her dream, surrounded by lavender, newly cut and dried, making lavender bags, bed pillows, and lavender essences. The sun was shining. She was sitting outside her cottage while the children she knew were her grandchildren played in the lavender fields. She was totally happy and was sorry when the dream ended.

DREAM BACKGROUND AND MEANING

Catherine and her husband had downsized to run an herb-growing business. Their family and friends said they were crazy to give up successful careers, as their idyll could not last. Catherine had been asked by her previous company to return, but she was content. Catherine experienced a timeless dream that could have occurred in any age and in many cultures and suggests she may once have been a wise woman.

INTERPRETATIONS AND FORTUNE-TELLING MEANINGS

* To dream about growing lavender flowers says someone who has been unkind may try to make amends.
* If you are looking for love, being given lavender flowers or any lavender product promises a gentle, kind lover who will always care for you.
* Walking through growing lavender fields is a sign of increasing prosperity through your own efforts.
* Dried lavender indicates love later in life and enduring love through the years.
* Applying lavender oil anywhere on the body signifies improving health and the reduction of pain and stress.
* Dreaming of dying or trampled lavender plants says that you are wasting your time trying to please someone or achieve reconciliation. Give up before you become hurt further.

OUTCOME OF CATHERINE'S DREAM

The dream helped Catherine to see that she was happy and that the happiness could go on through the years. She turned down the offer from her old workplace, and she and her husband are planning to expand into herbal oils and fragrances. Some dreams can confirm we are on the right path and that we may have all we need for that happiness.

Lawn

Alberto, sixty-one, whose pride and joy is his garden, dreamed it had been vandalized. His prize lawn had been dug up, and the orderly flowerbeds were ripped up. He woke devastated.

DREAM BACKGROUND AND MEANING

Alberto takes pride in his lawn, which he regularly mows into a checkerboard pattern, removing daisies and dandelions seeded from his neighbor's unkempt patch. His wife complains that he thinks more of the lawn than of her. The grandchildren have stopped coming because he complains if they play ball on his manicured lawn or kick the ball into his flowerbeds. Manicured lawns represent nature under strict control and a general lack of spontaneity in life.

INTERPRETATIONS AND FORTUNE-TELLING MEANINGS

* If a dream lawn is perfect, life follows a rigid orderly fashion with no surprises, good or bad.
* When a normally immaculate lawn has been dug up or grows wild in a dream, all may not be as smooth domestically as it appears on the surface.
* If every time you cut the lawn it starts springing up, you may be losing a battle to keep life and emotions under control.
* Neglected or dying lawns show that you are not paying enough attention to the people in your life.
* If you spend the entire dream cutting grass, it's time to ease up trying to overregulate yourself and others.
* If you dream you are cutting a seemingly never-ending meadow, you are trying to compensate for emptiness in your life.

OUTCOME OF ALBERTO'S DREAM

Alberto's wife found him a job keeping the local baseball field grass cut, as he had become bored since retirement. They used the extra money to travel around to horticultural shows. He created a games area for the grandchildren on his no-longer-immaculate lawn. The state of a lawn—out of control, manicured, or a family asset—reflects how you view ideal domestic life. Do others agree?

Leaks

Dixie, twenty-four, dreamed that while working for a television company she had been entrusted with a celebrity list of who would take part in a reality television show located on a cruise ship. While being interviewed on a morning TV show, she inadvertently revealed the name of the biggest star, and the secret was out. She was dismissed, as the star now refused to appear on the show.

DREAM BACKGROUND AND MEANING

Dixie and her siblings had booked a surprise cruise for their parents' golden wedding anniversary. Trixie was not very good at keeping secrets, so she was warned to not say a single word. At lunch she blurted out she had heard the cruise ship on which her parents were sailing was to be used on a television show. The secret was out in the open. Leaking secrets in dreams alerts the dreamer that they have a secret that they are likely to leak without extra care.

INTERPRETATIONS AND FORTUNE-TELLING MEANINGS

* If you dream of someone leaking information, your dream may reveal the culprit.
* If in the dream there is a small water leak from a dripping faucet, small irritations are building up that may cause an out-of-proportion response.
* If there is a minor gas leak in the dream, check your appliances, as your unconscious may have noticed a problem.
* If your dream gas or water leaks are more serious, someone is spilling secrets or stirring up trouble behind your back.
* If the ceiling leaks in the dream, repressed resentment will be dripping as sarcastic or reproachful remarks.
* If your shoes or umbrella leaks in the dream, you should step up preparations and precautions and fix potential glitches to avoid ongoing minor setbacks.

OUTCOME OF DIXIE'S DREAM

Dixie's mother was happy that the secret was revealed because she suffered from seasickness. They exchanged the cruise for a vacation on land. Leaks dreams occur when repressed information needs a safe outlet to avoid bursting forth at an inappropriate place or time.

Learning Later in Life

Jill, seventy, often dreamed she was walking through the cloisters of an Oxford college on her way to a lecture, listening to the chatter of the younger students. She was wearing a gown and carrying her lecture notes. Her children were calling through the closed gate for her to act her age and come home.

DREAM BACKGROUND AND MEANING

Jill had always wanted to study at Oxford and live in one of the old colleges, but she had left school at fifteen after her father lost his job. Now that she was retired with a substantial lump sum and pension, she had revived her dream to study at Oxford. Her children told her she was far too old. Learning dreams can express a desire to learn for its own sake in later years or to start a new career we may formerly have dismissed as impractical.

INTERPRETATIONS AND FORTUNE-TELLING MEANINGS

★ If you are learning something new in your dream and enjoying it, it's time to expand your knowledge base, whatever your age.

★ If you learn something unfamiliar in a dream and can recall it the next day, this may be learning from a past world.

★ Mastering a new skill in a dream that you are struggling with in everyday life says, "Relax, for you only lack confidence."

★ If you dream that learning material is either inaudible or the words are jumbled, people in your present life may be deterring you.

★ If you are graduating from a university, whatever your age, dreams promise it is never too late.

OUTCOME OF JILL'S DREAM

Jill applied to various Oxford colleges and found one that accepted mature students to an undergraduate course and assisted with study techniques. Dreams of learning can fill a gap in our lives where we missed out and offer reassurance that mature dedication and determination more than compensate for the often less-focused enthusiasm of youth.

Leaves

Trixie, sixty-six, dreamed it was fall in New England and the leaves were brilliant paintbox colors. As she scrunched through the fallen leaves, she was totally content. Trixie could hear the voices of her family and friends calling her. But the wind in the trees was whispering urgently over and over, "Trixie, you are free, just be."

DREAM BACKGROUND AND MEANING

Trixie had recently retired. Her family had plans for her to babysit for the grandchildren to save childcare expenses. Her friends wanted her to join the gym and work in the local charity store they had organized. She would be busier than ever. All Trixie wanted was to see New England in the fall and to rediscover herself, having worked all her life. Leaves in the fall are still vibrant, marking an interim in the natural progression of the life cycle.

INTERPRETATIONS AND FORTUNE-TELLING MEANINGS

★ Dreaming of jumping in a pile of leaves indicates a chance for spontaneous pleasure or fortune coming in small ways.

★ Falling leaves herald a natural change point, letting go of what has run its course.

★ Green or unfurling leaves promise new beginnings and the ending of stagnation.

★ Salad or vegetable leaves foretell a health boost if fresh, especially if you have been exhausted or unwell.

★ Dead or wilting leaves on a tree advise you to leave the past behind without regrets.

★ Listening to leaves in the wind reveals a message for you from your spirit guide or inner voice.

OUTCOME OF TRIXIE'S DREAM

Trixie told her family she was taking a step back and spending six months exploring what *she* wanted to do with the next phase of her life. Since her husband was not interested in travel, Trixie booked a solo trip to New England to see the fall leaves, and she was inspired to take up painting for pleasure. Voices of leaves in the trees can offer wiser advice than human voices, which have their own agenda.

Leaving the Parental Home

Belinda, twenty, dreamed she was standing outside the main campus, catching a bus to her home, which was hundreds of miles away. The journey passed in a flash. Belinda knocked on her door, but her father, who answered, said, "This isn't a good time." Belinda went to her room, wondering why she had bothered.

DREAM BACKGROUND AND MEANING

Belinda found making new friends at college hard. She phoned her parents regularly but felt they were eager to end the call. She was desperately homesick and asked her parents if she could attend a college where she could live at home. They refused. Leaving-home dreams can sometimes reflect the ideal of home that becomes frozen in a perfect life that never was (see "Nest," p. 327).

INTERPRETATIONS AND FORTUNE-TELLING MEANINGS

* ★ To have happy dreams of home when you are far away suggests a telepathic link with family, who may be missing you too.
* ★ If you dream of returning home and being unwelcome, you may need to accept that it's time to make a home life of your own.
* ★ If you see former neighbors and friends in the dream, you should create a new camaraderie.
* ★ If you are instantly transported in dreams to the home you are missing, this may be astral projection or teleportation (see p. 464).
* ★ If a small child talks of another home when they have never lived anywhere else or with anyone else, this is probably a past-life dream in which younger children experience overlap between worlds (see "Children's Past-Life Homes," p. 99).
* ★ If you constantly dream of being rejected when you return home, there is unfinished business to be cleared.

OUTCOME OF BELINDA'S DREAM

After the dream, Belinda moved into a student dorm that she made homey, and she was very happy there. Leaving-the-parental-home dreams can take us back to childhood homes, happy or not, whatever our age, as a reminder that a home can be re-created anywhere.

Leftovers

Rex, eighteen, in a recurring dream was standing outside the kitchen door of a big manor house, waiting for the kitchen boys to bring out the leftovers from the high table. He came every week so his family could have a decent meal, though the leftovers were often scraps and scrapings. Then in one dream he decided he was going to the feast, sneaked in through the open door, and sat at one of the lower tables. But he was recognized as an intruder and was chased out.

DREAM BACKGROUND AND MEANING

This may have been a past-life dream or ancestral memory. Rex was fed leftovers from the restaurant where his father, a single parent, worked. Rex vowed he would be so wealthy that he would own his own restaurant and dine on whatever he wished. On his father's birthday, Rex took him to the restaurant his father worked at, but they were refused admission because his father was an employee, and they were offered leftovers to take home.

INTERPRETATIONS AND FORTUNE-TELLING MEANINGS

* ★ If you dream you are eating leftovers after a party, you were not given due recognition socially or given status at work.
* ★ If you dream you are eating leftovers of a meal you made, you are too generous in what you offer others.
* ★ If you are reheating leftovers, you may feel second-best in a family or relationship.
* ★ If you dream you are carpeting a room with leftover squares, you are trying to patch together a relationship or family but are aware you may be the only one trying.
* ★ If you dream you are offering leftovers to others, you may be considered responsible for their well-being when they could care for themselves.

OUTCOME OF REX'S DREAM

Rex worked until he was wealthy enough to buy the restaurant. He insisted that the staff be given proper meals to take home to their families and not just leftovers, and could eat there cheaply on special occasions. Leftover dreams can act as a spur for the dreamer to aim for the best.

Lemons, Lemon Tree

Katya, forty-four, dreamed that her garden in an army camp was filled with blossoming lemon trees as the sun shone. Through the gate was her village, and jugs of the local drink with slices of lemons floating on top were being passed around. Her husband was walking through the grove toward her. She ran to meet him, filled with joy.

DREAM BACKGROUND AND MEANING

Katya was upset that the lemon tree in her garden was withering, and shriveled lemons lay on the ground. Her husband, Kevin, had bought it for an anniversary present, but it was too cold a climate for it to flourish where they were based. They had met in Cyprus, where lemon trees grow in profusion. Since they had moved to the United Kingdom, Katya was constantly unwell and exhausted, though her physician could not find the cause. Lemon trees not flourishing in dreams indicate that enthusiasm and health are deteriorating, but an abundance of lemon trees in the right environment talks of new life and regeneration.

INTERPRETATIONS AND FORTUNE-TELLING MEANINGS

* Dreaming of lemon groves rich with lemons says old resentment and unfinished business will clear from your life.
* Picking lemons from a tree says you need to tackle jealousy and gossip.
* Squeezing lemons says someone is extracting every possible benefit from a situation.
* If you are offered a sour lemon, a relationship or friendship will turn sour.
* A shriveled lemon says that you should start to care for your own happiness, as health and happiness are closely linked within the lemon symbol.
* To be eating lemons or cooking with them in a dream warns that a resentful elderly relative may try to interfere in your life.

OUTCOME OF KATYA'S DREAM

Like her lemon tree, Katya was not flourishing away from her natural environment. Kevin went on leave, and they spent a month in Cyprus. Her health dramatically improved, and her husband sought and received a long-term posting in Cyprus. Lemons above all signify healing through renewed enthusiasm for life.

Lemuria

Autumn, twenty-five, dreamed that her mottled Aboriginal mookaite stone, which she had recently acquired locally, carried her across the waves to the lost land of Lemuria, a Garden of Eden on Earth. She saw holy people with shimmering halos casting crystals, sparkling and earth-hued, into the sea. A holy man told her the crystals would carry the wisdom of the earth to indigenous people throughout the world.

DREAM BACKGROUND AND MEANING

Autumn loved crystals and was learning crystal healing in Sydney, Australia. But something was missing, and formal techniques were taking her away from her instinctive connection with indigenous earth crystals that worked so well for her. Her teacher said that she should focus on working with the Westernized polished crystals clients expected. Lemurian wisdom, unlike Atlantean, is directly Earth-based.

INTERPRETATIONS AND FORTUNE-TELLING MEANINGS

* If you dream of crystals floating in the sea or washed up onshore, you are linking with lost Lemuria and should look to the indigenous wisdom of your homeland.
* If you dream of a Lemurian Garden of Eden, nature will transfer healing powers through a direct Mother Earth connection, not through theory.
* If you dream of lemurs, said to be the magical creatures of Lemuria, now surviving only in Madagascar, they remind you to take a chance on life and seek new experiences.
* If you dream of healing with the crystals and plants from your present locality, allow them to guide you rather than seeking secondhand knowledge.
* If you dream of attending a master class with one of the holy men or women, they will become your special guide.

OUTCOME OF AUTUMN'S DREAM

Autumn quit her classes to study the indigenous stones of Australia. She joined courses organized by indigenous women. If you are formally studying spirituality and feeling jaded, Lemurian dreams can inspire you with direct contact with the earth and its healing.

Leopard

Hollie, twenty-eight, dreamed she was driving through a safari park. Despite warning notices, she opened the window to get a photo of a leopard, which had wandered close. It put its head through the window and was tearing at her clothes. She managed to close the window, but the leopard ran alongside the car, clawing at the outside. She woke terrified.

DREAM BACKGROUND AND MEANING

Hollie had been fascinated but scared of leopards since she was a child, when one entered the enclosure of their home when her family was living in rural India. Ever since then, she had nightmares of leopards pursuing her. Dreaming of these solitary creatures can indicate feeling isolated and overwhelmed by powerful feelings that others may not share.

INTERPRETATIONS AND FORTUNE-TELLING MEANINGS

* If you dream of seeing a leopard on city streets, the fierceness and the predatory nature of the leopard may be telling you to be more assertive.
* If you dream you are attacked by a leopard, you may be afraid of expressing strong views and challenging the status quo.
* If you are running with a leopard, you need freedom from someone who is trying to hold you back.
* If you see a solitary leopard climbing a tree, you should stand alone and express your unique gifts.
* Since leopards are associated with African storm deities and Fujin, the Shinto Japanese god of the wind, who carries the winds in a leopard-skin bag, a leaping leopard indicates the need for swift action.
* Staring down a leopard that backs away says that if you show courage and determination, you can overcome any obstacles.

OUTCOME OF HOLLIE'S DREAM

After the dream, Hollie realized that the leopard was her totem creature and could give her the courage she lacked to stand up for herself. As she worked with leopards in meditation, her leopard dreams became empowering. A creature feared by the dreamer, even if for no logical reason, represents buried or denied strengths of the dreamer, which if released give confidence and power.

Leprechaun

Sean, twenty-four, dreamed he was a child, taking part in the annual St. Patrick's Day parade, dressed as a leprechaun carrying his pot of pretend gold. In the crowd, he saw a small real leprechaun who beckoned him. He blinked in disbelief and was no longer in the American steelmaking town where he lived, but at the edge of a forest. Sean seized the leprechaun to make him hand over his gold. The leprechaun pointed to a stone pub from which fiddle music could be heard. Then the leprechaun disappeared, saying, "Go inside and find your own gold."

DREAM BACKGROUND AND MEANING

Sean was a steelworker in a Midwestern town. His late great-uncle had bequeathed him a pub in southern Ireland. Sean had always wanted to return to the homeland of his ancestors. Could he uproot his family for a venture about which he knew nothing?

INTERPRETATIONS AND FORTUNE-TELLING MEANINGS

* Leprechaun dreams are invariably lucky, especially for those of Irish heritage, but also for anyone attempting a risky, exciting venture.
* If you dream of catching a leprechaun, he will reveal his hidden gold in the place where your opportunities lie, as long as you do not lose focus.
* Taking a leprechaun's silver coin purse indicates building up financial resources through being in the right place at the right time.
* Beware of a leprechaun offering a gold coin purse, as seemingly lucrative ventures will be short-lived.
* See where the leprechaun leads you, even if the location is unknown, as sooner or later you will find it in life.

OUTCOME OF SEAN'S DREAM

Sean accepted the offer of the Irish pub. He and his family worked hard, and soon the pub was thriving. Leprechauns are solitary visionary beings and favor ventures where you attempt a private enterprise. They are also tricksters, so beware those in life who would try to deceive you.

Levitation

Maria, eighteen, started to dream about levitating horizontally and then standing up with her arms outstretched, just off the ground. She was too scared to try to fly. In her dreams she saw an old-fashioned Spanish-looking nun also levitating, who told her, "Come home and I will teach you."

DREAM BACKGROUND AND MEANING

Maria was half Spanish, but since her parents' divorce she had lost touch with her father's Spanish relatives. Her mother and stepfather discouraged her growing interest in the spiritual world and were pressuring her to work in her stepfather's business. Levitation in dreams can be a first sign of growing spiritual and healing powers.

INTERPRETATIONS AND FORTUNE-TELLING MEANINGS

★ A dream of rising above the ground, often slowly and horizontally, may be an out-of-body experience.

★ Rising slowly and remaining levitated indicates success in any ambition or deep-felt desire that may involve going against convention.

★ Often part of a mystical or spiritual experience, levitation is part of your initially random ability to control your thoughts and manifestation powers.

★ If you are frightened of levitating in your dream, you may be afraid of losing control emotionally or sexually.

★ If you dream that you fall while levitating, you may find it hard to maintain self-belief if challenged.

★ If you dream that your levitation is followed by flying (see p. 198) in a dream, you are ready to let go of restrictions and inhibitions in your own time.

OUTCOME OF MARIA'S DREAM

After research on the Internet, Maria discovered sixteenth-century Santa Teresa de Ávila, who, according to witnesses, had regularly levitated about a foot from the ground during spiritual ecstasy. Maria went to visit her relatives in Ávila and discovered they were all healers and diviners. She decided to stay and often dreamed of the saint. Her dreams progressed to flying as her spirituality developed. Levitation dreams can herald a growing deeper connection with spiritual learning.

Ley Energy Lines

Drew, forty-five, dreamed that beneath his house and leading to and from it were two wide lines of light and fire, crossing in the middle of his home. He could see them shining through the floor. When he stood on the cross, a surge of electricity shot through his body. Once off the lines, Drew was calm.

DREAM BACKGROUND AND MEANING

Drew had bought an old house but could not settle in, especially in the center of the house, where the dog howled, plants wilted, and the children often quarreled over nothing. A friend who was skilled in the use of a dowsing rod told him his house was built on crossing subterranean energies. This excessive energy was causing the problems. Drew, who was very logical, just laughed at the idea.

INTERPRETATIONS AND FORTUNE-TELLING MEANINGS

★ If you dream of straight lines of light entering and leaving your home, these are psychic manifestations of the ley energies.

★ If you dream of black vein-like streams penetrating beneath your home, these are blocked energy streams, experienced as inertia.

★ If you live in an area that was once the homeland of indigenous people, you may dream of them passing down the psychic tracks on their way to their ceremonies.

★ If you are standing on top of a hill and can see or sense energy tracks between ancient sites, you are naturally intuitive and a healer.

★ If you dream of a missing pet with lights extending from the animal to you, follow the direction in reality, as the lights are the telepathic energy link between you.

OUTCOME OF DREW'S DREAM

Despite his skepticism, Drew allowed his friend to place amethyst crystals around the home and hammer stakes on either side of the entrances and exits. Since his friend was also a feng shui expert, he balanced and freed the chi life force. The energies of the home dramatically improved and, though still convinced it was all coincidental, Drew noticed he was becoming more intuitive. Energy line dreams link dreamers with the energies of their home and environment and, if balanced, can improve domestic well-being.

Library

Audrey, thirty-one, dreamed she was in her local library, where she had worked since leaving college. She was tidying the books when suddenly they all cascaded around her. As she tried to catch them, she saw they were written in ancient Middle Eastern scripts she had studied at college in her archeology course. The books turned into sand and she was half-buried, but not hurt. When she escaped, she was staring at the pyramids; one had an open door. Audrey ran toward it and started to translate the inscription. She woke, wanting to stay in the dream forever.

DREAM BACKGROUND AND MEANING

After college, Audrey had not accepted the ancient-languages research post she had been offered, but worked in the local library, becoming chief librarian and living at home. Recently she had seen a post advertised at a university two hundred miles away, interpreting ancient scripts. But dare she go back into that world? When an orderly library changes into turmoil, life must be seized.

INTERPRETATIONS AND FORTUNE-TELLING MEANINGS

* If you dream you are tidying books, you may choose peace at the risk of stagnation.
* A library signifies that you know more than you think, so trust your own judgment.
* If you dream a library building is closed, postpone decisions, as hidden factors will emerge in the ensuing weeks.
* If you are told to be quiet by a librarian, you may be pressured into complying by a controlling person.
* If the books fly or fall off shelves, there will be new opportunities involving disruption.
* If you dream a library has no books or the book pages are blank, you cannot rely on the advice of others or previous solutions.
* An open book in a dream library will contain a message you should read.

OUTCOME OF AUDREY'S DREAM

Audrey applied for and obtained the post and has had the chance to travel, analyzing inscriptions at ancient sites in the Middle East.

License

Kennedy, sixty-five, dreamed he was speeding down the highway. In the dream he was eighteen, with no driver's license or insurance, not even license plates. He parked the vehicle, which he had found unlocked with the key in the ignition, at a wilderness campsite for which he did not have a permit. He was living totally outside regulated life and loved it.

DREAM BACKGROUND AND MEANING

Kennedy had been law-abiding all his life following a clash with the law when he stole an unlicensed car at age eighteen and was put in detention. Since then, he had become obsessive about making sure he had all the necessary licenses and permits and they were up-to-date. Now that he had retired, he often dreamed of the thrill of pursuing a life of crime. Dreams about licenses often occur when living a conventional life has brought neither satisfaction nor reward.

INTERPRETATIONS AND FORTUNE-TELLING MEANINGS

* To dream of applying for a license, whether to drive or for other official purposes, is a good indication that what are now just plans will become reality.
* Dreaming of signing a marriage license, even if you are not getting married, indicates a present or future happy relationship.
* If you are refused or lose a license for an infringement, you are taking chances and may be discovered.
* If you do not have a required license or permit for an activity in your dream, you may be subject to petty regulations or restrictions at work or with authority, and you need more spontaneity.
* If you dream you forget to renew a license, you may be ready to step outside convention.

OUTCOME OF KENNEDY'S DREAM

Kennedy saw a post for volunteer work teaching young offenders to become self-reliant and live within the law without sacrificing their identity. He learned as much from the boys as he taught them. Dreams about licenses can show the necessity of keeping within regulations without losing the self in excess conformity.

Life Review

Lindsey, fifty, in the dream was in her teens, being interviewed by her headmistress for some misdeed. Unusually, Lindsey interrupted the tirade and calmly listed her many remarkable achievements through the years, up to the present date. The woman's face became misty. The dream ended.

DREAM BACKGROUND AND MEANING

Lindsey had recently been invited to a memorial service at her old school for her former headmistress, who had constantly warned Lindsey that she would achieve nothing. The invite had stirred up feelings of inadequacy. In dreams, life reviews are generally a chance to reassess unfulfilled desires or regrets.

INTERPRETATIONS AND FORTUNE-TELLING MEANINGS

* Dreaming of handwriting a job application listing your life achievements where you keep smudging the page, or typing a computerized application where keys stick, suggests it may not be the job for you.
* If in the dream you are a child receiving a bad school report, it is a reminder for you to ignore past denigrating voices in your head that hold you back.
* Dreaming of being given an award for achievements in the area of life to which you most aspire—for example, an Oscar for acting—assures that you are heading in the right direction.
* If you dream of attending a school or college reunion years later, ask what you most want to revive of the past self that maybe has become buried.
* Should you dream of reconnecting with a once-significant person on social media, trace that person, who may be thinking of you.
* If you dream you are writing your autobiography or signing copies, reevaluate your achievements and use your experience to make a major leap.

OUTCOME OF LINDSEY'S DREAM

Lindsey decided to not return to a place with unhappy memories. In the dream, she had justified herself and could at last finally dismiss the denigrating headmistress's voice in her head.

If you are constantly defending your life choices, accept that your critics, especially older relatives, may be biased or their judgment flawed. Assess your own achievements.

Lifeboat

Ken, fifty-five, dreamed he was in the middle of the ocean, having escaped from a sinking ship. He swam toward the nearest lifeboat. His ex-wife reached out from the lifeboat for a box he was swimming with, containing the deeds of his home and stock certificates. She refused to allow him into the boat until he handed them over. He let the box float away and swam toward another, more distant lifeboat.

DREAM BACKGROUND AND MEANING

In order to be free, Ken had been prepared to agree to all his ex-wife's divorce settlement demands, though it would ruin him financially. She was already wealthy in her own right. Lifeboat dreams are about survival, especially if people already in the lifeboat are pushing you away.

INTERPRETATIONS AND FORTUNE-TELLING MEANINGS

* If you dream there are stormy waters, hold firm against emotional or financial pressures.
* If the lifeboat is overcrowded, there may be too many demands, and you may have to put yourself first.
* If the boat is filling with water or sinking, consider what and who are your priorities to save in the relevant area of life.
* Should you dream a rescue boat is in sight, a solution to a problem is at hand if you do not give up.
* Trying to reach a lifeboat suggests you may need to actively seek help or support if a situation or relationship is pulling you under.
* To dream you are cast adrift in a lifeboat in the middle of the ocean offers a choice: start paddling the boat or wait and hope to be rescued.

OUTCOME OF KEN'S DREAM

Ken realized that if he continued to fight legally, he would never be free of his ex. He placed a large proportion of his personal assets in trust for his children, so neither he nor his ex-wife could benefit. Water is a symbol of feelings. Lifeboat dreams suggest the matter from which you need rescuing is complicated by emotions.

Lightbulbs

Phil, twenty-eight, dreamed he was gazing up at a huge chandelier made of hundreds of tiny lightbulbs that sparkled and spun. The ballroom was empty, but music was playing and the girl of his dreams, Eleanor, who worked in the same office, but who he had never dared talk to, came in, wearing a sparkling dress. They danced beneath the chandelier and, as they spun around, the lights illuminated her, so she was made of light. The music stopped, she disappeared, and the lights went out.

DREAM BACKGROUND AND MEANING

Phil wanted to ask Eleanor out, but she was popular with all the guys, and he felt she was out of his league. An annual awards event was held in a big ballroom with the chandelier in his dream. Eleanor wore a sparkling dress that shimmered in the light.

INTERPRETATIONS AND FORTUNE-TELLING MEANINGS

★ If in a dream a lightbulb becomes brilliant, it heralds a lightbulb moment of inspiration when an answer to a troublesome question suddenly comes.

★ To change lightbulbs says that an idea has run its course and a new approach or source is needed.

★ If you dream a lightbulb breaks or explodes, beware of a volatile person or situation escalating out of control.

★ If a room or entrance has red lightbulbs, this indicates illicit passion or temptation offering instant gratification but longer-term consequences.

★ If a series of lightbulbs illuminate, one after the other, or form a chandelier, positive results in business, love, or finances soon follow.

OUTCOME OF PHIL'S DREAM

Because of the dream, Phil approached Eleanor, who was standing under the chandelier in her sparkling dress. But, as he was going to ask her to dance, one of the account executives whisked her off. Disappointed, Phil turned and bumped into Shelley, who worked in the next department. It was as if a lightbulb had gone on, and he saw how beautiful she was. Together they whirled around under the chandelier, and they are now engaged. Sometimes we can be dazzled by radiance and miss the true light.

Lighthouse

Tony, forty, dreamed he was in an old-fashioned lighthouse. Through the fog, huge waves surged. He had to switch on the light and activate the siren to warn ships. He saw his girlfriend, Avril, rowing a boat through gigantic waves and a sea monster trying to push her onto rocks that she could not see. He raced up seemingly endless steps to switch on the light, and the monster disappeared. The waves subsided, and Avril rowed safely ashore.

DREAM BACKGROUND AND MEANING

All of Tony's relationships had been wrecked by his mother. A dominating older woman can be symbolized by a turbulent ocean and sea monsters. Tony loved Avril, but his mother was already causing trouble. Tony knew he had to be more aware of his mother's hidden manipulation. Lighthouses alert you to difficulties ahead and offer clear signs for avoidance.

INTERPRETATIONS AND FORTUNE-TELLING MEANINGS

★ The dream of a lighthouse (a phallic symbol) engulfed by waves indicates a man trying to escape the influence of a controlling mother or older dominating lover.

★ If you climb steep steps to the top of the lighthouse and switch on the light, you will overcome potential hazards.

★ If you are in a boat and see and hear a lighthouse through fog, seek the guidance of someone wise rather than blindly pressing ahead.

★ If you dream you are the lighthouse keeper and are trying to switch on the light, be aware that a loved one may be entering dangerous emotional territory.

★ If you dream that you see a lighthouse too late and your boat ends up on the rocks, regard it as a warning sign that you are about to act unwisely.

★ Seeing a lighthouse in calm, bright weather says a problem you feared will not occur.

OUTCOME OF TONY'S DREAM

Tony moved in with Avril and resisted his mother's emotional blackmail. His mother is starting to back off. When lighthouses appear in dreams, it may be necessary to be prepared and counteract emerging known hazards in advance.

Lilacs

Sue-Ellen, thirty, dreamed she was in an English garden in early summer, and the lilacs were in full bloom. Suddenly she was back home in America, and her grandmother was tending her lilacs. Her grandmother looked very old and frail. Sue-Ellen reached out to her grandmother, but, as she touched her, she found herself in the English garden again, desperately longing for home.

DREAM BACKGROUND AND MEANING

Sue-Ellen's grandmother had brought her up since she had been a small child. Sue-Ellen, whose home was in England, was halfway through a world trip, working as a nurse in different countries. But after the dream, she needed to see her grandmother again, though her grandmother had encouraged her to travel. Lilacs, by their fragrance, which is often sensed in a dream, evoke memories of home, especially ones connected with a happy childhood.

INTERPRETATIONS AND FORTUNE-TELLING MEANINGS

* Lilacs growing on a bush or cut in a vase are a sign of domestic happiness.
* Lilacs are a good omen for older people, indicating a long and happy life.
* If you are far from home and dream of lilacs, contact your family, as they are missing you.
* Pale purple lilacs in dreams signify first love or trust after betrayal.
* Picking lilacs suggests a lasting love and the birth of children, or a lasting relationship with someone who has children already.
* White lilacs in a dream represent awakening or growth of spirituality and an innocent love with someone who is young or young at heart.

OUTCOME OF SUE-ELLEN'S DREAM

Sue-Ellen went home on an extended visit. She found her grandmother in the garden, tending her beloved lilacs. Shocked at how frail her grandmother was, she took her for a medical checkup. Her grandmother was severely anemic and had a minor heart problem. Sue-Ellen became fascinated by nursing older people and trained at the local hospital where her grandmother was treated. Lilacs act in dreams as a telepathic link of love, especially where a family member is not admitting to being ill to someone far away.

Lingerie, Underwear

Marina, twenty-nine, dreamed she was in a local shopping mall wearing nothing but black see-through underwear. Different men propositioned her. She told them she was married. But she made no attempt to hide herself. Marina went to her husband's gym, told him about the propositions, and made love with him in a shower.

DREAM BACKGROUND AND MEANING

Marina was married to Lou, a gym owner who often worked until midnight seven days a week. Lou was always too tired for lovemaking. Marina was worried that loneliness could entice her into being unfaithful. Dreams where sexy underwear is flaunted are a sign of erotic frustration and the need for a more exciting love life.

INTERPRETATIONS AND FORTUNE-TELLING MEANINGS

* If you dream you are in a public place wearing shabby underwear, you may be embarrassed about revealing your true self.
* If you are performing a striptease onstage, you are ready to spice up your existing love life or to find romance with passion.
* If you are a woman, dreaming of buying exotic underwear for yourself says you are complete in yourself and do not need to impress anyone.
* If you are a man and dreaming of buying underwear for a partner, your partner may feel neglected and need appreciation and care, not just passion.
* If in your dream you are committed in love but buying underwear for someone other than your lover, beware of the temptation to stray.
* If you are unwilling to let anyone see you in your underwear, others may be intruding on your personal space.

OUTCOME OF MARINA'S DREAM

Marina created an online store and held parties in women's homes to sell exotic lingerie and sex toys. She shocked her husband, who realized he was taking her for granted. He employed extra staff so he could spend more time with her. Dreaming of parading in your underwear in inappropriate settings alerts you to behaving unwisely with someone who may already be present in your work or daily life.

Lion

Louis, fifty-five, dreamed he was sleeping in a tent on safari in Africa. In the distance he could hear lions roaring. He followed the direction of the sound. Then he realized he was surrounded by lions and lionesses. A lion with a huge mane came bounding toward him. Losing all fear, Louis stroked the lion's mane, and the lion said, "Do not be afraid. We will come through this together." Louis woke totally reassured.

DREAM BACKGROUND AND MEANING

Louis had always loved lions, and as a child he had a lion as an invisible friend. He was saving for a safari when he was informed he would need extensive treatment for cancer. Now he was dreaming of his childhood lion. Power or totem animals often appear in dreams to offer a particular strength we need; in Louis's case, courage.

INTERPRETATIONS AND FORTUNE-TELLING MEANINGS

★ Lions appear in dreams at times when we must focus single-mindedly on a goal.

★ If you dream of a lion, you may be asked to take the lead in the workplace or community, in issues involving ethics or justice.

★ Dreaming of being attacked by lions indicates powerful opposition. Rescuing a lion among them represents your own strength to triumph.

★ A benign protective lion signifies a powerful ally entering your life and work.

★ If a lion appears in your garden, old fears or former enemies may reemerge but, if tackled, will fade away.

★ A lion is a sign of growing authority, confidence, and a successful bid for the top.

OUTCOME OF LOUIS'S DREAM

Louis responded positively to treatment and was well enough to book a safari. He never doubted that his lion would see him through. Often a connection with a power animal in adulthood harks back to childhood, where many sensitive children have invisible animal friends. The lion reminds you of your power.

Lioness

Belinda, thirty-eight, dreamed she was a lioness, hunting on the savannah, surrounded by other lionesses. They were rivals, fighting among one another as the prey scattered in all directions. Belinda drew the pride of females together, assigning each a role so as a team they drove the prey into a gully and each lioness gained enough food for her cubs.

DREAM BACKGROUND AND MEANING

Belinda held a senior position in a large company but after she had children she had been marginalized, as were other mothers, though officially the company had a strong equality policy. Since lionesses are the main hunters, a dream lioness needs to work with her fellow lionesses, not against them.

INTERPRETATIONS AND FORTUNE-TELLING MEANINGS

★ If you see your dream lioness defending her cubs, you will be called on to rescue a family member.

★ Lionesses hunting as a pack suggest that you should combine with other women to overcome prejudice or inequality.

★ If you dream a lioness attacks you, resist overpossessiveness in the mothering relationship.

★ A lioness choosing her mate advises you to know your own value and not settle for second best.

★ Becoming a lioness in your dream is called shape-shifting; you assume her psyche and power.

★ If your partner or boss (of either sex) in the dream assumes an autocratic role, reflected in daily life, it's time to show your claws and roar.

OUTCOME OF BELINDA'S DREAM

Belinda organized an association for women in the company for better childcare facilities, the removal of hidden competition, and mutual encouragement for women aiming for the top. Sekhmet, the fierce solar lion-headed goddess of Ancient Egypt who protected women, became their logo. Female executive productivity dramatically increased, and the workplace over time became female-friendly. The lioness represents equal respect not only among lionesses but with lions as well, recognizing that the lion may be king of the beasts, but she feeds the pride.

Lipstick

Scarlett, thirty-two, dreamed she was in Milan, preparing to star in a Milan Fashion Week event. She realized that she was not wearing any lipstick. Her makeup artist was nowhere to be seen. She could not find any lipstick in her bag and asked the other models to lend her theirs, but they refused. She had no choice but to go onto the catwalk without lipstick. Afterward, when she went backstage, she was sacked.

DREAM BACKGROUND AND MEANING

Scarlett, a catwalk model from New Hampshire, had worked for the same high-profile modeling agency since she was eighteen. Now in her thirties, Scarlett feared that her time as a leading model might be coming to an end, as her body and skin were no longer as taut as they once had been and makeup was increasingly necessary to hide their flaws. Lipstick represents the image of physical attractiveness we present to the world.

INTERPRETATIONS AND FORTUNE-TELLING MEANINGS

⋆ A dream of brightly colored or scarlet lipstick is a sign of sexual attraction toward someone off-limits, or the development or renewal of passion in an existing relationship.

⋆ A pink or pastel lipstick indicates a new relationship or seeking romance.

⋆ A broken lipstick warns of unrequited love and that it is time to move on.

⋆ A lost lipstick highlights worrying about losing youth and physical attributes instead of welcoming mature beauty.

⋆ Smudged lipstick warns of misplaced sexual attraction, which may lack love and care and end badly.

⋆ Perfectly applied lipstick says that what you wish to communicate will attract and enhance positive attention and media interest.

OUTCOME OF SCARLETT'S DREAM

The dream reminded Scarlett it was time to move on. She started her own successful modeling agency, training older and curvier women. Not wearing lipstick marks a new phase in a woman's life where she focuses on her intelligence, experience, and personality, rather than relying on physical appearance to advance her career.

Locked Out

Stan, seventy-four, dreamed he went out the front door of his isolated house to put out the garbage. The wind slammed the door shut. He had no coat, no phone, no wallet, and he had left the spare key inside. Sitting on the doorstep in the rain, he heard his deceased wife's voice say, "Silly old fool, there's a spare back door key in the pot of soil next to the tomato plants." When he looked, there was the key.

DREAM BACKGROUND AND MEANING

Stan's wife had died suddenly twelve months earlier. Stan had become increasingly forgetful and twice before had locked himself out. Though he did not believe in an afterlife, he was sure it was her voice he heard. Dreaming of locking yourself out warns you that home may no longer feel like home.

INTERPRETATIONS AND FORTUNE-TELLING MEANINGS

⋆ If the dreamer locks themselves out of their home, the dreamer is shutting away the isolation felt within the home.

⋆ If a door or gate denies entry in a dream, an opportunity you had hoped for may not materialize.

⋆ To find a spare key to unlock a door indicates the regrowth of happiness, whether in love or in a revived lifestyle.

⋆ If the lock is jammed and the door will not open, life may have reached a standstill, and returning to old ways is no longer possible.

⋆ If you dream you remember where the spare key is or find an open window or door, consider moving life forward by making positive changes in your present location and lifestyle so you feel settled.

OUTCOME OF STAN'S DREAM

After the dream, Stan realized he had to go forward with his life, rather than remaining locked in the past. He moved into the local town, where he had friends, and hid a key where he would not forget it. Locked-door dreams represent barriers, whether closed by the dreamer or barred by others and circumstances, prompting the dreamer to consider alternatives to avoid remaining locked out of life.

Locket

Magda, twenty-three, dreamed she was opening her Christmas present from her boyfriend and knew it would be an engagement ring, but to her dismay when she tore off the wrapping paper, inside was a velvet box containing a gold locket with a picture of her on one side, her boyfriend on the other, and the message "I will love you forever." Disappointed, she tossed the locket aside. Her boyfriend left, taking the locket.

DREAM BACKGROUND AND MEANING

Magda's best friend Suella's boyfriend had promised Suella an engagement ring for Christmas. Magda had pestered her boyfriend about what he was buying. He told her "something shiny," so she was certain it was a ring. She and her friend had always done everything together. Lockets are ways of carrying loved ones close to the heart, whether they hold a lover, children, or a beloved grandparent perhaps no longer on Earth. Locket dreams may be a much-needed reminder of that love.

INTERPRETATIONS AND FORTUNE-TELLING MEANINGS

* To dream of wearing a locket promises lasting happiness in love, marriage, or a loving family.
* If you dream you put on a locket, someone from the past may return, perhaps connected with a love interest.
* If you are wearing your locket beneath your clothes, this represents a secret or yet-unfulfilled love, or a secret admirer.
* If you dream you are given a locket by your partner, it is a sign of lasting love and fidelity. If you dream you are given the locket by a stranger, you have yet to meet that love.
* If you are wearing a gold locket, good fortune will be yours in love and life; if silver, romance and beautiful, loving children.

OUTCOME OF MAGDA'S DREAM

Following the dream, Magda realized she wanted a ring for the wrong reasons—to compete with her friend. Her boyfriend asked Magda what she really wanted for Christmas, and she said a locket containing their pictures. She was thrilled with it and they became engaged on her birthday, later the following year. Lockets are an inner expression of love for the person pictured inside, rather than an outer show to impress the world.

Loneliness

Tamsin, seventy-two, dreamed she was in a brightly lit room, attending a party filled with family, former friends, and neighbors. But each time she approached someone they said, "Got to go, speak to you later," and moved on. No one responded to her. The lights went out, and she was alone in the room.

DREAM BACKGROUND AND MEANING

Tamsin's family was busy with their own lives. Friends would make vague arrangements to meet her, which rarely materialized. Tamsin followed the usual remedies: volunteering and going on holidays for senior citizens. But she felt isolated from people who shared her life view.

INTERPRETATIONS AND FORTUNE-TELLING MEANINGS

* Dreams of being alone in a crowd suggest you feel isolated from the environment in which you find yourself.
* Dreaming of loneliness if you have recently retired or are about to retire may indicate that, for you, purposeful activities are more important than social contact.
* Dreaming of feeling isolated in a crowd of familiar people implies that communication has broken down because of the fast pace of modern life.
* If you dream of being rejected by family or former friends, you should seek the company of those who share your interests.
* Dreaming of being physically isolated because of the remoteness of your home and becoming ill or dependent with no support system advises you to relocate in preparation for possible future needs.
* If you are estranged from friends or family and dream of their welcoming you, it is time to build bridges.

OUTCOME OF TAMSIN'S DREAM

Tamsin realized she had mistaken others' busy lives for rejection and had become reproachful, so people felt a duty to see her. As an ex-university lecturer, she applied to take students from her former university into her home, offered tutoring to new history scholars, and started a local history group. Loneliness dreams can imply that the dreamer feels rejected but at the same time is pushing others away by fearing to be alone, and so becoming uncharacteristically needy.

Loop Dreams

Peggy, sixty, still recalled a dream from when she was about eight that she was in a game and she was running. An old man she knew was chasing her. He had an axe, and he threw it into her back. She

ended up facedown in grass and the dream started again. The terrifying game was on a loop, with no breaks in between, and eventually she woke, crying and terrified.

DREAM BACKGROUND AND MEANING

When Peggy was young, she had to pass a neighbor's house to get home from school. He would always be waiting and asked her to go inside. When she refused, he started swinging an axe menacingly. She told her mother, who did not believe her. Peggy lived in terror that he would drag her inside and kill her. Loop dreams involve instant repetition of a single action and result, and then return back to the action until the dreamer wakes.

INTERPRETATIONS AND FORTUNE-TELLING MEANINGS

* If you are caught in a dream loop, you may imagine you have woken up, only to be back in the loop.
* If your loop dream is close to a real-life situation but with dire consequences, this is a strong message that urgent remedial action is needed.
* If you overcome the threat, the loop action is broken.
* Sometimes in loop dreams there is an actual loop or rope catching you by the foot or hand.
* What distinguishes a loop dream from a Groundhog Day repetition dream (see p. 228) is the urgency and immediacy of the loop dream, often accompanied by a whirring sound.

OUTCOME OF PEGGY'S DREAM

So intense were Peggy's fears as a child and the repeated loop dreams that she refused to go to school unless her mother walked with her past the neighbor's house. Her mother saw the old man with the axe and informed the police, who discovered he had been terrorizing and abusing children for years. Loop dreams often can deter the dreamer from going to sleep.

Losing Control

Johannes, thirty-five, dreamed he was sitting in the back seat of his car, but there was no front seat. He was trying to reach the steering wheel and pedals as the car sped down the highway. At first he thought it was a driverless car, but then he realized he was supposed to be controlling it. He panicked because he was heading for a traffic jam and feared he would crash.

DREAM BACKGROUND AND MEANING

Johannes was in charge of the family company while his parents were on a long vacation. However, the other workers, most of whom had known him since he was a boy, totally ignored his instructions. They came in late, left early, and took days off for trivial reasons, causing orders to fall behind. When a dream shows the dreamer having only partial control, the symbolic vehicle's company or finances are potentially in danger of failing.

INTERPRETATIONS AND FORTUNE-TELLING MEANINGS

* If you dream of struggling to reach the controls of a vehicle representing your journey through life, you are allowing others who are not as competent to take over.
* If in a dream a child is behaving wildly and antisocially, the adult may often feel like a child, unable to assert their authority.
* If someone close gets their own way through anger, it's time to reassert the boundaries of what is acceptable behavior.
* If you feel disoriented in a dream, step back from a situation until you know what you want to do or say.
* If you cannot reach the pedals or move from the back seat of your dream car to the front, you may have been allowing matters to drift that need decisive action.

OUTCOME OF JOHANNES'S DREAM

After a dream in which Johannes was able to slide the back seat forward, he called all the workers together and explained that the company was losing orders and receiving complaints. If the workers did not respond, he would close the firm till his parents returned, but the workers could not be paid. Losing-control dreams usually reflect an actual situation that needs to be brought firmly under control in everyday life.

Loss of a Child

Norah, thirty-eight and six months pregnant, dreamed regularly of a little girl with a big smile and beautiful white teeth. She knew the little girl was her daughter, and Norah woke happy.

DREAM BACKGROUND AND MEANING

Norah's first infant, a baby girl, had died soon after birth, and the medical cause was never established. Norah was afraid to have another baby, in case a death happened again. The second pregnancy was a total surprise, and Norah was very anxious. Dreams are a way of reassuring a grieving parent that all will be well with the next child.

INTERPRETATIONS AND FORTUNE-TELLING MEANINGS

★ If you dream of a little child after a late miscarriage, stillbirth, or baby's death from sudden infant death syndrome (SIDS), some believe this is your lost infant's way of telling you that they may return as a healthy infant, whether as a son, daughter, or grandchild.

★ If you dream regularly of your baby dying, this is an anxiety dream, perhaps because the baby took a long time being conceived or you had a prior bad birth experience.

★ If you wake suddenly from a nightmare that your baby is in danger, this is your maternal radar in overdrive (see "Adoption," p. 22), which may alert you to the baby needing you before it cries.

★ If you are estranged from an adult child and not allowed to see your new grandchild, this represents your natural grief at being excluded but is a sign to keep trying, as the adult child may be regretting it.

★ If you dream of a baby dying in an accident or war zone, this is a predictive dream linking you to a tragedy in another location, a sign that your psychic powers should be channeled into healing.

★ If you dream of a baby dying and you are experiencing perimenopause, this signifies regrets at the loss of your fertility.

OUTCOME OF NORAH'S DREAM

The little girl was showing her teeth as a way of reassuring Norah that she would not die at birth, but would grow up normally. A baby dying, if in an old-fashioned scene or unknown cultural setting, may be a past-life memory, reawakened by hearing of the death of an infant belonging to someone you know.

Lost Child (Finding)

Megan, forty-one, dreamed she was crossing an airport concourse when she saw a small girl alone, crying. The child was too young to talk and had no identification. Though Megan was in a hurry, she took the child's hand and approached a security guard, who walked away. The information and flight desks closed, the lights went out, and everyone left. Megan took the child home.

DREAM BACKGROUND AND MEANING

Megan's marriage had broken up when she was pregnant. Her partner told her she had to choose between him and the child. It might have been her last chance to have a baby, but she wondered if she could cope alone. If you dream of encountering a lost child, your unconscious mind says you are ready to assume responsibility for a baby.

INTERPRETATIONS AND FORTUNE-TELLING MEANINGS

★ If you are a parent, dreaming of losing or having your child snatched in a crowded place, it is a normal parental anxiety dream and not predictive. Just take extra care.

★ If you are trying for a baby and have recurring dreams of finding a lost child, this may be your spirit baby making contact, ready to be conceived.

★ If you find a lost dream child that attaches itself to you, you have unconscious maternal or paternal instincts that will grow stronger.

★ If you dream that you conceal a lost child, you may be suppressing parenting desires because you know your partner or lifestyle could cause problems.

★ If you are accused of kidnapping a lost child, you may feel unworthy to rear a child.

★ If you dream that you hand the child to a security guard or find the parent, this is a good time to try for a baby.

OUTCOME OF MEGAN'S DREAM

Megan decided she would bring up her baby as a single parent. When the dream indicates that no one will take responsibility for the lost child except you, it reassures you that you can manage on your own.

Lost Items

Olive, twenty-eight, dreamed she was frantically searching for her engagement ring, which she had mislaid. She saw a circle of small stars dancing just above the ground.

Olive followed the dancing lights, which eventually rose and stopped above a set of drawers where she kept spare linen. As she opened the top drawer, the ring sparkled in full view. She woke happy.

DREAM BACKGROUND AND MEANING

Olive had searched the house for the ring in vain. She had been engaged for three years, as she and her fiancé were saving for a big wedding. She did not like the showy ring her fiancé insisted on buying, and sometimes she did not believe the wedding would happen. Dreaming of losing something valuable can question whether we really want what it represents at all, especially when an actual loss appears in a dream.

INTERPRETATIONS AND FORTUNE-TELLING MEANINGS

* Losing an item suggests something missing in your life, connected with the object.
* Searching and finding the item buried under papers or linens reveals a need to deal with unacknowledged resentments.
* Losing keys indicates fears about not feeling emotionally or physically safe in the place the keys open.
* Losing car keys raises questions of the purpose of your life plans.
* Losing an unwanted gift or valuable item you dislike in a dream represents shedding an unwanted obligation.
* Finding a lost item when you had given up hope says a lost connection with someone special will be restored.

OUTCOME OF OLIVE'S DREAM

Olive pulled out the drawer contents and found the ring wedged at the back. She told her fiancé they should sell the ring and use the proceeds and the money they had already saved to enjoy a more modest wedding straightaway. He was relieved, as he was also feeling pressured by the delays. When an item is lost, dreams may reveal our unconscious awareness of its location.

Lotus

Polly, sixty-five, dreamed of a huge blue lotus opening at sunrise on a clear pool and a young god emerging from it, offering her a jeweled phial containing what looked like oil but had a glorious fragrance. The dream ended with Polly trying to track where this perfume was made.

DREAM BACKGROUND AND MEANING

Polly owned an exclusive perfume store in London. She had wanted to go to Egypt all her life but was very disappointed with the Nile cruise she was on. Polly asked her guide what he knew about perfume that was pure oil, containing no alcohol. Her guide said such perfume had been made in Egypt for thousands of years and introduced her to a perfumer. The blue lotus represents the cycle of birth, death, and rebirth because it opens in the morning and closes before nightfall.

INTERPRETATIONS AND FORTUNE-TELLING MEANINGS

* Dreaming of a lotus floating in water says omens and symbols in dreams will give you your desired answers.
* A lotus in full bloom indicates success in business, career, finances, and love.
* If you are offered a lotus flower, the giver has great admiration for you, and this could grow into lasting commitment.
* A fading lotus says to give yourself time to grieve for what has ended, especially love. Do not rush into another relationship.
* The lotus is a sacred symbol of peace and enlightenment—in its pink form, in Hinduism, and purple in Buddhism.
* Two lotuses side by side in water indicate the growth of twin-soul passion.

OUTCOME OF POLLY'S DREAM

Polly returned to Egypt and commissioned special perfume oils. She learned to make them herself, possibly an art she had learned in a past world. This is suggested by her dream, since in Ancient Egypt, both Nefertem, the young god of perfection and fragrance, and the sun god Ra rose from the first lotus at the first sunrise. The lotus has for thousands of years in dreams represented perfume and the striving for lasting perfection.

Mafia

Bart, twenty-five, dreamed he was manager of a new casino in Las Vegas. Another branch of the Mafia had come to town and offered him a large bribe to turn a blind eye to their dealings. The existing Mafia also made him an offer. Should he bargain for the best payoff, as he was broke, or walk away? Suddenly he was caught in the middle of crossfire between the rival mobs, but he managed to reach a getaway car outside, which had a red dragon logo on the side.

DREAM BACKGROUND AND MEANING

Bart had taken a loan at a high rate of interest with a dubious company, which was now demanding repayment. Mafia dreams often occur when the dreamer is in financial or official trouble and cannot see an immediate way out. In the dream there usually will be a symbol or name that offers a possible solution that is considered but rejected.

INTERPRETATIONS AND FORTUNE-TELLING MEANINGS

★ If you dream you are a Mafia member, you may gain power over a situation where you were crushed by officialdom or an inflexible organization. Beware of acting unethically.

★ If you dream you are threatened by the Mafia, you may be afraid that forces beyond your control will threaten your well-being.

★ If two Mafia mobs are fighting and you are trapped in the middle, you may have two choices, neither of which is satisfactory. Look for another option.

★ If you are concerned about injustice at work or financially, assess how much power you have to put it right without harming your reputation or security.

★ If you are asked to join a dream Mafia organization, you may gain swift temporary advantage, but have long-term risks.

OUTCOME OF BART'S DREAM

The dream rescue made no sense until Bart remembered a debt charity called Red Dragon, which he had previously contacted but had dismissed as taking too long to pay his debt off. He recontacted Red Dragon, which established a legal charge through the court so the loan shark could no longer threaten Bart. Mafia dreams can represent a quick-fix solution to problems, but without care they can lead to a more precarious position.

Maggot

Mason, thirty-five, dreamed she opened her refrigerator to take out the elaborate salad she had prepared for her health-conscious boyfriend's first meal together when she noticed to her horror that it was crawling with maggots. Feeling sick, she tried to remove them, but her whole refrigerator was covered with them. She threw everything away. She woke as her boyfriend arrived.

DREAM BACKGROUND AND MEANING

Mason was trying to impress her new boyfriend, who was a committed vegan, by pretending she was also a vegan. A number of times he asked her to prepare him a meal, but she kept making excuses. With her demanding job, she ate whatever she could pick up from the late-night supermarket. Maggots can represent our confidence and credibility being eaten away if we pretend to be what we are not.

INTERPRETATIONS AND FORTUNE-TELLING MEANINGS

★ Maggots crawling on a dead animal represent someone in your life you are subsidizing or supporting who should be dropped from your life.

★ If you dream a maggot appears in a salad you are serving, you may be afraid of someone critical considering you inadequate.

★ To see maggots crawling over food suggests that a matter concerning someone you are feeding in the dream is eating away at you.

★ Dreaming of killing maggots represents overcoming fears of endings and changes that you may have been holding back.

★ Fishing with maggots says that to achieve an aim you may have to make difficult choices or work with people you consider unworthy.

OUTCOME OF MASON'S DREAM

Mason decided to be honest and told her boyfriend that she ate anything after a long day. He explained that he had become vegan because he had grown up on a farm where animals were regularly slaughtered for the table, but he did not expect her to be vegan unless she wanted to be. Maggots are considered shameful by many people, but in dreams they may occur when we imagine someone is disapproving of us, when they just have a different lifestyle.

Magic Carpet

Molly, seventeen, dreamed she was riding on a rainbow-colored carpet over turrets and minarets. She was able to guide the carpet just by naming a place and was going to a beautiful palace where her prince was waiting. There was a rush of wind, and the dream ended before she reached the palace.

DREAM BACKGROUND AND MEANING

Molly was very excited about the eleventh-grade dance, as her parents had bought her a fairy-tale dress. But she did not have a partner. Should she give up her fantasy of having a prince waiting in a palace to lead her into the first and last dance and not attend? Magic-carpet dreams suggest that we sometimes need to help make our own dreams come true and steer our carpet where we most want to go.

INTERPRETATIONS AND FORTUNE-TELLING MEANINGS

★ If you dream of flying on a magic carpet, you need to escape from routine, worries, or responsibility.

★ If you are flying on a magic carpet with a lover, there may be high romance, but you need to settle day-to-day matters.

★ Dreaming of a genie conjuring up a magic carpet says your wishes will be fulfilled in an unexpected way.

★ If you dream that your magic carpet is not flying high or crashes, there are practical matters that need sorting out.

★ If your carpet ends up at a different destination from the one you had planned, consider the alternatives available in terms of career or lifestyle.

★ If your carpet does not move when you say the magic words, you may need to make more earthly efforts and not rely on good luck and others.

OUTCOME OF MOLLY'S DREAM

Molly decided the excitement of the eleventh-grade dance was what mattered. She started a social-media group for others who were going to the dance alone, so they could arrive as a group. One of the guys from her year, who joined the group and had been too shy to ask her to be his partner, shared the first and last dance. Magic carpets can give a new perspective to see ingenious solutions by showing that the magic is within us already.

Magic Tricks

Gordon, seventeen, dreamed of a magician performing amazing tricks. He pulled all the things Gordon most wanted out of his hat, which seemed impossible—a new iPhone, the latest iPad—and gave them to Gordon. The magician disappeared when he heard police sirens, leaving Gordon to explain about all the goods.

DREAM BACKGROUND AND MEANING

A slightly older guy joined the group who hung around the local recreation ground. He did not have a job, but had plenty of money, and he sold the younger guys electronic goods at cut prices. Gordon had been saving for a racing bike, and his new friend said he could get him one at a rock-bottom price. Gordon knew his parents would ask questions, but he badly wanted the bike. A magician whose tricks seem inexplicable warns against someone in your life not to be trusted with your money or your heart.

INTERPRETATIONS AND FORTUNE-TELLING MEANINGS

★ A dream of a box of magic tricks advises against taking the easy option or accepting a too-good-to-be-true offer.

★ If you dream you successfully demonstrate magic tricks, you may get away with a risky plan. If the tricks go wrong, you will be caught.

★ Should you dream you are the victim of a magic trick, you may feel intimidated by a work colleague trying to humiliate you.

★ If you are a famous dream magician, you can attain success in an entertainment or media career.

★ If you succeed in demonstrating a difficult magic trick, you will receive an unexpected pleasant surprise.

OUTCOME OF GORDON'S DREAM

Gordon took his money and paid the guy, who promised to deliver the next day. But he never turned up, and the local police quizzed the boys. The older guy was a known thief. Gordon lost his money but did not dare say anything. A dream about a magician with exciting, frightening tricks warns of a con merchant.

Magnet

Gwen, fifty-five, dreamed she was being dragged toward a giant horseshoe magnet by her wedding ring, which had turned into an iron chain. She was powerless to resist. She ripped off the ring just before she hit the magnet. Everything went black. When Gwen woke, she realized she had almost died in the dream.

DREAM BACKGROUND AND MEANING

Many times, Gwen had left her abusive husband, and as many times she had returned for one more try. He said he loved her and would change. After the last attack, which put her in the hospital, Gwen knew she must go, although she still shielded her husband. But she loved him and the good times were good. A magnetic force may prove irresistible, even though the attraction brings danger.

INTERPRETATIONS AND FORTUNE-TELLING MEANINGS

* ★ A dream of a positive powerful attraction, to either a person or a particular course of action, if acknowledged will bring happiness.
* ★ If you are drawn against your will, you should extricate yourself from a potentially destructive situation you have experienced many times.
* ★ Malign influences may hold a fatal attraction in the name of love or codependency.
* ★ Drawing something or someone to you that you desire indicates a manifestation of your wishes.
* ★ A dream of a magnet with different metal items attached says you have choices in love or career.
* ★ Magnets that repel speak to incompatibilities or needing a change of perspective. Magnets attracting each other are a good omen for love.

OUTCOME OF GWEN'S DREAM

Gwen contacted her older sister, Catherine. Shocked at Gwen's injuries, Catherine insisted on taking Gwen to her home on the other side of the country and encouraged her to press charges. The dream had warned Gwen that her life was in danger and that the violence would escalate. Moving away from a magnetic force, or turning the poles of twin magnets to repel where the attraction is destructive and potentially codependent, may be necessary to break the cycle.

Magnifying Glass

Don, eighteen, dreamed he was making a fire by holding a magnifying glass over paper in bright sunlight, to impress his friends. At last, the paper smoldered, and Don took the glass away. But it was too late. The nearby bushes and trees caught fire in the hot, dry weather. His friends fled, leaving Don trying to beat out the fire in vain. He woke terrified and choking.

DREAM BACKGROUND AND MEANING

Don had made exciting but dangerous friends since starting his apprenticeship. They would steal cars to go joyriding. Now they were breaking into premises and starting fires. Don was out of his depth but knew they would not let him walk away. Magnifying-glass dreams reveal not only fears but danger as well, and clearly magnify possible consequences.

INTERPRETATIONS AND FORTUNE-TELLING MEANINGS

* ★ If you dream of looking through a magnifying glass, you may be worrying unnecessarily about a particular problem or person.
* ★ If you have a magnifying glass and can see a large eye staring back, someone familiar is taking an undue interest in your affairs. Resist their intrusion.
* ★ If you dream a magnifying glass is lying on top of official papers, contracts, or financial documents, double-check in case some detail has been overlooked.
* ★ Dreaming of looking at money through a magnifying glass reflects investments or financial speculation that may yield increasing profits.
* ★ Holding a magnifying glass in front of your face reveals unjustified fears that others will notice your inadequacies.
* ★ A broken magnifying glass reassures you that secrets remain safe or that any official investigation will be dropped with no further action.

OUTCOME OF DON'S DREAM

Don confessed to his father, who arranged for Don's apprenticeship to be transferred to the garage of a friend of his out of state. Don moved the next week. He could not stay safely in the area once he left the gang. Magnifying-glass dreams reveal to the dreamer the true situation and so accelerate the opportunity for necessary change.

Magpie

Lois, fifty-five, dreamed she was watching seven magpies, in the old rhyme linked with a secret that must never be told, sitting on a wall. One came and perched on her shoulder and to her amusement tugged at her ears and flew off with Lois's earrings. The magpie buried the earrings. The other magpies gathered around and started to peck Lois when she tried to retrieve her earrings.

DREAM BACKGROUND AND MEANING

Lois was known for her witty observations and had been popular at work. But since the arrival of Karen, who was appointed to work as her deputy, people were avoiding Lois and saying she was untrustworthy. Unexpectedly, Karen was promoted over Lois, and her boss excluded Lois from confidential memos. Magpies warn about careless chatter with someone you think you can trust, as they may use it against you.

INTERPRETATIONS AND FORTUNE-TELLING MEANINGS

★ If you dream that five or six magpies fly toward you with silver or gold in their beaks, you will gain unexpected advantage, leading to prosperity.

★ A magpie burying shiny treasure warns of a friend who may try to damage your reputation.

★ Two magpies indicate happiness in love and good fortune.

★ Although a single magpie is considered unlucky, as soon as you wake, greet the dream magpie to attract good luck.

★ If magpies are sitting on a fence, chattering, beware of idle gossip and those whose loyalty changes according to their best interests.

★ Magpies flying overhead chattering herald unexpected good news or someone advantageous coming into or returning to your life.

OUTCOME OF LOIS'S DREAM

Lois realized everything she had confided in Karen jokingly about colleagues had been twisted and reported to them. Karen had also been using Lois's comments about the boss against her. Lois changed departments and keeps her humor in check. Magpies are natural tricksters, and stealing earrings is especially indicative of eavesdropping or twisting innocent words for personal gain.

Mailbox

Gareth, thirty, dreamed he was posting in a mailbox in the mall all the unpaid bills, final demands, and official judgments concerning his forthcoming divorce with the words "Return to Sender, not known at this address." But every time he posted one, it came back out, as the mailbox was full.

DREAM BACKGROUND AND MEANING

Gareth disconnected his email address and telephone so his creditors and court officials could contact him only by post. That way he could return the mail unopened via the nearest mailbox. But now Gareth was getting visits from officials. Mailbox dreams represent a welcome buffer from unpleasant communications, but only as a postponement tactic.

INTERPRETATIONS AND FORTUNE-TELLING MEANINGS

★ A full mailbox indicates that you need to read and sign official documents, as vital details may be overlooked in online communication.

★ A letter sticking out of your mailbox says there is an important message, whether from your unconscious or from someone close who you should not ignore.

★ A mailbox full of junk mail warns that people are wasting your time with trivia.

★ An empty mailbox says you should reconnect with friends and family personally.

★ If you are posting a letter or parcel in a street or work mailbox, a matter you thought secret could be revealed.

★ If your mailbox is crammed with bills you cannot pay, beware of avoiding tackling financial, relationship, or business decisions by assigning them to snail mail in your dream—and in your life.

OUTCOME OF GARETH'S DREAM

Eventually the bailiffs arrived and a court official came with a summons to attend a divorce hearing. Gareth had been using his mailbox as a barrier to unwanted communication, but if the dream mailbox is too full, hard resolution may be unavoidable. However, mailbox dreams positively can suggest that, if the dreamer is overwhelmed by online communication and texts, the slower communication method allows time to study options and choices, rather than fulfilling the sender's expectations for an instant response.

Making Amends

Eamonn, forty-nine, often dreamed he was in jail, sentenced to five years' imprisonment for driving a getaway car in a jewelry-store raid in which the owner had been injured. Eamonn woke praying for forgiveness.

DREAM BACKGROUND AND MEANING

Eamonn had found a wallet filled with cash, with the owner's name inside. It was nearly Christmas and Eamonn had lost his job, so he used the money to give his children the best time ever. He always felt guilty that he might have ruined some other children's Christmas. Expressing regrets in a dream for something that has haunted you suggests that an opportunity is coming to make an altruistic gesture to balance the cosmic books.

INTERPRETATIONS AND FORTUNE-TELLING MEANINGS

★ If you dream about being jailed for a serious crime that was in fact relatively minor, you may have high standards of right and wrong and may be unnecessarily punishing yourself.

★ If you are scared that an old omission may be revived, it may be an anxiety dream because life is going well and you feel you do not deserve good fortune.

★ If an old problem with which you dealt badly recurs in a dream, accept that you are now a different person.

★ If you have a past-life dream of harming someone you dislike, there may be a reason, and the dream may reveal that you have unfairly taken all the blame.

★ If you dream of something nasty you did to a former friend or colleague when you both were young, try to contact them as they may also want to fix things.

★ If you feel angry about an injustice for which you were unfairly blamed, it's time to let it go.

OUTCOME OF EAMONN'S DREAM

Eamonn tried to track down the man, whose name he clearly recalled, but he had died. Eamonn donated the same amount of money plus interest to a children's charity. When consciences are troubled in dreams, take practical steps to put right the guilt and then let it go.

Mandala

Bertrand, sixty-six, had recurring dreams of wearing orange robes and sitting in an open mountaintop temple, painting a mandala, totally at peace. No one spoke, no one checked his progress, and one dream sequence flowed into another.

DREAM BACKGROUND AND MEANING

Bertrand had been a graphic designer known for his accuracy and speed. His company wanted him to stay on, but he was tired and wanted to live quietly, creating and selling mandalas, which had always excited him since his time living in Thailand. His friends and colleagues said he would go mad after a week, as he had been the life and soul of every party.

INTERPRETATIONS AND FORTUNE-TELLING MEANINGS

★ If you dream you are making a sand-and-crystal mandala, you will gain awareness of your life purpose if you have been contemplating it.

★ If you are pregnant or want to conceive, a labyrinth-like mandala or yantra (a geometric diagram used as a meditation aid) is an excellent traditional omen for a good birth.

★ If someone destroys a mandala you are creating, beware of a person you may recognize in the dream trying to upset your equilibrium.

★ If you are dismantling a mandala with running water after healing, pain will lessen in the days after the dream.

★ If you smudge your mandala, you may be trying too hard to attain perfect spiritual techniques, so relax.

★ If you dream you see a person meditating on a mandala and you hesitate to join them, you may have been intimidated by those who use spirituality as an ego trip.

OUTCOME OF BERTRAND'S DREAM

Bertrand visited a Tibetan Buddhist temple in Thailand and found the place from his dreams and the beautiful mandalas. He has taken up painting them in his Arkansas woodland retreat. The timelessness of mandalas triggers connections with ancient spiritual traditions and preserves them in the modern world.

Map

Roger, thirty-six, dreamed he found an old treasure map of an island in an antiques store. It was very dusty and tied with strong knots. Since he knew the island was a deserted one in the middle of an estuary and there were legends of pirates being there, he decided to hire a boat and explore. He dug where the map indicated and found a treasure chest filled with gold coins.

DREAM BACKGROUND AND MEANING

Roger had been offered a piece of land near a remote river where it was rumored that gold could be extracted. He had been sent a map by the owner. Roger was bored with his job in the local library and was excited at the possibility of such a challenge. Maps in dreams and in actuality offer a possible route to riches, but, even if riches are not there, provide adventure in return for risk.

INTERPRETATIONS AND FORTUNE-TELLING MEANINGS

★ If you are using a GPS, or satellite-based navigation system, in your dream, you may be relying too much on the expertise and advice of others.

★ Finding a map indicates imminent travel. See where the map is guiding you, perhaps somewhere totally unexpected.

★ If you dream you cannot locate where you are on a map, there may be a period of indecision ahead when you need to wait for signs of the best path forward.

★ If you dream you are looking at a photo of your home on a satellite map, you may be restless and unconsciously preparing for a move.

★ If you dream you are given a map by a boss, partner, or family member, they may be trying to direct your future path. Decide if this is in your best interests.

OUTCOME OF ROGER'S DREAM

Roger bought the land but did not find gold. However, he set up a business in which he buried treasure chests all over the area. Tourists followed maps to find them. Some chests held crystals and just one contained a piece of gold. A map can lead a dreamer to a positive life change, even if not to the original objective of the dream quest.

Maple

Rula, thirty-four, dreamed she was collecting maple sap to create maple syrup for the morning pancakes. Her young daughter would soon be awake for breakfast in their cozy cabin, and her husband back from his early-morning conservation work, where he protected trees and wildlife from illicit loggers and hunters. The maple leaves were falling, and Rula knew a good life lay ahead.

DREAM BACKGROUND AND MEANING

Rula and her husband, Pete, had applied to emigrate to Canada from the United Kingdom. She had no problems obtaining a job as a nurse, but it was harder for Pete to find work as a wildlife conservator. But they were determined to go. Since the maple leaf has been a symbol of Canada since 1868, and the eleven-lobed red sugar maple leaf is on the national flag, maple trees often appear in dreams of those who live in or seek to emigrate to Canada.

INTERPRETATIONS AND FORTUNE-TELLING MEANINGS

★ If you dream of tapping maple sap, this is a powerful fertility symbol for a baby, especially by late fall.

★ If you dream you are in a maple forest, especially if the leaves are red or gold, prosperity and job opportunities will come to you.

★ Dreaming of finding an old maple tree, which can live up to four hundred years, assures good health and a good quality of life, especially for older relatives you are concerned about.

★ If someone is cutting down a maple tree, this foretells family quarrels and disloyalty.

★ Making love beneath a maple tree in a dream promises lasting passion and many children.

OUTCOME OF RULA'S DREAM

Pete took a job as a trucker and they emigrated to Canada. By the time Rula was ready for maternity leave, Pete had obtained a job as a forester. They live in a log cabin similar to the one Rula saw in the dream. Maples are naturally protective trees and traditionally proof against demons, and so dreams involving them are almost always good omens, especially for those connected with Canada.

Marathon

Ginny, thirty-eight, dreamed she was completing her fourth marathon of the month with her lover running by her side. On the home stretch she made a final sprint but slipped, felt her calf muscle rip, and knew it was the end of her running career—and probably her romance.

DREAM BACKGROUND AND MEANING

Ginny had taken up marathon running because she really liked a guy in the running group who was a champion marathon runner. She increasingly found the practice sessions a chore and noticed that marathons were all he talked about. Marathon dreams are about dedication and perseverance and represent single-mindedness in working toward any long-term goal.

INTERPRETATIONS AND FORTUNE-TELLING MEANINGS

★ If you dream of running a marathon, you may have a mammoth task or struggle ahead in some area of your life that will require perseverance.

★ If you are struggling to keep up in your dream, you may be trying to achieve too much, too fast.

★ If you win in the dream, persevere in any venture and you will end up ahead.

★ If in your dream you are constantly pushing yourself in marathon after marathon, you may be exhausting yourself for the wrong reasons.

★ If you undertake any marathon task in life, you must commit to a long-term approach.

★ If you are watching someone close to you run a marathon, you know they are reliable and will stick by you but may be slow to declare their intentions in love.

OUTCOME OF GINNY'S DREAM

After the dream, Ginny acknowledged that she was pushing her body too hard, and it was only a matter of time before she seriously injured herself. She took up organizing refreshments and cheering the team on, but she realized that persevering with her love target was a marathon she was not going to win. Any marathon dream emphasizes the need for endurance but, for some, the effort outweighs the reward.

Marble

Faye, forty, dreamed she was in a room made entirely of white marble, with no windows and a marble door without a handle. She was terrified that she was trapped in a tomb. She banged on the door, and at last it swung open, leading to the slums of the area surrounding her home. She was free.

DREAM BACKGROUND AND MEANING

Faye was from a wealthy family. She was desperate to work with the street children living outside her marble walls, saving girls from prostitution and educating them. But her family would not hear of it.

INTERPRETATIONS AND FORTUNE-TELLING MEANINGS

★ To dream of marble buildings may be an indication that you will soon visit a place with ancient buildings that will bring you great pleasure.

★ To dream of marble statues, whether indoors or in a garden, suggests that your lifestyle is frozen in set expectations.

★ A marble table set for a banquet speaks of a rise in status or finances through a traditional source, profession, or organization.

★ Broken marble, especially white marble, suggests that traditional lifestyles are no longer relevant.

★ If you dream you are carving marble, as Michelangelo said, "The marble not yet carved can hold the form of every thought the greatest artist has." Creatively and in helping others, opportunities yet unknown lie ahead.

★ If you are playing marbles and winning, especially as a child in the dream, immature competition at work or socially demands a mature, detached response.

★ If you dream the marble is fake, beware of a friend or colleague who is all surface show.

OUTCOME OF FAYE'S DREAM

Following the dream, Faye realized she was trapped in her opulence and had to find the way into the real world. Defying her parents, she went to work in the young girls' rescue and education program, raising money from her rich friends. Marble is smooth, used for tombs to enclose the deceased. But it also can be carved into drinking vessels and bowls for nourishment.

Marital Financial Disputes

Shirley, forty-three, a senior physician at the local hospital, dreamed that she was told to discipline her husband, Byron, twenty-nine, who worked as a junior doctor at the same hospital, for a mistake he had made. She also had to reduce his salary as a result. He accused Shirley of stage-managing the incident to show her power over him and said that if she went ahead, the marriage was over.

DREAM BACKGROUND AND MEANING

Shirley and Byron had been married for three years and, despite their age difference, were very happy. Shirley was offered a promotion, making her in effect Byron's boss. Though the salary increase would be beneficial, Byron said that unless she refused the promotion he would leave her. Shirley knew that to not accept the offer would seriously damage her career, but she did not want to lose Byron. Often a partner who considers themselves the traditional breadwinner can resent the other one earning more. Dream scenarios express the not-always-desirable options.

INTERPRETATIONS AND FORTUNE-TELLING MEANINGS

* Dream disputes between a couple over earnings can reveal a deeper power conflict within the marriage.
* If the couple is in business together and one member of the couple makes executive decisions, a dream can show hidden resentments.
* If you dream of being promoted over your partner or vice versa, one of the couple may secretly feel insecure about those arrangements.
* If you are contemplating starting a business with your marriage partner, a dream suggests possible pitfalls, especially if one partner is domestically dominant.
* If money is an issue within a committed relationship, dream conflicts show potential flashpoints to be defused.
* If a dream shows a couple working in harmony and profitably, this is an excellent omen for starting a joint venture.

OUTCOME OF SHIRLEY'S DREAM

Shirley declined the promotion to save her marriage. She moved to another hospital in a lower position. After Shirley left, Byron was demoted for making another mistake. Dreams can alert and warn, but only the dreamer can weigh up the consequences of acting on the dream.

Marshmallows

Sally, twenty-five, dreamed she opened her kitchen cupboard to prepare lunch for her mother-in-law and sisters-in-law, but the cupboard was full of marshmallows. She checked the refrigerator, and that also was full of marshmallows. They rang the doorbell, so Sally hastily set the marshmallows in a dish and handed them around. Her in-laws were unusually nice to her. When the marshmallows were eaten, they left without a word.

DREAM BACKGROUND AND MEANING

Sally's mother-in-law and sisters-in-law were overfriendly and gushing to her face when Sally's husband, George, was present. George insisted they loved her. But when he was out of the room, they became spiteful and sarcastic toward Sally. They provoked her to anger, tears, or complaining. George accused Sally of not trying, when his family was so loving to her. This was causing problems in their marriage. Marshmallows in dreams represent soft words, but they can be used as a weapon concealing malice.

INTERPRETATIONS AND FORTUNE-TELLING MEANINGS

* If you dream you are toasting marshmallows around a campfire, you may want or need to create or re-create informal celebrations with friends and family.
* If you are buying marshmallows, you may have to be the one to bring the family closer.
* If you ate too many marshmallows and feel sick, someone at work or socially is overdoing sweet words and needs watching.
* If a store is closed and you cannot buy marshmallows for a party or dessert, you may have been neglecting your social life in favor of working.
* Sharing marshmallows with a loved one indicates romance and intimate times together.
* If you dream marshmallows are tasteless, there may be hidden spite or malice hidden behind loving words.

OUTCOME OF SALLY'S DREAM

After the dream, Sally responded to her in-laws' unpleasantness with over-the-top sweetness. George was pleased that she was making such an effort, and the in-laws gave up their nastiness. Marshmallows in dreams herald unexpected happy get-togethers and spontaneous fun celebrations.

Maternal Responsibility

Jana, forty-eight, dreamed her son, Hans, was waiting at a bus stop with his possessions in a garbage sack. Jana knew the sack would split, but he would not listen. The bus came, and Jana realized she and Hans were attached by a heavy cord. There was a violent pain in her stomach as they both let go.

DREAM BACKGROUND AND MEANING

Jana's nineteen-year-old son was planning to travel around Europe for six months and had quit college mid-term. Her husband said they were not subsidizing him, but how could she let her only child go so unprepared? Maternal protectiveness that begins in the womb should evolve naturally into mutual caring as the child becomes adult.

INTERPRETATIONS AND FORTUNE-TELLING MEANINGS

★ If a mother dreams of her adult child as a young child or baby, one or both are holding on to the dependent relationship in a restrictive way.

★ If a mother dreams of an adult child's danger or vice versa, check on them, as the telepathic bond remains throughout life.

★ If you are estranged from your mother or adult child, try to mend the breach so you can go forward free.

★ If your mother is no longer in your life through death or abandonment, parent yourself.

★ If an adult child constantly uses guilt to ask you for money or help, remember you are no longer responsible for their lives.

★ If you are suffering from empty-nest syndrome, rather than waiting for grandchildren to fill the gap, rekindle ambitions and desires set aside by parenthood.

OUTCOME OF JANA'S DREAM

Hans went on his trip, and Jana ensured that he had an emergency Visa card and a ticket home. The dream told her she must allow him to experience the consequences of being an adult for both their sakes. While mothers worry all their lives about children, dreams reveal where mother and child hold each other back in mutual dependency.

Maze

Rachel, thirty-five, had a recurring dream she and her husband, Raúl, were exploring a huge maze with high walls. They became separated and could not find each other, although they could hear the other calling. Eventually, Rachel found her way out, still calling, but didn't find Raúl.

DREAM BACKGROUND AND MEANING

Rachel and Raúl recently had visited the famous Hampton Court Maze near London. They became lost within the maze and eventually sought help from a security guard. Rachel wanted to give up work and try for a baby. But Raúl was giving mixed messages: one moment, planning the nursery; the next, talking about their taking a year off work to trek across Asia. Rachel's biological clock was ticking. Maze dreams reflect major issues where there are changing viewpoints and no clear consensus.

INTERPRETATIONS AND FORTUNE-TELLING MEANINGS

★ To dream of being lost in a maze or arguing about direction mirrors confusion and mixed messages that are causing an impasse.

★ If you are following or see a map in the maze, matters will soon be resolved and dilemmas cleared.

★ If you are in the center moving outward, you are on the right track.

★ If a maze has high walls, there are inner fears you can overcome if you face them.

★ If you dream you lose your partner in a maze, you are taking different directions, avoiding the main issue.

★ If you dream you can hear but not see your partner in the maze, you are not listening to the other's viewpoint.

OUTCOME OF RACHEL'S DREAM

Raúl admitted he feared becoming a father because his own father had moved out soon after his birth. Once Rachel was reassured that they were traveling the same path at different speeds, they agreed to go on a three-month Asian trek and then try for a baby.

Discuss options with anyone following life's maze with you. Stick together on the course you have decided, dismissing doubts and doubters.

Medication

Winston, forty-eight, dreamed he was walking through a rain forest whose floor was carpeted with small purple flowers. Louisa, his wife, who had mobility problems, was striding through the forest, clambering over tree roots. She looked twenty years younger. Louisa picked bunches of the flowers and told Winston they must take them home, as they made her feel so much better.

DREAM BACKGROUND AND MEANING

Winston's wife, Louisa, was resistant to conventional treatments for her deteriorating condition. Winston was skeptical of plant remedies but had heard that rain forests were increasingly turning up ancient remedies for modern ills. Since Egyptian and Greco-Roman times, dreams have been interpreted to reveal healing remedies.

INTERPRETATIONS AND FORTUNE-TELLING MEANINGS

* Taking medication in a dream reflects the necessity to settle down to unwelcome chores or detailed official forms you have been avoiding.
* If you see medicines being made from plants in a dream, identify the plants, as these may be helpful in relieving a stubborn illness for you or a loved one.
* If you dream you forget or lose an essential medication, even if you do not take it in everyday life, you feel vulnerable without help and support.
* If you dream the medicine tastes foul, there are difficult decisions and steps to take to overcome problems.
* If medicine is sweetened, someone may be trying to persuade you to take extra responsibilities with sweet words.
* If you dream you were given the wrong medication at a pharmacy, beware of misleading or false information.

OUTCOME OF WINSTON'S DREAM

After the dream, Winston decided to research clinics near rain forests that dealt with his wife's condition. He found that a clinic in Mexico was having success with a new flower found in the nearby Mexican rain forest. When he researched further, he discovered the plant had purple flowers. They took a loan and traveled to Mexico, where treatments improved Louisa's health. Medication dreams are a way of tuning in to the healing powers of plants that harmonize with our self-healing system.

Medicine Wheel

Duncan, sixty-six, dreamed he was standing in his favorite medicine wheel, Bighorn, high above sea level on remote Medicine Mountain in Wyoming, which is free of snow for only a small part of the year. The snow was deep. But suddenly the sun rose, the snows melted, and Duncan knew he would return by the next summer solstice.

DREAM BACKGROUND AND MEANING

Duncan was having major heart surgery and was scared he might not survive, as his parents had died young with heart problems. He had always felt an affinity with the Bighorn medicine wheel and returned every summer when the snows melted. But would he return this year?

INTERPRETATIONS AND FORTUNE-TELLING MEANINGS

* If you dream about standing in the center of a medicine wheel, your life is coming together in all aspects.
* If you dream you are a medicine woman or man carrying out a ritual with others, this may be a past-life dream, revealing you are ready to further develop your spirituality.
* If you are alone in a medicine wheel, you may need to develop your spiritual beliefs as a solitary practitioner.
* If the medicine wheel has been dismantled or is covered in snow, put plans for a spiritual vacation or course on hold until circumstances are more favorable.
* If the sun is rising on the solstices or equinoxes over a wheel, flow with life and its changes, trusting that all will be well.
* If you dream you are walking clockwise around the spokes of the wheel, it predicts life following its expected path. If counterclockwise, adapt to temporary setbacks.

OUTCOME OF DUNCAN'S DREAM

Duncan knew that because the snow melted over the Bighorn medicine wheel so startlingly, all would be well and after his operation he would visit again. Medicine wheels reassure that life will go on in spite of illness, loss, or major surgery.

Medicine Woman or Man, Shaman

Christian, thirty-five, dreamed he was a medicine man performing a ceremony on a reservation with his partner, the medicine woman. They were dancing and chanting at Midsummer sunrise around a medicine wheel made in the dusty earth. Christian woke as the sun rose in the dream, and he knew he had succeeded in keeping the old ways alive.

DREAM BACKGROUND AND MEANING

Christian and his partner, Bess, had Native North American roots, and both were qualified as lawyers. Now Beth was pregnant and wanted them to return to the communities they had left years earlier. Christian believed their children should have a comfortable, modern city lifestyle. Yet he felt something was missing. Being a dream medicine woman, man, or shaman represents a deep calling to a spiritual system, not necessarily your own, which holds the wisdom you need.

INTERPRETATIONS AND FORTUNE-TELLING MEANINGS

★ To dream you are healed by a medicine woman, man, or shaman indicates you have a wise spirit guardian.

★ If you are a dream shaman, your healing and mystical powers, rooted in nature, are growing.

★ If you identify the shamanic dream culture, it may link you to a past world that has a message for you.

★ If you sense something missing from your life, your dream shaman scenario will restore a sense of harmony.

★ If your medicine woman or man shows you special plants or flowers, their essences or oils may offer a remedy to a current physical or emotional problem.

★ If in the dream you take hallucinogenic substances, you may seek escape from a reality that needs resolution.

OUTCOME OF CHRISTIAN'S DREAM

The couple was introduced to a successful lawyer with indigenous roots who asked them to set up and maintain legal facilities, which involved traveling to different indigenous communities, a career that enabled their children to experience both ways of life. An archetypal shamanic keeper of wisdom in dreams or appearing soon after heralds a mentor.

Meditation

Coral, twenty-eight, dreamed she was in a temple, meditating with her friends among Buddhist monks and nuns, but she could not stop fidgeting, first at an itch on her nose, then a cramp, and finally at the antics of the temple cat. She was asked to leave. Outside, Coral watched trees swaying in the wind and tall white birds with long necks moving in harmony. She joined their dance and felt her mind soaring.

DREAM BACKGROUND AND MEANING

Coral's friends were planning a ten-day meditation retreat. Coral was an active person and found not moving for hours a huge strain and not at all spiritual. Her friends said she had to try harder. Meditative states in dreams offer powerful restoration, but there are other ways of attaining harmony.

INTERPRETATIONS AND FORTUNE-TELLING MEANINGS

★ If you dream of ashrams or temples and meditating people wearing robes, this may be a past-life dream, using methods you have not consciously learned.

★ If you dream of happily meditating with friends and family, you are entering a harmonious period in your personal life.

★ If you are constantly facing interruptions when meditating, others' demands are intruding on your personal space.

★ If you are also practicing yoga, tai chi, or other energy transference methods in your dreams, you are entering a period of being at home in yourself.

★ If you cannot focus on meditation in your dream but others around you are focusing, you may be seeking the wrong kind of spiritual enlightenment.

★ If you are meditating happily alone, you need more self-time, but if lonely you may need support from those who understand your life aims.

OUTCOME OF CORAL'S DREAM

Coral realized she was doing meditation to please her friends and switched to sacred dance. As she moved rhythmically, she entered the elusive meditation state. Meditation can by its nature impose rules, but dreams may free the dreamer to discover more creative ways of expressing spirituality.

Megaphone

Norman, forty-five, dreamed he was shouting through a megaphone to rally his supporters to vote for him. His brother, also with a megaphone, at the same time was calling them in the opposite direction to sponsor his cause. Norman shouted even louder so his voice drowned out his brother's. But, because of the conflicting noise, neither was heard clearly.

DREAM BACKGROUND AND MEANING

Norman was determined that his point of view would be heard in the business he ran with his brother, who took an opposing stand on almost every issue. The workers used the dissension to ignore them both. The business was suffering, but neither would listen to the other. Megaphone dreams reinforce an opinion but can lose effectiveness if another megaphone is used at the same time.

INTERPRETATIONS AND FORTUNE-TELLING MEANINGS

* To shout through a megaphone says you are becoming impatient that others will not listen.
* If your voice is muffled coming from the megaphone, your communication is being suppressed by someone with a different agenda.
* Do not ignore a message amplified through a megaphone, but consider what is being offered, as it may differ from what you think is being said.
* If you can hear a message through a megaphone but cannot see the speaker, this may be a message from your guardian angel, spirit guide, or ancestor that you are disregarding.
* If more than one megaphone is being used at the same time, the effectiveness of both will be diminished.
* If you are speaking through a megaphone from a moving vehicle, be sure you are not spreading your influence too widely.

OUTCOME OF NORMAN'S DREAM

Norman realized he and his brother were wrecking their livelihood and agreed to listen to each other without shouting. Megaphone dreams often contain an important message for the dreamer, but amplifying the intensity does not necessarily make it truer or even mean that it is taken more seriously.

Menu

Arnie, twenty-seven, dreamed he was having dinner for the first time at an expensive restaurant with his future in-laws. The menu was in French, which he did not speak. His future in-laws were very rich and sophisticated, so he chose three dishes at random, not knowing what they were. When they were served, he realized he hated them all, but did not want to waste them as they were so expensive.

DREAM BACKGROUND AND MEANING

Arnie came from an ordinary working-class family and was self-conscious that the family of his fiancée, Greta, would hold that against him. Greta was getting impatient because Arnie kept putting off meeting her family. Menus represent all the choices we have at the time of the dream, and the more extensive the menu, the more life options the dreamer has.

INTERPRETATIONS AND FORTUNE-TELLING MEANINGS

* If you dream that a menu lists your favorite dishes, the choices you make will be the right ones and bring happiness.
* If a dream menu is in a language you do not understand, you may not have the full facts about a decision you are making and should seek advice.
* If a menu contains nothing you like, it may be that none of the options or the locations on offer are right for you.
* If a menu is torn or stained, you may be offered second best, so hold out for what you want.
* If you cannot afford anything on the menu, you may be overstretching yourself financially in life or for a particular potential purpose.
* Sometimes if a menu in the dream is too small to be read or has obscure fancy writing, it suggests the dreamer should be open about a situation or offer, as it may be more favorable than anticipated.

OUTCOME OF ARNIE'S DREAM

Greta's parents invited him for a meal at their house. It was home-cooked like his mother made. Her father explained how he had worked his way up and was delighted Greta was marrying someone genuine, without pretensions.

Mermaid, Merman

Ellen, thirty-five, dreamed of a beautiful mermaid sitting on a rock, combing her long hair, sending resentful looks toward her. Ellen was a mermaid too. She saw her boyfriend, Hugh, clinging to wreckage and the young mermaid swimming toward him, holding out her hand. But he swam instead toward Ellen. The young mermaid was furious and created a storm. Ellen and Hugh clung together and the mermaid was gone.

DREAM BACKGROUND AND MEANING

Ellen was jealous because her best friend, Penny, had been flirting with Hugh and was constantly with them. Hugh insisted he was not interested and tried to avoid her. Ellen's suspicions were starting to come between her and Hugh. Mermaids or mermen represent an ideal romance. If the merpeople are threatening, they represent fears or danger of a partner straying.

INTERPRETATIONS AND FORTUNE-TELLING MEANINGS

* If your mermaid dream is happy and you are swimming with them or are one of them, let your heart rule your head.
* If mermaids are surrounded by mist, you may be tempted toward an exciting chance or passionate but risky relationship.
* If a mermaid or merman offers you treasure, be alert to an unexpected opportunity for prosperity.
* If mermaids or mermen are luring you onto rocks or mesmerizing you with their songs, it's time for an everyday reality check.
* If you dream you are in the mermaids' mystical kingdom and are one of them, your psychic and magical gifts are emerging.
* Dreaming of the song of mermaids or mermen reminds you to listen to your inner voice when deciding if a relationship or offer is genuine.

OUTCOME OF ELLEN'S DREAM

Ellen realized Penny was encouraging division between herself and Hugh, and Hugh was entirely innocent. They presented a united front and Penny discovered she was wasting her time. Mermaid and merman dreams warn that choosing temporary excitement over long-term happiness can lead to spite and revenge if it goes wrong.

Meteor, Meteorite

William, thirty-two, dreamed he found a meteorite in a crater, filled with gold and gems. As he held it, a cascade of light appeared. He was in the middle of an asteroid shower, illuminating the suddenly dark sky. Then it was gone and he was holding his glinting gray stone.

DREAM BACKGROUND AND MEANING

William was in the ancient tourist area of a big city, having gone alone on his honeymoon after his fiancée had called off the wedding at the last minute. The day after the dream he had on impulse bought a similar small meteorite he saw in the window of a mineral store. The owner assured him it would bring him great good fortune.

INTERPRETATIONS AND FORTUNE-TELLING MEANINGS

* A dream meteor creating a crater as it lands says, "Seize the moment, for a sudden opportunity may not come again."
* To dream of finding a meteorite filled with crystals or gems was in past times considered a gift from deities to humankind.
* A meteor falling and changing the shape of the landscape says feared disruption brings freedom from old outworn patterns.
* If a meteor is streaking across the skies, expect a sudden bonus, windfall, or lucky meeting.
* If you dream that a meteor causes a great deal of damage when it lands, anticipate and take diversionary action.
* If a meteor contains rare or valuable metals, this is an extraterrestrial dream saying that you are having an astral dream, and life-changing events may happen.

OUTCOME OF WILLIAM'S DREAM

William's luck changed almost instantly when he purchased the dream meteorite. He saw a good job advertised so he could start a new life and found a cheap but comfortable apartment in the old town. By the end of the week, he had become friendly with the owner of the mineral store, who shared his fascination with the extraterrestrial. William realized he had dropped his meteorite, but since his luck had changed, he decided he no longer needed it. Dreaming of a meteorite seems to activate the dreamer's own capacity for generating their own good luck.

Microphone

Alan, thirty-one, dreamed he was interviewing a politician he despised. Before the broadcast he was highly sarcastic about the interviewee. Suddenly he realized his radio mike was switched on. His words were heard all over the auditorium and network. Alan woke horrified, knowing it was the end of his career.

DREAM BACKGROUND AND MEANING

Alan was marrying the daughter of a wealthy property developer. As a wedding present, Alan's father in-law had offered him a senior position in the company with a good salary and their choice of property. Alan worked in social housing and had expressed views in the media criticizing his father-in-law's ethics. His fiancée said it was an offer too good to turn down. Microphones ensure views are heard, which have consequences if they are controversial.

INTERPRETATIONS AND FORTUNE-TELLING MEANINGS

★ Dreaming of being offered a roving or radio microphone says your influence will reach a wider audience. A fixed microphone indicates success in specific expertise.

★ Broadcasting in a studio, singing, or acting on stage indicates success in the performing arts; the larger the stage or better known the network, the higher you can fly.

★ If you dream your words are not clear through a microphone, express your ideas more assertively or in a different way.

★ If the microphone is muted, you are wasting your time communicating with those who have their own agenda.

★ Dreaming of karaoke indicates pleasurable, easy communication with friends, while sharing a mike with a lover promises harmony between you.

★ A hidden microphone warns against speaking too freely with those you do not know or expressing views that may prove unpopular.

★ Echoing microphones suggest that you express views of others with which you don't necessarily agree in order to keep the peace.

OUTCOME OF ALAN'S DREAM

Alan knew that, should he accept the job, he and his father-in-law would clash in major ways that would strain family relations. His fiancée gave Alan an ultimatum and they ended the relationship.

Midnight

Joachim, twenty-one, dreamed he was in a darkened room in a totally dark building and could hear a clock in the distance chiming midnight. He had no idea where he was or if he could find a way out. Then, directly ahead, a large circle of light appeared in the wall with a bright sun within it. A voice said, "This is the sun on the other side of the world that still shines. It is the sun shining at your midnight here." The circle became a doorway and Joachim walked out as the new day began.

DREAM BACKGROUND AND MEANING

Joachim had gone to the United Kingdom from Australia but had been able to obtain only casual work and was living in a small room in a run-down house with no friends and no money. His family, sensing he was unhappy, offered to send him a ticket home. But he was too proud to admit he had failed. Midnight represents a transition between two days, two weeks, or even months where positive change is overdue.

INTERPRETATIONS AND FORTUNE-TELLING MEANINGS

★ A dream set at midnight advises an ending that offers a solution to an unsatisfactory situation.

★ If the dream midnight is dark with no moon or stars, the dreamer may be losing hope, but the message is that morning will come.

★ If you see in the dream the sun shining on the other side of the world, usually as a circle of light, this is a reminder that there are always alternatives if sought.

★ If you are unwell or depressed, dreaming of seeing a safe, comfortable sleeping place says you will be restored by the healing tides of midnight.

★ If you dream you are at a party listening for the chimes of the new year at midnight, the twelve months ahead will be happy and prosperous.

★ If your midnight dream also features midwinter or Christmas, light and life will come into or return to your life very soon.

OUTCOME OF JOACHIM'S DREAM

Joachim realized that his life in Australia and his parents were still waiting. He accepted the ticket home and is studying astronomy. Midnight dreams are not gloomy; rather, they suggest a favorable transition.

Midsummer

Saga, fifty-five, dreamed she was young again in her Swedish village, dancing around the midsummer tree and decorating it with garlands of flowers. She knew her true love was coming at the end of the celebrations to claim her wreath and declare lasting love. But at the end of the festival her flowery wreath remained on the tree.

DREAM BACKGROUND AND MEANING

Saga had one true love in her youth who had suddenly gone away, and his family refused to tell her where he went. She married another young man from the village. After her husband died, she decided to find out what happened to her first love. Midsummer in many lands is a time for pledging love, and dreams of a former love may occur.

INTERPRETATIONS AND FORTUNE-TELLING MEANINGS

★ If you dream of traditional midsummer celebrations, you are linked with the old cycles of the year and should live according to the seasons.

★ If you dream of a beautiful sunrise around midsummer, the year ahead will bring prosperity and success.

★ If close to midsummer you dream of the rising sun being obscured, find new outlets for talents and new sources of income.

★ If you dream of finding or renewing love in your midsummer dream, this is a good omen for a lasting relationship.

★ If you dream of gold or golden ferns at midsummer, you will be led to new money-making opportunities and enjoy renewed health.

★ If at midsummer you dream of a baby in a cradle, this is a strong fertility symbol.

OUTCOME OF SAGA'S DREAM

Saga found her first love online and learned he had been taken north to work with his uncle to stop their romance, of which his mother disapproved. He had left Saga a letter with his address, but his mother had destroyed it. They are getting to know each other again, as he never married. Midsummer is a time of pledging loyalty, sometimes to reappear years later in dreams of midsummer.

Midwife

Constance, twenty-six, dreamed an older midwife in an old-fashioned uniform with a diamond brooch on top of her badge entered the labor room. She reassured Constance that she would soon have her strong, healthy daughter. Constance woke, and her daughter was born not long afterward following an easy labor.

DREAM BACKGROUND AND MEANING

Constance was in a labor room alone and scared and was given a sleeping pill, as her contractions had ceased. The dream was so real, she asked the midwife if the older midwife was relief staff, and commented on her beautiful brooch. The midwife said she was the only one on duty and staff were not allowed to wear jewelry. Midwife dreams during pregnancy or labor give the mother-to-be a sense of being protected, especially if the birthing mother is unsupported.

INTERPRETATIONS AND FORTUNE-TELLING MEANINGS

★ If a dream midwife is delivering your child, even if you are not pregnant, you will receive help in furthering an ambition or dream.

★ If you dream of three priestesses or mother figures delivering a child, this is an ancient symbol connected with annual rebirth of the sun and a good omen for any woman trying to become pregnant or expecting a baby.

★ If you are arguing with or dismissing a midwife and you are not pregnant, you are seeking independence from someone intruding on your private life.

★ If you are resisting help from a midwife, you may feel that your wishes about your birth and delivery are ignored by the medical profession.

★ If you dream of a midwife delivering your baby in different circumstances from your birth plan, your unconscious may be guiding you to be adaptable.

OUTCOME OF CONSTANCE'S DREAM

Constance forgot about the dream until years later, when a relative came from overseas with family photos of the branch of the family who had emigrated. In one of the photographs, Constance recognized the woman who was wearing the diamond brooch. She had been a midwife until her retirement. Midwife dreams, where the midwife has a biological connection with the family, continue the link of midwifery from earlier times.

Midwinter

Juliana, seventy, dreamed she was holding the only light at a ceremony of white-clad nature priests and priestesses, celebrating the return of light after the shortest day. She was beckoned to the center of the circle to take the part of the wise old woman of winter. Once she stepped into the circle, she would have to accept that she was getting older. She lit everyone's flame from her own and brought back the light of the sun.

DREAM BACKGROUND AND MEANING

Juliana was struggling because her company had a policy that no one could remain after seventy. She felt she was walking into the darkness of old age and could see no light ahead. Dreams of midwinter, and of other festivals of light returning, celebrate the wisdom and value of age as well as the regeneration of youth.

INTERPRETATIONS AND FORTUNE-TELLING MEANINGS

- ★ If you dream of a candle being relit in the darkness during the declining days of the year, it means that, whatever your age, the coming year will restore light and life.
- ★ If you dream of one of the old winter celebrations, this may be a past-life memory if you need encouragement to make new plans.
- ★ If you dream of a single light penetrating darkness, you may need to face an ending to find a new beginning.
- ★ If you see a calendar in your dream marking the shortest day, any flagged days after it represent new opportunities.
- ★ If you dream of the old woman of winter offering you a flame, this is a spiritual sign to use your wisdom and experience to guide others.
- ★ If you are retiring around midwinter, your dream will reveal ways to reinvent yourself.

OUTCOME OF JULIANA'S DREAM

Juliana decided to use the psychic and healing gifts she had not yet developed to help other retirees develop theirs. She is also learning about nature religions. Midwinter at any stage of life symbolizes a transition to hope.

Milk

Maura, thirty, dreamed she was carrying a jug of milk out to the garden to the barbecue her husband was preparing. Her hand slipped and the milk spilled everywhere. She started to clean it up, as she knew it would rapidly start to smell foul. She could hear her husband calling. There was no milk left, so she went outside empty-handed, and he ridiculed her in front of his friends and family.

DREAM BACKGROUND AND MEANING

Maura was the third wife of Edwin, a minor politician who had left his second wife for Maura when Maura became pregnant. She felt fat and incompetent and was terrified of making a mistake. Edwin complained that she was not up to the domestic standards of his previous wives. She realized that instead of being the cherished mistress, she was now expected to be a domestic goddess. Milk is a sign of nurturing guests and family alike, and spilling milk may be viewed as a sign of inadequacy.

INTERPRETATIONS AND FORTUNE-TELLING MEANINGS

- ★ Drinking milk is a fertility symbol if you want to conceive a baby.
- ★ Dreaming of pouring milk for others is a sign you are being too generous or understanding.
- ★ If in the dream your own mother or a maternal figure in your life insists you drink milk, you are being smothered.
- ★ Milking a herd of cows promises continuing and growing resources and prosperity.
- ★ If you dream milk is sour, a gesture of love or kindness will not be appreciated.

OUTCOME OF MAURA'S DREAM

Maura told Edwin she was not his mother or a domestic and, when the baby was born, she was going back to work and he could employ domestic staff. For fear of adverse publicity, he reluctantly accepted Maura's terms. Maura knows he is looking for a new domestic goddess. Milk dreams can be emotional, especially when a partner may be seeking a mother substitute as a mate.

Millionaire, Billionaire

Monica, sixty, dreamed she won millions of dollars on the lottery and wanted to share her good fortune. Immediately, people she had not heard from for years contacted her with hard-luck stories, as well as family members, who arrived with shopping lists for cars and new homes. She knew her windfall would rapidly disappear and gave it to charity.

DREAM BACKGROUND AND MEANING

Since Monica received a large retirement income, her children had each visited her separately, insisting that they would best care for her in old age. Monica was disappointed in their behavior.

INTERPRETATIONS AND FORTUNE-TELLING MEANINGS

* If you marry a wealthy person in your dream, you will meet someone rich in love.
* If you are the millionaire, your work or investments will pay off, albeit in a more modest way.
* If you dream of meeting someone who says they are a millionaire, be cautious in encountering a stranger promising wealth or a quick fix to financial problems.
* If you dream of winning a million dollars or more, it is a sign of good fortune, reflecting an underlying desire for a quick fix.
* If in the dream you are living in luxury as a millionaire or billionaire, this is wish-fulfillment. However, if you have been saving hard, take a break and spend some on yourself.
* If you acquire a great deal of money in the dream and everyone is demanding a share, note who they are.

OUTCOME OF MONICA'S DREAM

Monica had intended to invest her lump sum so the children would be provided for, but now she felt differently. She treated herself to a small chalet by the ocean, gave each of the children a modest equal sum, donated to charity, and saved the rest for her own old age. Millionaire or billionaire dreams can be wish-fulfillment, but they can also enable you to see who is more interested in your money than in you, which is usually borne out in life.

Mine, Underground, Claustrophobia

Edward, forty-five, dreamed he was a small boy pulling a heavy coal cart through tunnels where he could not stand upright. He was exhausted, and the heavy chains of the cart were cutting into his flesh. A rumbling indicated a tunnel collapse, and Edward found himself alone in the dark, for his lamp had gone out. He shouted, but no one answered. Then he heard a knocking. He had heard of mine spirits, as the older men tried to frighten him with tales of them. He followed the knocking and realized there was a small tunnel with a faint light at the end. Following the knocking, he reached the surface via a disused shaft.

DREAM BACKGROUND AND MEANING

Edward had a terror of enclosed spaces he had never understood. His claustrophobia interfered with his work as a structural engineer. Therapies had failed. Tales of mine spirits are found from Europe to South America. In times of crisis, anecdotes tell that the spirits have helped trapped miners, and represent the need to follow unconscious instincts when logic fails.

INTERPRETATIONS AND FORTUNE-TELLING MEANINGS

* Mines represent hidden potential that will soon emerge. If you persist, this will bring success in your chosen venture.
* Depending on the kind of mine—gem, gold, silver, base minerals, or fossil fuel—the dream meaning indicates the degree of prosperity that awaits.
* If you are working an exhausted mine, your natural optimism is being suppressed by someone seeking to emotionally control you.
* A mine that is closed represents resources, relationships, or directions no longer available.
* Owning a mine, whether small like an individual opal mine or a major mineral mine, promises prosperity unknown until fully explored.

OUTCOME OF EDWARD'S DREAM

By thinking about his dream escape, Edward was able to understand and overcome his phobia. Mine dreams are quite common in helping people to understand and overcome claustrophobia.

Miniature

Emerald, fifty-five, dreamed she was small enough to enter one of the Victorian dollhouses she collected. She stayed hidden as her parents called with some need or request. She walked past the nursery where the baby waited in the cradle, past the kitchen and the tiny groceries to be cooked. She sat undisturbed at the tiny desk in the book-lined study as her family rushed around, complaining that she must have gone out without telling them. At last, she returned full size to deal with the chaos.

DREAM BACKGROUND AND MEANING

Two of Emerald's adult children still lived at home, and her married daughter frequently brought her grandchildren over to be cared for. Emerald struggled as she worked full-time at home, but everyone assumed she was available 24/7. In dreams, a world in miniature represents a means of escape.

INTERPRETATIONS AND FORTUNE-TELLING MEANINGS

* A miniature house in which the dreamer is also tiny signifies domestic happiness, peace, and order.
* A miniature doll in a cradle symbolizes pregnancy soon to be attained.
* If the dreamer is large and everyone else is small in the dream, the dreamer will triumph over intimidation and those who try to diminish confidence.
* If the dreamer is small and everyone else is large, the dreamer may feel overwhelmed by others' needs and want to hide (see "Disappearing," p. 143).
* If the dreamer is small, trying to function in a full-sized world, the dreamer's identity needs reestablishing.
* If the whole world is miniature and threatened by giant invaders, the dreamer may feel under threat from external forces and circumstances beyond their control. Step back.

OUTCOME OF EMERALD'S DREAM

After the dream, Emerald put her home office out of bounds during working hours, left her cell phone and main phone on voicemail, gave herself time on weekends when she was not available to the family, and made the resident children share a room so she could create her own sanctuary. Her adult children moved in with her married daughter in return for doing babysitting duties. A miniature dream reflects the place the dreamer accords themself in relation to others and helps establish a life where their needs form the boundaries.

Mint

Beverley, sixteen, dreamed she was making peppermint tea in a glass, using chopped fresh mint and sprinkling the cooled liquid around a photo of her boyfriend and herself. She had read online that that would prevent a jealous rival's curse from breaking them up. But she could hear laughter and knew the curse was too strong. Beverley woke herself, knocking a glass of drinking water off her bedside table.

DREAM BACKGROUND AND MEANING

Beverley was fascinated by magick and used her mother's cooking herbs to cast folk spells, especially mint for love and protection. But Sophie, Beverley's former best friend, told Beverley she had cursed Beverley's relationship with her boyfriend using an online mint hexing, because she wanted Yves for herself. Ordinary herbs like mint, traditionally used for centuries in remedies, folk spells, and cooking, are sometimes used in online occultism.

INTERPRETATIONS AND FORTUNE-TELLING MEANINGS

* Drinking mint tea signifies freedom from the malice of jealous people.
* Making mint tea for someone you would like to know better traditionally attracts love.
* If in your dream you are adding mint to cooking, in folklore that represents increasing prosperity.
* Using peppermint candles or oil in the dream indicates happy, trouble-free travel, if you do not want to go on a particular journey.
* Walking in a dream garden with growing mint is a sign that psychic powers are likewise growing.
* If you buy a mint remedy in your dream, your health or a loved one's will improve or remain strong.

OUTCOME OF BEVERLEY'S DREAM

Beverley's mother was curious about Beverley's sudden obsession with mint tea. Beverley told her mother about the curse. Beverley's mother spoke to Sophie's mother, who had been worried about her daughter's preoccupation with online magick. They took the girls to see a reputable herbal healer, who straightened matters out. Beverley and Yves's relationship is thriving.

Mirror, Looking Glass

Phyllis, thirty-five, dreamed she was lost in a maze of mirrors. Each mirror distorted her image, making her seem ugly or overweight. There seemed no way out. At last, Phyllis saw a huge mirror and daylight beyond. In this mirror she was tiny, with her ex-husband totally enclosing her. Phyllis heard her new partner calling. The image disappeared, and she and her new partner stood together side by side, totally themselves.

DREAM BACKGROUND AND MEANING

Phyllis was divorced from her ex-husband, who had constantly diminished her, convincing her that she was fat, ugly, and stupid. Her new partner was loving, but Phyllis was sabotaging the relationship by accusing him of her ex's negative behavior, which had diminished her confidence to nothing. Viewing oneself in a distorted mirror reflects a poor self-image imposed by someone set to destroy.

INTERPRETATIONS AND FORTUNE-TELLING MEANINGS

★ Being happy with your image in a dream mirror confirms your high self-esteem and confidence.

★ If you are brushing your hair and gazing in a dream mirror, you may see your present or future love, known or unknown, standing behind you.

★ If the mirror is dark, you will be aware of an ancestor or spirit guide looking over your shoulder in the dream, protecting you.

★ To dream you are lost in a maze of mirrors indicates confusion about future plans and direction. Ignore conflicting messages.

★ A broken mirror or breaking a mirror does not foretell bad luck; rather, it expresses fears that your real self has disappeared through the demands of others.

★ Dreaming you are asked to lend your hand mirror warns that someone wants to steal your ideas or tempt your partner away.

OUTCOME OF PHYLLIS'S DREAM

Phyllis realized she was projecting onto her new partner the hurtful experiences of the previous relationship. She now listens to her partner's actual words, and the relationship is flourishing. In a mirror, everything is in reverse. Do not mistake illusion for reality.

Miscarriage

In her dream, Charmaine, twenty-five, who was twelve weeks pregnant, was having an ultrasound scan and was heartbroken to learn she was losing the infant. She phoned Mitchell, the baby's father, who hung up on her. His phone went to voicemail when she rang back. Charmaine woke in tears.

DREAM BACKGROUND AND MEANING

Charmaine was thrilled about being pregnant, even though Mitchell had left her when she told him the news, saying he was not ready for fatherhood. He promised to look after Charmaine and the baby financially, but she still hoped he would return. The evening before the dream, she started suffering pains and was offered a scan the following morning. She had asked Mitchell to come but was not sure he would turn up.

INTERPRETATIONS AND FORTUNE-TELLING MEANINGS

★ Dreams of a miscarriage can reflect natural anxieties if it is a first baby or if they happen around the time of an earlier miscarriage.

★ If a miscarriage dream remains with you all day, it rarely predicts a miscarriage, but a checkup may avert fears or give you early warning about problems.

★ If you dream of a miscarriage and you are not pregnant, a relationship may be going wrong that needs action to see if it can be saved.

★ If you are stuck on a project, as is common with authors or people in a job going nowhere, a miscarriage dream says it is time to try a new approach.

★ A miscarriage of justice that remains unresolved can be manifested as recurring miscarriage dreams until the unfairness is tackled.

OUTCOME OF CHARMAINE'S DREAM

On the scan, they saw that the baby was fine. Charmaine delivered a healthy girl at full term. Mitchell turned up and was so shaken that they might have lost the baby that he and Charmaine reconciled after the scan. He now is a devoted father. Dreams of miscarriages are emotional and can occur years after an actual miscarriage, especially if the dreamer is late in the pregnancy.

Mismatching

Cora, thirty-five, dreamed she turned up at what she thought was a costume party but was in fact a formal gown and black-tie occasion. Everyone was staring at her Batwoman costume, and she realized her boss and colleagues were present, along with her in-laws and everyone she had so wanted to impress in her Boston city life. She left, to their laughter.

DREAM BACKGROUND AND MEANING

Cora had obtained a good job in the city, a stockbroker boyfriend, and an upscale apartment she paid for by working 24/7. She had everything she had longed for as a teenager. Cora had won a scholarship that took her away from her small farming world. She missed her old life, but when she went home she felt like a fish out of water. However, she felt she did not fit in her new, sophisticated life either. Some people can slip easily between worlds, but for others there is a constant mismatch.

INTERPRETATIONS AND FORTUNE-TELLING MEANINGS

★ If you dream you have mismatched shoes, you may be uncertain which direction to take, especially if one is flat and the other high-heeled.

★ If you have mismatching gloves, there is a dilemma between showing your true self and fitting into a world where you seek a welcome.

★ If you dream your clothes are mismatching, for example a tiara with ripped jeans, you may want to break out of restrictions, become spontaneous, and not have to monitor your actions and words to obtain approval.

★ If you dream you are sitting on a low chair at a high table or vice versa, you may be trying to fit in socially or in a relationship where you fear you do not belong.

★ If you are in a workplace where your skills are the opposite of what is needed to succeed, you may be in the wrong career.

OUTCOME OF CORA'S DREAM

Cora went home and, while she could no longer fit back into farm life, took a job in a local town and rented a small apartment so she could go home more frequently and help around the place. She married a local attorney, also from farming stock, who she had known since childhood. A dream can reveal where we cannot fit in without constant effort, and then the dreamer can decide what really constitutes a life that matches expectations.

Missed Opportunities

Alf, seventy-one, for many years had dreamed that he was a participant in competitive sports. He ran out onto the field and waved to the adoring spectators. Suddenly, a ball hit him in the face, and he fell to the ground. He was carried off the field on a stretcher.

DREAM BACKGROUND AND MEANING

Alf, a retired accountant, had been a sports fanatic all his adult life. Whether for baseball, basketball, ice hockey, or soccer, he spent his days in front of a giant television screen, watching his sporting heroes. The dream was a reality check *hitting him in the face* to get out of his chair and strive for what was still attainable.

INTERPRETATIONS AND FORTUNE-TELLING MEANINGS

★ If you dream you are starring or scoring goals, it may not be too late to take up a modified active form of your spectator passion.

★ If you dream you get knocked down or booed, are you wasting time and energy regretting missed opportunities rather than enjoying the positive aspects of your life?

★ If you are sitting on the reserve bench or watching others win accolades, ask if you held back through fear of failure, or was it always fantasy?

★ Should you dream of a happy-ever-after in a past relationship that ended badly, make contact so you can rekindle love or friendship, or be glad it did not happen.

★ If you are successful at a career or creative art you abandoned or never pursued, consider if you could study in that area, even for pleasure.

★ If you are traveling in your dream to places you always wanted to see, go now.

OUTCOME OF ALF'S DREAM

Alf decided to travel interstate to support his favorite teams. He also joined a group of seniors learning new sports and raised his fitness levels. Look at a seemingly negative dream for what it is offering in terms of attainable opportunities.

Missing Pages

Anita, fifty, dreamed she was reading the story of her life up to the present day on loose handwritten pages. A huge wind then blew the pages everywhere. After collecting them all, she realized the last two pages were missing, so she did not know if there was a happy ending or if she, the heroine, went off alone.

DREAM BACKGROUND AND MEANING

Anita was at a crossroads in her life, whether she should use her layoff money to rent a remote cottage for six months and write the novel she'd always known was in her or get another job in the same town and continue the romance with a middle-aged divorcé in the hope that he would one day propose to her. Losing part of a dream novel, especially one mirroring the dreamer's life, means the answer is not as clear-cut as desired.

INTERPRETATIONS AND FORTUNE-TELLING MEANINGS

* If you dream the beginning pages are missing, there is uncertainty about whether the venture should be started at all.
* Pages missing in the middle, especially dialogue about a character's motives, indicate delays in a project or venture you are initiating, caused by other participants' indecision.
* If the end is missing, the anticipated outcome is by no means certain. It may be necessary to wait until matters and people's intentions become clearer.
* If pages are crossed out, illegible, or smudged, you may encounter unhelpfulness and need to make your own decision.
* If the book has blank pages intermittently throughout, a plan may have been put together too hastily and may need rethinking.
* If you dream the book is entirely empty inside, plans are unrealistic or based on empty promises.

OUTCOME OF ANITA'S DREAM

After the dream, Anita realized there was no clear answer, as her would-be partner was noncommittal about her going. She rented a cottage for three months to see how viable her novel was; if it was going well, she would extend the lease. Missing pages alert the dreamer to uncertain outcomes that only time will resolve.

Mistrust

Leon, fifty-four, dreamed he was alone at home when three masked robbers burst in. They knew the location and combination of the safe and cleaned out his gold bars and deceased mother's precious jewelry. His wife, Lorraine, arrived home as he was calling the police, and he noticed she was wearing his late mother's diamond earrings, which had been in the safe. He put down the phone and woke as he was confronting her.

DREAM BACKGROUND AND MEANING

Leon and Lorraine had been married for eight years. Recently, Lorraine had told him she had spent much of her youth in juvenile detention centers, and later in adult prison for burglary and online fraud. She assured Leon that she had changed, but after this dream Leon now had grave doubts, as he had noticed jewelry and cash disappearing from the safe. The only person he had confided in was his adult daughter, who said she did not trust Lorraine because of her criminal background. Mistrust, deliberately fueled in the everyday world, can creep into dreams as seeming proof.

INTERPRETATIONS AND FORTUNE-TELLING MEANINGS

* A dream may be the first sign of existing mistrust, and it alerts you to immediately confront the issue.
* If you dream of someone you mistrust misappropriating valuables, investigate before making accusations.
* If you hear whispering in your ear, doubts about someone close, the whisperer may have a motive in discrediting that person.
* If the mistrusted person is shadowy, be aware that the most obvious perpetrator may be used as a scapegoat.
* With any mistrust issue, ask who is likely to be trustworthy and who generates mistrust for their own gain.

OUTCOME OF LEON'S DREAM

After the dream, Leon confronted Lorraine, who said his daughter had recently had plenty of money and no job and had been wearing her grandmother's jewelry. Leon confronted his daughter, who confessed she wanted to discredit Lorraine. Leon banned his daughter, but, because of his suspicions, Lorraine left him. Dreams are excellent for picking up information missed by the conscious mind but can be clouded by prejudgment.

Mob

Liza, thirty-one, dreamed that outside the window a mob was running down the street, throwing bottles and stones and smashing windows. They broke in. Liza tried to hold them back but felt an intense pain in her neck and realized she had been shot in the neck. Her partner, Trudy, was trying to stop the bleeding. Everything went black.

DREAM BACKGROUND AND MEANING

Liza and her partner were expecting a baby. They lived in a fashionable city-center apartment. Liza was worried it was not a good place to bring up a baby. She wanted to move out to the suburbs. But Trudy was reluctant to leave. Liza was also secretly worried about the responsibilities of keeping a child safe in a dangerous world. Dreams about a mob can represent a worry about lifestyle changes that may not have been expressed or even acknowledged.

INTERPRETATIONS AND FORTUNE-TELLING MEANINGS

★ If you dream a mob breaks into your home, you may worry about break-ins and should check security.

★ If you dream a mob is running riot through a city, you are repressing hidden fears that your daily life is spinning out of control.

★ If you are trapped in a protesting mob, beware that you do not become caught in family, neighborhood, or workplace conflicts.

★ If you are injured in mob violence and someone is helping you, that person can help resolve fears of not coping.

★ Mobs are unpredictable. You need to decide who or what potential disturbance the dream mob represents and resolve worries.

OUTCOME OF LIZA'S DREAM

After the dream, there were reported break-ins and vandalism in their area. Trudy agreed that they needed a safer environment to bring up their child. They both obtained jobs working from home and have made an offer on a rural property. Mob dreams can bring to the surface seemingly unrelated issues that disappear when brought into the open.

Mold (Fungus)

Frank, fifty-six, dreamed he was sitting in the living room of his recently purchased home as thunderstorms raged. Water was entering the house through light fittings and under the front door. He saw mold growing on the ceiling that spread until the whole house was covered. He phoned his brother, a builder, who said, "I told you so" and hung up. Frank woke up, worried he had made an unwise purchase, as his brother had warned against buying the house.

DREAM BACKGROUND AND MEANING

Frank had recently purchased a historic home with his inheritance from his late mother. His brother wanted Frank to invest the money in a small apartment block his brother was building, in return for Frank getting a small apartment for life. But Frank loved the house, and a surveyor said there were no major problems. If mold covers your home in a dream, you may have growing anxieties about where and how you live, which may have been created by others with a hidden agenda.

INTERPRETATIONS AND FORTUNE-TELLING MEANINGS

★ If you dream of money in a safe covered in mold, it is time to start enjoying your money rather than saving it for others to inherit.

★ If you dream someone expresses disgust because you have mold in your home, they are seeking to make you feel insecure by pointing out your inadequacies.

★ If you dream that after cleaning off the mold it instantly returns, fears will overwhelm you unless you take action to confront them.

★ If you dream you eat moldy food without complaint, you should no longer accept second best in life or love.

★ If you dream your clothes have gone moldy, you have put your own feelings and needs second for too long and need to care for yourself.

OUTCOME OF FRANK'S DREAM

After the dream, Frank called in an independent builder, who assured him there were no damp issues and said he had made a wise purchase. His brother continued to find fault with the house and offered to buy it cheaply. Mold, a creeping fungus, represents continuing subtle undermining by those who have their own reasons to make you doubt your lifestyle.

Monkey

Anton, thirty-six, dreamed he was walking through a forest. Monkeys were flying through the trees, diving and playfully leaping on him and making no attempt to bite. He then realized that the monkeys had taken his wallet, phone, and even the hat that shielded him from the sun. When he tried to retrieve his possessions, a mass of tangled trees blocked the way.

DREAM BACKGROUND AND MEANING

Anton spent a month on a beautiful island. He had fallen in love and had been accepted by his new partner's family. He intended to return and gave his lover a substantial amount of money to invest in a bar they were going to run. But once he returned home, the family had cut off all contact. Anton had the dream once on vacation and again when he returned home. Monkeys can be delightful, but are unpredictable. Monkey dreams can warn not to be too trusting.

INTERPRETATIONS AND FORTUNE-TELLING MEANINGS

★ A monkey sitting on your shoulder warns of a fickle friend or lover who is fun but not reliable.

★ If you dream a monkey is watching you, he represents your own ingenuity and enterprise in solving problems.

★ Monkeys dancing around you indicate overcuriosity by work colleagues or neighbors into your private or financial life.

★ If you dream of a caged monkey, you may be restricted by others from expressing your ideas or initiating a plan.

★ If you see the mythical three wise monkeys—see no evil, hear no evil, speak no evil—you should keep your own counsel, as you may be tempted to act on rumors.

OUTCOME OF ANTON'S DREAM

It was not until Anton reached home that he realized the significance of the dream. After the second dream, he tried to retrieve his money, but in the flush of love he had signed no paperwork. He is working hard to rebuild his savings. Monkey dreams express the need for balancing the heart and head.

Monotony

Maggie, thirty-five, dreamed she was planting turnips in rows because the men had gone to war. The horizon extended flat and endless under gray skies. All she could see were other women silently planting. Even the children sat silently by their mothers. The full moon rose, and when it was too dark to work, they took the children home. But from her cottage door she could see other women coming outdoors and lighting candles to the moon. For the first time in ages, she felt hope and vowed that the next day they would sing while they worked and encourage the children to play together.

DREAM BACKGROUND AND MEANING

Maggie was a single parent with three young children and was always short of money. Her only outing was to the park, and she was too shy to talk to the other mothers. Her life was totally monotonous, and she could not see how it could improve. This may have been a past-life dream or one from the cosmic memory that can reflect the dreamer's present predicament. However, it ended optimistically.

INTERPRETATIONS AND FORTUNE-TELLING MEANINGS

★ Even if a dream reflects unchanging monotony, it may offer clues to the dreamer to make life as good as possible, knowing monotony will not last forever.

★ If a monotony dream does offer a solution, this may alert the dreamer to new energies, even within a seemingly unpromising situation.

★ If a superhero or superheroine arrives to relieve monotony, there may be a sudden opportunity and good fortune just over the horizon.

★ If the full moon is seen, this heralds inspiration that, if acted on, promises good changes.

★ If a monotony dream reflects a situation that could be changed by changing lifestyle, it may be a wake-up call.

OUTCOME OF MAGGIE'S DREAM

After the dream, Maggie started a local single-parent group for sharing babysitting and childcare, exchanging toys and clothes, and joining forces for birthdays, Thanksgiving, and Christmas if people were alone. Her group was adopted by a local charity, and Maggie was paid to organize it. Monotony dreams can alert the dreamer to alternatives, however limited, to bring new energies into life.

Monster

Michelle, seventeen, had a recurring dream of a monster stalking her, but one she could only see as an outline shadow. As she ran away, she could hear the heavy tread and the labored breathing. She tripped, and the black shadow engulfed her. She woke screaming.

DREAM BACKGROUND AND MEANING

Michelle was working at her first job as a trainee personal assistant. Though her manager, a man in his fifties, was courteous when others were present, when alone with Michelle he groped her. Older staff laughed, saying it was his regular initiation of new personal assistants and she should not make a fuss. Michelle needed her job but dreaded hearing the heavy footsteps approaching. Children often dream of monsters because their vivid imaginations clothe fears, especially fears of the dark, in storybook or cartoon form.

INTERPRETATIONS AND FORTUNE-TELLING MEANINGS

* When you are caught by a dream monster, you are being controlled, or fear being controlled, by a bully or sexual predator.
* Being chased by a monster talks of fears you have about your own inadequacies being uncovered.
* Being absorbed or engulfed by a shadow monster says there is a seemingly negative part of yourself that, if channeled into action, will increase your power.
* Hiding from a monster indicates a secret you dread being exposed.
* To defeat the dream monster says that you will overcome problems if you confront them.
* Dreams of a shadowy monster, especially if others cannot see it, represent feeling alone with your fears or abuse and helpless because of not being believed or taken seriously.

OUTCOME OF MICHELLE'S DREAM

Michelle's external training supervisor, arriving unexpectedly, caught the manager groping Michelle. She made an official complaint on Michelle's behalf. Other complaints had been registered but ignored. The manager was dismissed. Discovering the identity of a shadowy dream monster can give strength in real life to seek help to resolve the problem.

Moon

Alice, forty-two, dreamed she and her husband were standing in the water in a lagoon in the place they had spent their honeymoon, with a bright full moon overhead. Suddenly they were surrounded by shimmering moonbeams and bathed in their brilliance. Alice felt totally filled with joy as the largest moonbeam entered her womb. She woke laughing, and she and her husband spontaneously made love for the first time in ages.

DREAM BACKGROUND AND MEANING

Alice and her husband were trying for a baby using in vitro fertilization (IVF), so far without success. They had to decide whether to continue, as the treatment was draining their savings and negatively affecting their intimacy. Moon dreams, especially of the full moon, are symbols of fertility, motherhood, and mothers.

INTERPRETATIONS AND FORTUNE-TELLING MEANINGS

* To dream of the crescent moon foretells increasing success in love or business and a new or growing romance and commitment.
* A waxing moon indicates the increase of money-making opportunities within a month of the dream.
* A misshapen, blood, or orange moon warns of unrequited love, domestic quarrels, and disappointing business dealings.
* The full moon represents the conception of a child or a proposal of marriage, especially if you are bathed in moonlight.
* The waning moon is the end of a phase, or relief from pain or sickness.
* If you dream you are walking on the moon, follow your dreams, as they will materialize.
* If you dream you are in a rocket and fail to reach the moon, you are aiming too high too soon.

OUTCOME OF ALICE'S DREAM

Alice booked a vacation to their honeymoon destination instead of the next IVF treatment. She discovered she was pregnant not long after returning home.

If you feel confused over choices, listen to intuition and messages in moon dreams, and if still in doubt seek the advice of a wise older woman.

Moonlighting
(Holding Two Jobs at Once)

Denice, thirty, dreamed she was moonlighting at her nightclub job. When she was serving drinks, a customer grabbed her. She slipped on a spilled drink and hurt her leg badly. She was reluctant to go to the hospital in case her daytime employer found out.

DREAM BACKGROUND AND MEANING

Denice had a second job in a club, which was not permitted by the company for which she worked. She was being paid in cash for her club job, and she was not declaring the income. She was saving for a deposit on an apartment and was aware that she was becoming less efficient in her day job. Moonlighting dreams usually occur when the dreamer is multitasking; they signify overload in career or finances.

INTERPRETATIONS AND FORTUNE-TELLING MEANINGS

★ If you are moonlighting at an exotic second job in your dream, you may need more stimulation in your day job.
★ If in your dream you are caught moonlighting, you may secretly want a way out of a dull day job.
★ If in your dream your moonlighting job is lucrative, your talents might be better expressed in a change of career.
★ If in the dream someone at your day job reports you for moonlighting, you may be subject to unfair scrutiny.
★ If you discover in the dream that a colleague is moonlighting and you report them, are you resentful because rule breakers seem to flourish?
★ If you dream of gaining extra money from your day employment, is it possible to do overtime or start a business that will not clash?

OUTCOME OF DENICE'S DREAM

Denice took the dream as a warning that she was exhausted and getting careless. She quit the second job and is taking extra work, covering for sick or absent colleagues on her days off. Moonlighting dreams generally relate to earning extra money fast, and so can refer to any overload situation.

Moose

Helga, forty-five, dreamed of a young moose in the middle of a forest road bellowing in distress. Its mother was nowhere to be seen. Helga knew yearling male moose were abandoned by their mothers when the mothers were pregnant again. Most young moose survived alone. But Helga woke crying because she had not been able to rescue it.

DREAM BACKGROUND AND MEANING

Helga's nineteen-year-old son from her first marriage, Christer, had returned home. He was a heroin addict and was stealing money and selling valuable ornaments. Her husband said Christer must go, as his drug-taking was a serious threat to the younger children. But could she abandon her child? When a dreamer sees an abandoned young moose, they must show tough love, as this is generally a parenting issue being expressed.

INTERPRETATIONS AND FORTUNE-TELLING MEANINGS

★ If an adult moose hits a moving object such as a car, it keeps running, and so represents the inadvisability of taking on a major unpredictable challenge that may crush you.
★ A moose represents wild primal emotions that, if untamed, become a danger to self and others.
★ If you dream of a moose cull, you may be torn between head and heart.
★ If you see a mother moose with a baby calf, you may be called upon to defend those who are vulnerable at the expense of others who can care for themselves.
★ If you dream you see a solitary moose, you need the courage of your convictions and the determination to carry them through.

OUTCOME OF HELGA'S DREAM

Helga paid for her son to attend a private clinic in Stockholm, but made it known it was his last chance. He left the clinic after a few weeks and is living in an empty house with other squatters. The moose, by its sheer size and strength, is a creature of wonder but can use that power, often unintentionally, for destruction or self-destruction. A dream of it warns you to be wary.

Mosquito

Jeremy, thirty, dreamed he was on a tropical island on vacation but was plagued by giant mosquitoes. He had not taken any sprays or repellents, so they continued to bite him. At last, he immersed himself in the sea and the mosquitoes and bites were gone.

DREAM BACKGROUND AND MEANING

Jeremy, self-employed, was planning a vacation with his partner. He told her he would have to remain on call. She complained that there was always some crisis that took his attention away and doubted he was ready for commitment. Sometimes mosquitoes can represent willing interruptions that distract from having to ask crucial emotional questions, symbolized by the sea in the dream.

INTERPRETATIONS AND FORTUNE-TELLING MEANINGS

★ If you dream you are sleeping under a mosquito net, you will be protected from others' pettiness and unreasonable demands.

★ If your mosquito net has holes, daily problems and irritating people are intruding unnecessarily on your peace of mind.

★ To be covered in mosquito bites warns that people are draining your energy and resources.

★ If you dream that a mosquito bite becomes infected or makes you sick, exclude a particular person at work or in your social life who is constantly criticizing and provoking you.

★ If a plague of mosquitoes is buzzing around you, you have underlying conflicts to address.

★ If in your dream you are covering yourself with anti-mosquito cream or spray or using a repellent candle or incense in advance, the issues will not arise.

OUTCOME OF JEREMY'S DREAM

Jeremy wondered whether it was the distractions of his life or emotional commitment he was avoiding. Were the mosquitoes present to keep love at arm's length? He went on vacation alone and felt lonely. The irritation of mosquitoes prompts the question of the purpose they serve in the dream and who or what are the distractions in our lives.

Motel

Chris, thirty-eight, dreamed he was a trucker, traveling along a highway he knew well. He pulled into a motel he did not recognize, as it looked old-fashioned. As he entered reception, he felt he had come home. The receptionist asked, "Your usual room?" Chris went to the diner, and the waitress brought him a steak, saying, "Just how you like it, Chris." The diner was full of truckers, who greeted him. He put a fifties song on the jukebox. He felt he was in a time warp he could not escape.

DREAM BACKGROUND AND MEANING

Chris traveled a lot with his company. He was sure his wife was having an affair. Time-warp dreams can occur when we link into the anniversary of an event at a time we share emotions with the person whose life we temporarily assume.

INTERPRETATIONS AND FORTUNE-TELLING MEANINGS

★ If you dream that a motel, by its nature a staging post, feels homey, you may be in a necessary transition emotionally or commitment-wise.

★ If the motel is run-down, you may be accepting second best rather than figuring out what you are escaping from.

★ If you dream all the motels are full, you may have to move farther away to find a permanent job or home.

★ If you dream you are living permanently in a motel, your present life may involve insecurity, which you should tackle.

★ If you dream you are on a long vacation and staying in different motels, it is time to break domestic or career monotony and consider vacation or relocation.

OUTCOME OF CHRIS'S DREAM

Chris researched old journals about the highway and discovered that on the night he had dreamed about, in the 1950s, a trucker also named Chris had crashed his truck, it was suspected deliberately, while entering the parking lot of a motel. The trucker had discovered that his wife was having an affair with another trucker. Chris moved out of his home and quit his job, which he hated, to train as a trucker. It may be time to reconsider your domestic arrangements and lifestyle if a dream motel feels more like home.

Moth

Olive, forty, dreamed she was sitting at a table piled high with her favorite foods. Checking that no one was around, Olive ate until she felt sick. The door blew open and hundreds of moths flew in out of the darkness, covering Olive, the food, and the table. She then realized she was being filmed for a reality show called Greedy People. She woke utterly humiliated.

DREAM BACKGROUND AND MEANING

Olive had been unloved as a child and had compensated by eating whatever she could forage. As an adult, food had become an obsession for her. Her husband resented her being overweight and forced her to join a weight-loss club. Olive was a secret eater who, though she followed her weight-loss club menu to the letter, ate during the night. Moths represent irrational impulses that, once faced, can be released by direct action.

INTERPRETATIONS AND FORTUNE-TELLING MEANINGS

⋆ Dreaming of a moth fluttering too close to a flame suggests you should fight against a destructive relationship or a bad habit spoiling your life.

⋆ Moths flying out of stored clothes indicate unresolved past matters affecting present reactions.

⋆ As creatures of the night, moths represent hidden fears, secrets, and buried anger.

⋆ A dream of lots of moths coming indoors at night suggests accumulating small worries, guilt, and hurt marring domestic contentment.

⋆ An alter ego of the butterfly, a single moth at twilight in a dream is a message from a newly departed soul we are struggling to grieve for.

⋆ A moth banging against a closed window for entry represents denial of powerful sexual feelings toward an unattainable love.

OUTCOME OF OLIVE'S DREAM

Olive vowed to stop dieting and cut down her nighttime bingeing, but told her husband he needed to accept her as she was or not at all. Once the pressure was off, Olive's weight dropped slowly but consistently. When she was slim, she left her husband. Moths are symbols of transition between phases, when one door must close before another can open.

Mother's Day

Josie, fifty, dreamed it was Mother's Day and she was a child again. She and her friends were performing a song at the Mother's Day church celebration. Josie was not expecting her mother, because she worked Sundays, but to her amazement her mother was there. Josie vowed she would always be there on this day for her children.

DREAM AND BACKGROUND MEANING

Josie woke on Mother's Day anticipating the lunch she had prepared for her two daughters, who were in their twenties. She phoned them and was met with excuses about other plans. She was heartbroken. Mother's Day concentrates in one day all the expectations of demonstrations of maternal love that dreams can offer, an ideal hard to match.

INTERPRETATIONS AND FORTUNE-TELLING MEANINGS

⋆ If you have a happy dream of Mother's Day, or of the earlier Mothering Sunday in the United Kingdom, traditions are important to you as an annual affirmation of maternal love.

⋆ If you dream of happy Mother's Days but your own mothering or being-mothered experiences are less than joyous, enjoy the wish-fulfillment dream without expectations.

⋆ If you dream of an unhappy Mother's Day and your own mother is less than appreciative, focus on self-nurturing.

⋆ If your own children are self-focused and you are alone in the dream, remember that mothering can be celebrated any day of the year.

⋆ If you dream of reconciliation on Mother's Day and your own mother or children are far away or estranged, make a loving gesture, as the dream energies may reach them.

⋆ If you do not have children and your own mother is deceased or unloving, use the dream energies to focus on other blessings in your life.

OUTCOME OF JOSIE'S DREAM

After the dream, Josie realized she had done everything for her daughters. Mother's Day dreams, happy or otherwise, are almost always rooted in childhood Mother's Day experiences and express a desire for affirmation of our worthiness. Unfortunately, they can sometimes lead to disappointment.

Motorcycle

Lily, twenty-eight, dreamed she was waiting for the bus for work when a tattooed rider in a leather jacket pulled up on his motorcycle and offered her a lift. They roared through the

countryside. Then she was driving and loved the speed and freedom, though she was afraid of crashing. She woke, feeling disappointed that the adventure had ended.

DREAM BACKGROUND AND MEANING

Lily had been given a working visa for Australia. Her boyfriend, Saul, wanted them to settle in the small English town where they had always lived. She was restless and feared Saul was too conventional in his ways to emigrate, her greatest desire. Motorcycle dreams talk about taking a chance on life and going against convention.

INTERPRETATIONS AND FORTUNE-TELLING MEANINGS

* If you dream you are driving the motorcycle, you are willing to take a chance on life and adventure. Be aware that there may be a price to pay for freedom.
* If you dream you want to drive but are scared, is fear holding you back from breaking free, especially relating to traveling?
* Solo riding indicates you may need to go it alone if others do not share your vision.
* Not wearing a helmet or driving too fast suggests taking unnecessary risks.
* Crashing shows you may lose security, but also the restrictions of life in the slow lane.
* Refusing a ride or choosing a moped or scooter instead of a more powerful machine says you may need time to leave your comfort zone.

OUTCOME OF LILY'S DREAM

Lily asked her boyfriend to come for a vacation to Australia to see if they could settle into a new life. She is aware it might be the end of their relationship, but right now they have different priorities. Maybe she will meet her Australian biker. Motorcycle dreams alert the dreamer to opportunities that lie further afield. Playing it safe now may later bring regrets.

Mouse

Lucille, forty-five, dreamed she opened the back door of her house and hundreds of field mice came scurrying in from the fields. She called for help. A gang of young men arrived who emptied her pantry and then moved in. She locked herself in her bedroom, but the mice had followed her.

DREAM BACKGROUND AND MEANING

Lucille had moved alone, after a breakup, into a house that backed onto fields, and she started to hear mice scratching under the floorboards and behind the kitchen appliances. She was afraid to open the doors in case more came in. She hated the house because it was so isolated, and at night youths on motorbikes roared up and down the tracks. Mice in dreams reflect fears of actual infestations and being invaded by hidden enemies.

INTERPRETATIONS AND FORTUNE-TELLING MEANINGS

* To dream of mice running everywhere in a house represents fear of being overwhelmed by numerous small problems out of your control.
* A mouse running over you talks about an invasion of your privacy at home by uninvited visitors.
* Because mice are smaller than rats, they more easily stay hidden. You may be aware of someone undermining your efforts and self-esteem.
* Because of their ability to breed fast and frequently, mice are a fertility symbol for twins or babies close together in age.
* Because mice are known as timid creatures but are believed to frighten elephants, dreaming of a mouse in your workplace or socially warns you not to be fooled by someone who acts reticently.

OUTCOME OF LUCILLE'S DREAM

After the dream, Lucille contacted the local police, but they did not have spare patrols to deal with the youths. The rodent catcher said the mice would return, as Lucille was so near the fields and the house was very old. Lucille gave up her deposit and returned to a modern apartment in the city. Mice have both actual and symbolic meanings of the dreamer being taken over. Sometimes, although the foe is so tiny and logically defeatable, only quitting can bring peace of mind.

Moving Van

Destiny, fifty-five, dreamed she arrived home to find a large moving van outside her home and her husband, Jim, and the movers loading the furniture. She called out for them to stop, but her husband climbed in the front and they drove off. She woke clinging to her husband.

DREAM BACKGROUND AND MEANING

Since retiring, Jim wanted to own a small campground for camper vans and tents in his favorite mountain location. He had found exactly the right one. Destiny was not ready to give up work or leave her grandchildren, but Jim was adamant. Moving vans in dreams stir up major emotions and require deep discussions.

INTERPRETATIONS AND FORTUNE-TELLING MEANINGS

★ If your possessions are being packed into a moving van in a dream, there are strong pressures for you to move; the larger the van, the more distant the move.

★ If you dream you are happy about the move, you will take with you happy memories and experiences to form the foundation for a new life.

★ If you see a van in the dream and are not planning or wanting to move, events in your life may carry you in a new direction.

★ If your partner is moving without you, or you without your partner in the dream, this could be a warning you may need to compromise or separate.

★ If everything will not fit in the van or items get broken during loading and unloading, this signifies possible regrets, depending on the items left behind or broken.

★ If you dream you are traveling in the van and cannot find the new home, you may have serious doubts that should be resolved before moving.

OUTCOME OF DESTINY'S DREAM

Destiny realized Jim would always regret it, and maybe blame her, if he did not follow his desire. Plans are afoot for the grandchildren to have wonderful long vacations on the site. Destiny enjoys running the bookings and office. Moving-van dreams bring up major questions regarding location and lifestyle changes.

Murder, Killing

Trevelyan, forty-eight, dreamed he was running through the darkness, pursued by a man with a knife. He could not outrun him. His only chance was to confront the murderer, seize the knife, and use it. He tackled the pursuer and called the police. Trevelyan looked into the face of the murderer and saw it was the man who had him unfairly dismissed from work because of his own wrongdoing.

DREAM BACKGROUND AND MEANING

Trevelyan was angry that he had been unfairly dismissed from work and that the man responsible, the real wrongdoer, was still working for the company. The person trying to murder the dreamer may represent a great wrong the dreamer has suppressed, maybe over years, but discovers in dreams the injustice that burns within.

INTERPRETATIONS AND FORTUNE-TELLING MEANINGS

★ If you dream you are committing murder, you may be trying to kill off a part of your life that has caused you pain.

★ If you are the victim, you may be afraid of someone more powerful or a situation threatening your identity, reputation, or personal freedom.

★ If you dream you are unfairly accused of murder, you should be careful of those you trust, who may blame you for their own omissions or misdeeds.

★ If you dream you are being executed for a murder, this may be a past-life dream and you may have met the same adversary in this life, who both attracts and repels you.

★ If you dream you are murdering or being murdered by someone close, such as a partner, there are underlying anger issues that need resolving before they spiral out of control.

OUTCOME OF TREVELYAN'S DREAM

Trevelyan realized that the murder of his reputation had to be resisted, and he made a claim against the company for unfair dismissal, citing the wrongdoer as the cause. A tribunal vindicated him, and he accepted compensation instead of getting his job back. Murder dreams should not be ignored, as they represent potential character assassination against you, or wrongs that need to be acknowledged.

Names

Violet Mary, twenty-eight, dreamed she was six and her mother was dressing her in frilly frocks with ribbons in her braids. At school she was subject to gibes about her name, and was called Sweet Violet Mary, originating from a popular song of the 1950s called "Sweet Violet." The teachers expected her to be sweet-natured. She grew tired of the teasing and punched one of the girls in the nose. She was sent home in disgrace.

DREAM BACKGROUND AND MEANING

Violet Mary was named after a great-aunt and had always hated her name, as she was teased mercilessly at school. When she left home she adopted the name "Vee." Recently she had been dreaming of her childhood teasing, as someone at work had seen her real name on an official document and had sarcastically called her "sweet Violet Mary." It spread around the office. Names radiate an image that may be at odds with how a person perceives themselves.

INTERPRETATIONS AND FORTUNE-TELLING MEANINGS

★ Changing one's name or acquiring a secret name in a dream reflects your authentic self.

★ If you dream you are using a name of power, this may reveal potential and hidden strengths.

★ Forgetting the names of significant people to whom you have previously been introduced suggests you are overwhelmed by too many people demanding your attention.

★ If someone is calling you rude names, often in a childhood or teen dream recurring years later, it reminds you that your identity and self-esteem have been dented by others' past unkindness.

★ If you dream of an affectionate nickname you no longer like, you have outgrown that phase.

★ If you dream you revisit the disliked name, it may hold advantages yet untapped.

OUTCOME OF VIOLET MARY'S DREAM

Since she could not punch her detractors, Vee left and started a candy store for adults called Sweet Violet Mary. She was very successful. What we call ourselves or others name us defines the energies we project.

Narrow Spaces, Narrow Ledges

Loretta, forty-five, dreamed she was a child again and had found a cave with a narrow opening. She squeezed through the gap, but inside it was pitch black, and she could not find the opening to get out. She panicked and screamed. Her brother, who was playing outside, shone his flashlight and put his hand through to guide Loretta out. But she never forgot the terror.

DREAM BACKGROUND AND MEANING

Loretta's dream was a rerun of a childhood experience, and she had had a fear of narrow spaces from that day on. As part of her training for the security services, Loretta had to crawl through a low narrow smoke-filled tunnel. She knew she would fail the test. A childhood or past-world experience can recur as a dream when a similar experience occurs in adult life.

INTERPRETATIONS AND FORTUNE-TELLING MEANINGS

★ Dreaming of being stuck or having to pass through a narrow passage can reflect fears of overcoming seemingly insurmountable restrictions in life.

★ Walking across a narrow ledge with a drop below represents surmounting a potentially confrontational work situation or relationship.

★ Dreaming of walking down narrow steps with a drop on either side is an insecurity dream of feeling unsupported.

★ Walking up narrow steps between high walls indicates the need to accept uncertainty and proceed cautiously to achieve a goal, advantage, or promotion.

★ Narrow paths warn of a person or situation restricting your progress, freedom, or free expression.

OUTCOME OF LORETTA'S DREAM

Loretta knew she had to pass the test to qualify for her desired career. She went to meditation classes and practiced breathing while she visualized the dream, until she could picture it without panicking. The dream changed and she was able to get out of the cave without giving way to fear. She still hated the test but succeeded by focusing on her breathing. Narrow-spaces dreams can rekindle primeval fears of being trapped if confined, and need to be acknowledged and so overcome.

Nature Trail

Clive, sixty-five, dreamed that the nature trail he had loved all his life was covered in garbage and barbed wire. He tried to remove the wire and clear the garbage, but he tore his hands. The garbage kept piling up. As he despaired, he saw a beautiful blue butterfly and woke filled with hope.

DREAM BACKGROUND AND MEANING

After the dream, Clive phoned the local council to complain that the trail was neglected. The council replied they could do nothing as the builder had acquired rights to the path for vehicle access to the estate. The hedgerows were full of wildflowers, birds, and small animals. Nature trails appear in dreams if they are under threat, or because they have significance in the dreamer's life.

INTERPRETATIONS AND FORTUNE-TELLING MEANINGS

* If you dream of a spoiled nature trail in its original beauty, there is hope it will be restored.
* If you dream you are shown a particular plant or wildlife on the trail, note it, as it may have significance in preserving the trail.
* If you dream of showing children its beauty, the trail will be shared by future generations.
* If the trail disappears in the dream, there will be a fight to preserve it, but a single plant remaining is a sign of future regeneration.
* An unknown nature trail reminds the dreamer to follow new pathways if life has become mundane.
* Dreaming of clearing a garbage-filled beautiful place tells the dreamer it is vital to fight for what is of worth.

OUTCOME OF CLIVE'S DREAM

Clive met a walker who was hunting a rare blue butterfly in the area. Clive showed him where they were found, and the butterfly enthusiast remarked that they were a protected species. Clive used that information to save the trail. He now takes local school parties on guided nature-trail walks in return for their clearing the litter. To a sensitive dreamer, dreams of nature trails reveal a unique quality that ensures their survival for future generations.

Near-Death Experience

Bobbie, thirty-three, dreamed she was traveling along a tunnel of light to a beautiful garden filled with flowers and heard choral music. Her grandmother, who had died ten years earlier, was waiting. Bobbie wanted to stay forever. But her grandmother told Bobbie that her children back on Earth and her husband needed her, and she woke in her hospital bed.

DREAM BACKGROUND AND MEANING

Bobbie had an operation that went wrong. During the operation she was clinically dead for a short time. She had what is called a *near-death experience*, when someone momentarily dies during an operation or at an accident scene. Descriptions of the experience are remarkably consistent, even among children, who may later identify a relative they have never met from a faded photo.

INTERPRETATIONS AND FORTUNE-TELLING MEANINGS

* If you experience a near-death dream, you may see angels or a deceased relative who sends you back or gives you the choice to return.
* A near-death experience changes a person so they lose fear of death and may seek a more meaningful life.
* You may have a life review when memories flash past as you float up the tunnel, enabling mistakes to be put right.
* You may sense that you are rising from your body and may see it below on the operating table or at the crash scene, and may be able to describe what could not have been viewed physically during consciousness.
* The near-death dream is far clearer and seems longer than ordinary dreams, though it may have lasted only a minute or two.
* The experience invariably involves a beautiful place where the dreamer experiences peace and happiness.

OUTCOME OF BOBBIE'S DREAM

After the experience, Bobbie gave up her high-powered job to spend more time with the family. Bobbie discovered a gift for art, a talent that her grandmother also had possessed. Near-death experiences, though rare, seem to affirm an afterlife.

Necklace

Celine, forty-two, dreamed she was wearing a pearl necklace, a family heirloom that had disappeared after her grandmother's death. Suddenly, her grandmother appeared and snapped the string. The pearls rolled everywhere. Her grandmother said she wished she had left everything to charity. Celine woke crying, with an overwhelming sense of her grandmother's presence.

DREAM BACKGROUND AND MEANING

After the death of Celine's grandmother, there was great family conflict over property, money, and jewelry because she had not made a will. The family members, once close, were no longer speaking and were threatening legal action against one another. Celine had remained silent, but everyone used to complain to her about the others. Necklaces represent honest, loving communication with partners, family members, and close friends.

INTERPRETATIONS AND FORTUNE-TELLING MEANINGS

* Dreaming of putting on or wearing a necklace indicates the need to speak out clearly to resolve an issue, as a necklace covers the throat's speech energy center.
* Wearing a family heirloom says this is a psychic dream, and the deceased owner of the necklace is communicating with the dreamer.
* A broken or lost necklace reflects or heralds a fixable family or marital quarrel.
* To be given a gold necklace signifies lasting love.
* Silver necklaces signify fertility, especially if there are difficulties conceiving.
* Pearl necklaces promise strengthening or restoring of family unity, as the pearls represent tears and regrets for unkind words spoken.

OUTCOME OF CELINE'S DREAM

Celine called a family meeting in which everyone was allowed to express an opinion while the others listened. Celine put forward a solution of equal division, saying that her grandmother had sent them a message in a dream, wishing she had left everything to charity. Shocked, the family reached an agreement. Some weeks later, the necklace, which had been missing since her grandmother's passing, was found in a drawer and was given to the youngest niece on her eighteenth birthday. Necklace dreams suggest gathering old or new friends or family who offer loyalty.

Neckties

Jacob, seventeen, dreamed he was going for an interview for his first job and his parents said he must wear a tie. He struggled to knot it and felt he was choking. On arriving at the interview room, he could not breathe and threw the tie in the garbage. All the other interviewees were wearing ties. He got the job because he was told he was a freethinker.

DREAM BACKGROUND AND MEANING

In fact, Jacob did not get the job, and he decided to start his own business where he could wear what he liked. He tried various ventures but failed. He had never worn a tie. Now he had an interview with an enterprise board for a business he was sure would succeed, but knew he had to dress smartly to impress them. Ties represent formality and conforming to obtain rewards at the cost of accepting social norms.

INTERPRETATIONS AND FORTUNE-TELLING MEANINGS

* To wear a tie in a dream represents doing things the world's way, which can be difficult for a freethinker.
* To wear a standard college, military, or company tie in a dream indicates accepting the values of others.
* To dream you put on a tie to go to work says you will rise in prestige.
* If in the dream you cannot fasten your tie properly and give up, you prefer to go your own way.
* Since tying can represent either being bound or made secure, your feelings in the dream suggest whether deep down you desire security.
* If you buy a tie, this indicates that a new financial commitment or loan will be worthwhile.

OUTCOME OF JACOB'S DREAM

Jacob compromised and wore a tie to meet the enterprise board and was praised for his smart appearance and by implication reliability, and he was given the grant. A tie is a small but significant sign to others of fitting in with the world.

Neighbors

Douglas, fifty-seven, dreamed of his neighbor's garden, which was filled with heaps of garbage, scaffolding, and noise, and saw his neighbor loading his car with suitcases. Douglas ran after the car, but his neighbor drove off.

DREAM BACKGROUND AND MEANING

Douglas had never had trouble with his rather unfriendly neighbor. Recently, Douglas had noticed a lot of builders' vans outside the large house, and builders walking around the garden. When Douglas asked his neighbor, he insisted he was getting estimates of some minor repairs. But Douglas was suspicious. Neighbors have an intimacy in our lives because of their physical proximity, at best based on friendship and emotional commitment to our well-being.

INTERPRETATIONS AND FORTUNE-TELLING MEANINGS

★ To dream of a friendly get-together with good neighbors indicates a settled phase in your community life and practical help and support from neighbors for mutually beneficial undertakings.

★ Dreams of neighborhood disputes or a court case warn of unsettled times ahead, needing careful negotiations for maintaining rights under threat.

★ If in a dream you see a neighbor peering into your window or mailbox, they are taking an unwarranted interest in your life and should be politely deterred.

★ If your neighbors move out in a dream, and ideal or nightmare new ones replace them, this may be a premonition, even if your present neighbors seem settled.

★ If in a dream your neighbors are spreading gossip about other neighbors, be aware that they are also talking about you behind your back.

★ If your neighbors are abusive in a dream, even if not currently so in your life, they may be planning changes to their property or lifestyle that are disadvantageous to you.

OUTCOME OF DOUGLAS'S DREAM

After the dream, Douglas contacted the planning department of his housing complex and discovered that his neighbor was planning to create multioccupancy high-rise apartments on his land. Douglas and the other immediate neighbors objected and blocked the development. Neighbor dreams can express doubts and worries that are repressed because of trying to keep the peace.

Nest

Trevor, fifty-two, dreamed of a nest swaying on its tree with a huge overgrown baby bird unbalancing the nest, its mouth opening and closing for food, which its mother could not offer fast enough. The male bird was sitting on a distant tree,  *but suddenly flew over and tipped the nest. The parents left the overgrown baby bird clinging on, until, seeing no rescue, it slowly extended its wings and flew away. A swaying nest suggests the structure is no longer safe or may be overloaded.*

DREAM BACKGROUND AND MEANING

Trevor was becoming increasingly angry with his twenty-two-year-old graduate son staying at home, expecting room service, and refusing to get a job. Jane, Trevor's wife, was reluctant to ask her son to leave, although Trevor and his wife were planning to sell the house and travel. Trevor was spending time away from home alone.

INTERPRETATIONS AND FORTUNE-TELLING MEANINGS

★ Dreams of birds making a nest suggest it is a good time to settle down and seek the right home.

★ Birds sitting on eggs indicate that a domestic situation is secure for now, but not permanently.

★ Newly hatched chicks being fed are symbols of fertility and of a welcoming, nurturing home.

★ If a bird leaves a half-finished nest, a desired home may not bring anticipated happiness.

★ Smashed eggs on the ground or eggs being stolen by a predator mark a situation that cannot be fixed and warn that further input will be wasted.

★ The dream of an empty nest indicates regrets by a parent for a family becoming independent and leaving home.

OUTCOME OF TREVOR'S DREAM

Trevor paid a deposit and three months' rent on a studio apartment for his son, on the condition that his son go to the employment agency and sort out his life. Trevor and Jane put their home on the market. While baby birds in nests represent domestic bliss, a dream of an overgrown baby bird shows it may be time for that baby to fly before the nest is destroyed.

Nettles

Rosie, thirty-two, dreamed she was pushed and fell into a huge bed of nettles. She screamed but, to her amazement, she was not hurt. Her boyfriend, Josh, appeared and helped her climb out. Rosie recognized her assailant as her best friend, Sara. Sara insisted that it was Josh who had pushed Rosie into the nettles. Rosie did not know what to believe.

DREAM BACKGROUND AND MEANING

Sara told Rosie that Josh was cheating on her. Josh had strayed once, but Rosie knew he was sorry, and she trusted him to not do it again. The nettle dream she understood as Sara's jealousy, as she did not have a boyfriend, but not being stung was strange. Traditionally, if nettles you touch do not sting you, you will be protected from someone attacking your love or spreading false rumors.

INTERPRETATIONS AND FORTUNE-TELLING MEANINGS

- ★ If you dream of a nettle bed in your path, this is a sign you should protect yourself or a vulnerable family member from potential spite or bullying.
- ★ If nettles are growing in the garden, your home and family are safe, so you should not worry as they are a symbol of defense against harm.
- ★ If you are stung by nettles, beware that someone close to you at work, or a friend or neighbor, is spreading malicious gossip.
- ★ Hidden nettles in the grass advise you to check financial or business investments for hidden hazards.
- ★ If you dream you are cutting down nettles, it's time to take decisive action to quell rumors and misinformation that are causing unnecessary loss of trust.

OUTCOME OF ROSIE'S DREAM

After the dream, Rosie told Josh what Sara was saying, and he told Rosie that Sara had been messaging him, saying Rosie was cheating. He showed Rosie the evidence. Rosie dropped Sara as a friend. Nettle dreams recall the popular expression "grasping the nettle." Once doubts or rumors are confronted head-on, they can be either dismissed or acted upon.

New Year's Eve

Mike, sixty-four, dreamed it was New Year's Eve, and he and his wife and family were celebrating with one of their special parties for friends and neighbors. The only person who never joined in was the man opposite they called "the Hermit." But they just laughed and carried on. Then Mike woke to realize he was alone.

DREAM BACKGROUND AND MEANING

Mike's children were busy, and he was separated from his wife. His friends had drifted away, and for the first time he dreaded witnessing the celebrations. New Year's Eve is a great time for joy in the year ahead, but it can also be a sad reminder of what has been lost.

INTERPRETATIONS AND FORTUNE-TELLING MEANINGS

- ★ To dream of happy New Year's celebrations is a symbol of good luck in the year ahead.
- ★ If you dream of friends and family sharing New Year's Eve and you are not with them, it is time to send out invitations and maybe an olive branch or two.
- ★ If in the dream you are sweeping the doorstep and removing the old clutter on New Year's Eve, you are opening the way for new energies in the year ahead.
- ★ If, however, you are putting out garbage or sweeping up on New Year's Day, be careful not to squander the opportunities ahead.
- ★ It is said that whatever you dream of doing on New Year's Eve will become your main priority in the year ahead.

OUTCOME OF MIKE'S DREAM

Mike did not want to celebrate, but he saw the twitching of the curtains of the man who lived opposite and on impulse knocked on his door. He suggested they go to the local pub together. Mike had a surprisingly good time and learned that his neighbor was just shy but was good company. Dreams of New Year's Eve can awaken a desire to welcome the coming year, maybe in a new way.

Nomads

Mack, sixty-five, dreamed he was sitting on a mountain of red earth in the Australian Outback, watching the sun set. Below he could see a circle of camper vans and people around an open fire. He often came there in his dreams, and after sunset he would return to the camp, where other travelers were waiting to share their food.

DREAM BACKGROUND AND MEANING

Mack lived in the center of Melbourne, but when he retired he planned to sell up, buy a van, and travel as one of the "gray nomads"—Australian retirees who travel for weeks or months at a time. Now this plan was more urgent because he was slowly losing his sight and had only a couple of years left when he would be able to drive. A nomadic lifestyle represents the chance to experience freedom from the constraints of convention, often later in life.

INTERPRETATIONS AND FORTUNE-TELLING MEANINGS

★ If you dream that you keep seeing the same van or boat and locations you have not visited, the open spaces are calling you.

★ If you have a conventional life but dream of the open road, you may need more unstructured vacations to learn if you want a temporary or more permanent life change.

★ If you dream of a traditional nomadic people in the modern world, their culture and lifestyle may have a message for you.

★ If you have family and a partner but are alone in your nomadic dream, you or they may have become out of touch with one another.

★ If you dream that your vehicle breaks down in the middle of the desert and there is no help in sight, the idea of freedom may be more appealing than the reality.

★ If you dream that you are hijacked or kidnapped on the road, someone may be trying to restrict your future.

OUTCOME OF MACK'S DREAM

Mack realized it was now or never to experience those beautiful wild places while he was physically able. He rented out his home and set off with no fixed plans to return. Nomad dreams herald an inner free spirit.

Noon

Stuart, thirty-eight, dreamed he was racing across the desert on foot to reach the oasis where he knew treasure was buried, and that others were seeking to get there first. He threw off his sun hat and even abandoned his tent and water container so he could move unencumbered. But as the heat increased and the sun blazed down, he became weak and collapsed in sight of the oasis, seeing others already there who had traveled more slowly.

DREAM BACKGROUND AND MEANING

Stuart was a senior executive aiming for the CEO position before he was forty. He never switched off his work phone or took vacations. Recently, he had been feeling extremely tired and was worried he was losing his edge and would be overtaken by his rivals. If you are in the blazing desert heat in your dream, beware that you do not suffer burnout from 24/7 exposure to the fast lane in life.

INTERPRETATIONS AND FORTUNE-TELLING MEANINGS

★ Dreams of the noonday sun indicate moving into a powerful time of life, often during the middle years.

★ Standing bathed in brilliant noonday sunshine in a dream speaks of major success or recognition coming soon.

★ If you hear a clock striking twelve, the window of opportunity is close but will not last forever.

★ If it is cloudy at noon, beware of rivals stealing your glory or sabotaging your efforts.

★ If it becomes hotter in your dream after noon, you are moving toward the 3 p.m. peak, so conserve energy rather than expending it all at noon.

OUTCOME OF STUART'S DREAM

Stuart stayed up all night before an interview for the next promotion, studying the latest projections. He closed his eyes for half an hour, having set all his alarms, but was so exhausted that he slept through them. He was late for the interview and was flustered because he had rushed through the noonday heat. He was not offered the post. Noonday dreams herald leadership and success but also represent obsession with success, which can cause downfall.

North Star (Pole Star)

Philippa, nineteen, dreamed she was in a coracle guided by the North Star, exiled from Old Ireland because she would not become a Christian. She floated toward the Northern Isles of Scotland and was taken in, half-drowned, by a family whose eldest son she married.

DREAM BACKGROUND AND MEANING

Philippa's family had lived in Boston for more than two hundred years. She knew nothing about her ancestry except that there were Celtic or Gaelic roots. Then she met Charlie from the Scottish Northern Isles. He felt so familiar that she agreed to move into his home with him. Her family tried to persuade her to stay, but to no avail. The North Star carries a magick unlike any other star as a true guide to what may be only inner promptings.

INTERPRETATIONS AND FORTUNE-TELLING MEANINGS

* ★ To dream of following the North Star over water in the Northern Hemisphere says you will reach your goal if you do not waver.
* ★ Seeing the North Star in a dream signifies coming good fortune.
* ★ Because it symbolized the direction of freedom to enslaved African Americans in the southern United States, it is often regarded as a symbol of liberation.
* ★ Since the North Star mythologically marks the top of the world tree, the axis of the world, seeing it through the branches of a tall tree is a spiritual dream, connecting with wise ancestors.
* ★ If the North Star suddenly dims, beware of being tempted off course by others.

OUTCOME OF PHILIPPA'S DREAM

When Philippa reached Charlie's land, she instantly felt at home. Curious, she went to the local history museum to research her name and found that people of that name had emigrated from a nearby island and were never heard of again. She tracked down one or two distant relatives and reconnected her mother with her past. Dreams of the North Star occur at a time when significant travel is indicated.

Nuclear Plant

In a recurring dream, Brenda, sixty-five, heard a massive explosion from the nearby nuclear plant. She looked out of the window and saw fire all around as far as the eye could see. She frantically ran around the house looking for her daughter and grandchildren, who lived with her, but they were nowhere to be found. She woke in a cold sweat.

DREAM BACKGROUND AND MEANING

Since Brenda's husband had recently passed away, her domineering though well-meaning daughter Edwina had suggested they buy a house together. The house on which Edwina had set her heart was less than ten miles away from a nuclear plant. This worried Brenda, as accidents could happen and toxic fallout from such sites had been implicated in long-term illness. Nuclear plants may move an emotionally toxic problem out of view but do not solve it.

INTERPRETATIONS AND FORTUNE-TELLING MEANINGS

* ★ If you live near a nuclear plant and frequently dream of fires or leaks, these are anxiety dreams picking up negative energies from the land.
* ★ If you have an urgent one-off dream, you should remain vigilant and check safety precautions at home.
* ★ If you dream of a nuclear plant being built near your home, you may fear that your present lifestyle will be disturbed by others' control and intrusion.
* ★ If you are protesting about the opening of a nuclear plant, you may need to deal with a problem from the past that still affects you.
* ★ If you dream of a nuclear plant being shut down, toxic neighbors or work colleagues may move out of your life.

OUTCOME OF BRENDA'S DREAM

After the dream, there was a minor fire at the plant. More importantly, Brenda realized that living with her controlling daughter was fraught with problems. They bought two separate homes where the air was pure. Dreaming of nuclear waste reflects the need to move away from toxic or emotionally sensitive situations, rather than hoping they will go away.

Nudist

Leanne, twenty-nine, dreamed she and her new partner, Joannie, went on vacation. A few minutes after arriving, Leanne saw that Joannie had taken off her clothes, and a lot of Joannie's friends, who Leanne did not know, were also nude. They crowded around Leanne, who backed away, embarrassed. Joannie said Leanne was a prude. Leanne left.

DREAM BACKGROUND AND MEANING

Leanne had known that Joannie was enthusiastic about nudism, but she had made it clear that she would not be joining in. Joannie was planning a vacation for them at a nudist resort and Leanne did not want to go, but Joannie insisted that she would love it when she got there. Nudist dreams are significant in a relationship where there are different views of appropriate intimacy.

INTERPRETATIONS AND FORTUNE-TELLING MEANINGS

★ If in your dream you are enjoying being on vacation without clothes, you may want to shed inhibitions and reveal your real self.

★ If a nudist dream becomes a nightmare, you may have a strong sense of privacy and should not be pressured to reveal any more of your personal feelings than you are comfortable offering.

★ If you are pressured in a dream to visit a nudist club, be aware of the motives of the person pressuring you.

★ If you dream of finding yourself in a nudist resort by mistake, you may be feeling vulnerable if relative strangers are encroaching on your daily life.

★ If you are aroused in the dream by being nude with people you know, there may be someone with whom you would like to sexually connect.

★ If you dream you are chased from a beach for not wearing clothes, you may face disapproval in your life for being your true self.

OUTCOME OF LEANNE'S DREAM

Leanne explained to Joannie that for her, her body was something to be shared with those you love, and that nudism debased that personal intimacy between them. Nudist dreams can reveal deeper issues of trust that go beyond whether or not clothes are worn.

Numbers

Fiona, thirty-four, dreamed she was adding together the number values of her birth name to find her lucky number using this formula: A = 1, B = 2, C = 3, D = 4, E = 5, F = 6, G = 7, H = 8, I = 9, J = 1, K = 2, L = 3, M = 4, N = 5, O = 6, P = 7, Q = 8, R = 9, S = 1, T = 2, U = 3, V = 4, W = 5, X = 6, Y = 7, Z = 8. Her total number came to 29. By adding the 2 and the 9 she got 11; finally, she added 1 and 1 to equal 2, the number of balance and harmony. But Fiona wanted to be viewed as dynamic. Then her middle name changed into her first name, and she ended up with 9, the number of action, power, and change. She woke full of confidence.

DREAM BACKGROUND AND MEANING

Fiona's birth name brought out her compliant, eager-to-please persona. She felt unnoticed at work and too shy to ask the guy she met at the gym on a date. Dreams can reveal the birth numbers that resonate with who we are at our core.

INTERPRETATIONS AND FORTUNE-TELLING MEANINGS

★ Certain numbers repeated three times in dreams and then seen in daily life, such as the Master Numbers 11, 22, and 33, or the traditionally lucky 7, indicate good times ahead.

★ If you consistently dream of a particular sequence of numbers, are these lotto or gaming numbers? They may be a sign from a guardian or deceased relative of winning numbers.

★ If numbers are seen behind dollar, pound sterling, or other currency signs, the higher the numbers, the more money coming your way.

★ If you dream of the number 1, this indicates a new beginning and leadership; 2, harmony; 3, prosperity; 4, property; 5, healing and business.

★ If 6 (forget the negative 666 meaning), it indicates love and friendship; 7, fertility, good fortune, and psychic powers; 8, transformation; 9, courage and victory.

★ If you see a million or billion, it's time to speculate or invest.

★ A house with your lucky number is favorable if you are house-hunting.

OUTCOME OF FIONA'S DREAM

Fiona officially changed her middle name to her first name and became more confident. The guy at the gym had the same name number, promising compatibility. Dreams can often reveal both lucky and compatible numbers.

Nursing

Vernon, twenty-one, dreamed his father was seriously unfit and collapsed on his building site. He gave his father emergency treatment and stayed with him until he was admitted to the hospital. The consultant told Vernon's father he might have died before the ambulance arrived had Vernon not known what to do.

DREAM BACKGROUND AND MEANING

Vernon was studying first aid in his spare time, as he wanted to become an emergency nurse. His father said men shouldn't be nurses, so Vernon joined his father's building firm to keep the peace. Dreams of nursing and saving lives, if you are or wish to become a nurse, confirm the rightness of your choice.

INTERPRETATIONS AND FORTUNE-TELLING MEANINGS

★ If you dream you are a nurse in an old-fashioned hospital, this may be a past-life dream.

★ To be a nurse in a present-day setting says you have a talent for the caring professions.

★ To be cared for by a nurse in the dream is an indication that too many people are demanding your attention.

★ To be incredibly overworked as a nurse says you are trying to be all things to all people.

★ If you are one of several nurses trying to care for the same patient, there may be family rivalries to control a particular family member.

★ If you dream you faint or are sick at the sight of blood, your intentions may outweigh what you can offer to revive an ailing relationship or crisis.

OUTCOME OF VERNON'S DREAM

Vernon instinctively felt his father was unwell and took him to the physician, who admitted him to the hospital, as he was on the verge of having a stroke. His father withdrew his opposition to Vernon's training as a nurse after he received excellent care from nurses of both sexes in the hospital. Nursing dreams alert the dreamer to persuade a family member taken ill in the dream to seek medical advice before a problem becomes acute.

Oak Tree

Perdita, thirty, dreamed she was planting an acorn in her garden, though she knew an oak tree would take many years to grow. To her amazement, a tree immediately started to spring up, tall and green. She felt protected, as though she needed no one.

DREAM BACKGROUND AND MEANING

Perdita had moved out of army accommodations after her husband had mailed her from an overseas posting to say he had met someone else and wanted a divorce. After receiving a grant, Perdita bought a tumbledown pottery studio with living accommodations in order to renovate and market her historic clay reproductions. But since it was the first time she had ever lived alone, she was scared, especially as there was much to rebuild. Planting an acorn represents a successful long-term move, investment, or creative venture. The oak's speed of growth in the dream provided double assurance.

INTERPRETATIONS AND FORTUNE-TELLING MEANINGS

★ If you are in a grove of oaks, this magical tree, sacred to the Celtic Druids, assures success in long-term study or by following a traditional path, rather than by innovation.

★ A single thriving oak represents a wise man or woman whose advice you should take, or resolution of official or legal matters.

★ A tree mythologically said to resist storms, the oak indicates you have the strength to overcome challenges if you do not doubt the rightness of your path.

★ The oak promises growing prosperity through secure ventures that will continue to grow.

★ If you dream that an oak is diseased or dead, seemingly trustworthy support may prove unreliable.

★ Dreaming of an oak tree in winter, stripped of leaves, advises choosing independence rather than accepting help that brings restrictions.

OUTCOME OF PERDITA'S DREAM

The dream assured Perdita that she was on the right track, that her decision was the right one, and that she had a secure future and needed no one else in order to succeed. Oak-tree dreams almost always reassure that you can stand independently through your own efforts.

Oasis

Bill, twenty-five, dreamed he was exhausted, and walking through the desert. But ahead was an oasis with silken tents, and he was greeted as an honored guest, having his every need met. Suddenly, the Bedouin chief told Bill to clean and feed the camels. Bill was horrified. Everything disappeared and he was at a dried-up water hole.

DREAM BACKGROUND AND MEANING

Bill was unemployed because he was seeking the perfect job in television. He had been rejected by major broadcasters and had lived at home since leaving college.

He had been offered a role in a three-person cable company as general assistant. But Bill considered this a waste of his talents. His father said he had a month to get a job or he would be homeless. Oasis dreams can connect with past lives, assuring you that you can overcome present difficulties.

INTERPRETATIONS AND FORTUNE-TELLING MEANINGS

★ If you dream the oasis is a mirage, do not trust a cheap offer or loan with incredibly low interest rates without checking details.

★ Finding an oasis after wandering lost through the desert indicates that whatever is most lacking in your life—love, money, career success, a new home, or travel—will soon appear.

★ If you dream of romancing in a modern oasis resort, the person with you, known or unknown, can offer lasting love.

★ If the water in the oasis has dried up, your current objective may not materialize.

★ If you decide to live at the oasis, you may be idealizing a perfect future home, career, or ideal person and not making the most of the here and now.

OUTCOME OF BILL'S DREAM

Bill realized that his father was serious and so reluctantly accepted the offer. He learned everything, from making good coffee, to production, to presenting. As a result, he was able to get a job in a larger company's training program in production. Oasis dreams are often about mirages and ideals and assist the dreamer in separating the two.

Observatory

Caitlin, nineteen, dreamed she was looking through a giant telescope as the stars and constellations wheeled overhead. The observatory was made totally of glass, like a giant bubble, and below her she could see endless stars and Earth. The observatory was static, but the galaxies wheeled around. Caitlin was totally alone, completely happy, and wished the dream would last forever.

DREAM BACKGROUND AND MEANING

Her dream is sometimes called a "peak experience dream," in which we are totally in harmony with ourselves and the cosmos. Caitlin had quit art college and was living in a small studio at the back of her mother's house, wondering what was next. She loved the stars, using them to inspire pottery, star people statues, and other art.

INTERPRETATIONS AND FORTUNE-TELLING MEANINGS

★ To dream of being in an observatory is a sign that you will gain momentary or longer-lasting fame or celebrity status.

★ Explaining the stars to an audience indicates that you could become an astronomer or astrologer, or could obtain a job in the media or creative arts.

★ Being in a glass observatory in outer space is an astral dream involving mind travel or time travel.

★ If you dream that you are in an observatory on a strange planet, you may always have felt different and may be a star soul visiting home.

★ If skies are cloudy, you may experience doubts and uncertainty. Hold on.

★ If you dream that you discover a new star, planet, or galaxy, new opportunities and perspectives will soon be open to you.

OUTCOME OF CAITLIN'S DREAM

Caitlin's amazing dream stopped her from worrying about the future. She obtained a youth enterprise loan, bought a cheap camper van, and traveled to craft fairs, selling the star-inspired pottery, photos, and paintings of the night skies that she had been creating since she quit art college. While Caitlin did not make an instant fortune, her dream inspired her. Caitlin often camped in the wilderness to track the stars. Observatory dreams reflect new perspectives and that you are part of the wider picture.

Obsessive-Compulsive Disorder

Lottie, forty-two, dreamed that each time she finished cleaning the kitchen there was more mess than when she had started. She was in a frenzy because her sister, who was equally meticulous, was coming to lunch. Just as her sister arrived, Lottie spilled a jar of sugar all over the floor. She pretended to not be home.

DREAM BACKGROUND AND MEANING

Lottie and her sister had been brought up by their late mother to believe cleanliness was next to godliness. Lottie was a frenetic cleaner, haranguing her husband for leaving a wet towel on the bathroom floor. He accused her of being obsessive and told her she should see a doctor. But she was worried about germs in the doctor's office. Recurring dreams about keeping a house clean may reveal anxieties bordering on obsessiveness.

INTERPRETATIONS AND FORTUNE-TELLING MEANINGS

* Dreams of a house becoming dirty no matter how hard you try to clean are insecurity dreams reflecting a fear of losing control over the family, a partner, or finances.
* If you dream of being locked in a cycle of repeating actions ritually, this may alert you to similar actions in daily life.
* Dreaming of being in a germ-warfare laboratory reflects a fear that you or loved ones may catch germs and illnesses due to poor hygiene.
* If in a dream someone is sabotaging your efforts to clean, you may resent their presence in your life.
* If your home is dirty or messy in a dream, you may have had impossibly high standards imposed on you in childhood.
* If in a dream you or your family are wearing dirty clothes, you may fear being labeled a bad mother or a neglectful partner.

OUTCOME OF LOTTIE'S DREAM

After the dream, Lottie realized she and her sister were bordering on obsession. She found a job cleaning other people's houses and as a result is more relaxed about her own domestic standards. Obsessive-compulsive dreams often contain guilt about past inadequacies or failures, whether actual or imagined.

Octopus

Lionel, forty-eight, dreamed he was swimming in a reef, his favorite relaxation, when he saw a group of octopuses. One was attempting to tangle the tentacles of the central octopus, pulled off one of the central octopus's tentacles, and swam away with it, leaving the central one unable to swim.

DREAM BACKGROUND AND MEANING

Lionel was working on a joint project at work, but it was going nowhere. Data seemed to be changed overnight and crucial facts went missing. Lionel's boss was becoming impatient and was questioning Lionel's competence. Lionel noticed that whenever one team member was absent, things ran smoothly. Yet the guy seemed helpful. Lionel was suspicious.

INTERPRETATIONS AND FORTUNE-TELLING MEANINGS

* If you dream that the octopus squirts ink at you, someone is concealing their emotions and their intentions.
* If the tentacles of a giant octopus are entangling you, you should distance yourself from emotional blackmail or overpossessiveness and maybe leave a secure but stifling situation.
* If the octopus is swimming through clear water, then it's a time when multitasking is needed.
* If you dream an octopus tries to crush you, take action against someone who is intimidating you by groping you at work or socially.
* A number of octopuses swimming in the same direction indicates that you will find the right people to help with a joint endeavor.
* If they are swimming in different directions or attacking you, current help may prove counterproductive and may involve different agendas or even sabotage.

OUTCOME OF LIONEL'S DREAM

Lionel did what he never usually did—he looked on the computer of the guy who he suspected. There were all the missing data and the original correct work, formed into an alternative project, obviously to be presented to the boss after the guy discredited Lionel. Lionel showed the boss the evidence. The guy was dismissed, and the project ran smoothly to completion. Octopus dreams often involve entanglements that need to be understood, whether strangleholds, friendships, loves, or attacks.

Offering

In his dream, Jimmy, forty-five, was touring the Far East, seeking a site for building a tourist resort. He found a perfect location with a small golden Buddha surrounded by a village of small houses and rice fields. His guide said the same families had farmed for centuries but could be bought off cheaply. On Buddha's offerings table, Jimmy, with no flowers or fruit to give, left his gold watch. Instantly a monk appeared, gave Jimmy fruit to offer, and returned his watch, saying, "We need only tributes of the heart." Jimmy awoke feeling cleansed and at peace.

DREAM BACKGROUND AND MEANING

For the first time, Jimmy had become disturbed about his materially focused lifestyle. He realized he could compensate the villagers but feared he would be destroying a traditional way of life (see "Buddha," p. 73). An offering in a dream marks a need to stop and reflect on what is being sought and what is promised in its place.

INTERPRETATIONS AND FORTUNE-TELLING MEANINGS

★ If you dream of a sacred statue, the dream may be questioning if you have lost sight of meaning in exchange for material acquisitions.

★ If you dream you are making an offering at a public shrine, ask if what you are offering is of value to you and why.

★ If you meet a significant figure at a shrine or the focal statue gives you a message, you are contacting a higher source for an answer.

★ If your shrine icon is small, grandiose plans need to be set in the context of people who will be affected by your project.

★ If you dream you revive a neglected shrine, you may be able to restore life and purpose to a personal or even commercial venture to add spiritual value.

OUTCOME OF JIMMY'S DREAM

Jimmy became much more thoughtful about areas he was changing, introducing education programs and welfare facilities and making sure that no one lost the means to support their family. An offering does not depend on its material value but on the pledge made as an honorable exchange for favors sought.

Oil Spill

Pammie, fifty, dreamed she found a seabird on the shore, covered in oil and barely alive. As she followed the deserted shoreline toward the cave where the seabirds nested, she noticed oil on the sand. Inside the cave was a barrel of oil that had split on the rocks and was covering the nesting birds.

DREAM BACKGROUND AND MEANING

Pammie was a warden on an island bird sanctuary just off the Irish coast. There had been problems, as overseas tankers had been mooring near the island, jeopardizing the safety of the seabirds.

INTERPRETATIONS AND FORTUNE-TELLING MEANINGS

★ If you dream that there is an oil spill in the ocean and seabirds are covered in it, someone in your daily life is abusing their wealth, status, and power.

★ If in the dream your boat is leaking oil into the water, take precautions in everyday life to plug a financial hole or wasted resource.

★ If you dream you are trying to clear up spilled oil anywhere, you will be asked to sort out problems not of your making.

★ If you dream that oil spills over your hands, do not take the blame for others' carelessness.

★ If you are cleaning up the results of a major oil spill, you are more powerful than you realize in making a difference to environmental issues.

★ If you are organizing volunteers, seek support in causes that matter to you, whether in the environment, workplace, or community.

OUTCOME OF PAMMIE'S DREAM

Pammie checked, and all the nests were safe. However, there was a barrel of crude oil on the island shore that could have easily split open. She confronted the councilors at the next meeting and, while denying they had given permission for the change, the ships moored near the island no more. Dreams can cut through falsehood by alerting the dreamer to information not accessible to the dreamer's consciousness, in this case with a protective purpose.

Olives

Suzy, thirty-six, dreamed she searched from store to store for olive oil, but there was none. She wanted to cook her ex-husband's favorite meal, as he was coming for dinner to discuss the future. She went home. To her amazement, an olive tree full of fruit was growing in the garden. Her husband arrived and together they created enough olive oil for dinner. Afterward he gave her a silver brooch with tiny jade stones, representing growing olives. He told her he had booked a vacation to their honeymoon destination, an olive farm in California. She woke, sad that he was not there.

DREAM BACKGROUND AND MEANING

Suzy and her husband, Jeff, had been separated for three months. She missed him and knew he missed her. Olive dreams are full of hope and are a good omen if there is estrangement.

INTERPRETATIONS AND FORTUNE-TELLING MEANINGS

* To dream of eating olives (if you like them) foretells happy parties, gatherings, and vacations, especially to sunny places.
* If an olive branch brushes your face, there will soon be reconciliation with an estranged family member, lover, or close friend.
* If you dream of olive trees bearing ripe fruit, you will gain rewards and recognition for previous hard work. They are a good symbol of fertility.
* If olive trees are empty or olives are crushed on the ground, you need to revive a missed business opportunity or moneymaking venture.
* If you dream you are making olive oil, poor health and emotional worries will disappear.
* If you dream that you share sweet olives with someone, that relationship will flourish. If they are sour, the relationship needs compromise to survive.

OUTCOME OF SUZY'S DREAM

Suzy booked a make-or-break holiday on the olive farm where they had honeymooned. She and Jeff revived an abandoned joint passion to buy an olive farm, making their own produce. Dreaming about olives suggests that solutions can be extracted from the dream of moneymaking with those sharing a vision.

Olympics

Rob, forty-four, dreamed he was competing in an Olympic race, dressed in a white toga-like garment. Everyone said he had great talent. He raced ahead, but a fellow competitor deliberately tripped him. Furious, Rob leapt up, raced to the winning post, and received a gold medal.

DREAM BACKGROUND AND MEANING

Rob was a teacher who, with a number of his colleagues, had applied for the position of deputy head of the school. Rob recognized his rivals in the dream race. The one who tripped him always seemed to denigrate Rob when they were in the company of the head teacher. Rob had never worried about that until the dream. Olympic and general sporting dreams occur when there is real-life competition or serious opposition, and they are a good omen for the dreamer.

INTERPRETATIONS AND FORTUNE-TELLING MEANINGS

* If you dream you are entering the Olympics, you are seriously competing in some area of your life where there may be hidden aggression in others.
* If there is fierce competition and others are pushing or jostling in the dream, beware of unfair competition.
* If you dream you are carrying the Olympic torch, you have a desire for a person or cause that will be realized if you keep trying.
* If you win a medal, you will gain recognition for an achievement.
* If you lose a race or Olympic competition, do not allow others to destroy your confidence in your own talents.
* If you dream of white-clad athletes, you may be linking to the old Olympic world and may find yourself in competition with people you now know who you knew in a past life.
* If you dream you are practicing for the Olympics, keep trying in whatever aspect of your life you most want to succeed, as your chances of success are excellent.

OUTCOME OF ROB'S DREAM

Rob was alerted to the fact that his dream rival would try to disrupt his equilibrium in the group interview that the applicants had with the head teacher and board of governors. Rob was polite but assertive and obtained the post. Olympic dreams are a reassurance that if you let no one or nothing distract you, you can succeed.

Onions

Beryl, sixty, dreamed of being a child in fields of onions in Spain. The men were carrying onions in strings on their backs. An older woman gave Beryl a doll with a black mantilla and a flamenco dress. Beryl woke feeling a connection with the people in the fields.

DREAM BACKGROUND AND MEANING

Beryl remembered her father taking her to the annual onion fair when families from Spain went to the UK Midland town where she lived, sold their onions, had sideshows, and did flamenco dancing. One year, her father won her a doll with a mantilla and flamenco dress. It was the last time they went. Beryl's father recently had died. Her mother had dementia and was in a nursing home. Beryl's father was Spanish but never spoke of his family. Onions are primarily a domestic symbol and can form a timeless link with members of subsequent family generations.

INTERPRETATIONS AND FORTUNE-TELLING MEANINGS

★ Dreaming of cooking onions, especially white ones, speaks of removing obstacles and dispelling domestic disputes.

★ Red onions in dreams represent passionate love and male virility.

★ Eating onions says that poor health concerning yourself or a family member will soon disappear.

★ If someone is peeling onions and crying, the feelings they express can be superficial.

★ Dreaming of peeling an onion layer by layer says you may need to probe deep to get to the truth of a matter.

★ Planting onions with shoots is a symbol of future prosperity.

OUTCOME OF BERYL'S DREAM

On impulse, Beryl took her childhood doll to show her mother who, in a rare lucid moment, told Beryl she had met her late father at the onion fair when he came with his family to sell onions. He stayed with Beryl's mother, but his family cast him out. Every year he went to the onion fair with Beryl. Beryl decided it was too late to trace her Spanish family. Onions with their multiple layers can represent family secrets that may one day be revealed.

Online Dating

Pam, fifty-five, dreamed she was waiting for the handsome ex-captain she met online to take her to their new ranch. Getting no answer on his phone, she phoned the website on which they had first made contact. She saw a scruffy office with men crouched over computers. Her bank details were on the screen of an old ugly man. She woke, panicking.

DREAM BACKGROUND AND MEANING

Pam had been dating online for many months and intended to buy a small ranch with the man of her dreams. He had apparently been detained overseas because of a disputed family inheritance, delaying their wedding. Pam was told there were numerous expenses, which she had been paying until his money was freed up. Online dating dreams pick up information hidden or consciously ignored.

INTERPRETATIONS AND FORTUNE-TELLING MEANINGS

★ If you dream you see your real-life partner on a dating site, you may be insecure due to lack of attention.

★ If you dream of an online guy or gal having dinner with your family or in mundane settings, this could be the one.

★ If you dream that your online date is wearing a mask, check their identity on social media.

★ If the screen flickers on and off or you can't hear their words clearly, the online date may be married or be multiple-dating.

★ If you dream that your online date is commanding a regiment in battle, take a reality check if your date claims elevated status.

★ If you dream that you are marrying your online date on a tropical island, make plans to meet in a safe, mundane setting to reassure yourself that the fairy tale is true.

OUTCOME OF PAM'S DREAM

When she woke, Pam checked the details of the ranch. She discovered it was a piece of unsold, abandoned land. She contacted her bank and stopped the transfer of her remaining savings to a foreign-owned company. Though many romances flourish on dating sites, online dating dreams advise you to use caution before parting with your heart or savings.

Online Sales

Toby, thirty-one, dreamed that an online company had offered to market his custom-built calculators for the visually impaired. After receiving no orders, he saw cheap substandard versions on sale by the same company. Unable to afford to sue them, he woke feeling cheated.

DREAM BACKGROUND AND MEANING

Toby was having problems marketing his new product via his website. A large online sales company had offered to market his product in return for a 30 percent profit share. He hesitated, as he considered their commission excessive. Online sales dreams can open doors to a wider market, but extreme caution is advised.

INTERPRETATIONS AND FORTUNE-TELLING MEANINGS

★ If you dream of selling products or services online, you should expand an existing face-to-face commercial or creative venture by advertising or increasing advertising on the Internet.

★ If you successfully launch a new website in your dream, this is a good time for marketing an original product internationally.

★ If your online sales in the dream increase as part of a global sales website, you would benefit from joining forces.

★ If your dream online business fails, concentrate on face-to-face communications.

★ If in your dream you buy from a commercial site and are sent something inferior, do not trust people you do not know.

★ If in your dream you are head of a major online sales organization, remain undeterred if initially the odds seem against you.

OUTCOME OF TOBY'S DREAM

Toby found another online agent, which was prepared to take 10 percent of every sale through its site. Toby was able to maintain total control. Though he initially made less money, he was able to build up his online business. Online sales dreams can refer to commercial or financial enterprises using online advertising, but they raise questions if an expanding customer base can be achieved without surrendering control.

Open Relationship

Candace, thirty, dreamed she was at a swingers' party. She was approached by a man who invited her into one of the rooms with him. They made love for the rest of the evening. When Candace awoke, she and her live-in partner, Jeff, experienced the best lovemaking for months.

DREAM BACKGROUND AND MEANING

Candace and Jeff were living in an apartment paid for by Candace's wealthy parents, who also had given them a new car and subsidized expensive holidays. Candace was sexually dissatisfied, as Jeff had lost interest. Candace felt if they each enjoyed sexual encounters outside their relationship, the excitement would return to them. Sometimes dreams of open relationships are enough to stimulate fantasies to spice up an existing relationship.

INTERPRETATIONS AND FORTUNE-TELLING MEANINGS

★ If you dream of an open relationship and you know the third person well, there may be temptations to stray emotionally as well as sexually.

★ If you dream you are making love with a stranger at a party, examine what is missing in your current sex life, and see if you can put it right without adding extra complications.

★ If in a dream you and your partner are happily participating in a swingers' party, a more open sex life may bring more excitement and fantasy if your sex life has become routine.

★ If your dream of swinging ends disastrously, there may be underlying insecurity issues in your current relationship that need resolving.

★ If you dream that your partner is participating and you are not, is that person making you feel undesirable or flirting as a means of control?

★ If you are participating and your partner is not, are you outgrowing the relationship or feeling neglected?

OUTCOME OF CANDACE'S DREAM

Jeff was horrified at Candace's suggestion and for the first time spoke of his unhappiness that they were constantly subsidized by her parents, as that made him feel inadequate in every way. She realized their lack of sex life was a symptom of Jeff's loss of confidence. Frequent sexually explicit dreams need careful examination to see whether a quick sexual fix is the answer or the problem is more deep-seated.

Oranges

Bonnie, thirty-five, dreamed she was walking through an orange grove and the wind was blowing the petals like fragrant snow. She picked an orange from a tree. But as she peeled the orange, it tasted sour and was starting to rot. The wind blew so fiercely that even the evergreen leaves were shaken from the tree. Bonnie saw another grove ahead, untouched by the wind, where the blossoms were intact and the fruit sweet.

DREAM BACKGROUND AND MEANING

Bonnie was getting married and wanted to have orange blossoms in her hair and to carry a small basket of oranges instead of a bouquet. Her fiancé never wanted children, but she intended to secretly not use contraception and pretend that a pregnancy was an accident. Blossoming orange trees with growing fruit are a powerful symbol of conception, but sour or rotting oranges warn that deception will spoil happiness.

INTERPRETATIONS AND FORTUNE-TELLING MEANINGS

★ Oranges are a symbol of the sun, health, fertility, prosperity, and travel.

★ The orange blossom has been a good omen for betrothals, marriages, and children from Ancient China onward.

★ A basket of oranges indicates many opportunities for prosperity in career and fertility in every way. Eating the orange is especially fortuitous.

★ If you are wearing the color orange, you will gain popularity with others and your creativity will bring tangible rewards.

★ Dreaming of squeezing oranges to make juice suggests that you may be asked to give too much of yourself.

OUTCOME OF BONNIE'S DREAM

Bonnie realized after the dream that her deception would only bring heartache. Since her fiancé remained adamant that he would not bring up children whatever the circumstances, she broke off the engagement. The second orange grove in the dream reassured her that if she did not find someone to share her desire for parenthood, she could have a child as a single parent. Oranges have almost entirely positive dream meanings but, as symbols of the sun, they demand truth and honesty.

Orchard

Patrick, forty, dreamed he was walking through blossoming trees toward where an orchard had been uprooted by a storm. His wife, Bella, pointed to partially damaged trees that could be replanted and others that could be trimmed, where blossoming branches had survived. Patrick didn't want to try, but she insisted that between them they could fix it. He woke, after dreaming of replanting the roots of a tree heavy with blossom into the ground.

DREAM BACKGROUND AND MEANING

Patrick and his wife had invested all their savings in a vintage-car restoration business and had their first orders almost completed. Then a fire started, Patrick believed by a jealous rival, partially destroying the premises and badly damaging some of the cars. Patrick wanted to take the insurance money and forget the venture. Bella insisted he should not give up on their lifelong ambition, which could blossom again. Orchard dreams indicate growth at a time when you may doubt it is worth continuing.

INTERPRETATIONS AND FORTUNE-TELLING MEANINGS

★ A dream of an orchard with plentiful fruit indicates long-term profitable results for any enterprise; from small beginnings, promising efforts will be rewarded.

★ A blossoming orchard signifies love and romance that will grow with encouragement and perseverance, even in hard times.

★ A cherry orchard with ripe fruit heralds pregnancy and healthy good-natured children.

★ An olive orchard brings wealth through the fulfillment of a lifetime ambition in any area of life.

★ A barren orchard or one with rotting fruit on the ground warns of missed opportunities because action was too late.

★ Storm damage to an orchard offers reassurance that an endeavor can be revived and flourish.

★ As-yet-unripe fruit advises patience and perseverance in long-term ventures.

OUTCOME OF PATRICK'S DREAM

Patrick's wife encouraged him to rent temporary premises and complete and sell the undamaged cars. They created custom-built premises themselves that were better than before and used the insurance money to invest in the business. They have an order for the first reconstructed car.

Orchestra

Maurice, twenty-five, dreamed he was listening to an orchestra when suddenly the lead violinist was taken ill. The spotlight fell on Maurice, and he was invited to the stage to play the violin solo. But Maurice had stage fright and was unable to play a single note. The audience booed. Spurred on, Maurice started playing brilliantly, and the spotlight remained on him throughout the evening.

DREAM BACKGROUND AND MEANING

Maurice, who had a junior role in a design team, produced a winning original idea for the company's next major advertising campaign. He was afraid to present it, although it would bring him recognition.

The key to orchestra dreams is whether you are listening or participating and whether that role is what you want.

INTERPRETATIONS AND FORTUNE-TELLING MEANINGS

* If you dream that an orchestra plays in harmony, success lies in joint ventures and cooperating with others.
* If one player drowns out the others, beware of someone trying to dominate the family, workplace, or community.
* Dreaming of conducting an orchestra says you will be called upon to coordinate a joint project, whether at work or in the community.
* If the orchestra is discordant, you may be trying too hard to fit in with others and should follow your own path.
* Since an orchestra blends different instruments, orchestra dreams are a good omen for combining two families or different views in the workplace or community.
* If you are denied a place in an orchestra, it may be the wrong setting for you to fit in.

OUTCOME OF MAURICE'S DREAM

Encouraged by the dream, Maurice had his presentation ready for the next design meeting. But at the last minute his courage failed. At the following meeting, another member of the team suggested a similar idea that was enthusiastically adopted. Orchestra dreams not only involve blending different skills but also give members chances to demonstrate individual talents; the chances should be seized before they become lost in the collective sound.

Orchid

Astrid, twenty-two, dreamed that she found dark red and white Lady Orchids growing wild, and she wanted to pick them, as she loved orchids but never seemed able to grow them. But when she tried picking them, needle-like shocks surged through her fingers and so she gave up. Then her ex-boyfriend appeared and offered her a beautiful flowering orchid, growing in a pot.

DREAM BACKGROUND AND MEANING

Astrid had recently split up with her boyfriend, Joe. Her job resulted in a lot of after-hours solo socializing, and Joe was unhappy about it. He was desperate to reconcile, but she refused and went straight back to dating. None of the men she was seeing made her feel happy. However, she did not want to give in. Orchids are associated with love, romance, and sexual awakening and are often called "the woman's flower." Being given an orchid by a known or unknown lover says this is your twin soul.

INTERPRETATIONS AND FORTUNE-TELLING MEANINGS

* Flowering orchids represent riches and the acquisition of beautiful things, but they warn against undue extravagance.
* Purple orchids may appear in dreams when you need more personal time and space if others are wearing you out, or when you desire more money or a more fulfilling, luxurious lifestyle.
* Dreaming of flowering orchids in your home reassures you of protection for your family and by those you love.
* White orchids foretell a lasting marriage or relationship commitment. All orchids are fertility symbols.
* Red orchids assure success in new fitness and diet regimes.
* Yellow orchids promise profitable business dealings, especially for women, but warn against listening to gossip.

OUTCOME OF ASTRID'S DREAM

When Astrid woke, she saw that the orchids she had been planning to throw away were starting to bud, and she realized she had been neglecting them. Astrid contacted her boyfriend, and they decided to reconcile. Caring for an orchid that is starting to bud says you need to spend extra care on a project or relationship for lasting results.

Orgasm

Tansy, thirty-two, dreamed she was in bed with a man she had picked up in a bar in Paris and was experiencing orgasm after orgasm in his hotel room. She woke next to her husband, Steven, in rainy England, but when she moved toward him, he gently pushed her away and continued snoring.

DREAM BACKGROUND AND MEANING

Tansy and Steven were celibate until their wedding. But after they were married, Tansy faked orgasms, as Steven showed little interest in sex. Tansy feared it was her fault. Since she was pretending ecstasy, she could not say anything and did not want to hurt his feelings. Orgasm dreams are not only sexual but recognize that reaching the height of sharing pleasure spiritually, psychologically, or as an intense life experience with a partner may have not yet been found.

INTERPRETATIONS AND FORTUNE-TELLING MEANINGS

* If you dream of reaching orgasm with your partner, this is an excellent sign for a passionate relationship and, if desired, children.
* If you experience orgasm with a stranger in your dream but have a partner, you may be feeling emotionally and sexually unfulfilled.
* If you have multiple orgasms in a dream with someone you know but neither of you is free, be careful, as there is great risk.
* If you dream of having an orgasm as part of an orgy, you may have inhibitions about sex more easily expressed in fantasy.
* If ejaculation occurs only in the dream state, resentments, fear of vulnerability, or lack of trust toward a partner may prevent spontaneity.
* If there is perfect lovemaking in a dream, the dreamer may need to re-create the dream scenario to release inhibitions.

OUTCOME OF TANSY'S DREAM

After the dream, Tansy booked a long weekend in Paris with the intention of seducing her husband. However, Steven arranged a full cultural itinerary and even the Museum of Erotica failed to excite him. Tansy has the choice of staying with Steven and accepting his low sex drive, finding a lover, or maybe moving on. Orgasm dreams can spice up a mundane sex life, but if there is no spark between the couple, they may only serve to accentuate differences.

Ornaments

Bessie, sixty-six, dreamed she was surrounded by boxes of ornaments from her childhood and her children's childhoods. She was trying to fit the boxes into her small car to move them home, but there were just too many. At last, she left all of them with the garbage and drove off.

DREAM BACKGROUND AND MEANING

Bessie, a widow, wanted to downsize from her old, overly large home in a seaside town and buy a small city apartment so she could travel without worrying about repairs. But her children and grandchildren refused to hear of it, as Bessie's house was the center of the family's vacations, long weekends, and, increasingly, a second home for the grandchildren. They were all attached to her collection of memorabilia, although Bessie wanted to get rid of everything as they were dust magnets. Ornaments reflect either valued memories or accumulated and redundant responsibilities that hold us back.

INTERPRETATIONS AND FORTUNE-TELLING MEANINGS

* A dream of a home with well-dusted ornaments on shelves indicates a settled home or the opportunity to settle down in the near future.
* Dusty ornaments or ones piled in boxes say you have unfinished business distracting you from moving forward.
* Broken ornaments suggest that tact may be needed in settling inheritance disputes.
* If you dream you are given a new ornament and you like it, it confirms that the giver is in tune with your needs. If you hate it, others are imposing their views on you.
* Ornaments filling every surface imply a life or work overloaded with too many small demands.
* If you are throwing away ornaments or giving them to charity, the energies are right to move on to a new phase in your life and leave the past behind.

OUTCOME OF BESSIE'S DREAM

Bessie downsized to her city apartment and distributed the ornaments among the children. Ornaments have emotions attached to them according to the memories they hold. But they can represent a need to prioritize and declutter a lifestyle in order to attain freedom.

Oscars, Awards Ceremonies

Perdita, twenty-eight, dreamed she was making her Oscar acceptance speech, thanking everyone for their encouragement. When she mentioned her parents, she realized they were not present. She rushed outside to where they were waiting in the crowd. Perdita had left her Oscar behind and knew it would be given to someone else.

DREAM BACKGROUND AND MEANING

Perdita had achieved some minor successes in her acting career. She had recently been accepted by a new agent, who promised her an Oscar. However, the agent said she needed reimaging from the girl from the small-town steelworks whose parents had sacrificed to send her to acting school. She would become the abandoned child of drug-addict parents who had been rescued by her agent and given stardom. Perdita wanted to succeed, but at what price? Oscars represent fame and attainment in your chosen world, especially in the field of entertainment or creativity, but may exact a price.

INTERPRETATIONS AND FORTUNE-TELLING MEANINGS

* If you dream of receiving an Oscar, you should aim high in your chosen field. You will soon receive an award or acclaim.
* If you are nominated for an Oscar in your dream, it's time to push extra hard, as opportunities for recognition are increasing.
* If you dream that you mess up your acceptance speech, you may not feel worthy of success and may need a confidence boost.
* If you dream you are barred from the ceremony though you are due for an Oscar, you need some new contacts, as there is jealousy and resentment in your way.
* If you dream that your Oscar is stolen or given to someone else, beware of rivals stealing your limelight.

OUTCOME OF PERDITA'S DREAM

Perdita told the new agent she was proud of her parents and her background, and she stayed with her present agent. Before too long she was nominated for an award for a supporting role and took her parents to the ceremony. Oscar dreams signify high acclaim in your chosen profession and positive publicity. However, they should be based on unique talent, not attained at the cost of integrity.

Ostrich

Barrington, twenty-two, dreamed he was in Africa, watching a flock of ostriches with their young. He approached as he wanted to take photographs but, too late, he realized a huge male was advancing toward him, ready to protect his young. Knowing he could not outrun the ostrich, Barrington backed slowly away and hid in the bushes until the ostriches moved on.

DREAM BACKGROUND AND MEANING

Barrington had never known his father, as his mother had not told the man she was pregnant and refused to talk about him to Barrington. She had remarried when he was young, and he had never fit in with his younger siblings and stepfather. Now Barrington wanted to find his birth father, but he was afraid of being rejected.

According to myth, rather than fact, to dream of an ostrich burying its head represents fears of facing reality.

INTERPRETATIONS AND FORTUNE-TELLING MEANINGS

* Dreaming of an ostrich's egg is a powerful fertility symbol. If seen when the baby is due, it can indicate an imminent birth.
* Dreaming of being given an ostrich egg, the largest of all eggs, predicts an unexpected gift.
* A single ostrich feather is associated with receiving justice, because one was worn in the headdress of Maat, Ancient Egyptian goddess of wisdom and justice.
* As a symbol of perpetual light and motion in African magick, seeing an ostrich running in a dream is a sign of moving forward to success and sometimes relocation.
* Since ostriches make good fathers from the egg-incubating stage on, ostrich dreams signify good or improved relationships with a father figure and strong paternal instincts toward children.

OUTCOME OF BARRINGTON'S DREAM

Barrington contacted his mother's sister, who was able to tell him the identity of his father, and Barrington contacted him. His father was delighted to discover he had a son, as he had no living family. Since they both shared a fascination with Africa, Barrington's father took him on a safari.

Overambitious Parents

Jimmy, eighteen, dreamed he was sleeping rough in a doorway in London's West End when his parents walked past him. Even though he knew they saw him, they completely ignored him. Jimmy woke very upset.

DREAM BACKGROUND AND MEANING

Since the family's arrival in the United Kingdom from northern Xinjiang, China, Jimmy's brother and two sisters had attended college and graduated with degrees in medicine. This placed a lot of pressure on Jimmy, as his parents insisted that he also study medicine. But he wanted to work relieving homelessness. His parents threatened to abandon him without a cent and said he could live on the streets. Parental ambition dreams closely mirror real life and express fears of going against the demands of ambitious parents.

INTERPRETATIONS AND FORTUNE-TELLING MEANINGS

★ If in the dream you are young and a parent or teacher is pressuring you to finish your homework, someone older is trying to control you.

★ Barred windows and doors represent restrictions to keep you within the conventions of a family firm or profession.

★ Past-world scenarios of starving on the streets or being cast out by cruel parents may rekindle fears in the present world.

★ Should you dream of a deceased parent asking you to keep the family firm or name going, be aware that we cannot remain frozen in time and must move forward.

★ Seeing your parents as children holding a golden trophy with your name on it means that they are living their own unfulfilled ambitions through you.

★ If you see yourself returning home in triumph to a feast, you know your independence will bring you eventual reconciliation.

OUTCOME OF JIMMY'S DREAM

Jimmy enrolled in a scheme in which he studied for a social work certificate part-time while helping organize and live in a hostel for rejected teenagers. Overambitious-parent dreams, by drawing attention to the child's stifling, can assist in bringing it to an end.

Overcrowding

Peggy, thirty-five, dreamed she, her husband, and their four children had been at a fireworks display. Afterward, their car would not start. A neighbor offered them a lift home. But the neighbor also had three children, and so the car was seriously overcrowded. There were not enough seat belts and Peggy was terrified the car would crash. Then she saw lights on the wrong side of the road and knew her fears were materializing.

DREAM BACKGROUND AND MEANING

Peggy was worried as her sister Jill, who had separated from her husband, had moved into Peggy's small house with her three children. Peggy's own children were doubling up in the bedrooms, and there had been minor accidents because of the confined space. Peggy knew her sister had to go. But could she ask her sister to leave? Overcrowding dreams show the dreamer how much disruption, physical or emotional, is building up.

INTERPRETATIONS AND FORTUNE-TELLING MEANINGS

★ If you dream you are crammed in an overcrowded elevator or bar, you need more space in your work or social life.

★ If your home is full of friends and neighbors in the dream, your home life is intruded on by people outstaying their welcome. Impose boundaries.

★ If a train, subway, or bus is overcrowded, do not feel obliged to go along with others' plans.

★ If you are in an overcrowded place and fighting breaks out, you are probably overwhelmed by trying to maintain peace between warring factions.

★ If you dream there is an accident because of overcrowding in an arena or sports event, you are ignoring personal danger signs of overload. Be wary also of safety factors at forthcoming large events.

OUTCOME OF PEGGY'S DREAM

Peggy realized she was no longer at home in her own home and her younger children were also feeling lost. Peggy told her sister she must look for her own place, after Peggy's youngest wandered through an open gate into the road. Her sister went back to her husband. Overcrowding dreams reflect feeling overwhelmed by demands of others and lacking solitude.

Overflowing

Trinny, forty-five, dreamed she was filling the bath with scented water when she realized she had left a cake in the oven and needed to take it out. Then her mother called and they had a long, complicated conversation. She forgot all about the bath till she saw water dripping through the kitchen ceiling and, dashing upstairs, found the bathtub was overflowing. The bathroom carpet was ruined.

DREAM BACKGROUND AND MEANING

Trinny was always busy with a full-time job, an absentee husband, teenage children, and a demanding mother, as well as her charity work. She was not sleeping because her mind was full of unfulfilled tasks. Unlike flood dreams (see p. 195), overflowing dreams reflect a life overload that warns of the consequences of not slowing down.

INTERPRETATIONS AND FORTUNE-TELLING MEANINGS

* If a drain, sink, or shower becomes blocked in a dream, someone or some situation is standing in the way of the smooth running of your life.
* If you dream that you left a pot on the stove that overflowed and burned dry, you are suppressing resentment that if not tackled may burst out as anger in an inappropriate setting or against an innocent person.
* If you dream that you let a sink or bath overflow, you may be drowning under suppressed emotions or simply too much to do.
* If you see an overflowing drain outside your home, others may be intruding too much on your time.
* If you are drinking champagne or wine and the bottle is overflowing, expect a happy event or celebration.
* If you dream that your purse or wallet is overflowing with money, you may receive a windfall or bonus; but if it is overflowing with credit cards, you may be overstretching yourself financially, subsidizing others.

OUTCOME OF TRINNY'S DREAM

After the dream, Trinny cut down on her work for two days a week and on those two days refused to cook for the family, meet her mother's demands, or do charity work. She had no more overflowing dreams or near misses in life. Overflowing dreams are a graphic way of saying slow down and avoid having life overflow with even more problems to resolve.

Overseas

Tobias, fifty-eight, dreamed he walked out of his front door into a different world. The heat was blazing and market stalls at the end of the street were piled high with exotic fruit and vegetables. He slammed the door, but his future daughter-in-law took his hand and introduced him to people in the street, who welcomed him.

DREAM BACKGROUND AND MEANING

Tobias, who had lived in the same English village all his life, was due to fly to India for his only son's wedding. He was worried, as he would know no one there except his son. For some people, overseas dreams represent adventure and new experiences, but for others the unknown can seem terrifying.

INTERPRETATIONS AND FORTUNE-TELLING MEANINGS

* Dreaming of having a vacation overseas, if pleasurable, suggests widening horizons, new experiences, and a good vacation farther afield.
* If you are living overseas in your dream, this may predict opportunities to relocate.
* If lost in an unfamiliar country, you may fear intrusion by others in your familiar world.
* If you cannot speak the language and no one understands you in your dream, you may be suffering from miscommunication from colleagues or family members who cannot see your point of view.
* If you belong to a different culture and are living in a different country in your dream, you will need to adapt to unfamiliar innovative ideas or be left behind.
* If in your dream you are denied entry to a country because of incorrect paperwork, you may not be ready for big changes in your life.

OUTCOME OF TOBIAS'S DREAM

After the dream Tobias felt less frightened. He was met at the airport by his son and his fiancée's family, and he stayed in their house. He had such a good time that he plans another visit. Overseas dreams, even if the dreamer is not planning on traveling, signify leaving a comfort zone, which almost always leads to a widening of horizons if embraced.

Owl

Most Thursday nights, Celia, forty-five, dreamed of two owls swooping into her home, the smaller flying away with something shiny in its beak. Celia tried to catch it, but the larger owl pecked Celia until she retreated, bleeding.

DREAM BACKGROUND AND MEANING

Celia recently noticed that on Fridays, when her cleaner came, pieces of jewelry went missing, including a valuable brooch. When questioned, the cleaner became angry and Celia backed down. But the thefts continued. An owl can indicate concern regarding the behavior of someone close at home or work.

INTERPRETATIONS AND FORTUNE-TELLING MEANINGS

★ A white owl never heralds death, but alerts you to unexpected opposition from a previously helpful source.

★ An owl flying in front of your vehicle or face says that suppressed negative fears and feelings, which you try to deny, are valid.

★ Dreaming of an owl flying in the dark warns that someone is deceiving you or keeping secrets.

★ The owl goddess of the Celts is a bird of the grandmother goddess and the waning moon. A large brown or gray dream owl suggests talking over domestic worries with a wise older woman. This is also a symbol of fertility for an older couple.

★ Since the little white owl was sacred to Athena, Greek goddess of wisdom, and the Roman Minerva, a small white owl flying high is an excellent omen for any court cases or tribunals.

★ If you dream of an owl before a change point, consider if you really want the change or are being pressured.

OUTCOME OF CELIA'S DREAM

Celia, using a hidden camera, discovered that the cleaner's daughter was accompanying her mother on the Fridays that jewelry went missing. When Celia confronted her cleaner with the video evidence of her daughter pocketing items, the cleaner stormed out with a torrent of abuse. Celia did not prosecute. Repeated owl dreams alert us that we are ignoring problems that will resolve only when we tackle them.

Oyster

Megan, forty-one, dreamed she was in an expensive restaurant with her married lover. She ordered oysters, but he said he did not need an aphrodisiac when he was with her. The oysters tasted off, but she ate them without complaining as she did not want to make a fuss. Almost immediately she felt sick and had to excuse herself to go to the bathroom. On the way to the hotel, she vomited all over the leather seats of his new car. She knew he would not ask her out again.

DREAM BACKGROUND AND MEANING

Megan was in love with Roger, the husband of her best friend, Cy. Roger told Megan he dreamed every night of making love to her. He asked Megan to go with him to a hotel farther up the coast where they could stay overnight and visit the best seafood restaurant in the state. Oysters often appear in temptation dreams, because of their fabled aphrodisiac properties.

INTERPRETATIONS AND FORTUNE-TELLING MEANINGS

★ A closed oyster represents secrets and confidences that should not be revealed, or a woman who is uncertain about lovemaking.

★ An open empty oyster shell says an opportunity has been lost, or another person has taken what is rightfully yours.

★ An oyster containing a pearl represents the profitable results of hard work, patience, and usually hard times on the way.

★ If you are allergic to oysters in a dream or the oysters taste bad, a temptation in love may ultimately prove toxic or destructive.

★ A pile of oyster shells is a good omen for building up a successful business by using resources wisely.

OUTCOME OF MEGAN'S DREAM

Megan did not like seafood. More significantly, after the dream she realized that having an affair with her best friend's husband would only lead to heartache and loss of a precious friendship (see "Pearls," p. 357). She turned down the offer. Oyster dreams may hold promises of hidden treasure, but the nature of the dream may show the likelihood of ending up with an empty shell or a pearl.

Packing

Max, forty-one, had a recurring dream that he was packing for a vacation with a restricted luggage allowance. He could not decide what to take or leave. Every time he closed his suitcase, he thought of something essential, until at last the case would not close. He woke, tipping the contents on the floor, and canceled the vacation.

DREAM BACKGROUND AND MEANING

Max was newly separated and had met a woman named Valerie on the Internet who lived in a distant state. But every time they set a date to meet, he postponed the trip, though he wanted to see her. Valerie was tired of excuses. As she had small children, it was hard for her to travel. Emotional baggage can be hard to leave behind and often features in packing dreams.

INTERPRETATIONS AND FORTUNE-TELLING MEANINGS

* Dreaming of packing boxes for a new location or a home can, according to whether the dream is exciting or fearful, reveal true feelings about a change.
* Having too much to fit in suitcases indicates guilt about leaving behind an old attachment where there are still pressures to return or stay.
* Realizing at the airport that you have packed the wrong clothes or forgotten something vital raises doubts about the wisdom of your choices to move on in life.
* Dreaming that you are watching someone else packing suggests you fear being left behind in a relationship, friendship, or career, according to who is packing.
* A broken or battered suitcase says you may be stuck in a rut and need to regain your spirit of adventure.
* Delaying packing at the end of a vacation so you miss the plane says something is lacking from your everyday life that you need to rekindle or discover.

OUTCOME OF MAX'S DREAM

Max booked his ticket and traveled light. The relationship is progressing. Overattention to packing dreams reveals a need to anticipate problems in advance, which may not be possible or desirable.

Padlock

Simone, twenty-two, dreamed she was entering a championship cycling race and had padlocked her wheels while she went for breakfast the morning of the race. When she returned, the combination numbers to her lock no longer worked. Her friend Jess, seeing her struggling, offered to lend Simone her spare bicycle. Simone gratefully accepted as the race was starting, but it was much heavier, and Jess won.

DREAM BACKGROUND AND MEANING

Simone only had one main rival, Jess, who lent her the losing bicycle for the dream race. There had been minor sabotage to cycles in the competition village. The only other person who knew her combination was Jess, who had taken Simone's bike with her own for a pre-race servicing when Simone had a migraine. But surely Jess was Simone's friend and played fair? Padlocks symbolize the need for security on many levels, whether guarding an important item, knowledge, or secrets.

INTERPRETATIONS AND FORTUNE-TELLING MEANINGS

* An open padlock symbolizes an opportunity to extricate oneself from a difficult situation or to end restrictions.
* If the lock is closed, you need to keep something precious or a special secret involving love or money safe from prying eyes.
* If the key is missing, you or someone close may find it hard to express emotions or are inhibited in a sexual relationship.
* If someone is undoing your padlock, whether by combination code or by key, beware of intrusion on your privacy. The identity of the dream person holds the clue.
* Dreaming of changing combination numbers or replacing a padlock says you need to take matters into your own hands.
* To dream that you forgot combination numbers reveals that information or an opportunity is not available. This may be temporary.

OUTCOME OF SIMONE'S DREAM

Simone realized that Jess was in fact the one sabotaging Simone's bicycle. Simone replaced her padlock with an extra-secure one and did not tell Jess the new combination. Simone easily won the next race. Padlocks represent both security and blocking the way.

Paganism

Astrid, fifty-five, dreamed she was in the center of a slowly turning wheel, decorated with flowers of all seasons. She reached out for the first buds of spring, May blossoms, and golden sunflowers, dancing and singing at each change point. She knew that she was connected with the wheel's turning and with herself for the first time.

DREAM BACKGROUND AND MEANING

Astrid's best friend, Caitlin, had become a pagan. Caitlin had taken Astrid along to the seasonal celebrations and invited her to join the group. But Astrid's husband warned her that she was indulging a weird fantasy. Dreaming about the cycles of the seasons and their rituals draws upon an ancient instinctive link to live in harmony with Earth.

INTERPRETATIONS AND FORTUNE-TELLING MEANINGS

* If you dream of performing rituals in an ancient stone circle to bring growth to the land, this may be an old world you once shared.
* If you dream of being part of a circle of others celebrating nature, you will be drawn to the right natural magick group at the right time.
* If you are affected by the different cycles of the moon, you are already linking your natural cycles with those of the cosmos.
* If you cast stones into water, listen to the rustle of leaves or birdcalls, as you are receiving messages from your inner psyche.
* If you dream of an old wise figure, she is your nature guardian, connecting with you.
* If you see shadowy figures around a fire and are afraid, ignore those who do not understand.

OUTCOME OF ASTRID'S DREAM

Astrid joined the group and became more tuned in to the everyday as well as the natural world. Astrid's daughter joined her mother in the group. Dreams of paganism, whether or not you have knowledge or experience of seasonal celebrations, tap into our deep instinctive souls, but may not be understood by those who are afraid of their own instincts.

Pagoda

Alison, fifty-five, dreamed she saw a pagoda with its door swinging open. When she entered, the altar and relics box were empty. Disappointed, she climbed the rickety ladder-type stairs and reached the top. She saw pagoda upon pagoda leading into the distance. When she climbed down, an old Tibetan nun showed her a secret passage where the relics were hidden. She said, "Seek beyond the immediate," and then disappeared. Alison woke feeling blessed.

DREAM BACKGROUND AND MEANING

Alison had taken early retirement, but her life seemed meaningless. She was a mathematician and had always despised Westerners who became students of ancient Far Eastern faiths. Recently, however, she had attended a lecture on Far Eastern spiritual architecture and was fascinated by its symmetry. Pagodas, as symbols of ascending to the heavens, represent a tangible entry to the old spiritual world.

INTERPRETATIONS AND FORTUNE-TELLING MEANINGS

* To dream you see a pagoda or many-tiered stupa foretells a long happy journey within the next year.
* To be welcomed into a pagoda says you will be given a beautiful present that will become more valuable over the years, along with the affection of the giver.
* If you are shown sacred Tibetan Buddhist, Taoist, Hindu, or Japanese relics within the pagoda or stupa, you have a spirit guide from one of these ancient cultures with you.
* If you dream that you enter a pagoda with a lover, known or unknown, you desire a spiritual as well as sexual relationship and may be lacking this.
* If the pagoda is locked, you are unconsciously seeking creative or spiritual inspiration, but may need to explore the wisdom of an ancient culture to attain it.
* If you see many pagodas, your spiritual journey will be long but fruitful.

OUTCOME OF ALISON'S DREAM

After the dream, Alison booked a tour of Far Eastern temples and became fascinated. She is planning more pilgrimages. Pagodas represent magical journeys, actual and through learning, into the heart of spirituality.

Painkillers

Della, fifty, dreamed she dropped her bag in a busy shopping mall and it spilled open, dropping packet after packet of painkillers. People rushed to help her pick them up, but she was so ashamed that she ran away, leaving them on the floor and vowing to never take a painkiller again.

DREAM BACKGROUND AND MEANING

Della had been prescribed painkillers for a chronic condition, but over time they had become less effective, and now she was overdosing every day and could not do without them. She was suffering from severe stomach pains and shaking but was too ashamed to visit the physician. While painkillers are a temporary fix, a dream can alert us when they are becoming an addiction (see "Medication," p. 304).

INTERPRETATIONS AND FORTUNE-TELLING MEANINGS

★ If in a dream you are handed prescribed painkillers by a physician or pharmacist, you may be hoping someone else will fix your emotional issues.

★ If you are secretly taking too many painkillers or another anesthetic, such as excess alcohol, to blunt negative reactions, a dream may reveal that you are getting careless and are in danger of discovery.

★ If in your dream you are hiding painkillers, you are seeking to hide unhappiness or anger from others.

★ If you have lost your painkillers and can't get more in the dream, you may be scared of facing up to what is making you unhappy.

★ If you dream you are giving painkillers to an unwilling partner, you may be trying to avoid dealing with their discontentment, fears, or worries.

★ If you dream that you cannot swallow a painkiller, you are finding it increasingly hard to accept other people's views and opinions without protest.

OUTCOME OF DELLA'S DREAM

After the dream, Della realized her symptoms were worse than the original pain. She went to an addiction unit. The dream radar warns that excesses may cause emotional as well as physical problems to escalate.

Palmistry

Clara, fifty-two, dreamed she was in a clairvoyant's tent, so dimly lit that Clara could see neither the fortune-teller nor her own palms. The old woman was saying that Clara's palms revealed an ancient death curse on the whole family. She could remove it, but it would cost ten thousand dollars. Terrified, Clara gave her a check. Suddenly, the lights came on and the fortune-teller, surrounded by thousands of dollars, was reading her predictions by flashlight from a palmistry book. Clara seized her check and walked out.

DREAM BACKGROUND AND MEANING

Clara had been visiting a local palmist every week. Each time, the palmist discovered bad luck in Clara's palms, and Clara bought numerous amulets to protect her loved ones. Clara was scared to stop going or buying amulets, in case the palmist cursed her family. Dreams are like a protective radar, revealing who or what is genuine.

INTERPRETATIONS AND FORTUNE-TELLING MEANINGS

★ To read another's palm in a dream indicates emerging psychic ability, especially in palmistry.

★ To read your own palm advises that you listen to your intuition and take a chance on life.

★ A dream of a palm reading promising instant great fortune warns you that a stranger or acquaintance may persuade you to part with your money.

★ If your dream palm is totally blank, create your own path and ignore others trying to influence you.

★ If a dream palmist foretells death and disaster, this is never predictive but a sign of your unacknowledged stress overload.

★ If you see your actual palmist surrounded by light in a dream, you can trust their palm readings.

OUTCOME OF CLARA'S DREAM

As the dreams and money demands occurred more regularly, Clara realized she was being exploited. She bought a good palmistry book and is learning to read palms herself. Palmistry, like other psychic arts, has both talented practitioners and charlatans. If palmistry dreams are ringing alarm bells, take your common sense, not your purse, to the palmist's.

Pancakes

Dora, fifty-five, dreamed she was making pancakes, her specialty, for the family. All her colleagues from work arrived and demanded pancakes too. She was making pancakes as fast as she could, but everyone was complaining they were still hungry. She was getting hot and bothered and started dropping them. At last, she aimed one pancake at the ceiling, where it stuck. Then she walked out and went to a pancake house in the mall for her own breakfast.

DREAM BACKGROUND AND MEANING

Because of an original offer she had meant kindly, Dora was now expected to take the daily orders for everyone's lunch at work, and bring back the lunches from the sandwich bar. But often she was not paid the full amount people owed her. If she did not offer to take the orders, her colleagues asked if she was in a bad mood. It was becoming a chore and taking time out of her workday, which she had to make up. Pancakes represent nurturing others, but excessive quantities in a dream can suggest that the dreamer is being exploited.

INTERPRETATIONS AND FORTUNE-TELLING MEANINGS

★ Dreaming you are tossing or turning pancakes is a sign that you have a determined independent streak that will overcome any criticism.

★ Eating pancakes with friends and family signifies family unity and spending more informal time together.

★ Maple syrup pancakes represent good fortune and the acquisition of money, but if they are oversweet, beware of flattery.

★ If you burn or drop pancakes, a dominant woman may try to undermine your confidence.

★ Dreaming you are making pancakes but not getting to eat any yourself says you need to stand up for your rights, as you are being taken for granted.

OUTCOME OF DORA'S DREAM

Dora announced at work that she was on a special diet and bringing her food from home, so she wouldn't go to the sandwich bar anymore. Her colleagues rapidly created a rotating list of people to fetch the lunches, as no one wanted sole responsibility. Pancake dreams are sociable unless the dreamer does all the making and none of the eating.

Pantomime

Tessie, twenty-one, dreamed she was cast in the annual pantomime at the town's main theater. As she was about to step on stage, the pantomime villain waved his wand and told her she would lose her voice and end up like him, a loser. She lost her voice, but realized the villain had no real power unless she accepted his fantasy. She seized the wand and declared, "I am the winner." She was a great success.

DREAM BACKGROUND AND MEANING

Tessie had been attending local drama classes for years and had applied to go to stage school. But Zed, her acting coach, the dream villain, discouraged her, saying she would probably end up teaching young hopefuls. Dreams about pantomimes, performed mostly during the Christmas and New Year season in the United Kingdom, vividly set out a situation in story form, revealing everyone's true roles.

INTERPRETATIONS AND FORTUNE-TELLING MEANINGS

★ If you dream you are in a pantomime, your future possibly lies in the performing arts, media, or communication.

★ If the pantomime villain casting evil spells is someone in your daily life, they are undermining your confidence because of jealousy.

★ If you marry your prince or princess in the dream pantomime, there's a good chance you will meet the right person or your present relationship will last.

★ If you are cast as one of the ugly sisters or in the wicked-stepmother role, you may be accepting the fall-guy role in someone else's real-life drama.

★ If you dream of watching a pantomime around Christmas, it signifies good times ahead.

OUTCOME OF TESSIE'S DREAM

After the dream, Tessie recalled all the times Zed had discouraged her. She knew she must prove Zed wrong and decided that if she failed to get into stage school, she would apply to a university to study the performing arts. Pantomime dreams allow the hero or heroine to rehearse a happy ending and use the dream energies to translate fantasy into reality.

Paper, Parchment

Jasper, fifteen, dreamed he was writing on parchment with a quill, but was smudging the words and figures and longing to be outdoors. He could see a carpenter on the grounds struggling to build a chair. As the heir to the property, Jasper was tutored to take over the estate. He drew detailed plans on the parchment for making the chair and joined the carpenter. Jasper woke incredibly happy.

DREAM BACKGROUND AND MEANING

Jasper was not academic, but he had designed and created many beautiful carvings. His father had sent him to a high-achievers' school, where he was regarded as a failure. He contemplated running away. In what was probably a past-life dream, the parchment paper only came to life when it was used to create meaningful designs.

INTERPRETATIONS AND FORTUNE-TELLING MEANINGS

* To dream of blank paper says you will come up with original ideas or solutions to a problem you should see through.
* A dream of crumpled and discarded paper says plans or ideas will not work out in practice.
* Papers blowing in the wind, scattering everywhere, indicate that you should go against convention.
* An unfilled official form warns that you may be storing up trouble if you delay answering legal or government paperwork.
* An unanswered examination paper suggests you need to prepare more in some aspect of life to demonstrate your worth.
* Dreaming of a pile of papers to be sorted and read advises that you organize your time and cut down on nonessentials.

OUTCOME OF JASPER'S DREAM

The school principal showed Jasper's father the fabulous woodworking Jasper had drawn and created in the only lesson he enjoyed. He explained that Jasper would never be an academic. Jasper's father was disappointed, as he wanted his son to take over the family's business one day. However, he transferred Jasper to a school where the emphasis was on creativity, and Jasper flourished. Paper can represent restricting talents and ideas to an intellectual context and theory unless the written plans are brought to actuality in the dream.

Parachute

Daphne, twenty-six, dreamed she was standing at the altar, waiting for her husband-to-be, Stewart, to join her. He had promised he would be home on army leave, but she was afraid he would not make it in time. Suddenly, there was a commotion outside the church, and Stewart made a perfect parachute landing, wearing his ceremonial military uniform.

DREAM BACKGROUND AND MEANING

Daphne had postponed her wedding several times because of urgent last-minute missions on which her fiancé, Stewart, had been sent. She had booked a date at the local church three months ahead and warned him he had better show up this time. Parachute dreams inevitably involve excitement and challenge, but also have built-in uncertainty, which may be worse for those left on the ground.

INTERPRETATIONS AND FORTUNE-TELLING MEANINGS

* Dreaming of floating down on a parachute is a good sign that if you aim high, you will not fall or fail.
* If you smoothly parachute to the ground, you have a lot more control of the future than it may seem.
* If your lover smoothly parachutes to the ground, it is a sexual dream of surrendering to passion and deep commitment in a relationship regardless of uncertainties.
* If you dream that a parachute does not unfold until the last minute or the ropes tangle in the air, do not rely on others to help you with money or in your career.
* If you dream of a parachute not opening at all, you may need to build in security factors and escape clauses if you are taking a major risk.
* If you dream your parachute gets tangled in trees, you may need a backup plan, as complications may arise because of unavoidable obstacles rather than ill will.

OUTCOME OF DAPHNE'S DREAM

Stewart brought home some beautiful parachute silk to make Daphne's wedding dress. For the ceremony, he and his honor guard arranged to be dropped outside the church on parachutes, as in her dream. Parachute dreams, whether about a relationship or a cause, predict both hazards and happy landings, according to their nature and outcome.

Parallel Life

Antonio, forty-five, a Londoner, had regular dreams of living in the center of an American city, catching the bus home, watching the crowds, and admiring the tall buildings. He brought home takeout from an Italian restaurant similar to the one in which he worked in London. He ate it watching his favorite sitcom. He heard a buzzing and felt a sense of leaving his body before these particular dreams, and following them he gently returned to his waking British life.

DREAM BACKGROUND AND MEANING

Antonio was totally content with his life in London, though he knew he was in a rut. He had an open invitation to manage his cousin's Italian restaurant in Chicago. Dreams in which we live a remarkably similar life to our own in another location suggest an alternative lifestyle that would not involve disruption.

INTERPRETATIONS AND FORTUNE-TELLING MEANINGS

★ If you experience a buzzing and lifting sensation in dreams, this indicates astral or spirit travel during sleep to a particular world, whether actual or created on the dream plane.

★ If we dream of ourselves in a parallel life, we might be linking with someone far away who shares our energies, and we might superimpose ourselves temporarily on their life.

★ If you see someone else living a similar life, they may be your astral twin or another part of yourself.

★ If you make a major change in the dream of the parallel world, a similar action or decision in the waking world would be advantageous.

★ If you dream that a lover is waiting in the parallel life, that may be where true love waits.

★ If you have a connection with the dream place, it is calling you to move or vacation there.

OUTCOME OF ANTONIO'S DREAM

The dreams continued. Antonio went on a long vacation to stay with his cousin in Chicago and to see what the prospects were. Parallel dream lives can ease a transition between an old life and a new one, reassuring those reluctant to embrace change because of fears that they would lose the lifestyle they love.

Paranormal Nightmares

Soon after moving to coastal Christchurch in Hampshire, United Kingdom, Keith, twelve, experienced horrendous nightmares, which recurred every full moon. There was an abandoned metal boat tied to the riverbank in the harbor. Keith sensed evil but was forced to go belowdecks by an invisible force. The far left-hand corner of the boat was in shadow, and there was a shadow within it, darker than the outer shadow. There was no shape to it. The shadow rose up, getting larger as it did so. Eventually it filled the room, towering over Keith. Then it swooped down, enveloping him. He screamed and woke.

DREAM BACKGROUND AND MEANING

Keith had never been to the harbor of his dream, but he later discovered that the World War II vintage metal boat in his dream was a minesweeper and was moored there. By moving to the area, Keith may have triggered some past-world memory or may have linked with a disturbed spirit.

INTERPRETATIONS AND FORTUNE-TELLING MEANINGS

★ Psychic children may suffer nightmares in places where the paranormal energies are strong.

★ A child experiencing personal trauma may attract in dreams free-flowing negative energies that hook onto personal distress.

★ Keith's nightmare recurred on full moons, and there seems to be a link between moons and paranormal energies.

★ Psychic nightmares are strongest before the age of seven and again in adolescence, when a child's psychic energies surge.

★ Whether psychic or psychological, recurring nightmares are a manifestation of repressed fears and anxieties, and need reassurance for the dreamer, unlike what happened to Keith, who was punished.

OUTCOME OF KEITH'S DREAM

A few weeks after the nightmares had started, there was a storm. The metal minesweeper was torn from its moorings on the far side of the river. Keith was further traumatized by this. Psychic children need extra care at night until the nightmares lessen.

Parental Rejection

Chloe, nine, had many nightmares in which her mother would leave her in the middle of nowhere and drive off. In the most vivid, Chloe saw her mother getting into a car, and she rushed to try to pry the driver's door open. But her mother was acting as if Chloe was not there.

DREAM BACKGROUND AND MEANING

Chloe had lived alone with her mother since she was two, but her father had intermittently entered her life, bringing elaborate gifts. When Chloe was seven, he remarried and all contact ceased. Chloe knew her mother would still be there, but the dreams began. Fear of being abandoned by a parent is a primeval instinct, designed to ensure that the baby is nourished while vulnerable, but such instincts can end up being misplaced.

INTERPRETATIONS AND FORTUNE-TELLING MEANINGS

* If you dream of being a child again, abandoned by one or both parents, there may be an issue in a current relationship that makes you feel insecure and vulnerable.
* If at any age you dream you see someone driving away without you, you may fear that you are being left behind at work or socially. Do you want to catch up?
* If in your dream you are being abandoned at whatever your age by a father, mother, or grandparent, examine what is going on in the current relationship that makes the person act coldly toward you, maybe a personal insecurity of theirs.
* If the person rejecting stops and waits for the dreamer, fears of abandonment are groundless, but clingy behavior may eventually drive the other person away.
* If both parties are amicably driving in different directions in the dream, having more space may fix any sense of being possessed or of codependency.

OUTCOME OF CHLOE'S DREAM

Time and reassurance by Chloe's mother, plus a discussion of who would care for Chloe if her mother died, a hidden fear for a single-parent child, cured the dreams. Where children are rejected by a parent, the sense of rejection can reemerge at crisis times in adulthood (see "Abandonment," p. 18).

Parents

In his dream, Peter, twenty-seven, was five years old, being taken to his first day at school by both parents. They hugged him and said that after school, as a treat, they would go to a café for dinner. He woke filled with longing for those days.

DREAM BACKGROUND AND MEANING

Peter had been raised by an abusive father. His mother left when he was four. A neighbor took him to school on the first day, but there was no one there to meet him later in the day. Now Peter was married to Anne, who wanted to start a family. But Peter feared turning into his father. Dreams about parents can create ideal scenarios if the reality was not ideal. If the parents were bad role models, dreams can show that we are not our parents and can change history.

INTERPRETATIONS AND FORTUNE-TELLING MEANINGS

* To dream of your parents, whether alive or not, suggests that you feel you need permission from an authority figure, actual or in your head, to make a major decision.
* If you dream of a deceased parent or parents, they may have a message for you or may seek reconciliation.
* To dream of a dominant parent, alive or deceased, says that you are striving to overcome dependency on the approval of others.
* To dream of an indulgent parent or parents means you are seeking permission to opt out of responsibility in a tricky situation.
* If you have happy relationships with your parents, living or deceased, dreams of gatherings in your childhood home recall aspects of growing up that you would like to recapture in your present life and relationships.
* If you never knew your birth parents, you may dream of them and gain clues that you can follow if you wish.

OUTCOME OF PETER'S DREAM

After the dream, Peter went to counseling to express his fears and suppressed anger. He links the dream with the future, when he and Anne will take their eldest child to school. Parental dreams are common, especially if the dreamer is contemplating becoming a parent, or is already one; the dreams can overwrite traumas and fears with positive images.

Parking

Mark, thirty-eight, dreamed he was running late for a job interview. The first parking lot he tried was too small. The nearby multistory had no spaces. Panicking, Mark parked outside the interview building, though it was a no-parking zone. Halfway through the interview, a law enforcement officer arrived to say that unless Mark moved the car it would be towed away. Torn, Mark stayed at the interview, and his car was gone when he returned.

DREAM BACKGROUND AND MEANING

Mark had applied for a new job involving promotion but was not certain he could manage it, as he shared childcare with his wife. He always seemed to be late and rushing. Since a car represents the journey through life, leaving parking or scheduled events to chance causes unnecessary stress.

INTERPRETATIONS AND FORTUNE-TELLING MEANINGS

* If you dream you find the perfect parking spot, the day after the dream will run smoothly, with desired results.
* If you dream you cannot park your car in a small lot or full parking lot, you are struggling against restrictions.
* A dream of a parking fine or of being towed away is an authority dream where old failures and criticism may hold you back from making a change in lifestyle that could be advantageous.
* To park illegally suggests that you are prepared to take a risk for short-term advantage.
* Losing your car in a parking lot, or being in an unlit scary one, is a safety dream, reflecting concerns about security when you travel.
* Having your parking space taken as you try to park warns against underhanded and ruthless dealings.
* Parking a car when you are desperately racing against time says you may be trying to do too many things at once and should slow down.

OUTCOME OF MARK'S DREAM

Mark allowed time to park before the interview and was offered the job. The company had a day-care facility where he could take the children. A dream of successful parking says we need to plan self-time out of a busy schedule.

Parrot

Harry, forty-eight, dreamed he was in a rain forest with beautiful parrots flying free. His own parrot was in a cage on a tree, squawking as the others flew by. Harry set his parrot free and it flew to join the others.

DREAM BACKGROUND AND MEANING

Harry had inherited a parrot from his aunt that took a dislike to him and would peck and squawk incessantly. He was tempted to take the parrot and set it free, but he knew it would not survive, having been caged all its life. In Pueblo Indian mythology, the parrot is a bird of the sun and a bringer of abundance, and parrots in their natural habitat promise travel and a chance to shine once you find your right place in the world.

INTERPRETATIONS AND FORTUNE-TELLING MEANINGS

* Parrots are messengers and bringers of news in Afro-Caribbean lore. One appearing in a dream says you will hear from someone who you have lost touch with.
* Chattering parrots indicate gossip and idle rumor, best ignored in the workplace or among neighbors.
* Teaching a parrot to talk in a dream suggests that you are lacking new ideas and bored with present activities.
* If a parrot is incessantly chattering, you need more privacy and self-time.
* A dream of a silent parrot says petty quarrels among family, friends, or colleagues will at last be resolved.

OUTCOME OF HARRY'S DREAM

After the dream, Harry realized that the bird was lonely. He took the parrot to a rescue center, where it was gradually introduced to other parrots in a huge aviary. It started to talk and mimic visitors and became a great attraction. If the parrot is confined in a cage in your dream, it can warn you that you may need to find your own voice rather than echoing the status quo you may not believe in.

Passing Over

Juliet, thirty-nine, dreamed she was in a waiting room filled with light that had two doors, one she had come through and one closed, leading out. Her mother was sitting white-faced, and Juliet realized that she was waiting to pass over. She held her mother's hands and explained gently that she had died and now had to go through the door to the other side. Juliet promised to take care of the family. Juliet opened the second door, and there was a rushing wind and brilliance, and her mother was gone.

DREAM BACKGROUND AND MEANING

Juliet's mother had died unexpectedly at home. Juliet and her father were both in shock. Juliet had sensed that her mother had not fully passed. If you dream of a newly deceased relative in a corridor or waiting room, or outside gates, they may not have yet made the transition to the afterlife (see "Dying," p. 157).

INTERPRETATIONS AND FORTUNE-TELLING MEANINGS

* If you dream of a newly deceased agitated relative, they need to tell you a message of unfinished business, and then you will sense that their presence has moved on.
* If a death was sudden or traumatic, there may be several dreams in the days after the death when the deceased is seeking a familiar presence.
* If in the dream the relative refuses to leave Earth, there may be a close living relative unconsciously holding them back because of grief or guilt.
* If you can see a beautiful garden through golden gates or a tunnel of light in your dream, you are helping your relative to pass over.
* If a relative died traumatically, you may see them in the dream as younger and fit, a reassurance the relative needs to give.

OUTCOME OF JULIET'S DREAM

After the dream, Juliet sensed her mother was no longer around, and she was able to help her father to grieve. Passing-over dreams are very significant, as some spirits seem reluctant to leave the family, especially if there has been estrangement. These dreams can play an important part of mourning and letting go for both deceased and bereaved.

Passport

Roland, thirty, dreamed he had lost his passport overseas on the last day of his vacation. He located the embassy but waited for hours, only to be told he had the wrong documentation to prove his identity. He left, anxious that he would not return before the passport section closed. A man outside told Roland he could buy a new passport in any identity he wished. Roland handed over his money and disappeared into the streets with a new identity.

DREAM BACKGROUND AND MEANING

Roland wanted to go to the airport, pick a destination at random, and continue life from there. What was to stop him? Passports represent a doorway to infinite possibility, and dreams about them are a reminder that there is a whole world waiting.

INTERPRETATIONS AND FORTUNE-TELLING MEANINGS

* If you dream you are passing through customs with your passport en route to vacation or business, you will experience successful, happy travel.
* If your passport is rejected, you may doubt your self-worth, and anxiety may block your progress to a less limited lifestyle.
* If you dream that your passport is torn or wet, a rival may try to deter you from applying for promotion.
* If you dream you are traveling on a forged passport, you may be worried that your knowledge or expertise may be challenged.
* If you dream that you have a brand-new passport with no stamps in it, there is a chance to reinvent your image.

OUTCOME OF ROLAND'S DREAM

Roland booked an open-return ticket, initially around the Americas and Canada, and, for the first time in his life since enrolling in college, he had no agenda. He returned after a year of traveling the world and taking casual work as he needed to, settled in his original location in his former profession as a surveyor, and married his childhood sweetheart. Even if you have no definite plans to travel, passport dreams can reflect an unacknowledged desire to widen your horizons by traveling or changing your location or career.

Pathways

Addison, twenty-eight, dreamed he had reached a crossroads with a signpost. One way said PAST, the one he had traveled; the second said PRESENT UNCERTAINTY; and the third, UNKNOWN FUTURE. He was tempted to go back the way he had come but he knew it was a dead end. The PRESENT was flooded and the third, the FUTURE, was brambly, stony, and uphill. He woke trying to decide.

DREAM BACKGROUND AND MEANING

Addison had walked away from a loveless marriage and a career that was going nowhere. It was not too late to go back. He had given his ex all their savings and was in effect homeless. He knew he could easily get work in the mines and earn enough to save for a deep-sea diving and snorkeling course to open his adventure school. But the work would be hard. Would that path be worth the effort?

A path represents your personal journey through life. Though others have trodden the same way and erected signposts, ultimately you must choose your own direction.

INTERPRETATIONS AND FORTUNE-TELLING MEANINGS

* Dreaming of a choice of paths indicates you do have options but have to decide.
* A sunny, flower-strewn path heralds opportunity that, if followed, will lead to success and fulfillment.
* If a path is shrouded in mist, it represents initial uncertainty, but once the mist clears it may prove worth the risk.
* A path whose way is blocked by barbed wire suggests that others have interests in deterring you from what may be to your advantage.
* A flooded footpath says that the decision of which path to follow in life is filled with emotion but should not exclude logic and common sense.
* Fallen signposts in dreams tell us we have to make our own decisions, looking at the actual paths ahead, not just accepting others' advice.

OUTCOME OF ADDISON'S DREAM

Addison instinctively knew his dream was telling him to take the hard path so he could have a fulfilling life ahead, though the present was uncertain.

Pawnbroker, Pawnshop

Linda, twenty-five, dreamed her fiancé, Roger, proposed and took her to a pawnbroker, showed her a tray of rings, and told her she could have her pick. She felt a bit cheated, but was glad he had proposed at last. He told her the engagement was secret as his family would not approve, but she could wear the ring when they were alone.

DREAM BACKGROUND AND MEANING

Linda thought she was lucky Roger was her boyfriend, as he came from a wealthy family and she was an ordinary working girl. She knew his family did not approve because of her background, but he said they could get engaged if she did not tell his family. He told her the ring he gave her was a valuable family heirloom.

INTERPRETATIONS AND FORTUNE-TELLING MEANINGS

* If you dream that you see three gold balls suspended from a bar, the sign of a pawnshop, whether set in a past or present world, look carefully at financial or love offers to ensure that you are not fobbed off cheaply.
* If you dream you are visiting a pawnbroker shop to leave what is of value to you, be careful with current finances or a secret relationship, to avoid losses.
* If in the dream you are bought a gift from a pawnbroker, consider if you are being given due respect in your career or relationship.
* If you are a pawnbroker in the dream, you may be asked for a loan by a friend or family member. Check that your money will be returned.
* If you dream you are looking for a bargain in a pawnbroker, be reassured that a second or subsequent relationship can work well if you go in with your eyes open.

OUTCOME OF LINDA'S DREAM

After six months, Roger's parents announced his engagement to their best friends' daughter. Linda took the ring to a pawnbroker, who told her it was worthless. Pawnbroker dreams can occur when the dreamer is being undervalued in love or career.

Peacemaking

Patrick, sixty-five, dreamed he was riding toward the enemy, holding the flag of truce in what seemed to be the late fifteenth century. Everyone was shooting arrows, and he feared for his life. Finally they stopped, and he was admitted to the tent of the rival fighting for the crown. Patrick's terms of peace were accepted. However, as the would-be king returned with Patrick, the king's army began firing again, killing the leader and wounding Patrick.

DREAM BACKGROUND AND MEANING

Patrick was involved in a bitter neighborhood dispute in which half the village supported a new traffic bypass while the other half said it would destroy passing trade. Patrick, a retired attorney, was unofficial mediator. Each side accused him of supporting the other. He believed each argument had merit, but all meetings thus far had ended in shouting matches. Peacemaking dreams, when positive, can indicate bringing or restoring harmony to the out-of-balance area of your life. If neither side will compromise, your dream may be saying you have undertaken a thankless task.

INTERPRETATIONS AND FORTUNE-TELLING MEANINGS

* If you dream you are negotiating a peace settlement between relatives or friends, be careful both sides do not turn on you.
* If you are trying to pacify a hostage-taker in a dream, you may fear that psychological pressure means neither side wants resolution any longer.
* If you are involved in peacemaking where armies are fighting, there exist far bigger issues than there seem.
* If you are being asked to make a peace that will involve unfair compromise, do not give in to pressure.
* If you dream you are acting as official peacemaker or mediator in the dream, you may want to detach yourself.
* If you dream the feuding parties refuse to make peace in a long-standing dispute, walk away or end the quarrel.

OUTCOME OF PATRICK'S DREAM

After the dream and a broken window the next day, Patrick quit and put his house on the market. Peacemaking dreams may reveal factors that indicate that stepping back may be the answer, as peacemaking may be escalating a problem.

Peach

Ariadne, thirty-five, dreamed she found a magic peach tree, and when she ate a peach was granted three wishes. She wished for her husband, Pete, to love her forever; for her baby daughter to remain healthy; and finally that their lovely house would be protected from disasters. But, while she was wishing, a tornado destroyed the blossoming peach trees and the house, and she could not find Pete or the baby in the darkness.

DREAM BACKGROUND AND MEANING

Ariadne had a husband who adored her, a beautiful baby, and a lovely house, bought by both sets of parents. But Ariadne was terrified that it was all too perfect, and she could not sleep at night, worried about disaster taking it all away. She was deliberately arguing with Pete to drive him away so life would not be too perfect. Pete was confused about her sudden hostility. Peach dreams can be double-edged swords, promising a lasting happiness that the dreamer may worry will be snatched away.

INTERPRETATIONS AND FORTUNE-TELLING MEANINGS

* The peach dream is a fertility symbol for natural conception if lovemaking is marred by ovulation charts or tests.
* The peach blossom represents growing prosperity, improved health, and romance or revival of romance.
* In China and Japan, the peach is a symbol of immortality. To be offered one says that you will prove invincible in a particular ambition.
* A peach surrounded by leaves is a symbol of passion and compatibility in love, especially for those who are bisexual or seek a same-sex relationship.
* A rotting peach warns that a friend or lover may not be all that they seem.

OUTCOME OF ARIADNE'S DREAM

Pete was about to leave her when Ariadne explained why she was pushing him away. They realized she was depressed and sought help. They also made practical plans for any contingency, including taking out extra insurance on their lives and the home. Ariadne is learning to appreciate every moment of happiness. Peach dreams should be seen as symbols not only of worldly good fortune, but also of emotional riches daily renewed.

Peacock

Mandy, nineteen, saw a peacock with incredible colors surrounded by other peacocks with painted feathers, of which she was one. She fought off the pecks of the others to be next to the fabulous peacock. It rained, and her colors washed away. She realized she was just a small brown peahen, as were the others, except for the glorious peacock, who strutted away.

DREAM BACKGROUND AND MEANING

Mandy wanted to be the girlfriend of Declan, the captain of the baseball team. She went on a diet, spent her money on new clothes, and spent hours over her appearance. At last she was noticed and trailed along as his adoring decorative girlfriend. But she had to compete for her place against the jealous women who surrounded him, who he encouraged. Dream peacocks almost always signify people in your life. Make sure there is inner beauty as well as veneer.

INTERPRETATIONS AND FORTUNE-TELLING MEANINGS

* A beautiful peacock surrounded by brown peahens represents a vain friend, family member, or lover.
* Having a peacock strutting away represents ambitious plans that do not materialize.
* If you dream you turn into a brown peahen, value your true self, rather than pretending to be what you are not.
* A peacock feather with an eye is not unlucky, rather a symbol of protection against jealousy, traditionally repelling the evil eye.
* If a peacock is screeching, someone is causing discord and is not reliable.
* A peacock spreading its plumed tail promises success, fame, and fortune if you display your talents.

OUTCOME OF MANDY'S DREAM

Mandy was broke, her work suffering, and Declan was using her as a foil for his vanity. Mandy dropped the hard-to-maintain image and became herself again.

The peacock is the creature of the goddess of women, the Greek Hera and Roman Juno, representing the power and beauty of the true woman.

Pearls

Juliana, twenty-eight, dreamed of her great-grandmother, who she had only seen in faded photographs, coming to her and offering her a string of pearls to wear on her wedding day. Her great-grandmother, who Juliana resembled, told Juliana the pearls had been in the family for generations and always brought the bridal couple happiness and good fortune. She woke, feeling that her great-grandmother was blessing her marriage to Janice. Juliana was happy, because some of the elderly relatives disapproved of her choice and had refused to attend the wedding.

DREAM BACKGROUND AND MEANING

Juliana woke puzzled and contacted her mother, who sent a picture of her great-grandmother as a bride wearing the pearls. Since a few of the pearls were cracked and fading, her mother had not offered the pearls to Juliana. Pearls are often borrowed by a bride from a happy couple to transfer the happiness.

INTERPRETATIONS AND FORTUNE-TELLING MEANINGS

* Pearls are a symbol of romance, love, and marriage, especially as a string of pearls.
* As a necklace, pearls are a sign of happiness if worn at a wedding, promising that a bride will never cry during her marriage, because the pearls represent the tears of the angels or sea goddesses that have been shed so humanity might always smile.
* A broken string of pearls indicates growing disappointment in a love match that you knew in your heart was not right.
* A jar of pearls in a dream signifies fertility and the health and safety of a baby throughout their life.
* If pearls are seen falling from the sky, they represent prosperity and healing.

OUTCOME OF JULIANA'S DREAM

Juliana had the pearls restored and wore them on her wedding day. She felt her great-grandmother close all day. Juliana had the old photo restored and printed on the front of the wedding invitations.

Pearls belonging to ancestors have special significance, as they are supposed to absorb and transmit the love of the family through the generations. Because a pearl is created from a grain of sand in the oyster shell, they represent the growth of love through good times and bad.

People from the Past

Christabel, forty-five, dreamed she had returned to the school in her hometown where she first worked as a teacher twenty years earlier. The same headmistress, Miss Harrison, was there. To her amazement, Christabel, normally a very private person, asked for her job back while pouring out her life story and being comforted. She woke feeling reassured.

DREAM BACKGROUND AND MEANING

Christabel had left teaching years earlier and was now a successful author. She did not want to return to teaching. But she had no one to talk with, as she was divorced and childless and her parents had died. Dreaming of people from the past, usually former mentors, can form a sounding board for a life review at a time when we need change, even if the person is no longer alive or part of your life.

INTERPRETATIONS AND FORTUNE-TELLING MEANINGS

* If you dream of someone you have not heard of for years who is much older, they may be passing over and you may have appeared in their mind.
* If you are pouring out your life story to a former mentor, you are seeking validation of your experiences and acknowledgment of your feelings.
* If you dream of receiving comfort from a person you do not know, especially one dressed in the clothes of a former century, they may be a spirit guide who shared a past world with you.
* If you dream of someone from the past who you parted from in anger, you may be connecting with them telepathically to close a chapter.
* If you regularly dream of a contemporary who you have lost touch with, they may want to restore the connection.
* If your dream connection is healing or reassuring, it is time to rediscover your roots.

OUTCOME OF CHRISTABEL'S DREAM

Christabel rented out her city center apartment and returned to her hometown area. Though it had changed, there was still a sense of community with familiar people. Dreaming of people from the past does not necessarily mean contact will be resumed, but it offers a safe place to plan a new future and maybe a return to the area.

Pepper (Spice)

Susie, twenty-eight, dreamed she was cooking dinner for her girlfriends. She had run out of many spices and so added extra pepper to give the dish flavor. But when they ate it, her friends said it burned their tongues. A quarrel broke out in which they all said things they would later regret. Susie woke, realizing it was the end of the friendships.

DREAM BACKGROUND AND MEANING

Susie had suspected for some months that, since she had been promoted at work over her friends, they were less comfortable in her company, had started excluding her from outings, and would test her authority. Should she resign her promotion and win her friends back? The right amount of pepper in a dream represents lively verbal exchanges and stimulating friendship, since it is associated with hospitality without rancor.

INTERPRETATIONS AND FORTUNE-TELLING MEANINGS

* If you dream you see peppercorns growing on their woody vines, excitement and good fortune will enter your life, especially involving overseas travel.
* If you dream that pepper is being ground, your natural wit and humor will need to be toned down to avoid quarrels with people eager to pick a fight.
* If a riot squad is using pepper spray to disarm a crowd, you may find yourself temporarily blinded to the true situation at work or in your community.
* If you dream you are sprinkling pepper on the doorstep, this is a traditional protective remedy for banishing unwanted visitors and gossips.
* A broken or spilled pepper jar indicates hidden spite or sarcasm without provocation.

OUTCOME OF SUSIE'S DREAM

Susie realized that she could not go back to what was before and needed her promotion so she could enter the next level of her training. The words spoken in the dream were actually said the day after the dream when Susie asserted her authority, speaking to her friends about their unwillingness to follow instructions.

Pepper dreams walk the line between humor, wit, honest speaking, and allowing jealousy to sour words with harshness.

Phantom Pregnancy

Rhoda, twenty-four, dreamed that she was busy preparing her baby's nursery for the birth when, through the window, she saw a white stork with a bassinet in its beak. She woke truly happy.

DREAM BACKGROUND AND MEANING

Twice previously, Rhoda had had morning sickness and tender breasts. When she had an ultrasound, she was told they were phantom pregnancies. Since then, she had refused to see a doctor, despite having more symptoms of pregnancy.

INTERPRETATIONS AND FORTUNE-TELLING MEANINGS

* If a woman has experienced phantom pregnancies and loses faith in carrying a child, a symbol personal to the dreamer, connected with birth, reassures the mother-to-be that this time should be the real thing.
* If a woman or her partner is anxious to conceive, a dream of a baby surrounded by mist may indicate that there may not be a baby this time.
* If you are not trying for a baby, a phantom pregnancy can mean it is not the right time for that new project.
* If you or your partner dreams of a phantom pregnancy, and you are pregnant with a thriving baby, you may have natural anxieties about the pregnancy or about parenting.
* If you are a man and dream of being pregnant at the same time as a pregnant partner or surrogate, you will make an exceptionally sensitive father.
* If you are beyond childbearing years and dream of having a child, you may be linked with the unborn child of your pregnant daughter or daughter-in-law.

OUTCOME OF RHODA'S DREAM

As a child, Rhoda had loved the Disney film where storks were carrying babies in baskets in their beaks to expectant mothers. After the dream, she was reassured that she really was pregnant and ultimately had healthy twins. If a woman has suffered a phantom pregnancy, dreams with symbols of babies can be reassuring that this time it is different.

Phoenix (Golden)

Polly, thirty, dreamed she saw her golden phoenix rising into the sky from a fire. She showed her small children the wondrous creature as the sun rose over the deserted street. It turned, indicating that Polly should follow. As they struggled with their bags, Polly saw ahead a golden doorway opening. Inside was her childhood home and her room, waiting unchanged. She woke happy, until she remembered her dire circumstances.

DREAM BACKGROUND AND MEANING

Polly left her violent husband and was living with her children in a women's shelter. She had left home with only what she and the children could carry. Polly had not seen her own family for years, as they had quarreled over her marriage. She had written to them without much hope.

The legend of the golden phoenix describes the bird preparing a funeral pyre of aromatic spices every five hundred years, which is ignited by the first rays of the sun. From the ashes, a golden young bird emerges.

INTERPRETATIONS AND FORTUNE-TELLING MEANINGS

* The phoenix is a rare, precious dream symbol indicating major transformation and hoped-for opportunities.
* An alchemical sign, any golden phoenix dream heralds fame and fortune through total dedication and single-mindedness.
* The young bird foretells a chance to put a bad experience, business failure, or relationship behind you.
* The bird framed in the sun is a spiritual sign to change emphasis from achievement to fulfillment.
* A flying phoenix indicates it is time to travel or relocate.
* A phoenix rising is a good omen for the restoration of health and a better quality of life, even if the prognosis is not encouraging.

OUTCOME OF POLLY'S DREAM

Polly's mother arrived at the shelter to take the family home. Polly's bedroom was the same. On the bookshelf was her magical book of animals, recounting the story of the phoenix.

In various cultures, the phoenix is linked with the sun and with creation out of destruction, while recognizing that success or happiness comes at a price.

Phone-Sex Line

Fleur, fifty-five, dreamed she was working on a phone-sex line. The guys and women who used the line were getting very excited at her talk. Then she recognized her husband's voice on the line and, without revealing she knew his identity or who she was, they had a thrilling conversation, which amazed her. She hung up, anxiously awaiting his arrival home so they could make passionate love.

DREAM BACKGROUND AND MEANING

Fleur's sex life with her husband, Jim, had been nonexistent for years, and she had been having increasingly erotic dreams. Fleur did not want to have an affair, as she was otherwise happily married. She worried that the dream was saying that Jim sought satisfaction elsewhere. Phone-sex line dreams reveal a secret desire to shed respectability anonymously and share intimate secrets with strangers.

INTERPRETATIONS AND FORTUNE-TELLING MEANINGS

* If your love partner dials a phone-sex line and you are answering in your dream, you may already suspect they are seeking satisfaction elsewhere.
* If you dial in to or work on a dream phone-sex line, you will benefit from more fantasy within your relationship.
* If you are earning money on a high-class phone-sex line in your dream, you might consider writing racy novels.
* If you dream of being on the receiving end of a sex chat and you hate it, you need more romance in your existing or future love life.
* If in your dream you are questioned by the authorities for running a phone-sex line, you may be feeling guilty about your sexual fantasies and repress natural passion.

OUTCOME OF FLEUR'S DREAM

Fleur told her husband about her dream, and he said he had thought about phoning one of those lines but lacked the courage. They acted out phone line fantasies, and their sex life instantly improved. Phone-sex line dreams can reveal to the dreamer the desire for a richer, more exciting sex life, concealed from a partner through embarrassment or guilt.

Piano

Gloria, fifty-two, dreamed she was a child trying to play scales, but her piano teacher smacked her fingers when she played a wrong note. At last the teacher left and, to her amazement, Gloria discovered she could play songs and classical tunes without looking at the music or piano keys. She woke filled with joy.

DREAM BACKGROUND AND MEANING

Gloria had always wanted to play the piano, but as a child she had a piano teacher, the one in the dream, who told her she was useless. Gloria recently inherited her aunt's piano and regretted that it stood silent at family parties. Was she too old to learn? Pianos are symbols of harmony and togetherness if playing is treated as a pleasure, not a chore.

INTERPRETATIONS AND FORTUNE-TELLING MEANINGS

* If you dream of family or friends standing around a piano, singing, any spontaneous social gatherings will be a great success.
* If you dream you are a famous concert pianist, you have gifts in the performing arts you could develop professionally.
* If the piano is out of tune, there may be discord at a family gathering.
* If you dream a piano lid will not open or the keys do not play, it is not time to try to bring people together or resolve difficulties.
* If you are unwillingly playing scales, persevere with routine tasks or tedious study to lead to more fulfilling opportunities.
* If you dream of people gathered around a piano singing wartime or music-hall songs, you may be linking into family history and should contact older relatives or research ancestors.

OUTCOME OF GLORIA'S DREAM

After the dream, Gloria took lessons from a teacher who was used to nervous pupils. The teacher discovered that Gloria played by ear and did not read the sheet music. Gloria now plays at family parties and for the local school at their concerts. Whether you want to play as a concert pianist or socially, it is never too late to learn the piano for pure pleasure and to pass that pleasure on.

Picnic

Rachael, twenty-eight, dreamed she packed a romantic picnic to share with her boyfriend, Tai. She waited for him, but time was passing and he was not answering his cell phone. At last, he reported that the highway was blocked and there was no way he could reach her, so they would have to reschedule. It began to rain as she dumped her carefully prepared canapés.

DREAM BACKGROUND AND MEANING

Tai was working 24/7 so he could reach the top. Rachael hardly ever saw him, and their planned weekends or days together were often canceled at the last minute. Picnics can represent an away-from-it-all romantic occasion. If one participant does not show up in the dream, there may be underlying issues about commitment.

INTERPRETATIONS AND FORTUNE-TELLING MEANINGS

* Enjoying an impromptu picnic indicates a break from work and pleasurable time outdoors.
* Ants or wasps spoiling a picnic warn that someone in the family or a friend may make trouble at an informal social event.
* If the dream picnic is for two with champagne, a wicker hamper, and delicacies in a beautiful spot, you need more romance, time, and space alone with your love.
* If you arrive at the picnic place, but the picnic has been left at home, the person who forgot it may not want to socialize with whoever else is present.
* If you dream a rain shower or storm breaks up a picnic, troubles you left behind still need resolving.

OUTCOME OF RACHAEL'S DREAM

After the dream, followed by yet another canceled date together, Rachael realized that the only time they met was when she accompanied him to a formal business dinner. Tai admitted that work was most important and that he needed a girlfriend to fit in. She found a less-ambitious partner and is planning her romantic picnic for two, now that they are seriously dating. Picnics can represent valuing a relaxing lifestyle rather than striving for luxury.

Pigeon

Flora, thirty, dreamed that a snow-white pigeon flew out of the sun with a message from her husband, George, a soldier serving overseas, that he had been wounded but was safe. Flora felt strangely reassured since she knew pigeons had been used to send messages for many centuries, especially by soldiers on the battlefront.

DREAM BACKGROUND AND MEANING

Flora's husband was missing in action, but there was no news. She did not believe he was dead. She had had her pigeon dream many times since George had been missing and found it reassuring. She kept seeing pure white pigeons settling on her roof.

INTERPRETATIONS AND FORTUNE-TELLING MEANINGS

* Dreaming of sending a pigeon with a message indicates you can trust a friend or family member to act as a messenger or arbitrator in a family dispute, especially with someone estranged.
* Dreaming of a pigeon flying toward you with a message strapped to its leg indicates unexpected communication from afar or the revival of an old friendship or love.
* Seeing a pigeon shot in a dream warns against acting as a go-between with warring factions or relatives.
* Pigeons flying in a flock and returning to their nest say you or a loved one will travel far but always return home.
* A carrier pigeon that gets lost or injured says there may be a misunderstanding via social media. If possible, communicate face to face.
* Pigeons nesting foretell happy family days and vacations and are an excellent omen if you are creating your first home or planning a family.

OUTCOME OF FLORA'S DREAM

Against all odds, George returned home, though he was wounded. Though pigeons are not used in modern warfare, in Flora's dreams the pigeons brought telepathic hope from George. Pigeons mate for life and so can form a powerful love link, especially where lovers are parted over many miles.

Pile, Heap

Duncan, fifty-eight, dreamed he was looking at a pile of gold he had acquired. But he realized that if he took any off the pile, it might collapse, and so he continued to stare at it. Then it changed into a pile of salt. He was devastated after all his saving. It rained, and the salt pile was washed away.

DREAM BACKGROUND AND MEANING

Duncan had saved all his life for his retirement and had a considerable pension pot into which he could dip although he was still working. He had developed a heart condition not covered by his medical insurance, which could be fixed if he paid for a private operation and ongoing treatment that would take a substantial amount of his savings. He hesitated to spend so much money. A heap of salt represents good health; for hundreds of years salt has been valued as currency because of its value in preserving food and, so, life.

INTERPRETATIONS AND FORTUNE-TELLING MEANINGS

* If you dream of a pile of sugar, beware flattery, unwise investments, or overspending.
* If you dream you have a pile of unwashed laundry, you may be expected to fix the problems of others. If it is washed and neatly folded, you will complete a seemingly endless task by being methodical.
* If you dream that a building collapses into a pile of bricks, a property venture may prove an expensive mistake.
* If you are building a tower with a pile of toy bricks, go back to an earlier idea and see how you can give it substance.
* If you are given a pile of presents on your birthday or Christmas, you are appreciated by others. Beware if you heap gifts on others and do not receive some.
* A dream of a heap of money or gold indicates prosperity, but a rubbish heap suggests you may be overwhelmed by others' quarrels.

OUTCOME OF DUNCAN'S DREAM

Duncan's daughter, who he told about the dream, said his pile of money was no use if he was not there to enjoy it. He had the operation and, when he recovered, splurged on a world cruise. Piling up whatever the commodity is in the dream can suggest new priorities and the balance between accumulating and enjoying what has been saved.

Pilgrimage, Sacred Quest

Drusilla, fifty, dreamed she was high among the mountains, following a pilgrim trail with hundreds of other people. An old woman in a brown robe gave her a very old scallop shell, a symbol of the pilgrimage. She said it was no good having the experience if you missed the meaning. Drusilla woke, knowing she had met her sacred guide.

DREAM BACKGROUND AND MEANING

Drusilla's new partner, Alan, was on a constant quest for spiritual fulfillment. They had visited ashrams in India, temples throughout Indonesia, ancient stones, pilgrimage trails throughout the world, sacred indigenous routes in America, and song lines in Aboriginal Australia. But she felt frustrated, irritable, and exhausted. Alan complained that Drusilla lacked spirituality and questioned whether she was the right partner for his sacred life quest.

INTERPRETATIONS AND FORTUNE-TELLING MEANINGS

* A pilgrim walking beside you indicates unexpected communication from afar.
* Being greeted by a pilgrim wearing brown robes with a staff says you have a wise spirit guide who protects you.
* If you dream you are alone, walking an established pilgrimage route such as one of the St. James of Compostela roads to Santiago in Spain, you need inner peace, not others' spirituality imposed on you.
* If you are in a medieval scenario, pursuing the legendary Grail Chalice, you may soon find romance and twin-soul love.
* If you are walking between sacred sites on energy lines or ancient tracks, and in your dream feel vibrations, you are connecting with Earth energies in a powerful way and should visit similar places in the everyday world.
* If you dream you get lost on your pilgrimage route, fulfill your everyday needs before focusing on spirituality.

OUTCOME OF DRUSILLA'S DREAM

Drusilla declined Alan's planned sacred quest, and he went off with another woman from the healing group to race around the world, seeking fulfillment. Drusilla bought a scallop shell, which she holds to experience connection with her pilgrim guide. Sacred quests can be inner journeys in the most mundane places if we focus on the meaning and not just on the outward experience.

Pineapples

Dulcie, fifty-five, dreamed she was chopping pineapples in an open-air cocktail bar on a tropical island, making piña colada cocktails. The local boys were chatting to the new arrivals, eager for romance and passion. The older male tourists were being offered a good time by the local girls. Dulcie counted her profits and went home with her latest young lover.

DREAM BACKGROUND AND MEANING

Dulcie had come to an exotic island to find romance and she predictably met a young man, Juan, who complimented her on her beauty. She enjoyed two weeks of sun and amazing sex. She was contemplating buying the highly profitable beach bar where they had romanced, which was for sale. Pineapple dreams are the ultimate fantasies and, if taken at face value, can bring joy and an escape from reality.

INTERPRETATIONS AND FORTUNE-TELLING MEANINGS

★ If you dream you are sipping piña coladas in luxurious surroundings, you are seeking a more exotic lifestyle.

★ If you are cutting open a fresh pineapple to eat the fruit, extra effort in any area of life will bring rewards.

★ If you hurt your hand on the sharp pineapple skin, take extra care, as the price of satisfaction may be higher than anticipated.

★ If you dream the fruit is overripe inside, do not hesitate too long before reaching for what you desire.

★ If a pineapple has withered on the plant, you may have neglected seizing a chance because of illusion.

★ If you dream you are being given a pineapple, the giver may promise happiness, but buying it yourself enables you to be independent.

OUTCOME OF DULCIE'S DREAM

Dulcie heard that Juan captivated older women and tried to pull the beach-bar scam, in which the down payment disappeared into his pocket. However, Dulcie was not going to be fooled, and she purchased the bar. She now has it under management and periodically visits the island for vacations and a new lover. Pineapple dreams promise sweetness if handled carefully.

Pins

Gilda, forty-four, often dreamed about a woman making pins in a workshop at the side of a small cottage. After her husband's death, the woman, who seemed to know Gilda and talked to her in dreams, was struggling to pay the rent. The  *bailiffs arrived and threw the woman and her children out. They walked along the road with their bundles toward the distant workhouse. The woman gave Gilda a box of pins.*

DREAM BACKGROUND AND MEANING

Gilda had heard of a pinmaker in the family two hundred years earlier but knew nothing about her. Now a widow herself, Gilda was living in a leased cottage that her husband had said was theirs for life. A local landowner told Gilda she must pay him a large sum to renew the lease or leave. Being given a box of pins in a dream says you will be offered the right help if you go back to the original source.

INTERPRETATIONS AND FORTUNE-TELLING MEANINGS

★ Pinning together ripped clothes says a permanent solution to problems will need to be found.

★ A spilled box of pins represents the buildup of petty irritations and spite.

★ Ornamental silver or gold hatpins promise success and prosperity, given persistence.

★ Making pins by hand or with old-fashioned tools may be a past-life dream, saying a solution to problems will be found in checking small details.

★ To stand or sit on a pin or have one pierce your skin warns about the need to guard against trickery.

OUTCOME OF GILDA'S DREAM

Gilda consulted the attorney who had witnessed the original lease signing. Under the terms of an ancient trust, which was the legal owner of her land—not the local landowner—the cottage was Gilda's if she wanted it, in return for the present land rent. Gilda discovered the woman in the dream to be her missing pinmaker relative.

Finding a dropped pin represents overcoming vulnerability by searching for the answer, which may be very close.

Pizza

Luigi, thirty-five, dreamed he was cooking a pizza in an outdoor oven under the olive trees in his home village in Italy. His wife and cousins were waiting on tables. Then he walked away and caught a plane to London, despite remembering that inheriting the family business had been his father's dying wish for him.

DREAM BACKGROUND AND MEANING

As the only child, Luigi had inherited the traditional family pizza business in a smart part of London. A large upmarket pizza chain had offered to buy the restaurant, which would give Luigi and his wife enough money to buy a house outright and a new taxi for his expanding business. Pizza symbolizes family unity and sociability, but only if it is what the dreamer wants.

INTERPRETATIONS AND FORTUNE-TELLING MEANINGS

* If you dream you are sharing a pizza with friends or family, happy informal meetings and family ventures are favored.
* If you defrost a pizza in a dream, you may need to devote more time to leisure and family.
* If you agree on the ingredients of a takeout pizza with those who are sharing, there will be harmonious business and personal relationships.
* If you disagree over ingredients or are served the wrong ones, you may be pressured to go along with others' preferences.
* If your pizza is only half-cooked or burned, you are being offered second-best in life.
* If you dream you are making pizza, you will have increased prosperity and good fortune, particularly in business and love.

OUTCOME OF LUIGI'S DREAM

Luigi went to see the family in Italy whose village pizza business, where his father had started, was not thriving. He offered to help them raise a loan to buy his father's London business at a far lower price than the consortium had offered. They accepted and are re-creating the village atmosphere in London. Pizza imagery involves compromise so everyone can maintain that unity in their own way.

Plants (Indoor)

Edith, eighty-nine, dreamed she was watering her indoor plants. But as she poured the water into the pots, each plant wilted and died before her eyes. She tried everything she knew to revive them, without success. Distraught, she sat in her favorite chair, crying, as she looked around her living room at her beloved plants, which she had nurtured and loved for so long.

DREAM BACKGROUND AND MEANING

Edith lived in a small one-bedroom apartment, in which she was unable to keep animals, so her plants were her company. Edith had no children and very few visitors. Without her plants, Edith believed she would have little to live for. Plants, especially indoor ones, in dreams reflect the well-being of their owners, emotional as well as physical, and can warn when the owner is feeling isolated.

INTERPRETATIONS AND FORTUNE-TELLING MEANINGS

* Watering plants indicates nourishing your own life and expanding in new directions.
* If indoor plants begin to grow or regrow dramatically in a dream, this is a sign of good or improving health and domestic stability.
* If in the dream indoor plants die, this is not an omen that the dreamer will suffer illness or death, but it represents the dreamer restricting their horizons rather than exploring beyond their four walls.
* Indoor plants that in dreams fail to thrive may also suggest that they are set over a spot with negative Earth energies beneath and need to be moved before they wilt (see "Ley Energy Lines," p. 284).
* If indoor plants are taking over every space, the dreamer is allowing thoughts, regrets, and worries from the past to dominate their life.
* A profusion of indoor plants represents seeking an insulated life, free from external pressure, but the price may be loneliness.

OUTCOME OF EDITH'S DREAM

After the dream, Edith joined a local horticultural society, made new friends, and was able to exhibit her plants, which flourished. Since research has suggested that plants respond to human emotions, the condition of your dream plants and actual plants can mirror feelings you may not have acknowledged.

Poison

Jacques, twenty, dreamed he was in a sixteenth-century French court as an apprentice to an alchemist who made poisons for nobles and royalty with which to get rid of their enemies. But Jacques was unhappy, as many of the victims were good, kind people, and so he secretly worked on antidotes. However, a jealous senior apprentice told the alchemist, and Jacques was cast out from the court with a price on his head. He fled south; on waking, he knew he could use his gifts for good.

DREAM BACKGROUND AND MEANING

Jacques was working as an apprentice automotive technician in a very poisonous atmosphere. The boss did not train him properly and the senior apprentice, Simon, bullied Jacques continually. Simon was diverting profitable work from the garage, though he was not qualified. Jacques tried to check on Simon's private repairs, but the boss caught him. Simon denied involvement, and Jacques was dismissed. What was his future? Poison dreams are usually warnings, so look for an escape or remedy.

INTERPRETATIONS AND FORTUNE-TELLING MEANINGS

* To dream of poison indicates spite and malice at work or a relation who causes dissent.
* To dream that you make or are given an antidote says you can survive a toxic atmosphere if you avoid rivalry or dishonest dealing.
* To be bitten by a venomous snake warns that a hidden enemy or rival may betray you.
* Dreaming of drinking poison advises that you not listen to spite or gossip, however plausible, about someone you trust.
* Dreaming of making or mixing poisons implies that you may be swept up in others' agendas.
* Where there are poisonous plants growing, beware that you are not conned by someone charismatic who is destructive behind the charm.

OUTCOME OF JACQUES'S DREAM

Jacques realized that he was better off out of the destructive atmosphere. He returned to college so he could eventually become an apprentice trainer. Since venom is also an antidote, see what positive aspects can be salvaged from your poison dream.

Poker (Game)

Maurice, forty-eight, dreamed he was gambling on a nineteenth-century Mississippi paddleboat steamer and using his system for winning at poker and other card games. He made a sizable bet and won a poker game against a wealthy professional gambler. As Maurice picked up his winnings, he was surrounded by thugs and threatened that unless he handed over the secrets of his system, he would be thrown overboard. He woke as he hit the water.

DREAM BACKGROUND AND MEANING

Maurice had developed a system for playing poker that seemed to overcome many odds. He realized that if he raised his gambling stakes, he could probably make a good living using his system. But Maurice feared repercussions from ruthless professional gamblers. When a similar scenario reappears in someone's daily life, dreams can trigger memories of past worlds.

INTERPRETATIONS AND FORTUNE-TELLING MEANINGS

* Dreaming of playing poker indicates the need to keep your intentions secret from those you can identify in daily life with whom you are playing dream poker.
* If you dream you win at poker, especially with a royal flush, be patient, as your present strategy will bring desired results.
* If you dream you lose at poker, others are concealing their intentions from you. Again, study the identity of other players.
* Dreaming you are playing poker for high stakes says you have reached an all-or-nothing decision and need to take a chance.
* If you dream you are playing poker with strangers, you should be more open with someone trustworthy close to you.
* If someone calls your bluff in the dream, beware of promising what you cannot deliver.

OUTCOME OF MAURICE'S DREAM

Maurice has been commissioned for a series of books on narrowing the odds in gambling. In the meantime, he plays poker at different casinos, especially ones on Mississippi paddleboat steamers, and he is making a good living. A warning dream can inspire an interest in an alternative approach to using a talent.

Pole Dancing

Becky, twenty-three, often dreamed she was a pole dancer in an exclusive club. After the show, she went outside, where her car and chauffeur were waiting to take her to her beachside apartment, where her maid would have champagne ready on ice. Becky never wanted to leave her dream.

DREAM INTERPRETATION AND MEANING

Becky was struggling to pay for her method-acting classes in Hollywood by waitressing at a down-market nightclub. The manager said she should work as a pole dancer in the club, as the money was good, with perks if she went home with clients. Pole-dancing dreams are often rooted in sexual fantasies but can have a more materialistic aspect involving moral choices.

INTERPRETATIONS AND FORTUNE-TELLING MEANINGS

★ If you dream you are pole dancing in an exclusive club and you feel beautiful and totally sexy, you are aware of your sensuality and confident in your body.

★ If you are visiting a pole-dancing venue in your dream, you may be bored with or unfulfilled in your love life.

★ If you dream you are tempted to make money or gain advantage through your sensual charms, whether in the workplace or socially, you should be aware that the price may be high.

★ If you are pole dancing in an inappropriate setting, for example in the office or in the street, you may have a desire to shock to get the attention you need.

★ If you are pole dancing exclusively for your current partner, you may not be sexually fulfilled in your relationship.

OUTCOME OF BECKY'S DREAM

Becky tried pole dancing at the club but found it demeaning and quit the club. She was offered work at the method-acting school as a receptionist and general assistant, and through connections there she obtained her first minor role. The pole used in pole dancing is often considered a phallic symbol, and can reveal a lack of emotional connection with a partner as well as a lack of sexual connection, which can be harder to fix.

Politics

Erika, thirty-eight, dreamed she was at a polling station in the north of England, surrounded by giant posters of herself, watching people lining up to vote. Strangers stopped and told Erika that they would be voting for her. Erika woke excited at her prospective election, then realized it was just a dream.

DREAM BACKGROUND AND MEANING

Erika had always wanted to enter politics, but married and had children when she was young, abandoning her politics degree. Now that her children were independent, her political ambition had returned. She wondered if it was too late to enter government. She recently had led a successful campaign to save an area of outstanding beauty from indiscriminate fracking. Political dreams can trigger or revive a dormant personal interest in politics or can represent a desire to influence a common cause.

INTERPRETATIONS AND FORTUNE-TELLING MEANINGS

★ If you dream that you address the Senate or Parliament, you will be asked to take the lead on behalf of other workers or in a community dispute.

★ If you dream you are participating in a political rally or demonstration, you feel strongly about a matter or injustice in some area of your life where you need to speak out.

★ If you dream that a famous politician is listening to you, your opinions will influence outcomes at a high level in a matter of great importance to you.

★ If a dream crowd heckles you, your opinions will be unpopular, but stick to your beliefs.

★ If you dream you are helping someone else be elected, you may not immediately gain the promotion or recognition you deserve.

★ If you are prime minister, president, or leader of the United Nations in your dream, you can rise high in your chosen field of expertise.

OUTCOME OF ERIKA'S DREAM

Erika returned to studying politics and at the same time became involved more closely in local politics to make a name for herself as an eventual candidate. Dreams of politics that include intrigue are warnings to beware of double-dealings in any negotiations.

Poltergeists

Olivia, forty-six, had a recurring dream that she and her teenage daughter were in the kitchen. Plates and cups, pots, and pans were flying in the air around them, as if tossed by invisible hands. The kitchen window shattered.

DREAM BACKGROUND AND MEANING

Olivia's husband was violent toward her, and the attacks terrified her daughter. Olivia had noticed that after an incident and when her daughter was upset, crockery would break, seemingly by itself, doors would bang, and electrical appliances would fall from shelves. Poltergeist activity is believed to be from malevolent spirits, energized by troubled adolescents reacting to conflict.

INTERPRETATIONS AND FORTUNE-TELLING MEANINGS

★ If you dream of poltergeist activity, it may be a warning picked up by your subconscious that if disturbing relationship dynamics are ignored, they may manifest as poltergeist activity and amplified violence.

★ If you dream of shadowy whispering figures, you are suppressing anger or fear that is building up into malevolent energy, whether through you or the catalyst of a psychic teenager.

★ If you dream that your workplace or home is haunted by strange energy disturbances, even if all is well, your psyche may be tuning in to negative events that occurred before you entered the environment.

★ If you dream of malfunctioning technological equipment that invariably malfunctions the next day in real life, you are unconsciously releasing past bad memories.

★ If in your dream you defeat a poltergeist with prayer, a cross, or ritual, opportunities will come to set past sorrows to rest.

★ Poltergeist dreams can be associated with sexual abuse or intimidation that needs to be reported, whether in the present or the past.

OUTCOME OF OLIVIA'S DREAM

The dreams became more frequent, and poltergeist activity involving her daughter increased, as did the domestic violence. Olivia obtained a restraining order against her husband. After he left, the poltergeist dreams ceased. Poltergeist dreams are occasionally caused by dabbling with ouija boards or practicing black magick. If so, call a healer.

Pop-Up Shop

The night before opening her Halloween pop-up shop, Lois, forty-two, dreamed that she unloaded her stock with the help of her friend. But her friend did not put down the shutters of the store as she had promised. In the morning, the stock was all gone. Her friend told her to give up and said she would run the shop herself and buy new stock. Lois handed the keys to her friend and walked away.

DREAM BACKGROUND AND MEANING

Lois had been offered old Halloween stock from the previous year and had rented an empty shop for a month before the festival. But she had few customers and even fewer sales. After two weeks, her friend offered to take over the store and buy the stock for half of what Lois had paid. Lois saw that everything started selling fast, for double the prices. Pop-up shop dreams represent enterprise, but can warn the dreamer to beware of hidden trickery.

INTERPRETATIONS AND FORTUNE-TELLING MEANINGS

★ If in your dream you are opening a temporary shop for a festival, you are focusing on short-term aims in life generally.

★ If you are publicizing your special craft or arts in your dream pop-up shop, you have creative ideas that you are ready to market.

★ If you dream that a pop-up shop is empty, your goals may work better long-term than instantly.

★ If you make a profit in the dream and take over the shop permanently, you have a good business head and moneymaking ideas worth developing.

★ If you dream you are left with excess stock, you may have overly ambitious expectations about a current venture, or perhaps you have unfair competition in the real world.

OUTCOME OF LOIS'S DREAM

Lois discovered that her friend, who had offered to handle the shop's advertising, had listed opening dates that were two weeks after the shop opened. After Lois gave up ownership of the business, she realized that the sign advertising the shop, which she had firmly attached to a wall at the end of the road, had been turned around the wrong way. Lois's friend denied trickery. When Lois opened a successful Christmas shop, she handled everything herself. Pop-up shops by their nature suggest uncertainty, but dreams act as a warning to check details for quick profit in short-term projects.

Portrait

Kenneth, forty-four, dreamed he was painting a portrait of a famous general. No matter how hard he tried to portray the subject in a flattering way, the general had cruel eyes and a wolfish grimace. The general was furious at the results and threw paint over the finished canvas.

DREAM BACKGROUND AND MEANING

Kenneth was working for a political publicity organization but did not trust a wealthy new client. There were rumors the client had financial interests in dubious and illegal clubs, though he was being presented as an ideal politician and respectable family man. So strongly did Kenneth feel, he asked to be taken off the campaign. His boss was furious, as was the client. Should Kenneth risk damaging his career? Portraits, even more than photographs, capture the energies of the real person, and so portrait dreams are often about authenticity.

INTERPRETATIONS AND FORTUNE-TELLING MEANINGS

* If you dream that the portrait is a good likeness, you will soon be recognized for a unique achievement.
* If you dream of a happy family portrait or one with a lover, this is a sign of secure, untroubled times ahead in home and relationships.
* If you dream you are part of an old-fashioned formal portrait, you may need to break free of the others in the portrait.
* If your dream self-portrait bears no resemblance to you, there is a difference between your true self and the image shown to the world.
* If you dream that a portrait is stolen, beware of someone taking your ideas or draining your energies.
* If you dream that a portrait falls from a wall or is damaged, beware of challenges to your authority or expertise. Stand firm.

OUTCOME OF KENNETH'S DREAM

Kenneth was dismissed and went freelance. Within a few months, the wealthy client was embroiled in a major sex and drugs scandal and ruined the former employers who had fired Kenneth. Having dreams of painting portraits can indicate efforts to sell the virtues of something or someone you do not believe in.

Potatoes

Seamus, twenty-eight, dreamed he was digging in the potato fields in old Ireland. Most of the crop was already rotting. He knew the family had to deliver the potatoes or be evicted. The dream ended with his present family carrying their bundles to the docks.

DREAM BACKGROUND AND MEANING

Seamus was fascinated by the Irish potato famine, which happened from the 1840s to the early 1870s, when a million people died and two million emigrated. Every few years Seamus's family returned to Ireland from America. Seamus was collecting the family history and hoped one day to restore the abandoned family cottage. His dream may have been an ancestral memory. If you have a heritage where peasants were displaced from their land, dreams may link you with a deep longing to reconnect to your spiritual roots.

INTERPRETATIONS AND FORTUNE-TELLING MEANINGS

* Dreaming of peeling and cooking potatoes, if you are happy in the dream, predicts a stable family life with sufficient resources.
* If you dream you have mounds of potatoes to peel and cook, your routine and responsibilities may be wearing you down.
* If you dream you are growing potatoes, your finances and savings will likewise grow slowly but remain stable.
* If you are enjoying eating sweet new potatoes, appreciate life as it is now, and do not worry about tomorrow.
* If you dream you are carrying a heavy sack of potatoes, this may be a past-world memory and suggests you are taking on too many practical burdens for others.

OUTCOME OF SEAMUS'S DREAM

Seamus went to Ireland on the family pilgrimage and discovered his family were leaders of the potato famine resistance and some were imprisoned. He found a local historical society, which offered him a grant to restore the family cottage as a museum to those times.

If you dream of leaving Ireland for America, the United Kingdom, Australia, or New Zealand on a sailing ship, any relocation in this present life will offer new opportunities, but you may eventually be drawn home.

Potpourri

Henry, fifty, dreamed he was in his garden, which was filled with fragrant flowers. Butterflies were settling on the plants, and birds were flying around. He saw an unfamiliar shack and pushed open the door. Instantly he was overwhelmed by the sickly smell of cheap dried flowers sprayed with perfumed chemicals. A man handed him a sealed pack and said, "They will never tell the difference." Henry ran to the store he owned, where he could smell the same sickly fragrance.

DREAM BACKGROUND AND MEANING

Henry was famed for making a unique potpourri from his garden, which he sold in his gift store. But he had become tired and overwhelmed by the day-to-day running of the store and knew he was cutting corners. He found a wholesale company that sold prepackaged potpourri for a fraction of the price. Sales had dropped off, and he was contemplating selling up. Cheap potpourri in a dream suggests you are offering and accepting second best in life.

INTERPRETATIONS AND FORTUNE-TELLING MEANINGS

★ If you dream you are surrounded with fragrant potpourri, stress will diminish and pleasure in life will return.

★ If the fragrance of the potpourri is overpowering, someone in your life who is excessively friendly should be viewed with caution.

★ Making your own potpourri says you have many talents to combine to create both success and fulfillment.

★ If dream potpourri loses its fragrance, you need to discover what is missing from your life and restore it.

★ If you dream you are selling different kinds of potpourri, you may be in demand as a peacemaker. Be careful you do not get too involved and lose your own identity.

OUTCOME OF HENRY'S DREAM

After the dream, Henry opened the prepackaged potpourri and realized how overwhelming the smell was. Henry took on a manager and focused on making his signature potpourri and expanding the range of fragrances. His business thrived once more. Potpourri represents our essential self, what we give out and so receive from life in return.

Powerball, Lottery

Julian, fifty-nine, dreamed he met a man dressed in the costume of the owner of a famous chain of fast-food chicken restaurants. The man told Julian it was Julian's lucky day. Julian bought 100 dollars' worth of Powerball tickets. The television was on when he reached home. His wife was furious at his wastefulness, but Julian saw he had all the jackpot numbers.

DREAM BACKGROUND AND MEANING

Julian owned a small café in downtown Dallas, Texas. The café had been successful for many years, enabling them to buy a house and put money aside for their son's college. However, three years earlier, a large mall that opened just a hundred yards from their café resulted in a 75 percent reduction in the café's turnover.

Although a dream heralding good fortune may not mean it will materialize precisely, the dream will hold clues to winning good fortune.

INTERPRETATIONS AND FORTUNE-TELLING MEANINGS

★ If you dream of buying a Powerball ticket, it is a lucky time generally if life is tough.

★ If you buy more tickets than usual in the dream, winning odds are with you, though not necessarily via Powerball.

★ If you dream that you lose, you need to find other practical ways to improve your fortunes, as chance is not with you right now.

★ If a deceased relative or living celebrity gives you Powerball numbers, use them whenever you feel lucky.

★ Dreaming of winning the Powerball jackpot may herald a substantial win in the weeks ahead. However, it also advises you to use your initiative to further a money-making idea.

OUTCOME OF JULIAN'S DREAM

Julian bet on Powerball and won a small amount. More significantly, he saw on local television that there was a controversy because the fast-food chain in his dream had lost its space in the mall, as the mall owner had bought shares in a rival company. Julian contacted the chicken restaurant's headquarters. They bought his restaurant, giving Julian enough money to start a diner in his hometown in South Carolina.

Power Outage, Power Cut

Todd, seventy, dreamed he was walking home when all the streetlights went out and the houses on the road were plunged into darkness. He found his way by the light of his phone battery and opened the door of his home, but there was still a major outage. Todd sat in total darkness and silence, perfectly content in his favorite chair. Then the power was restored and he woke disappointed, as he had loved the dream darkness and serenity.

DREAM BACKGROUND AND MEANING

Todd had rejected the offer of retirement, as he wanted to boost his pension. But he was no longer enjoying his job and found himself switching off and having blank moments. His physician said his blood pressure was high, medication was not helping, and that he should either retire or find a stress-free job. But Todd needed the extra pension.

INTERPRETATIONS AND FORTUNE-TELLING MEANINGS

* If the power goes out totally in your dream, you may be on overload and your mind may be telling you to step off the treadmill.
* If you dream you stop the electricity supply by deliberately cutting through wires, you are excluding some activity or person who is draining your energy.
* If you dream that a fuse has blown, a frustration at work, domestically, or in a relationship is building up and should be dealt with before full shutdown.
* If power lines have come down, you may have become entangled in others' conflicts or in quarrels you cannot win.
* If you dream that the power supply is intermittent, a person or situation is proving unreliable. Consider alternatives.

OUTCOME OF TODD'S DREAM

Todd woke from the dream realizing he had been asleep in his chair all night and could not remember coming home. Considering the other mini-blackouts that had happened to him, he realized it was time to quit his job. Todd found a part-time position in a DIY superstore, advising on power tools, an interest of his. Power outage dreams can be early warning signals that it may be time to cut back on stress.

Predictive Warnings

David, fifty-five, had a dream in which a car came hurtling out of a field and smashed into the family car. The dream was so vivid that David told his wife, but they were not planning any travel that day.

DREAM BACKGROUND AND MEANING

David, an Anglican priest, was asked unexpectedly to make a journey, and he and his family set off in the car. David came to a spot he recognized from the dream. He told his wife this was where the dream accident had occurred. She reassured him that there was not any other traffic. At that moment a car did come hurtling out of the field. True predictive dreams have been described as more real than even a vivid dream and are said to remain with the dreamer long after an ordinary dream would be forgotten.

INTERPRETATIONS AND FORTUNE-TELLING MEANINGS

* You may have only one of these true-warning dreams in your lifetime, if at all. But you will know a predictive warning by its urgency.
* Waking with nagging anxiety after dreaming of disaster indicates that you are feeling generally jittery about life, and this is not a prediction.
* If the dream is of an unexpected place or unplanned journey, you should take it seriously and change plans.
* Events in predictive-warning dreams seem to occur mainly within forty-eight hours of the dream.
* If you have a psychic child or teenager and they have regular unspecified dreams about major disasters, reassure them that they are just tuning into a potential incident they cannot prevent.
* If you are regularly tuning into global disasters, your psychic powers are emerging and should be channeled into healing.

OUTCOME OF DAVID'S DREAM

As a result of the dream, David was alert and swerved into the ditch to avoid the speeding car. The dream scene in premonitions usually feels like real life, and dreamers awake instantly.

Pregnancy

When Tracey, thirty-one, was pregnant for the first time, she dreamed three times that her baby would be a boy, blond, born two months early, and perfectly all right. Soon after the birth she became pregnant again and dreamed she was having twin girls.

DREAM BACKGROUND AND MEANING

After the first pregnancy dream, Tracey worried, as she knew babies born two months early were not always fine. With the second pregnancy she became convinced the dream was right and that they were twin girls. Tracey said she was not particularly psychic, but the dreams were incredibly vivid. Pregnancy dreams are the forerunner of maternal or paternal radar, alerting the parent to the needs of the newborn infant.

INTERPRETATIONS AND FORTUNE-TELLING MEANINGS

* Pregnant women seem to become psychic, connecting through dreams with the unborn children.
* Seeing a healthy baby during a pregnancy dream encourages parents if there are medical doubts about the future well-being of the infant.
* Pregnancy dreams of the delivery reassure parents that the actual birth may turn out differently but well.
* If a dream baby has teeth or is older, this can be comforting for an anxious mother who has previously experienced miscarriages.
* Dreaming of the baby establishes the maternal or paternal link, if either parent is anxious about the birth or about being able to be a good parent.
* If it is hard conceiving and if you are wondering whether to carry on, seeing the mother pregnant in a dream is an excellent omen for a successful pregnancy.

OUTCOME OF TRACEY'S DREAM

Tracey's first baby, Simon, was born just before thirty-three weeks and, as the dream foretold, he was blond and healthy. In her next pregnancy, at fourteen weeks' gestation, twins were detected and indeed proved to be twin girls. Dreaming consistently of the same child being born can occur even before the mother-to-be decides to become pregnant, and some believe the little soul is making contact from the heavens.

Preschool-Age Nightmares

Oliver, four, woke crying because he dreamed of a huge sheep with big horns outside the house. It was eating the garden plants and getting bigger. Oliver was afraid it would come inside and eat him and his family.

DREAM BACKGROUND AND MEANING

Oliver had recently started school and was finding it hard to settle in. He cried when he was left there because he was afraid his mother would not come for him at the end of the day. The week before he started school, Oliver had been knocked over by a boisterous sheep at a farm park. Afterward, Oliver refused to watch his former favorite cartoon about an enormous talking sheep. Young children can see projected characters from books or television as three-dimensional and real.

INTERPRETATIONS AND FORTUNE-TELLING MEANINGS

* If a child refuses to watch a previously loved cartoon or film with talking creatures or monsters, they may be having nightmares about them, even if they cannot explain.
* If a child is in an unfamiliar daytime environment or sleeping away from home, they may associate the separation with fears of storybook or cartoon characters.
* If a preschool child is afraid of the dark or talks about people in their room, they may be psychic and seeing benign deceased relatives.
* If the child suddenly starts bedwetting, sleepwalking, or screaming with eyes wide open, they may be experiencing nightmares or terrors they cannot explain.
* If the child refuses to go to bed or sleep alone, they may benefit from extra quiet time before bed, a night-light, and gentle music.

OUTCOME OF OLIVER'S DREAM

Oliver refused to go into the farm park the following weekend, though he had previously loved it, and he started crying about the sheep eating him. His mother made the connection between Oliver being knocked over and starting school. She bought Oliver a cuddly sheep toy to drive the scary one away at night. Children's nightmares and night terrors can be overcome once the trigger is known by dealing with the problem on the child's terms.

President

In her dream, Stella, thirty-six, was at the National Convention, seeking nomination for the US presidency. Her opponent, Gillian, was making a speech that was enthusiastically received. When it was Stella's turn to speak, she realized she was still only a teenager and Gillian was a confident, sophisticated candidate. The crowd was laughing at her.

DREAM BACKGROUND AND MEANING

At school, Gillian had been Stella's best friend. However, their friendship ended when, at age sixteen, Gillian took Stella's boyfriend away. Gillian never forgave her, even though she was now married with two children. Now they were rivals for the presidency of the local Democratic Party Electoral Committee, and Stella feared she would be defeated by her former friend again. Presidential dreams can encompass any leadership ambitions where there are fears about inadequacy.

INTERPRETATIONS AND FORTUNE-TELLING MEANINGS

★ If you dream of becoming president of the United States and are entering the political arena, your ambition is worth pursuing. You may have the right energies to rise to a senior political position, even if not as president.

★ If you dream you are riding in the presidential car or Air Force One, applying for an official role in any area of life says that promised status and rewards may be the driving force behind your ambition. Consider whether you also want the responsibility that comes with the job.

★ If you are against an old rival for a leadership position, the dream reminds you that it is important to not let past failure deter you.

★ If you dream you are a child or teen running against an adult version of your rival, you may still think of yourself in a vulnerable or inferior position.

★ If you successfully challenge a rival in your dream for a leadership bid, this confidence will reflect in everyday life.

OUTCOME OF STELLA'S DREAM

After the dream, Stella decided it was time they put teenage insecurities behind them. She met Gillian and they agreed, since they both had strengths, they should share the post. Presidential dreams can say quite as much about the way we judge ourselves as about the actual leadership positions.

Princess

Trinny, fourteen, dreamed she was a princess who, as in fairy tales, had been reclaimed by the royal family in her teens after being stolen by a wicked enchantress. She was given beautiful clothes and a fabulous bedroom. Then she woke with her sister raiding her wardrobe.

DREAM BACKGROUND AND MEANING

Trinny was the third of five sisters and always felt left out of family recognition. Her older sisters participated in beauty pageants and the younger ones were child models. Trinny was the quiet, academic one. Princess dreams can be compensatory for younger and sometimes older women when others, seemingly no more deserving, are singled out for acclaim.

INTERPRETATIONS AND FORTUNE-TELLING MEANINGS

★ If you dream constantly of a little princess, you may, if you are trying for a baby, have a daughter; or the dream may be reassurance if you are worrying about an existing daughter.

★ If you dream you are a princess locked in a tower, waiting for rescue, you may need to strike out for independence yourself.

★ If you dream of a departed princess, such as Princess Grace of Monaco or Diana, Princess of Wales, there may be something unfulfilled in your earlier life that you regret.

★ If your princess is someone you know and is over twenty-five, they may be using their helplessness as a power play.

★ If you dream of living with royalty or being a princess, you may feel you are being overlooked by your waking family.

★ Your dream princess represents new beginnings, or maybe returning to a childhood location, or reviving an earlier desire for fame and fortune.

OUTCOME OF TRINNY'S DREAM

After the dream, Trinny put herself forward to represent her school in a major knowledge quiz, and the team won all the way through to the interstate finals. She continued to represent the school in academic competitions. Sometimes a dream can give a reluctant princess the confidence to shine.

Procession

Frederick, forty, dreamed he was driving his son's class float, which he had decorated for the school carnival. All the decorations were falling off, leaving the bare trailer. A father he recognized climbed on board and secured the flowers and decorations back into place to the cheers of the crowd, as Frederick kept driving. The float won a prize.

DREAM BACKGROUND AND MEANING

Frederick was a single parent. Though he tried hard, he was aware that his son did not have the right costumes for theme days or have homemade contributions for the school snack shop. Frederick constantly worried that he was a bad father, though he and his son were very close. Procession dreams can reveal worries about keeping up with others' expectations.

INTERPRETATIONS AND FORTUNE-TELLING MEANINGS

★ Dreaming of taking part in a procession says that you will be given credit for successful completion of a project or invited to a celebration.

★ If you are watching a procession, you may feel unfairly excluded from recognition of achievements or from a social event to which you expected to be invited.

★ A carnival procession heralds a period of spontaneous pleasure when you should break from routine and 24/7 working.

★ A Thanksgiving parade is a reminder to contact friends and family if you have been too busy.

★ A military procession suggests you may be coerced into going along with opinions of which you are not certain.

OUTCOME OF FREDERICK'S DREAM

After the dream, Frederick posted a notice at the school, offering to trade bookkeeping in return for making costumes and baking. Another single parent with a child in an older class said he was a master baker and designed costumes for the local theater, but his accounts were in a dreadful mess. They traded skills, and life is running smoothly. The kind of procession you dream of—religious, military, Gay Pride, victory, or celebratory—signifies coming together with like-minded people in friendship as well as for a common cause.

Property Investment

Rhona, forty-two, dreamed that a property backing onto fields that she was contemplating buying was surrounded by earth-moving machines. A man in construction gear came to the door, offering her a ridiculously low price to move, though she had not long before taken possession. She woke disturbed.

DREAM BACKGROUND AND MEANING

Rhona fell in love with a seemingly perfect house, one of the few in the area not surrounded by modern houses, which was offered at an incredibly low price. She contemplated making a quick offer before it was sold. Rhona checked that there were no planning applications nearby. Property in dreams can represent any long-term major investment where the head as well as the heart is needed.

INTERPRETATIONS AND FORTUNE-TELLING MEANINGS

★ To buy or sell property in a dream says it is a good time to initiate house moves, redecoration, extensions, or renovations.

★ If an existing property is abandoned in a dream but not in reality, plans in any area of life that are not bearing fruit should be abandoned.

★ If you are extending a house or business premises in a dream, you may be offered a business investment that with effort will pay longer-term dividends.

★ If you are contemplating buying or selling property and you dream of a major increase or crash in prices, this may be a prediction of an imminent local price change because of as-yet-unrevealed circumstances.

★ If in a dream you see your perfect property, you will come across it before too long, as your inner radar is guiding you.

★ If you are contemplating buying a property and snags appear in the dream, check them out, as your unconscious may have picked up problems.

OUTCOME OF RHONA'S DREAM

Rhona questioned neighbors and was told the fields were owned by a man who lived overseas. There had been previous attempts to buy them by developers to build a small estate. Rhona held off making an offer, as she did not want complications now or in the future. Property dreams can indicate good or otherwise investments where awareness of problems may be overlooked because of a desire to own the property.

Psychic Adults

Joseph, eighty-two, did not know where his newly deceased wife had put the rent money. She suddenly broke into his dream. He saw her in the distance and heard her voice say, "It's behind the red galleon in the wooden box." When he woke, there it was.

DREAM BACKGROUND AND MEANING

Joseph had left paying all the household expenses to his wife, and as he was alone after her death, he had no clue where she kept the money to pay the bills. A retired biologist, he had been a skeptic all his life, but it is thought that everyone has psychic abilities. In logical people these are often activated at the time of a bereavement, childbirth, or crisis.

INTERPRETATIONS AND FORTUNE-TELLING MEANINGS

* If information you are seeking comes from a deceased person through a dream, this is a sign that the love and the essence of the person live on.
* If you frequently have psychic dreams, this may be a sign of emerging psychic or healing powers.
* If your psychic dreams are disturbing, channel these energies into learning healing or divination, and the random dreams will cease.
* If you receive an urgent warning in a dream that remains with you as vividly when you wake, this should be taken seriously.
* If you were psychic as a child, the reemergence of these powers usually occurs first in dreams, so note down information received to check its accuracy, whether these are actual powers or enhanced intuition.
* If you dream of someone close to you or your family as dangerous in the dream, there may be concealed characteristics in their personality they keep hidden.

OUTCOME OF JOSEPH'S DREAM

Not only was the rent money where his wife told him in the dream, but there was also a list of other payments and where the money for each was kept. Sometimes psychic links can emerge as a one-off when the dreamer urgently needs information.

Psychic Children

Suzy, eighty-four, recalled a dream she had when she was seven years old. She dreamed that her uncle, who was in the navy, was swimming in the water and was picked up by a dinghy with soldiers in it and taken to the shore. The dream was so vivid, she talked about it all day. She had been close to her uncle.

DREAM BACKGROUND AND MEANING

Suzy's uncle had been pronounced dead in World War II when his frigate was torpedoed, and no survivors were listed. This made Suzy's dream even more disturbing, since she insisted her uncle was alive. Children can connect telepathically when a close relative is in distress and thinks of home.

INTERPRETATIONS AND FORTUNE-TELLING MEANINGS

* If a child dreams of a relative far away who may be in trouble, their dream should be taken seriously.
* If a child's dream goes against the known facts, it should be accepted that all the information available conventionally may not be accurate.
* If a child is afraid of their psychic dreams, they should be reassured that those just mean the person is sending them love and checking that they are okay.
* Since these dreams are spontaneous and cannot be called up at will, it is important to accept them as proof of the wonder of the human mind and maybe survival after death, and not to pressure the child for more information.
* If a child does not want to talk about these special dreams, they should be given plenty of mundane and physical stimuli to bring the child back to Earth.
* If it is possible to check the information psychically revealed by the child, useful knowledge can be gained that may make reconnection with a missing person or even a missing pet possible.

OUTCOME OF SUZY'S DREAM

After the war, Suzy's uncle returned home, after having been picked up by the Japanese army with one or two other sailors who had survived. They had been imprisoned in an internment camp till the end of the war. Children's psychic experiences often manifest in dreams and seem to occur because children's minds are less cluttered by logic and disbelief than adults' minds. Wartime dreams are especially common.

Psychic Pets

Maureen, forty, dreamed of her dog Bojo running away, leaping into the back of a delivery van, and, when the doors opened, bolting for an open shed whose door swung shut. She saw a detached house with a shed at the bottom of the garden and heard Bojo barking. The shed was next to open land and a footpath sign with half the name covered.

DREAM BACKGROUND AND MEANING
Maureen's dog had been attacked and had run away. She advertised everywhere and scoured the district without success. She felt Bojo was alive, as the dream was so clear. Pets, both living and deceased, frequently connect with us on the dream plane, at the unconscious level where psychic links take place.

INTERPRETATIONS AND FORTUNE-TELLING MEANINGS
* If you dream of your pet, be aware of warnings about a forthcoming outing. Pet dreams can have predictive purposes.
* If you dream of a lost pet and the connection is clear, follow the clues, however unlikely, to the dream location.
* If your missing pet seems surrounded by mist, they may have passed over.
* If you are not looking for a pet but dream of a specific one, it may come into your life in a totally unexpected way.
* If your pet is unwell in a dream, get them checked to make sure they are well.

OUTCOME OF MAUREEN'S DREAM
Maureen went to the town named in the dream, trying paths until she found one with the sign and the shed backing onto the path. No one answered the front door, so she phoned the local dog-rescue organization. They found Bojo, exhausted and dehydrated, too weak to bark. Pets have a psychic radar linking to us, strongest in sleep, which should be trusted.

Pumpkin

Joel, twenty-eight, dreamed he was making a special pumpkin pie to take to the home of his partner, Jez, to meet Jez's parents. Though he was trained as a pastry chef, Joel was anxious to make a good impression with his cooking. He baked the pie to perfection. But as they were setting out, he tripped, and the pie was ruined. Joel felt his chance of approval slipping away.

DREAM BACKGROUND AND MEANING
Joel was going to meet his prospective in-laws for the first time, and he was worried, as he knew they were very wealthy. He did not know what to take as a gift for a couple who had everything.

INTERPRETATIONS AND FORTUNE-TELLING MEANINGS
* If you dream you are making a pumpkin pie for Thanksgiving or Christmas, you will enjoy a happy occasion.
* If you dream of a jack-o'-lantern, you may need to take a chance on love or life. (Jack was condemned at Halloween to carry his pumpkin lantern between worlds because he was too afraid to cross the river of immortality.)
* If you dream that your pumpkin is sour, do not let anyone's criticism sabotage your efforts to succeed.
* Since a fairy godmother created Cinderella's coach from a pumpkin, dreaming of carving a pumpkin predicts that your wishes will come true.
* Dreaming of a good pumpkin harvest in the fields says your financial efforts during the previous six months will come to fruition.

OUTCOME OF JOEL'S DREAM
After the dream, Joel decided to take some mini pumpkin pies, carefully packed, to the meeting, as it was nearly Halloween. Jez's parents were incredibly pleased, as Jez's father said it reminded him of his boyhood, when his father was struggling as a chef and would bring treats home. Jez's parents backed Joel to start his own specialty cake store based on homemade recipes of childhood. Pumpkins, because they are associated with celebrations, are a good omen in dreams for happy family gatherings, representing togetherness and not material possessions.

Puppet

Victoria, thirty-two, dreamed she was watching a puppet show. Her new partner, Steve, was a giant harlequin puppet, being made to dance by the wicked witch puppeteer. The witch resembled his ex-partner. Victoria was booing. But then, to her amazement, the wicked witch dropped the strings. Steve did not run away, but danced hand in hand with the wicked witch. Victoria was confused.

DREAM BACKGROUND AND MEANING

Steve had told Victoria he could not live with her openly, because if his ex found out she would stop him from seeing the children. Victoria accepted that they could not have children or buy a home because the *wicked witch* constantly demanded money. Puppets, like clowns (see p. 107), can be tricksters. Some claim to be manipulated when they are codependent with the puppeteer.

INTERPRETATIONS AND FORTUNE-TELLING MEANINGS

★ If you dream you are the puppet or one of several in a puppet show, you are being manipulated or part of someone's grand plan. Beware of trickery.

★ If you dream you are the puppeteer, is a partner or relative too dependent on you?

★ Organizing a puppet show indicates a successful business transaction. Ensure that coworkers or employees do their share.

★ When you dream that puppet strings tangle, too many people are interfering in your affairs.

★ Dreaming of watching a puppet show suggests that you are aware that a friend, colleague, or family member is putting on an act. Who is the puppeteer?

★ If you dream of a Punch and Judy show, there may be issues of control in your partnership, home, or workplace. Assert your right to respect.

OUTCOME OF VICTORIA'S DREAM

Victoria by chance saw Steve with his very pregnant wife and three children, laughing in a shopping mall. She realized that *she* was the puppet in his double-life drama.

Puppet shows are based around illusion. The puppet needs the puppeteer to animate him or her, and the puppeteer needs the puppet so the show goes on.

Purse, Wallet

Elsie, seventy-five, dreamed her son arrived at her home with a van and took her possessions. He left her outside. She looked for her wallet in her bag, but it was gone. Elsie woke shaking.

DREAM BACKGROUND AND MEANING

Large quantities of money had been disappearing from Elsie's purse. But when Elsie told her son, he said she was losing her memory and had lost the money. He suggested she give him power of attorney. It seemed strange that money disappeared only when he came. Purses and wallets represent personal portable financial resources. Dreams can alert your radar to potential fraud or loss.

INTERPRETATIONS AND FORTUNE-TELLING MEANINGS

★ If you dream that your purse is full of money (see "Credit/ Debit Cards," p. 120), you will enjoy abundant times and see results of earlier labor flow in.

★ If you dream that you lose your purse or wallet, you may have been careless with money due to life overload.

★ If you dream that your purse or wallet or money from it is stolen, it could be a warning to beware of financial cheats in the days ahead.

★ If you dream that a family member or friend is spending freely with your purse or wallet, you may be overgenerous. Be sure you are not taken advantage of.

★ If your purse is empty, assess whether what you are giving to others in time as well as resources is too much.

★ If there is a single coin in your dream purse or wallet, it is an excellent sign that your fortunes will slowly revive.

OUTCOME OF ELSIE'S DREAM

Elsie knew her mind was as sharp as ever, so she set a trap and discovered that her son was stealing money and valuables from the house. He was planning to apply for power of attorney by saying she was mentally incapacitated. Elsie gave power of attorney to her trusted daughter, and her son stopped visiting. Purse and wallet dreams frequently occur when there are emotional factors involved.

Puzzles

Fergus, twenty-six, dreamed he was sitting in front of a 500-piece jigsaw puzzle of a bunch of rainbow-colored flowers. He hated jigsaw puzzles and was struggling, as many of the pieces looked the same. Some were missing. Fergus became increasingly frustrated. As he put in the final piece, a whirlwind blew through the open window, carrying the pieces to form a rainbow mural on the outside wall opposite. He woke feeling excited.

DREAM BACKGROUND AND MEANING

Fergus is a graphic designer working on incredibly detailed technical projects, which he dislikes. He has been offered promotion. His lifelong dream is to paint murals. His art tutor had dissuaded him, saying there was no future in such work. Puzzles of all kinds—mathematical, crossword, or jigsaw puzzles—represent rewards gained by attention to detail in career, official, or legal matters, or when studying.

INTERPRETATIONS AND FORTUNE-TELLING MEANINGS

★ If you successfully complete any kind of dream puzzle, the solution to problems lies in using logic, not your heart.

★ If pieces or clues are missing in any puzzle, look for concealed information before going further in a confusing situation.

★ Scattered jigsaw pieces ask if attention to detail is limiting you creatively, or if you are trying to focus on too many trivial matters.

★ A puzzle with many pieces says a matter may take much longer than expected. Do you want to complete the task it represents?

★ Dreaming about puzzles if you do not enjoy doing them suggests you need more freedom and spontaneity in life.

★ If completing the dream puzzle is a welcome challenge, you will untangle a financial problem, though it will take time and patience.

OUTCOME OF FERGUS'S DREAM

Fergus turned down a promotion and began painting murals for charity in run-down parts of town. He has been offered commissions as a result. Puzzles demand patience and persistence in life, heralding success through a step-by-step approach.

Pyramid

Dylan, forty-two, dreamed he was a Mayan priest, but hated the sacrifice of prisoners at the top of the stepped Pyramid of the Sun. He knew his life would be forfeit if he disobeyed. His wife had just given birth, and he did not want his son growing up accepting sacrifice. They and the prisoners escaped through the pyramid's underground passage into the rain forest, where they were free.

DREAM BACKGROUND AND MEANING

Dylan's wife had just given birth. As they lived close to a freeway, he worried about the baby's health. But they had prestigious jobs and a luxurious lifestyle. Pyramids represent earthly glory but also spiritual pathways to other dimensions. Choosing may require sacrifice.

INTERPRETATIONS AND FORTUNE-TELLING MEANINGS

★ If you are inside an ancient Egyptian or Mayan pyramid, it may be a past-life dream at a time of present choice.

★ Pyramid dreams indicate you have healing and psychic abilities you can develop.

★ Being inside a full-size crystal pyramid is a good omen if you or a loved one need healing, particularly the squat shape of the Pyramid of King Cheops at Giza near Cairo.

★ Dreaming of being trapped in an ancient pyramid suggests you are restricted by obligations or guilt that should be let go.

★ A dark or stone pyramid says pain, sorrow, and sickness will be relieved. Clear ones restore energy.

★ As ancient Egyptian pyramids represent the first mound of earth that rose from the primal waters at creation, dreaming of building or painting pyramids suggests you will succeed in creative ventures, but success will not be immediate.

OUTCOME OF DYLAN'S DREAM

Dylan and his wife moved into the wilderness, built their own home, fostered refugee children, and are working on self-sufficiency.

Pyramids reach for the stars, but in history they represented suffering of living Egyptian slaves, buried with their deceased owners, and the bloody power-bringing sacrifices made on the Mayan structures.

Quarantine

Johannes, twenty-five, dreamed he was traveling to a country with strict quarantine regulations owing to a pandemic. He felt ill but did not inform the airline. He was stopped on arrival and, when tested, was placed into quarantine in a run-down hotel, where he spent his entire vacation.

DREAM BACKGROUND AND MEANING

Johannes was planning a backpacking adventure and refused to postpone it because of travel restrictions. However, travel insurance was now very expensive. This meant he had to cut way back on the trip to pay for it. Friends with whom he was traveling said they would take a chance and buy minimum insurance coverage. Quarantine dreams can be warnings of restrictions that should be anticipated whether regarding travel, financial, or health matters.

INTERPRETATIONS AND FORTUNE-TELLING MEANINGS

★ To be placed in quarantine in a dream because you are carrying an illness means you feel helpless about malice and gossip someone is spreading about you.

★ If you are going into dream quarantine, withdraw immediately from a situation where you doubt the good intentions of others.

★ If you dream you are in self-imposed emotional isolation, you may feel drained by the negativity of others.

★ If you sense trouble brewing in a relationship or workplace, it is time to avoid being drawn into others' disputes.

★ Dreaming of quarantine restrictions in international travel is a warning that this is not a time for major changes without backup plans.

★ If you dream of being quarantined because of travel restrictions, avoid taking risks with your health, as you may not be as resistant as you believe.

OUTCOME OF JOHANNES'S DREAM

Johannes's parents paid for full insurance covering the quarantine, but his friends bought the cheapest. When his friends became sick, they faced costs of many thousands of dollars for repatriation. Quarantine dreams at any time in any situation can alert the dreamer to step back for now and avoid unnecessary stress and risks.

Quayside (Dock)

Debra, thirty, dreamed she disembarked from a ferry, expecting her fiancé, Greg, to meet her on the quayside. The quay was deserted and there was no border patrol, no taxis, and no one to ask for help. She phoned her fiancé, but his phone was disconnected. She walked to his address, where a young woman said she was his girlfriend and shut the door.

DREAM BACKGROUND AND MEANING

Debra had met Greg, a young Canadian, on the Internet. He proposed marriage and suggested she come over to Canada on a vacation paid for by him while they sorted out visas and work permits prior to the wedding. But, as the departure date neared, Greg became harder to contact and the tickets never arrived. She booked herself an air fare and emailed him with her arrival date. But recurring dreams of the deserted quayside started. A quay in a dream signifies a welcome to a new location, a personal adventure, or abandonment, according to the dream's nature.

INTERPRETATIONS AND FORTUNE-TELLING MEANINGS

★ To dream that you stand on a quayside watching boats arrive and depart says you should put long-anticipated travel plans into action.

★ A dream of fishing boats unloading their catch indicates money or a wealthy relation arriving from overseas.

★ If you are waiting on a quay for a lover or family member to arrive, it depends, according to your dream scenario, if this is a good omen.

★ If the quay is deserted and no ships are on the horizon, a hoped-for result may be delayed or lost.

★ If you are disembarking on a quay, and carrying your own luggage, you are going on an independent venture, or need to embark on one.

OUTCOME OF DEBRA'S DREAM

After the dreams became more frequent, Debra phoned Greg's workplace, but they did not know him. His phone was disconnected, and his photo appeared on another dating site, seeking a bride to emigrate, all expenses paid. Debra did not hear from Greg again. Quayside dreams signify entry into a new life, but can also give signs of what is waiting in reality.

Queen

Howard, forty-four, dreamed he caught the elderly female personal assistant everyone called "Mother" clearing away his papers from his workspace. To his horror, she had shredded notes he had scribbled down that were the basis of a major project worth millions. He seized her hand and she slipped and hit her head.

DREAM BACKGROUND AND MEANING

Bessie, or "Mother," as she insisted on being called, had organized the office to the last postage stamp, but had no idea of personal space. The other workers said the CEO had a soft spot for her. But she was causing chaos and costing the company time and money. Queens like to rule their domains and may take over territory not rightly theirs.

INTERPRETATIONS AND FORTUNE-TELLING MEANINGS

* The queen may represent your mother or an older or more powerful woman in your workplace. The nature of the dream reveals your feelings toward her.
* If in the dream the queen is aggressive, or aggression boils over, you may need to stand up to your mother figure if she hides control under nurturing.
* If you dream of your deceased mother as a queen and you the suppliant or prisoner, it's time to let the relationship go in peace.
* If you pick a playing card or tarot card queen, if she is diamonds or pentacles/coins, there will be financial gain; hearts or cups, love and fertility; clubs or wands, career success; and spades or swords, overcoming obstacles or resentment. Is she you?
* If you see your love partner as a queen in the dream, she is emotionally mature, a supportive help, and a good mother if you both choose.
* If your queen is riding out to battle, she will be loyal to you and the family.

OUTCOME OF HOWARD'S DREAM

Howard requested that Bessie leave his workspace to him. She was very offended. They have an uneasy truce. A nurturing figure in a workplace can be endearing, but a dream will warn when underlying emotions are reaching the boiling point.

Questionnaire

Vlad, forty-two, dreamed that he arrived at the airport with the correct paperwork for his flight to Cambodia to meet his girlfriend, Chantrea. But he was given a twelve-page questionnaire and told that if he did not fill in the questions correctly he would not be allowed on the plane. An airline official stood over him and changed each question after Vlad had answered it, so he had to answer them again. At last Vlad finished, but all the answers he had written disappeared, and his visa was canceled.

DREAM BACKGROUND AND MEANING

Vlad was worried about a job interview he was having to send him to the Cambodian branch of his company. Despite being well-qualified, Vlad was told he had to fill in a psychological multichoice profile. He was worried that he might answer incorrectly. Questionnaires and profiles are often answered inaccurately to conceal the dreamer's true feelings, but dreams reveal what the dreamer does not want to show the world.

INTERPRETATIONS AND FORTUNE-TELLING MEANINGS

* If dream questions are intrusive, they may touch on secrets the dreamer is concealing from themselves.
* If the dreamer lies on the dream questionnaire, they may fear their application being refused.
* If questions and answers change or disappear while the dreamer is writing, the dreamer has mixed feelings about the future.
* If the questionnaire is feedback on service, it may refer to a relationship and assess the dreamer's true feelings about that relationship.
* If a questionnaire has multiple choices, the dreamer may not be ready to make decisions.
* If the dreamer writes on or marks the questionnaire, they may be questioning if whoever filled in the questionnaire is honest.

OUTCOME OF VLAD'S DREAM

Vlad answered the psychological profile questions honestly and was offered the job. However, he was still troubled by the dream and wondered if he really wanted to live in Cambodia and marry his girlfriend. He put the job on hold and went on vacation to Cambodia, where all his doubts were resolved. Questionnaires where the questions alter in the dream can cast doubts whether the dreamer is asking the right questions.

Questions

In her dream, Louise, twenty-eight, was being questioned by the parents of her boyfriend, Ken, about her background, previous boyfriends, if she went to church, and her view on how *soon she would have children. They fired off questions one after the other until at last she said she was answering no more.*

DREAM BACKGROUND AND MEANING

Ken's family ran a business in which his brothers' wives were expected to work. They all lived in houses within the grounds of the main house and vacationed together. Louise was staying on the weekend after the dream, and Ken said his family would want to know all about her. Questions can be a good icebreaker with people you do not know well, but can become intrusive if they overstep boundaries.

INTERPRETATIONS AND FORTUNE-TELLING MEANINGS

* If you dream you are answering questions in a quiz, you have a chance to use your knowledge and expertise for profit, whether in a competition or in the workplace.
* If you are answering examination questions, especially if you are a child in the dream, you may feel or be under scrutiny.
* If you are questioned under oath in a court of law, you may feel guilty about a mistake from the past you concealed.
* If you are asking questions and not getting answers, you may have unvoiced doubts about the reliability of an offer or the trustworthiness of the person you are seeking answers from.
* If you are filling in a questionnaire, you are not able to express your views freely.
* If in the dream you are questioning someone you suspect has done you wrong, your own fears may give an inaccurate dream answer.

OUTCOME OF LOUISE'S DREAM

Louise's weekend with her prospective in-laws was a rerun of the dream, except that she was prepared by the dream and refused to be quizzed. This made for an uncomfortable weekend, and Louise was quietly dropped by Ken. Questioning indicates confidence and a desire for truth, but being questioned suggests insecurity and fear of giving the wrong answer.

Quicksand

Katarina, twenty-five, dreamed she was racing along the shore with her boyfriend, Seb. As always, he was desperate to get ahead. Too late, they saw the quicksand warning, and Seb was sucked down. Using all her strength, Katarina released him, but in doing so became trapped herself. To her horror, Seb ran off, leaving her sinking fast. Then she saw Paul, a guy she had known all her life, tying up his boat and coming to her aid.

DREAM BACKGROUND AND MEANING

Seb was athletic, an all-action man. But he was reluctant to commit and would frequently let Katarina down if something more exciting came up. Paul had always been in her life—kind, supportive, but he did not make her heart somersault. Quicksand can alert you to difficulties you had not anticipated and so can prepare you to avoid them.

INTERPRETATIONS AND FORTUNE-TELLING MEANINGS

* Dreaming of sinking in quicksand refers to money, debt, or emotional worries that may require advice and support.
* To be rescued from quicksand says your rescuer, who may not be the person you expected, will save you from a perilous or unwise situation.
* If you dream you escape by your own efforts, you will move away from a potentially destructive situation involving someone draining your energies.
* Should you see signs warning of quicksand, you need stability in a relationship or career and should not ignore imminent danger signs.
* If you rescue someone from quicksand, make sure you do not become drawn into another person's problems at a cost to yourself.
* If you miss the signs and only stop yourself from falling in at the last minute, you may be underestimating a financial situation that needs fixing now.

OUTCOME OF KATARINA'S DREAM

The dream alerted Katarina to the contrast between the two guys. She let Seb go, and she and Paul are planning a future. Avoiding a number of quicksand beds represents that you acknowledge and are dealing with underlying fears and insecurities.

Quilt

Deanne, forty-five, dreamed she was sewing a memory quilt for her daughter for her wedding, made of pieces of fabric from memorable occasions from her daughter's childhood. Her daughter picked up the quilt, laughed, and asked who the hideous bedcover was for. Hurt and humiliated, Deanne pushed it into a cupboard.

DREAM BACKGROUND AND MEANING

Deanne's only daughter was ultraminimalist and had definite ideas about the furnishings and fabrics for her new home. But Deanne was determined to make a quilt to transfer her love to her daughter's new life. However, her daughter already had rejected several suggestions and asked her mother to back off from interfering. Quilts are an expression of love, but for some they represent an old-fashioned sentiment, so it's important to be sure any interventions in a family member's life are welcome.

INTERPRETATIONS AND FORTUNE-TELLING MEANINGS

- ★ If you dream you are given a handmade quilt by a friend or family member, you are assured of their love and devotion.
- ★ If you are wrapping a family member, especially an adult child, tightly in a quilt, be sure you are not smothering them with well-intentioned possessiveness.
- ★ If you are hiding under a quilt, you need to nurture yourself, as you are in danger of burnout.
- ★ If a quilt is ripped or dirty in your dream, you have been neglecting your own needs to care for others.
- ★ If you dream you are sewing a quilt, you will be required to devote extra time to domestic or family matters.

OUTCOME OF DEANNE'S DREAM

Following the dream, Deanne asked her daughter what she would like as a wedding gift, and her daughter said a gift certificate for furnishings. Deanne showed the half-finished quilt to a neighbor, who asked if Deanne would make one for a special commission. Deanne has set up a successful online business making memory quilts. Sometimes quilts given or made for another can represent a desire by the donor or maker to hold on to family togetherness, which can stifle everyone concerned.

Quiz

Henry, twenty, dreamed he was in a televised quiz as a member of his college team. When the camera lights came on, his mind went blank, and he struggled over basic questions. Suddenly, a voice in his ear gave the answers clearly, and his hand was swiftly on the answer buzzer, almost prior to the question having been asked. His team won easily, but he could not explain how he had known the right answers almost before hearing the entire question.

DREAM BACKGROUND AND MEANING

Henry's late great-uncle had been a walking encyclopedia and had taught Henry what his family said were useless facts but which Henry absorbed like a sponge. Henry had been offered a place in a televised college quiz game. Quiz dreams occur when the dreamer feels they are on trial in a specific area of their life and are afraid of failing.

INTERPRETATIONS AND FORTUNE-TELLING MEANINGS

- ★ If you do well in a solo dream quiz, trust in your expertise to pass an interview, examination, or test.
- ★ If you dream you win a fortune in a television quiz, your knowledge will bring prosperity where most needed.
- ★ If you do badly in a dream quiz, pay more attention to small details.
- ★ If you are taking part in a team quiz, do not let seeming experts intimidate you.
- ★ If you dream you are being questioned over financial or official matters, do not be bullied into incriminating yourself.
- ★ If in your dream you discover another person cheating on a quiz, beware of taking answers at face value.

OUTCOME OF HENRY'S DREAM

After the dream Henry felt confident and entered the quiz. His team won through to the semifinals and, though he heard no voices in his ear, he answered every question correctly. Quiz dreams seem to release a store of knowledge acquired through life and indicate that the dreamer is ready to test themself in the world.

Rabbit

Trudy, forty-three, dreamed she was in a field surrounded by rabbits running in all directions. One family of rabbits stayed close and hopped into a big cage she had brought to capture pet rabbits for her son. But Trudy knew in her heart that they should be free and so opened the cage. Trudy woke for the first time in ages without pressure.

DREAM BACKGROUND AND MEANING

Trudy had a son from her first marriage and wanted children with her new partner, Bill. But she had a high-powered job in the city and Bill ran a small property in a rural area, so they could not often be together. Bill offered to give up his business, but she realized he would be unhappy as a city dweller. Time was passing; if they were going to start a family, it had to be soon. A caged rabbit represents the trade-off between security and fulfillment.

INTERPRETATIONS AND FORTUNE-TELLING MEANINGS

⋆ The ultimate fertility symbol, dream rabbits represent babies, children, and togetherness.

⋆ A family of rabbits is a good omen if you want a larger family and conception is slow to occur.

⋆ Rabbits racing across a field indicate the need for speed to attain a goal or to escape from a difficult situation.

⋆ White rabbits, especially in pairs, are a sign of faithful, lasting love, whether known or unknown.

⋆ All rabbits in a dream near the beginning of a month, particularly white ones, are a symbol of growing good fortune.

⋆ Rabbits disappearing down a hole suggest that avoiding facing family problems will not make them go away.

⋆ Rabbits frozen in headlights or attacked by hunters advise that a sudden change in direction may be necessary.

OUTCOME OF TRUDY'S DREAM

Trudy quit her job, and she and her son went to live on the property with Bill. Trudy is pregnant and, for the first time in years, feels free. Rabbits represent abundance in life quality.

Radiation

Lennox, forty-eight, in his dream was on duty at a nuclear power station while a party was going on. He noticed the dials were moving toward danger levels. But it was the power station's party and no one would listen to him. He watched in horror as the warning dials rose and the alarms were activated. Still the partying continued. He shut the system down and fled to the bunker.

DREAM BACKGROUND AND MEANING

Lennox was a director in an engineering firm. But the company was not making money. The senior director and owner, Adam, treated the finances like a personal ATM, buying new cars, expensive holidays, and luxurious clothes, while Lennox took as little as possible. Radiation dreams can reflect fears that may or may not materialize but need careful examining.

INTERPRETATIONS AND FORTUNE-TELLING MEANINGS

⋆ If you dream that radiation is used in investigative or interventional radiography, you may need to take risks for positive results.

⋆ To see danger signs warning of a radioactive leak says you should guard private projects and confidential mails.

⋆ If you dream you are infected by radiation, you may be subject to others' toxic attitudes and should keep your distance.

⋆ If you dream you detect a radioactive cloud approaching in the distance and run rather than shelter, beware of panicking in a crisis.

⋆ If you dream of nuclear attack, you have unresolved fears caused by others' malice or carelessness.

⋆ If in your dream you or someone close is suffering from radiation sickness, shed negative situations and people who are damaging your confidence.

OUTCOME OF LENNOX'S DREAM

Lennox withdrew as a director and left the company. He took a job in the same field, and when Adam could borrow no more money to fund his extravagant lifestyle, he went bankrupt. Radiation can have positive uses for generating power but, unwisely used or disregarded, it is a double-edged sword.

Raffle

Hilary, thirty, dreamed she was on a tropical island with her future husband, having won first prize in a lottery. The hotel was cramped and dirty, the island overrun with mosquitoes, and they caught a stomach bug on the first day.

DREAM BACKGROUND AND MEANING

Hilary was hoping to win a luxury vacation for two for her honeymoon in the sweepstakes at the hospital where she worked. She bought several books of raffle tickets. Raffle dreams can indicate good fortune ahead but, unlike other predictive dreams, do retain the element of chance both in winning and in satisfaction with the prize.

INTERPRETATIONS AND FORTUNE-TELLING MEANINGS

★ If you dream of winning a raffle but have not entered one, this says you have a good chance of reward.

★ If you have already entered a raffle or competition, or intend to, this is a good omen.

★ If in your dream you buy a lot of raffle tickets for a specific prize, you will have an opportunity to take a risk in speculation or in an uncertain investment and should calculate the odds.

★ If your name is chosen in a work or community raffle in the dream, you may need to allow fate or others to determine the future in a particular venture.

★ If you dream you donate an unwanted item to a raffle, you may be thinking of giving up on a relationship or activity.

★ If you dream you win a consolation prize in a raffle but you only wanted the main one, use initiative rather than relying on luck.

OUTCOME OF HILARY'S DREAM

Hilary googled the island and hotel and found it was all she hoped and more. But her future husband said he would prefer going somewhere cooler. She won the runner-up prize of a hundred-dollar voucher. Raffle dreams can indicate lucky breaks but may question if winning or succeeding delivers what is wanted, or if the winning is the ultimate goal.

Raft

In his dream, Louis, sixty, was a teenager building a raft with a group of friends as part of a competition. In the competition, the opposing team was trying to tip their raft over. He realized that his two teammates, in adulthood partners in his business, were assisting to destabilize his raft. He dived overboard and swam to the opposite shore.

DREAM BACKGROUND AND MEANING

Louis ran a business with two friends he had known since school. He discovered they had been negotiating behind his back to sell the business. He was not ready to retire but could not afford to buy his partners out. Raft dreams involve team-building and cooperation. If that cooperation is withheld or removed, the raft is in danger of sinking (see "Whitewater Rafting, Rapids," p. 508).

INTERPRETATIONS AND FORTUNE-TELLING MEANINGS

★ To dream you make a raft from driftwood found near water indicates that if you use your initiative, you can reach your goal with or without assistance.

★ If you dream you are successfully sailing a raft on a river or the sea, you will find success in another part of the country or in a new venture, even if not in your first choice.

★ Making a raft yourself to cross a body of water is a good sign of your going it alone, as difficulties will be overcome.

★ Dreaming of being cast adrift in a raft may occur after a loss or betrayal. Allow events to take their course.

★ If you dream you are sailing a raft with someone you love, you will have a happy relationship together.

★ If you dream someone you know is trying to tip the raft over or refuses to help sail it, you may be in danger of being exploited.

OUTCOME OF LOUIS'S DREAM

Louis decided to set himself up working from home with his wife helping with administration. Raft dreams occur at points in life where the contribution of others is in question and the dreamer may do better sailing his own raft.

Rain

Maxine, forty-five, dreamed she was balancing trays of party food in the pouring rain, and she and the food were soaked. She knocked on the door of her older sister's house, where the party was being held. All her relatives were watching through the window, but no one would help. She was crying, because the food and party would be spoiled. Then she became angry, threw the trays into the front garden, and walked away. The rain stopped. Maxine woke feeling powerful.

DREAM BACKGROUND AND MEANING

Since her mother's death, Maxine had assumed responsibility for organizing family get-togethers, with no practical or financial help or appreciation from the family. She has acted as go-between, peacemaker, and cheerleader and was increasingly resentful. She had said nothing. Rainstorms represent the necessary outpouring of sorrow or resentment to clear the air.

INTERPRETATIONS AND FORTUNE-TELLING MEANINGS

* If you dream you have an umbrella or are watching rain from indoors, step away from emotional demands on you.
* Rain coming through the roof warns against ignoring tensions building up that may escalate out of control. It alternatively warns of an illicit affair being discovered.
* If you are offered shelter from the rain, you will learn who you can trust in times of trouble.
* A rainstorm soaking you through is a powerful symbol of fertility and male potency in many cultures and ages.
* A shower falling from a clear sky is an excellent omen for the success of new ideas, new beginnings, and the rapid growth of a new business.
* Dreaming of rain spoiling an event or catering warns that you have been trying too hard to please others at a cost to yourself.
* If you are longing for rain, you may feel stifled by an unemotional partner and need to express your feelings.

OUTCOME OF MAXINE'S DREAM

Maxine told her family that in the future they had to take their share of organizing family events. She made herself less available and responsible for family happiness.

Rain Forest

Drew, thirty, was walking through the rain forest, looking for healing plants. He came across loggers cutting down the trees. The loggers offered Drew money to not reveal their presence. When he refused, they threatened him with machetes. He woke as they closed in.

DREAM BACKGROUND AND MEANING

Drew worked for a major pharmaceutical company, which made synthetic products with large profit margins. While on vacation in the Amazonian rain forest, Drew learned about a plant that was a natural antibiotic. Drew told his bosses, but they said it was too expensive to get a license or produce it commercially. Rain-forest dreams occur when you feel you need to put into practice any concerns you have about climate change and the environment.

INTERPRETATIONS AND FORTUNE-TELLING MEANINGS

* If you dream of finding a special plant in a rain forest, it or a derivative may provide relief for yourself or a relative if modern medicine is not giving answers.
* If you dream you are an indigenous person in a rain forest, this may be a past-life experience. Revise your lifestyle to spend more time close to nature.
* If you dream you see a rain forest being destroyed, in some aspect of your life you will need to defend a principle against powerful interests.
* You may be made a tempting offer for short-term profit that will cause problems in the longer term.
* Rain forests filled with flowers and exotic birds predict that your creative side will emerge if you leave convention behind.
* Rain forests represent deep primal instincts that, if expressed, enable you to live authentically.

OUTCOME OF DREW'S DREAM

Drew discovered that the company was working on a new, very lucrative synthetic antibiotic. His expected promotion was blocked when he expressed concerns about its concealed side effects. Drew joined a less-profitable organization that researched natural rain forest remedies. As rain forests are the lungs of the earth, concern for their preservation is, through dreams, entering the consciousness of many people not normally motivated to fight for their survival.

Rainbow

Julio, forty-five, dreamed he was walking in a torrential rain, pushing a wheelbarrow of brightly colored crystals. Suddenly, the sun came out and a brilliant arched rainbow appeared directly ahead. As Julio walked toward the rainbow, he found himself in a market where there was an empty stall. The market became crowded, and Julio sold all the crystals he had in the vacant stall. The dream ended with Julio wheeling home a golden ceramic pot, filled with money, and with the rainbow following him overhead. He woke bemused.

DREAM BACKGROUND AND MEANING

Julio had recently closed his crystal store because of an increase in rent, and another store had offered to buy his stock. But crystals were Julio's passion, and he had collected them since childhood. Rainbows often appear in dreams after a major setback saying, "Hold on, for better times are coming."

INTERPRETATIONS AND FORTUNE-TELLING MEANINGS

★ Rainbows are among the most predictive dream signs for new beginnings, opportunities appearing seemingly out of the blue, acquiring money, and good fortune.

★ A bright complete rainbow heralds an unexpected windfall or the turnaround of an unpromising venture.

★ A fading rainbow indicates the need to instantly seize a chance.

★ If you are estranged from a relative or close friend, the rainbow promises reconciliation.

★ Any rainbow dream alerts the dreamer to previously unconsidered ideas and brings happiness in the area of life of most concern to the dreamer. Success comes by taking a chance.

★ Double rainbows, or those that begin and end in the sea, represent incredible good fortune.

OUTCOME OF JULIO'S DREAM

Julio rented a stall at a local market to sell his crystals, and the venture was very profitable. He now trades at several markets where overheads are low and the turnover fast, and he has hired an assistant. Rainbow dreams are always positive, if you act fast according to the dream omen.

Rainbow Bridge

James, thirty-five, dreamed he was on a bridge with his best friend, Paul. Overhead was an arched rainbow, coloring the bridge. Paul told James to go back, but look for shining pebbles on the way, each a plan that James now needed to complete. Paul headed toward huge golden gates. James turned back. As promised, as he found each pebble, he remembered a goal he and Paul had been going to fulfill.

DREAM BACKGROUND AND MEANING

Paul, thirty-eight, had died suddenly, though he had seemed 100 percent fit. James suddenly questioned what he had done with his life. He and Paul had been intending to travel around Southeast Asia. Dreams about rainbow bridges between dimensions occur in many cultures and ages, triggered by a major unsought loss, whether an unexpected bereavement or a lifestyle taken away.

INTERPRETATIONS AND FORTUNE-TELLING MEANINGS

★ If you dream of a rainbow bridge at a point of major change, it's time to put travel or movement plans into action.

★ If you are on the bridge with someone you have lost in death, you may be sharing their transition to the afterlife.

★ If you dream of deceased pets on a rainbow bridge that has become associated with the place they waited for owners, you will know their love is still with you.

★ If you are walking across a rainbow bridge and are told, whether by a deceased person or spirit guide, that you must go back to fulfill your destiny, this is equivalent to a near-death experience (see p. 325) but experienced during a life crisis when you may not want to go on.

★ If a rainbow bridge fades before you can cross it, you may not be ready yet for a new life.

OUTCOME OF JAMES'S DREAM

After the dream, James was released from the inertia that had hit him immediately after his friend's untimely death. He booked an open ticket to Indonesia to visit those places he and Paul had talked about. Rainbow-bridge dreams do not necessarily follow a bereavement, but almost always mark an ending or the need for an ending to prepare for a new life purpose.

Rat

Helena, forty-two, dreamed she had been given a pet rat in a cage for her children, which she hated as she had a fear of rats. The door of the cage opened, and it escaped. It tried to bite the children. Overcoming her revulsion, she chased it out of the apartment.

DREAM BACKGROUND AND MEANING

Helena's new boyfriend moved in, and she rapidly felt it was not her home, as he took over. She was worried about the effect on the children, as she had discovered child pornography on the family computer. Her boyfriend told her she was making a fuss about nothing. Rat dreams, like real rats, represent a destructive factor that needs to be tackled before it escalates.

INTERPRETATIONS AND FORTUNE-TELLING MEANINGS

* Being overrun by small vicious aggressors in a dream signifies feeling attacked on many fronts by demands that seem to constantly multiply.
* Dreams of rats attacking you or your family warn you to be wary of who you invite into your family or friendship circle, as they may turn on you.
* Killing rats in a dream says you can overcome those trying to interfere in your life by tackling issues and not allowing them to go unchallenged.
* Driving rats away, especially into water, represents acknowledging deep-seated fears about a relationship if you are feeling uneasy, rather than denying your feelings.
* If you dream that rats are contaminating food, others are twisting your words or misrepresenting your intentions. Speak up for yourself.

OUTCOME OF HELENA'S DREAM

Helena told her boyfriend to go. When he refused, she told him she would report him to the police. He moved out after damaging the place, and Helena reclaimed her territory.

Rats, if allowed to spread their malign influence, represent in dreams a problem that will not go away but brings to the surface primal fears of this universal and ageless predator.

Reality Show

Gaynor, twenty-five, dreamed she was on a reality TV show, competing for a vacation with a gorgeous celebrity. The show producer deliberately did not deliver her suitcase of glamorous outfits, and the other competitors would not lend her any. Gaynor stripped down to her underwear while washing the jeans she arrived in, paraded around half naked for much of the show—and won.

DREAM BACKGROUND AND MEANING

Gaynor was an avid fan of reality shows. But she was engaged to a respectable corporate funds manager who insisted she dress discreetly and expected her to stay home once they were married. She craved fame but also the respectability and security her fiancé offered, as Gaynor had experienced a chaotic childhood. Reality-show dreams reveal an often-buried desire for public notoriety in the seemingly most reticent people.

INTERPRETATIONS AND FORTUNE-TELLING MEANINGS

* If you are appearing in a reality show in your dream, you may be seeking positive recognition and a higher profile in your work life or social life.
* If you win a reality show in your dream, you are aiming for fame and should persist, as you have star quality.
* If you are watching a reality show in your dream but not participating, you may feel that life is passing you by and you are living through family or friends.
* If you dream you are being set extra-challenging or dangerous tasks in the reality show, you may be prepared to take more risks in life to attain your goals.
* If in your dream you are voted off a reality show, you are lacking confidence in your abilities to come out on top.

OUTCOME OF GAYNOR'S DREAM

After the dream, Gaynor realized that the price of security was too high, and she wanted to be noticed. She sent show reels to various reality shows, which in part reconstructed her dream. She was offered a place on a desert-island show, and her fiancé told her she had to choose. She chose the show. Reality-show dreams can represent any high-profile event where there is a need to act flamboyantly to succeed.

Rearranging Furniture

Lynette, fifty-five, dreamed she was back in her childhood home, helping with her mother's regular rearranging of the furniture. Her mother would haul everything into the backyard, try the furniture in different positions, and always put the furniture back in its original places. Lynette never argued, but it seemed so pointless. She woke frustrated.

DREAM BACKGROUND AND MEANING

Lynette feared she was turning into her mother, continually rearranging the furniture but never satisfied. Her husband was living with his mistress, so Lynette could live as she liked, but she always rearranged the furniture and returned it to where it had been. Rearranging furniture represents an underlying discontentment.

INTERPRETATIONS AND FORTUNE-TELLING MEANINGS

* If rearranging furniture in your dream solves the problem, it is only the outer facade of a situation that needs fixing, but this tends to be a dream with a deeper meaning.
* If, as usually occurs, moving the furniture in the dream or in actuality does not resolve the issue, there may be a deeper restlessness being overlooked.
* If in the dream the furniture is too heavy to move, you may be weighed down by worries you have not acknowledged.
* If an item of furniture cracks or breaks, there may be issues that cannot be resolved with a quick fix.
* If you dream you permanently replace the furniture, you are ready for a new start in life and should not hesitate.

OUTCOME OF LYNETTE'S DREAM

Lynette realized that her own mother had settled for second best in life, and Lynette vowed she would not do the same. She insisted that her husband sell the house so she could have her share. She no longer wanted him back when he tired of his latest mistress, as he had previously done. She realized that all the furniture had been chosen by him. When she moved, she got rid of it all. The dreams ceased. Furniture is a symbol of what makes us feel settled at home or otherwise, and sometimes rearranging it is not sufficient.

Recapturing Lost Youth

Rod, sixty-one, dreamed he was seated at a table, enjoying a cherry soda with chocolate ice cream. To his amazement, in walked the characters from his favorite movie, Grease: Sandy, Danny, and their friends from Rydell High. They sat at his table and included Rod in all their conversations. They were all the same age as they had been in the movie, and Rod was also a high-school teen again.

DREAM BACKGROUND AND MEANING

Since high-school movies were all the rage in the 1970s, Rod had shown a devotion that had, if anything, increased through the years. He had filled the bedroom with posters and enjoyed his weekly sessions with cherry soda and ice cream while watching reruns of the movies. Being obsessed with the past can signify reluctance to accept the aging process.

INTERPRETATIONS AND FORTUNE-TELLING MEANINGS

* If in a dream you meet characters from old movies, there may be a lack of spontaneity in your present life.
* If regular dreams are about high-school or bubblegum movies, the carefree ideal may be the attraction, especially if the dreamer's high-school experiences were unhappy.
* If the dream is full of camaraderie and belonging to a group, there may be a lack of like-minded people in the dreamer's current life.
* If the dreamer dreams they are young again, there may be teen ambitions unfulfilled or a craving for a first young love.
* If the connection with the dream world is no longer possible in the present world, maybe it should be left behind.
* If the dreamer keeps returning to a period typified by special music and movies, they should find others who share the interest instead of seeking dream fulfillment.

OUTCOME OF ROD'S DREAM

Rod's wife found a society not many miles distant that had 1970s revival nights and vacations. Rod took along his old posters and videos. Dreams of carefree days that maybe once existed are a good rejuvenator but should be shared.

Recipe

Holly, thirty, dreamed she had been entrusted with handwritten recipes from her new husband's family so she could bake his birthday cake according to tradition. She opened the window, and all the pages blew out onto the street. There was only the one copy, which was sacrosanct to the family.

DREAM BACKGROUND AND MEANING

Holly worked long hours at her job and was horrified to discover that she was expected to follow a special recipe handed down through the generations for her husband's birthday cake. She knew everyone, including her husband, would be judging her. Recipes, especially family ones, can have a lot of expectations attached involving issues of conformity, which may be at odds with the dreamer's lifestyle.

INTERPRETATIONS AND FORTUNE-TELLING MEANINGS

★ If you dream you are following a recipe, using precise ingredients and measurements, you will successfully—though resentfully—fulfill a task precisely as asked.

★ If in your dream you create your own recipe, using what you have in the pantry, you need to live your own way rather than going along with others' demands.

★ If you are using a ready-to-make mix where you just need to add the contents and cook, you may tend to take shortcuts in life.

★ If you dream you are missing a vital ingredient from a recipe, you may be going along with a decision or relationship out of duty, disregarding your own feelings.

★ If you dream you are following a traditional family recipe, you may be pressured to please the family, even against your own preferences.

★ If you dream of devising a recipe on a television competition, your success will determine how far a unique creative venture will succeed in your waking life.

OUTCOME OF HOLLY'S DREAM

Holly photocopied the recipe book and gave the copy to a friend who ran a private cake-making company and secretly created the cake on Holly's behalf. Recipes represent blending different viewpoints and lifestyles where creativity may fight with conformity.

Reconciliation

Caleb, forty, dreamed he was returning to his childhood home for the first time in twenty years. He was holding his small baby. He knocked at the door. His father said Caleb was dead to them and slammed the door. His mother chased after Caleb and told him she wanted to know her grandson. She said she would talk his father around.

DREAM BACKGROUND AND MEANING

Caleb had not seen nor heard from his parents since becoming involved with a bad crowd, resulting in his serving a lengthy prison sentence for armed robbery. He had left his life of crime behind him when he was released from jail ten years earlier, and now had stable employment. He desperately wanted to reestablish a connection with his family, as this is their first grandchild. Reconciliation dreams make telepathic links with those we are estranged from, if they are thinking of us.

INTERPRETATIONS AND FORTUNE-TELLING MEANINGS

★ If you dream of being reconciled with a family member, friend, or ex-lover, this may be a good time to make initial contact, as the energies are right.

★ If in a dream you connect with a friend or lover from the distant past, look for them on social media, if only to make peace.

★ If you dream of reconciliation with a departed spirit who you were not able to say goodbye to, visit a place you were happy together and you may feel peace.

★ If someone you are estranged from appears angry, contact them through an intermediary or accept that this is not the time.

★ If someone, living or deceased, walks away from you through a door or gateway, let go, as attempts at peace will be rejected.

★ If in the dream someone estranged contacts you, they may seek peace but fear it is too late. Make contact and see if they respond.

OUTCOME OF CALEB'S DREAM

After the dream, Caleb realized that reconciliation would only come through his mother. He wrote her a letter and enclosed photos of her grandson. She contacted Caleb and suggested they meet and said that she could in time win his father around. Dreams about reconciliation can pick up the energies of those involved with the dreamer and so ease the process.

Recycling

Juliana, twenty-five, dreamed that outside the house she had bought with her partner were piles of serviceable furniture, carpets, cutlery, and crockery with a sign HELP YOURSELF. Juliana was thrilled, but her partner, Tess, said there was no way they were using other people's castoffs. Juliana had been brought up in a thrifty household, sharing school uniforms, bicycles, and toys that were outgrown. She woke disappointed in Tess.

DREAM BACKGROUND AND MEANING

Though they were already stretched financially, Tess wanted to take out a bank loan to furnish their new home. Juliana hated waste and would always buy products made from recycled waste and spend weekends looking in discount clothes stores and charity stores for bargains. Recycling dreams often have underlying theme issues of sharing, the basis of generosity.

INTERPRETATIONS AND FORTUNE-TELLING MEANINGS

⋆ To be recycling paper, cardboard, glass, and other renewables in a dream suggests the need to assess what is of worth and what should be left behind.

⋆ To dream of emptying a recycling bin represents letting go rather than holding on to outgrown memories.

⋆ To visit a recycling center in a dream, where waste is transformed into other products, signifies the need for exchange, whether of ideas, resources, or services.

⋆ If recycling items are mixed with garbage, beware of materially focused folk who value only what is new.

⋆ If you dream that recycling gets spoiled or polluted, you may be wasting your time and energy trying to revive a project. Start again with more environmentally focused people.

⋆ If you dream you are recycling clothes or household items, have another try at regenerating a relationship.

OUTCOME OF JULIANA'S DREAM

Tess's family had a home furnished with valuable antiques, and Juliana pointed out that they were recycled items. Juliana made a point of stopping the car at a local landfill site where acrid smoke was pouring from bonfires, and she asked Tess if she wanted their future children to grow up with damaged lungs. In dreams, recycling, a principle going back thousands of years, may appear when the dreamer is trying to persuade a partner or family to preserve rather than squander.

Redwood Trees

Edwardo, twenty-one, dreamed he was walking in a redwood forest and noticed how interconnected and tall the trees were. He could see his family walking in the distance through the trees but could not reach them, as the trees were so close together. He called out, but they could not hear him. The closer he moved, the faster they went away. He realized he did not want to lose sight of them.

DREAM BACKGROUND AND MEANING

Edwardo had quarreled with his family and stormed out of the home, vowing to never return. But now the argument seemed trivial and he was missing his folks, but too proud to call them. Though the roots of redwoods are shallow, they gain strength from bonding together, and the redwood is a sign of unity.

INTERPRETATIONS AND FORTUNE-TELLING MEANINGS

⋆ Dreaming of redwood trees is an excellent omen for rising high in any career, profession, or finances, as they are the tallest trees in the world.

⋆ Because redwoods live more than a thousand years, a redwood forest is a sign that your family will be healthy and any unwell members will find healing.

⋆ Because redwoods have interlinking supportive roots, to dream of seeing their strong roots extending through the earth says you will find support from others.

⋆ If you see felled or dying redwoods, you may feel desperately overwhelmed by the odds against you, but you will rise again, since a new redwood grows from the old roots.

⋆ To dream of a redwood opal created from fossilized redwood says that you will find an old friend or lover from the past reemerging in a way that can bring happiness.

⋆ Planting or replanting a redwood forest brings reconnection with family members you may have lost touch with.

OUTCOME OF EDWARDO'S DREAM

After the dream, Edwardo realized that the family meant more to him than his pride. They reconnected, and he has moved back home. Redwoods are above all a symbol of reconciliation and, as they are resistant to fire, can overcome many difficulties.

Refuge, Refugee

Ivan, twenty, dreamed he was trekking across mountains to return to the land of his birth when a sudden snowstorm obscured everything. Ahead was a hut. When he opened the door, he saw that it was equipped with logs, firelighters, water, and basic canned foods. He never wanted to leave, as he did not know whether to go forward or return to the place he now called home.

DREAM BACKGROUND AND MEANING

Ivan had been living in the United Kingdom with his family for many years after they had been granted asylum from their former homeland. Now Ivan wanted to return home, as he had never felt like he belonged in the United Kingdom. A refuge or refugee in a dream shows that the dreamer may not feel that they fit in their current lifestyle.

INTERPRETATIONS AND FORTUNE-TELLING MEANINGS

* If you dream you are a refugee escaping to a new world, you may presently be living on other people's terms.
* If you find a refuge away from everything and everybody in your dream, you may need to leave behind what is familiar and start again.
* If in your dream you are a refugee taken in by your current family, you may need to find new ways of living in your career, spiritual life, or social life.
* If you dream you are a refugee denied entry to a country of safety, you may be looking in the wrong place for kindred spirits.
* If you do not wish to leave a temporary refuge to go either forward or backward, delay making a decision, as a third path may appear.
* If you are constantly seeking a better home in your dream, the restlessness may be within you and not caused by external circumstances.

OUTCOME OF IVAN'S DREAM

Ivan returned to his birth country and took up a residential job in a state orphanage where he knew conditions needed improving. Refuge and refugee dreams may be closely linked if the dreamer in whatever situation or potential life change needs to find where their true inner home is, to bring harmony.

Reinventing Life

In her dream, Marie, thirty-three, was sitting in the sunshine in a town square in Spain, drinking coffee while her five-year-old twins played in the fountain with the local children. She threw her antidepressants in the garbage.

DREAM BACKGROUND AND MEANING

Marie was struggling as a single parent teaching English in a gray city in the United Kingdom. Her husband had abandoned her and the children for a woman young enough to be his daughter. He handed over custody, paid nothing, and never saw the children, and Marie had to take antidepressants to get through the day. A friend who ran a language school in Spain invited Marie to come and work there. But how could she? A dream can sometimes show that a seemingly impossible plan could work.

INTERPRETATIONS AND FORTUNE-TELLING MEANINGS

* If a dream regularly reveals the same reinvention of your life at a time when change is needed, study how it could become possible.
* If you dream you are surrounded by dense fog but see a tiny patch of light ahead, your circumstances may be obscuring possibilities.
* If you see yourself in a particular location with which you have even vague connections, the dream may be guiding you to a new future there.
* If you are older and living a completely different lifestyle, investigate the dream location, and you may find a longer-term future waiting.
* If you are alone and dream of yourself with another partner and maybe children, or more children than you have, this may be a predictive dream.
* If the dream shows a reinvented life and you are not ready, begin with small lifestyle improvements.

OUTCOME OF MARIE'S DREAM

Marie took three months off work, rented out her UK house, and went with the children to Spain to work in the language school. She loved it, and her children thrived and were learning the language. She is planning to resettle there. Happiness in a reinvented life is not guaranteed, but it may offer a temporary or permanent way out of a seemingly endless cycle of gloom.

Relocation

Teresa, forty-eight, dreamed she was trying to hold a globe of the world that spun round and round, stopping over Thailand. Then it began spinning again, always directing her to Thailand. She found herself young again, walking along the street of temples in the ancient city of Chiang Mai, and felt she had come home.

DREAM BACKGROUND AND MEANING

Teresa worked for a United Kingdom broadcasting service that was relocating to the north of England. She had been offered relocation or layoff pay to stay in London, where she had built her life since her divorce. She did not want to go north but feared that at her age she might not get another announcing job in broadcasting.

INTERPRETATIONS AND FORTUNE-TELLING MEANINGS

★ If you are planning relocation to a specific area and the dream shows it beautiful with wide, prosperous streets, you will be happy there. But if in the dream it has dirty, narrow streets, you will not settle in.

★ If you are not planning to relocate but have this dream, you may be ready for changes in other parts of your life or relationships.

★ If you see an unexpected dream location, it may offer advantages. Explore the area on vacation, and the dream may be explained.

★ If you do not recognize the place of the dream, research its location, as it may hold a new love or career beginning.

★ If you dream of a compulsory relocation and you are unhappy, explore alternatives, as the relocation area, not the move, may be the problem.

OUTCOME OF TERESA'S DREAM

Teresa had the dream night after night. She had lived in Chiang Mai with her ex-husband, and they had held good positions in the university. After the breakup she had not returned for twenty years. As a result of the dream, she revisited the Chiang Mai University and was offered a job. She met her ex-husband again. Relocation can involve returning to a place where we were once happy, if our present location no longer offers the opportunities we need.

Renovations

Matt, forty, dreamed he was renovating an abandoned barn in his favorite area of France. But the harder he worked on it, the more it crumbled, and more and more problems emerged. As Matt tried to shore up a dangerously leaning wall, the whole property collapsed. Matt woke disappointed but knowing he had done his best.

DREAM BACKGROUND AND MEANING

Matt was planning to give his marriage yet another chance. However, his partner was very possessive, constantly checking his mail and phone, telephoning him several times a day at work, and accusing him of affairs if he came home late. This had already started again during their first week back together. Renovation dreams talk about attempts to repair damaged situations that may or may not be fixable.

INTERPRETATIONS AND FORTUNE-TELLING MEANINGS

★ Renovating or rebuilding a structure with a love partner or business partner that is going well in the dream is a good omen for a continuing and growing relationship between you.

★ If, despite every effort, you are not progressing or keep hitting the same dream problems, the venture or relationship is probably not worth the input.

★ If you dream that the structure collapses, however much you put into it, it will fail.

★ If you dream you are working alone and making little progress, you are putting in all the effort. This mirrors the relationship or situation you are trying to save.

★ If you are renovating or repairing a real structure, a dream showing progress or the completed structure is a good omen.

★ If you dream someone is sabotaging your renovations, a third party has an interest in your failing.

OUTCOME OF MATT'S DREAM

Matt realized the reconciliation was not going to work, no matter how hard he tried. He moved to Central France alone and is building a house on land he bought. Sometimes demolishing an unstable structure, representing a crumbling relationship or situations, and building something new may be the solution.

Rescue Pilot

In her dream, Melanie, twenty-six, was taking her AirTanker over a bush fire to drop fire retardant in front of a raging fire to slow it down. As she approached the fire, she dropped the retardant and hit the target. But she saw someone looking remarkably like herself trapped on a hilltop, swooped in, and rescued her. When they reached the airport, the alter ego began servicing the other planes.

DREAM BACKGROUND AND MEANING

Melanie wanted all her life to be a rescue pilot. She had almost qualified as a basic pilot but needed specialized training to obtain her rescue pilot's license. But her regular work hours had been cut, and she could no longer afford the course. Rescue-pilot dreams indicate the power to attain success with satisfaction if we persevere.

INTERPRETATIONS AND FORTUNE-TELLING MEANINGS

★ If you dream of being a rescue pilot and you are connected with aviation, you will rise above any obstacles if you are adaptable as to how you reach the goal.

★ If you are a rescue pilot in your dream but not in life, aim for the top in a career or business that brings fulfillment as well as material rewards.

★ Relieving trouble from the air suggests you will be of more use in a difficult situation by remaining detached and focusing on the bigger picture.

★ If you dream your rescue plane crashes or spins out of control, you may have offered to do more than is advisable and may be getting too involved in others' conflicts.

★ If you dream you are asked to pilot a rescue mission and have never flown before, have faith that you can resolve a major problem at work or in the community.

OUTCOME OF MELANIE'S DREAM

After the dream, Melanie volunteered to help around the rescue base in her now-increased spare time, in return for free training as a rescue pilot. She is now qualified and working full-time for the service. Rescue-pilot dreams suggest ingenious ways we can fulfill seemingly impossible goals by allowing our unconscious self to take control.

Reservoir

Gaynor, twenty-five, dreamed the local reservoir was polluted with chemicals and all the fish had died. The townspeople who relied on the water source became very ill. She phoned the local media, and they featured it on the news, but afterward no one would speak to her.

DREAM BACKGROUND AND MEANING

Gaynor worked for a local water company and knew that the local chemical works were bribing the water board to overlook chemical leaks into the local river. Her dream warned her that, if the matter was unchecked, catastrophe would follow. The company said she was a troublemaker. Polluted reservoir-water dreams represent corruption that may go deep in any area of life.

INTERPRETATIONS AND FORTUNE-TELLING MEANINGS

★ A full reservoir is an assurance of sufficient resources for the future and a period of emotional contentment.

★ A reservoir brimming with fish is a powerful sign of fertility and of health in the dreamer.

★ If you dream that a reservoir dam bursts, words may be spoken and actions taken that may be later regretted but cannot be undone.

★ If a reservoir is low or empty, you have no more to give emotionally to an overdemanding person and should take a step back.

★ If you dream you are mending a reservoir dam, you may be called upon to negotiate between people of very differing views or generations.

OUTCOME OF GAYNOR'S DREAM

Gaynor tested the reservoir water and found it to be seriously polluted. She leaked the information to an investigative television network, which found her accusations to be true. But it was all hushed up by higher government sources, and Gaynor was unfairly dismissed. Dreams about reservoirs can indicate trouble stored for the future if the dream water is not clear.

Resignation

Phillipa, twenty-six, dreamed she stood up in the office at the call center where she worked and said, "I quit." Then everyone stood up and declared they were quitting. The senior manager offered them a small bonus to stay, and they all sat down and continued work, except for Phillipa, who was escorted from the premises.

DREAM BACKGROUND AND MEANING

Phillipa was tired of dire working conditions and was trying to persuade her colleagues to join her in a mass resignation at the call center's busiest time, to get what they wanted. Most agreed with her, but she sensed reluctance to act. Sometimes resignations on matters of principle lack support from those for whom personal preservation comes first.

INTERPRETATIONS AND FORTUNE-TELLING MEANINGS

★ If in your dream you make a dramatic resignation exit, you have made up your mind but should choose your time.

★ If in your dream you are asked to resign from a committee or official organization, you are picking up double-dealing from people who may superficially seem supportive.

★ If in your dream you are composing a detailed written resignation, this reveals problems that you may not have realized were troubling you.

★ If you often dream about resigning from your job, start looking for something new before doing anything radical.

★ If you dream you are resigned to an injustice or a bad work practice, seek the best possible outcome for you, which may not be immediate resignation.

★ If you unexpectedly resign from a job that seemingly was going well, beware of gossip or rumor unsettling you into acting impulsively.

OUTCOME OF PHILLIPA'S DREAM

On the morning of the planned mass resignation, Phillipa realized that everyone was avoiding her, and she knew if she resigned she would do it alone. She got another job before making her protest and, as the dream predicted, no one backed her. Resignation dreams may offer strategies and tactics that prevent impulsive, self-damaging actions.

Responsibilities

Tomas, seventy-two, dreamed he was standing by an open window, holding his baby daughter. In the dream he was a young father again. The baby became heavier and heavier and larger and larger. Eventually he could no longer hold the baby, who fell out of the window onto the sidewalk below. He knew she was dead and shut the window.

DREAM BACKGROUND AND MEANING

Tomas was his wife's caregiver, and his daughter lived on the other side of the world. His wife had dementia and mobility issues, and Tomas was finding it increasingly hard to lift her. Dreaming about failing responsibilities toward someone vulnerable is an anxiety dream but, because it is bound up in feeling a failure, the symbolism can become confused.

INTERPRETATIONS AND FORTUNE-TELLING MEANINGS

★ If in a dream a baby becomes suddenly larger and heavier, the baby represents anxieties about caring for a vulnerable someone.

★ If you drop a baby or a symbolic baby in a dream, your mind is saying it can no longer cope with the burden of responsibility.

★ If you see yourself abandoning a baby, child, or elderly person in a dream, it does not mean you will, but indicates an overload of caring or carrying others' burdens.

★ If the dreamer deliberately drops, throws, or pushes the baby or symbolic baby from a height or a moving car, this is an ultimate guilt dream in which a person gives form to negative thoughts.

★ If the dreamer walks or drives away, leaving the vulnerable baby or other person alone, they may be seeking to offload responsibilities not necessarily linked with caring, perhaps too heavy a load at work or financially.

OUTCOME OF TOMAS'S DREAM

The nurse who visited weekly discovered Tomas had fallen and broken his arm while lifting his wife. Help was sent in to take Tomas's wife to a residential care facility and Tomas to the hospital. Dreams of responsibility are a mixture of anxiety and guilt, inner cries for help. Sadly, by the time the dream situation materializes, external intervention may be too late.

Restroom, Toilet

Annette, fifty-four, dreamed she was desperate to find a restroom. The public restrooms were closed. She entered a big department store and found their only toilet was in the middle of the dress department and completely open. In desperation, she used it. There was no way to flush, and the contents overflowed onto the carpet and on her outfit. She fled in total humiliation.

DREAM BACKGROUND AND MEANING

Annette had been harshly toilet-trained as a child and remembered being humiliated in a department store because she could not get to the restroom in time. Now she had met a man who left the bathroom door open while he was using the toilet and also walked in on her. She loved him but was loath to have sex with him. Unpleasant restroom experiences signify fear of a loss of control over the behavior of others and may be linked with subconscious fears of sex being dirty and sinful.

INTERPRETATIONS AND FORTUNE-TELLING MEANINGS

* Defecation in a clean restroom represents ridding yourself of all in your life weighing you down, including toxic people.
* Overflowing or clogged toilets suggest you are being flooded with others' negativity and problems and are reaching overload.
* Defecation and feces dreams are traditionally symbols of coming wealth or the release of unexpected funds.
* If you dream you are forced to use a toilet with no privacy, you may find it hard to let go of sexual inhibitions, especially if you have been celibate for a while.
* An overflowing or nonflushing toilet signifies fears of others discovering your mistakes.
* If in your dream you cannot find a restroom when you urgently need one, you are trapped by feelings you cannot safely express.

OUTCOME OF ANNETTE'S DREAM

Since Annette had been living alone for ten years, she found any physical intimacy hard. Her partner promised to better respect her private moments. Dreams of restrooms are very common anxiety dreams of being humiliated in public by people seeing who you really are.

Retirement

Melvyn, fifty-five, dreamed he went in to work at his insurance office and the other employees were dressed in school uniforms. They told him he was too old to work there anymore and had been retired without pension. There was a single present on his desk with a yachting cap inside and the words "Happy Sailing."

DREAM BACKGROUND AND MEANING

Melvyn was not due for retirement but was aware that most of his colleagues were young college graduates with impressive qualifications and he was being more and more sidelined. Should he go before he was pushed? Retirement dreams are not predictive, but they can reveal underlying dissatisfaction with career if colleagues or work practices are changing.

INTERPRETATIONS AND FORTUNE-TELLING MEANINGS

* If you dream of retiring and are not of retirement age, you are ready for a career change where you may start your own business.
* If you dream you are being forced to retire, you may have worries about getting old or being replaced, whether in someone's affections or by being overtaken by a younger person at work.
* If you dream of continuing to work in retirement, there is unfinished business to resolve, or work may have become an emotional fulfillment in your life.
* If you see yourself retiring early in your dream and moving away, reassess what it is you have not completed in your working life.
* If you are asking for retirement, you may need to end an aspect of your life not necessarily connected with work in order to move to the next phase.

OUTCOME OF MELVYN'S DREAM

Melvyn contacted his brother, who had a boatyard selling craft to tourists and especially to retirees. He offered to set up a marine insurance business specializing in those who wanted to go on long voyages in retirement, giving practical advice as part of the service, as Melvyn was an experienced sailor. Retirement at any age can open a doorway to half-forgotten or abandoned ambitions that offer a new lease on life.

Reunion

Alfred, forty-five, dreamed he was seventeen at a high school reunion where everyone else was adult. He met George, who Alfred remembered as the teen who had stolen his girlfriend because George's parents had provided a stretch limo to take them to the graduation ball. Though Alfred was smaller than George in the dream, he started punching and kicking George and was thrown out.

DREAM BACKGROUND AND MEANING

Alfred always regretted losing the love of his life, and George had married her. Reunions, whether for school, college, family, or the workplace, tend to bring up bad old memories as well as good ones, especially since obnoxious people are generally still obnoxious.

INTERPRETATIONS AND FORTUNE-TELLING MEANINGS

⋆ If you attend a reunion or link up with old friends online, this can revive old friendships and draw a line under unfinished business.

⋆ If at the dream reunion you are a child, this suggests you still have resentments toward people who made you feel inferior years ago.

⋆ If you decline an invitation in the dream to a reunion, it may be that returning to a school or organization where you were not particularly happy would serve no positive purpose in reality.

⋆ If you are singled out as a success or given an award at a dream reunion, this may vindicate in your mind that the path you took through life was the right one.

⋆ If you are organizing a reunion for family, former colleagues, or peers, is there someone you have not seen for a while who you would like to reconnect with?

OUTCOME OF ALFRED'S DREAM

After the dream, Alfred found his former rival on Facebook and discovered that George had done nothing useful with his life and was divorced, whereas Alfred had a successful business, a wife, and a family he was devoted to. Soon after, Alfred was invited to a high school reunion, which he declined. Reunion dreams can bring to the surface resentments and insecurities that have no basis in reality and may be best left in the past.

Revenge Porn

Belinda, nineteen, dreamed she was at home with her parents when her young brother walked in with his iPad and showed her parents nude photos of his sister that were all over social media. They were furious and told Belinda to leave the house and to never return.

DREAM BACKGROUND AND MEANING

Belinda had an intimate relationship with Rocky, a man ten years her senior. They shared nude photos with each other online, promising that they would not show the photos to anyone else. Belinda had recently told her online lover that she no longer wished to continue the relationship. He threatened that if she left him, he would publish her photos on social media.

INTERPRETATIONS AND FORTUNE-TELLING MEANINGS

⋆ If this dream occurs while you are still in the early stages of a relationship, take it as a warning that the person you are dating is not trustworthy.

⋆ If you want to end a relationship and your partner has compromising material, ask for the deletion of erotic images before having a potential confrontation over the relationship.

⋆ If your partner has pictures and you are regretting them, talk over your fears with your partner, and you may be reassured.

⋆ If you dream of racy pictures even if there are not any, you may worry that family and friends will not approve of your new partner. Ask why.

⋆ If you have sexy glamour photos in your dream that you consider disastrous for public display, examine the insecurity or love of danger that makes you take risks of being found out.

OUTCOME OF BELINDA'S DREAM

Belinda's dream was a forewarning. She retaliated by threatening to go to the police and make a blackmailing complaint. Since Rocky had a very respectable job, he backed down. Such dreams may be expressing fears over a current or anticipated sexually demanding relationship. Consider what motivates you to press this potential self-destruct button.

Revisiting Unfamiliar Places

Bill, thirty-four, dreamed frequently of the same castle, built in the side of a hill with a tunnel leading down to the river. Whenever he visited this place, it seemed so familiar. In the most vivid dream, he was a young boy in danger because the owner's son wanted him killed because Bill was the rightful heir. One of the servants hid Bill in the kitchen until it was safe to lead him down the tunnel to the river to escape.

DREAM BACKGROUND AND MEANING

Bill had been working at the same hospitality venue for ten years. Though the job was safe, it stifled him. Bill wanted to go traveling but feared that if he did not go soon, he would never go. It is common to regularly revisit an unknown place in dreams, and it is sometimes possible to trace its location.

INTERPRETATIONS AND FORTUNE-TELLING MEANINGS

★ If you keep returning to an unfamiliar location in dreams, perhaps a past-life memory, there is unfinished business you need to resolve so you can move on in the present.

★ If you escape or overcome obstacles in your dream location, it is a good omen that you will escape restrictions in your present life.

★ If you encounter someone harmful or helpful in this place, be aware of their identities in your current life, especially if you had not suspected malice.

★ If one dream visit is especially vivid, this may predict a coming challenge and the built-in solution.

★ If there is a special feature you love in this world you revisit, it may be something missing from your present life that you need to find.

★ If you meet the same people who span several time frames, you will, if you do not already know them, discover your twin soul, soul family, and a soul enemy you need to finally confront and overcome in your present life.

OUTCOME OF BILL'S DREAM

Bill realized it was time to escape, and he made plans to travel overseas. He believes he will discover his dream place and what waits there to complete his life search. Till then he continues to dream. To keep revisiting the same location in dreams indicates you have not yet reached your true home and must seek it, not wait for it to appear.

Revolution

Sebastian, twenty, dreamed he was fighting for the Republicans in the Spanish Civil War of 1936 against fascist principles. He had studied the war in college and was horrified by the slaughter on both sides. He was hiding in the mountains, but he knew he could not abandon the cause. There was an explosion. His family shipped him home, as he was badly wounded. His family was angry at what they saw as his needless sacrifice.

DREAM BACKGROUND AND MEANING

Sebastian was no longer allowed to attend college after he led a movement protesting about impoverished students rarely being admitted to that institution. His wealthy parents were furious that he had wrecked his future prospects. Winning a revolution says the dreamer may achieve freedom and independence, but at a price.

INTERPRETATIONS AND FORTUNE-TELLING MEANINGS

★ If you are leading a historic revolution like the Russian or French revolutions, this may be a past-life memory and you may want to right a major injustice.

★ Dreaming of watching a revolution at any age says you need change in life, whether of your career, home life, or relationship, but should consider the consequences before acting or speaking.

★ If you dream you are listening to a revolutionary speech or singing revolutionary songs, you may enjoy the idea of rebellion, but may be constrained by convention.

★ If you are dreaming of joining a cause of which your family disapproves, you may feel they are restricting you from being yourself.

★ If in your dream you fail in a protest or revolution, you may be fighting a lost cause but going ahead anyway.

OUTCOME OF SEBASTIAN'S DREAM

Sebastian got a job training underprivileged young people so they could have further education. His parents always expressed their disappointment, and eventually he left his privileged but restricted home. Revolutionary dreams are often very dramatic and stem from the dreamer's own desire to not merely escape from a narrow home or work life, but for wider freedom and justice—and they mark the dreamer for noble purposes.

Rice

Laboni, twenty-six, dreamed she was in her mother-in-law's kitchen in the home they shared in India, and the half-empty rice jars were contaminated with weevils. Then she was boarding a plane to London. Her mother-in-law was at the departure gate, holding Laboni's husband, Aanan, tightly and telling Laboni to get on the plane, out of their lives. A heavily veiled woman at the departure gate was also clinging to Aanan, and Laboni knew this was her intended replacement.

DREAM BACKGROUND AND MEANING

Laboni's husband had been offered a job in the United Kingdom in her family's rice-exporting business. But his mother was set against the idea and had been inviting Aanan's former girlfriend to the house, saying that Laboni was unfaithful and the marriage could be made void.

INTERPRETATIONS AND FORTUNE-TELLING MEANINGS

* ★ Cooking and eating rice at family meals is a symbol of conception, births, and marriages.
* ★ Rice dreams are rooted in family life and, with well-cooked, abundant rice, ample stores of happiness are assured.
* ★ Storage jars filled with rice herald coming and increasing prosperity.
* ★ Growing green rice fields represent succeeding in an area of your life that is of great emotional significance as well as practical advantage.
* ★ Rice containing weevils represents others spoiling our efforts or reputation.
* ★ Making rice offerings on an altar in a dream defines what is most desired. Empty jars and spoiled rice are warnings that the goodness has been taken out of a situation or relationship and may need fighting to restore happiness.

OUTCOME OF LABONI'S DREAM

After the dream, Laboni realized that she must not agree to her husband's suggestion that she should go to the United Kingdom first and he follow. Her mother-in-law would do her best to break up the marriage. Laboni insisted that he come with her and, though her mother-in-law created a scene at the airport, they settled in England.

Ring

Gillian, fifty-eight, mother of four adult children, wanted to buy herself a ring. She immediately saw in an antique store a three-stone diamond baguette ring, almost identical to her late mother's engagement ring. Her mother's ring had been sold after her death, though it had been promised to Gillian. Gillian tried it on, and it was a perfect fit. She knew she might never see another like it, but she hesitated to spend so much money on herself. She woke, regretting that she had not bought it.

DREAM BACKGROUND AND MEANING

Gillian heavily subsidizes her children and grandchildren, rarely spending money on herself. Recently she has been feeling secretly resentful of her frequently unappreciated generosity.

INTERPRETATIONS AND FORTUNE-TELLING MEANINGS

* ★ An engagement or wedding ring indicates the rightness of a relationship or, if you are not in a committed relationship, is a premonition of your forthcoming engagement and marriage.
* ★ Being given an eternity ring symbolizes the renewal of trust and fidelity after doubts or betrayal.
* ★ Dreaming of buying yourself a ring indicates you are learning to value yourself and meet your own needs, and above all considering yourself complete without a partner.
* ★ Wearing a ring you bought yourself on your heart finger, the fourth finger on your left hand, represents a commitment to an idea, a project, or a career path involving single-mindedness.
* ★ Refusing or trying to fix a broken ring reveals underlying doubts or fears about an existing relationship.
* ★ Beware of a dream person trying on your engagement or wedding ring, as they may be jealous of your relationship in real life.
* ★ A ring that does not fit suggests you are making all the concessions.

OUTCOME OF GILLIAN'S DREAM

Gillian decided to look for a ring like the dream diamond, to plan solo holidays, and to be less available to the family's financial and emotional demands.

Ripping

Goldie, seventeen, dreamed she was wearing her new prom dress and was getting into the limo. Somehow her best friend's heel got stuck in Goldie's hem and the whole dress was ripped apart at the back. Everyone waiting in the limo laughed, and Goldie went back inside the house in tears.

DREAM BACKGROUND AND MEANING

Goldie had bought a beautiful pink floor-length frilled dress for the prom. But her best friend said she looked ridiculous in it and that everyone would laugh at her. The store would not take the dress back, and she had to wear a bridesmaid's dress she already had. If you dream that someone is ripping something of yours, watch out for anger or resentment in that person, who may want to sabotage your efforts.

INTERPRETATIONS AND FORTUNE-TELLING MEANINGS

* While a rip or tear is often considered an unfortunate omen, sometimes ripping up an out-of-date rule book is necessary for spontaneity and new beginnings to shine through.
* To dream you accidentally rip a new or much-loved garment suggests an unfortunate loss due to carelessness.
* To rip up a contract or official document in a dream suggests defiance of the status quo.
* To repair a rip or tear says that a situation caused by impulsive action can be fixed with care.
* To see a rip getting bigger despite efforts to mend it suggests that a situation is not retrievable and should be left alone.
* If you dream you find something precious ripped, someone may be trying to rip you off or sell you short.

OUTCOME OF GOLDIE'S DREAM

Goldie's boyfriend said she looked beautiful. To Goldie's surprise, her friend was wearing the identical dress to her pink one. The dream was a premonition, because her friend got her heel stuck in the hem of her own dress and had to wear it all night with a huge rip in the bottom. Although a rip can be an annoying accident, sometimes the dream can reveal jealousy that generally rebounds on the person causing the dilemma.

Risks

Ruth, nineteen, dreamed she was in the passenger seat of her boyfriend Ed's old car, which was his pride and joy. They went faster and faster until they reached a ramp. He drove up it. She screamed at him to stop, but he ignored her. They flew through the air and somersaulted, landing upside down. She heard sirens and thought her mother had been right.

DREAM BACKGROUND AND MEANING

Since he had passed his driving test and had been bought an old car by his parents, Ed had been modifying it to go faster. He was always showing off with new stunts. Ruth's mother was seriously worried. Ruth was sometimes scared but did not want to lose Ed. Dreams can predict a likely outcome, especially where road safety is ignored.

INTERPRETATIONS AND FORTUNE-TELLING MEANINGS

* If you are a natural risk-taker and the dream highlights potential disasters, it's time to modify the risks.
* If in the dream you are taking risks to please someone else, consider whether the person has your interests and safety at heart.
* If your life is routine and you dream of dangerous activities, explore how your lifestyle can safely become more challenging.
* If you are deliberately risking a relationship in a dream because you are angry or bored with a lover, giving way to temptation may not be the best way to resolve suppressed resentment.
* If innocent people are involved in your risk-taking in a dream, are you seeking revenge against them or have you not thought through the consequences to others?

OUTCOME OF RUTH'S DREAM

Ruth continued to ignore the dreams until an accident did happen and the car ended upside down in a ditch. Ed was charged with dangerous driving. Ruth no longer sees him. Dreams can be warnings the dreamer can override if the risk is considered worthwhile. In this case Ruth wanted to keep her boyfriend, but at the cost of risking her life.

Riverbank

Bernie, fifty-three, dreamed he was sitting on a riverbank, watching otters, water voles, and other small water creatures, when a deluge of brown sludge washed into the river and over the banks, covering their holes. Bernie woke, knowing the wildlife on the riverbank was lost.

DREAM BACKGROUND AND MEANING

Because of the pollution it would cause to the riverbank habitat, Bernie was opposing a new chemical plant being built on land upriver. His son-in-law had a major stake in the new development, and hostility between the households was making it hard for Bernie and his wife to see their grandchildren. Dreams of much-loved riverbanks can occur at a time when an actual riverbank is threatened or when there is intense emotional pressure being applied in any area of life.

INTERPRETATIONS AND FORTUNE-TELLING MEANINGS

* Steep riverbanks suggest you are holding back your feelings, especially in love or sexuality.
* Crumbling riverbanks say others are breaking down your resistance with emotional blackmail.
* Railed-off or bricked-up riverbanks in dreams deny you access to affection from a partner or parent who does not express love or approval.
* If you dream the river has dried up and the banks are all that are left, your enthusiasm has been drained away, and you may no longer be content with the outer form of a relationship or situation.
* If a sudden flood breaches the banks, beware of others getting their own way through tantrums or threats.
* If riverbanks are set in fertile land with teeming wildlife, it augurs well for love and fertility.
* If you dream the land is barren or frozen, you may be pouring love and emotional effort into a relationship with barriers that are too great to overcome.

OUTCOME OF BERNIE'S DREAM

For his wife's sake, Bernie withdrew his opposition because of her fear of not seeing the grandchildren. The scheme went through with guarantees from his son-in-law's company that the environment would not be harmed, but Bernie anticipated a disaster. Riverbanks can represent the dividing line between expediency and practicality, and emotions.

Robbery

Eliza, twenty, dreamed she and her friends broke into an electronics store and were helping themselves to the most expensive goods. When they were dividing the loot, Eliza asked if she could have a top-of-the-line computer. The leader, Susie, sneered and said Eliza was too dumb to use it. Eliza grabbed the computer and ran, but the police were waiting. The others disappeared with the stolen goods, and she was blamed.

DREAM BACKGROUND AND MEANING

Eliza had worked as a data entry operator since leaving school at seventeen. The work was boring and low-paying. She had been a D-grade student because she had constantly been moved from school to school. Eliza wanted to learn computer programming but could not afford a computer. Her friends had told her they could get hold of a stolen computer, which she could buy cheaply, but they would laugh behind her back and say she is so stupid she will probably get caught. Robbery, whether actual or psychological, destroying a reputation or confidence, promises instant results but also has risks.

INTERPRETATIONS AND FORTUNE-TELLING MEANINGS

* If you dream of taking part in a robbery, are you seeking an easy way to advance your career or finances or to cheat officialdom?
* If you know the people in your dream encouraging you to take part in a robbery, they may be robbing you of your self-esteem.
* If a dream robbery succeeds, you may escape detection, but at what personal cost?
* If you dream you witness a robbery, you may secretly wish you had the boldness to steal someone's partner, but fear rejection.
* If you take part in a robbery in your dream but try to stop it, you may pull back from stealing data, petty pilfering, or taking credit for ideas that are not yours.

OUTCOME OF ELIZA'S DREAM

Eliza refused the offer of the stolen computer and worked evenings till she saved enough to buy one. She is now training at college in the evenings in computer science and has amazed herself at how fast she is learning. Her friends told her she would fail, and so she dumped them. Robbery dreams can refer to anything in the dreamer's life that is taken from them or that they take, rarely without consequences.

Robots

Lenny, sixty, dreamed that the hospital pharmacy he ran had been taken over by robots overnight. When he tried to reach his workstation, two robots demanded his entry code in metallic voices. He could not remember it, and glass walls came down, enclosing him. More robots approached and changed him into a robot.

DREAM BACKGROUND AND MEANING

Lenny had become increasingly frustrated that more and more of the pharmacy dispensing work was performed by robots. While it was fast and efficient, it reduced his role to delivery boy. His fellow pharmacist had been laid off, and Lenny knew he would any day be offered early retirement. If we dream of being changed into a robot, we may be unconsciously worried that our expertise is not appreciated.

INTERPRETATIONS AND FORTUNE-TELLING MEANINGS

★ If you dream of being married to a robot and that your children and pets are robots, you may be struggling to express your true emotions and feel taken for granted.

★ If you dream of your workplace dominated by robot bosses controlling you with disembodied voices, your work may become increasingly depersonalized.

★ If you dream of your home and garden filled with robot gadgets that have a mind of their own, you may fear that family members no longer take your opinions seriously.

★ If you dream you are being chased or attacked by robots or barred from entering your home or workplace, you may be feeling underappreciated.

★ If you dream the world is taken over by robots, who is reducing your life to routine and making you feel old or useless?

★ Conversely, if you dream you are hiding against an attack and using robots as a shield, you may be struggling with those seriously resistant to change.

OUTCOME OF LENNY'S DREAM

The robotic system of dispensing medications broke down, but hospital management had dismantled the old system. Only thanks to Lenny's initiative was disaster averted. Thereafter, Lenny's job was secure. Robots are valuable in many fields of life, but ultimately they must be controlled by humans, as they are brilliant as servants but not as masters.

Roller Coaster

Molly, thirty-nine, dreamed she was in a fairground, wanting to ride the roller coaster with her husband, Joel. But he was too scared. She was disappointed and said she would go alone. Then she saw Rick from work sitting in a carriage, calling her to join him. As she was about to get in, she realized there were no safety bars in his carriage. She rode in her own car, which had a seat belt, and woke excited as she completed the circuits.

DREAM BACKGROUND AND MEANING

Joel never did anything adventurous and, though Molly loved him, she was increasingly frustrated with their boring life. Molly had been flattered by the office Don Juan, Rick, flirting with her. He had invited her to go white-water rafting. She hesitated because of his bad reputation with women. A roller coaster injects much-needed excitement and spontaneity into a predictable life.

INTERPRETATIONS AND FORTUNE-TELLING MEANINGS

★ Dreaming of riding a roller coaster indicates the dreamer seeks drastic changes involving unpredictability in love or a financial gamble.

★ If a roller coaster ride ends safely and uneventfully, all will turn out well.

★ Being on a high roller coaster with a new partner tells there will be passion, quarrels, and reconciliations, but not security.

★ No safety bars or deliberately leaving off a seat belt warns that you are taking undue risks, especially in love.

★ A stuck or broken roller coaster that suddenly lurches forward or leaves the tracks says you are taking chances by relying on others to fulfill your excitement quotient.

★ Walking away from a roller coaster before the ride or going solo involves choosing security and independence over unwise temptation.

OUTCOME OF MOLLY'S DREAM

Molly refused Rick's offer and booked herself into an extreme sports weekend. To her surprise, Joel joined her. Although he was scared, he tried everything. Transferring the thrill of the roller coaster to a safer form of excitement maintains the impetus of the dream without the risks.

Roof

Pandora, twenty-five, dreamed she was jumping from roof to roof on tall houses with chimney pots, looking down on the world and the lights in the late evening, feeling total freedom and possibility in her life. At last, she came to what was her house in the dream and entered through a skylight, knowing she could explore the rooftops any time she wanted.

DREAM BACKGROUND AND MEANING

Pandora was living in a tiny top-floor studio apartment overlooking the rooftops of Paris, studying Impressionist art at Sorbonne University, painting, and working as a waitress to pay the rent. She loved France and aimed to move there permanently from the United Kingdom and work in a gallery on the Left Bank. Rooftop dreams represent ambitions not easy to fulfill but which should be pursued without allowing fears of limitations to intrude.

INTERPRETATIONS AND FORTUNE-TELLING MEANINGS

* A roof in good repair represents protection against others' discouragement or intrusion.
* Dreaming of sitting or climbing on a roof warns that it may be risky to attempt to achieve an ambition, but if you succeed it will open a whole new world to you.
* If you dream you fall from a roof, you may be afraid to pursue an ambition because of fear of failure.
* If you dream your roof is falling in, it's time to examine insecurities about your home life and, if necessary, repair relationships.
* A dream of a leaking roof suggests that others are gradually draining your resources and neighbors or colleagues are taking too much interest in your private life.
* A dream of a roof terrace or garden offers an overview of life and says you are confident enough to reveal your thoughts to the world.

OUTCOME OF PANDORA'S DREAM

Pandora discovered there was access outside her apartment that led through a skylight onto the rooftops. The view inspired many paintings, one of which she has sold. A small gallery has taken others. Roofs represent protective limits that, once ascended, open the dreamer to infinite possibility.

Rooster, Cockerel

Ellie, twenty-seven, dreamed that two roosters were fighting, and feathers were flying everywhere. They were seriously wounding each other. Ellie tried to part them, but they stuck their claws into her and began viciously pecking her. She broke free, covered in blood. As she escaped, the roosters stopped fighting.

DREAM BACKGROUND AND MEANING

Ellie was constantly trying to keep the peace between her domineering father and equally combative husband, and she was being asked to judge who was right in their daily disputes. Ellie's husband worked for her father, and they clashed over every decision. Ellie became increasingly distressed, since she also worked at the company and had no peace at home or work. Her mother refused to get involved. Two roosters fighting indicates serious rivalries made worse by an audience.

INTERPRETATIONS AND FORTUNE-TELLING MEANINGS

* If you dream of a rooster strutting with hens, a guy is seeking admiration and flattery and loves himself most.
* If you dream that a rooster crows before dawn, there may be difficulties the day after the dream.
* If a rooster continually crows, you are feeding someone's ego at the expense of your own peace of mind.
* If two roosters are fighting to the death, they are competing for your attention and may both turn on you.
* Seeing a single rooster in a dream signifies that you will be successful and prosperous if you are not deterred by others with big egos.
* A dream of a chorus of many roosters' cries at dawn foretells a significant day, when you will need to make your opinions heard.

OUTCOME OF ELLIE'S DREAM

Ellie realized she was the one getting hurt and had adopted her mother's approach. She resigned from the firm and refused to become a referee in the men's personal vendettas.

Dream roosters at their best represent people close to us who are protective. However, they are insistent that they are always right and should be prevented from making others their cheerleaders.

Roses

Marianne, twenty-three, dreamed that her boss presented her with an exquisite white rose on her birthday. Her best friend, Tim, who worked in the same office, gave her a bunch of slightly wilting yellow roses from his garden. She tossed them in the trash. Marianne rushed down to the parking lot to thank her boss, only to see her boss driving off with his wife. She realized the rose he had given her was artificial.

DREAM BACKGROUND AND MEANING

Marianne was having an affair with her boss, who had told her many times he was going to leave his wife. But just as many times, he let her down at the last minute. Tim had made it clear that he would like to be more than a friend.

The rose is the flower most associated with love and romance. The color and condition of the rose offers reassurance or warning about an existing love, especially if it is surrounded by thorns, which can also indicate a jealous rival.

INTERPRETATIONS AND FORTUNE-TELLING MEANINGS

* Dreams of pink roses, especially rosebuds, tell of coming love and romance, especially after a previous betrayal has destroyed trust.
* Red roses, particularly full-blooming ones, indicate lasting love, fidelity, and passion.
* Yellow roses promise love in later years or a loyal friendship at any age that may develop into love.
* White roses are associated with weddings, but also with secret love.
* Fading roses represent love that will not last, and wilting roses show the need to devote more time to love or friendship.
* A rose garden with flourishing flowers promises happiness and good fortune in love and life. An empty rosebush indicates that love will not develop.

OUTCOME OF MARIANNE'S DREAM

Marianne realized she would always be second to her boss's wife and family, and so resigned from her job. She is dating Tim and seeing what develops. Artificial roses, however beautiful, indicate that the giver may be less sincere and devoted than they say.

Royal Wedding

Rosanna, twenty-six, dreamed she was marrying the prince of a small Mediterranean kingdom and was having the ultimate fantasy wedding. She wore his family's tiara and a magnificent wedding dress, and rose petals showered from the roof of the cathedral. Then Rosanna realized that her grandmother, who was living in a nursing home, was not present. She asked her future in-laws where her grandmother was. They said she was outside in a bus and was not allowed in. Rosanna went out and brought her grandmother inside and pushed her wheelchair up the aisle. The wedding broke up in disarray.

DREAM BACKGROUND AND MEANING

Rosanna's grandma had dementia, and Rosanna's wealthy in-laws, who were paying for everything, said she would ruin the occasion if she were present. Rosanna's grandmother, who still recognized Rosanna, was getting very excited about the wedding.

INTERPRETATIONS AND FORTUNE-TELLING MEANINGS

* If in the dream you do not recognize your fiancé, are you questioning whether the wedding event and status of your fiancé are more important than the marriage, or if perhaps you have not yet met the right one?
* If you dream you are worried about someone being banned from the wedding, examine whether the person or people imposing the ban are expressing your own doubts.
* If you dream that the royal wedding ends in chaos, maybe status matters more than personalities.
* If you originally had a small, informal wedding, you may decide to have a new blessing or renewal of vows with a more elaborate ceremony.
* If you feel the occasion is running out of control, whether anniversary, engagement, or wedding, decide what you and your future partner want.
* If you dream of a royal wedding and you are not getting married, you may need more excitement and indulgence in your life.

OUTCOME OF ROSANNA'S DREAM

Rosanna decided to have a much simpler ceremony, and then go to the nursing home for a blessing that her grandmother would enjoy. Royal wedding dreams are more about spectators and glitz and glamour, and often the wishes of the bride and groom can be forgotten.

Royalty

Judith, forty, dreamed she was invited onto the balcony with the royal family after a parade and was waving to the cheering crowds. She was pleased that everyone must be envying her for being an intimate friend or member of royalty. One of the senior members of the group asked her advice. Judith felt valued and respected and did not want the dream to end.

DREAM BACKGROUND AND MEANING

Judith had been sidelined at work by a new member of the staff. Her husband had been given a promotion at his work, and she now was expected to mix with the wives of the senior managers, who were immaculately groomed and super-confident. Royalty dreams can occur at a time when our confidence is low and we need acclaim from someone whose prestige we can borrow.

INTERPRETATIONS AND FORTUNE-TELLING MEANINGS

★ Kings and queens in dreams may stand for the dreamer's parents or socially superior figures, while princes and princesses are often the dreamer's siblings, peers, or people of the same age who are super-confident (see "King," p. 269; "Queen," p. 379; and "Princess," p. 372).

★ If in the dream you see yourself as royalty, you may not be receiving due recognition of your worth.

★ If you dream you are mixing with royalty and talking to them on intimate terms, you desire a more glamorous, prestigious lifestyle.

★ If you dream that you marry into royalty, you desire more from your current relationships.

★ If you become a confidant of a particular member of the royal family in recurring dreams, you may identify with their problems and seek to have someone listen to you and speak up on your behalf.

★ Dreams about royalty, like dreams about celebrities (see p. 89), are fantasy dreams in which we receive the acclaim we are lacking by those whose opinions matter to us.

OUTCOME OF JUDITH'S DREAM

After the dream, Judith started to raise her own profile by having a makeover, expressing ideas at work, and steering the wives to activities at which she excelled. Royalty dreams are a warning that it is time to step into the limelight and not seek the reflected glory of others.

Ruby

Layla, forty-five, dreamed her fiancé, Gerard, had given her a huge ruby ring. But when she tried it on, it was too big and slipped off. The stone was slightly cracked. Her fiancé assured her the ring could be fixed. But she knew it belonged to his deceased wife and gave it back. She woke feeling betrayed.

DREAM BACKGROUND AND MEANING

Gerard was very attentive but constantly extolled the virtues of his deceased wife. After they were married, he wanted Layla to move into the home he had shared with his former wife. He had twice called her by his deceased wife's name. She had seen the ring in various photographs of Gerard's wife. Being given a ruby belonging to someone else in a dream suggests you are being made to feel second-best to the original owner.

INTERPRETATIONS AND FORTUNE-TELLING MEANINGS

★ Rubies represent health and strength. A ruby becoming brighter, especially in the dream of a woman from middle years onward, is a sign of recovery of health and happiness.

★ A dream of a glowing ruby ring is a pledge in a relationship of lasting fidelity, especially in a second or third major love.

★ A dull or fading ruby is a sign that love needs reviving or extra care should be taken with health.

★ Losing a ruby ring in a dream suggests acknowledging fears of betrayal that may be due to personal insecurity.

★ Dreaming of being given a bag of rubies indicates future lasting prosperity greater than anticipated.

★ A dream of a ruby surrounded by smaller rubies says you have an important role in uniting the family if there is dissension.

OUTCOME OF LAYLA'S DREAM

Gerard did suggest that the ruby ring would be an ideal engagement ring, as it was valuable, and the slight crack could be fixed. Layla called off the engagement, as her dream fears seemed confirmed. A cracked dream ruby suggests imperfection in a relationship that, even if fixed, is present in the background.

Ruins

Astrid, forty-four, constantly dreamed of finding an old, ruined village in the middle of the hills, where everything was left as if time had suddenly stopped. She vowed that one day she would restore it.

DREAM BACKGROUND AND MEANING

Astrid had lost her home when her job contract ended and a global financial crisis sent house prices plummeting so she could not sell her home for enough to cover the loans. She had been traveling around Denmark excavating villages lost to plague or raids. Though the salary was low, archeology jobs were few during the Recession, and basic accommodations were included. Ruins in dreams can represent the loss of hope but may contain the capacity to salvage part of what is lost in a new way.

INTERPRETATIONS AND FORTUNE-TELLING MEANINGS

★ If you dream of a ruined castle, you no longer need to maintain your emotional defenses, as the threat has gone away.

★ If you find a ruined stone circle in a dream, it is a sign to rediscover and rebuild your spiritual life.

★ If you see your childhood home in ruins, there may be people from your earlier years with whom you can rebuild a relationship or friendship.

★ To walk among the ruins of an ancient civilization says we can learn from what is enduring and of value from the past, rather than closing the door totally on painful memories.

★ If you are sad when you see the ruins of your childhood home in a dream, ask yourself what you have let crumble away of your earlier desires that you could rebuild.

OUTCOME OF ASTRID'S DREAM

Astrid knew the dream was telling her to take the job. Eventually she became warden of a reconstructed village similar to the one in her dream. Though ruins may represent what can be no more, they contain the essence of the original builders and those who lived, worked, or worshipped there.

Running

Cory, fifty-five, had a recurring dream he was running through woods and then along a path through open fields. The sun was shining, the temperature was perfect. He was not getting at all tired and could have kept running. This was his favorite local route. But the dream ended, and he felt so disappointed when he was aware of his painful, stiff muscles and that he had not run his favorite circuit for many months.

DREAM BACKGROUND AND MEANING

Cory had always been fit and had enjoyed running. But since a recent operation on his knees, he had been barely able to walk. His surgeon said time and exercise would bring some improvement, but it was unlikely that he would return to running. Running dreams can be pure pleasure dreams in which the dreamer, especially if less mobile than previously, enjoys freedom and movement.

INTERPRETATIONS AND FORTUNE-TELLING MEANINGS

★ Running for pleasure through pleasant surroundings without effort can be a wish-fulfillment dream and enable the dreamer to wake refreshed.

★ Running with a good rhythm and pace in dreams indicates smooth progress and swift results in any venture.

★ If you dream you are running a race or marathon, you may be striving to overtake rivals or reach the top in your career ahead of others.

★ If you are running to catch a bus or train, or to catch up with someone in a dream, you may need to put in more effort and impetus to achieve the target.

★ If you dream you are running away from a situation or person, you may fear being caught against your will in obligations that will slow you down.

OUTCOME OF CORY'S DREAM

Cory vowed to improve his mobility and, through a gentle daily exercise regime, he can now do a slow jog through his favorite haunts, but he still enjoys the dreams. If running dreams are frequent, they may act as a spur for improving mobility in the daily world.

Rust

Gerard, twenty, dreamed he was in his grandfather's shed. Beneath a cover was a shiny red motorcycle. Thinking it was an early birthday present, he climbed on it and revved it. But, to his disappointment, it turned into a rusty old model with an engine that sounded as if it had a cough. Only the handlebars shone.

DREAM BACKGROUND AND MEANING

Gerard desperately wanted a motorcycle but could not afford one, as he was struggling through college. His grandfather had offered him a rusty motorcycle he had once ridden but said Gerard would have to help him restore it. Gerard refused, as he wanted a shiny new model. Rust can conceal great potential if the dreamer can see beyond the surface.

INTERPRETATIONS AND FORTUNE-TELLING MEANINGS

* If you have a rusty vehicle in a dream, it suggests that you have not taken care of your health and body.
* A dream of rusty tools says you are making do with second best in life, which may not last or prove durable.
* Dreaming of rusty nails warns that you are letting a relationship or friendship deteriorate and eventually break.
* If you dream you are cutting with a rusty knife, you will not make an impression on any situation or end a relationship with a clean break.
* A rusty key warns that you have been neglecting resources and talents that will be hard to revive.
* A dream of a heap of rusty metal indicates worries about the health of an older person, or a disappointment that has temporarily clouded your enthusiasm for life.

OUTCOME OF GERARD'S DREAM

Next time Gerard visited his grandfather, his grandfather had started to restore the bike and, as the rust was removed, Gerard saw that a shining motorcycle lay beneath. He helped his grandfather, and when it was finished his grandfather said Gerard could sell it and, as it was a vintage model, he would get more than enough money to buy a brand-new model of his choice. But Gerard chose to keep it. Rust in a dream speaks of what has been ignored or neglected. However, if rust has not eaten away the metal, it shows that many situations and relationships as well as objects can with care be restored.

Sabotage, Saboteur

Clemence, thirty, dreamed she was a saboteur in the French Resistance during World War II, sent to sabotage a bridge used for transporting supplies to the front. She was approaching the bridge when a patrol challenged her. But her fiancé, Gerard, hiding beneath the bridge, protected her and sacrificed his own life, giving her the chance to escape while he detonated the charges.

DREAM BACKGROUND AND MEANING

Clemence was fascinated by the Resistance and knew that her uncle had been shot as a saboteur for defending France in the movement. However, in her present life sabotage was more subtle. Her mother deliberately sabotaged Clemence's relationships by lying about her. Clemence had met Gerard, a man she really loved, who she believed was from the French Resistance world and who had died for her in a past life. Sabotage dreams take many forms, but often emotional issues are at the root.

INTERPRETATIONS AND FORTUNE-TELLING MEANINGS

* If you dream of a wartime experience in which you were a saboteur, especially if someone significant reappears, this may be a past-life dream.
* If you are sabotaging something potentially dangerous in your dream, you may need to act decisively to deflect harm away from yourself or a loved one.
* If you dream someone is sabotaging your happiness, question their motives and resist having your life wrecked by them.
* If, in your dream, you sabotage your own relationships or career opportunities, this may be caused by fear of failure.
* If, in your dream, there are people in your life who sow seeds of doubt in your mind and others', be aware they may be doing this so you wreck your own chances while they innocently stand by.
* If you know the dream saboteur, your dream alerts you that someone you think is loving may have malicious intentions.

OUTCOME OF CLEMENCE'S DREAM

When Clemence finally introduced Gerard to her mother, Gerard fiercely defended Clemence, and Clemence's mother realized her ploys would not work. Sabotage dreams are often rooted in jealousy and fear of being left alone.

Sacred Books

Antoinette, thirty, dreamed she was in a white marble building with tall, white-dressed figures, walking through mist. In the center was an open book from which poured light. On one page was Antoinette's life so far; on the second, her future. But as she went to read the future, the page became covered in gold light. Antoinette woke desperate to get back into the dream, but she could not.

DREAM BACKGROUND AND MEANING

Antoinette, a physician, was at a crossroads in her life. Should she travel with Doctors Without Borders or go home, marry her childhood sweetheart, and take over her father's general practice? If the future is hidden when a person is dreaming of the Akashic Records—the repository of our past, present, and future—it is still to be decided.

INTERPRETATIONS AND FORTUNE-TELLING MEANINGS

★ If you dream of a sacred book open at a specific page, whether or not it is familiar to you, discovering the actual sacred book will reveal answers relevant to your present dilemma.

★ If you are studying a sacred book in your dream, you may have past-life connections with that world.

★ If you are a devotee of a particular culture in your dream, there may be an aspect of that culture that is relevant to your current life stage.

★ If you can identify your sacred book from the dream, but it is still closed, obtain a copy and open the book anywhere at random to find your personal message.

★ If the words in the book are obscured, the dream is telling you to wait, as this is not the time to make a decision.

OUTCOME OF ANTOINETTE'S DREAM

Antoinette realized that she had to make that golden future and that no one else could make up her mind. She told her boyfriend she would come home after a year if he would wait. Her father took in a temporary assistant to help out while she traveled. Sacred books can offer advice and wisdom but cannot substitute for making our own destiny.

Sacrifice

Abigail, fifty, dreamed she was a queen in an ancient Mesoamerican culture and, having produced many children, was being asked to sacrifice herself to transfer her fertility to the land, where there was a drought. She ran into the rain forest with her pursuers following. She woke, uncertain whether she had escaped.

DREAM BACKGROUND AND MEANING

Abigail had sacrificed a successful career as a roving reporter because she had been unable to leave her small children. Instead, she took a part-time desk job. Now the children were teenagers, and she had been offered a job as a foreign correspondent. Her family said she was selfish to even contemplate leaving them. Often past-life sacrifice dreams emerge when the dreamer is considering putting themself first.

INTERPRETATIONS AND FORTUNE-TELLING MEANINGS

★ If you dream you are making a willing sacrifice of your life at an altar, it represents giving up a part of yourself to move to the next stage of life.

★ Making an offering at an altar of something precious to you symbolizes the need for temporary sacrifice for a greater gain.

★ A dream of offering your body sexually to a high priest or priestess appears if you are contemplating a deep sexual relationship or exploring sacred sex.

★ If you dream you are not willing to sacrifice your life, there are buried fears and resentments of sacrificing your own needs and happiness.

★ If you dream of sacrificing an animal, you are contemplating going against your instincts to gain approval.

★ If you are making sacrifices on behalf of others or they for you, is this expected, demanded, or your or their choice? Is there a payoff?

OUTCOME OF ABIGAIL'S DREAM

Abigail turned the job down as impractical, knowing that by the time the children were totally independent she would be too old. She resented the family for holding her back. Sacrifice dreams are complex, where the rewards of giving up freedom or independence must be weighed against obligations and duty.

Safe (Security Box)

Sandi, sixty-five, dreamed she discovered a safe with a key. Inside was ten thousand dollars. Sandi took the money and rushed to the travel agent, who told her that if she hurried she could reach the docks in time for the last unsold cabin on a Caribbean cruise. It was only as she was boarding that she realized she had no extra clothes and had not told her daughter. She laughed and ran onboard.

DREAM BACKGROUND AND MEANING

Sandi had won ten thousand dollars on Powerball and realized she could go on the holiday of a lifetime. But her daughter had found several investment accounts with good interest to save for Sandi's old age. Sandi was torn, as she felt life was passing her by. A safe is useful to conserve resources but can restrict pleasure or developing talents.

INTERPRETATIONS AND FORTUNE-TELLING MEANINGS

★ To dream of putting money or valuables in a safe indicates a period of stable and increasing finances ahead.

★ An empty safe warns that you should be careful who you trust with money, love, or secrets.

★ To dream that you rob a safe says you may profit from someone else's mistakes or careless actions.

★ To open a safe or safety deposit box offers an opportunity to reveal your hidden talents for profit or pleasure.

★ If you are considering a sexual encounter, a dream of a locked safe says you should be sure the experience will enrich you.

★ Should your dream safe not open when you use the combination or key, this may not be the time for a major purchase or investment.

OUTCOME OF SANDI'S DREAM

Sandi booked her dream holiday despite her daughter's disapproval and had a wonderful time. She took many photographs and realized this was a talent she could develop. Safes represent securing what or who is truly valuable to us, whether savings, extra effort in career, happiness, or love.

Saint

Delphine, forty-two, dreamed she was riding in armor behind Saint Joan of Arc. They were heading into a walled city. Delphine was afraid. Saint Joan stopped and said she would go on alone. Everyone but Delphine turned back. As the two of them entered the town, everyone welcomed them.

DREAM BACKGROUND AND MEANING

Delphine had volunteered to drive a truck to a war zone in Eastern Europe, as her company in the United Kingdom was seeking experienced drivers for a convoy of medicines. She had recently been vacationing in Rouen in France where Joan of Arc was martyred and had bought a Saint Joan medallion, though she was not religious. Saints, identifiable by halos of light around their heads, appear to religious and nonreligious dreamers alike, heralding a special event and a chance to make a difference to others.

INTERPRETATIONS AND FORTUNE-TELLING MEANINGS

★ To dream about meeting saints is a sign that your spiritual and healing powers are growing.

★ If a saint is blessing you, expect practical help from someone altruistic if you are despairing.

★ If the saint is surrounded by brilliant light, someone may be asking you to sacrifice too much by appealing to your conscience.

★ If a saint's halo is missing, you may be expecting too much of someone you have idealized.

★ Dreaming of following a procession of saints says you need to take a moral stand and risk losing approval.

★ A saint can be a messenger from higher realms, offering to guide or to connect you with a principled deceased relative you are mourning.

OUTCOME OF DELPHINE'S DREAM

As a result of the dream, Delphine felt the presence of her late aunt, a former member of the wartime French Resistance, and overcame her fears. She wore her Saint Joan medallion and returned safely. If you recognize a particular saint connected with you, such as Saint Joan of Arc for female courage, you are being offered that strength.

Salary Inequality

Lindy, forty-five, dreamed she was in a conference hall filled with staff from the television company for which she worked. She saw a pile of pay slips in an open briefcase in the spare seat next to hers. She started to read them and saw that the men were paid far more than the women and that male presenters received almost double what their female counterparts got. She marched onto the stage, seized the microphone, and announced that the company was guilty of discrimination against women. She was told her employment was terminated.

DREAM BACKGROUND AND MEANING

Lindy was slowly gathering evidence that men were paid more than the women in her company for the same work. However, many of the women refused to speak openly because they were afraid of losing their jobs. Paycheck dreams may reveal inequalities in life generally, as well as in career, by confirming justified suspicions through the dreamer's unconscious radar.

INTERPRETATIONS AND FORTUNE-TELLING MEANINGS

* If you dream that you open your paycheck and there is a big increase in the amount, it is a good omen that you are in line for promotion or a major raise.
* If you dream you are given the wrong paycheck, you may be insecure about a colleague being more highly regarded than you.
* If your dream paycheck is considerably lower than usual, you may feel emotionally undervalued in a relationship or within the family.
* If your dream paycheck is blank or missing, or if you protest about poor wages and conditions, are you in danger of being fired on another pretext?
* If your paycheck contains a huge amount you could not possibly have earned, it might be a chance to make fast money if you accept the risks.

OUTCOME OF LINDY'S DREAM

Lindy took a job with another production company, known for equal opportunities, and exposed the scandal at her previous job as a news item, having collected enough evidence before leaving. Paycheck dreams are significant at times when the dreamer's value in their workplace may be under question.

Salmon

Judith, thirty-four, dreamed that a salmon swam toward her in a river thousands of miles from home and told her she must go home for the birth of her baby. The salmon promised the baby would be blessed with health, intelligence, and wisdom. She left a note telling her husband she was going home for the birth.

DREAM BACKGROUND AND MEANING

Judith was six months pregnant and was worried because a scan had picked up some possible problems. She was booked into a very expensive hospital near their new home in the Far East for the birth, but she felt uneasy. Though the hospital had a good reputation, it was not a specialist maternity hospital.

Salmon is the most magical of fish. It is believed in parts of the Northwest United States and Canada that once a year, if a magical salmon is eaten, it will bring good fortune and ensure that any children subsequently born understand the language of fish, animals, and birds.

INTERPRETATIONS AND FORTUNE-TELLING MEANINGS

* If you dream of a salmon spawning, this is a powerful maternal and fertility sign.
* If the salmon is swimming upstream, you will find your right home if you persist.
* As a symbol of wisdom in the Celtic world, a salmon rising to the surface suggests taking expert advice for a major decision.
* Since Pacific salmon, unlike Atlantic salmon, die after spawning, you may be asked to make sacrifices to fulfill an ambition.
* Since salmon travel hundreds of miles from their home stream to the ocean, seeing a shoal of salmon indicates long-distance travel with the intention of someday returning home.

OUTCOME OF JUDITH'S DREAM

Judith flew home and booked into a maternity hospital near her parents' home. Though the baby was premature, there were excellent facilities and she and the baby, once it had a good weight, returned to the Far East. Salmon dreams, while *never* predicting that a mother or baby is going to die, can pick up parental anxieties about a forthcoming pregnancy or birth and encourage the mother to give birth where she feels at home.

Salt

Barry, forty-one, dreamed he was extracting salt from the local marshes to sell in the markets. His neighbors were working on their salt pans. Men with fierce dogs drove them off the marshes and burned their cottages. But the salt panners, led by Barry, fought back and at last drove them away.

DREAM BACKGROUND AND MEANING

Barry lived near beautiful salt marshes, but the area was under threat by developers to build luxury homes and compulsorily purchase the local cottages, including Barry's, which dated back centuries. This was possible despite environmental protests because of corruption and bribery of the local council. A past-life dream, a salt dream centers around the concept of preservation, and that can include environmental or historical conservation.

INTERPRETATIONS AND FORTUNE-TELLING MEANINGS

★ A universal symbol of life, health, and healing, salt indicates that your healing powers are evolving, or your health or that of a loved one is improving.

★ Spilled or spilling salt is a traditional sign for treachery in someone who pretended to be a friend.

★ If you dream you run out of salt while cooking, you may need to nurture yourself more or ask more support of others.

★ A heap of salt, sometimes called white gold, represents growing prosperity; the greater the amount of salt, the more the gain.

★ Making circles of salt or using it in a magick spell may be indicative of a past world where you were a wise woman or man.

★ Dreaming of sprinkling salt on the doorstep says your home and family will be protected from all harm and malice.

OUTCOME OF BARRY'S DREAM

Prompted by the vividness of the dream, Barry investigated local historical archives, which revealed that each of the cottages had ancient rights over the salt marshes, which effectively protected the area from development once the claims were staked. Dreams can link us with the energies of an area in which we live, and salt represents not just financial gain, but spiritual gold as well.

Samples

Wilhelmina, forty, dreamed she was going from door to door in her neighborhood, offering samples of canapés she made for her home-catering business. But the neighbors crushed her offerings on the path and slammed the door. She could not understand why, as she was a professional chef and had prepared beautiful samples.

DREAM BACKGROUND AND MEANING

Wilhelmina had moved to a new area and asked the neighbors on the street to a canapés party to meet her and advertise her catering business. They refused, seemingly without reason. Wilhelmina discovered that one of the locals also ran a home-catering business, and the neighbors saw becoming friends with a rival as disloyalty. Sample dreams represent putting forward talents and goodwill to attract business or friendship, but success may be resented by those less enterprising.

INTERPRETATIONS AND FORTUNE-TELLING MEANINGS

★ If in the dream you are offered samples of food or beauty products, your business or plans will grow from small beginnings with increasing profitability.

★ If a family member or partner dreams of sampling different foods and rejecting some, they may need to try several jobs or training before they settle.

★ If you are giving away samples in a store or mall, you may feel people are taking advantage of your generosity in everyday life and not offering anything in return.

★ If you dream you are asked to rate different samples, you may have to make a choice, none of which feels right.

★ If you dream that people refuse the samples you are offering, your efforts may seem wasted, whether in the workplace or in relationships.

★ If you dream that you drop your samples or they are crushed, you may be offering too much or offering them to the wrong people and should not blame yourself.

OUTCOME OF WILHELMINA'S DREAM

Wilhelmina spoke with her rival, who admitted she was struggling to complete orders and the last thing she wanted was competition. Wilhelmina suggested they join forces and created their own specialties. Wilhelmina is now accepted by the neighbors, and both businesses are flourishing. Samples dreams indicate the need to explore opportunities step by step and to keep offering, even if you are at first discouraged.

Sanctuary

Harry, twenty-two, dreamed he was in an ancient sanctuary on top of a mountain in Tibet, surrounded by chanting monks, and he was totally at peace. Then he saw soldiers ascending the mountain and knew they were coming to arrest him. He picked up his small pack and went down the mountain to meet them.

DREAM BACKGROUND AND MEANING

Harry was studying theology at an exclusive college, following his parents' ambition that he would eventually become an Anglican priest and rise high in the church. But his girlfriend had become pregnant. On his parents' advice, Harry had denied all responsibility, as they said it would ruin his future career. However, Harry loved his girlfriend and wanted to be part of his newborn child's life, whatever the price. Sanctuaries can represent a refuge, but when they become an escape from life they no longer serve their purpose.

INTERPRETATIONS AND FORTUNE-TELLING MEANINGS

* If you dream of a secret temple in beautiful gardens, you may need to move out of life's fast lane for a while.
* If you are creating a healing sanctuary for others, your healing powers are gaining strength.
* If a sanctuary is abandoned, you may no longer feel safe in a formerly secure environment or situation.
* If you dream you are building a private sanctuary behind high walls, you may need to exclude those intruding on your private space.
* If you are claiming sanctuary in a church from attackers, this may be a past-life dream. Your present life is under attack from hostile people, so seek support.
* If you dream you are refused admission to a sanctuary, people you formerly trusted may prove less than reliable.

OUTCOME OF HARRY'S DREAM

Harry left his insulated college life, found a job, and asked his girlfriend if he could be part of his son's life. She is wary, but they are starting to build a future for themselves in the everyday world. His parents have disowned him. Seeking sanctuary does not take away unresolved issues, which may appear in dreams in the form of attackers.

Sandy Beach

Amy, twenty-five, dreamed she was trying to sunbathe, but her young stepchildren were constantly bothering her. She closed her eyes, but when she opened them minutes later, the children were at the top of a huge sandhill, which was starting to shift. She climbed the dune and safely brought them down, realizing that where they had been standing had collapsed.

DREAM BACKGROUND AND MEANING

Amy had taken her two stepchildren to the beach while her partner, as usual, had stayed at the chalet to answer business emails. The children constantly asked for their father, fought, and bickered, and she was unable to relax. Sandy beaches in dreams may revive happy memories, but these may filter out the effort adults made to generate the happiness.

INTERPRETATIONS AND FORTUNE-TELLING MEANINGS

* A dream of an expanse of empty sandy beach is a sign of undisturbed time needed to reflect on life or recover energy.
* A dream of a sandy beach filled with children making sandcastles is nostalgia for a simpler lifestyle.
* If sand blows into food or people's eyes, minor irritations will result in angry exchanges, unless tackled.
* If you dream you are sliding down a sand dune, be careful of your facts and the security of your position before acting impulsively.
* If sand is coarse and patches of shingle are washed in by the tide, a seemingly idyllic situation may have to be adapted to reality.
* If in your dream the sandy beach is totally covered by the tide, you may need to deal with recurring emotional demands.

OUTCOME OF AMY'S DREAM

The following weekend, Amy built sandcastles with the children. The dream made her realize how much she cared for them. She told her partner he must join in if they were to form a family and not leave it all to her. Sandy-beach dreams represent childhood fun, but they reveal that happy families do not happen by chance but through creating those memories and putting personal desires aside.

Santa Claus

Meggie, now sixty-eight, recalled a vivid dream she had when she was six years old. It was so vivid that it had remained clear through the years. In her childhood dream, she saw Santa Claus in his sleigh rising higher and higher in the sky. She followed him, calling, "Don't go, don't go." Then she heard her father's voice say, "Meggie, Meggie, don't go." She woke in pain with her father by her bedside. It was almost Christmas.

DREAM BACKGROUND AND MEANING

When she was six, Meggie was having a serious operation to mend an arm damaged at birth. The operation went wrong, and she almost died. While Santa Claus dreams are primarily experienced by younger children like Meggie, adults can have them too, as they reflect a longing for childhood innocence when adults could fix anything.

INTERPRETATIONS AND FORTUNE-TELLING MEANINGS

★ If an older child dreams of Santa Claus around Christmas or Thanksgiving, they may be struggling with the destruction of their belief in magick and Santa Claus.

★ If a child dreams of Santa bringing gifts way beyond the parental budget, it is time to change the emphasis away from consumerism.

★ If an adult dreams of being a child and seeing Santa on Christmas Eve, it is a reminder of the magick of Christmas if they have become jaded with life and need more spontaneous fun.

★ If you dream of being a child and of Santa not turning up because you have been bad, you may still be relying too much on the approval of others.

★ If you dream of a parent or grandparent dressing up as Santa on Christmas Eve in your childhood, it is time to start fulfilling your own needs and wishes.

OUTCOME OF MEGGIE'S DREAM

It may be that Meggie had a near-death experience, when the soul temporarily leaves the body (see p. 325), or had an anesthetic-induced dream. Meggie was brought up by her father. Santa is an archetype of the ideal all-giving father who can perform the seemingly impossible. Santa Claus dreams in adulthood often represent the need for moving past idolizing a father figure, which may be preventing any partner from seeming good enough.

Sapphire

Daphne, twenty-five, dreamed she found her missing blue sapphire ring in the shirt pocket of her husband, Stefan, as she was preparing the laundry. Stefan said he was borrowing it to check the size for her birthday surprise. Now she had spoiled it. He stormed out and, upset, she put the ring on her finger. The stone fell out and she saw the sapphire was a fake. It was not her ring at all.

DREAM BACKGROUND AND MEANING

Recently, several pieces of Daphne's late mother's jewelry had gone missing. There had been strange phone calls, which Stefan went outside to answer, and she heard raised voices. Was there another woman Stefan was giving her jewelry to? A fake sapphire warns that there may be falsehood and hidden matters that should be investigated.

INTERPRETATIONS AND FORTUNE-TELLING MEANINGS

★ Being given a blue sapphire in the dream is a symbol of lasting fidelity by the giver.

★ A dream of wearing or admiring a sapphire on an engagement finger foretells a betrothal or precious gift by a lover or partner.

★ A ring on the index finger of the writing hand says justice will be done and dishonesty uncovered.

★ A dream of a tray of sapphires in a jewelry store or window suggests that you will be made an advantageous offer in your career or financially that will lead to prosperity.

★ Dreaming of prospecting for sapphires in a mine says you will need to probe to get the answers or justice you deserve.

★ If sapphire jewelry is stolen or missing in a dream, be careful who you lend money to or do favors for, as they may prove untrustworthy.

OUTCOME OF DAPHNE'S DREAM

After the dream, Daphne confronted her husband, and he admitted he had become involved with a high-stakes gambling syndicate and had been pawning her jewelry to pay debts. As the stone of purity and truth, sapphires in dreams appear when the unconscious mind is questioning truth.

Satin, Silk

May, forty-five, dreamed she was a young woman making silk garments in a temple. She was secretly saving leftover fabric in exotic patterns for her forthcoming marriage. May intended to blend them together to make her wedding dress. But her secret hoard was discovered and destroyed. She was dismissed, and her fiancé left her.

DREAM BACKGROUND AND MEANING

May was in love with her boss, who gave her erotic, expensive presents and promised to leave his wife and marry her. He was siphoning money from the company for their future. May agreed to keep the money in an account in her name, to which he had access. But recently she worried that he was using her as a means of hiding money. Her dream may have been a past-life dream containing subconscious warnings about her present life.

INTERPRETATIONS AND FORTUNE-TELLING MEANINGS

* To dream you are wearing satin or silk says that you want more luxury and indulgence in your life. If necessary, indulge yourself.
* Weaving silk indicates profitable work and fulfillment of ambitions through your own efforts.
* Dreaming you are sleeping alone in satin sheets reveals that you lack romance in your present sex life or crave an exciting new lover.
* To be given a silk garment says the dream donor will cherish you, and silk underwear promises passionate love.
* Bales of silk foretell a wealthy lover.
* Dreaming of ripped or dirty silk or satin speaks of deception in love or an ambition unfulfilled through lack of support.

OUTCOME OF MAY'S DREAM

After the dream, May accepted that she would be the one blamed for the fraud. She returned all the money and told the CEO. Because May had been honest, she was dismissed without a reference rather than prosecuted. Her boss, who denied everything, was arrested and convicted. In dreams, silk can speak of being seduced by promises of material love and luxury, suggesting that you examine what lies behind extravagant offers or gifts.

Saving Lives

Jenny, nineteen, dreamed two older women came into her bedroom. One she recognized as her deceased grandmother. They told her to wake up quickly, as there was great danger. Jenny woke and saw smoke pouring under the door.

DREAM BACKGROUND AND MEANING

Jenny's parents had been decorating her teenage brother's room. Her brother's mattress had accidentally slipped against a light and started to smolder. There were gas cylinders downstairs. Deceased grandmothers especially act as guardians to the family in times of danger and contact the person most likely to respond fast.

INTERPRETATIONS AND FORTUNE-TELLING MEANINGS

* If you wake from a dream warning you of a fire, check that no plugs are overheating or cigarettes were left smoldering.
* If you wake after dreaming about a fire, flood, or intruder and you are generally feeling worried, check to reassure yourself. Most likely this is an anxiety dream.
* If you consistently dream of a domestic or workplace accident, use the forewarning to check emergency procedures and security.
* If you dream of someone putting you or a family member in potential danger—for example, by joyriding—take this as a warning to change your company.
* If you dream regularly of an elderly relative suffering a fatal fall or accident, it may be time to consider their ongoing safety and security.
* If you dream of becoming a firefighter or paramedic and saving lives, explore the practicalities of taking training, at least as a volunteer.

OUTCOME OF JENNY'S DREAM

Jenny woke her mother and they were able to call the fire department just before the phone went dead. Jenny's mother later asked what had woken her. Jenny described the two women. The second unknown woman was Jenny's other grandmother, who had died before she was born. Our unconscious radar remains active during sleep. Many potential catastrophes have been avoided by a dream so vivid that it wakes the dreamer.

Saying Goodbye

Diane, forty, was living in the United Kingdom and dreamed her grandfather died. In the dream, she flew to Australia to break the news to her cousin David. The dream was so real that Diane felt David's hand in hers as she told him the news. Diane's grandfather had indeed died at the time of the dream.

DREAM BACKGROUND AND MEANING

Diane's grandfather appeared to Diane in her dream so she could send David, the strongest family member, to be with his family. When she was officially informed the next day and phoned the family in Perth, her cousin David had just arrived home on compassionate leave, after telling his commanding officer that his grandfather had died, though he had not received any news. In their dying moments, many relatives appear in dreams to kin, so the dreamer can spare the family from finding out from a stranger.

INTERPRETATIONS AND FORTUNE-TELLING MEANINGS

★ If you dream of a relative dying in a vivid dream, previously unknown personal information may confirm astral travel as the soul leaves the body.

★ If there has been an estrangement, a relative may come back at the point of death to make peace.

★ If a dying relative comes to you in a dream surrounded by deceased loved ones, they may be seeking permission to let go of life.

★ If you are emotionally close to a dying relative and keeping a bedside vigil, you may fall asleep and see them moving toward the light.

★ If a relative is missing or in a coma, you may see them in a dream well and strong at the time of passing.

★ If a child dreams of a great-grandparent saying goodbye, this affirms that love goes on after death.

OUTCOME OF DIANE'S DREAM

Diane's dream was immensely comforting to the family overseas. In wartime, many service personnel appear to loved ones at the moment of death, and the timings invariably prove accurate.

Scabs, Skin Conditions

Sunita, twenty-five, dreamed she was the beautiful daughter of a medieval knight and she was promised to a wealthy duke because of her fabulous looks and beautiful skin. But she caught smallpox and, though she survived, her skin was covered in scabs and pustules. She knew she would be badly scarred and the only future for her was in a convent. She woke crying.

DREAM BACKGROUND AND MEANING

Sunita had a great future as a makeup model on television and had a contract with a famous cosmetics company, but she developed rosacea. Her face and arms turned bright red with silver scales. Her fiancé dropped her, she lost her contracts overnight, and none of the conventional treatments worked. When success depends on appearance, scabs, scars, and skin problems can prove catastrophic but can also alter the sufferer's perspective on priorities.

INTERPRETATIONS AND FORTUNE-TELLING MEANINGS

★ To dream about being covered in scabs is an expression of worry about your imperfections generally, often because of overcritical or jealous people.

★ A child covered in scabs in your dream expresses worries that you are not caring for them well enough.

★ If you dream you pull the head off a scab, you are reliving an earlier hurt or unfairness and not letting it heal.

★ If in the dream scabs are healing, you are starting to move forward from a setback.

★ If scabs have left scars in the dream, you may find it hard to forgive or reconcile past wrongs.

★ If you are rejected in the dream because of your scabs, the person who leaves you is interested only in a superficial relationship.

OUTCOME OF SUNITA'S DREAM

Sunita found an alternative remedy that made her rosacea fade, and with makeup it was virtually undetectable. However, she no longer wanted to go back to a world where success depended purely on appearance, and she trained as a makeup artist for people with scars and disfigurements. Scabs can represent rejection by others, but scars heal, and the value of people who stick around is revealed.

Scaffolding

Florence, sixty, dreamed she found a ruined structure resembling a Sleeping Beauty castle covered in flimsy wooden scaffolding. Florence entered and wandered through beautifully furnished rooms. But when she reached the central courtyard, she heard rumbling, cracking, and roaring. The scaffolding was collapsing, and the whole castle was crumbling inward. Choking, Florence escaped as the castle vanished beneath the dust.

DREAM BACKGROUND AND MEANING

Florence, an interior designer, had discovered her dream home, an unconverted watermill, and was determined to live in it once the building was shored up by scaffolding; she planned to renovate room by room. She ignored the surveyor's and architect's warnings, as she was totally enchanted by her fairy-tale home and was seeking a bank loan for the work. The dream will indicate the viability of repairing the existing structure, replacing it, or not doing anything at all, depending upon whether the subject is a building, an emotional situation, or a financial deal.

INTERPRETATIONS AND FORTUNE-TELLING MEANINGS

★ Dreaming of solid scaffolding tells you to seek support with family or relationship problems, or when in need of financial advice.

★ If dream scaffolding is flimsy or unsound, question if you are paying too high a price for support.

★ If scaffolding collapses, but the building remains, you are seeking help from the wrong person.

★ If the whole dream structure collapses, beware of major problems and wasted investment, whether emotional or financial.

★ If you are erecting scaffolding or climbing it, a loan, deal, or bailout promises success in a project, especially one concerned with property.

★ If you dream you descend or fall off scaffolding, you have only a temporary solution to give you breathing space while you find a permanent answer.

OUTCOME OF FLORENCE'S DREAM

Florence pulled out, as she realized that her dream property was a money pit and learned that the only loan she was offered was at extortionate rates. Scaffolding dreams often pick up signals of unacknowledged actual property problems to be taken seriously.

Scales (Weighing)

In her dream, Carina, thirty-four, was weighing herself as she did every morning, and to her horror saw she had put on a large amount of weight. Carina was very focused on her weight and fitness, and if she put on even a pound would not eat until it had gone. Suddenly, she tired of having her scales dictate her happiness, threw them in the garbage, and went off to buy a chocolate bar.

DREAM BACKGROUND AND MEANING

Carina constantly worried about her weight. When she was younger she had been slightly overweight. Her mother put her on a strict diet. Her husband would question her weight every day. Though with careful dieting and exercise she kept her weight under control, Carina obsessed about food and dreaded her morning weigh-in. If you dream about weighing yourself, this represents an external form of control for measuring your self-worth.

INTERPRETATIONS AND FORTUNE-TELLING MEANINGS

★ If in your dream your weight increases dramatically, it is clearly an emotional as well as a fitness issue, making you insulate yourself.

★ If you throw your scales away in the dream, you are freeing yourself from what may be an obsession with perfection.

★ If your partner or a parent is weighing you in the dream, they are seeking to state your value in their eyes.

★ If you are in a restaurant and weighing yourself and your food, you may have guilt issues about sensual pleasures of all kinds.

★ If you are on a diet and dream of being ecstatic when you have lost weight overnight, you may be expecting a weight loss to fix everything in your life.

OUTCOME OF CARINA'S DREAM

After the dream, Carina decided she would weigh herself no more, would eat what she wanted when she was hungry, and told her husband and mother that her weight was her business. Scales dreams can alert the dreamer that they do not need anyone or anything to regulate their life.

Scapegoat

Raimon, thirty-five, came from a very religious family who read the Bible every night. He regularly dreamed of a scapegoat carrying the sins of the people into the wilderness. Then Raimon turned into the goat and his family was heaping huge weights onto his back, saying everything was his fault. He was turned out onto the hills of the Scottish island where they lived, but he threw off the burdens and roamed free.

DREAM BACKGROUND AND MEANING

Raimon was second-youngest of six children, and from early childhood he was always blamed for any family trouble. His siblings taught his peers at school to despise him. Now he was married. His family was turning his wife against him. If you dream of being excluded from your family, peers, and colleagues, you may be continuing the role that a dysfunctional nuclear family has created for you.

INTERPRETATIONS AND FORTUNE-TELLING MEANINGS

* If you dream of staggering along carrying everything on a family trip, you should stop trying to please your family.
* If you are excluded from the family table in a dream, you are denied a chance to express your own gifts and strengths.
* If your family is haranguing you in a dream for what is not your fault, this is not a sign of your guilt, but rather a continuance of victimhood imposed on you, probably from childhood.
* If in your dream you see a new scapegoat in your family, as happens when one scapegoat leaves, note who it is, as they may prove an ally in your fight.
* If you see yourself happy and respected within your own family, you know you can break this destructive pattern.

OUTCOME OF RAIMON'S DREAM

Raimon told his wife she could either move away with him immediately or stay with his family and he would go. She left the island with him, and they have broken contact with his family. Scapegoating is etched in the subconscious through generations. Dreams are especially helpful to the dreamer in discovering his or her own self-worth.

Scarab Beetle

Rudy, seventy, dreamed he was in an Ancient Egyptian tomb in the Valley of the Queens, and his late wife was with him. They watched the burial of a beloved queen. Most precious of all the amulets to protect her on her afterlife journey was a red-and-gold–winged heart scarab. In an instant, the burial scene was gone, along with his wife. He saw the heart-shaped scarab on the floor and heard her voice saying, "You too must travel to rebirth."

DREAM BACKGROUND AND MEANING

Rudy was on his first vacation alone in forty-five years, after the death of his wife. A Nile cruise and even the fabulous amulets in the Cairo Museum did not inspire him. The scarab is an ancient reminder of new life transformed from the old, and often occurs in dreams after a bereavement, not necessarily set in Egypt.

INTERPRETATIONS AND FORTUNE-TELLING MEANINGS

* Khepri, the scarab-headed god, was the Ancient Egyptian god of the sun at dawn. Seeing the scarab-headed god, or an altar dedicated to him, in a dream offers assurance of major transformation in your life.
* If you see a blue scarab beetle amulet in your dream, you carry within you the seeds of new, undeveloped talents you'd set aside.
* Seeing scarab beetles running everywhere, B-movie style, in an Egyptian tomb dream, predicts maximizing opportunities.
* Dreaming of scarab beetles rolling their eggs, which they lay in a ball of dung, promises that within twenty-eight days of the dream—the time it takes for the eggs to hatch—improvements will be felt.
* Dreaming of a heart-shaped scarab with wings being placed in the heart cavity of a mummy says you will be protected against sorrow and those who would deceive.
* A golden dream scarab promises wealth and esteem and overcomes fears of aging and mortality.

OUTCOME OF RUDY'S DREAM

The morning after the dream, Rudy returned to the Cairo Museum and found the winged scarab among the amulets. He bought one, a reminder that love never dies. The scarab is a reminder of the little beetle, rolling its eggs ceaselessly toward new beginnings.

Scholarship

Alain, thirty, was eighteen again in his dream and arriving at the college where his father, grandfather, and three older brothers had all won scholarships. When he arrived, the huge iron gates were barred. He woke feeling ashamed he had let his family down.

DREAM BACKGROUND AND MEANING

Alain's family were all academics, but Alain had been an average student. While they all had high-powered jobs and beautiful houses, he had a modest condo with his wife and two children and worked as a supervisor in a local supermarket. His family was pressuring him to make something of his life and had found a scholarship for late starters, for which he could apply. Scholarships in dreams indicate attainment academically and in life generally, but they are not everyone's road to happiness.

INTERPRETATIONS AND FORTUNE-TELLING MEANINGS

* Dreaming of winning a scholarship, whatever your circumstances, says you will attain success.
* If you are trying for a scholarship, winning one in a dream is a good omen for achieving this, as the energies are right.
* If in the dream you are offered an alternative scholarship to the one you wanted, this can refer to any aspect of your life where you are taken down a different path.
* If in the dream you fail to get a scholarship, you may doubt your ability in your career, finances, or business.
* If you are praised for your learning or scholarship in a dream, you should believe in your own talents, which can take many forms.
* If you dream you are criticized for lack of knowledge or scholarship, you may have felt inadequate earlier and may still be listening to those voices from the past.

OUTCOME OF ALAIN'S DREAM

Alain accepted that academic attainment was not for him and turned down the late scholarship. Scholarship dreams can represent attaining dizzying heights and gaining sponsorship to advance, but can cause undue pressure for people with different priorities.

School, Classroom

Perdita, twenty-four, dreamed she was in the classroom of her old school, alone, writing out a hundred times, "I will never succeed if I question everything." Her friends were playing in the sunshine. She got out of her chair, left the classroom, and walked out through the gates. She then hesitated, turned around, and went back to finish her detention.

DREAM BACKGROUND AND MEANING

Perdita was working for a company that dismissed all her ideas and suggestions for righting the many inefficiencies and developing new avenues. She was constantly planning to leave, but at the last minute changed her mind. School dreams suggest you are held back by voices and limitations imposed in the past that no longer are relevant.

INTERPRETATIONS AND FORTUNE-TELLING MEANINGS

* If you dream you are looking out the classroom window at everyone else playing, fears of unworthiness are holding you back.
* If you are being rewarded with a prize, you will have the chance to learn a new skill based on gifts you have that were not encouraged at school.
* Dreams about school are a good omen if you worry about your children's education and for all who study or work in teaching or childcare.
* A return to unhappy or humiliating school scenes indicates lack of confidence in your abilities. Ignore unjustified criticism and carping by a current authority figure at work.
* If you dream you walk out of the school in frustration but then return, you need a definite plan for leaving your comfort zone.
* If you dream that you keep walking, you are ready to go forward and claim your power.

OUTCOME OF PERDITA'S DREAM

Perdita realized that fear was holding her back from using her talents and initiative. She took a loan and went to college to study forensic psychology, where she could use her questioning mind and ability to voice her insights. Sometimes it is necessary to go back to the schoolroom in dreams, pick up your abandoned plans, and leave behind forever the restrictions imposed in the classroom.

School Excursion

Heather, sixty-six, dreamed she was trying to wake teenagers who were sleeping on the floor in large mobile homes. The bus was leaving for the ferry for the first stage of a school excursion, so they could not miss it. But everyone refused to wake and said they would sooner sleep in. Heather was becoming increasingly angry.

DREAM BACKGROUND AND MEANING

Heather, a retired teacher, had been responsible for organizing school excursions. It had been so much easier than controlling her teenage grandchildren while their parents were overseas. Heather was constantly reminding them not to be late and to remember what they needed to take with them each day. School excursion dreams represent set timetables that must be followed.

INTERPRETATIONS AND FORTUNE-TELLING MEANINGS

* If you are successfully organizing a school excursion in your dream, you will find younger people in your life very cooperative.
* If you are struggling to organize unwilling children or teenagers in your dream, change tactics from coercion to persuasion regarding the young people in your life.
* If you are unwillingly participating in a school excursion and are young in the dream, extra responsibility for younger people may be burdensome.
* If you are enjoying a dream school excursion as a child or teenager, you may benefit from organized travel where your needs are catered for.
* If you dream of a school excursion and an authority figure imposes unnecessary restrictions, you may recognize a controlling person in your life.

OUTCOME OF HEATHER'S DREAM

Heather explained essential timekeeping to her grandchildren and told them that from then on they would be responsible for organizing themselves. With a few hiccups, her grandchildren assumed more responsibility, which they had not been encouraged to do by their parents. School excursions can represent necessary responsibilities in daily life. Once the responsible adult eases up, the burden falls on the younger people to organize their own life journey or accept the consequences.

Scissors

Gundrid, twenty-six, dreamed she was in Gotland, an island off Sweden known for its magical stones and myths. She was defending her cottage door against a tall, evil troll who wanted to steal her son away. Gundrid remembered a tale her grandmother told her that Gotland trolls were afraid of scissors. Gundrid seized her scissors and brandished them at the troll, who shrank in size and disappeared into the forest.

DREAM BACKGROUND AND MEANING

Gundrid was fighting for her son, as her ex-husband, Erik, was entitled to equal custody but left their son alone in the evenings though he was only ten. Erik also drank heavily and had drugs in open view. The courts would not believe Gundrid, as Erik put on a good act as a caring father. Erik's live-in girlfriend also had a ten-year-old son who was neglected by Erik, but she was afraid to complain, as Erik controlled her drugs. Scissors are useful in sewing and mending but also can cut through wrongdoing and injustice.

INTERPRETATIONS AND FORTUNE-TELLING MEANINGS

* Dreaming of cutting with scissors says you should cut through other people's inertia, indecision, or bad behavior.
* Broken scissors can indicate quarrels between two people who are competing for your attention.
* If you dream you cut yourself with scissors, someone around you is being unduly critical or malicious.
* If you dream that the scissors are blunt, you may be unnecessarily tactful and reticent in order to not offend.
* Cutting through a cord, thread, or string represents a bid for independence, even symbolically cutting the umbilical cord with a possessive mother in adulthood.

OUTCOME OF GUNDRID'S DREAM

After the dream, Gundrid realized she had to get tough. She contacted Pehr, the former partner of Erik's new girlfriend, who was also worried. He had been collecting evidence against the couple, and together Gundrid and Pehr threatened to expose them over the drugs unless they gave up the children, except for supervised access. Even a bully is afraid of something, and the dream alerted Gundrid to the fact that her seemingly untouchable husband had his weak spot, the girlfriend. Scissors dreams are about either domestic happiness or a bid for independence involving swift, decisive action.

Scorpion

Steve, forty-one, dreamed he was inside a dimly lit tomb, wearing a headdress, The tomb was sealed. People were screaming because they were trapped underground with a nobleman's mummy. Next to the mummy was a statue of Selket, the Ancient Egyptian scorpion goddess, who administered both a death sting and an antidote. Suddenly, hundreds of scorpions emerged from the statue, not attacking but escaping down a narrow passageway in the wall. Only Steve was brave enough to follow. He found himself among the sandhills, free.

DREAM BACKGROUND AND MEANING

Since visiting Egypt, Steve had felt a strong connection, so this could be a past-world dream. He had been feeling pressured at work since the takeover of the publishing group where he had worked for the past twenty years, with fierce competition and rivalry, even among former friends. Already people had been dismissed for failing to achieve unreasonable targets. Scorpion dreams indicate the buildup of small but toxic threats.

INTERPRETATIONS AND FORTUNE-TELLING MEANINGS

* If your dream scorpion does not harm you, you will escape attack even if others are affected.
* If you see Scorpio as a starry glyph in the sky or see the Scorpio symbol in your dream, your psychic powers are rapidly emerging.
* If you sense but cannot see a scorpion, beware a hidden enemy attacking your reputation.
* If you dream you kill a scorpion, you will outface a direct threat, but if the scorpion escapes be aware that the threat may return.
* Should you dream you are stung, take extra care to protect your own interests in the weeks ahead and prepare for sudden spite or viciousness.
* If you dream that there are a lot of scorpions, see if they, like the scorpion goddess, hold the antidote to a problem, perhaps by indicating an escape route.

OUTCOME OF STEVE'S DREAM

Steve realized how toxic the workplace was and knew that now was the time to seek a new job, as the stress was making him dread going to work. Scorpion dreams are inevitably warnings, so be vigilant.

Screaming

Mia, twenty-five, had a recurring dream of being in a dark place and knowing someone was waiting in the darkness to attack. She would wake herself, screaming aloud, "Where are you? I know you are there. Leave me alone."

DREAM BACKGROUND AND MEANING

Mia was afraid to go to sleep because of her screaming dreams and, when staying with friends, she had awakened them. During the day Mia was a calm, reassuring person who as a counselor absorbed the sorrows of others and was always the person to whom her family turned for advice. But as she was the newcomer and eager to please, Mia's work colleagues were taking advantage of her junior position. Screaming dreams represent letting go of control of negative feelings that are being repressed.

INTERPRETATIONS AND FORTUNE-TELLING MEANINGS

* If you scream aloud in your dream and wake yourself, you have valid fears, resentment, or anger that you need to acknowledge and express.
* If your screaming is part of the dream of a human assailant, you are feeling insecure about your life, whether in a relationship or the workplace. No harm in checking your personal security.
* If you dream that you scream but no sound comes out, you are feeling intimidated about expressing a grievance.
* If you scream at a paranormal threat, your psychic powers need channeling into healing or divination, as you are overwhelmed by psychic energies during sleep.
* If someone you know is screaming in your dreams, they may have unexpressed worries that they need to share.
* If you hear screams in your dream but cannot identify the source, you are picking up psychic signals of someone in distress.

OUTCOME OF MIA'S DREAM

Mia realized the screaming dreams occurred on days when she was given an extra-heavy caseload, and she acknowledged that she resented the others for not taking their share. She complained and, once her workload was eased, she no longer had the screaming nightmares. Screaming nightmares where the dreamer screams are a sign of stress overload.

Seagull

Tristen, fifty-five, dreamed of a solitary seagull trapped in a gully at the side of a lake. He tried to rescue it, but it pecked fiercely in fear. Once freed, the bird stood at the side of the lake, screeching. Tristen put the bird in a container and drove to the sea to release it. It died on the journey. Tristen realized it was too late for the bird to adapt to the ocean.

DREAM BACKGROUND AND MEANING

Tristen lived in the center of a city and sailed his yacht on an inland lake. He sold boat supplies from a hut at the lakeside and did repairs. But he felt increasingly hemmed in, as he was five hundred miles from the ocean and rarely went there. He had a substantial payout from a damaged boat and had paid off his home loan. Should he move to the ocean or was it too late?

INTERPRETATIONS AND FORTUNE-TELLING MEANINGS

* A dream of seagulls flying over the ocean indicates the freedom to spread your wings and live your own way.
* A seagull flying to shore heralds an absent family member or lover returning.
* Seagulls perched on masts of yachts predict overseas travel or moving closer to the ocean.
* Seagulls on inland waters suggest you may be in the wrong place or career.
* Seagulls eating fish are signs of abundance and the resources you need.
* Scavenging seagulls recommend a new lifestyle, as your present one is not fulfilling.
* Seagulls attacking in the dream warn of hidden opposition caused by resentment at your success or freedom.

OUTCOME OF TRISTEN'S DREAM

Tristen sold his boat-supplies business and started another business, which involved being out on the ocean, sailing ocean craft. He discovered there was much to learn about the business and a great deal of competition. But he knew there was more to life, and that it was not too late for change. Seagulls as creatures of air and water reflect an inspirational or spiritual leap of faith.

Seahorse

Eric, twenty-five, dreamed he was scuba diving and became trapped in a coral reef. He had been searching for the elusive seahorses that often blended among similarly colored plants. He was trapped, and his air was running out. Then he saw hundreds of seahorses, which guided him toward a break in the reef. To his sorrow, they disappeared.

DREAM BACKGROUND AND MEANING

Eric was a first-class baseball player but was secretive about his private life. Eric was gay, and he and his partner desperately wanted children. He knew that a particular journalist was on his trail. Should he tell his fans of his sexuality and accept that he might encounter prejudice? Seahorses are a reminder that uniqueness is wondrous; they appear in dreams when the dreamer is contemplating revealing a secret that not all may accept.

INTERPRETATIONS AND FORTUNE-TELLING MEANINGS

* Dreaming of baby seahorses indicates potential success for artificial insemination, or sperm or egg donation.
* Seeing seahorses swimming in pairs reveals a very special kind of love, where twin souls find lasting security in their daily life.
* If you are worried, swimming with or on the back of a giant seahorse promises small miracles and the fulfillment of wishes.
* Because Poseidon, ancient Greek god of the sea, rode a chariot pulled by seahorses, steering a chariot of seahorses promises a happy vacation or relocation overseas.
* Since the Undines, small ancient Greek water spirits, changed into tiny seahorses whenever they wished to be unobserved, seahorses hiding say you can keep love or major life change secret until the time is right to reveal it.

OUTCOME OF ERIC'S DREAM

After the dream, Eric realized that the beautiful seahorses were guiding him to reveal his true self. He encouraged the journalist to publish an article, complete with photos of his partner. Other baseball players revealed that they were gay, too, but had held back from admitting it. When Eric's daughter grew up, she established an all-female baseball team. The unique magick of the swimming seahorse promises in dreams and actuality that uniqueness should be celebrated.

Seal (Sea Creature)

Antonia, twenty-eight, dreamed she was walking along the shore of a Scottish island and found a sealskin. She knew the legend of the Selkies, magical seals who could become women by taking off their sealskins. She put the skin on and dived into the waves, but could not breathe and, as she struggled back to shore, she saw the true Selkie claim it.

DREAM BACKGROUND AND MEANING

Antonia had an actor boyfriend she wanted to impress. She pretended she had a theater background in her homeland, Canada. On his recommendation, his company had offered her an audition, but she had never before acted. The other girl auditioning, an experienced actor, was successful. Should Antonia confess to her boyfriend and risk losing him? Since a seal is graceful and swift in the water, a seal dream says you will be happiest in your natural environment rather than trying to deceive.

INTERPRETATIONS AND FORTUNE-TELLING MEANINGS

★ Seals are in legend shapeshifters and can become mortals, but without their sealskins they lose strength, a reminder that you should be your own authentic self.

★ Seal dreams in which seals are performing in animal shows reveal the dreamer following a path that is based on illusion to impress someone, which rarely works.

★ Seals sunning on rocks suggest you need to touch base and temporarily abandon hunting for desired results.

★ Dreams of baby seals being hunted for their fur warn that someone from your past who you would sooner forget may try to make contact but has not changed.

★ A dream of an abandoned sealskin warns of trying to claim gifts or expertise not naturally yours.

OUTCOME OF ANTONIA'S DREAM

Antonia told her boyfriend the truth, and he was hurt by her deception. He and the other female actor are dating. Antonia has returned to Canada, where she is very successful. Seals are messengers telling us that what we are is what we are meant to be, and that we should fulfill that destiny the best we can.

Searchlights, Spotlights

Keith, twenty-seven, dreamed he had been captured by enemy soldiers. He was surrounded by searchlights and realized that they were revolving. There was a brief interval where, if he timed it right, he could use the temporary darkness to climb over the wall. He ran and, when the lights were not on the nearest section of the wall, he leaped to freedom.

DREAM BACKGROUND AND MEANING

Keith knew that the soccer team he played for was reducing the squad. He realized that his best chance of surviving was to not make a spectacular show of individual skills, but to merge into the team and avoid mistakes. The chance would come when the owners would be watching the last match of the season. Searchlights or spotlights in dreams represent coming under scrutiny, which is positive if you are searching for someone or seeking to impress; but sometimes avoiding scrutiny is necessary to emerge unscathed.

INTERPRETATIONS AND FORTUNE-TELLING MEANINGS

★ Searchlights that highlight a particular pathway or person in your dream tell you to pay attention to this part of your life.

★ If you have lost something precious, searchlight dreams can help you to locate it.

★ A broken searchlight suggests temporary relief from unfair scrutiny or from feeling on trial in any situation.

★ Dreaming of searchlights that are too dim reveals that you are not aware of the full facts, especially pitfalls to avoid.

★ Searchlights flashing on and off can indicate a relationship that is blowing hot and cold, which may be exciting or exhausting. Ask which.

★ A searchlight shining directly into your eyes says someone is trying to blind you to the truth or is creating an illusion.

OUTCOME OF KEITH'S DREAM

As Keith predicted, his teammates were trying to outshine one another and hold the spotlight and as a result made mistakes. Keith took his moment, while the others were occupied trying to stop one another from shining, to score just one spectacular goal, which was noticed by the opposing team's manager for Keith's excellent timing. Revolving searchlights in a dream can indicate when best to take a chance to escape, if their pattern of light is understood and followed.

Seasons

Eleanor, forty, dreamed she was lying on the ground outside a tepee and the seasons were whirling overhead, one after the other: the golden leaves of fall, winter snow that made her shiver, soft spring sunshine and the migrating geese returning, and the hot summer sun in the clear blue sky. She raised her arms but could not catch or slow down the seasons and knew she had to let them pass in their own time.

DREAM BACKGROUND AND MEANING

Eleanor had retired from being a top athlete because she had slowed with the passing years. Her friends said she should take up coaching or sports commentating, but she was not ready for a passive role. She had the chance to rent a home in the mountains, where the four seasons followed a definite pattern. But was she running away from life? Dreams about rapidly changing seasons herald a major transition and advise letting time take its course.

INTERPRETATIONS AND FORTUNE-TELLING MEANINGS

★ If you dream of a particular season, it will have significance: the fall for reaping rewards or letting go, winter for stepping back, spring for new beginnings, and summer for a surge of power.

★ If you dream of the monsoon season, stagnation will be automatically swept away; the dry season says it's time to grow or regrow relationships and business.

★ If you are dreaming of seasonal conditions at the wrong time, such as drought in spring, life needs reordering to restore balance.

★ If a dream season is particularly extreme, you may need to adapt your usual lifestyle to fit unusual circumstances.

★ If you allow the seasons to flow, you will move into harmony with yourself and others.

OUTCOME OF ELEANOR'S DREAM

Eleanor realized she was in transit and should not rush to the next phase of her life. She moved to the mountains to watch the changing year until she is ready to step back on life's wheel. Seasonal dreams occur when we need to reconnect with a different season of our lives.

Secrets

Penny, forty-one, dreamed she was clearing her late adoptive mother's house and discovered in the attic a secret box labeled with her own name, to be opened after her adoptive mother's death. In it were her birth certificate, her adoption certificate, old family photos she had never seen, and papers from an orphanage in Ireland. As she touched each, it crumbled.

DREAM BACKGROUND AND MEANING

Penny knew she had been adopted, but there were no photos with the family before she was three. In the dream box were pictures of her as a young child with a lot of other children and nurses. She knew the name of the orphanage from the dream, as it had recently been in the media. Often secrets will be revealed in dreams when a missing birth-family member is thinking of the dreamer or trying to find them.

INTERPRETATIONS AND FORTUNE-TELLING MEANINGS

★ If you dream you discover a secret garden, you are ready to enter or develop a secret love or forbidden passion.

★ If you find a secret doorway or entrance, a new opportunity that involves leaving a familiar place or comfort zone will unexpectedly appear.

★ If you dream someone close is hiding a secret, your suspicions are justified and the dream will offer clues.

★ If you dream of your secret love, you are telepathically connecting with them. If you dream that the person is as yet unknown, your family and friends may not approve.

★ If your secret love is revealed to others in the dream, you may be taking risks or may welcome your secret being revealed.

OUTCOME OF PENNY'S DREAM

Penny researched the orphanage and discovered a recent scandal that had come to light, concerning children placed there after abuse of their mothers by close relatives, some of whom were clergy. The orphanage was closed down about the time of Penny's adoption. Penny decided to not probe further. Secrets, especially surrounding a birth, may be imprinted on the dreamer's subconscious.

Seeds

Judy, thirty-eight, dreamed she was reseeding her lawn by hand, but every time she scattered a row, the birds swooped down and ate the seeds. She tried to scare the birds away, but they ignored her. Eventually, she gave up.

DREAM BACKGROUND AND MEANING

Judy was living on her own after her husband moved out. The garden had died after a hot summer of neglect. Judy wanted to move to the forest lands and run a retreat for newly divorced people to recover and plan a future in peace. But though the present house was her half of the settlement, she hesitated, hoping her husband would return. How seeds grow, the kind of land, and the nurturing they get can predict the viability and timing of a venture.

INTERPRETATIONS AND FORTUNE-TELLING MEANINGS

★ Dreaming of planting seeds that instantly grow into flowers or plants indicates great rapid returns from small beginnings.

★ If you dream that a plant is completely different from the kind of seeds you planted, the results of your endeavors will be unexpected but positive.

★ Growing seeds in a beautiful garden is a sign of male potency if there have been sexual worries.

★ If you dream you scatter seeds on dry, barren earth, you may be wasting your endeavors and should look for richer soil.

★ Dreaming of eating seeds as part of a salad says you are absorbing desired energies according to the type of seeds: mustard seeds for prosperity; pumpkin seeds for wishes; sunflower seeds for health and happiness; and sesame seeds for passion.

★ Seeds floating on water represent new beginnings and female fertility.

OUTCOME OF JUDY'S DREAM

The dream showed Judy that replanting the old land was not working, so it was time to move on and plant anew. She found her woodland retreat and planted a garden of healing seeds that, within a few weeks, were shooting out of the earth. Sometimes seeds that can't take root in a dream are a good omen for planting elsewhere.

Seesaw

Charlene, forty-five, dreamed she was a small child struggling to balance on a gigantic seesaw. Her sister, Becky, an adult in the dream, was at the other end, doing nothing. Suddenly, Becky gave a huge leap. Charlene was thrown off the seesaw, landing on the concrete. Her sister laughed and walked away.

DREAM BACKGROUND AND MEANING

Becky had bipolar disorder but refused to take medication, resulting in her being increasingly hyperactive and sometimes cruel. Becky lived with her sister, as Charlene had promised their mother before her death to care for Becky. Charlene's marriage had broken up because of her sister. Now Charlene had a new relationship, but her future partner refused to allow Becky to live with them. Seesaw dreams represent issues of balance in relationships, sometimes revealing imbalances that maintain an unsatisfactory status quo.

INTERPRETATIONS AND FORTUNE-TELLING MEANINGS

★ A dream of a giant seesaw, whatever your age, talks about the difficulties of keeping life in balance, especially if the person on the other end is bigger or inert.

★ A perfectly balanced seesaw indicates harmonious relationships in business, love, family, or friendship.

★ If you dream you are an adult on a children's seesaw, you are trying unsuccessfully to contain someone's destructive or petty behavior.

★ If no one is on the other end, you need to demand more help and support generally.

★ If you dream that a seesaw is broken, no more can be done to restore a bad situation or relationship.

★ Dreaming of falling off or being propelled from a seesaw warns of opposition to maintaining harmony.

OUTCOME OF CHARLENE'S DREAM

Charlene decided she could no longer sacrifice her life if her sister was unwilling to help herself by taking her medication. Her sister's social worker offered Becky counseling and supported housing, but Becky refused. Charlene walked away. Left to her own devices, Becky started taking her medication. If one person is working extra hard to balance the seesaw, the other person may take no responsibility for the problem.

Self-Consciousness

James, twenty, dreamed he was at a soccer match, watching his favorite team. To his amazement, he realized he had an uninterrupted view of the field and all the players. Normally, because he was so short, he had to peer around the heads of those in front of him, but not today. He received a tap on the shoulder from a spectator sitting behind him who said, "I can't see a thing, as you are so tall." James woke, wishing it was not just a dream.

DREAM BACKGROUND AND MEANING
Because of his height, James had been teased mercilessly by peers and had avoided sports as well as asking girls out. But a coach at college asked him to try out for the soccer team as James was fast and, being shorter than many players, good at evading attack. If you dream of what is sometimes perceived a physical deficiency in yourself, this can prove to be an advantage, given a change of perspective.

INTERPRETATIONS AND FORTUNE-TELLING MEANINGS
* If you dream of being short or small in a dream compared with others, if you are not in everyday life, you may feel inferior socially or in sports.
* If you are self-conscious about your actual lack of height and are tall in the dream, you may unconsciously radiate unrealized power and confidence.
* If someone in your dream asks you to stoop down because you are blocking their view, especially if you are short, they may be jealous of your potential to succeed.
* If the dream is linked with a favorite sport or activity, you may have unique abilities because of your physique.
* If a dream shows you life from another angle, expand your horizons and refuse to be labeled.
* If those who see your talents draw them to your attention, do not allow self-consciousness to stop you from testing these new expectations.

OUTCOME OF JAMES'S DREAM
James went for a soccer tryout and found he could slip through gaps in play and run like the wind. Almost everyone has a burden of inadequacy to overcome, which other people who are insecure may focus on to take away attention from their own drawbacks.

Self-Employment Success

David, thirty-eight, dreamed he was walking through a shopping mall and saw a large well-stocked shop with his name emblazoned across the windows. Business was booming. Upon waking, David wondered if this dream was a good omen or just a fantasy of his ambitions for the future.

DREAM BACKGROUND AND MEANING
Since leaving school at seventeen, David had worked for a major department store in Los Angeles. He worked his way up to assistant buyer of soft furnishings for the entire group. His job paid him a sizable income, but he was dissatisfied with the restrictions of working for such a large organization. He had been thinking about handing in his notice and putting his savings toward opening up his own business. Dreams of working for oneself provide the incentive to project the right energies to succeed.

INTERPRETATIONS AND FORTUNE-TELLING MEANINGS
* If you see your name in lights or across a window in a dream, this is manifesting on the astral plane what can be achieved with initiative and hard work.
* If you see someone in the dream who presently gives you a hard time at work, you should not let them intimidate you, as you will outperform them.
* If your dream reflects a current ambition or half-formed plan, the successful dream suggests you should be developing the idea now for when everything comes together.
* If you repeatedly have the dream, you are moving closer. Note special features of your own business that would make it stand out.
* If you use dream energies to boost your self-belief, this new confidence will open doors that make ambitions more possible.

OUTCOME OF DAVID'S DREAM
David gave himself a year to learn aspects of the business he did not know. At the same time, he worked toward a master's degree in business administration in the evenings. He then approached the CEO of the company he worked for with a proposal for a franchise to personalize soft furnishings with an at-home service. He was given six months' trial and is working toward the fulfillment of his dream.

Self-Fulfilling Prophecy

Anita, twenty-one, dreamed she was being physically held back by her mother at the starting line of a major cycling competition. Her mother said it was for Anita's own good, as she would come in last. Anita pedaled for her life and came in first.

DREAM BACKGROUND AND MEANING

Anita was a first-rate racing cyclist. Her sports coach had offered to prepare her for interstate competitions, as her practice times were outstanding. But her mother had always told her she lacked the talent to succeed. Self-fulfilling sabotage emerging in dreams often stems from childhood, where seeds of failure years later were sown by a disapproving adult.

INTERPRETATIONS AND FORTUNE-TELLING MEANINGS

★ If you dream of repeating a humiliating situation from earlier in your life, you may anticipate and attract failure by your reactions.

★ If you dream that a marriage or career will fail, you may unconsciously fulfill the prophecy.

★ If in your dream you see yourself as successful or happy in love, that is what you will attract toward you in the daily world.

★ If someone in the dream points out negative characteristics in your partner out of jealousy, beware of looking for evidence to justify the opinion.

★ If you are predicting a bad outcome for a younger or dependent person in your dream, you are setting them up to fail.

OUTCOME OF ANITA'S DREAM

Anita realized after the dream that her mother was jealous of her because she herself had failed as a cyclist in her youth. Anita chose to attend a sports college on the other side of the country, where she could make and fulfill her own prophecies. Self-fulfilling prophecy dreams are remarkably common, revealing faulty programing by oneself or others, which sets the dreamer up to fail.

Selfishness

Cathy, forty, dreamed there was a family dinner, for which she cooked a huge meal. When she sat down to eat, there was nothing left. Annoyed, Cathy said to her family, "You are so selfish. Get out." The family accused her of always being the selfish one. She was about to run after them and apologize. But when they came back, she refused to answer the door.

DREAM BACKGROUND AND MEANING

Following a family member's death, it was assumed that the wake would be at Cathy's house. To refuse would mean the family would turn on her and call her selfish. If we dream of standing up to unfair situations, it may be a rehearsal for becoming more assertive in our waking life.

INTERPRETATIONS AND FORTUNE-TELLING MEANINGS

★ If in your dream you are accused of being selfish and protest, your unconscious is warning you to not unfairly accept responsibility when others are unreasonable.

★ If you run after a partner, family, friends, or colleagues to apologize when they behave unreasonably, you may believe, from your childhood experiences, that your needs were of secondary importance.

★ If you are allowing others to impose on your good nature in a dream, you may want to feel needed.

★ If you are asserting your rights in a dream and everyone protests, have you created an expectation that has contributed to others' selfish attitudes?

★ If you dream of your parents or grandparents being taken advantage of, you may have inherited the family role of martyr and service provider.

★ If in your dream you refuse an unreasonable request and others back down, the dream will help you radiate more assertive energies in real-life situations.

OUTCOME OF CATHY'S DREAM

After the dream, Cathy sent a list of suitable venues to the executor of the will and said she would be happy to attend. Breaking the patterns of selfish behavior can be as hard for the victim as for the perpetrators, if the victim subconsciously encourages the behavior.

Separation

Colin, forty, dreamed he was a child at a big-city railway station, being separated from his mother and evacuated to the countryside because there were bombing raids. But he hid until the train left and found his way home. His mother was angry but did not send him away.

DREAM BACKGROUND AND MEANING

Colin's father had been traumatized when, as a small boy during World War II, he was evacuated and sent to a farm where he was mistreated. Colin's father had lived alone since Colin's mother had died and was unable to look after himself, but he refused to be separated from his old dog, who could not come to a nursing home. Colin worked far away and could no longer care for his father or the dog. Separation anxiety begins when a baby realizes the mother is no longer in view and the anxiety can reemerge at times of adult uncertainty.

INTERPRETATIONS AND FORTUNE-TELLING MEANINGS

★ If the dreamer is walking away from a familiar career, relationship, or situation, they are ready to break away in everyday life.

★ To dream of becoming accidentally separated from family as a child, or separated from friends in an unfamiliar country, indicates overdependency on loved ones.

★ Seeing the self in two different personas in a dream says it may be necessary to separate different parts of life or commitments.

★ Dreaming that you separate from someone in a permanent relationship can reveal differences that need resolving or acceptance that the relationship should end.

★ Dreaming of leaving home, perhaps as a younger self, suggests a desire for independence from others' emotions.

OUTCOME OF COLIN'S DREAM

Colin was experiencing his father's childhood fears in his dream, and he knew that he had to resolve the question of the dog. He persuaded an animal-loving nephew to take the dog and found a nursing home where Colin could take the dog every week to visit the old man. Neither man nor dog survived long without each other, but they had many happy days. Separation dreams, because they are so deeply rooted in the dreamer, need attention in daily life, especially if recurring.

Serialized Dreams

Lucinda, thirty-one, dreamed she was on a bus with other tourists, heading for a ruined castle on lovely grounds. When she arrived at the castle, Lucinda woke but went straight back to sleep. In the second, overlapping part of the dream, she re-entered the bus to visit the old stone town down the hill, where there was a special tea shop that sold delicious cakes, which she knew about from other dreams. As she walked in, she woke, but for a third time went back into the dream, finished her tea, and walked down the steep street to the museum, where they had Roman artifacts she had read about. She woke, having enjoyed her dreams.

DREAM BACKGROUND AND MEANING

Lucinda often had happy serial-like dreams that seem to last all night. It is not known whether the dreamer constructs the world on the dream plane or visits an existing dream setting, selected according to the dreamer's current needs. Either way, if, like Lucinda, you do not have much time for actual leisure, these remarkably common dreams refresh the dreamer as a real-life trip might do.

INTERPRETATIONS AND FORTUNE-TELLING MEANINGS

★ If you frequently dream of the same pleasurable scenario, it may be a future place you will visit that will bring great happiness.

★ If you are trying to escape the dream location, it may hold an antidote to present stress or dissatisfaction if you persist.

★ Even if you are in modern dress in the dream, you may be experiencing a past life. Most past lives are remarkably uneventful.

★ If you are just observing in your dream, you may have opted out of daily experiences because of 24/7 work.

★ If in the dream you are organizing others, it's time to let others take more responsibility in the everyday world.

OUTCOME OF LUCINDA'S DREAM

Lucinda now pictures her favorite dreams before sleep or in meditation and is able to reenter them for the next episode. Serial dreams give our inner self a chance to experience fun of our choosing.

Sex in the Golden Years

Arthur, sixty-nine, dreamed he and his wife, Patricia, sixty-eight, were holidaying on a tropical island. In this romantic setting, it was like recapturing their honeymoon forty years earlier. On their first night, they ordered champagne in their suite. That night they made passionate love and fell asleep in each other's arms. Arthur woke wishing the dream had never ended.

DREAM BACKGROUND AND MEANING

Arthur and Patricia had enjoyed an active sex life until about five years earlier. It was then that Patricia announced, "It's time we stopped doing that silly stuff." Arthur continued to want to be intimate with Patricia, but she insisted it was not going to happen. Dreams of passionate sex by one member of a couple in their golden years may reveal emotional, psychological, or physical problems in their partner, of which the dreamer may be unaware.

INTERPRETATIONS AND FORTUNE-TELLING MEANINGS

★ If you dream of passionate sex with your partner in the golden years, there is still a strong sexual connection, but circumstances must be right.

★ If you dream of having sex with a prostitute or younger stranger, you may have lost the emotional connection necessary for good sex.

★ If you dream of your partner in the golden years having sex with someone else, you may have personal insecurities about your libido.

★ If you dream of being caught with pornography by your partner, you may need to make more effort if sex is routine or nonexistent.

★ If you dream of not being able to make love, consider other means of intimacy together, which can be equally as satisfying as intercourse.

OUTCOME OF ARTHUR'S DREAM

After the dream, Arthur asked his wife what was wrong, and she replied that the last time they had sex he had made remarks about her gaining weight, and he had expected her to have an instant orgasm. He realized that he had been largely at fault and arranged romantic weekends with no pressure to have sex. Dreams of sex in the golden years can often reveal crossed wires in a relationship where expressions of love have become lost.

Sex Tourism

Josh, twenty-two, dreamed he was in a beach bar. A beautiful local girl started flirting. They went back to his hotel room, but while his mind was willing, his body was uncooperative. After just a few minutes she got dressed, demanded a large sum of money, and said her minders were outside and would hurt Josh if he did not pay up.

DREAM BACKGROUND AND MEANING

Josh was going on his first all-male holiday to the Far East and had heard he could choose a different exotic woman every night for just a few dollars. He was excited but also scared, as he had not previously experienced sexual intimacy. He could not pull out of the trip and was afraid his friends would call him cowardly if he did. Dreaming of sex tourism can be part of the vacation anticipation, but a bad dream warns the dreamer that they may not be as ready for commercial sex as they think.

INTERPRETATIONS AND FORTUNE-TELLING MEANINGS

★ Dreams about sex tourism before a planned vacation are often wish-fulfillment for a novice traveler.

★ If in the dream sex is expensive, emotional costs of the experience may be higher than anticipated if the dreamer is sensitive or inexperienced.

★ If the dream ends dangerously, this may be a warning to exercise caution.

★ If you dream of being or having a sex slave in the encounter, the actual experience may awaken feelings for which the dreamer is not ready.

★ If you dream you are offering sex for money in a vacation destination, this may be telling you that you need to prove your sexual prowess to friends.

OUTCOME OF JOSH'S DREAM

Josh discovered that his friends were all talk, like he was. But they had a good time clubbing, drinking in the sun, and arguing who would be the best sex partner to rent. Josh met a girl on the vacation and is dating her back home. Sex-tourism dreams can indicate a desire for exotic sex that may remain best as fantasies.

Shampoo

Carrie, twenty, dreamed she was in the salon where she worked. An open shampoo bottle spilled foam and bubbles, half covering the clients and chairs. The owner insisted that Carrie do something to stop the bubbles, which continued to flood the salon. Carrie refused until the owner promised to treat her fairly. The owner agreed, and Carrie put the lid on the bottle.

DREAM BACKGROUND AND MEANING

Carrie, despite being very gifted, was allowed to do only menial tasks in the salon. Her promised training and courses at the local college rarely materialized, as the salon was always short-staffed. When shampoo spills everywhere, it is a sign that the dreamer is starting to reclaim her power and reveals problems coming to the surface.

INTERPRETATIONS AND FORTUNE-TELLING MEANINGS

* If you dream you are shampooing your own hair, you are cleansing yourself of past influences or others' negativity.
* If you dream you accidentally leave shampoo in your hair, you haven't entirely removed an old problem or regret, whose effects may linger.
* If you dream someone is shampooing your hair, you are handing over your power, unless it is to someone you trust, as hair represents your strength.
* If you dream you are shampooing other people's hair, you are taking too much responsibility for others' inadequacies.
* If the shampoo fails to bubble, rewards may not materialize as promised.
* If shampoo in the dream gets in your eyes, you are not being told the truth.

OUTCOME OF CARRIE'S DREAM

Carrie confronted her boss with evidence recorded on her phone and written records of absenteeism from college and threatened to expose the exploitation to the college. The boss admitted she was in financial trouble and had been using Carrie as cheap labor. She then started to teach her and made sure Carrie was able to fulfill all her college requirements. Carrie is now a senior stylist. Shampoo dreams are more about control than about beauty, and the shampooing process shows where the real power is and should lie.

Shared Dreams

Linda, sixty-five, dreamed she was at the airport, waving goodbye to William, her husband, as she went through passport control. William looked unhappy, but she did not turn back. As the plane took off, she felt excited. When she woke, William asked, "You wouldn't really go without me, would you?"

DREAM BACKGROUND AND MEANING

Linda had been married for forty years and wanted to live in Spain for the winters. But her newly retired husband refused to discuss moving and wouldn't even look at the brochures. Dreams you share with a partner may not be romantic, but they are valuable in revealing differences that need compromise.

INTERPRETATIONS AND FORTUNE-TELLING MEANINGS

* Shared dreams can occur with total strangers, guiding both people to a location where, as twin souls, they meet.
* Dream lovers may regularly meet in a dream past world and years later may discover the encounters, even if they are not together in this lifetime.
* Dreaming conversations with a loved one far away or someone estranged can rekindle a connection so one or both make contact.
* If you call a lover before sleep, they may share your dream or sleep experience so you can deepen your soul connection.
* If you and a lover share erotic dreams when you are far apart, you may be meeting astrally.
* If you are aware of observing a partner's dream but not participating, there may be secrets or worries to resolve.

OUTCOME OF LINDA'S DREAM

William, embarrassed, admitted he had dreamed about Linda catching a plane to Spain and leaving him behind. Linda explained that she would go alone if necessary to get away from the winters that made her arthritis worse. All their lives she had done what William wanted. That morning, William suggested they go to Spain for a fortnight initially to see how they liked it. Long-standing partners may move close on a psychic as well as psychological level and pick up each other's needs in dreams.

Sheep

Gillian, twenty-three, dreamed she was a high-flying graduate in agricultural biotechnology, working in her laboratory. Each time she picked up a test tube, it broke, and the contents were ruined. Gillian cleared up the mess. Ignoring questions, she left the laboratory. Outside the laboratory was a flock of beautiful curly-haired sheep. Gillian found herself expertly shearing the sheep and spinning wool. She woke totally happy. The dream was occurring more frequently.

DREAM BACKGROUND AND MEANING

Gillian had been promised a great career in research like her parents, who were successful scientists. But she felt penned in and unfulfilled. Gillian spent her free time on her aunt's Merino sheep farm, where her aunt spun and wove the wool into beautiful garments. Her aunt had suggested that Gillian join her, as she showed great creative talent and gifts with animals. Sheep and agriculture dreams can represent a more natural—rather than achievement-focused—lifestyle.

INTERPRETATIONS AND FORTUNE-TELLING MEANINGS

* If you dream that sheep are walking in a line, beware being led on a preordained path because you are following a family tradition or what is viewed as success, which may not be for you.
* Dreaming of shearing sheep or spinning wool assures prosperity and success through creativity and hands-on work.
* If you are successfully herding sheep in your dream, you should take control of your destiny, even if others do not approve.
* A dream of sheep worried or injured by dogs indicates that others may pressure you if you break free.
* A dream of shorn sheep suggests that you have gained everything you can from a situation and should move on.
* A large flock of unshorn sheep represents resources and talents to be utilized.

OUTCOME OF GILLIAN'S DREAM

Gillian moved to the farm permanently, despite her parents' and professors' disapproval. Twelve months later she was running the farm with her aunt and exhibiting woven garments at international fairs. Sheep dreams question who is leading, and who is following, and whether this order feels right.

Shells

Lorna, thirty-two, dreamed she was walking along the shore, looking for shells to add to her collection for the jewelry she created from shells and sea glass. But, unusually, there were hardly any shells, and those that were there were broken. A huge wave crashed on shore and receded, leaving a perfect rainbow shell. Lorna put it to her ear and heard, "Time to move on," and then she woke.

DREAM BACKGROUND AND MEANING

Lorna was staying in the family beach shack on her favorite deserted shore after her contract as an advertising executive was suddenly terminated when a major client pulled out. She could no longer afford her apartment and had been staying in the shack for two months. Lorna was no nearer to deciding her future, whether to launch with her jewelry or go back to the rat race. Shells are carried by the sea at times when we need to flow with life, guided by fate.

INTERPRETATIONS AND FORTUNE-TELLING MEANINGS

* Dreams of putting a conch shell to your ear say, "Listen to your inner voice when making a decision."
* Dreaming of a living creature within a shell advises you to seek protection at home and to temporarily withdraw from the world.
* A dream of a hermit crab in a shell indicates that you may discover that a new colleague or friend is not what they seem.
* Collecting shells on the shore symbolizes memories from the past that still have power to influence or cause hurt.
* A dream of empty or broken shells reveals that an opportunity or key moment to act has passed.

OUTCOME OF LORNA'S DREAM

After the dream, Lorna realized that she wanted to stay near the coast. She obtained a job in a nearby tourist resort, in the craft store. She is creating shell and sea-glass jewelry to see if she has the talent to make a living from it.

Ship's Cabin

Benjamin, thirty-five, dreamed he was in an old-fashioned wooden cabin in a tea clipper traveling from old Ceylon, now Sri Lanka. The woman he loved was a plantation worker. He was being sent home in disgrace after a night of passion. He felt that his life was like the cabin, a comfortable prison.

DREAM BACKGROUND AND MEANING

Benjamin was due to go on a cruise with his wife, paid for by his in-laws to fix the marriage after he had an affair. The thought of being trapped with his wife for six months filled him with dread. Recently, he had been dreaming of tea plantations of Sri Lanka, and the ship was going there.

INTERPRETATIONS AND FORTUNE-TELLING MEANINGS

★ If you dream of an old world that has a meaning you may not understand, you may be linking with a past with the power to change your life.

★ If you are in a luxurious cabin, it represents a desire to travel without the risk of sacrificing comfort.

★ If you dream you are in a cramped cabin without a porthole, you may be confined in a restrictive relationship.

★ If you are reluctantly sharing a cabin with someone, have you traded freedom for approval?

★ If you dream you jump ship in a place in the dream to which you feel strong connections, you may be ready to take a risk.

★ If you dream of a person waiting where your ship is heading and you leave everything behind in the cabin, you are ready to start living again.

OUTCOME OF BENJAMIN'S DREAM

After the trip, Benjamin took only his personal belongings and got a temporary job in a tea-plantation museum in Sri Lanka. He has not met the girl of his dreams and has no future plans. For some people, a ship's cabin represents a safe way of viewing the world. For others, it is a cramped prison from which the world is seen through a porthole (see "Cruise," p. 123).

Shipwreck

Patrick, seventeen, dreamed he found a wrecked motor yacht. When he clambered onboard, the seats and lockers were slashed as though someone had been searching it. Wedged behind a berth, he found a bag of white powder and knew it was drugs with a street value that would set him up for life. But as he tugged it free, the boat lurched. The powder washed away.

DREAM BACKGROUND AND MEANING

Patrick lived in an English coastal village where there was high youth unemployment. A couple asked if he would like to earn cash guiding small boats to shore and unloading them. Patrick knew they were drug smugglers but was tempted by the easy money. Shipwrecks may offer rich pickings, but there may be major hidden costs.

INTERPRETATIONS AND FORTUNE-TELLING MEANINGS

★ Beware that others do not sabotage a plan or financial arrangement through ineptitude or lack of commitment.

★ A shipwreck can represent a disruptive influence who may encourage a family member to become involved in dubious dealings.

★ Where the ship is smashed on rocks, it is important to see what remains in the wreckage to form a basis for rebuilding love or a business, though a situation may seem irretrievable.

★ If you dream that a friend or family member is shipwrecked, they may seek support, but be careful that you do not get dragged down with them.

★ If you dream you are seeking to escape from a shipwreck, you may feel emotionally overwhelmed. Is the situation worth salvaging or should it be abandoned?

★ If you dream you survive a shipwreck, you will escape from emotional blackmail but may need to move on to be free.

OUTCOME OF PATRICK'S DREAM

After the dream, Patrick knew he was out of his depth, and if he was caught it would destroy his life. He moved to a fishing fleet farther along the coast with better pay. Since ships represent our emotional path through life, shipwreck dreams are warnings to not ignore hazards that might take the dreamer out of their depth.

Shoes

Myra, forty, dreamed she was in a shoe store because the heel had dropped off one of her evening shoes. She was on the way to meeting her partner's boss for the first time. The first pair of shoes she tried on were too big; the second, so small she could not walk. Myra decided to go barefoot. Her partner was horrified and insisted she buy the ones that were too small. They hurt, and Myra threw them across the store and said she went barefoot or went home. He left without her.

DREAM BACKGROUND AND MEANING

Myra had an ambitious boyfriend, Mike. With him she had to maintain a sophisticated act, instead of being herself. He was constantly criticizing the way she looked, acted, and spoke. Shoe dreams are linked with the life direction we are taking, and so the shoes must be comfortable in the dream.

INTERPRETATIONS AND FORTUNE-TELLING MEANINGS

* Dream shoes that are too tight or too loose suggest that we are trying to fit into someone else's image of how we should be, at the risk of losing our true self.
* A broken strap or heel suggests that the part of life represented by the shoes needs fixing.
* To lose a shoe warns that you may be avoiding following a direction you do not really want to go in.
* Going barefoot represents spontaneity, freedom, and independence.
* Mismatched pairs of shoes show confusion over which is the right course of action and lifestyle.
* Worn-out shoes in a dream suggest that you have reached the end of the road with a particular person or life situation. Walk away.
* If the dream shoes are old-fashioned, they can be ancestral past-life experiences suggesting where your life path runs parallel with an ancestor's.

OUTCOME OF MYRA'S DREAM

Myra realized that she had to be herself and not the image Mike created for her. They parted, and he married the elegant CEO's daughter. Myra opened a store that sold stylish, comfortable shoes for women to walk free.

Shoplifting

Celia, thirty-two, dreamed she was stealing bread and fruit for her children from market stalls in the Middle Ages. She knew if she was caught she would lose a hand and her family would starve. A well-dressed woman touched Celia's shoulder, paid the vendor, and handed the bread to Celia. Celia ran.

DREAM BACKGROUND AND MEANING

Celia was short of money and sometimes shoplifted to supplement her welfare benefits. She had almost been caught several times. Celia enjoyed the excitement in her dull world, living in substandard accommodations with three small children. Dreams of shoplifting may go back to a past-world experience and appear at a time the dreamer is about to take a risk, sometimes out of need, but more usually because of something missing emotionally.

INTERPRETATIONS AND FORTUNE-TELLING MEANINGS

* If in a dream you see someone you know shoplifting, they may not be as honest as they seem.
* If in your dream you are shoplifting on impulse, you are feeling unappreciated and this is a self-compensatory dream.
* If you dream you have a whole hoard of hidden goods you have taken, you have something missing in your life and are always giving to others.
* If you dream you are caught shoplifting by a security guard or police officer, or are taken to court, you may still feel worried about being found out for some past omission or minor infringement.
* If in your dream you are taking luxury goods, you are unfulfilled sexually or romantically, maybe both.
* If you dream you are stealing anything connected with work, such as computers, you may be feeling angry that you have been overlooked for a raise.

OUTCOME OF CELIA'S DREAM

The day after the dream, Celia discovered a woman's group where members could borrow stylish clothes, brush up on their skills, and get help with childcare. Shoplifting dreams are a cry, not necessarily for financial help, but for whatever you need, and may attract you to the place, time, and person where help awaits.

Shopping Channels

Phyllida, forty-five, dreamed she was in a magical grotto for adults with tubs of jewelry, sparkling party clothes, and every imaginable electrical gadget. Best of all, everything was free. Then she realized that she was trapped inside a giant television screen and there was no way out.

DREAM BACKGROUND AND MEANING

Since she had been at home after a serious fall, Phyllida had become obsessed with the shopping channels on daytime television. She loved bidding for the goods, many of which she had not opened and would never use. Every day was like Christmas. Shopping-channel dreams represent the desire to be nurtured and indulged if feeling neglected.

INTERPRETATIONS AND FORTUNE-TELLING MEANINGS

★ If you dream of amazing goods for sale on the television screen but do not buy any, this is a wish-fulfillment dream for more excitement.

★ If you dream you are buying from shopping channels for friends and family, this may be in the hope that others will give to you emotionally.

★ If you dream you are buying expensive items you do not need, you are considering an unwise financial action.

★ If you dream that goods from the shopping channel you ordered do not arrive, widen your horizons to explore new pleasures.

★ If the goods arrive and you are not charged, you may hope financial problems, probably caused by overspending, will disappear.

★ If you dream that items from the shopping channels are broken or inferior, you may be accepting second-best from a relationship.

OUTCOME OF PHYLLIDA'S DREAM

After the dream, Phyllida became aware her credit card was maxed out. She started an online sale of her unwanted goods to recoup some of her expenditure. This was successful, so she started a small online-trading business. Shopping-channel dreams can be a warning that you are compensating for an unsatisfactory lifestyle. Think about using your love of material goods to make, not lose, money.

Shouting and Swearing

Ashley, forty, dreamed she booked a vacation for her partner and teenage children to drive to Disney World. She packed and prepared for the vacation, but, to her fury, the family drove off without her. She shouted and swore. Her anger spent, she bought a first-class flight to Paris, emptying the family credit card of the vacation spending money.

DREAM BACKGROUND AND MEANING

Ashley was soft-spoken and never raised her voice or swore, unlike her family, who communicated through yelling at the tops of their voices. Now her family was arguing over where they should go for the annual vacation, which meant she stood in the middle of the battleground and kept the peace before sorting everything out for the trip. If you have an abusive partner or family members who get their own way by shouting and swearing, your dream retaliation will strengthen your resolve to resist.

INTERPRETATIONS AND FORTUNE-TELLING MEANINGS

★ If you do not normally shout and swear, doing so in a dream suggests that you are bottling up angry resentful feelings that may be turned inward on yourself.

★ If you dream you are shouting to be heard over a combative family, in daily life repeat your needs quietly but firmly till you are heard.

★ If in a dream you are swearing under your breath, you may be afraid of losing the approval of others if you express negative feelings.

★ If you dream you are shouting for help but no sound emerges, act decisively to get attention.

★ If you are shouting to warn others of danger in a dream, this is a forewarning to them of a crisis in the workplace or home that is avoidable, if they listen.

★ If others do not listen, they are on a collision course. Save yourself.

OUTCOME OF ASHLEY'S DREAM

After the dream, when the vacation-choice battle began, something snapped in Ashley. She shouted at her amazed family, using swear words they never realized she knew. Taking the family credit card, she booked herself a first-class flight to Paris and left the next day. In dreams and life, shouting and swearing are a powerful release valve to regain your voice, when they are used sparingly.

Shower (Rain, Bathroom)

Wilhelmina, forty-two, dreamed she was heading for a business lunch with her boss. Without warning, the sky darkened and she was caught in a heavy rain shower. Wilhelmina arrived at the restaurant drenched. Her boss said, "You do not seriously think I am going to offer you promotion looking like that." To her own amazement, Wilhelmina awoke laughing.

DREAM BACKGROUND AND MEANING

Wilhelmina was in line for a promotion that would involve a move of hundreds of miles, but with a big expense account, a company car, and an apartment. So why was she not excited? Shower dreams, whether in the rain or bathroom, represent an infusion of fresh energies into life that may lead to consideration of a freer lifestyle.

INTERPRETATIONS AND FORTUNE-TELLING MEANINGS

★ If in your dream you are caught in a rain shower, expect unannounced temporary disruption or interference with plans.

★ If you dream the showers are frequent or develop into a deluge, unsought change and renewal will be of benefit.

★ If you dream you are enjoying a refreshing shower in the bathroom, you need to free yourself of old burdens.

★ If a bathroom shower is cold, this may be a necessary but unwelcome reality check.

★ If you dream that a showerhead is inefficient or broken, clear away lingering problems, resentments, or unhelpful people.

★ If you dream your bathroom shower will not turn off, are you trying to cram too many activities into your schedule?

★ Sharing a shower with a partner or desired lover represents a new stage in love where adventure may override convention.

OUTCOME OF WILHELMINA'S DREAM

After the dream, Wilhelmina realized that life in the fast track no longer appealed, and she could see herself in the years ahead, striving for the top with the pressure of constantly being on show. Her dream had made her feel happy for the first time in ages. She booked a vacation to Niagara Falls. Afterward, she resigned her position and took a job as a tourist guide at the Falls until she decided what she wanted to do with her future.

Sibling Rivalry

Lorna, seventeen, in her last year of high school, dreamed she was about to receive an award for her science project when her younger sister came onstage and took the award, to tumultuous applause. Lorna walked off the stage, unnoticed.

DREAM BACKGROUND AND MEANING

Lorna was an A-grade student in high school, but her younger sister, Lia, constantly outshone her in every way. Whatever Lorna achieved was disregarded by her parents, who encouraged the rivalry. Sibling competition is inevitable and in moderation can be healthy, but dreams can reveal the depth of resentment in the less-appreciated sibling, often fueled by others.

INTERPRETATIONS AND FORTUNE-TELLING MEANINGS

★ If you dream of being young and in competition with a sibling for success or family favor, it may be that the problem still needs resolving in adult life.

★ If you do not have a sibling, the dream may refer to a friend or work colleague who outshines you in achievements.

★ If you outshine a sibling in the dream, and that is unusual in real life, you may need to focus on your unique talents rather than trying to match the sibling.

★ If you dream of a popular friend stealing your boyfriend or girlfriend, you may lack confidence in your own worth, but need to beware of underhanded dealings.

★ If you consistently have dreams about being outshone by a sibling, whether or not you have one, you should ask who is applying the pressure, maybe yourself.

★ If you have a reward or award taken in the dream by a sibling, friend, or colleague, assert your rights to respect.

OUTCOME OF LORNA'S DREAM

Lorna decided to finish her final year at another high school some distance away, where she would not be compared to her sister. Rivalry between people of similar ages and abilities for who is best loved, whether at home, the workplace, or even among friends, is often fueled by outside sources, and the competitors become victims of a power game.

Silent Movies

Louis, twenty-five, dreamed he was playing the piano in a silent-movie theater. The dream was black-and-white and grainy. Then the lights came on, and Louis was playing in a 1920s café with the audience sitting at tables and his fiancée serving food.

DREAM BACKGROUND AND MEANING

Louis's great-grandfather had played the piano in a silent-movie theater. Louis had inherited the movie reels and projector. As a child, Louis played the upright piano along with the movies. He and his fiancée, Sonia, were buying an apartment with no room for his movie equipment. To Louis's dismay, Sonia was adamant that it all had to go. If you dream of a hobby that seems lifelike, the dream may suggest a previously unconsidered way of turning the hobby into a lucrative solution.

INTERPRETATIONS AND FORTUNE-TELLING MEANINGS

* If you dream of an earlier era, this may show a strong affinity with a world that you value preserving.
* If you are watching silent movies in your dream and have no connection with them, the dream is saying you may need to help a friend or family member.
* If you are starring in a silent movie, you may need to initiate action if others are promising but not delivering.
* If you are the villain in your dream silent movie, you need to break out of a rut and rewrite the rules.
* If you are the hero or heroine in a silent movie, an opportunity will come to take the initiative if you have been hesitant.
* If you are the victim in the silent movie, you may be relying on others to fix your problem.

OUTCOME OF LOUIS'S DREAM

After the dream, Louis found premises in which to open a 1920s silent movie–themed café with Sonia. Black-and-white dreams often reveal a stark contrast between the present world and what might be achievable by using existing resources in a novel way.

Silver

Spencer, thirty-five, saw a silver pathway across the ocean under a full moon. Rising from the sea was the moon goddess, Diana. Unafraid, Spencer crossed the silver pathway. He felt no passion for Diana, who indicated a silver figure waiting on the shore. He realized it was his best friend, Tony, and they exchanged silver rings.

DREAM BACKGROUND AND MEANING

Spencer's parents were desperate for him to settle down with a nice girl and insisted it was just a phase when he told them he was gay. He worked in a very macho environment on the family ranch. The only person who understood was his friend Tony, whose parents, also ranchers, were denying *his* sexuality. Both were gifted in animal healing. As silver is the metal of the moon, silver dreams represent mystical spiritual love based on soul connections.

INTERPRETATIONS AND FORTUNE-TELLING MEANINGS

* Silver shimmering is a way guardian angels make their presence known, especially Gabriel, archangel of the moon.
* Dreaming of turning over silver coins on the crescent moon heralds the granting of wishes and growth of good fortune.
* If you dream you are wearing or have been given a silver heart locket by a lover, known or unknown, you will find romance or have romance rekindled.
* Dreaming of making love under a full moon is a sign of conception occurring soon.
* If you dream you are giving your mother or grandmother a silver gift or receiving one from children or grandchildren, mothering worries will be resolved.
* Dreaming of wearing a silver St. Christopher medal, or of giving one to a family member, is a good omen for safe traveling, especially overseas.

OUTCOME OF SPENCER'S DREAM

Spencer and Tony had a heart-to-heart and realized they had always loved each other. They told their parents and moved away from the ranching world to set up an alternative animal-health clinic. Silver for men and women is the metal of fidelity and gentle love.

Singing

Jade, forty-two, who had been a professional nightclub singer and backing vocalist since she was a teenager, regularly dreamed she was singing in an exclusive nightclub. However, when she began singing no sound came out. She left the stage crying, to the sound of the audience booing.

DREAM BACKGROUND AND MEANING

Recently, Jade had become aware that younger singers were taking the nightclub starring spots, and she feared being left behind. However, Jade had an exceptional voice and was considering applying for a place in an operetta company. Whether or not you are a singer, a dream in which you lose your power to sing, or your written or spoken words no longer impress, means it's time to explore new ways of expressing your talents.

INTERPRETATIONS AND FORTUNE-TELLING MEANINGS

★ Dreaming of singing before an audience indicates that you feel passionately about a matter or opinion and should not be silenced for fear of disapproval.

★ If you dream you are part of a group of people singing together, there will be harmony at a family gathering, workplace meeting, social event, or party.

★ If you dream you are singing in a talent contest, you need to take center stage and promote yourself, as there will be fierce competition in the relevant area of your life.

★ If you dream that people do not listen to your singing, you may need to find the right audience, outlet, or location where you are appreciated, rather than those who take you for granted.

★ If you dream you are starring in a big musical, you will gain recognition and the success you deserve for your talents.

★ If you dream you are pushed to the back of a choir or singing group, move to the front and make sure you are heard, whatever the situation or personalities the singers represent in your life.

OUTCOME OF JADE'S DREAM

Jade is studying drama and operetta singing. She has won a role and new career with a traveling operetta company. Expand horizons and sing louder if old limits contract.

Skeleton

Wilf, thirty-five, dreamed he found a memento mori in an antique store, a medieval silver skull carried as a reminder to value life, which would not go on forever. It was strangely comforting. He proudly showed this rare treasure to his wife, Jenny, waiting outside. She said it was disgusting and threw it in a trash can. He woke, realizing they had nothing in common.

DREAM BACKGROUND AND MEANING

Wilf's ex-wife was dying. Wilf promised he and Jenny would take care of his young children, but Jenny refused, saying someone else could take them and that was final. Wilf knew he could not abandon them. Skeletons in dreams may represent stark choices, where the dreamer is faced with questions of what will endure and what must be let go.

INTERPRETATIONS AND FORTUNE-TELLING MEANINGS

★ Skeleton dreams, whether of human or ancient animal remains, do not predict death, evil, or misfortune but reflect basic core values and priorities in any area of life that requires tough decisions.

★ Talking to a skull in a dream represents intellectual achievement and recognition of your knowledge.

★ If you dream you dig up a skeleton, people or memories from the past may return, but they have lost their power to trouble you.

★ If you dream you are trying to conceal a skeleton, but it keeps falling out of its hiding place, there is a secret or mistake from the past you fear may reemerge.

★ If you are having a nightmare of being chased by skeletons, you are suppressing fears of personal health and mortality, often at a time when you have lost a loved one.

★ Dreaming of dancing skeletons, like spooky Halloween figures, indicates acknowledging rather than denying hidden fears.

OUTCOME OF WILF'S DREAM

The dream was a reminder that Wilf's children were his priority. Wilf realized that his relationship with Jenny had to end. Dreams of skeletons can express the need to strip down dilemmas to the bare bones, which may involve painful but necessary choices.

Skiing

Marama, thirty-four, frequently dreamed of skiing down the slopes of Mt. Ruapehu, one of New Zealand's largest ski fields, though she had never skied. In the dream she fell but was rescued by a tall, handsome stranger who set her on her skis and then disappeared. She despaired, thinking she would always be alone.

DREAM BACKGROUND AND MEANING

Marama was the eldest of nine children in a Maori family living on New Zealand's North Island and was a journalist on a local paper. She had never had a love relationship, as she had devoted most of her time rearing her younger siblings since their mother died. Now her father was remarrying and the children were independent. Skiing represents freedom and widening of horizons, but with it the risk of getting hurt.

INTERPRETATIONS AND FORTUNE-TELLING MEANINGS

★ If you dream you are skiing alone down a mountain, you are ready to spread your wings and to take chances.

★ If you dream you fall, you may be afraid of venturing into the fast lane of life.

★ Dreaming of being rescued by a romantic stranger indicates you are seeking someone adventurous to support your bid for freedom. If the person disappears, you are unconsciously waiting for an ideal partner.

★ If you dream you are engulfed in a snowdrift, your desire for freedom and excitement is becoming overwhelming.

★ Skiing with a partner symbolizes embarking on a passionate sexual relationship involving uncertainty, which adds to the excitement.

★ Dreaming of winning a skiing competition says, "Take a chance and go all out for what you want." If you dream of losing, you may not actually want the opportunity but feel obliged to make an effort.

OUTCOME OF MARAMA'S DREAM

Marama took up skiing and applied for a reporter's job in New South Wales, Australia, where there were ski fields. Marama did not need rescuing by her tall, handsome stranger but met a fellow journalist who enjoys snowboarding. A skiing dream is an open-ended one where anything is possible.

Skinny-Dipping

Phoebe, fifty-eight, dreamed she was seventeen and on vacation near a lake with a group of friends. It was a hot night, and someone suggested they take off their clothes and skinny-dip in the waterfall. They were having a marvelous time when the camp warden arrived, and they fled into the woods, laughing.

DREAM BACKGROUND AND MEANING

In reality, Phoebe had been the only one too shy to go skinny-dipping, which she now regretted. She was now a wife, mother, and organizer of the village Women's Club. Through the international wing of the club, she had been invited on a trek for charity through the Amazon rain forest to raise money for street children in Peru. Skinny-dipping dreams reveal or revive a desire to take a chance on life and express your true self, risking the consequences.

INTERPRETATIONS AND FORTUNE-TELLING MEANINGS

★ If you dream of skinny-dipping when you were younger, you have an opportunity to recapture that freedom.

★ If you are self-conscious about taking off your clothes in the dream and diving into the water, you may fear expressing emotional and sexual desires.

★ If you are caught skinny-dipping in the dream, take a risk to become your authentic self.

★ If you do not go skinny-dipping in your dream but others do, you may hesitate to abandon convention and approval.

★ If you overcome your inhibitions in the dream, your suppressed adventurous self should not be silenced.

★ If you are skinny-dipping in the dream with someone who tempts you sexually, you may be considering abandoning a safe path for excitement. If the dream ends happily, go for it.

OUTCOME OF PHOEBE'S DREAM

Phoebe decided she was not missing her chance for adventure and went on the trek. The group camped by a waterfall, and Phoebe initiated skinny-dipping in the bright moonlight. Skinny-dipping dreams advocate taking a chance on life and sometimes on love, if the dreamer has held back for fear of losing the approval of others.

Smoke

Gloria, forty-five, dreamed she was smudging the house with a sage smoke stick after a screaming match with her seventeen-year-old daughter, Trixie. Gloria was not concentrating. The smudge set her daughter's curtains on fire. The room filled with choking smoke. Trixie screamed that she was suffocating. Gloria woke, dragging her daughter to safety.

DREAM BACKGROUND AND MEANING

Gloria's daughter had recently left home to live with her boyfriend. Trixie had forbidden her mother to contact her. But Gloria was convinced that the dream was a message that Trixie needed her urgently. Smoke can represent a call for help, as with indigenous smoke signals, a culture from which Gloria and Trixie are descended.

INTERPRETATIONS AND FORTUNE-TELLING MEANINGS

★ A dream of smoke rising upward is a good omen for instant results; smoke pouring in all directions indicates delays, and spiraling smoke indicates a spirit guide with a message.

★ A dream of a smoke-filled room is a warning that tensions and tempers are rising. Defuse a volatile situation before it escalates.

★ If you are a nonsmoker, dreaming of smoking is a sign that your needs are not being met or you are swallowing anger.

★ If in your dream you are carrying out a smoking ceremony with an herbal smudge stick or incense, you need to clear the air after an argument or simmering resentment.

★ If you dream that smoke rises from a domestic chimney, you may be seeking an ideal homelife while not fixing existing domestic issues. This may be a past-life dream.

★ If you dream that smoke is pouring from your home, check fire precautions, as you may have unconsciously noticed a problem with the electrical system or gas. Alternatively, it may mean that someone close is playing with fire emotionally.

OUTCOME OF GLORIA'S DREAM

Gloria went straight to the apartment when she woke, and she found her daughter hysterical. Her boyfriend had persuaded Trixie to smoke marijuana and she had experienced a bad reaction. She asked her mother to take her home. Smoke can cleanse, but sometimes at the cost of destruction.

Snake, Serpent

Bella, eighteen, feared snakes. In her dream, a huge snake blocked her path. She realized it was not going to bite her, as it held in its coils a golden vial. Bella reached for the vial. Instantly the snake shed its skin and became a fabulous rainbow serpent, coiling upward to become a rainbow in the sky. Bella rubbed the contents of the vial on her arms and cheeks and they shone golden.

DREAM BACKGROUND AND MEANING

From adolescence, Bella had suffered from a skin complaint that physicians could not cure. She had been invited to stay with her aunt and uncle in Australia for three months but was too self-conscious of her appearance to accept. The snake or serpent represents both the creative, regenerative power of the Australian Aboriginal creator Rainbow Serpent, and the tempter of the Bible. Your dream will reveal the most relevant.

INTERPRETATIONS AND FORTUNE-TELLING MEANINGS

★ A dream of a snake shedding its skin is a symbol of new beginnings and transformation.

★ If you are afraid of snakes, your dream snake reflects fears of betrayal or facing temptations yourself.

★ Entwined snakes represent healing, physical or emotional, and indicate that you have healing abilities.

★ To be trapped in a pit of snakes in a dream warns of hidden spite and jealousy around you.

★ If you dream you are bitten by a snake, a jealous rival may be preparing to strike. You will survive the attack, since snake venom is also curative.

★ A snake that shows no fear but does not attack represents sexual potency and fertility.

OUTCOME OF BELLA'S DREAM

Intrigued by the rainbow snake, Bella discovered it was the creator in Australian Aboriginal lore and so saw it as a sign that she should go to Australia. There she used indigenous bush essences, and her skin is much better. The snake, with strong Mother Goddess associations, harnesses the source of the inner kundalini energy center to give power to turn around any situation or overcome any opposition.

Sneezing

Hayley, twenty-three, dreamed she was boarding a plane to her dream destination with her boyfriend, Patrick. But on the way to the gate she saw a beautiful display of fragrant flowers and impulsively smelled them. Immediately, she started sneezing, and her eyes were streaming. Hayley realized that this had triggered her plant allergy, and she was denied access to the plane. Patrick went without her.

DREAM BACKGROUND AND MEANING

Hayley's boyfriend would stay away from Hayley if she had even a mild cold. Hayley had suffered from allergies since she was a small child, and Patrick was obsessively disinfecting her kitchen surfaces if she so much as coughed. Sneezing, which from Roman times was believed to release the soul via the mouth, can occur in a dream when the dreamer has problems holding back words they want to say.

INTERPRETATIONS AND FORTUNE-TELLING MEANINGS

★ If you dream that you sneeze continuously at an airport or business meeting, you are worried about drawing attention to yourself.

★ If you dream that someone else is sneezing, they may be unsuccessfully trying to hide their true feelings.

★ If in the dream you have the desire to sneeze but hold it back, you may worry about creating a bad impression by acting spontaneously.

★ If an allergy makes you sneeze, others in the dream may be toxic, and their opinions ultimately may make life hard for you.

★ If you dream that you inhale pepper and it makes you sneeze, you may be offended or hurt by someone's sarcastic manner and should not tolerate it.

★ If you dream of sneezing ruining a holiday or preventing travel, you may have doubts about your travel companion.

OUTCOME OF HAYLEY'S DREAM

Hayley decided she did not want to go on vacation with her boyfriend, who would be fussing about hygiene the whole time. When he returned, she met his mother, who suffered from obsessive-compulsive disorder, for the first time. Hayley then understood why Patrick was so obsessed with illness. He is trying to compromise, and Hayley is trying to be more tolerant of his phobia. Sneezing dreams can free inhibitions where sneezing represents threat of loss of control.

Snow

James, thirty-eight, dreamed he was due to spend the weekend with his girlfriend's parents to discuss wedding arrangements. Thick snow was falling outside the window. James went outside and started digging snow off the driveway. But the snow became even deeper. The car was half-buried. James walked toward the main road, but a huge snowdrift blocked the way. Totally unfazed, he started to build a snowman.

DREAM BACKGROUND AND MEANING

James was being pressured by his girlfriend into marriage and children before he was ready. He felt relieved in the dream that he could not travel. He knew he would be buried under his girlfriend's and her parents' smothering plans that cast him as bridegroom in their drama. The meaning of snow dreams depends on whether snow is a barrier to a desired action or a welcome relief from the need to act or make a decision.

INTERPRETATIONS AND FORTUNE-TELLING MEANINGS

★ Dreaming of driving or walking through deep snow or being caught in a blizzard advises postponing a planned journey, life change, or decision until matters are clearer.

★ Dreaming of being buried in a snowdrift reflects being snowed under with demands that have piled up and may need time to clear.

★ A dream of playing in the snow or making a snowman is a sign to devote more time to leisure and pleasure and rediscover your spontaneous inner child.

★ A dream of being hurt by snowballs suggests that there is petty childish spite against you or that you are being frozen out by envy and rivalry.

★ A dream of melting snow brings the thawing of a relationship or personal isolation.

★ Dreaming of watching snow fall from inside the home says, "Do not fight against restrictions but enjoy the breathing space."

OUTCOME OF JAMES'S DREAM

James put a brake on his relationship. His girlfriend refused to wait and rapidly found someone else to fulfill her family's dream. James is planning a snowboarding vacation with friends. Snow dreams advise taking a step backward if life or others are pushing you too fast.

Snow Globe

Layla, twenty-five, dreamed she found herself back in her childhood bedroom and saw her once-treasured snow globe. She shook the glass sphere, and the snow inside began to fall. She could see the family inside pulling a sledge through the snow toward the house lit with twinkling Christmas lights. Santa's sleigh was on the roof. She felt excited again at memories of opening her Christmas stocking and finding the snow globe inside.

DREAM BACKGROUND AND MEANING

Layla had been invited to spend Christmas Day with her boyfriend, Jules, and his young daughter, as he was a single parent. But her friends wanted her to go snowboarding. Layla found the little girl hard work and resented the attention Jules paid to her. The scene within your dream snow globe will determine the area of your life where you seek peace and harmony.

INTERPRETATIONS AND FORTUNE-TELLING MEANINGS

* Dreaming of seeing a scene within a snow globe indicates thoughts that have not yet emerged and the stored energy to fulfill desires in that area.
* If you drop a snow globe in the dream and it breaks, your illusions may be shattered.
* If you dream you are a child holding a snow globe, the globe reveals the area of your life where you seek to revive the past or a former connection.
* If you dream you are trapped in a snow globe, you are denying or not expressing your emotions and may feel restricted by pretending to be happy about a matter.
* If you dream you offer a snow globe as a gift, you are opening your vulnerable self to the person receiving it.
* If you dream you are given a snow globe, you can trust the donor with your heart and emotions.

OUTCOME OF LAYLA'S DREAM

After the dream, Layla understood that Jules was a devoted father and would be the same with their children. Next time they met, Layla gave his daughter the snow globe, and they are planning a family Christmas. Snow globes in dreams are a reminder of childhood magick and of reconnecting with simple pleasures instead of needing sophisticated entertainment.

Soap

Mabel, sixty-six, dreamed she was back in the orphanage where she and her sister had been brought up, and her mouth was being washed out with carbolic soap, because she protested while being abused. Mabel was choking and vowed she would expose the abuse. She woke still tasting the soap.

DREAM BACKGROUND AND MEANING

Mabel and her sister never discussed those days. Neither had married, as they could not bear being touched. An inquiry into abuse in the home revived her memories, but Mabel was reluctant to bring it all up again. Mabel had worked as a hospital cleaner where they used rough soap. When she came home, she would bathe with expensive rose soap, scrubbing her skin hard. Soap dreams may have a deeper meaning, especially if the dreamer was made to feel dirty as a child.

INTERPRETATIONS AND FORTUNE-TELLING MEANINGS

* If you hesitate to buy yourself beautiful soaps in your dream, cherish your body more and acknowledge yourself worthy of love.
* If you dream you buy beautiful fragrant soaps for others and no one buys some for you, you are giving too much and receiving too little.
* If you are bathing in expensive, fragrant soap, you may be washing away unresolved memories.
* If in a dream you are constantly washing your hands, you may be overly worried about germs, your own or someone else's.
* If you dream the soap produces no suds, do not accept second best.
* If in your dream someone has worn away your last bar of soap, others may be taking advantage of you.

OUTCOME OF MABEL'S DREAM

Mabel acted as a witness at the inquiry and delighted in seeing the abusive woman, now old and frail, publicly disgraced. Mabel and her sister finally discussed the past. Mabel now luxuriates in fragrant bubbles. Soap dreams involve cleansing, but sometimes bad memories caused by others, maybe long ago, need purifying.

Soccer (Football)

In her recurring dream, Emily, sixteen, was running onto the soccer field. Her parents and relatives were in the crowd, cheering her on. One of the team was injured on the pitch and was taken off. Emily was called on as substitute and immediately scored.

DREAM BACKGROUND AND MEANING

Emily had been an avid soccer follower since she was a small child. Now her school had announced that it was starting an all-girl soccer team. Emily immediately signed up, but her parents said it was not a suitable sport for females and wrote to the school principal expressing opposition to their daughter joining. This caused unrest in the family, and Emily was threatening to leave home. Sporting dreams can reinforce belief in a natural talent that should be manifest in the real world.

INTERPRETATIONS AND FORTUNE-TELLING MEANINGS

★ A recurring sporting performance dream indicates that a chance will come to participate if this has not been possible before.

★ If you see yourself as very successful in the dream, with practice and perseverance you can make progress to reach stardom.

★ If you face opposition because of stereotypes, the dream can refer to any career or interest where there are strong ageism and sexism barriers to be overcome.

★ If opposition is absent in the dream, it will be possible to overcome the obstacles in the real world.

★ If the team and even the location for a sporting event recur in a dream, this may be predictive, which your radar is picking up.

★ A success in a sporting dream can encourage persistence even when a cause seems hopeless, as it can change the energies around the dreamer to bring positive results.

OUTCOME OF EMILY'S DREAM

The principal contacted her parents and said that because Emily was considered a role model among her peers, her joining the team would do a great deal to overcome prejudice. Her parents withdrew their opposition, and Emily is already gaining a big reputation within the sport. Sporting-performance dreams that cut across barriers can open possibilities for both the dreamer and the sport, if it suffers from stereotypes.

Social Exclusion

Dana, fifty, dreamed she had driven to the home of her best friend, Chloe, but when she looked through the uncurtained window there was a party with all her friends in full swing. She drove home feeling rejected.

DREAM BACKGROUND AND MEANING

Dana had a good social life and organized the social events with her circle of friends. But after a recent hysterectomy, she had put on a lot of weight and was very depressed. Social-exclusion dreams can express being left out of friendship or workplace groups or may reflect unconsciously withdrawing because of circumstances or misread signals.

INTERPRETATIONS AND FORTUNE-TELLING MEANINGS

★ If you dream of being a child left out of playground games, a recent setback may have revived forgotten feelings of rejection.

★ If you dream you are in the darkness, walking away from a lighted social event, you may need to move on from former friends.

★ If you dream of being at work or in a neighborhood where everyone turns their backs on you, recall who was the ringleader and who the most helpful, so you can react accordingly.

★ If you dream you are helping friends build a high wall around your house, you need more self-time or need others to take more responsibility.

★ If in a dream you are excluding someone from your life, you may be rejecting the part of yourself you are projecting onto them.

★ If former friends do not open the door or answer your emails or phone calls in a dream, do the friendships need more time and effort on either or both sides?

OUTCOME OF DANA'S DREAM

Dana realized she had been pushing her friends away because she felt so bad about herself after her operation. She contacted them, and soon she was back in the center of social life. They realized they needed to share the responsibility for the social events. Social-exclusion dreams can express our own energies subconsciously pushing people away because of a present or past insecurity.

Social-Media Addiction

Mick, twenty-eight, dreamed that Sharelle, his wife, was at her computer as usual, chatting on social media. Suddenly, the whole room was filled with people he did not know. Sharelle told him these were her new online friends. She was going with them and had no idea when she would be back. The room was empty, and Mick had no idea if she would even return.

DREAM BACKGROUND AND MEANING

Mick and Sharelle have a nine-month-old daughter. Since the birth of the baby, as soon as Mick gets home, Sharelle spends two or three hours each night messaging people online. When asked about her online contacts, she becomes defensive. Mick fears she is losing interest in him and the baby. Social-media addiction arises when there is a gap in everyday satisfaction and can escalate as a substitute for real life.

INTERPRETATIONS AND FORTUNE-TELLING MEANINGS

★ If you dream that a partner or child of any age is glued to social media and this happens regularly in daily life, they are seeking ideal friendships divorced from everyday life's imperfections.

★ If they do not openly message others in your presence, the person in the dream may be hiding an obsession because they fear your disapproval.

★ If you dream you are threatened via social media by excessive contact with people you know, it's time to cut back on technology to regain your personal space.

★ If you dream you are desperately trying to connect with people on social media but no one is responding, your life may have become empty of meaningful connections.

OUTCOME OF MICK'S DREAM

Mick asked his wife how he could make her life easier. She said she had lost touch with her work friends, who were her social life pre-baby, and was lonely. Mick suggested she should go back to work, which she loved and missed. Social media was substituting for a social life for Sharelle. Social-media addiction often reflects a change in circumstances where the user is feeling isolated from actual friends and a face-to-face social life.

Southern Cross

Rohan, twenty-five, dreamed he was leaping from ice floe to ice floe. Ahead blazed the Southern Cross asterism with two of the brightest stars in the sky, Acrux and Gacrux, pointing due south. He noticed that the ice was melting. He knew he had to do something and woke determined to go to the Antarctic.

DREAM BACKGROUND AND MEANING

Rohan wanted to travel from Australia to the Antarctic to study global warming for his doctoral thesis. He would have to pay many thousands of dollars but knew the trip would make all the difference to his future. He had saved enough for the deposit on a house. His parents said he should buy the house, rather than waste it on a glorified vacation. The Southern Cross, being made up of five stars, the number of expansion, encourages following your stars whatever the financial cost.

INTERPRETATIONS AND FORTUNE-TELLING MEANINGS

★ If you dream of the Southern Cross shining bright in the southern sky, a good omen for people in the Southern Hemisphere or those wanting to go south, you are on the right track.

★ If in the dream the Southern Cross is barely visible, follow your own path to success.

★ If in the dream you see the Southern Cross from the Equator, possible for six months of the year, you will be in the right place at the right time.

★ Since the Southern Cross is part of the Crux constellation, if you want to shine you may have to accept others sharing your glory.

★ If the Southern Cross in your dream blots out every other star in the sky, be single-minded, as opportunities are increasing.

OUTCOME OF ROHAN'S DREAM

Rohan applied for a place on the trip. Some of his photographs were spectacular, and he was able to sell them. He joined the permanent field-trip staff after obtaining his doctorate and postponed buying a house. Following the Southern Cross in your dreams can offer reassurance if you are having doubts.

Sphinx

While he was still a prince and not directly in line to be the next ruler of Egypt, Thutmose IV, who was between twenty-five and twenty-eight years old at the time, dreamed he fell asleep, shaded by the Sphinx that was half buried in sand. The Sphinx told the prince that he would become king if he promised to clear away the sand. Thutmose agreed and, when he was made king, kept his promise.

DREAM BACKGROUND AND MEANING

The Sphinx, representing wisdom and the solar guardian who ensured the protection of the sun god, Ra, against the chaos serpent, Apep, in Egypt, appears in modern dreams of those with past lives in Old Egypt and those seeking answers in traditional wisdom and being prepared to work for it.

INTERPRETATIONS AND FORTUNE-TELLING MEANINGS

★ If you dream of seeing the ancient Egyptian Sphinx, you should look to the past to traditional knowledge or to a wise older person to resolve a dilemma.

★ If you see the Sphinx covered in sand, there may be major obstacles to overcome and a lack of belief by others.

★ If you dream of clearing sand from the Sphinx as Thutmose IV did, you will have to work hard to achieve your ambitions but will receive rewards.

★ If you dream of the Ancient Greek Sphinx, you may be reluctant to question a person or situation you do not fully trust, but to remain in ignorance may be unwise.

★ If the Ancient Greek Sphinx questions you in the dream, consider your motives and agenda, or those of someone close, to avoid making mistakes.

★ If you dream you successfully answer the Ancient Greek Sphinx's questions, you have the answers to a dilemma already and just need to trust your intuition.

OUTCOME OF THUTMOSE'S DREAM

Any Sphinx dream is by its nature challenging if you have been avoiding making major decisions. However, by avoiding impulsive decisions and easy fixes, rewards will be great. Sphinxes also appear in Asia.

Spiderwebs

Manny, eighteen, dreamed he was in a ruined tower, watching a huge spider spinning a web and hovering above the top of the staircase Manny had climbed. He did not try to escape, as the spider spun her rainbow-colored and shimmering web around him. Then the threads became tighter and tighter and the web turned into smothering bonds. He woke shaking.

DREAM BACKGROUND AND MEANING

Manny was in love with his history teacher, and they were having a secret affair. But the teacher had become increasingly possessive and resented the time Manny spent playing soccer and with friends. Now it seemed she just wanted him on her terms. How could he end it without getting into trouble with his parents, who were very strict? In love, webs represent possessiveness that can tip over from single-minded threads of devotion to stranglehold chains.

INTERPRETATIONS AND FORTUNE-TELLING MEANINGS

★ To dream of spiderwebs warns of deceit and manipulation by those you thought of as a devoted friend or lover, especially referring to an older woman.

★ If you dream you escape from a gigantic spiderweb, you will overcome emotional blackmail that seeks to entangle you.

★ If you dream of archetypal spider goddesses weaving the web of fate, who may appear as spiders or women covered in veils, you will take control of your destiny and have a lucky future.

★ To be in a room full of dusty spiderwebs warns against dwelling on or in the past for too long.

★ If you are sweeping or dusting away spiderwebs, you are marking a new creative or emotional beginning.

OUTCOME OF MANNY'S DREAM

Manny told his lover that the affair must end or he would report her to the head teacher. Since she had more to lose than Manny did, she unwillingly helped him change subjects and tutor groups. Webs are wondrous acts of creation, but ultimately carry dangers of entrapment for those they are woven around.

Spilling Wine

Anastasia, sixty-one, dreamed she was having dinner with a stranger she had met in the dream through a dating agency. Anastasia picked up her glass of red wine. To her horror, it slipped through her fingers and spilled all over her dress. Embarrassed, she excused herself and went to clean the stain. Upon her return to the table, her date had disappeared.

DREAM BACKGROUND AND MEANING

Anastasia's husband had died five years earlier and she had been contemplating joining a dating agency for older people. However, she felt guilty about dating another man. Spilling wine from a glass reveals not letting yourself relax socially or emotionally, as the glass limits the unbridled pleasure of free-flowing wine.

INTERPRETATIONS AND FORTUNE-TELLING MEANINGS

★ If you dream that someone you know pours wine over you, they may secretly resent you because you are more popular or successful.

★ If you dream you are drinking alone and spill your wine, you may feel guilty about indulging yourself if you normally put others first.

★ If you spill wine and you or your date leave as a result, you may be unconsciously self-sabotaging efforts, and you may need to give yourself more time.

★ If you dream you hide spilled-wine stains you did not make, you are worried about others blaming you for what is not your fault.

★ If you dream the spilled wine is white wine, a mistake is retrievable, but red wine has longer-term consequences and may leave emotional scars.

★ Deliberately breaking a bottle or throwing a glass of wine over a stranger represents a repressed desire to release sexual inhibitions. If you know the person, there are buried emotional issues in danger of spilling over as an excessive reaction.

OUTCOME OF ANASTASIA'S DREAM

Anastasia went on a date. Her date was nervous and spilled his wine. Anastasia made light of the incident and plans to meet him again.

If wine spills over from a bottle while you are pouring, welcome indulgence, passion, happiness, and spontaneous pleasure.

Spinning Around

Polly, thirty-five, dreamed she was in an aircraft, standing between two seats, when the plane started to spin. The emergency announcement warned passengers to put on their seat belts, but she was spinning around and around. The next thing she knew, she was outside the plane, examining the wreckage. Polly believed she had experienced a miracle.

DREAM BACKGROUND AND MEANING

Polly's life was in a total spin. She had been asked to permanently relocate to the Middle Eastern office of her company. Polly saw this as a big chance for promotion. Spinning dreams by their outcome predict the success or otherwise of life being suddenly turned upside down.

INTERPRETATIONS AND FORTUNE-TELLING MEANINGS

★ If you are dizzy in a dream and the world is spinning, you may be feeling overwhelmed by unexpected demands to change your life almost instantly.

★ If you dream you are in a spinning plane or car that has been hit and spins over, you should consider whether the rewards are worth the disruption to your life unless you emerge unscathed.

★ If you dream you are spinning a globe, there are going to be alternative locations and lifestyle choices not to be left to chance.

★ If you dream you are spinning upside down on a fairground ride, and if you are enjoying the sensation, leaving your comfort zone will open future doors.

★ If you dream you are terrified on a spinning ride or it breaks down, leaving you wildly spinning, this may not be the time to take risks.

OUTCOME OF POLLY'S DREAM

The next day, Polly heard that a plane going to the Middle East had crashed. The plane was described by witnesses on the ground as spinning out of control. Though she had survived in the dream, Polly felt the disruption of relocating would be too great at a time when her life was becoming secure. Prediction? Coincidence? Spinning dreams occur when there is a choice between excitement and disruption versus playing it safe. Check also for ear or blood-pressure issues if the dizziness transfers to the waking world.

Spiral Slide

Tara, twenty-three, dreamed she was a young woman in Victorian clothes at the top of a giant fairground spiral slide. The young man she was there with, who was behind her on the slide, thought it was amusing to push her hard without warning. Tara closed her eyes until she hit the ground, terrified but unhurt.

DREAM BACKGROUND AND MEANING

Tara was an attendant at a theme park, working in a reproduction Victorian fairground. While she was checking mats at the top of the large spiral slide when the park was closed, her supervisor backed her into a corner at the top and tried to assault her. She pushed him down the slide and realized that this was the man in the past-world dream. Sometimes nightmares about slides can act as forewarnings and reassurance of regaining control.

INTERPRETATIONS AND FORTUNE-TELLING MEANINGS

* Dreams of slides represent letting go of certainty and, if exciting, indicate you are ready to take major physical or financial risk.
* A dream of an old-fashioned spiral slide may be a past-world memory, whether happy or otherwise, of when you had control taken from you.
* A dream of a giant water slide represents deep emotion, letting go sexually, or making a commitment. If in your dream you cannot swim, you may struggle to express your deeper feelings.
* A dream of an adult stuck on a children's slide warns against an unwise choice or speculation.
* Dreaming of being a small child pushed unwillingly down a slide says you should confront bullies.
* Dreaming of happy experiences on a slide suggests that you will have opportunities to progress rapidly but need to be ready.

OUTCOME OF TARA'S DREAM

Tara decided to take swimming and lifesaving classes and transferred to the sister water park. She heard months later that the supervisor who assaulted her was dismissed for harassment of young employees. The dream revealed Tara's soul enemy from a past world, who she overcame in this world. Slide dreams are about choice versus coercion.

Squirrel

Gordon, forty-five, dreamed he was watching squirrels frantically collecting food, burying it, and stealing one another's hoards. He tried to stop them, but they turned on him, climbing on him and biting him. He woke defending himself and walking away.

DREAM BACKGROUND AND MEANING

Gordon was trade union leader in a large company. There were strong rumors of a takeover, but Gordon had been assured that the workforce would remain the same and pay and conditions would improve. He reassured his members, but they would not believe him. Chattering squirrels mindlessly running up and down trees suggest it may be hard but necessary to step back to distinguish between rumor and valuable warnings.

INTERPRETATIONS AND FORTUNE-TELLING MEANINGS

* A dream of squirrels burying food represents the need to conserve resources and time, as you may suddenly receive urgent demands on finances.
* A squirrel burying an excessive mound of food while other squirrels hang back represents an acquisitive person in your life at work, socially, or at home who refuses to share ideas and resources.
* Squirrels chattering in a circle warn of a clique at work or in the neighborhood that gossips about others and spreads rumors.
* A dream of a squirrel dashing around collecting food says you will be able to get out of debt and save money if you make a concentrated effort.
* Squirrels that are indoors, whether in the home or workplace, advise against taking work worries home and home worries to work.

OUTCOME OF GORDON'S DREAM

Gordon resigned as union leader and focused on building up the security of his own job so the takeover would be smooth for him. Others removed money from pension funds, began in-fighting, and threatened strikes. When the takeover happened, some were let go because of their hostility. Uncoordinated squirrel activity can indicate business arguments and unnecessary rivalry, so jobs and finances are put in jeopardy by destructive rather than cooperative behavior.

Stairs, Steps

Jack, thirty-five, had a recurring dream of being a servant in a large mansion, climbing the back uncarpeted stairs while carrying a bucket of coals. When he reached the top, he found himself at the bottom again.

However, in the most recent dream, he left the bucket at the bottom of the stairs, crossed the gardens, closed the gate, and waved at a wagon approaching along the road. Jack did not have the dream again.

DREAM BACKGROUND AND MEANING

This could have been a past-life dream. Jack had a secure but monotonous job with few prospects of promotion. A former school friend was planning on working his way around the world and running a tourist bar in Thailand. He had invited Jack along. Jack had refused, but he was regretting his decision. Stairs or steps represent upward or downward movement through life in career or personal ventures.

INTERPRETATIONS AND FORTUNE-TELLING MEANINGS

* Dreaming of walking upstairs says you will gain promotion and prosperity in the world.
* Walking down suggests loss of anticipated advancement, especially if the stairs are uncarpeted or are back stairs.
* Walking up a wide staircase with a red carpet promises increased opportunities and recognition, while a dark narrow one talks of family secrets that should be revealed.
* Dreaming of falling downstairs warns that your position is not secure, whether in love, finances, home, or career.
* Depending on the location of the stairs, to dream of continually walking upstairs and then down again means you may be trapped in a situation going nowhere that only you can remedy.
* Dreams of carrying others' luggage upstairs warns that you should shed what is not for your benefit.

OUTCOME OF JACK'S DREAM

Jack joined his friend in traveling, and they eventually obtained work in Thailand teaching English while they saved for their dream bar. If dream steps are not leading anywhere, it may be time to walk away, whether the stairs are related to home, work, or a social activity.

Stalker

In her dream, Fleur, seventeen, was approached in the street by a stranger with his face covered who told her he knew where she lived because he had been tracking her phone. Fleur ran away, but on the next corner she was approached by another stranger with a covered face, who said he also knew where she lived. He grabbed her, but she fought him off and woke crying.

DREAM BACKGROUND AND MEANING

Fleur has recently been receiving harassing phone calls and text messages from random numbers and is now afraid to look at her phone or take it with her in case she is tracked. Stalker dreams can mirror and magnify a real threat but give the victim advance warning to unconsciously prepare for any attack.

INTERPRETATIONS AND FORTUNE-TELLING MEANINGS

* Faceless or nameless dream stalkers represent fear of being constantly watched by a force more powerful because of its anonymity.
* Stalker dreams express a sense of helplessness and isolation in life generally. Share your fears.
* If you see a shadow stalking you, these are suppressed unresolved guilts.
* An ever-present dream stalker suggests that you are downplaying a problem, hoping it will go away.
* A phone or social-media dream stalker can be someone who, in everyday life, takes excessive interest in your love life or family life, and should be discouraged.
* An ex-lover stalking you in dreams indicates they are not over the relationship. Be careful to discourage them.

OUTCOME OF FLEUR'S DREAM

Fleur's stalker was waiting outside the college and tried to snatch her. The dream had forewarned her, and she kicked him hard. A lecturer ran to help. As he seized the assailant, his hood came off. The stalker was an ex-student and was arrested for harassing other girls as well as Fleur. Stalker dreams awaken primal fears of being abducted and harmed so deep that the victim may find it hard to report the actual crime.

NOTE: If you find yourself in this position, there is help available. Notify the police or a helpline in your local area.

Stars

Ellen, nineteen, dreamed she was standing under a galaxy of stars in an open field. One of the stars became brighter and moved across the sky, and she followed it. Suddenly, she was standing center stage under starry lights. The audience was applauding her. Ellen woke full of confidence.

DREAM BACKGROUND AND MEANING

Ellen was the best singer and musician at her drama college, but was self-conscious about the scars on her face from a recent traffic accident. There was a forthcoming audition for the starring role in the annual college performance at the local theater. A jealous rival told Ellen she was wasting her time, as her scars were too disfiguring. Ellen decided to not audition. Stars are a lucky omen representing a wish coming true and the fulfillment of ambitions if pursued. Let nothing or no one deter you.

INTERPRETATIONS AND FORTUNE-TELLING MEANINGS

★ A dream of a bright star overhead or one that moves close indicates future fame and fortune using your existing talents in the area where your gifts lie.

★ A dream of a shooting star heralds a sudden flash of inspiration or that a loving deceased relative is supporting you.

★ A single twinkling star foretells the conception and birth of a very gifted baby.

★ Two stars joined or close together signify a twin soul either in your life or coming into your life soon.

★ Stars that fade warn that an opportunity will be missed unless you actively pursue it.

★ Following a moving star will guide you to success and maybe the chance of overseas travel.

★ Dreams of traveling to or through the stars can be a form of out-of-body travel and indicate that you are a star soul.

OUTCOME OF ELLEN'S DREAM

Ellen attended the audition because of the dream, gained the starring role, and was a great success. She is using special makeup until the scars fade. A talent scout has offered her a small role at an international drama festival.

Starting a Business

Tuyet, twenty-seven, dreamed she was in the nail salon where she was working. She spilled all the nail polishes and knocked everyone's sterilized manicure sets onto the floor. The manager screamed at her to get out. Then Tuyet found herself in a beautiful, tranquil spa, directing other Vietnamese-born women, who were massaging clients' hands and feet with flower waters. She woke dreading going to work.

DREAM BACKGROUND AND MEANING

Tuyet moved to New Zealand from Da Nang, Vietnam, where she qualified as a beauty therapist. In her new salon she was required to work fast and focus on the nails, not on people. But she needed the work. A friend from Vietnam was experiencing similar problems in her salon. Sometimes dreams reveal how an alternative business could be created in a unique, viable way.

INTERPRETATIONS AND FORTUNE-TELLING MEANINGS

★ If you are having nightmares about your present employment, maybe you should become your own boss.

★ Dreaming of finding run-down premises says you will need determination and perseverance in the early days to overcome setbacks.

★ If you find the perfect dream premises, your rise will be rapid and easy.

★ If you dream of being cut off by inadequate Internet, you may need more direct initial contact with customers and suppliers.

★ If in the dream you identify a market or regular outlet for your creative output, your sleep radar is making connections.

★ If you dream that someone destroys your stock, beware of jealousy of an established company. This is a warning of underhanded dealings.

OUTCOME OF TUYET'S DREAM

Tuyet's parents and the parents of the other woman having problems agreed to set them up in business. Their spa, called *From Soul to Toe,* became an oasis for tranquil, holistic experiences, and soon they were able to repay their parents. Dreams of setting up a business expand the boundaries of possibility by revealing alternatives not considered or dismissed as impractical.

Starting School

Maureen, twenty-six, dreamed she was a small girl standing in a playground with big children rushing around, shouting and bumping into her. When the bell rang, they disappeared into the school, leaving her standing alone. She looked across the playground and saw her own young son, also alone. She rushed toward him, but he disappeared.

DREAM BACKGROUND AND MEANING

Maureen's only son was due to start school, and he had been confident about it but was getting nervous as the day approached. Recently, Maureen had been dreaming of her own first day at school, where she had been left alone in the playground by mistake. A dreamer's child starting school for the first time or moving to a new school may be picking up the dreamer's anxieties stemming from their own bad experiences.

INTERPRETATIONS AND FORTUNE-TELLING MEANINGS

★ If you dream of your child happily starting or changing schools, you are linking into their confidence vibes, ensuring a successful transition.

★ If you dream of your own early traumatic school experiences, your child starting has triggered memories from your past.

★ If you dream of your child not settling in at school, your unconscious radar may be telling you it's the wrong school.

★ You may be telepathically picking up hidden doubts or fears your child has.

★ If you see your own child present in your childhood school dream, you are psychically entangled, each amplifying the other's uncertainty about the parting.

★ If the school is large, your dream may be alerting you to rehearse safe zones where teachers and helpers are found, and the places you will drop off and collect your child.

OUTCOME OF MAUREEN'S DREAM

Maureen realized that she was reluctant to let her child go to school, due to the many happy times they enjoyed together. However, by boosting her son's confidence, he happily entered school. When a child starts school for the first time or changes schools, it can be traumatic for both parent and child.

Statues

Jeanette, thirty-five, dreamed she was locked in a museum filled with classical marble statues, which started changing into brilliantly colored fantastic mythical creatures of all shapes and sizes that whirled around her. Then the curator opened the door, and they were still and marble again.

DREAM BACKGROUND AND MEANING

Jeanette was a sculptor, but she was rejected for a series of bronze birds in flight for the town square for the centenary and was asked to work instead on creating a children's fantasy walkway around the town, which she did not consider real art. Statues represent a static phase when we are locked in a certain situation and mindset.

INTERPRETATIONS AND FORTUNE-TELLING MEANINGS

★ If you dream you are in a gallery or garden of beautiful statues, you are entering or are currently in a period of harmony.

★ If you see dancing or colorful statues, unexpected new life and opportunities will occur in a previously static situation.

★ If you dream a statue is broken, you may be getting only a partial picture of the truth.

★ A missing arm suggests you may have to reach out for an opportunity; a missing leg, being held back; lack of facial features, deceit; and missing genitals, a sense of powerlessness.

★ If you dream you are creating a statue from stone or clay, there will be a chance for you to express your creativity for profit.

★ If you dream you are locked in a hall of statues, you may be or may feel excluded from the action or the social or communication loop.

OUTCOME OF JEANETTE'S DREAM

Jeanette recalled her dream of the fantasy animals and created a multicolored walkway of unicorns, dragons, phoenixes, and other mythical creatures. Her creations received a lot of enthusiastic publicity. Jeanette has found herself in great demand for fantasy sculptures. Statues preserve what is of beauty, and that can vary according to those who seek its inspiration.

Stock Market

Aaron, thirty-six, dreamed he was in an overseas stock exchange, confused by brokers talking fast to each other in different languages and by boards flashing ever-changing information. He knew he could not afford to hesitate or make a mistake. A stranger was jostling him to act or get out of the way. The room went quiet; everyone had gone. Aaron realized he had left it too late.

DREAM BACKGROUND AND MEANING

Aaron was pressured to take a job in an international company that offered travel, a good salary, and a chance to invest his savings to share in the profits. Yet he hesitated at life in the fast lane. He was a country boy at heart and, despite his qualifications, was happy working in a small-town bank, living with his wife and two children in a house surrounded by fields. Stock market dreams reflect external pressure to make a fast decision. Your feelings in the dream are your wisest guide.

INTERPRETATIONS AND FORTUNE-TELLING MEANINGS

★ If you have a stocks-and-shares dream the night before a major transaction, it is an omen, either good or ill, according to the dream.

★ If you are buying shares in a dream, even if not relevant to your waking life, it's a good time to invest, whether in finances, career, or love.

★ If you dream you are selling shares for a profit, it's a favorable time for initiating changes in your life.

★ If you are selling shares at a loss or are ruined financially by dealings, rethink any major lifestyle decisions or changes.

★ If you dream you are on the floor of the stock market, slightly ahead of the fluctuating exchange rates, trust your instincts and follow intuition in life.

★ If you are given insider information in your dream, check before speculating, as there may be hidden conditions.

OUTCOME OF AARON'S DREAM

Aaron realized he and his family were happy and were making sufficient money. He turned down the job but started advising wealthy local clients about their investments. Stock-market dreams with fast decisions and potential rewards cast up warnings of what may be lost as a trade-off—in Aaron's case, his peace of mind.

Stork

Soraya, forty-five, had a Disney-like dream in which storks were carrying babies in baskets in their beaks to different houses. But they did not stop at her house. Then she saw a stork with two older children riding on its wings; it stopped outside her front door, and the children alighted. She said there was a mistake and shut the door. She woke, feeling cheated, because everyone else had a baby.

DREAM BACKGROUND AND MEANING

Soraya, who had married four years earlier, had been told after numerous failed IVF treatments that their chances of having their own baby were small, and they had run out of money. None of the alternative medical interventions gave guarantees. Must they give up?

INTERPRETATIONS AND FORTUNE-TELLING MEANINGS

★ A universal symbol of safe pregnancy and birth, stork dreams predict an addition to the family, whether by birth, adoption, or remarriage.

★ A stork carrying a baby in its beak, traditionally from the salt marshes, is an excellent omen if an older couple is trying to conceive a child.

★ A stork perching on a roof in a dream promises domestic happiness and an increase in good fortune.

★ A stork flying away from a home warns that more input is needed between partners if they are to maintain or revive love.

★ If a solitary stork appears in your dream, it indicates a new beginning or the launch of a personal creative venture.

OUTCOME OF SORAYA'S DREAM

After the dream, Soraya saw an advertisement for adopting older siblings in need of a permanent home. The ones in the picture looked remarkably like the children the dream stork brought her. Soraya and her husband are exploring the adoption route. A stork dream representing new beginnings can open viable alternatives to what is most desired, especially connected with children.

Storm

Paul, twenty, dreamed he was trekking across an open plain in Southeast Asia as a storm was approaching. He started to run. The people he shared a hostel room with called him to join them as they sheltered under the only tree for miles. But Paul felt it would be dangerous to shelter with them. They became angry when he kept running. Paul found a cave, from which he watched the storm pass over.

DREAM BACKGROUND AND MEANING

Paul had been traveling solo through Southeast Asia. At the hostel, he met a group of friendly travelers. However, he discovered one of them going through his backpack and repacking the contents. They said Paul should join them, as the area was dangerous and prone to have bandit raids. But Paul hesitated. A sudden fierce storm can warn of impending danger and suggest that shelter offered by others may not be safe.

INTERPRETATIONS AND FORTUNE-TELLING MEANINGS

* If you dream that a storm passes overhead quickly without damage, it predicts the end of a period of tension or waiting.
* If it is a noisy storm with pouring rain and loud thunder, you should speak and act decisively rather than internalizing resentment.
* If you dream that lightning destroys a building or tree, beware of sudden unreasonable anger from an authority figure or domineering family member.
* Flashes of lightning in the distance moving nearer indicate surging personal power for dramatic change.
* Dreaming of being safe in the eye of a storm suggests that disruption or unwelcome changes will not affect you.
* If you dream of an electric or tropical storm, there may be unexpressed passion or unrequited love.

OUTCOME OF PAUL'S DREAM

As a result of the dream, Paul decided to leave the hostel without warning and changed his route and his security details. Later he learned that a gang posing as backpackers was robbing tourists by obtaining their security information. Brewing storms in dreams are warnings that danger may be building, and deflecting action is needed.

Stranger

Toby, fifty-five, dreamed he was in a strange town. He could not understand what people were saying. The young people were trying to remove him, and he realized that to them he was the stranger. Then he saw his wife driving toward him, and she stopped the car to let him in.

DREAM BACKGROUND AND MEANING

Toby felt like a stranger at work, as his young trainees would laugh when he asserted his authority. At home his teenagers ignored him and played their loud music even louder when he reproached them. His wife told him he had forgotten what being young was like. Toby even felt alienated from his wife, who mixed happily with everybody whatever their age. When we suddenly become the stranger in our dreams, we may have lost or never explored part of ourselves that enables us to connect with others.

INTERPRETATIONS AND FORTUNE-TELLING MEANINGS

* If a stranger is chasing the dreamer, there may be a new strategy or aspect of your life needing recognition.
* If a stranger in the dream seems to know you, it may be part of yourself you have been denying through fear of change.
* A friendly, helpful stranger in a dream signifies a change of attitude to welcome others.
* An unpleasant or frightening stranger represents changes in home or workplace of which you disapprove.
* Falling in love with a stranger in a dream is a sign of approaching love from another location if you are unattached; if within a relationship, you may be seeking a stereotype and rejecting the reality.
* Being told by strangers that *you* are the stranger may turn your self-image upside down.

OUTCOME OF TOBY'S DREAM

After the dream, Toby realized that he had become a stranger, locked in outmoded prohibitions that prevented his reaching out to others. He started encouraging the younger people at work to share their ideas, which were like his own that he had abandoned. He took his children on an adventure vacation and talked to his wife about plans they still shared. Stranger dreams usually occur when the dreamer finds themself alienated from the world they live in while refusing to recognize that they have created barriers.

Strawberries

Ruth, forty-eight, was a young teenager in her dream, being fed strawberries by her first boyfriend, who vowed eternal love. They sat together in the strawberry fields in soft sunshine under blue skies, and she wished the dream would last forever.

DREAM BACKGROUND AND MEANING

Ruth had recently divorced and had discovered on social media that her first boyfriend was also divorced. She wondered whether to contact him to see if a love that had ended when her parents moved away from the area could be revived, as she had never forgotten him. Strawberries in dreams represent ideal, innocent love memories untouched by time and circumstances that, like strawberries, may retain their sweetness.

INTERPRETATIONS AND FORTUNE-TELLING MEANINGS

* Dreaming of eating strawberries says you should indulge yourself more and relax if you have been working too hard or devoting yourself to others.
* Dreaming of sharing strawberries with a lover, known or as yet not connected with, suggests that a lover from the past may return and revive happy memories or more.
* Making strawberry jam indicates domestic happiness and a permanent home if you do not already have one.
* If strawberries are tasteless or sour, you may be tempted into a love affair that will bring disillusion after the first taste of forbidden fruit.
* Strawberries and cream predict abundance, good fortune, and a chance to experience luxury.

OUTCOME OF RUTH'S DREAM

Ruth made online contact with her first boyfriend, posting a slightly faded photo of them together in the strawberry fields. He replied. They flirted online and met for a romantic picnic in which she took along strawberries. But though fun reminiscing, the magick had gone, and they lost contact again. However, the dream reminded her that she was still that young, romantic girl inside. Strawberry dreams can revive parts of ourselves that we have lost and remind us that what we want may lie in the future, not the past.

Street Girls

Anya, twenty-five, dreamed she was a young street girl in Thailand, sent there to support her impoverished farming family. Other girls told her she might find a rich protector or husband among the wealthy older tourists. Anya's first client was a surly elderly man. When she saw him, she fled for home.

DREAM INTERPRETATION AND MEANING

Anya felt great sympathy for the street girls. She was staying in Pattaya, Thailand, with an older man with extensive business interests in the Far East. He was very generous toward Anya, but she worried that in time her appeal would fade. If you dream of selling your body in an exotic setting, you are seeking romance, passion, and luxury in a maybe mundane relationship.

INTERPRETATIONS AND FORTUNE-TELLING MEANINGS

* Street-girl dreams reveal hidden doubts about the viability of a lifestyle where personal identity is compromised.
* If you run away in the dream before selling your body, your unconscious is warning you of the pitfalls of going ahead with using sex as coinage, however great the potential gains.
* If in the dream you are forced by economic need into selling your body, you may be questioning the price of a relationship where sex alone is the glue.
* If you are abused in the dream by a client or regular lover, you may have felt unworthy of respect from a partner.
* If in the dream money and sex have become inextricably linked, perhaps you are afraid to ask for what you need from a relationship for fear of rejection.
* If prostitution dreams portray your partner as a client, sleep fantasies can spice up your love life.

OUTCOME OF ANYA'S DREAM

After the dream, Anya told her lover she wanted a regular relationship with him. He already had his eye on an exotic young street girl, so Anya went home. She is pursuing a master's degree in women's studies.

Stroller

Lucy, twenty-five, in her dream was a little girl, sitting in a stroller. Her cousin Peg, a few years older, was pushing the stroller and refused to allow Lucy to get out of it at the playground, saying it was too dangerous. When Lucy insisted, Peg became angry, tipped Lucy out, and strapped in another little girl, who was alone in the playground.

DREAM BACKGROUND AND MEANING

Lucy had grown up with her older cousin Peg next door. Peg had protected her at school, chosen her clothes, and advised her on her love life. Lucy totally depended on Peg's approval. However, lately Peg would get annoyed if Lucy expressed a different opinion from Peg's. Stroller dreams question who is pushing, or controlling, and who is dependent.

INTERPRETATIONS AND FORTUNE-TELLING MEANINGS

★ If the person pushing the stroller in the dream is recognizable, you may willingly be handing over your power as the price for friendship or love.

★ If you dream you are too big to fit in the stroller, it may be time to quit being dependent.

★ If the person pushing the stroller refuses to let you walk, their self-image is tied up in others needing them.

★ If the stroller breaks or refuses to open in the dream, an unequal relationship is starting to unravel.

★ If the stroller is a child's toy and the pusher is pushing a doll, they will seek an instant replacement if the dreamer resists.

★ If you are happily pushing a stroller or full-size pram in the dream, this is an excellent omen for the future conception and health of a child.

OUTCOME OF LUCY'S DREAM

Lucy told Peg she was not going to share an apartment with her as they had previously planned. Peg was furious and severed all ties with Lucy. Now Peg has become a mentor to a young coworker. While stroller dreams herald happy pregnancies and families, if the dream child is oversize and the pusher is determined not to let go, a particular relationship or more than one should be examined for dependency issues.

Substitute

Cheryl, nineteen, dreamed she was preparing to lead a major cheerleading event with her squad, who she had known from childhood. Then she saw Sandra crying on the sidelines. Sandra told Cheryl that her mother was coming from another state because Sandra had said she would be one of the squad in the event. Cheryl laughed and said, "No chance." The others in the clique also laughed when Cheryl told them. But Cheryl woke uneasy.

DREAM BACKGROUND AND MEANING

Cheryl had known the cheerleading squad from childhood because their mothers had all been cheerleaders themselves at the same college. But Sandra was an outsider to the clique, and so Cheryl kept her as a substitute. Substitute dreams talk about replacing one person or item with another but can hide deep emotions about value.

INTERPRETATIONS AND FORTUNE-TELLING MEANINGS

★ If an item is broken and another of equal or greater value is substituted in the dream, an alternative plan or offer in your life can be advantageous.

★ If you dream you are offered a cheaper substitute for what is broken or not available, you may feel you are being asked to accept second best in life or in a relationship.

★ If in the dream you are always on the substitute bench in sports or cheerleading but know you are worth a place in the lineup, you may need to be more assertive.

★ If you substitute a healthy food or drink for an unhealthy one in a dream, it's time to quit a bad habit or to better take care of your well-being.

★ If you are acting as a substitute for someone who is absent, ill, or on leave at work, in sports, or in the performing arts in your dream, you will have an opportunity to shine, leading to more permanent advancement.

OUTCOME OF CHERYL'S DREAM

Cheryl felt guilty that they had never given Sandra a chance. Cheryl incorporated Sandra as an extra cheerleader in the event, and Sandra's mother was thrilled. Cheryl realized Sandra was talented and often substituted her for other cheerleaders, though they resented it because she was not *one of them*. In dreams and life, a substitute can be resisted for the wrong reasons or for fear of change.

Suicide

Nathaniel, twenty-two, dreamed he was borrowing his younger brother Sam's computer. He came across a site Sam had joined, describing ways of committing suicide. There was a forum encouraging other young members to coordinate their plans to end life. Nathaniel awoke worried, as the dream was so real.

DREAM BACKGROUND AND MEANING

Nathaniel's brother was depressed and stayed in his room on his computer all day, refusing to go to classes. His parents had high-powered jobs and had left the boys to be brought up by the housekeeper. But what could Nathaniel do, based on a dream? Suicide dreams can be a psychic call for help from someone we are close to, and Nathaniel had acted as a surrogate parent to his brother.

INTERPRETATIONS AND FORTUNE-TELLING MEANINGS

★ If you dream about a relative or friend committing suicide and you know they have emotional issues, you are linking into their energies and may be able to offer tactful support and point them toward professional counseling. If the dream is urgent and feels immediate, you should contact them, as you may be in time to prevent a tragedy.

★ If you dream of someone you know who has recently committed suicide, they may have thought of you as they were dying.

★ If you dream the person is no longer alive, all you can do is to send blessings, hoping that they have found peace.

★ If you dream of committing suicide, you may feel hopelessness in some area of your life or generally. Take the dream as a sign to seek support.

★ If you dream of your relatives, partner, or friends attending your funeral and weeping, you may feel angry about unfair treatment, which you need to express.

★ If you dream of a celebrity committing suicide, you may be fearing a loss of status or recognition through a mistake or someone's malice.

OUTCOME OF NATHANIEL'S DREAM

Nathaniel, who no longer lived at home, invited his brother to stay with him, looked at his computer, and found the suicide site of the nightmare. He took his brother under his care and enrolled him in a new high school with good pastoral care. Especially vivid and urgent life-and-death dreams should not be ignored, even at the risk of overreacting.

Suitcase, Travel Bag

Charlotte, thirty-five, dreamed she was waiting at the airport carousel for her suitcase. Many looked identical and when she tried to claim hers, she realized someone had taken her suitcase, leaving one with ripped, dirty clothes in it that were too small. She complained to security, but they said she should have marked her case so it stood out from similar ones.

DREAM BACKGROUND AND MEANING

Charlotte felt she had lost her identity since marrying into a large established family who had farmed the same land for generations. She wanted to return to her career as a teacher, but the family expected her to stay home, help in the kitchen feeding the workers, and produce an heir. If you end up with the wrong suitcase, you may be uncertain about your identity and place in the world.

INTERPRETATIONS AND FORTUNE-TELLING MEANINGS

★ A dream of a designer suitcase reveals that you have high ambitions that you can fulfill.

★ A suitcase packed for a vacation promises fun and happiness ahead. If you have no plans, take a spontaneous break, as the time is right for an adventure.

★ A fake designer case says you should value yourself as you are and not worry about creating an impression.

★ A lost suitcase warns you to guard your reputation and take care what you say to whom.

★ An empty or battered suitcase implies that you have been giving too much of yourself to others.

★ A suitcase or travel bag, its contents, and whether it is well used or unopened represents the unique qualities we should manifest in the world and not keep shut away.

OUTCOME OF CHARLOTTE'S DREAM

Charlotte went back to teaching, though her husband's family disapproved. She and her husband moved out of the farmhouse to a small house on nearby land and are planning their first vacation together.

A heavy suitcase can indicate that you carry burdens of responsibility that belong to others. Traveling light says you do not need anyone's permission to be yourself.

Sun

Ben, forty-seven, dreamed he was wearing white robes, guarding an old stone circle. Inside, women in white were performing a sun ceremony so that the sun would be reborn at Midwinter. Warriors with black helmets and spears came over the hill. Ben tried to drive them off but knew he was outnumbered. There was a huge explosion of light and heat from the center of the circle. The men fled. The sun rose over the horizon at the same moment the chief priestess announced that the sun was reborn. Ben woke puzzled. He was a logical accountant and fought against his spiritual side.

DREAM BACKGROUND AND MEANING

Ben had been very depressed, as his colleagues bullied him because he was gentle and helped impoverished clients for reduced fees. Dreaming of journeys to the sun, solar celebrations, or sun priests and priestesses may link with past worlds, indicating a spiritual nature, often hidden because of others' cynicism.

INTERPRETATIONS AND FORTUNE-TELLING MEANINGS

★ Enjoying sunshine among growing crops and flowers is a symbol of coming joy, fertility, and health, and a reminder to enjoy happiness each day.

★ Seeing the sun rise in a dream indicates new beginnings, especially if it is at a seasonal change point.

★ A bright or noonday sun is a sign of success, prosperity, and confidence.

★ Clouds in front of the sun conceal obstacles ahead to success. If the clouds clear, this delay is only temporary.

★ An overly bright sun in a desert indicates dangers of burnout.

★ The setting sun says it is time to move on to a new lifestyle if the 24/7 dash is proving unfulfilling.

OUTCOME OF BEN'S DREAM

Ben stood up to his colleagues, who backed off. He has started his own accountancy firm and is very successful and able to help those in need. He has also created his own healing group. Sun dreams are among the best for automatically relieving anxiety or depression.

Sunflowers

Lorraine, forty-five, dreamed she was standing in a field of sunflowers like a golden carpet, swaying as far as the eye could see. The sky was cloudless, and she never wanted the dream to end. Her husband waved to her as he came home from the fields to where they lived in France. Then he was gone. She woke and remembered, but the happiness of her surroundings remained.

DREAM BACKGROUND AND MEANING

Lorraine's husband had been killed in a car accident. Their manager was running the business, and the whole summer she had had a stream of visitors from the United Kingdom, telling her she should sell up and come home. Sunflowers represent a life cycle, releasing nutritious seeds with oils used in cooking and beauty products. Their annual replanting reminds of the continuation of love.

INTERPRETATIONS AND FORTUNE-TELLING MEANINGS

★ If in the dream the sunflowers are tall, straight, and plentiful, be confident that you will make or rebuild a happy future.

★ Planting sunflower seeds indicates a new venture based on experience, which will flourish in the months ahead.

★ Extracting or using sunflower oil promises abundance, healing, and the growth or return of enthusiasm.

★ Sunflowers turning toward the sun say, "Follow your own desires and do not be swayed by what others advise."

★ Sunflowers entwined represent combining business and home and the growth of new love when the time is right.

★ Fading sunflowers predict the regrowth of life and light by the releasing of the old.

OUTCOME OF LORRAINE'S DREAM

After the dream, Lorraine realized she had spent the whole summer catering to friends and relatives and could start her own bed-and-breakfast and create sunflower beauty products, as she wanted to stay in France. She went into partnership with the manager, and his wife helped her with her business. Sunflowers represent nutrition and healing, but also loyalty and devotion. Lorraine felt she owed it to her husband to complete their life plan.

Sunset

Gerda, seventy-five, dreamed of a beautiful bright sunset and a cruise ship sailing into it, its windows tinged red and purple. Gerda knew the ship would not wait, and she found herself swimming after it. Her children, grandchildren, and great-grandchildren were on the shore, trying to stop her. They pursued her in a boat, trying to persuade her to return to shore, saying she was too old and would drown. But Gerda kept swimming, and the ship lowered a ladder so she could climb aboard.

DREAM BACKGROUND AND MEANING

Gerda had been feeling tired and was worried she was getting old. She babysat her grandchildren after school and helped with the two young great-grandchildren. She had seen a world cruise advertised that she wanted to book, but her children said at her age it was too risky to go off alone. Gerda felt she should be in her golden and not sunset years. The traditional saying, "Red sky at night, shepherd's delight," promised that the days ahead would bring new opportunities.

INTERPRETATIONS AND FORTUNE-TELLING MEANINGS

* According to myth, if you see your dream sunset reflected in a mirror, you will glimpse yourself as the person you can still become.
* Watching a bright sunset in your dream indicates a successful completion of a project or action.
* If the sunset gradually fades in the dream, a phase of your life will come to an end naturally, preparing the way for the new sunrise.
* A cold gray sunset warns that you must care for your own interests and well-being, as others are draining you emotionally.
* A dream sunset with many clouds warns that your confidence is being held back by others who spread unnecessary doubts, but you will overcome this.

OUTCOME OF GERDA'S DREAM

Despite great opposition from the family, Gerda booked a Caribbean cruise to see if she enjoyed traveling. She took painting classes on the ship, and when she came home said she could not look after the children every day as she wanted to travel more and explore her art. Sunsets mark endings, but for every sunset there is a new sunrise to open new possibilities.

Supermarket

Lennart, forty, dreamed he was dashing to the supermarket to buy food for his parents' anniversary party. But he had stayed too late at work, and many of the shelves were empty. He filled a shopping cart with what he could find. As he was waiting at the checkout, he noticed that the supermarket prepared special instant buffet packs that could be ordered and delivered.

DREAM BACKGROUND AND MEANING

Lennart promised his parents he would do the shopping for their anniversary party, but time had run away from him. He went to the supermarket the morning after the dream and found that they sold pre-packaged party packs, consisting of a variety of salamis, cheeses, pretzels, salads, nuts, candy, and party decorations, which he had never noticed before. Supermarket dreams can alert us to instant fixes in different aspects of life, overlooked in our haste but registered on an unconscious level and revealed in dreams.

INTERPRETATIONS AND FORTUNE-TELLING MEANINGS

* A dream of a well-stocked supermarket with your favorite products promises happy, secure days ahead where you will have all you need.
* If you dream that a supermarket declines your credit card, you may need to revise your budget, as you may have overspent on luxuries.
* If you are forced to slow down in your dream, you may discover that this can actually save you time and effort.
* If the supermarket is empty of goods, your current life path may not instantly fulfill your needs, and you may have to find a slower alternative.
* If the checkout assistant or scanner is too fast, are you trying to fit too much into limited time?
* Should you dream your bags break and goods spill everywhere, beware of unreliable people who will break promises.

OUTCOME OF LENNART'S DREAM

Lennart ordered his instant party, and it was a great success with minimum effort. He discovered a lot of other time-saving services he had previously dashed past. Supermarket dreams suggest that we already have the resources we need and should explore existing opportunities before looking elsewhere.

Superstitions

Antonia, thirty-five, dreamed she was going for an interview to work on a cruise ship, but on her way she had to walk under a ladder to avoid road work. It was Friday the thirteenth, and a black cat crossed her path. Antonia was incredibly superstitious and decided not to bother to go to the interview, as luck was against her.

DREAM BACKGROUND AND MEANING

Antonia was anxious about the interview, and she had been looking for signs in her waking life of good fortune or otherwise. The dream confirmed that she was wasting her time applying. Breaking superstitions and so attracting bad luck can become a self-fulfilling prophecy.

INTERPRETATIONS AND FORTUNE-TELLING MEANINGS

* If you dream of breaking a superstition and do not carry out the remedial action, you may be unconsciously stacking the odds against yourself.
* If you see lucky symbols in your dream, such as two magpies for joy or six for gold, this is a good omen for success.
* If you are very superstitious and this penetrates your dreams, you are giving fate more credit than it deserves.
* If you are not normally superstitious and a dream is full of lucky or unlucky symbols, see which predominate so you can take advance precautions to stack the odds in your favor.
* If you dream of a lucky amulet, obtaining one may restore your confidence in your ability to positively influence a situation.
* If your dream worries you, check to see where the bad luck is centered so you can take diversionary action.

OUTCOME OF ANTONIA'S DREAM

After the dream, Antonia pictured herself taking the remedial actions needed for each piece of predicted bad luck, which gave her more confidence. She went to the interview and was offered the job. If superstition dreams are troubling you, accept that they are anxiety dreams and relate to your lack of self-esteem, not your predestined fortune.

Swallow (Bird)

Bernard, twenty-five, regularly dreamed he was watching the swallows migrating south in huge numbers, and he was filled with excitement. The sky was filled with the darting and swooping birds, and then they were gone, and he was in rain-swept London, going to the subway.

DREAM BACKGROUND AND MEANING

Bernard was disappointed because his work visa for Australia had been rejected. He had hoped to ultimately attain residency there. He had enough savings to go as a tourist for three months if he stayed in hostels, but he wanted a new life. Swallows migrate back in the warmer weather and so seeing them leaving for the winter favors travel, even if not ideal, sooner rather than later.

INTERPRETATIONS AND FORTUNE-TELLING MEANINGS

* Since swallows were sacred to Isis, the Ancient Egyptian Mother Goddess, and to Venus and Aphrodite, the classical goddesses of love, swallows nesting indicate a permanent relationship and, in future, children if wanted.
* It is said that swallows removed the thorns from Christ's head at the time of His Crucifixion, thus alleviating his pain. For this reason, swallows are seen as sacred animals. Hearing swallows calling is a reassurance that after disappointment, plans will materialize, albeit differently from planned.
* In a dream, swallows returning after the winter is a symbol of the renewal of life and a happy summer.
* If your dream swallows are building nests in the eaves of your house, success, happiness, and good fortune are promised to all who live there.
* Medieval superstition says that if your dream swallow brings you a ruby or black pearl, you will have wealth, protection, and good fortune.

OUTCOME OF BERNARD'S DREAM

Bernard followed the sun and traveled around Australia as a tourist. In the North he discovered there was a shortage of workers, and a hostel where he stayed offered to sponsor him to work there after his visa expired. Dream swallows, like real ones, follow their assigned path and encourage the dreamer to fly, trusting all will be well.

Swamp, Quagmire

Flynn, twenty-five, dreamed he was taking a shortcut at night across a swamp he knew well to meet a new guy who excited him. But he dropped his flashlight and lost his sense of direction and was up to his knees in muddy water, afraid to go forward because there were deep, treacherous areas. Then he saw his long-time partner coming toward him with a huge lantern, stepping carefully on the dry parts to lead him back to shore.

DREAM BACKGROUND AND MEANING

Flynn was bored with his relationship. Though he and his partner had a beautiful home, good careers, and plenty of money, he was aware that he was seeking more and intended to ask the new guy at the office for a date. Swamps in dreams hold dangers for the unwary.

INTERPRETATIONS AND FORTUNE-TELLING MEANINGS

★ If you dream you are negotiating your way across a swamp, decide if you want or need to cross the swamp, which represents risk in your daily life.

★ If you successfully cross a swamp, you will before long find yourself in a better position to decide if you want to return or go forward in life.

★ If the swamp is filled with beautiful flowers, growth can come out of a seemingly stagnant situation.

★ If you are bogged down in a swamp, you may be feeling held back by routine or by uninspiring people.

★ If you rescue someone you know from a swamp or they rescue you, you may be motivated to move forward together in a more exciting way.

OUTCOME OF FLYNN'S DREAM

After the dream, Flynn realized that he relied on his partner more than he had imagined. They talked honestly, and his partner was also feeling restless. They took a long vacation to the Everglades swamps in Florida and settled in the area, running tourist boats. A swamp dream points to the problem and also to a built-in solution.

Swan

Anya, thirty-two, had a magical dream of seeing an enchanted swan, which she identified as herself, in the center of a lake. Her fiancé, Antony, called to her from the bank of the lake. But the spell that held her in swan form was too strong. He started walking into the water, was transformed into a swan, and they flew away together.

DREAM BACKGROUND AND MEANING

Anya was engaged to Antony, an Australian she had met in Thailand. She was having problems getting a visa to join him in Australia, as she had Eastern European citizenship. Antony offered to live in her home country, but she could not ask him to give up his life and family. The dream mirrors a fairy tale Anya recalled from childhood. Old myths remain buried deep within us, emerging in dreams.

INTERPRETATIONS AND FORTUNE-TELLING MEANINGS

★ Swans represent harmony and stillness, achieved through prolonged, often hidden, effort.

★ Flying swans indicate a spiritual or inner transformation and also travel.

★ As the bird of the Greco-Roman god Apollo, a flock of swans is a good omen for singers, musicians, dancers, beauty businesses, and all who create beauty.

★ Dreaming of two swans swimming side by side says you will meet your soulmate or, if you already have, your partner will always be faithful.

★ Swans on lakes herald prosperity and smoother times ahead; on a river, gradual advantageous change through a home or career move.

★ Swans with cygnets suggest fertility, a safe pregnancy and delivery, a happy united family, and loyalty in those close.

OUTCOME OF ANYA'S DREAM

The pair decided to marry and live in Thailand until Anya's visa came through, which took almost a year. However, since Anya was a beautician, they stayed in Thailand and set up a beauty business for wealthy Westerners. Since swans stay together for life, they provide assurance for overcoming practical difficulties standing in the way of lasting love.

Swimming

Frances, twenty-five, dreamed she was being dragged in ropes toward the village duck pond. She was protesting, after being accused of being a witch for helping women to reduce the pain of childbirth using herbs, which the priest forbade. The Church, the priest told her, believed women should suffer for the sins of Eve. The priest walked in front, holding a cross and chanting. At the pond, her arms and legs were bound and she was pushed into the water. She knew that if she floated, she would be hanged as a witch. She put her head underwater, resisting the overwhelming desire to survive.

DREAM BACKGROUND AND MEANING

Frances had been accepted for the security services but was required to pass a test, swimming and diving underwater. The recurring dream from childhood had haunted her, and she had never been able to learn to swim. Fear of swimming can be linked with past-life drowning traumas.

INTERPRETATIONS AND FORTUNE-TELLING MEANINGS

★ Swimming, like floating, is an excellent dream omen, indicating life will flow along happily.

★ Swimming dreams with a lover, known or unknown, indicate a fulfilling sexual relationship.

★ Swimming to shore is a good sign if you have been struggling with life or worrying about the future.

★ The ease or otherwise of swimming and the depth of water indicate recognition and expression of deep emotions.

★ Staying in the shallows can represent fears of commitment in love or sexual passion.

★ Swimming in the open sea involves risks but offers freedom, while a swimming pool is safer but can be restrictive.

OUTCOME OF FRANCES'S DREAM

Frances found a teacher who specialized in nervous pupils and passed her tests, though she still does not enjoy swimming. Now that she has more confidence, the dreams have lessened. Swimming indicates control over emotions; sinking or drowning can indicate unresolved trauma.

Sword

Todd, nineteen, dreamed he was surrounded by soldiers, all taller and stronger than he was, with their swords drawn. They backed him against a stone containing an Excalibur-type sword. He pulled the sword, and it came away easily in his hands. Instantly, the attackers dropped to their knees. Todd walked through them to where a gorgeous princess was waiting.

DREAM BACKGROUND AND MEANING

At college Todd had been teased because he was small. He had been afraid to approach a beautiful girl in his year who he wanted to date. Todd had been secretly learning kung fu and wondered if he dared enter the college's annual kung fu competition. He was worried because some of the guys in his year, who were attacking him in the dream, were entering the contest and boasting about how good they were. Dreams of wielding swords advise the need for decisive, courageous action.

INTERPRETATIONS AND FORTUNE-TELLING MEANINGS

★ Wearing or being knighted with a sword represents recognition and increased authority and respect.

★ Dreaming of pulling a sword like Excalibur out of a stone involves fighting for a principle or justice. Assert your authority and opposition will fade.

★ Being attacked from all sides suggests you have a lot of opponents but should deal with them one at a time.

★ A sword knocked out of your hand or your being wounded talks about trickery and being stabbed in the back.

★ Tarot sword cards advise, according to the dream card picture, whether to respond logically, ignore the situation, or walk away.

★ Sword dreams are often past-life dreams, especially if they involve heraldic or fairy-tale qualities, and advise using tactics, not force, to overcome bullying.

OUTCOME OF TODD'S DREAM

Todd entered the competition and defeated several college guys who had bullied him. Though the girl he wanted to date showed interest after he reached the semifinals, he is now dating a girl from his kung fu class. Sword dreams occur when you feel on the defensive but in fact are more powerful than you realize.

Table

Lola, fifty-five, dreamed she was sitting at the kitchen table with her children and grandchildren, eating a special meal she had prepared. But her children and grandchildren each seized a large dish of food for themselves. In the argument that followed about who could eat the most food, most was spilled on the floor.

DREAM BACKGROUND AND MEANING

Lola had inherited the house when her husband died. Recently her children and grandchildren had demanded money when visiting Lola, which they never repaid. If Lola refused to give them money, they would call her selfish and would visit her less frequently. The dining table, the heart of the home and symbol of nurturing, holds great significance as the gathering place of family unity or discontent.

INTERPRETATIONS AND FORTUNE-TELLING MEANINGS

★ To dream of friends or family gathered around the kitchen or dining-room table talking happily heralds united, loving times ahead.

★ A table full of food indicates abundance, not only physical, but a sharing of love and caring.

★ An empty table in a dream warns of divisions over the sharing of resources and resentment toward the provider of food.

★ If a table contains only dirty dishes for you to clear, you may be neglecting your own needs and should seek more consideration.

★ If you dream of a picnic table, there are spontaneous fun outings and a vacation ahead.

OUTCOME OF LOLA'S DREAM

Lola stopped inviting her family for meals and refused to subsidize them. She started visiting a nursing home and encouraging older people to re-create traditional recipes to share. One by one, her children and grandchildren contacted her to say how they missed the meals around the kitchen table, and she explained that she would start them again, but money requests were off the agenda. She is slowly rebuilding family unity. When the table becomes not a place of togetherness but one of dissension in dreams, it may be necessary to consider whether in everyday life the dreamer is the one doing all the giving.

Tadpole

Estelle, eighteen, dreamed she was a little girl fishing for tadpoles with a jelly jar and net. She took them home proudly to put in a bowl. Her mother poured them down the drain, saying pond water was full of germs. Estelle returned to the pond and caught some more. This time she hid the tadpoles in the shed until they could be released as frogs.

DREAM BACKGROUND AND MEANING

Estelle wanted to be a dancer. Since her family disapproved, she took a weekend and evening job to pay for classes. Her parents insisted that she accept a place offered at a university to study math. But Estelle had secretly applied to a major dance academy and had been offered a scholarship. The tadpole dream was recalling a childhood memory. Childhood recollection dreams occur at key points, in this case to allow Estelle's transformation.

INTERPRETATIONS AND FORTUNE-TELLING MEANINGS

★ Tadpoles trapped in a small bowl represent teenage independence versus parental safety concerns.

★ Tadpoles beginning to change into frogs herald a period of transformation and reinventing your lifestyle.

★ A large number of tadpoles swimming in a pond is an excellent potency symbol for men wanting to become fathers or experiencing sexual difficulties.

★ Because tadpoles, unlike frogs, are not amphibious, tadpoles hiding in the reeds indicate the need to germinate ideas and plans before manifestation.

★ Tadpoles that are not changing into frogs when others do suggest reluctance to leave a comfort zone or an outgrown stage.

★ Tadpoles that are eaten by predatory fish alert the dreamer to the presence of ruthless or dishonest people.

OUTCOME OF ESTELLE'S DREAM

Estelle told her parents she was going to study dance. They were furious, but she was determined to unfold her own blueprint. She was offered paid dance roles as she trained, including the musical *The Frog Prince*. Like tadpoles, we need to allow our own blueprint to form if we are to be true to our destiny.

Talisman, Lucky Charm

Petra, thirty, had a recurring dream that she was frantically searching through long grass, trying to find her lucky ankh charm, which had slipped off the chain she always wore around her neck. When it became dark, she was ready to give up. Then she saw it lying golden at her feet; but, as she seized it, the charm faded. Petra woke crying.

DREAM BACKGROUND AND MEANING

Petra had worn the ankh since she was at school and it was irreplaceable. While overseas she had dropped it. Since she had returned, she was experiencing consistent bad luck. Now she had a vital interview, but without her charm she knew she would not succeed. Petra had the talents and qualifications to do well but had become overreliant on good fortune as symbolized by the charm.

INTERPRETATIONS AND FORTUNE-TELLING MEANINGS

- ⭑ To wear or carry a good-luck charm in a dream is a sign that you will have good fortune and perhaps a win on Powerball or the lottery, or in some other game of chance.
- ⭑ To dream that you make your own talisman promises that your luck will improve through your own efforts.
- ⭑ To dream that you buy a talisman or charm from a magical person such as a wizard suggests that you rely on others too much for your lucky breaks.
- ⭑ To dream you lose or break a precious talisman or charm reflects deep-seated fears that your good fortune is running out.
- ⭑ To see an unusual talisman says you should allow the charm to present itself naturally when most needed.
- ⭑ To dream you win a major talent contest or ideal job using your existing talisman alerts you to good fortune coming, most likely an opportunity to be seized.

OUTCOME OF PETRA'S DREAM

Petra went for her interview. Once she accepted that her charm, but not her luck, was gone forever, she obtained the job through her talents. Rely on your own abilities as well as talismans to attract your own good fortune.

Tantrums

Cybil, fifty-six, dreamed she was in a supermarket with her husband, George, and the store was sold out of his favorite barberry jam. He suddenly threw a tantrum, screaming abuse and stamping his feet. She tried to placate him, but he would not stop.

DREAM BACKGROUND AND MEANING

George would often throw tantrums. Cybil was tired of covering up for him with the family. She was starting to fear his outbursts. Some adults who were overindulged in childhood continue having tantrums, but when the tantrums appear in a loved one's dream, it suggests the dreamer is running out of patience.

INTERPRETATIONS AND FORTUNE-TELLING MEANINGS

- ⭑ If a close adult or teen relative is a child in your dream and having a tantrum, beware that they do not get their own way too often by expressing uncontrolled fury.
- ⭑ If in your dream your own child is having a tantrum in a public place and you are panicking, a family member may have criticized your parenting skills.
- ⭑ If you are a child having a tantrum in your dream, you may have been too patient with people taking advantage of you.
- ⭑ If you are an adult and having a tantrum in your dream, beware that others do not provoke you to act impulsively.
- ⭑ If family members are throwing tantrums in your dream, they are using you as audience and referee.
- ⭑ If you vent anger in a dream, but normally are restrained, tension building up may appear at an inappropriate time or against the wrong person.

OUTCOME OF CYBIL'S DREAM

George started a fight in the supermarket when someone pushed in front of him. Cybil said she would leave him unless he saw a counselor. George admitted he was haunted by memories of his father's continual anger, which had wrecked his childhood. He agreed to attend therapy. Dreams of adult temper tantrums give advance warning of escalating problems that need outside intervention.

Tasting

Flo, thirty-eight, dreamed she was eating her favorite chocolate dessert, which she had made for her husband and parents. But Flo could not taste the chocolate at all and left most of the dessert in her dish. She felt disappointed, as it was to be the highlight of the meal.

DREAM BACKGROUND AND MEANING

Flo was planning a special dinner party for the family to celebrate her promotion at the university. However, she had hoped her parents or husband would invite her to a restaurant, as this was an important occasion for her. But they had not even sent her a congratulatory card. If food is tasteless in a dream, you may need to speak out, whether in love or work, if you are feeling taken for granted (see "Dessert," p. 140).

INTERPRETATIONS AND FORTUNE-TELLING MEANINGS

★ If you dream you are eating chocolate and enjoying it, an unexpected reward or chance to indulge yourself will soon occur.

★ If you dream of food being too sweet, you may be falling for flattery to lull you into a false sense of security.

★ If food is spicy, expect excitement and a chance to explore new experiences and activities.

★ Salty food says there will be few flattering words but a chance to make a quick profit, maybe through speculation.

★ If you dream of eating lemons, beware of spiteful words spoken out of jealousy.

★ If you can always taste foods in dreams (some people can't), you have clairsentient abilities to sense psychic information through taste and fragrance in everyday life.

OUTCOME OF FLO'S DREAM

Flo was tired of always being the one to plan family treats. She told the family she was going out with friends to celebrate. They were shocked, as they assumed Flo enjoyed organizing treats. Her husband booked a special restaurant meal, and her parents brought gifts and a celebration cake. When in a dream you have a bad taste in your mouth or food tastes rotten, you may be swallowing resentment at others' inconsideration when they are totally unaware of their selfishness.

Tattoo

Conrad, thirty, dreamed his tattoo designs were everywhere, in books, as pictures on walls, and printed on T-shirts as well as on skin. Companies were offering him big money for exclusive rights to them. The boss at the tattoo parlor where he worked placed his designs in a plastic folder, the one they showed customers. When Conrad opened it, his designs had disappeared.

DREAM BACKGROUND AND MEANING

Conrad was a gifted tattooist, but he wanted to design body art and fantasy designs from different ages and cultures. His boss, an older woman, told him he was to follow her set designs or quit. It was a well-paid job and, despite customers loving his work, he feared failing.

INTERPRETATIONS AND FORTUNE-TELLING MEANINGS

★ If in the dream you are a tattoo artist, you may desire greater open commitment, love, or loyalty from the person you are tattooing.

★ If you are having a temporary stick-on or henna tattoo, you need time to make a decision with longer-term implications.

★ If you dream you are being tattooed, beware that a close friend or lover does not become overpossessive, especially if you are having their name tattooed on you.

★ The design you have chosen reveals what it is you most desire to express about yourself or attract to yourself.

★ If you dream you are having a tattoo removed, you are having doubts about a person or situation you thought would last forever.

★ A hidden tattoo suggests you are not yet ready to reveal your true self to the world in general.

OUTCOME OF CONRAD'S DREAM

After the dream, Conrad decided to send his designs to a fantasy book and print publisher and to sell designs to other tattooists. Conrad was successful and was offered a position in a prestigious tattoo parlor. Tattooing is a major statement to the world, as it is generally permanent. Dreams may give the incentive to go ahead with being tattooed or learning tattooing.

Tea, Coffee

Millie, forty-two, dreamed she was serving tea and reading the teacups. Present-life friends were wearing Victorian clothes. She was afraid her husband might come home early, as he disapproved of anything psychic. He suddenly burst in. Millie dropped the teapot and the cups, which smashed.

DREAM BACKGROUND AND MEANING

Millie started a weekly psychic party after meeting a group of local women she was convinced she had known in past worlds. Her dream might be a flashback. Her husband, the local minister, forbade her from dabbling in the metaphysical and told her to concentrate on organizing church coffee mornings, which she hated. She agreed to host them, but missed her psychic parties. Tea and coffee dreams are about drawing together people with spiritual and emotional affinities (see "Coffee," p. 108).

INTERPRETATIONS AND FORTUNE-TELLING MEANINGS

★ If you dream you are serving tea or coffee on formal china, ask yourself who you want to welcome into your tea party and your life.

★ Stirring takeout tea or coffee for someone else in a dream indicates you wish to know them better.

★ If you dream you are reading tea leaves or coffee grounds, your psychic powers are emerging.

★ If you spill the liquid and the cup or pot breaks, you are suppressing feelings you should more openly express.

★ A dream of a tea or coffee party or ceremony, especially in an old culture, like ancient China, advises you to take time for your spiritual needs.

★ Dreaming of refilling the kettle or pot says there is a lot remaining unsaid.

OUTCOME OF MILLIE'S DREAM

After the dream, Millie decided she was not going to allow her husband to dictate her friends and interests. Her magical evenings proved popular with the villagers. For the first time in her marriage, she prioritized her own needs and offloaded the coffee mornings on the churchwarden's wife, who loved church minutiae. Tea and coffee sessions represent creating a personal oasis of harmony.

Teacher, Educator

Yolande, twenty-five, dreamed she was eighteen and having an affair with her history professor. He insisted they must keep their affair secret or the college authorities would fire him. She announced to everyone that they were going to get married, only to discover he was already married.

DREAM BACKGROUND AND MEANING

Yolande did have a brief affair with her college professor. Now she was in love with the senior executive who ran her fast-track training program. When away on weekend seminars, they shared a passionate affair. She threatened to tell his wife unless he upped the tempo of their relationship, but he said he would throw her off the company training program if she did.

INTERPRETATIONS AND FORTUNE-TELLING MEANINGS

★ If you wake up speaking aloud what you are currently teaching or learning, called somniloquy, you have important information to impart.

★ If you dream you lose track of what you are supposed to be teaching, or the students or audience walk out while you are speaking, you worry no one is listening to you.

★ If you dream you are a teacher at your childhood school, you may be in danger of repeating old mistakes.

★ If a teacher or educator from your teens returns in dreams, you have issues on which you need wise advice.

★ If you dream that a former teacher is criticizing you, an authority figure in your present life makes you feel inadequate.

★ If you are having a romance or affair with a former teacher or educator in your dream, you may be unconsciously seeking an older, wiser parent figure to protect and nurture you.

OUTCOME OF YOLANDE'S DREAM

Yolande realized her lover had no intention of including her in his personal life, except for sex on trips. She transferred her studies to another company. The nurturing role of an educator can create an emotional dependency in a student. A dream reveals whether this is love, or the teacher or student is inappropriately taking advantage of the closeness.

Teddy Bear

Laurence, fifty-six, had a dream he was a small child again, looking for his teddy bear, without which he could not sleep. Suddenly, he saw the bear perched on the window ledge outside his first-floor bedroom. He clambered out and woke, realizing he had let the bear go to save himself.

DREAM BACKGROUND AND MEANING

Laurence was a successful businessman, ruthless in the boardroom. In his private life he depended on Craig, his partner of twenty years, who stayed at home and took care of domestic trivia. Craig wanted Laurence to sell his business interests and move to rural France. Laurence said no, but Craig was threatening to go alone. Dreaming of a teddy bear from childhood implies an emotional dependency on another person that may, at the time of the dream, become coercion.

INTERPRETATIONS AND FORTUNE-TELLING MEANINGS

★ To be a child looking for a comforter says that the dreamer is seeking approval and reassurance from someone who may withhold it as a weapon.

★ If a teddy bear is torn or battered, the dependency has outworn its usefulness.

★ If a teddy is lost or thrown away in the dream, the dreamer is moving out of the comfort zone and may need to make hard decisions.

★ If you dream you are looking for your childhood teddy bear, you may have transferred the need for parental approval to a love partner.

★ If you give a teddy bear away to a child, whether known or unknown, you are comforting your inner uncertain self and assuming independence.

OUTCOME OF LAURENCE'S DREAM

Since Laurence ultimately was the breadwinner, for the first time ever he refused to go along with Craig. They did, however, buy a small vacation home in France. Teddy bears in dreams heighten emotional dependency issues that can reveal untested independence in the dreamer if teddy is abandoned.

Teenage Friendship

Sonia, fourteen, dreamed she was with her friends in an abandoned building. She saw two lionesses approaching. The girls tried to shut the door, but it was rusted and the lionesses were poking their claws through the entrance, snarling. To save her friends, Sonia leaped forward into the jaws of the lionesses.

DREAM BACKGROUND AND MEANING

Sonia had been friends with the same group of girls since elementary school, and they had sworn lifetime friendship. But recently she had been excluded because she had a boyfriend and they did not. She was desperate to prove to them their importance to her. Dreams about teenage friendships tend to be very intense, as emotions run high over loyalty issues.

INTERPRETATIONS AND FORTUNE-TELLING MEANINGS

★ If you dream of sacrificing yourself for your friends, they may have been giving you a hard time. How far are you prepared to go to demonstrate the strength of your friendship?

★ If you dream of your friends sacrificing you or treating you badly, question if the friendship is worth pursuing.

★ If you are an adult dreaming of a particular teenage friendship, you may be contacted by that friend from the past via social media.

★ If you dream of a lifelong friend, still part of your life, the nature of the dream can reveal underlying issues to be resolved or can help you to accept it is time to move on.

★ If you are adult, dreaming of unknown teenage friends, this may alert you to what is going on in the current workplace or friendship group.

OUTCOME OF SONIA'S DREAM

After the dream, Sonia wondered if her friends would have saved her, and she knew the answer. She made other friends and, after a period of spite from her former best-buddy group, she realized she had been outgrowing them for a time. Teenage friendship dreams, especially if occurring in adulthood, can reveal childishness or pettiness in a social situation best avoided.

Teenage Problems

In her dream, Francesca, thirty-eight, witnessed her thirteen-year-old stepdaughter, Lollie, encircled by teen bullies who were stamping on her smartphone and pushing her to the ground. Francesca waded in, as she was a kickboxer, and the bullies scattered.

DREAM BACKGROUND AND MEANING

Lollie constantly caused trouble between Francesca and her husband, Jo. Francesca loved Jo but was at the end of her tether with her stepdaughter. Her instincts told her something was wrong in Lollie's life. Dreams about teenagers can offer an understanding of the real issues causing a teen's bad behavior.

INTERPRETATIONS AND FORTUNE-TELLING MEANINGS

- ⋆ If you are a teenager in the dream, you need to just relax and have fun.
- ⋆ If in the dream you are a teenager behaving irresponsibly, you may be ready to buck the status quo and insist on what you want.
- ⋆ If you are coping with difficult adolescents in your dream, they could represent people of any age behaving immaturely.
- ⋆ If you dream you are being threatened by a teenage gang, you may fear intimidation at work or socially.
- ⋆ If you are a teenager madly in love in your dream, you may be tempted by a chance for a fling without considering the consequences.
- ⋆ If you know the badly behaved teenager in your dream, look for clues in the dream world for what's behind their misbehavior.

OUTCOME OF FRANCESCA'S DREAM

Francesca was concerned, as her stepdaughter sometimes came home with torn clothes and once made up an excuse about her broken phone, which her father had instantly replaced, which infuriated Francesca. Francesca watched from outside the school gate and saw six girls attacking her stepdaughter. Remembering the dream, she ran in, executed a few showy kickboxing moves, and they fled. Her stepdaughter has been far more cooperative with Francesca since then. Dreams about teenagers pick up unconscious clues when all is not well and offer a door into a more positive relationship.

Teenage Sex

In her dream, Pearl, seventeen, decided to let her former boyfriend make love to her, as she wanted him back at any cost. But during lovemaking she felt absolutely nothing, and afterward she thought, "Well I have got that over now."

DREAM BACKGROUND AND MEANING

Pearl had been dumped by her boyfriend, Matthew, because she refused to have sex with him. Pearl was still a virgin, and she wanted to wait until her wedding day. But she desperately missed having a boyfriend and wondered if she should have sex with Matthew to win him back. The dream allowed Pearl to experience sex with her former boyfriend on the astral plane. Teenage sex dreams are often rehearsals, but sometimes can give the teen courage to resist sex before they are ready.

INTERPRETATIONS AND FORTUNE-TELLING MEANINGS

- ⋆ If a teen is having erotic dreams about their boyfriend, they are probably ready for lovemaking.
- ⋆ If the teen dreams of making love to a stranger, it is the idea of sex rather than the reality that is appealing.
- ⋆ If a teen, pressured to have sex with a boyfriend or girlfriend, finds it disappointing in the dream, the person may not be the right one.
- ⋆ If a teen dreams of having sex with an unwilling partner, that may be the right partner but the wrong time.
- ⋆ If a teen dreams of having sex with a teacher, their present partner may benefit from the fantasy, as long as it remains as such.
- ⋆ If a teen is forced in a dream to have sex with someone who makes them afraid in real life, it is time to take precautions about not going out alone to unsafe places.

OUTCOME OF PEARL'S DREAM

The dream warned Pearl that her virginity was too precious to give away just to please her boyfriend, and that it was a shame to rush what should be a meaningful experience. Pearl has met another guy who is very respectful, and she is experiencing growing passion for him.

Teenage Vacation

Bonny, fifteen, dreamed she was on vacation on a tropical island with her school friends, and there were no adults present. They were having a brilliant time. Then Bonny heard screaming and realized her best friend was being attacked by a shark. They dragged her onto land, but the wound needed stitching. A large wave swept in. Two helicopters were putting down ladders to rescue them, but Bonny's friends refused to leave as they wanted to watch the tsunami. The helicopters left and there was a rush of water.

DREAM BACKGROUND AND MEANING

Some of Bonny's friends persuaded their parents to let them stay in a holiday complex for the vacation, supervised by the older sister of one of the girls, a teen herself. Bonnie's parents refused to let her go, as she would be relatively unsupervised. A teen vacation dream casts up fears for parents and children of letting go versus ensuring safety, looming beneath the surface.

INTERPRETATIONS AND FORTUNE-TELLING MEANINGS

* If you dream of disasters on your vacation with friends, examine hidden security worries about your independent trip.
* If in the dream you rescue friends, are your companions reliable away from home base?
* If you dream of disasters occurring on your teenager's projected adventure, this is an anxiety dream but may represent valid precautions you need to put in place.
* If you have a sudden urgent dream of disaster while your teen is away, you may be telepathically picking up a situation they are insufficiently mature to handle. Make contact.
* If you see your teen safely vacationing with friends in a supervised environment, consider compromise. Your teen may not be as confident as they appear.

OUTCOME OF BONNY'S DREAM

Bonny told her parents about the dream, and they suggested that she and her friends camp near the family's vacation home but live independently. After the first night, Bonnie and her friends moved into the vacation property garden, as they did not like the dark. Dramatic teen vacation dreams may express doubts parents and children find hard to express that, when spoken, open the way to compromise.

Teeth

Marina, forty-eight, dreamed she was receiving a media award at a ceremony when suddenly her teeth started to fall out one by one. She attempted to hide them in her hand. The presenter took back the award. Everybody watched in silence as she left. Outside there was no car waiting at the end of the red carpet, and she knew her career was over.

DREAM BACKGROUND AND MEANING

Marina was a newscaster on a satellite channel. She was aware that she was being increasingly passed over for younger, less experienced, physically glamorous female colleagues. It had been suggested that Marina should take an off-screen role.

INTERPRETATIONS AND FORTUNE-TELLING MEANINGS

* If teeth fall out in a dream or are missing, they reflect fears of waning power and physical admiration, or their actual waning, often because of prejudice about aging, professionally, socially, or in a relationship where physical appearance is prized above all.
* False teeth represent someone lying. The more ill-fitting the teeth, the greater the falsehood.
* Dreaming you are unable to bite through food because of loose teeth suggests you are afraid to speak out.
* A dream of someone you know smiling slyly, hiding their teeth, or snarling means their apparently benign intentions may be hiding malice.
* If you are surrounded by smiling people and you are smiling back, your popularity and approval rating will increase for who you are and what you do and not for your physical appearance.
* A dream of a dentist hurting you or refusing anesthetic warns of someone in authority intruding on your personal space with inappropriate sexual or malicious remarks or behavior.
* Teeth falling out can forewarn of actual problems with teeth and gums, especially if checkups have been missed.

OUTCOME OF MARINA'S DREAM

Marina found a new post researching, producing, and presenting hard-hitting documentaries and did get her high-profile award ceremony, which went off without a hitch. Sometimes loss-of-power dreams involving physical appearance can spur success in other ways.

Telepathic Dreams

Lily, forty-eight, whose daughter, Grace, was a new recruit in the navy, dreamed of Grace in distress. An older enlisted woman backed her against the cabin wall, and the door was blocked by other senior enlisted women. They were pressuring her for money. Lily woke very concerned.

DREAM BACKGROUND AND MEANING

Grace wrote happy emails home. But Lily had been feeling uneasy for some time, and the dream confirmed her fears. Telepathic dreams between parents and children, partners, or close family are more vivid than ordinary dreams.

INTERPRETATIONS AND FORTUNE-TELLING MEANINGS

★ If you have telepathic dreams featuring a deceased relative, they may have a useful message for you or may be sending love and reassurance.

★ If you regularly dream of your child or absent partner in distress, the problem may be an ongoing one they have not revealed.

★ If a dream is sudden and urgent, especially if the child is small and in another room, even if they are making no sound, it is well worth checking, as the dream invariably wakes you.

★ If you are constantly dreaming of an adult child and their unspoken problems, after a tactful inquiry, it is time to reclaim your personal space by blocking worries before sleep.

★ If you pick up happy information, for example that a daughter is pregnant before she herself knows it, your unconscious mind is connecting you with her through the family link of love.

OUTCOME OF LILY'S DREAM

Lily called Grace, who admitted that she was experiencing severe financial problems. She had been gambling with older enlisted women and had lost a lot of money. The women had been cheating young recruits at cards and threatening them to make them pay with interest. Lily paid Grace's debts and persuaded her to complain to a trusted officer. The women were discharged from the navy. Telepathic dreams seem especially strong between mother and child of any age.

Teleportation

Victor, seventeen, often teleported in his sleep to the same star, where he witnessed himself living a completely different life with loving star parents. He saw inventions not yet created in his current world. He never wanted to go home. When he traveled in sleep, his body disintegrated into stars and he instantly found himself in the star world and, at the same time, watching his other self.

DREAM BACKGROUND AND MEANING

Victor was obsessed with science fiction and fantasy and attended every convention possible. He was regarded as a geek and an oddity at his school and by his parents, though he never talked about his teleportation dreams. But sometimes he drew inventions he had seen. He decided he would send the best to an aeronautic laboratory. His friends and family said he should take a reality check. Teleportation dreams, whether actual or within the mind, open the psyche to ideas beyond the mundane world.

INTERPRETATIONS AND FORTUNE-TELLING MEANINGS

★ To dream of instantly teleporting from one place to another suggests a desire to move away from restrictions and obstacles as fast as possible.

★ Teleporting dreams are a form of instant astral projection without experiencing the sensation of traveling.

★ Teleporting dreams involving extraterrestrials or visiting other galaxies may seem to last days or weeks but in fact may last only minutes.

★ Teleportation dreams where the dreamer seems to disintegrate and appear as a replica elsewhere (see "Double, Doppelgänger," p. 151) are a way twin souls who live far away or have never met can come together on the dream plane.

★ If you teleport to an earthly unknown place where you are at home, your mind may be moving ahead to guide you to the right location to settle.

OUTCOME OF VICTOR'S DREAM

Victor received a reply to his inventions mail and was invited to the laboratory for the day. He was told he could apply for an apprenticeship once he completed his examinations. Teleportation dreams widen the horizons of possibility for the dreamer and confirm that it is possible to see beyond the immediate.

Television Dating Show

Melanie, twenty-nine, dreamed she was on a television dating show and twelve hunky guys were competing for her favors. She was shocked to see one of the contestants was John, her husband. She was to spend time with each man and then decide who she wished to take to a deserted island for a romantic weekend. One guy, Anthony, was her clear choice of fantasy dating. John, expressionless, walked away, seemingly unmoved.

DREAM BACKGROUND AND MEANING

Though Melanie loved John, at times he seemed staid and boring. Melanie was concerned with why she chose another man over her husband in her dream. Was John the man she was meant to spend the rest of her life with? Should she consider an affair or accept John's lack of romance as the price of security? When a partner becomes part of a dream television dating show, especially if rejected, it may be time to put a new spin on the relationship.

INTERPRETATIONS AND FORTUNE-TELLING MEANINGS

- ✳ If you dream of starring on a television dating show, this is a fantasy-fulfillment dream to brighten up a less-than-exciting relationship.
- ✳ If you are in a relationship but choose an exotic television lover in your partner's place, there may be something missing from the relationship.
- ✳ If you love the world of glamour in the dream, you may be seeking a more fulfilling career or lifestyle.
- ✳ If the dream recurs, there may be factors in the chosen lover that warn of a growing restlessness, which could tip over into an affair.
- ✳ If in the dream you are enjoying the limelight, you may be ready to become more out there in your love life.
- ✳ As long as fantasy stays fantasy, such dreams are good to revive a relationship.

OUTCOME OF MELANIE'S DREAM

Melanie booked a holiday to an exotic island for herself and John and sent a show reel to a series where partners get a make-over. Television dating dreams can enliven relationships that have been getting dull.

Television Soap Opera

Almost every night, Marsha, sixty-four, dreamed of being one of the characters in her favorite soap opera, a wealthy widow living alone in a mansion in Florida who has retreated from the world after the death of her husband. The character grieves for her estranged son but is too proud to contact him.

DREAM BACKGROUND AND MEANING

Marsha lost her husband during a pandemic and had become reclusive since then, rarely leaving the house. She had one son who lived overseas, who she had not been in contact with for many years. Marsha spent all her waking hours watching television soaps and went to bed early and slept long hours, as the life she loved was now found in her dreams. Soap operas can be a relief from mundane reality; however, if they dominate your waking thoughts, you need to seek a more fulfilling daily life.

INTERPRETATIONS AND FORTUNE-TELLING MEANINGS

- ✳ If you regularly dream of your favorite soap operas and are one of the characters, their life may mirror an idealized or dramatized version of your own.
- ✳ If you are your present self in the soap-opera dream, interacting with the characters, there may be people in the soap opera who mirror the characteristics of people around you who you find it hard to interact with.
- ✳ If you are dreaming of soap operas most nights and the dreams linger all day, you may be in danger of losing touch with reality.
- ✳ If there is a particular relationship in the soap opera that troubles you, identify the similar scenario or character in your own life and try to bring it to fruition or closure.
- ✳ If you dream accurately of advance events in the soap opera, maybe you should consider either writing fiction yourself or learning clairvoyance.

OUTCOME OF MARSHA'S DREAM

Marsha realized the dreams were taking over, especially the life of the widow and her estranged son. She decided to attend bereavement counseling and contact her real-life son, and she is now training as a bereavement counselor.

Temptation to Stray

Amelia, forty-three, dreamed she was having a dinner date with a new colleague. He suggested they go away for the weekend. Across the room, her husband, Noah, was having an intimate dinner with his personal assistant. Amelia left her date and told the assistant to leave her husband alone. She woke, and they made love for the first time in ages.

DREAM BACKGROUND AND MEANING

Amelia had been married to Noah for nineteen years. They had two children and among their friends were known as the perfect couple. However, Amelia had become convinced that her husband was having an affair. Rather than confront him, she had been flirting with a colleague at work, and it had now escalated to being invited on a date. Temptation dreams may reflect dissatisfaction with the current circumstances, rather than proof of infidelity.

INTERPRETATIONS AND FORTUNE-TELLING MEANINGS

⋆ If in a dream the dreamer is responding sexually or romantically to someone not their partner, it is time to talk through problems.

⋆ If in a dream you retaliate to a partner's apparent infidelity by being unfaithful yourself, it is a warning that urgent action is needed to put on the brakes.

⋆ If in the dream you are flirting, it may be necessary to revive not just the sex life, but also the companionship you and your partner once shared.

⋆ If you are making emotional connections with a colleague at work or vice versa, there may be insecurity in the workplace that needs an ego boost.

⋆ If you are jealous when you see your partner with someone else in the dream, you may decide that the relationship is worth saving.

⋆ Even if you are both happily with other people in a dream, you may be tempted to hold on to the security of the familiar.

OUTCOME OF AMELIA'S DREAM

After the dream, Amelia realized that she did not want to risk her marriage by starting her own affair. They both admitted that they had been close to straying. They went away for a vacation without the children and revived the passion that had become lost. Temptation dreams are a valuable early warning system that a relationship needs attention.

Termite

Joseph, forty-five, dreamed he was sitting on the veranda of his new home. There was a rumbling, and the floor beneath him collapsed, followed by the living area, which crumbled like paper. Every surface was covered by hundreds of insects running over him and getting into his hair and clothes.

DREAM BACKGROUND AND MEANING

Joseph was negotiating to buy a beautiful wooden house with a veranda all around it. It was a private cash sale by the person who had inherited it. A few insects were crawling across the floor. The man said beetles were to be expected, as the house had been empty a while. He offered Joseph a very low price for the house, sold as is. Termite dreams can represent bargains that need deeper investigation.

INTERPRETATIONS AND FORTUNE-TELLING MEANINGS

⋆ Since termites destroy the inside of a structure, leaving the outside intact, termite dreams indicate a problem eating away at your confidence.

⋆ If you dream of a few termites and then see a whole lot more eating away at wood, a bad habit that seems not to have affected you will start to have visible effects if you do not stop.

⋆ Killing termites says you will get rid of a toxic atmosphere or relationship in your life.

⋆ Your house represents the self, so there will be room for changes and new beginnings.

⋆ If you dream of the fabulously shaped castle-like termite mounds, sometimes more than 6½ feet high, found in Australia, Africa, and South America, nature's Stonehenge, you will overcome unjust officialdom.

⋆ If termites appear and disappear down cracks in the floor, someone close is concealing underhanded plans.

OUTCOME OF JOSEPH'S DREAM

Using his phone, Joseph secretly photographed the insects and showed them to a surveyor, who said they were termites, not beetles. After a survey, Joseph found that the house was being eaten away and would cost a fortune to fix. Termite dreams represent any problem eating away under the surface of your life, and they warrant deeper probing.

Text-Messaging

Fenella, fifteen, dreamed her cell phone text-messaging was not working, neither was her tablet, and she lost her voice, so she could not phone her friends. She worried she was being talked about. Her friends were too busy texting to notice that she was missing. She woke, immediately checking if her phone still worked.

DREAM BACKGROUND AND MEANING

Fenella was constantly using her phone to text everyone. Her boyfriend complained that she spent all her time texting rather than focusing on him. Fenella rejected the criticism and became annoyed when he did not instantly reply to her frequent texts. Text messages disappearing indicate that you worry about being out of touch in case someone is saying nasty things about you.

INTERPRETATIONS AND FORTUNE-TELLING MEANINGS

★ If in your dream you cannot read a text message because the writing is jumbled, you may be overmonitoring trivia rather than communicating directly with people who matter to you.

★ If you dream that your phone's battery goes flat in the middle of an important text message, consider what you are planning to text, as you may regret it later.

★ If you and a lover or family member far away text at the same time, the connection between you may be telepathic.

★ If you dream you are waiting for a text message that does not come, communication with the sender needs more thought and care.

★ If you dream that someone receives a message different from the one you intended to send, there may be mixed messages or underlying misunderstandings between you.

★ If you receive malicious dream texts from someone you thought was a friend, beware of hidden jealousy.

OUTCOME OF FENELLA'S DREAM

After the dream, Fenella realized she needed to communicate directly with people important to her rather than by impersonal text-speak. She left her cell phone at home when she was seeing her boyfriend. Texts are of great value for instant communication, but dreams can indicate when they are becoming a substitute for love and meaningful friendships.

Thanksgiving

Hetty, eighteen, dreamed she was back at the first Thanksgiving, when the Plymouth colonists and the Wampanoag indigenous people came together in a feast. Her family was happy because the harvest was good, and she made friends with the local children. She vowed she would always spend Thanksgiving with her family.

DREAM BACKGROUND AND MEANING

Hetty was planning on spending Thanksgiving with her family, who came from all parts of the States for a giant family celebration. But her wealthy new boyfriend had been given two tickets to a luxury all-inclusive resort and wanted her to come with him. She had invited him to her family celebration, but he said he was not into tradition. Dreams about Thanksgiving are a reminder of the blessings of family coming together through the generations.

INTERPRETATIONS AND FORTUNE-TELLING MEANINGS

★ If you dream of a happy Thanksgiving, you will have abundance through the coming year based on the efforts you have already put in.

★ If you dream of a past-world Thanksgiving, you are connecting with tradition and will draw pleasure from older family members and friends.

★ If you dream of a family Thanksgiving but have or are offered alternative plans, you may feel pressured to choose between two people or families and cannot please both.

★ If in your dream there is dissension, or family members are absent through estrangement, reach out in the spirit of unity.

★ If in the dream the meal is a culinary disaster, you may worry too much about perfection rather than the pleasure of togetherness.

★ If the past year has been a disaster, a happy Thanksgiving dream marks a healthier, more joyous phase ahead.

OUTCOME OF HETTY'S DREAM

Hetty went with her boyfriend. She missed her family and found his constant boasting about his wealth tedious. The following Thanksgiving she had a new boyfriend, who came along to the family feast. Thanksgiving dreams are a reminder not just of achievement but also of the real treasure of a family together in celebration.

Thanksgiving Tree (Gratitude Tree)

Paulette, twenty-five, dreamed she was home for Thanksgiving. Her mom had made a Thanksgiving tree out of branches and leaves in their many colors that were found near their home. Paulette was hanging her special Thanksgiving message on the tree, expressing gratitude for the support the family had offered for her first job in the big city and for being able to come home for the festival.

DREAM BACKGROUND AND MEANING

Paulette was not really going home for Thanksgiving, as her contract had not been renewed and she did not have the fare home. She purchased an artificial Thanksgiving tree in the colors of the leaves back home and filled it with messages of gratitude. Finally, she added a wish, a family tradition. Dreaming of a Thanksgiving tree in the place you most want to be means you are reaching out to those you miss.

INTERPRETATIONS AND FORTUNE-TELLING MEANINGS

* If you dream you are decorating a Thanksgiving tree and adding messages of gratitude for the previous year, this signifies a happy fulfilling love-filled year ahead.
* If your Thanksgiving tree is empty of messages from others, it's time to actively seek new contacts.
* If all the messages on the tree are negative, you may have false friends.
* If your Thanksgiving tree is a natural, living one, you will take forward existing relationships into the year ahead.
* If you dream that the leaves fall off a living tree, some ventures or relationships have run their course.
* If you add a special wish to your Gratitude tree, this will be fulfilled.

OUTCOME OF PAULETTE'S DREAM

Her wish was fulfilled when, the next day, she received a ticket home for Thanksgiving. She had come to really value her family and took a local job back home. Dreaming of Thanksgiving trees can generate or regenerate enthusiasm to persevere if life seems dire.

Theme Park

Dan, forty-eight, dreamed his family was arguing about which theme parks in Florida they should visit. Wanting to please them, he agreed they could visit them all. Immediately the family was on a gigantic roller coaster, whizzing over the different parks at top speed, and they did not stop at any of them. Afterward, the children blamed Dan for ruining their vacation.

DREAM BACKGROUND AND MEANING

As a new stepfather, Dan was desperate to please his new wife's children. But whatever he offered, they complained. It was affecting his relationship with their mother. Their father, his wife's ex, threw money at the problem, but little else. Theme parks represent concentrated experiences where the highs are intense but short-lived, leaving the often-unsatiated desire for more.

INTERPRETATIONS AND FORTUNE-TELLING MEANINGS

* If you dream of a theme park, this is telling you to introduce more fun into your life or your family's life.
* If you do not wish the dream to end, life will present new opportunities if you maintain the enthusiasm generated by the dream.
* If you realize in the dream you are in the wrong theme park, you may be focusing on superficially immediate impressions rather than on naturally evolving experiences and relationships.
* If you have a scary experience in the dream, there are fears and illusions you need to overcome; for example, performing sharks may represent predatory colleagues.
* If the theme park is closed in the dream, you may be pressured by others to join a risky venture promising a quick return. Be wary.
* If you wait seemingly endlessly for a popular ride in your dream, consider if what is being delayed or postponed in your life is worth waiting for.

OUTCOME OF DAN'S DREAM

Dan realized he could not compete with the children's birth father. But he could give them his time and his knowledge of the natural world. He took the children wilderness camping and orienteering, and they loved it. Theme parks in dreams represent occasional thrills but rarely long-term satisfaction or fulfillment.

Thirst

Trina, fifty, noticed an outbuilding in her garden she had not seen before, and inside were penned animals dying of thirst. She knew they were hers and she had totally forgotten them because she had been so busy. She was trying to revive them, but for many it was too late.

DREAM BACKGROUND AND MEANING

Trina had taken on the responsibility of looking after her frail elderly mother. But because Trina was a single mother with a full-time job and a teenage family, she was aware she could not offer her mother the care she needed. When Trina had suffered a fall recently, a neighbor had promised to look in on her mother. But her mother had refused to eat or drink, and Trina was reproached for neglect. Drink, a necessity of life, can appear in thirst dreams as an inability to satisfy everyone's overwhelming needs.

INTERPRETATIONS AND FORTUNE-TELLING MEANINGS

★ Assuming you are not physically thirsty, being thirsty in a dream says you are not being given enough affection or gratitude.

★ The dream may be a warning that a source of income may be drying up and you need to find a new outlet for your talents.

★ If you are thirsty and cannot find a drink, you are missing someone who makes you feel fulfilled emotionally or sexually.

★ If you are thirsty but cannot drink what you are given, what you are being offered in life or in a relationship is not satisfying you.

★ If you dream you are drinking but still feel thirsty, you are lacking necessary knowledge or being fobbed off with inadequate information.

★ If you dream others are thirsty and you are trying to find water for them, they may be overreliant on you.

OUTCOME OF TRINA'S DREAM

After the dream, Trina realized she could not care for her increasingly dependent mother as well as her family and work, and she did not have adequate room to house her mother. Reluctantly, Trina persuaded her mother to enter a nursing home, but she has ever since suffered guilt. Thirst dreams are rooted in basic needs but also in guilt when we feel responsible for the well-being of others.

Thorns

Michael, twenty-eight, dreamed he was in a Sleeping Beauty–like scenario where his fiancée was locked in a tower surrounded by high thorn hedges. He slashed at the thorns with his sword but was getting cut to pieces as more thorns sprang up. He knew he had to rescue her or lose her forever. At last, he broke through the hedge and rode off with her, pursued by men on horseback with scimitars.

DREAM BACKGROUND AND MEANING

Michael wanted to marry Sharmila, but her parents, from a traditional community, had forbidden her to see him. They were sending her to Delhi for a traditional arranged marriage with a cousin. Michael knew he and Sharmila had to go away immediately, where her parents would not find them. Fairy tale–like dream themes set out stark choices and consequences clearly and are common throughout the ages where a decision is life-changing.

INTERPRETATIONS AND FORTUNE-TELLING MEANINGS

★ A thorn hedge is a traditional symbol of magick and psychic defense. It indicates growing occult knowledge or spiritual practices.

★ Thorns provide a barrier against those who are critical or are draining your self-confidence, especially neighbors or relatives.

★ A rose protected by thorns says you may feel pressured into sex or sexual practices with which you are uncomfortable. Trust your protective instincts.

★ To be tangled in thorns indicates a difficult situation from which you need to extricate yourself carefully to avoid further pain.

★ Thorn bushes in blossom promise better times ahead after stagnation or an impasse.

★ If you dream that thorns are hidden in greenery, a seemingly supportive friend or family member will show secret spite or jealousy.

OUTCOME OF MICHAEL'S DREAM

Michael took Sharmila away and they changed their names. They are happy but hope someday they will be reconciled with Sharmila's family. Thorn-dream symbolism varies according to whether you need protection by the thorns or are being excluded by them.

Tides

Ollie, twenty-five, often dreamed of riding huge waves on his surfboard on the incoming tide on Australia's Bondi Beach, and winning large monetary prizes. Then a shark would appear and drag him under, and all he could see was blood in the darkness.

DREAM BACKGROUND AND MEANING

Ollie was a lifeguard on a beach in Southwest England, spending his days rescuing paddleboarders, children with inflatables, and holidaymakers cut off by sudden high tides. He was bored and did not have the chance to train in order to compete in international surfing events. Dreams of tides vary in meaning according to the nature and intensity of the tide.

INTERPRETATIONS AND FORTUNE-TELLING MEANINGS

★ If you dream of swimming at high tide, you are ready to meet challenges head-on.

★ The significance of an incoming tide depends on whether it brings garbage, symbolizing bad memories, or treasure, symbolizing the mending of estranged love or new beginnings.

★ An ebb tide represents the need to let go of what is no longer relevant in your life.

★ A slack tide, the space between the incoming and outgoing tides, says it is time to wait and see how life unfolds.

★ A tidal river is the meeting of two people in love and their mingling sexually and emotionally.

★ Struggling to swim against the current says you may be trying to buck the trend rather than going with the flow of life's energies and events.

OUTCOME OF OLLIE'S DREAM

Ollie realized the shark attack represented his own fears of failing if he competed on the world stage. He had an uncle in Australia who could sponsor him, so he took a chance working as a lifeguard on Bondi Beach and seriously pursued his surfing training. Since tides signify the ebb and flow of emotions in dreams and in actuality, tune into your own ongoing energy flows and changing moods so you swim with the optimal tide of life and not against it.

Tiles

Single mother Ambrosia, fifty-five, dreamed a tiler came to replace the tiles in her bathroom, as they were starting to come away from the wall. He removed the old tiles, then asked her for double the original quoted fee, as the bathroom needed waterproofing. Ambrosia didn't have any more money. He left with the first installment and never returned, leaving the bathroom untiled. She woke worried.

DREAM BACKGROUND AND MEANING

Ambrosia had found a tiler online to replace her bathroom surfaces. He had also pointed out that her roof had several cracked tiles and warned her that she could suffer serious leaks. He quoted a price for all the work that was way above what she could afford. What was the dream warning her about?

INTERPRETATIONS AND FORTUNE-TELLING MEANINGS

★ Having tiles replaced in a dream indicates the need for restoring order if life is chaotic.

★ If in your dream you are happy with the design and price of the new tiles, this promises a harmonious period.

★ Broken or cracked tiles suggest there may be cracks appearing in a once-untroubled relationship.

★ If you are uncertain about the honesty of the person replacing your tiles in the dream and you are contemplating having tiles replaced, check credentials and be sure that financial terms are fixed in advance.

★ If tiles on your wall do not match, there may be a mismatch with someone you are trying to fit into your life.

★ If you dream that the new tiles instantly fall off your wall, a new acquaintance may make your life more complicated.

OUTCOME OF AMBROSIA'S DREAM

Ambrosia mentioned her concerns to a neighbor, who sent her husband, a builder, to check the tiling. He told her there was nothing wrong with her roof tiles and he would fix her bathroom at a quarter of the price. Tile dreams can stress how important it is to ensure that a new relationship, career, or financial arrangement will not disrupt the order of your life.

Time Travel

Orlando, twenty-eight, dreamed he was in a tunnel with lights on the walls and doors marked with names of different centuries and lands. He had always been fascinated by tea clipper ships, which transported tea from China in the 1840s. He dreamed he entered that time and was sailing around the Cape of Good Hope when a huge storm blew up. He willed himself to wake from the dream.

DREAM BACKGROUND AND MEANING

Orlando was convinced that he had perished on a tea clipper in a past life. He had a good job in a shipping office, but he had been offered a chance to crew on a tall ship sailing around the world for two years, the time it had taken for a tea clipper to make the round-trip journey. Dreams are a natural vehicle for time travel. Dreams and past and future worlds share the ether energy field surrounding us.

INTERPRETATIONS AND FORTUNE-TELLING MEANINGS

* If a particular time period from the past appears frequently in your dreams, it may hold answers to present-day challenges.
* If you dream of future worlds, you may discover potential and talents you can develop in your present life.
* If you recognize foes or destructive lovers in time-travel dreams, you may become aware of strategies to deal with them and their memories today.
* If you travel to an unexpected time, a spirit guide may be waiting, or a twin soul, perhaps one not yet encountered in this life.
* If you meet your present family on your time travels, you may understand why they behave the way they do. It is a good omen if you have children in the past world and want them in the present.
* If you want to time travel in dreams, meditate or visualize your means of travel—time machine, staircase, or marble steps—and a doorway before sleep will in time become spontaneous.

OUTCOME OF ORLANDO'S DREAM

Orlando decided to crew on the tall ship and, since he had perished on the past-life tea clipper, he knew this time he would return safely. Time-travel dreams, however we view their source, are rich in insights for this life and confirm the rightness or otherwise of a course.

Tithes, Annual Contributions

Robert, thirty-nine, dreamed he was placing an envelope containing his annual contribution to the church's expenses into the collection box at church. His wife, Leonie, leaned across, removed the envelope from the box, placed it in her handbag, and then left the church, leaving Robert very embarrassed.

DREAM BACKGROUND AND MEANING

Robert was brought up in a devout Christian household. Tithing, contributing 10 percent of his annual income to the church, had been a part of his life since he first went to work. However, since marrying Leonie four years ago, who rarely attended church, they had argued over tithing, because they had suffered a major financial setback. Robert had told Leonie he was not prepared to reduce his payment to the church. Leonie had made threats to leave. Dreams of giving a church tithe or an annual contribution to another organization may reveal deep resentments if a partner does not share your beliefs.

INTERPRETATIONS AND FORTUNE-TELLING MEANINGS

* If you dream you are collecting tithes, prosperity will come through joint work or projects.
* If you dream of a medieval world where a tithe collector demands a portion of your grain, you may feel pressured to offer more than you can afford emotionally or financially.
* If you are asked for tithes you cannot afford, you may need to question old obligations to support others.
* If you dream you are happy giving tithes, what you give will come back as love, approval, tangible profits, or investments.
* If you dream you are reminding someone to pay their tithes, you may find others are less generous or prompt repaying debts.
* If you dream that someone close stops you from paying a tithe, you may have conflicting priorities and loyalties.

OUTCOME OF ROBERT'S DREAM

Robert did not want to lose Leonie but felt torn. He talked to the priest, who told Robert he should give only what he could afford and should not leave his household short. Dreams of traditional practices such as tithes or set annual contributions often can refer to family members who demand support year after year, whether in terms of practical help or financial input.

Toad

Alessandro, thirty-five, dreamed that he was joining an annual moon potency ceremony, where he touched a huge toad-shaped rock and was promised a child. He rushed down the mountain to tell his parents, who were delighted. He then went to tell his wife that they would be blessed, but all her possessions were gone and a note said she was going back to Madrid, where they had met.

DREAM BACKGROUND AND MEANING

Since Alessandro had married Juanita, they had been constantly pressured by his family, because a grandson was considered essential to carry on the family name. His mother had visited the local *bruja* (witch) to obtain a dried toad amulet, which she hid in their house. Alessandro could no longer make love, and Juanita was threatening to move out unless his parents backed off. The toad is linked with potency and virility but can represent undue coercion by relatives anxious to conceive.

INTERPRETATIONS AND FORTUNE-TELLING MEANINGS

★ To dream of a toad with a golden coin in its mouth foretells money from an unexpected source.

★ Because in lands from China to Africa the toad is associated with the moon, to dream of a toad during the full moon heralds immense good fortune.

★ If you have a burning wish or desire, dreaming of a toad on a crescent-moon night promises tangible steps toward fulfillment within three lunar cycles.

★ The alchemical involvement of the toad in creating the stone to turn metals into gold says that the dream of a toad in an old-fashioned laboratory advises you to persist.

★ Brightly colored toads in a dream rain forest warn of hidden venom and spite toward you from someone seemingly charismatic.

OUTCOME OF ALESSANDRO'S DREAM

After the dream and finding the dried toad, Alessandro realized that he and Juanita were being railroaded into a child for which they were not ready. They moved back to Madrid, their lovemaking became spontaneous, and several years later they had a daughter and son, to the delight of his parents. Toad dreams have strong magical associations with money and fertility but can sometimes reflect the ambitions of others to interfere in destiny.

Toadstools (Poisonous Mushrooms)

Daphne, eighteen, dreamed she was a child again dancing round a fairy ring of spotted toadstools. The fairies invited her in and offered her a feast on golden plates. They told her that if she ate a spotted toadstool, she would always be able to see the fairies. She was about to eat one when she heard her mother calling, and the dream faded.

DREAM BACKGROUND AND MEANING

Daphne was on a wilderness food-foraging trip, but her boyfriend said the leader was far too cautious and suggested they go off alone for real foraging. They found a field of fabulous spotted mushrooms like the ones in Daphne's dream and picked some to take back and cook. Daphne was dubious that they were safe, as they looked like ones on the warning chart the leader had given them. Her boyfriend assured her that she could trust him. Some exciting experiences can easily tip over into disaster if you do not set boundaries.

INTERPRETATIONS AND FORTUNE-TELLING MEANINGS

★ If you dream of a fairy-tale toadstool circle or an elf on a toadstool, beware of trusting someone who has all the answers.

★ If you are invited into a magick toadstool ring, be aware that exciting offers in everyday life need an opt-out clause.

★ Since some mushrooms can be poisonous, if you are not certain whether your dream mushroom represents danger, check in everyday life before committing yourself to what may be an unwise course.

★ If you find an empty fairy ring in your dream, the magick may have gone out of your life.

★ If you dream you stop someone from eating a toadstool, or poisonous mushroom, you may need to be a steadying influence to a friend heading for danger.

OUTCOME OF DAPHNE'S DREAM

After her dream, Daphne was more cautious than her boyfriend and checked with the leader before cooking the mushrooms, which turned out to be poisonous. Her boyfriend went home in a snit. Dreams can act as an inner radar, separating excitement from unwise risk.

Tomatoes

Benjamin, sixty, dreamed he was walking between his tomato plants and they were unripe and withered. Suddenly, a golden light appeared from the skies and within seconds the plants were fully grown and ripe. He tasted a tomato and it was the sweetest he had ever known.

DREAM BACKGROUND AND MEANING

Benjamin's tomato plants had failed because of a late frost. Since tomatoes were a major part of his business, he was not making any profit. But he refused to allow his son, who was his business partner, to modernize the business, as he said fruit and vegetables tasted better without interference.

INTERPRETATIONS AND FORTUNE-TELLING MEANINGS

★ If you dream of a dish of ripe tomatoes, it predicts health and fertility in the way most needed.

★ If your dream tomatoes are near a source of heat, prosperity will spread through the home.

★ If you dream you are cooking a tomato-based dish for a lover or would-be lover, it is a good omen for romance and passion, as they were traditionally considered an aphrodisiac and were called *pommes d'amour*, love apples, in France.

★ Unripe tomatoes represent the need to wait for results to materialize. If you act too early, you will not get the full benefit.

★ Overripe tomatoes warn that the right moment to speak or act has passed.

★ Dreaming of throwing rotten tomatoes at a person or event indicates you are far angrier than you have acknowledged. Be careful that your actual protest does not put you in the wrong.

OUTCOME OF BENJAMIN'S DREAM

Benjamin told his son about the dream, and his son showed him a catalogue containing golden heat and light devices to set above the tomatoes. Benjamin decided to invest in the equipment, and profitability doubled. The following year Benjamin retired, moving back to his homeland, Italy, to grow tomatoes under the sun. Tomato dreams can create health and abundance in all kinds of ways, and tomatoes growing in dreams are a sign that your life will prosper and grow.

Tongue Stud

Amy, twenty-eight, dreamed she had come home with the tongue stud she had promised herself for her birthday since no one else had bought her anything. As she entered the front door, her father started yelling that she was late and he wanted his dinner. Then he saw the tongue stud as she replied and went berserk, hitting her and telling her that if she did not take it out she could get out. She left with what she was wearing and her guitar.

DREAM BACKGROUND AND MEANING

Amy had put her career as part of a traveling music backup group on hold since her mother had died six months earlier. Her father had always been abusive, but she had promised her mother to care for him. Now she felt she had to speak her mind and leave, or disappear beneath his control. Tongue studs are linked with the need and often suppression of clear communication (see "Body Piercing," p. 63).

INTERPRETATIONS AND FORTUNE-TELLING MEANINGS

★ Dreaming of having a tongue stud indicates that there is something the dreamer needs to say that is building up inside.

★ Having a tongue piercing in a dream and a stud fitted often precedes establishing or reestablishing assertiveness.

★ To remove a tongue stud because someone objects to it in the dream warns that keeping the peace may be at a personal cost of speaking freely.

★ A gold tongue stud indicates success through communication or in the performing industry.

★ A silver tongue stud says that necessary words will be moderated with tact and kindness at a sensitive time in a relationship.

OUTCOME OF AMY'S DREAM

Amy realized her father was not going to change and took a job with a backup group traveling overseas. She had a gold tongue stud fitted after leaving home. Tongue-stud dreams are of special significance because they deal with communication, and having one fitted may be an act of defiance if identity is being eroded.

Tourist Train

Monica, sixty-four, dreamed that just before Christmas she was riding around the town on a tourist train on which there was a Santa Claus in each carriage. Excited children boarded, and the train passed through brilliantly decorated streets, stopping at each child's house with a wrapped present. Then the train went back to the depot. The lights went off, leaving Monica in the darkness.

DREAM BACKGROUND AND MEANING

Recent Christmases for Monica had involved sitting in a corner while hordes of youngsters charged around screaming. Her dream reminded her of the Spanish Christmases she had had in her twenties, working in a Spanish bar and then hitching a lift home on the festive train passing by. Dreaming of a festive land train is a reminder that fun can be had at any age.

INTERPRETATIONS AND FORTUNE-TELLING MEANINGS

* If you dream you are a child on a train around town at Christmas or at a significant festival, it is now time for making new memories.
* Dreaming of riding on a train in an unknown location suggests you may be seeking freedom.
* If a train is full and you miss the ride, stop waiting for excitement to come to you.
* If the train goes in circles around a familiar town, it may be time to break the shackles of a bad relationship.
* Being left on the train when everyone else gets off suggests you need to start socializing.
* If you enjoy your train ride in a new city but do not have the desire to explore, you might be in need of a vacation.

OUTCOME OF MONICA'S DREAM

Monica is looking at using her pension lump sum to buy a bar in Spain, located near a stop for the train tour. A tourist train is limited by its set route but can remind the dreamer that they can get off at any stage in life, rather than watching it go endlessly around.

Tower

Bethany, forty-nine, dreamed she was on the highest level of the Eiffel Tower in Paris, waiting for her Internet lover, Kevan, to share a romantic weekend together. He arrived with his three sulky teenagers and said he was taking them sightseeing. Unnoticed, Bethany descended the tower, disillusioned.

DREAM BACKGROUND AND MEANING

Bethany had never wanted children. Her new love had three, but she had not considered that they would be part of their lives. She was having doubts, as she wanted the high life and never intended to bring up someone else's children. The Eiffel Tower is a symbol of rising to the heights of romance and passion, but descent alone can represent disillusionment.

INTERPRETATIONS AND FORTUNE-TELLING MEANINGS

* Dreaming of climbing a tower says you can aspire to a high position and have made the right choices.
* A dream of a church or clock tower heralds a family celebration, especially a wedding or birth.
* If you are in a watchtower, prepare yourself for approaching opportunities and avoidable challenges.
* Being locked in a tower speaks of restrictions or overwork preventing you from enjoying life.
* If you dream you have shut yourself in the tower because of betrayal or major setbacks, consider whether it is time to give the world another chance.
* If you dream you fall from a tower, it indicates you should beware of those who would undermine your ambitions.
* If the dream tower crumbles or is ruined, the heady heights of love or ambition may bring disillusion and unkept promises.

OUTCOME OF BETHANY'S DREAM

Bethany realized she was unrealistic in her expectations, as most people of her and Kevan's age would have ties from a previous relationship. She resolved to get to know his children before deciding if she wanted high romance or a more realistic kind of love. The kind of tower in our dream reveals a lot about what we seek to attain.

Toys

Pamela, seventy-five, had a movie-type dream in which all the toys in the attic left their boxes and marched out of the house. She tried to catch them, but each was claimed by a child and disappeared. Pamela woke crying.

DREAM BACKGROUND AND MEANING

When Pamela was fifteen, she was placed in a home for unmarried mothers and babies, and her son was taken from her at birth, for adoption. Since then, she had collected a toy every year for his birthday until he was eighteen. She had received a letter from him via an adoption reunion registry saying he had no wish to meet the woman who had abandoned him. Pamela was heartbroken. Toy dreams can revive wonderful memories of childhood or can be symbols of unrequited sorrow.

INTERPRETATIONS AND FORTUNE-TELLING MEANINGS

* If you dream of being a child, playing happily with your toys, you will enjoy precious family contact.
* If you dream of a toy you always wanted as a child but never had, it is time to leave the past behind and buy the toy for a child who would value it.
* If you are clearing out your children's toys, now that they are adults, focus on your own future beyond parenthood.
* If you dream of broken toys, you need to reconcile resentment for a less-than-ideal childhood or leave it behind.
* If toys come to life in your dream, some childhood desires can still be achieved, albeit modified.
* If you are longing to become a parent or grandparent and are buying or making toys in the dream, it is a good omen that you will have children in your life when the time is right.

OUTCOME OF PAMELA'S DREAM

After the dream, Pamela accepted that her son probably was not coming back. She took the toys to a charity store and volunteered at the local school, teaching children traditional crafts, her special gift. Toys hold great dream symbolism, for they can heal our inner child and override sometimes unsatisfactory childhood experiences by nurturing others.

Traffic Jam

Penelope, fifty-five, dreamed she was stuck in a traffic jam on her way to an urgent medical appointment. There was no chance of changing routes or turning around. Suddenly, her car elevated, flew over the traffic, and landed gently in the clear road ahead. She knew instantly that all would be well with her health, and she lost all fear.

DREAM BACKGROUND AND MEANING

Penelope had been postponing seeing her physician about worrying medical symptoms she had noticed, and had created a thousand and one reasons she should not go. But that did not stop her from worrying, and the symptoms were getting worse, which resulted in her avoiding appointments even more. Traffic jams in dreams may involve consciously or unconsciously putting obstacles in the way of unpleasant or worrying events.

INTERPRETATIONS AND FORTUNE-TELLING MEANINGS

* Dreams of traffic jams caused by an accident do not warn of actual crashes, but of potential problems in any venture caused by not checking plans ahead to avoid delays or mishaps.
* Traffic-jam dreams are anxiety dreams about being late or delayed, so allow extra time for reaching events or fulfilling projects soon after the dream.
* An endless traffic jam is a symbol of overload where one demand piles up on another and priorities need rethinking.
* A traffic jam suddenly clearing indicates the end of a slow or worrying situation.
* To cause a traffic jam by breaking down suggests that you may be seeking a postponement of a responsibility that was foisted on you and accepted unwillingly.
* If you dream that others cause a traffic jam by breaking down, you need to clear obstructive people and unhelpful advice from your life.

OUTCOME OF PENELOPE'S DREAM

After the dream, Penelope realized that her delays in booking an appointment were only postponing the problem. As the dream foretold when she flew over the traffic jam, scans showed that she only needed medication and a minor procedure to restore her to health. The nature and outcome of traffic-jam dreams can suggest that the dreamer may need to clear a blockage or uncertainty that prevents moving forward.

Traffic Ticket

Belinda, nineteen, regularly dreams of being stopped by a police officer, handed a traffic ticket, and told she must attend court and will lose her license. She protests that she does not know what she has done wrong and wakes fearful.

DREAM BACKGROUND AND MEANING

Belinda passed her driving test a few months earlier and had had no driving incidents. She was very worried about the dream, which she feared might be a warning, and was reluctant to drive. Her parents were very anxious and, when they were passengers in her car, constantly warned her of hazards she had already seen. All her life they had made her fearful. Belinda attended a local college, as she was reluctant to leave home. Now she had a chance to study overseas, but her parents said it was too dangerous. Traffic tickets symbolize fears of getting in trouble with authority, often traceable to overanxious parenting.

INTERPRETATIONS AND FORTUNE-TELLING MEANINGS

* Receiving a traffic ticket in a dream represents fears of other people judging you for perceived inadequacies.
* Should the dreams recur, the source of your anxiety is still influencing you.
* Dreaming of being given a traffic ticket for parking in the wrong place suggests you need to change unsatisfactory parts of your routine.
* Being given a traffic ticket for speeding says you are doing too much and should slow down.
* Dreaming of ripping up a traffic ticket says you are defying or need to go against convention and take more chances.
* Being unfairly given a traffic ticket says petty injustices should be challenged before they escalate.

OUTCOME OF BELINDA'S DREAM

Belinda realized that her parents were making her afraid not only of driving but of life and of the consequences of breaking the rules. She refused to drive with her parents anymore and applied for the overseas sabbatical. She now confidently drives and lives overseas. Traffic dreams can reveal fears of spontaneity and so can be positive.

Train

Paul, nineteen, dreamed he was catching a train to a university to study accountancy. He was burdened with mountains of luggage, some of which got left behind on the platform when the train suddenly pulled out. Paul picked up his guitar and got off the train at the next station, leaving the remaining mound of luggage on the train.

DREAM BACKGROUND AND MEANING

Paul was a gifted musician and had been offered an apprenticeship in a music studio. But his father, who owned an accountancy firm, insisted that Paul go to a university so he could join the family firm upon graduating. Train tracks offer a route that leads to a predetermined destination, unless you get off the train or do not get on.

INTERPRETATIONS AND FORTUNE-TELLING MEANINGS

* Dreaming of traveling by train promises happy days ahead if the journey is through lovely scenery to a desired destination.
* Luggage overload represents being weighed down by unwanted expectations, excess emotional baggage, or obligations to others.
* Trains that are late, are canceled, or do not arrive forewarn of problems in any actual planned journeys or in life changes where others are railroading you down a path that feels wrong.
* If you dream there is an emergency stop or derailment, your future plans are moving too fast. Put on the brakes.
* Entering tunnels is associated with an illicit passionate sexual relationship. Is it wise?
* A dream of a train station where you are waiting for a train represents a change point chosen or imposed according to your feelings about the journey in the dream.

OUTCOME OF PAUL'S DREAM

Paul realized that he did not want to be an accountant and was willing to take a chance on a musical career, even though his father would not help him financially.

Decide if the dream destination is what you want right now, whether a relationship, career, or location move, and whether accepting the ticket has too high a price in return for losing independence.

Transgender Concerns

Olivia, eighteen, who is very beautiful, dreamed she arrived at her estranged parents' house. In their hall mirror she saw a hideous monster with claws and fangs. Her parents screamed, pushed her out, and slammed the door. Her lover was waiting outside, and Olivia realized that she was lovely again.

DREAM BACKGROUND AND MEANING

Olivia, whose birth name was Michael, from a very early age experienced distress over a mismatch between her assigned sex and gender identity. Because of her parents' hostility, she left home to live with her favorite aunt. Olivia had had no contact with her parents since leaving and had recently transitioned. Olivia was scared to see them, because she feared they would still reject her.

Dreams in which you are ugly suggest that you are having identity issues caused by others who refuse to accept you as you are.

INTERPRETATIONS AND FORTUNE-TELLING MEANINGS

* If you frequently dream of adopting another gender, this affirms the rightness of your choice.
* If you dream that a friend appears to have changed sex, they may be suffering an identity crisis not necessarily linked with gender.
* If you dream that you are forced by family into a strongly feminine or macho role against your natural persona, you need to resist stereotyping.
* If in the dream you have transitioned and suddenly appear hideous, note those projecting their deep-seated prejudices.
* If you dream you are advising someone else who is transitioning, consider taking up counseling, informally or professionally.
* If you dream you are trying on male and female clothes and neither feels right, do not be rushed into making decisions or changes before you are ready.

OUTCOME OF OLIVIA'S DREAM

Olivia wrote to her parents, enclosing photographs of her new life and her lover. The letters were returned unopened. Olivia realized the dream was warning her that direct contact would end in heartbreak. The reaction of others in a dream to your changed persona picks up unconscious signals of their true feelings, and you may discover unexpected allies.

Transitions, Changes

Winifred, seventy, dreamed she was watching her childhood home being demolished as part of clearing out the backstreet slums. She retrieved a cutting from a rosebush that had survived, and it was the first flower planted in her new home. She woke feeling comforted.

DREAM BACKGROUND AND MEANING

Winifred remembered that when she was ten, her old community was razed to the ground and families were forcibly moved to impersonal new estates on the city's edge. As in the dream, she had gone back and retrieved the rose cutting from the rubble, and it had eased the transition to a new world that ultimately brought many advantages. Years later, as a widow, Winifred purchased a small apartment, as her marital home was too expensive to maintain, but she was having doubts. Transition dreams can focus on a symbol like the rose, reminding the dreamer that even unwelcome changes can turn out well.

INTERPRETATIONS AND FORTUNE-TELLING MEANINGS

* If you dream in later years of a successful childhood transition, it reminds you that going forward brings compensations, even if not sought.
* If a dream symbol like Winifred's rose offers continuity through transitions, it can offer reassurance of a good transition.
* If you dream of a rickety bridge that you are reluctant to cross, the transition may seem uncertain but offers a better life.
* If you dream of airports, bus stops, ferry ports, or crossroads, you need to be sure the transition is leading you where you want to be.
* If you dream of floating without a compass in a boat on the ocean, you may be allowing others or circumstances to dictate your future direction.

OUTCOME OF WINIFRED'S DREAM

The day Winifred moved, she took a cutting from the original rose retrieved after the childhood demolition and transplanted it outside her apartment window, and she grew to love her new home. Dreams can remind us of earlier transitions that, though unwanted, turned out well.

Trapdoor

Mark, thirty-eight, dreamed he was in a room full of trapdoors. As he stepped on a trapdoor, the one immediately in front of him opened and a pantomime demon figure in black popped up and asked a quiz question. Mark knew if he got the answer wrong the door beneath him would swallow him. The trapdoors seemed never-ending, and the questions got more obscure. At last, he stopped the game and made his way, avoiding the traps, to the door, hearing the mocking laugher of the pantomime kings.

DREAM BACKGROUND AND MEANING

Mark had been offered an interview at a prestigious company where the rewards were high but staff turnover was frequent. Mark was ambitious, but he had been concerned by reports of the pressure of intense and competitive sales targets. Trapdoors conceal or reveal hidden opportunities but also pitfalls to the unwary.

INTERPRETATIONS AND FORTUNE-TELLING MEANINGS

* If you dream that a hidden trapdoor is suddenly revealed, a secret or secret emotion will surface, representing danger if discovered.
* A dream of a trapdoor offering a hiding place enables you to escape scrutiny or attack in a hostile environment.
* A trapdoor can give access to buried treasure, an undeveloped talent, or unexpected opportunity.
* If you dream that an old trapdoor is filled with cobwebs, memories or faces from the past may bring an unfinished matter to its conclusion.
* If demonic figures lurk beneath a trapdoor, a primal fear rooted in guilt or undiscovered misdemeanors is still haunting you and should be faced.
* If you dream there is a series of trapdoors, you may feel under constant pressure to prove yourself at work, socially, or in a relationship and may need to opt out.

OUTCOME OF MARK'S DREAM

Mark withdrew from the job interview, as he felt the constant competition and pressures did not merit the extra salary and prospects. Beware if you suspect someone is trying to lure you into a commitment or purchase with a high hidden price.

Trapped Underwater in a Car

Stella, nineteen, dreamed that her mother was driving straight into the river, though Stella, the only passenger, screamed to warn her. The car became submerged, but Stella managed to remove her seat belt and escape. She tried to open her mother's door, but her mother pulled Stella farther underwater. Rescuers helped her mother, and Stella swam alone to the surface.

DREAM BACKGROUND AND MEANING

Stella wanted to join the security forces and travel the world. Her mother, Zoe, had plans for her daughter to go to a local college and marry the boy next door. Stella felt totally trapped.

INTERPRETATIONS AND FORTUNE-TELLING MEANINGS

* Being submerged by another's emotional needs may be represented in dreams by a car (your path through life) being driven by someone whose possessive love drowns you and them.
* If you know the driver, but they ignore your warnings, they are putting their own needs first, refusing to recognize reality.
* If you are driving the car that hits the water, avoid reacting to life only with your heart.
* If the driver is a stranger, you may be in danger of being influenced to make an unwise emotional or sexual decision.
* If you escape from a submerged car, you can attain independence.
* If you are rescuing someone in the car and they are pulling you under, beware of falling for emotional blackmail.
* If you dream that floods submerge the car or a bridge collapses, you may need to move away from a stifling influence.

OUTCOME OF STELLA'S DREAM

Stella realized she had to live her own life and that her mother would use any means to keep her at home. Stella applied to the armed forces and was accepted. Though Stella felt guilty, her mother developed a good social life in Stella's absence. Sometimes it is important to put your own survival first, if someone close is dragging you into their life fantasy.

Trash, Garbage

Spencer, thirty-two, dreamed he was emptying trash down the chute from his top-floor apartment when a large box became stuck. He slipped and hurtled down the chute into the trash cans at the bottom. Spencer was almost buried in trash. He shouted, but no one heard. Even more trash came down the chute and he feared he would suffocate. He woke choking.

DREAM BACKGROUND AND MEANING

Spencer shared an apartment with his younger brother, Colin, who refused to clear up his mess and constantly partied in the apartment. Spencer felt he was drowning in his brother's chaotic lifestyle, but their parents, who owned the apartment, said that as Spencer was the older brother, he should take care of Colin. Spencer's girlfriend suggested he should move in with her. But how would Colin cope? Trash or garbage dreams can refer to emotional as well as actual chaos.

INTERPRETATIONS AND FORTUNE-TELLING MEANINGS

✶ If you dream you have cleared trash, you are entering a harmonious, orderly time in your domestic or work life.

✶ To dream of piles of trash in or around your home advises that you resolve old issues and long-standing arguments.

✶ Dreaming of disposing of other people's trash means you are accepting problems others have created.

✶ If in your dream every time you clear trash from your home or yard it reappears, protest, as others are adding to your workload.

✶ If you dream you are searching through trash for something precious, value what you have in a relationship or risk losing it.

✶ If you dream someone is taking your trash away, you have escaped the consequences of a mistake.

OUTCOME OF SPENCER'S DREAM

Spencer told his parents and brother he was moving out. After Spencer left, his parents visited the apartment and were horrified by the chaos, for Spencer had always cleared up before they came. They gave Colin notice. Dreams in which you are drowning in trash suggest that a problem, whether actual or emotional, is becoming overwhelming and should be resolved.

Travel, Journey

Tricia, a forty-year-old divorced teacher, dreamed she was traveling on a Greyhound bus to an unknown destination. She asked the other passengers where the bus was heading, but no one knew. In sheer frustration, she asked the driver, but he was not able to hear her. The journey continued relentlessly along the freeway throughout the dream with no external road signs, and she woke in a panic.

DREAM BACKGROUND AND MEANING

Tricia had lost her job and had been traveling to out-of-state interviews without success. She was applying for multiple jobs, many of which did not fit her experience or expertise. One unsuccessful journey merged into another.

INTERPRETATIONS AND FORTUNE-TELLING MEANINGS

✶ Dreaming of being on or planning a journey indicates future profit, satisfaction, or disappointment, depending on how pleasing and successful the travel and destination are.

✶ Vivid travel dreams to a specific place may be a premonition of an unexpected chance to travel, move, or spend a vacation there, especially if the place was previously unconsidered.

✶ Travel dreams can be wish-fulfillment, indicating you need to broaden your physical horizons if life has become routine. The dream nudges you in the right direction.

✶ Delays and mishaps on the journey represent questions about the advisability of the travel.

✶ Dreaming of missing your destination or being on the wrong bus, train, or plane suggests you may be seeking change for its own sake but learn that the problem was lifestyle, not location.

✶ Dreaming of heading to an unknown destination and being unable to get information suggests you need to plan your desired future path rather than following every avenue available.

OUTCOME OF TRICIA'S DREAM

Tricia rewrote her job-search profile, and applied only for posts for which she was well qualified. She regained her direction and gained the right job.

Are you missing signals that would prevent you from going on wasted journeys, taking misguided career steps, or pursuing unsuitable relationships, instead of taking a chance that your plans will work?

Triplets

Georgia, thirty, dreamed she was walking down a path between fields when she saw identically dressed girl triplets running toward her, laughing. They put their fingers to their lips and raced off into the corn, only to appear again farther along the path, again indicating that she should be quiet. The third time this occurred, Georgia tried to catch them, but they called, "Wait, not yet, soon," and ran into the corn, laughing.

DREAM BACKGROUND AND MEANING

Georgia was waiting for three pieces of good news: first, that her house sale was going through; second, that the house of her dreams would be hers; and third, that she would get the promotion that would make it possible to manage the mortgage payments. All three occurrences were interdependent and uncertain. There had been numerous delays, and she was thinking of pulling out and staying in her rented apartment. Triplets, especially laughing ones, herald the favorable coming together of three related factors.

INTERPRETATIONS AND FORTUNE-TELLING MEANINGS

⋆ If you want a family, giving birth to triplet babies in your dream says you will, if you choose, have three children, not necessarily all together.

⋆ If you dream of being pregnant with triplets, no matter your age, your financial and business fortunes will increase threefold.

⋆ If you dream that three sisters are walking in a line or spinning or weaving, they are linked with the triple sisters of fate. Someone favorable from your past will return to the present and bring happiness.

⋆ If you dream of three mystical identical sisters dancing in a circle, this is a magical dream and says your healing, divinatory, and psychic powers will spontaneously grow together.

⋆ If you dream you are trying to take care of three babies at once, whether or not you are a parent or prospective parent, you have taken on too much and need to prioritize.

OUTCOME OF GEORGIA'S DREAM

The dream encouraged Georgia to persist. She obtained a promotion, made a good sale, and gained the ability to buy the house of her dreams. Triplet dreams almost always are omens of good fortune and of tripling what you most want.

Truth-or-Dare Game

Stacey, seventeen, dreamed she was balancing on the narrow ledge of the dorm window three floors above ground level as her Dare challenge after the bottle spun toward her. She was scared but did not want her new roommates to ask awkward questions about her life. She lost her balance and plunged down headfirst.

DREAM BACKGROUND AND MEANING

Stacey had won a scholarship. She was a year younger than her fellow students but wanted them to accept her. She had lived a sheltered life and never had a boyfriend. Stacey always picked dare, to avoid revealing her lack of sophistication. Recently her roommates had been making her dares more dangerous. Dreaming of Truth-or-Dare games may occur when you are under pressure to appear what you are not.

INTERPRETATIONS AND FORTUNE-TELLING MEANINGS

⋆ If you dream of undertaking dangerous games to impress friends, consider whether their approval is worth taking risks.

⋆ If you are asked to tell the truth in a dream game and those present make fun of you, avoid placing yourself in any situations where you feel under scrutiny.

⋆ If you dream that you lie in a game of Truth or Dare, you may fear revealing your authentic self and are perhaps in the wrong company.

⋆ If you dream of failing at a dare or refusing to try, you may test yourself beyond what is reasonable.

⋆ If you dream you are asking a question to which you really need the answer about the honesty of a person, note what they say and how sincere they are.

OUTCOME OF STACEY'S DREAM

Stacey realized that, though academically she was equal to the others, in terms of emotional and social development she did not fit in. She postponed her college entry for another year and enrolled in a program from home for gifted students. Truth-or-Dare dreams can reveal underlying pressures to express yourself in a way that may be at odds with your well-being.

Tug-of-War

Julian, twenty-eight, dreamed he was in a tug-of-war contest held on a local sports field. He and his wife were knotted in the middle of the rope; on one side was his family and on the other the family of his wife, Shona. He was afraid they would be torn apart, as each family was determined to win.

He shouted at them to untie them, and both families were furious at them for spoiling the contest.

DREAM BACKGROUND AND MEANING

Julian had a very close-knit family, as did his wife, and both families insisted the couple spend their first married Thanksgiving with them. Neither family would accept trading Christmas or accept Julian's suggestion that they all come to the newlyweds' house for Thanksgiving. Tug-of-war dreams represent any competing or conflicting interest, e.g., home versus work, two families, or talent versus career.

INTERPRETATIONS AND FORTUNE-TELLING MEANINGS

* If the dreamer is caught between the teams or asked to choose one over the other, the choice will be difficult and potentially cause ill feeling.
* If the tug-of-war represents two clear choices in the dreamer's mind, the results of the dream contest may offer a clear decision if the dreamer is wavering.
* If the rope breaks or contestants fall over, there may be unfair pressure from both sides, which should be resisted.
* If the tug-of-war takes place over a river or stream, hidden emotions are deep and the issue is about more than the surface choices.
* If the tug-of-war is over divided loyalties and the dreamer walks away, this may represent a major step to independence from the combatants.

OUTCOME OF JULIAN'S DREAM

Julian and his wife told both families that they were going on vacation for Thanksgiving. They would be holding an open house for Christmas if any or all wanted to join them, as they wanted to spend their first Christmas in their own home. Inevitably, in tug-of-war dreams one side will remain unsatisfied, and so in life it may be easier to avoid the contest in the first place.

Tunnels

Bo, twenty-five, dreamed he was working in a warehouse in the old part of a city in Victorian times, and there were tunnels running under the warehouse. The staff refused to go down there because they often heard screams. The owner insisted that Bo and a female worker go down after heavy rain to check for flooding. Bo saw a hideous spirit, and the woman froze, unable to move. Bo picked her up and carried her up the stairs, feeling the spirit pursuing him.

DREAM BACKGROUND AND MEANING

Bo worked as a security guard in an old warehouse beneath which there were many subterranean tunnels. He hated his job, which required him to patrol alone at night, as he could hear screams in the tunnels, though he never went down. Sometimes a dream from one lifetime offers the means to confront fears to escape from present restrictions.

INTERPRETATIONS AND FORTUNE-TELLING MEANINGS

* Tunnels beneath buildings, which exist in many old cities, represent in a dream memories or fears subconsciously buried.
* Spirits lurking in a tunnel in a dream may link the dreamer to a haunted site.
* Dreaming of subway, rail, or road tunnels speaks of transitions and the need to face uncertainty in order to reach a desired objective.
* Stairs leading down to the tunnel signify the need to tackle hidden feelings head-on.
* A blocked-off tunnel says past relationships or opportunities should be released.
* If you dream you are crawling through a narrow tunnel, you are right now restricted but must continue to edge forward.

OUTCOME OF BO'S DREAM

Bo went down into the tunnels and saw a Victorian female ghost cowering. He carried her upstairs and she disappeared. Bo was no longer tied to his job, as he had released his fear of moving on by rescuing the spirit girl. He started his own security firm. Tunnel dreams can offer the dreamer incentive to release what is holding them back.

Turtle

Becky, twenty-six, dreamed she was snorkeling through dying coral. A mother turtle and her young were trapped in the sharp coral. Becky went to help. Her boyfriend impatiently beckoned her, as they were due to attend a prestigious award ceremony that would lead to a lucrative career. But Becky ignored him.

DREAM BACKGROUND AND MEANING

Becky had been invited to become a volunteer tagging and observing endangered turtles in Australia's Great Barrier Reef. She graduated at the top of her class in marine biology and had been offered several well-paid posts. But this work touched her heart. Turtles can live on land and sea but are most agile in water and represent the heart ruling the head.

INTERPRETATIONS AND FORTUNE-TELLING MEANINGS

* If your dream turtle is laying eggs and burying them for safety, this is a powerful maternal fertility symbol in many cultures, including in Amerindian lore.
* If you dream that newly hatched turtles race for the ocean with seagulls swooping overhead, your embryo venture needs extra care to avoid stumbling in its early stages.
* If you dream of a turtle on its back, struggling to right itself, ask for assistance in overcoming a temporary setback, rather than struggling alone.
* If, however, you dream that a huge mother turtle flips over, it may be time to shed your caring role toward selfish dependents and make a few waves.
* If you dream of turtles in a small tank, resist restrictions in your home or work life and be prepared to leave your comfort zone.
* If you dream you are a turtle swimming free in the ocean, carrying its home on its back, there may be travel opportunities.

OUTCOME OF BECKY'S DREAM

Becky accepted the volunteer post. Becky's boyfriend insisted that they had to save for a house and said he would not wait for her. He did wait, but she met another volunteer. Together they are moving to an injured-turtle sanctuary. The long life of turtles indicates that any decisions have long-lasting results.

Twin Souls

Bill, thirty-five, had experienced the same dream for many years, of meeting the same person, looking into their eyes and saying, "Oh, it is you," knowing it was his twin soul. He had dreamed of being married to his twin soul in seventeenth-century colonial America and living as a New Zealand indigenous couple, and he once dreamed of her making eye contact from the top deck of a stationary bus as he walked by.

DREAM BACKGROUND AND MEANING

Although Bill had enjoyed various relationships, he was certain the twin-soul encounter would happen in real life and they would instantly know. The concept of the twin soul, where another person completes your life, dates to Ancient Greece and may often be initiated on the dream plane, where souls roam free.

INTERPRETATIONS AND FORTUNE-TELLING MEANINGS

* If you consistently dream of the same person in different settings and ages, this is probably your twin soul connecting with you telepathically.
* Though your twin soul may be connecting with you on the dream plane, some twin souls do not come together in every lifetime.
* If you have a sense of certainty and rightness when you dream of your twin soul, you will experience a sense of homecoming if you meet them.
* If you keep dreaming of meeting your twin soul in a particular location, it may be worthwhile visiting the place regularly, as they may also be drawn there.
* If you see your twin soul only in the distance in dreams, be open to other relationships rather than waiting for your dream lover.
* See if you can develop the relationship within the dream, as these may be out-of-body connections.

OUTCOME OF BILL'S DREAM

Bill is happily waiting for the meeting. Lovers who appear for years in dreams are making a soul connection but might appear in a different role—for example, as a best friend or mentor.

Twins

Joseph, twenty-one, had dreamed regularly throughout his life of meeting a twin brother on a seashore. But as they ran toward each other, the twin disappeared and the dream ended, leaving Joseph feeling bereft.

DREAM BACKGROUND AND MEANING

Joseph was an only child, adopted when he was a year old. He always felt someone was missing from his world. His adoptive parents became annoyed when Joseph talked about his dream and tried to dissuade him from probing into his birth family when he was eighteen. The dream continued, but Joseph did not want to upset his parents. Dreaming of a missing twin generally means someone or something major is absent from your life, whether it is a missing sibling, a parent you lost when young, or a birth family you don't know.

INTERPRETATIONS AND FORTUNE-TELLING MEANINGS

* If you regularly dream of having a loving twin, this confirms that you may have met your twin soul.
* If the twin is unfamiliar, a twin soul will soon come into your life.
* If in your dream you are fighting with your dream twin, there is conflict between your inner self and the image you show the world.
* Twins can also represent two talents, one of which may be emerging.
* If you are pregnant or trying to conceive a child, especially by in vitro fertilization (IVF), dreaming of twins can be a sign you will have twin babies.
* To dream of an evil twin suggests you are denying or trying to offload negative feelings instead of channeling them.

OUTCOME OF JOSEPH'S DREAM

Joseph's dream could have referred to his missing birth family, which often occurs with adoptees who cannot find their birth kin or who are dissuaded from searching. However, Joseph felt the dream had greater significance and probed his past. He discovered a twin brother who had died at birth. Though his birth family refused contact with him, Joseph was able to resolve his feelings and mourn his lost brother.

Ulcers

Tam, forty, dreamed his body was breaking out all over in painful ulcers. He covered each visible one with a Band-Aid, which made them hurt even more. His work colleagues were moving away from him, fearing that he was infectious. He was sent home and panicked because he was leading a major project and knew it could not go ahead without him.

DREAM BACKGROUND AND MEANING

Tam had a responsible position as team leader, but feared the team resented him because he was a newcomer. He worked hard but never delegated, thinking to do so would make him even less popular. He had developed a duodenal ulcer but refused to take time off. He told no one at work. Ulcers can represent the negativity of others eating away at the dreamer's confidence.

INTERPRETATIONS AND FORTUNE-TELLING MEANINGS

* Mouth ulcers in a dream represent angry words you are not speaking.
* Stomach ulcers signify a long-standing grievance or injustice, gnawing away at you, which needs resolving.
* Neck ulcers suggest you are maintaining a neutral position in a matter in which you rightly should intervene.
* Leg or foot ulcers suggest a fear of moving forward in a career or socially because envy by others is eating away your confidence.
* If in your dream you are sick with an internal ulcer, stress overload is eroding other parts of your life.
* If someone you know in the dream has an ulcer, but not in the real world, they may be jealous of you.

OUTCOME OF TAM'S DREAM

After ignoring the warning of the dream that his health was deteriorating, Tam collapsed at work and was taken to the hospital. His team rallied and the project was successfully completed without him. Tam learned that it was his refusal to allow team members to have responsibility that was at the root of their hostility. Dreams of ulcers can be warnings—if not of an ulcer, then that the dreamer is damaging their own well-being and sometimes overall health.

Umbrella

Aaliyah, twenty-six, dreamed she was on her way to a class to improve her language skills, having arrived from Lebanon a month earlier. It started to rain heavily. When she tried to put up her umbrella, it wouldn't open. Within seconds she was drenched and returned home. The rain stopped. By the time Aaliyah arrived home, her clothes were dry. Her mother was furious and accused her of making excuses to not attend the class.

DREAM BACKGROUND AND MEANING

Aaliyah was finding it hard to settle in the new land. She was due to start language classes the following week but was scared of making a fool of herself. Her mother did not speak the new language and was totally dependent on Aaliyah. Rain represents emotional demands pouring down, in this case from Aaliyah's mother.

INTERPRETATIONS AND FORTUNE-TELLING MEANINGS

* When we dream we turn back from a desired destination or necessary objective because an umbrella does not protect us from the rain, the message is to persist.
* If your umbrella fails to open in dreams or is broken, seek backup support for the demands pouring down on you.
* An open umbrella in rain is a lucky omen, assuring protection from harm, stress, and malice.
* Someone sharing their umbrella with you indicates a new or existing trustworthy protective lover or friend.
* If you share your umbrella but the person known or unknown leaves you getting wet, you are too easily taken advantage of.
* An umbrella blown inside out says, "Do not allow constant pressures on you to wear your resistance down and fall for emotional blackmail."
* Taking someone else's umbrella by mistake or accepting it indicates assuming others' burdens.

OUTCOME OF AALIYAH'S DREAM

Aaliyah joined an online Lebanese group and made new friends. She insisted that her mother come to language classes with her. She found her mother a volunteer worker who speaks Lebanese, to help with practical matters.

Umpire

Veronica, thirty-eight, dreamed she was umpiring the men's final of the American Open Tennis Championship, and the match result was close. But her husband was standing next to her, disputing every decision. She demanded video proof of her decisions. When she was proven correct every time, she had her husband removed from the court.

DREAM BACKGROUND AND MEANING

Veronica had a promising future as an umpire, but her husband said she should give up umpiring now that she had a baby. Her mother said she should pursue her career and offered to take care of the baby when her daughter was umpiring. Umpire dreams refer to any issue where a decision must be made between two options or opponents.

INTERPRETATIONS AND FORTUNE-TELLING MEANINGS

* If you dream you are questioning an umpire's decision, you may have been unfairly judged or criticized.
* If you are umpiring a sporting event in your dream, you may be asked to take sides in a dispute at work or among family and friends.
* If you are umpiring and someone is constantly questioning your decisions, they may have difficulty accepting your success and judgment.
* If you are umpiring a series of matches or a matter where viewpoints seem irreconcilable, a decisive judgment may be necessary, however unpopular.
* If you dream of more than one person umpiring the same match, you may be bombarded with conflicting opinions.
* If an umpire in your dream does not understand the rules, you may encounter someone in authority who does not know what they are doing.

OUTCOME OF VERONICA'S DREAM

Veronica was now being offered international matches. After the dream she knew she had a good future but that to go ahead would split the family. She stepped back from her career and hoped one day to revive it. Umpire dreams, unlike real-life umpiring, may not lead to a straightforward decision, as people's personalities and feelings must be considered.

Unattractiveness

Melanie, twenty-one, dreamed she was in a nightclub, dancing with her boyfriend, Ricky. A beautiful girl approached Ricky on the dance floor and said, "What's a guy like you doing dancing with her?" She pushed Melanie aside and started dancing with Ricky who, after the dance, took the girl for a drink, ignoring Melanie. Melanie left the nightclub alone, in tears.

DREAM BACKGROUND AND MEANING

Melanie had for many years believed she was unattractive. At school she was teased about the metal braces she wore, and later she developed a facial skin problem that erupted when she was stressed. Ricky constantly reassured her about how attractive she was to him. But her insecurity was making her clingy, which irritated Ricky. A negative self-image from early teen years may resurface in dreams at times when the dreamer is feeling insecure.

INTERPRETATIONS AND FORTUNE-TELLING MEANINGS

* To dream you are unattractive indicates worry about revealing your true self in case you are rejected.
* If you reject an unattractive person in a dream, you are off-loading your own image issues onto a dream figure rather than dealing with your own insecurity.
* If you are chased by an ugly monster in your dream, you have built your concern with physical appearance into a huge problem.
* If your mirror image becomes incredibly beautiful in a dream, you have the power to win admiration through your charisma.
* If your face becomes distorted in the mirror, it is a warning that your resentment of someone you would like to be may erupt suddenly in daily life.

OUTCOME OF MELANIE'S DREAM

Ricky did not want to lose Melanie and told her he loved her just as she was. Melanie realized *she* was projecting the image of being undesirable and started maximizing her good features. Sometimes constantly reassuring a person who is insecure about their beauty compounds the problem, rather than minimizing physical attractiveness as just one aspect of the person.

Unavoidable Disaster

Stuart was thirteen when he woke in great distress and told his mother he had dreamed of a big ferry that went out of the harbor, rolled over on its side, and capsized. He described people drowning. He begged her to do something. His mother said it was a nightmare, but he remained inconsolable.

DREAM BACKGROUND AND MEANING

Two days after the dream, a roll-on, roll-off car ferry, the *Herald of Free Enterprise,* set off from Zeebrugge in Belgium for Dover, hundreds of miles from where David lives. The bow doors were left open. The boat destabilized, rolled on its side, and capsized within ninety seconds. The date of the disaster was March 6, 1987, and 193 people lost their lives. Unavoidable disaster dreams may involve traveling into the future by connecting with the energies being built up by the approaching disaster.

INTERPRETATIONS AND FORTUNE-TELLING MEANINGS

* Sometimes a child may dream of a local disaster but may not be believed. For example, a ten-year-old girl in Aberfan, a Welsh village, dreamed about her school being covered in black and destroyed, and told her mother when she woke. Soon after, the school was engulfed by a black slag heap.
* If a premonition is definite and urgent with clues, it may be worthwhile changing a booking, as changing the energies means it may not happen.
* A child who has frequent premonitions may one day become a healer or clairvoyant but should not be pressured to perform.
* Some who continue to have premonitions may send advance blessings or a telepathic warning to those soon to be in distress.

OUTCOME OF STUART'S DREAM

Stuart continued to feel guilty for years. In his case he did not go on to develop his powers professionally. For many young people, disaster premonitions are one-time experiences, and the gift fades.

Unicorn

Roxanne, eighteen, who loved unicorns, dreamed she was in a misty field encircled by pure white unicorns. Her special unicorn asked her to sit on its back. Together they flew high in the sky and landed in an enchanted palace, where her devoted fans were waiting. She began to sign autographs but immediately found herself in her local fast-food restaurant, cleaning tables.

DREAM BACKGROUND AND MEANING

The dream was a reality check. Roxanne wanted to be a famous television celebrity. She could not see the point in studying or getting a vacation job. She applied for every reality show but had no response. Her parents were losing patience. Roxanne had been asked to go on vacation with friends in the summer, but her parents said she must find the money herself. Since a unicorn was described in 398 BC by the Greek physician Ctesias of Cnidus, who had been in Persia, unicorn dreams can suggest a yearning for a golden future to magically appear.

INTERPRETATIONS AND FORTUNE-TELLING MEANINGS

* A dream of a unicorn suggests a rare opportunity or unusual experience, which will bring you happiness.
* It might herald the emergence of psychic, healing, and magical powers.
* A dream unicorn is a symbol of increased libido, fertility, and potency.
* Flying on the back of a unicorn says you should spread your wings to make desires happen.
* Unicorns shrouded in mist warn against believing in illusions or waiting for the ideal moment to act.
* A herd of unicorns suggests that you seek an original solution or pursue an innovative creative idea rather than sticking to the tried and tested.

OUTCOME OF ROXANNE'S DREAM

Reluctantly, Roxanne took a part-time job but kept her ambitions alive by attending stage school, which her parents agreed to fund. She is writing a children's play about unicorns and realizes she has to develop magical star qualities to be accepted for reality television. Unicorn dreams keep alive possibility but warn that the dreamer must also further their ambitions in the real world.

Unrequited Love

Geraldine, forty-five, dreamed her son was young again. The head teacher of his boarding school told Geraldine that he had always loved her. They made love. She woke excited yet saddened that it had been just a dream.

DREAM BACKGROUND AND MEANING

Geraldine had always enjoyed a special relationship with her son's head teacher. He always chose to sit with her at concerts. Now that she was divorced and he had retired, she saw no reason they should not be together, though she had not heard from him since her son left school. An idealized dream relationship not tested by reality can be very sustaining in lonely times.

INTERPRETATIONS AND FORTUNE-TELLING MEANINGS

* If you dream constantly of being married to or making love with a celebrity or royalty, this is a fantasy dream to be enjoyed.
* If you dream of love with someone in authority—a physician, your bank manager, or the head teacher of your child's school—without their encouragement, you may need to make existing relationships more fulfilling.
* If you dream of a romantic lover, they or someone with the characteristics you admire in your dream love may be coming into your life.
* If you have dreams of a colleague or acquaintance being your lover and you would not welcome this, beware of flirtatious fun signals you may be giving out.
* If you dream of declaring your love to someone you know as a friend or colleague, approach the matter subtly in case the feeling is not reciprocal.
* If you frequently dream of an ex-lover, they may be telepathically connecting with you. Decide if you want to try to reconnect or if it is too late.

OUTCOME OF GERALDINE'S DREAM

Now that Geraldine was free of her marriage and her dream love also was free of professional restraints, she contacted him on social media, telling him she was divorced, and received a formal yet friendly reply, mentioning his new partner several times. Geraldine was saddened that she no longer had her dreams. Unrequited love is only problematic if it stops actual relationships from developing.

Unresolved Sexual Trauma

Barbara, fifty-two, had a recurring dream that she was a young teenager again, being repeatedly assaulted by her English teacher. She went to the police, but they did not believe her and threatened to have her charged with making a false statement. She woke in tears.

DREAM BACKGROUND AND MEANING

Barbara still recalled the trauma of being raped in her teens and how everyone disbelieved her. She wondered if it was too late to report her abuse. Her husband wanted her to let it go. Unresolved sexual trauma appearing regularly in dreams can reflect scars still present in life decades later.

INTERPRETATIONS AND FORTUNE-TELLING MEANINGS

* If present publicity about sexual abuse is causing flashback dreams, you may be recalling buried traumas that need resolution.
* If you fight back against the abuser in the dream, you are regaining your power, whether to retaliate against past or present abuse or move on.
* If you are having past-life dreams of abuse, explore them to uncover present seemingly inexplicable trauma.
* If there is a successful prosecution in your dream, find other sufferers to put a case together.
* If you are unsuccessful in your dream, or you cannot face court proceedings, seek counseling or join a therapy group.
* If in your dream no one believes you when you complain of current or past workplace or educational establishment abuse, seek impartial external sources of help.

OUTCOME OF BARBARA'S DREAM

Barbara contacted other women taught by the English teacher, and several had experienced similar trauma. They are seeing an attorney to discover the likelihood of bringing a successful prosecution as, though the teacher is in his late seventies, he still coaches teenagers. An unresolved sexual-abuse dream can trigger positive action that allows victims to express and gain justice or closure by having their traumatic experiences validated.

Upset Stomach, Diarrhea

Pauline, thirty-two, dreamed she had been invited to dinner with a new girlfriend she was eager to impress. But she felt her stomach churning and knew she would have bad bouts of diarrhea, caused by nerves. At the restaurant she ordered the plainest dishes, which upset her girlfriend, who had booked the exclusive restaurant as a treat. The evening was a disaster, as Pauline had to frequently leave the table to go to the bathroom.

DREAM BACKGROUND AND MEANING

Pauline suffered from irritable bowel syndrome (IBS), made worse by stress. She usually avoided eating out, but her new girlfriend insisted on booking a fine dining restaurant for Pauline's birthday. Embarrassment prevented Pauline from explaining her condition. Dreams about stomach upsets anticipate an imminent stressful event that may exacerbate the problem.

INTERPRETATIONS AND FORTUNE-TELLING MEANINGS

* If you dream of having a stomach upset at an event, you may be finding the coming situation unnecessarily stressful. Try to find alternatives.
* If you have a physical stomach problem, a dream can forewarn you to take preventive measures before an event.
* If in a dream you have a stomach upset unrelated to any coming event, a current situation may be hard to accept.
* If in your dream you have persistent diarrhea, a situation may seem out of your control.
* Diarrhea dreams can reflect a situation you wish to remove from your life.
* Diarrhea in recurring dreams suggests the need to cleanse yourself of negative feelings.

OUTCOME OF PAULINE'S DREAM

Pauline realized that she had to explain her condition to her new girlfriend. Her girlfriend revealed that her mother suffered from the same condition and said she could change the booking to a restaurant her mother loved, known for catering to all diets. They had a wonderful evening. Stomach upsets can signify fears of losing control. Since Pauline's previous relationship had been abusive, she had many fears to purge.

Useful Solutions

When he was twenty-seven, Elias Howe, the American who patented the sewing machine in 1846, dreamed he was attacked by cannibals who had spears with holes in the tips. He woke, realizing his dream had given him the solution to a dilemma he had with his invention.

DREAM BACKGROUND AND MEANING

Elias had been trying to discover how the needle on the sewing machine could effectively be used to hold the thread. Dreams offer space where the unconscious mind is able to sift through unrecognized information or ideas that are accessible only via psychic radar during sleep.

INTERPRETATIONS AND FORTUNE-TELLING MEANINGS

* When logic or known answers fail, the sleep plane widens the scope and range of the mind if solutions lie just out of conscious view.
* If a dreamer writes a question on a piece of paper, reads it, and puts it beneath their pillow, an unconsidered option may emerge in a dream the same night.
* If a dreamer is puzzling over a solution, the answer will come in symbols during the dream, which are easily unraveled, as Howe's dream spears did in a context that made him take notice.
* If the answer does not come in a dream, it may appear in the semiconscious awakening state first thing in the morning or in a clear symbol during the day.
* If no answers come but more questions arise, the dreamer is being told that the matter is more complex than originally realized and needs more time to resolve.
* If no solution comes in dreams or on the following day, do not consciously consider the question the subsequent night, as the dreaming mind may still be processing the original question.

OUTCOME OF ELIAS'S DREAM

The dream gave Elias the answer: the sewing-machine needle must have a hole in the tip for the thread to pass through. It is not uncommon for answers to come in dreams. There are many recorded examples through history. Alexander the Great dreamed of a snake with a plant in its mouth, and Alexander was able to identify the plant's location. This saved the life of his friend Ptolemy, who was dying of a poisoned arrow wound, and saved others with the same condition.

Utopia

Eli, thirty-five, dreamed he was living in a community of artists and craftspeople with their own family houses and communal workshops, sharing profits and expenses. Everyone shared in the care of the children. No one argued, and decisions were made jointly after discussion. Eli woke, wishing he could stay.

DREAM BACKGROUND AND MEANING

Eli had been offered workshop space in an artistic collective where everyone was paid out of the collective profits. But his partner said that he was asked only because he was making a name for himself and could subsidize the others. Idyllic wish-fulfillment dreams can sometimes work best free from reality.

INTERPRETATIONS AND FORTUNE-TELLING MEANINGS

* If you dream of living in total harmony with others on a beautiful island like the fictional one described by Sir Thomas More in his 1516 book *Utopia*, be aware that communal ventures need practical safeguards as well as goodwill.
* If you dream of your ideal workplace with total equality and sharing of hard work and results, you may be able to improve your present working conditions, but do not expect miracles.
* If you dream that others are leaving the Utopia of your dream, you may be expecting too much of family, friends, and colleagues.
* If you dream of working with supportive colleagues when the reality is very different, seek a workplace more in tune with your aims or start your own business.
* If you dream of an ideal partner and sugar-sweet children, you may need a reality check to avoid missing or rejecting a good enough lifestyle for a fantasy.
* If in the dream you are living in the middle of nature and are self-sufficient, explore how this may become at least partially possible.

OUTCOME OF ELI'S DREAM

Eli joined the craft workshop community as a guest artist for a month but was disillusioned at the pettiness and jealousy among the craftspeople and how some worked hard while others sat around doing nothing. Eli took on an apprentice in his existing business to pass on his expertise and ideals. Utopian ideas of sharing and equality are to be strived for but may work best within an existing framework.

U-Turn

Trent, forty-nine, dreamed he was driving down the highway in a hurry, as he was late for an important meeting. He realized he had missed his turn, so he did a U-turn at an opening in the road onto the other side and accelerated straight into the path of a truck.

DREAM BACKGROUND AND MEANING

Trent had made a major investment on behalf of his company. Everyone told him he had made a dreadful mistake, share prices were dropping, and he should get out while he could. Should he do a U-turn or stay on track? U-turns always need care and should not be undertaken impulsively or hastily.

INTERPRETATIONS AND FORTUNE-TELLING MEANINGS

- ★ If you dream that every vehicle is making a U-turn because of an accident or major jam ahead, you may need to go along with the majority view and hold back a decision or action till matters become clearer.
- ★ If your dream satellite navigation system tells you to make a U-turn but you know a shortcut, trust your intuition and wait before reversing any decisions.
- ★ If in the dream you are making a U-turn, ask yourself what previous action or words were a mistake and whether it is possible to reverse them.
- ★ Making a U-turn, even if there is no sign, says there is unfinished business or a relationship you need to resolve before you can go forward.
- ★ If you dream you are being directed by traffic control or a police officer to make a U-turn, there are new facts and factors that will change your opinion about an earlier decision.
- ★ If you dream there is no gap or side road on which to do a U-turn, you may have to live with the consequences of an earlier decision or words you regret.

OUTCOME OF TRENT'S DREAM

After the dream, Trent decided to cash in his investment, but waited a short while. During that time, the shares rose, making him a sizable profit. If he had sold when values fell, it would have been a major loss. U-turns are rarely without consequences, so they need a good reason to undertake them.

Vacation

In the dream, Lenny, twenty-five, was in an exotic resort hotel with his girlfriend, Shelley, lounging by the pool and sipping cocktails. He was bored stiff. To his delight, his family arrived in their battered camper van, unloaded all the beach paraphernalia, and started a game of volleyball in the middle of the sunbathers. Shelley was horrified and insisted Lenny tell the family to leave. They packed up, but Lenny went with them.

DREAM BACKGROUND AND MEANING

Lenny had agreed to vacation with his extended family as they did every year in their vacation home by the ocean. He had invited his new girlfriend. But Lenny quickly realized she was bored with their unsophisticated family fun and wanted to cut the vacation short. Lenny enjoyed the beach games and barbecues but was trying to please everyone. Vacations in dreams represent being our true selves, revealing what really matters.

INTERPRETATIONS AND FORTUNE-TELLING MEANINGS

- ★ A dream vacation indicates that a planned vacation will be enjoyable or that you should plan one soon.
- ★ The dream of a vacation delayed by travel hitches says life may have become a chore: slow down.
- ★ The dream of an exotic luxury vacation suggests that you should indulge yourself, if you usually do a lot for others.
- ★ A dream of a vacation romance predicts a romantic connection with someone exotic, who may be from overseas, and is not necessarily on vacation. It says you need to spice up your current love life.
- ★ A canceled vacation warns of disruption of plans generally, so have a backup strategy.
- ★ If in your dream you lose your ticket or luggage, or arrive at the wrong destination, details of a venture or adventure need careful planning or replanning.

OUTCOME OF LENNY'S DREAM

Lenny realized that he loved the extended family's lifestyle. Anyone he married and started a family with would need to have the same open attitude to life. Shortly afterward, he and Shelley split. Vacations can either confirm shared interests and views of a lover or companion or reveal incompatible differences in perspectives and aims.

Vaccination

Hal, twenty-five, dreamed he and his friend Simon were trekking through the Amazonian rain forest. Simon was bitten by a huge mosquito. His arm swelled up instantly and he could not breathe. Hal was half-carrying his friend, and their phones were out of range of help. Hal collapsed, totally lost, as the dream ended.

DREAM BACKGROUND AND MEANING

Hal and his friend Simon were going trekking and needed several expensive inoculations. Simon said Immigration did not check these. He told Hal he was fussing unnecessarily, as risk-taking was half the adventure. Hal was worried, as he did not know Simon well. Simon did not purchase travel insurance and was booking with obscure travel companies that were cheap and had poor online reviews. Vaccination dreams can symbolize the necessity of precautions generally, especially when traveling.

INTERPRETATIONS AND FORTUNE-TELLING MEANINGS

* If in your dream you are being vaccinated, this may be your body's way of saying, "Whether you agree with vaccination or not, it is the most advisable action to take."
* If you dream of getting sick and you did not get vaccinated because you do not believe in vaccination, the dream suggests you find alternative precautions.
* If in the dream you are vaccinated but still get sick, promises of help and support will not materialize.
* If you are working to create a new wonder vaccine, you may soon learn of a helpful treatment for a resistant condition for yourself or a loved one.
* If you dream you are refused a vaccine that you need for travel, there may be a delay in a trip that will afterward be seen as a blessing.

OUTCOME OF HAL'S DREAM

Hal decided to book on an established tour for his first trek. He spent money on his vaccinations, insurance, and secure accommodation. He experienced no problems but heard Simon had been stopped at the border for lack of certification. Vaccination dreams occur when you are contemplating or being persuaded to take chances to save money that may ultimately prove expensive.

Valentine's Day

Jill, sixteen, dreamed of the coming Valentine's Day dance at her high school. In the dream, everyone had a partner except her. A beautiful bouquet of red roses was delivered to her on the dance floor. The most popular girl in the year claimed they were hers and took the bouquet. Jill was sure her name had been on the card, but, humiliated, she went home alone.

DREAM BACKGROUND AND MEANING

Jill's boyfriend had abandoned her for the popular girl in the dream, and now everyone excluded her. The Valentine's Day dance was coming up, but she did not think she could go alone. Valentine dreams, good or bad, are about expectations and romance and not usually about real love at all.

INTERPRETATIONS AND FORTUNE-TELLING MEANINGS

* To dream of receiving a special valentine, whether or not you are in a relationship, promises romance and excitement.
* To send a Valentine's Day card in a dream means that you are still looking for someone special. If you are in a relationship, it may need spicing up.
* Dreaming of a box of old valentines says you may meet an old lover or unexpectedly hear from them.
* Dreaming anytime of receiving an anonymous valentine card suggests you may have a secret admirer.
* If you dream of receiving no Valentine's Day cards or presents, you may be seeking an ideal romance and missing a realistic relationship.
* If around Valentine's Day you dream of happy couples excluding you, it's time to start making yourself happy and letting love come in its own time.

OUTCOME OF JILL'S DREAM

Jill advertised on the class social media that people without partners should turn up as a group at the dance. She was astounded by the enthusiastic response. Jill is dating one of the solo guys, who bought her a red rose. The hype of Valentine's Day can cause a lot of insecurity, rejection, and anxiety, which may act as a spur to self-love.

Vampires

Ralph, forty-four, dreamed he was being pursued by a beautiful vampire through the darkness, and his lover was trying to shoot the vampire with a silver bullet to rescue him. But he did not want to be rescued. They entered the vampire's Gothic castle, barred the door, and made passionate love. Ralph reluctantly went home as it was becoming light, but his wife had gone and taken the children, leaving a discarded silver bullet on the ground.

DREAM BACKGROUND AND MEANING

Ralph had fallen in love with a beautiful, exotic woman he had met during his career as a theater agent. But she refused to live with him, as she had a rich husband. However, she was ambitious to use Ralph's connections to obtain starring parts. Ralph's wife had known about her husband's affair for some time, but believed that the marriage could be saved. Ralph had promised her that he would let his lover go. Sexual excitement with a tempter or temptress is closely bound in vampire myths and dreams.

INTERPRETATIONS AND FORTUNE-TELLING MEANINGS

★ Dreaming of being bitten by a vampire indicates that you are being emotionally blackmailed, though the relationship may be codependent.

★ Killing a vampire with a silver bullet or cross says you can overcome temptations, but it will not be easy.

★ If in a dream you are in love with a vampire, you are giving more in a relationship than you are receiving.

★ Being chased by vampires warns you that others are making too many demands on you, which ultimately will drag you down.

★ Dreaming of being a powerful vampire or pursuing one symbolizes seizing pleasure and satisfaction regardless of consequences.

★ If you dream you are a vampire but lose power in daily life (sunshine), a bad habit or addiction is draining you.

OUTCOME OF RALPH'S DREAM

Ralph realized that he could lose both his wife and lover, as his wife had reached a breaking point. He still hoped he could keep both women, but the discarded silver bullet suggests otherwise. Dreams can only advise, not compel.

Vanilla

Bethany, twenty-nine, dreamed she was soaking in a bath of vanilla foam, waiting for her lover, Brad, to arrive. She was certain this was the night he would propose, after a very long courtship. When he arrived, he presented her with a small box. She opened it, and inside was a ceramic vanilla orchid brooch, not the ring she expected. To her disappointment, she noticed it was not her name on the tag pledging love but a name she had seen on his phone. She woke confused.

DREAM BACKGROUND AND MEANING

Bethany had been dating Brad for five years, but he had never discussed moving in together or marrying. Bethany wondered if they would ever marry. Vanilla dreams can indicate lasting love but can, less positively, stand for divided or lukewarm affection.

INTERPRETATIONS AND FORTUNE-TELLING MEANINGS

★ If you dream you are baking with vanilla, a family or social get-together will be harmonious.

★ If you are offered vanilla ice cream but can see many other flavors, you may feel your life is boring and predictable.

★ Vanilla pods indicate wealth accumulated through family financial security and careful savings.

★ If you are given a vanilla fragrance by a lover, the relationship will be long-lasting but may be slow to ignite.

★ If in your dream you are burning vanilla-scented candles, you will soon find romance.

★ If you smell vanilla in a childhood home dream, you may be seeking the security of childhood, real or imagined.

OUTCOME OF BETHANY'S DREAM

Bethany had been suspicious for some time of Brad's intentions, especially as she had overheard conversations with the woman whose name was on the dream brooch gift tag. Finally, Brad admitted that he still saw a former girlfriend and was uncertain which of the two he loved more. Bethany broke off the relationship and replaced her vanilla essences with rose, the fragrance of committed love. If you are settled in a relationship, vanilla dreams can be very reassuring, but can lack passion.

Vasectomy

Trinny, twenty-six, dreamed of her new husband's ex-wife standing with him in a flowing stream, and all the water drained away as they stood there. His ex-wife told Trinny she would never have children, as Phil had had a vasectomy after the birth of their only son. Trinny woke heartbroken.

DREAM BACKGROUND AND MEANING

Trinny had been desperately trying for a baby, and the physician confirmed that she should be able to conceive. Phil refused to have tests, as he said he had already proved that he was potent. A dream can tap into unconscious concealed signals, even if there are no detectable signs of surgical intervention.

INTERPRETATIONS AND FORTUNE-TELLING MEANINGS

★ If you dream of having a vasectomy without your partner's knowledge, you may find being a father or contemplating fatherhood hard but be unable to say so.

★ If you are undergoing a vasectomy in the dream, you are contemplating a major relationship change.

★ If in your dream you change your mind about having a watercourses, you may fear the repercussions of an irrevocable change.

★ If you and your partner agree to a vasectomy in the dream, you need to discuss commitment issues to restore the emotional balance.

★ If you dream of branches broken from a tree, dried-up watercourses, or land suddenly becoming arid, these may be signs that your partner has had or is considering a vasectomy.

★ If you dream that a vasectomy is reversed and your partner becomes pregnant, your body is telling you that it may be possible to reverse a vasectomy.

OUTCOME OF TRINNY'S DREAM

Phil told Trinny his ex-wife had insisted on having children, despite there being little or no passion in the relationship. He had had a vasectomy after the first birth, after which she left him. Trinny reassured Phil that she loved him, with or without a baby. He had the vasectomy reversed and they are trying for a baby.

Vegetables

In his dream, Grenville, sixty-five, was a small boy again, being forced to eat his vegetables at boarding school. He was in a huge field of growing sweet corn. Grenville knew it was his farm and he would return there. He woke, gagging on the overcooked dream vegetables.

DREAM BACKGROUND AND MEANING

Grenville had been sent to boarding school at age seven, learning to conform and later becoming a colonel in the army, marrying a general's daughter, and having two children, who he actively encouraged to eat their vegetables. But he still longed for the boyhood sweet-corn fields he saw from the train on his way home on vacations. Now that he was a widower and his children had their own lives, it was now or never.

Planning to grow vegetables represents any slow-growing venture or ambition, reconnecting with the roots of who we truly are.

INTERPRETATIONS AND FORTUNE-TELLING MEANINGS

★ Dream vegetables represent money, health, and practical arrangements, and their condition and quantity are significant.

★ Fields of growing vegetables or a thriving vegetable garden represent financial potential, fulfilled in the months ahead.

★ Rotting vegetables symbolize practical ventures that need urgent intervention if we are to not fail.

★ If you dream you are eating a particular vegetable, your subconscious mind may be revealing that your body needs particular nutrients.

★ Dreaming of selling vegetables symbolizes gaining rewards for past efforts.

★ Overcooked vegetables indicate that you have spent too long on a grievance and need to move on.

★ Dreaming of buying vegetables advises you to invest more time and effort into health and fitness.

OUTCOME OF GRENVILLE'S DREAM

Grenville enrolled in agricultural college and plans to buy a sweet-corn farm. Since vegetables represent the basics of life, dreams involving planting and tending vegetables say, "Start long-term plans small, be patient, and persevere." Above all, they advise finding a more natural way of life if you have always followed convention.

Vendetta

Phil, fifty-six, dreamed he was in an old-fashioned Midwest town, having a shootout with a rival family who claimed rights over the land between their ranches. Phil seized the rival family's teenage son, who had crept up behind him with a gun. Phil disarmed him and released the boy. Both senior males set down their guns and agreed to end the vendetta between them for the sake of their children.

DREAM BACKGROUND AND MEANING

This may be a past-life dream. Since he recently moved in next door, Phil's neighbor had pursued a vendetta against Phil over parking and boundary rights in the suburb in which they live. Each had responded with legal action against the other. However, the vendetta had escalated, spilling into violence between the two sets of teenagers. A vendetta dream warns that a vendetta is getting out of control and must be stopped before real harm is done.

INTERPRETATIONS AND FORTUNE-TELLING MEANINGS

* If someone is waging a vendetta of words in the dream, the person is talking about you behind your back, no matter how friendly they seem.
* A gangland vendetta dream indicates major rivalries in your world, whether from office politicking or from branches of the family at war. Stay uninvolved.
* If there is a dream truce between you, take this as a positive indication to attempt peacemaking.
* Should one of the dream sides build high defenses, entrenched attitudes may be hard to overcome by force.
* If the police arrive in the dream, deal with any neighborhood disputes through the courts or mediation agencies, not force.
* If you are arrested in the dream, beware of a dispute adversely affecting other family members.

OUTCOME OF PHIL'S DREAM

Phil was seriously worried, as both sets of teens were resorting to criminal damage that had involved the police. Phil talked to his neighbor, and they agreed to mediation. Dream vendettas may give clues to reducing conflict when neither side admits to being wrong.

Ventriloquist's Dummy

Maisie, fifty-five, dreamed she was a ventriloquist's dummy with bright red lips, sitting on the knee of her husband, Kevin. When anyone spoke to her, she answered in his words. But suddenly she spoke in her own voice and said he was lying and cheating. Kevin was so angry, he dropped her and ripped off her head, and nothing but straw came out.

DREAM BACKGROUND AND MEANING

Maisie was very confident, but when she was with her husband she found herself echoing his opinions and following his wishes. If Maisie attempted to express opinions of her own, he made her look like a fool, and she lost her confidence and stuttered. In relationships where one partner is controlling the other, the manipulated half may be seen in the dream as a ventriloquist's dummy.

INTERPRETATIONS AND FORTUNE-TELLING MEANINGS

* If you are the ventriloquist in the dream, you may be trying to persuade someone to accept your opinion, even if you are not sure about it.
* If you are the dummy, you may be expressing views that are not your own to gain approval or keep the peace.
* If in the dream it is obvious that the ventriloquist is speaking the words, someone is trying to convince you of their honesty but should be viewed with caution.
* If no sound comes out of the dummy's mouth, whoever is the ventriloquist in your dream will soon be unmasked as a fraud.
* If the ventriloquist is mesmeric and charismatic, beware of a controlling lover who may steal your heart, reputation, and money.
* If the ventriloquist drops or breaks the dummy, they will lose their power over the person they are deceiving.

OUTCOME OF MAISIE'S DREAM

After the dream, Maisie realized that her husband was becoming increasingly manipulative. He was trying to persuade Maisie's elderly and confused mother that she should give Maisie's husband power of attorney over her affairs, under the pretext that her money would be safe. The identity of the dream ventriloquist and their behavior in daily life may explain the dream, but often trickery is involved (see "Puppet," p. 376).

Video Games

Marcus, twenty-five, dreamed he was the superhero in his video game, of which he had become a character. He was happily outmaneuvering the alien attack force when the gaming machine shattered. The aliens rained shots down on him with their weapons, unopposed. He woke desperately seeking shelter.

DREAM BACKGROUND AND MEANING

Marcus was obsessed with online gaming. He rushed home from work to begin gaming and would sometimes stay up all night. His boss had issued a final warning, as Marcus was always half asleep. Video games in dreams link the simulated world with what is happening beyond the game, sometimes as a warning to pay more attention to life.

INTERPRETATIONS AND FORTUNE-TELLING MEANINGS

★ If you frequently dream of video gaming, you may need to create a clear demarcation between gaming and sleep, if boundaries are becoming blurred.

★ If you are trapped inside a video-game dream and you escape, you may be rehearsing dream strategies to overcome restrictions in daily life.

★ If you become a video-game character, whether a villain or superhero, unexpressed aspects of your personality need bringing out or modifying in the everyday world.

★ If you dream repeatedly of a particular strategy in a war or fantasy world–building game, the same tactic can overcome real-life opposition or malice.

★ If your video game is full of monsters or enemies, consider who occupies those roles in your daily life and their symbolic dangers.

★ If you are role-playing in the dream game, is it difficult to be your authentic self in everyday life?

OUTCOME OF MARCUS'S DREAM

Marcus's gaming machine broke down and he could not afford to replace it. He suffered serious withdrawal symptoms and realized he was becoming addicted. His work performance improved, and he started to make friends outside the gaming community. Video games improve strategic thinking, but if we dream of them, it may suggest that a passion for them is becoming an obsession or even an addiction.

Violent Women

Mitchell, forty-six, had recurring dreams of his wife, Jeanette, stabbing him in a jealous rage. Jeanette was arrested. He was admitted to the hospital in danger of losing his life, and the children were taken into foster care. He woke fearful of what the day would bring.

DREAM BACKGROUND AND MEANING

Mitchell, a gentle guy, was married to Jeanette, an alcoholic who became violent toward Mitchell when she drank heavily and accused him of being unfaithful. He was too ashamed to admit that he was being attacked by a woman and never retaliated, believing it was his fault. He was afraid of the effect the violence was having on the children. Female domestic violence is hidden abuse. A dream can reveal the potential seriousness of the situation so the victim is forewarned.

INTERPRETATIONS AND FORTUNE-TELLING MEANINGS

★ If you are being attacked by your partner or a female relative in real life, dreams alert you to not deny the taboo subject.

★ If your female partner is not actually violent, the dream reveals resentment simmering within your partner on a taboo subject.

★ If you are female and attack your partner or a female relative in a dream, directly express justifiable anger calmly but assertively.

★ If you are a child in the dream being attacked by a maternal figure, you may feel helpless if a female boss or authority figure is bullying you.

★ If you are attacked by a female gang, do not be drawn into power games at work or socially by an overassertive clique.

★ If you are sexually play-fighting with a partner, be aware of tipping over into violence.

OUTCOME OF MITCHELL'S DREAM

After a vicious attack left him bleeding, Mitchell, forewarned by the dream knife attack, seized the knife. Mitchell told Jeanette that she must enter an alcohol abuse clinic or he would call the police. A dream with disastrous consequences helps the sufferer to see that they are not at fault.

Visas

Paola, thirty-eight, dreamed she was at the airport with her new partner, Ted, and her two young children from a previous marriage. Ted said he did not have visas for the children to enter the vacation country. He said her ex-husband could pick them up and hustled her through the gate. He said she had to choose between him and the children. She watched him leave.

DREAM BACKGROUND AND MEANING

Paola, a single parent, told Ted she was a package deal with the children. But he always excluded the children and insisted that she leave them behind when they go on vacation, when, she believed, he planned to propose. Visas represent acceptance in a new country and in dreams represent acceptance of existing commitments (see "Passport," p. 354).

INTERPRETATIONS AND FORTUNE-TELLING MEANINGS

★ If you obtain a visa in a dream, you will gain admission into an area of life from which you were previously excluded.

★ If you are applying for a visa for yourself and family to emigrate, if the dream application is favorable, you will be accepted.

★ If your application to emigrate or to work in another country is turned down in the dream, this may not be the time for such a move.

★ If you dream you are taking part in a visa interview, you may feel on trial in some area of your life and may lack confidence.

★ If you or the person traveling with you in the dream loses the visa at the last minute, check for obstacles in a planned change. Be sure the change is what you want.

★ If you dream you are in an endless line to obtain a visa, you may need to persevere to be accepted, as results could be slow.

OUTCOME OF PAOLA'S DREAM

Paola realized that the dream was questioning whether Ted would accept her children into his life. Since *love me, love my kids* was non-negotiable, they split. Visas can bring people together or divide them, especially where love is involved.

Visitors

Dora, sixty, dreamed she was selling tickets and teas to visitors in her picturesque cottage garden in the middle of the thatched village where she lived. Then she put the CLOSED sign on the gate and enjoyed the peace and solitude of her garden.

DREAM BACKGROUND AND MEANING

Though Dora was naturally sociable, she was tired of visitors to the village wandering around her garden uninvited and banging on the door to ask for information about local beauty spots. She had put a notice on her gate saying PRIVATE, but the visitors persisted and, as she worked from home, she was tired of the interruptions of uninvited guests. Visitor dreams suggest that you are giving too much to others and feeling isolated and uncared-for.

INTERPRETATIONS AND FORTUNE-TELLING MEANINGS

★ Visitors you know appearing in a dream may give advance warning of an unheralded arrival.

★ Unknown visitors who bring pleasure in the dream say that you will befriend new people, especially if you have moved to a new area.

★ If in your dream visitors, known or unknown, refuse to go home or outstay their welcome, you need to be more assertive.

★ If you feel like a visitor in your own home, friends and family may be taking advantage of your hospitable nature.

★ If visitors take over your home or workspace and prove menacing in the dream, beware of being deliberately unsettled by those jealous of your personal happiness or career success.

★ If you dream of a series of visitors, none of whom stays, your life may be filled with too many superficial connections.

OUTCOME OF DORA'S DREAM

After the dream, Dora applied to become the local visitor center, tea shop, and organizer of tours to local beauty spots. She was then able to regulate her private time and welcome visitors on her terms. Often a visitor dream reveals a natural sociability toward others and suggests regulating this rather than becoming overwhelmed.

Voice Mail

Lois, twenty-one, was trying to leave a loving message on the voice mail of her boyfriend, Geoff, because his phone was switched off. In the dream, Geoff was at the airport, flying out. But every time she tried to leave a message, everything she said came out with the opposite meaning. Her increasingly confused voice mails were broadcast all over the airport on the public address system, and she knew Geoff's plane would be taking off any minute, with Geoff thinking she didn't care.

DREAM BACKGROUND AND MEANING

Lois had a bad argument with her boyfriend and said she never wanted to see him again. He was going overseas for three months, and she was desperate to put things right before he left. But she feared it was too late after all the awful things she had said. Voice-mail dreams often occur when there is frustration over miscommunication and a recorded message does not express feelings clearly.

INTERPRETATIONS AND FORTUNE-TELLING MEANINGS

★ If in your dream you hear a message on voice mail, your subconscious has something important to tell you, and you should listen carefully.

★ If voice mails left on your phone or watch are deleted before you listen to them, you may be finding it hard to distinguish between what is true and what you are being told.

★ If you dream that you leave an important voice mail that only half records, you are misunderstood and need face-to-face or voice-to-voice communication.

★ If you dream that you keep failing to speak directly to someone close and communicate through a series of voice mails, you may be unconsciously avoiding direct contact of major significance.

★ If you leave an angry voice mail in a dream, expressing your fury openly in everyday life may involve unwise words that cannot be taken back.

OUTCOME OF LOIS'S DREAM

After the dream, Lois phoned her boyfriend and left a loving message. He came straight around to her apartment, and they were reconciled. Voice-mail messages are tied up with anxiety about failing to communicate clearly or sending the wrong message through anxiety.

Volcano

Theresa, thirty, dreamed she was living in a house in a beautiful valley with a volcano towering above. Rescuers suddenly arrived, telling her to move out, as the volcano was about to erupt. But though she could see sparks emerging and feel intense heat, she loved her home and could not bear to leave it. Then there was a huge explosion and fire came down the mountain. She ran and ran and woke still running.

DREAM BACKGROUND AND MEANING

Theresa had a live-in boyfriend who was incredibly passionate and romantic. However, he was easily roused to anger and had started to hit her, the violence escalating every time. Afterward he apologized and was extra-loving. Though her family insisted she should leave him, Theresa said he made her feel alive.

INTERPRETATIONS AND FORTUNE-TELLING MEANINGS

★ A dream of an active volcano is not a warning of danger, but signifies the release of buried emotions through creativity or heralds the consummation of love.

★ A dream of a sporadically spewing volcano where lava and sparks land on houses or people indicates a permanently angry person who uses bubbling fury to intimidate others.

★ An extinct volcano says an old relationship cannot or should not be revived.

★ An active volcano near houses or people warns of a potentially volatile, unpredictable situation or relationship, which, if not defused, could erupt destructively at any time.

★ A volcano spewing out lava says present or coming temptations in love or an attractive but uncertain investment should be avoided, as there are great risks.

★ Lava covering a town says angry or destructive words cannot be unspoken, so consider their effects before speaking out impulsively.

OUTCOME OF THERESA'S DREAM

Theresa realized she was playing with fire. She took out an injunction, since her boyfriend refused to leave her apartment and threatened to kill her. Her own survival instincts kicked in before she was seriously injured. Volcano dreams are often warnings that we are dancing with danger and ignoring the signals.

Vomiting

Ellie, forty-eight, dreamed she was on a transatlantic flight when she vomited all over herself, the seat, and the aisle. Though flight attendants cleared up the mess, the smell lingered, and her fellow passengers glared at her.

DREAM BACKGROUND AND MEANING

The day after the dream, Ellie was due to fly interstate to solve a problem with her mother, who was living in a nursing home. She was angry, because her sister lived close to her mother but always summoned Ellie when difficulties arose. Ellie said nothing, because she felt guilty for living so far away. Vomiting in a dream can reveal resentment and unspoken fury that bursts out suddenly in a way that causes problems for the dreamer.

INTERPRETATIONS AND FORTUNE-TELLING MEANINGS

★ If in a dream you vomit on someone you know, you may have suppressed issues that need expression before you speak or act in an inappropriate way.

★ If you vomit on a stranger, you may misdirect anger that rightfully should be addressed at the perpetrator.

★ If in a dream you vomit in a public place, you may be secretly afraid of revealing your true feelings.

★ If in a dream you suffer from motion sickness and you do not in everyday life, this may be a warning that an imminent trip will not yield desired results.

★ If you suffer from projectile vomiting in the dream, a matter about which you are avoiding talking will negatively affect more people than you realize.

★ If someone vomits on you, they may have a hidden grievance that is festering away, and you may need to investigate.

OUTCOME OF ELLIE'S DREAM

Ellie talked with her sister and cleared the air. They agreed on a schedule in which Ellie would spend a month a year staying near her mother. Her sister would deal with the daily crises. Vomiting dreams, unlike upset stomach/diarrhea dreams (see p. 487), deal with a sudden unplanned outburst of grievances that needs defusing.

Vultures

Mick, seventy-two, dreamed he came across three vultures sitting in the middle of a deserted road, eating roadkill. They refused to move, though he sounded the car horn and went up close. He could not steer the car around them. Mick was reluctant to run them over, but they turned aggressive and attacked the car. He reversed the car fast and returned home to his partner.

DREAM BACKGROUND AND MEANING

Mick was dreading going to see his three older sisters and telling them he was selling the family business, which he ran single-handedly, because his health was poor. He wanted to move overseas with his new partner, who his sisters didn't like. Mick was happy to give them all the proceeds of the sale. Vultures are powerful symbols of clearing the past when a particular life road is ending.

INTERPRETATIONS AND FORTUNE-TELLING MEANINGS

★ A flock of vultures represents gossip and troublemaking that you need to avoid.

★ A single vulture approaching close signifies someone rejoicing in another's misfortune. Be cautious who you tell your problems to.

★ Vultures eating dead creatures are a sign of leaving an old, outgrown situation behind, but not easily.

★ A vulture flying over a battlefield is, according to Middle Eastern tradition, a sign of victory. It is a good dream omen if you are engaged in a personal or professional conflict.

★ If you dream you are attacked by vultures, beware of the greed and constant demands of those who would drain your energies.

★ In Ancient Egypt, the vulture hieroglyph represented the protective power of the Divine Mother, Isis. Dreaming of seeing vultures outside your home or workplace window says a fierce, loving woman will defend you.

OUTCOME OF MICK'S DREAM

Mick's sisters were so unpleasant when Mick told them about his plan that he dealt with them through a lawyer. His new partner stood by him throughout. They are living overseas, poorer but happier.

Vultures embody many mythical fears of evildoing but are excellent for fighting malice and overcoming seemingly insurmountable odds.

Wading

Yolande, sixty, dreamed she was going to a lake in Almería in Spain, where thousands of bright pink flamingos were wading while waiting to migrate to Africa. She had wanted to see this for years, but her husband had refused, as he wanted to play golf at a well-known course en route, and when she arrived the lake was empty.

DREAM BACKGROUND AND MEANING

Yolande felt she had always waded in the shallows of life, trailing after her husband. She desperately wanted to see the flamingos, but he had always refused, as it would involve going miles out of their way on their regular vacation to Spain. For Yolande, seeing the wading birds fly became a symbol of overcoming her own limited life. But was it worth an argument? Sometimes a dream can highlight a desire that we postpone in the waking world but increasingly regret not fulfilling.

INTERPRETATIONS AND FORTUNE-TELLING MEANINGS

* Dreaming of walking in clear water is a good omen of rapid and easy progress, especially in dealing with people who may be difficult.
* Wading in muddy or weed-choked water warns of tangled communications or love affairs.
* To wade out of your depth says you should not get involved in others' emotional dissension, even if asked to do so.
* If you dream you wade into water but are afraid to swim, you may be uncertain about letting go of security.
* Dreaming of wading into a situation or argument suggests that you should be sure of your facts before speaking or acting.

OUTCOME OF YOLANDE'S DREAM

Yolande decided to go alone to Spain to see her flamingos. Her husband was shocked and said they could go together. She saw the flamingos take flight and planned all the things she would do once she left the shallows of her husband's shadow. Wading dreams can symbolize staying in the shallows to please others, but, like the flamingos, it is possible for people to fly.

Wagon, Cart

Hermione, seventy-five, dreamed she was driving a wagon in a wagon train on her way to the goldfields of California. Her husband had died with a fever, and she had children to support. Though she had never driven a wagon before, she knew she had to keep up with the others. At the goldfields, she accepted the help of a prospector who cheated her out of her gold. She took over the prospecting herself and soon got lucky. She woke ready for adventure.

DREAM BACKGROUND AND MEANING

Hermione, an artist of modest success, lived alone in her large, beautiful home. She had been cheated out of her savings by a pension scam. How could she afford to stay there? Sometimes wagon dreams say striking out alone with courage can turn disaster into opportunity.

INTERPRETATIONS AND FORTUNE-TELLING MEANINGS

* Dreaming of driving a wagon train suggests you are making a major speculation on future success that involves travel or a new venture.
* A wagon or wagon train under attack says you may need to defend your interests against the disruption of others.
* A wagon carrying hay or produce indicates good rewards for long-term efforts.
* An empty wagon warns that your efforts may be unfruitful, so consider alternatives.
* An upturned wagon, or one with a broken wheel, predicts unforeseen delays in plans, which you may need to fix yourself.
* A dream of wagons drawn together in a circle says that a venture may need a joint effort for security and support, even if people's agendas are not precisely the same.

OUTCOME OF HERMIONE'S DREAM

After the dream, Hermione brainstormed and decided to rent rooms to students from the local art college with facilities for them to share in her own extensive attached art studio. She started giving lessons to retirees and slowly increased her own sales. Wagon dreams talk about using resources we have and the pioneering spirit to adapt those resources to make a new better life.

Waiting

In the dream, Oscar, now twenty-eight, was fifteen, waiting for his father, who no longer lived at home, to take him to the first baseball game where Oscar was playing for the varsity team. Oscar was standing at the window, watching for the car, but, as time went on, he realized he had been let down again. He woke knowing he had missed the game and lost his chance of being asked to play again.

DREAM BACKGROUND AND MEANING

Oscar's dream actually had happened in real life, when young Oscar would wait all afternoon for his father, who would often fail to collect him. Now, after a silence of years, his father had asked Oscar to meet him. Oscar had tickets to take his girlfriend to a music festival the same weekend and did not want to let her down. Waiting dreams can either heighten excitement or anticipate disappointment if the wait is not worthwhile.

INTERPRETATIONS AND FORTUNE-TELLING MEANINGS

⋆ If you are a child in the dream waiting to see the principal for a misdemeanor, you may feel guilty about the consequences of some yet-undiscovered mistake.

⋆ If you dream you are waiting for a train or plane that is delayed, you may have doubts about the advisability of a journey or decision.

⋆ If you are waiting in an endless queue on the telephone or in person, you may need to follow up on a delayed matter or decision in everyday life.

⋆ If you are waiting for someone who does not turn up, you may be relying unduly on the approval or support of others.

⋆ If you dream you are waiting impatiently in a line, you may feel you are being treated second best; but if you are waiting patiently, you are happy to let matters unfold in their own time and way.

OUTCOME OF OSCAR'S DREAM

Oscar knew that his girlfriend had been waiting excitedly for the festival. He told his father they would have to arrange another time. Waiting dreams are often rooted in previous good or bad experiences and can reflect the attitude toward waiting that we express in daily life.

Walking

Scott, seventy-four, dreamed he was walking along a brambly path toward his daughter's new house. The path was not marked on his map. He pressed on but became bogged down in mud and could not go forward. Scott was reluctant to retrace his steps. He saw a grassy path leading in a different direction, which took him to a picturesque unfamiliar village with a tea shop. On the way he spotted many rare birds and bird blinds. He woke happy.

DREAM BACKGROUND AND MEANING

Scott's daughter wanted him to move into the custom-built chalet she intended to build for him in the garden of her new house. He had lived alone since his partner's death. He did not want to move, but the pressure was intense. Walking dreams involve traveling our own path in our own direction at our own pace.

INTERPRETATIONS AND FORTUNE-TELLING MEANINGS

⋆ To dream of enjoying a walk is a reminder to relax and enjoy life.

⋆ The people you dream you are walking with indicate those who will make you happy. Walking alone says right now you have your own agenda.

⋆ Tripping or getting bogged down in mud implies that the chosen direction may not be right.

⋆ Dreaming you are tangled in briars says you may be restricting your freedom due to fears of upsetting others.

⋆ Using a walking stick warns against relying on others' help and approval too much.

⋆ Dreaming of getting lost on a walk suggests that you are avoiding planning life your way. Try new things or rejoin your former activities.

OUTCOME OF SCOTT'S DREAM

Scott knew living so close to his daughter would be a disaster, as she would organize his life. He decided to buy a smaller home, join a walking club, and resume his former passion of bird-watching. Sometimes the direction in our dream walk will take us somewhere very different from the original planned destination and will give us signs of how and where we should be traveling.

Walls

Glenn, sixty-one, dreamed he was building a high wall around his home. But every time he put in bricks, they crumbled. He realized that his partner and a surgeon dressed in hospital scrubs were demolishing the wall as fast as he built it. He gave up and stepped into an ambulance waiting for him outside. Glenn woke panicking.

DREAM BACKGROUND AND MEANING

Glenn had been troubled by heart pains for months. He was afraid because his father died during a heart operation. Despite his partner's constant pressure to get him to see a doctor, Glenn refused and was building a new conservatory in his spare time, though lifting made the pains worse. Walls mark the boundaries between two parts of your life. If they are old, they may be keeping out the resolution of deep-seated fears or problems.

INTERPRETATIONS AND FORTUNE-TELLING MEANINGS

★ High walls can either represent security from attack or make you aware of self-imposed limitations, depending on the nature of the dream.

★ A door or gateway in a wall, especially if open, heralds approaching good fortune and opportunity.

★ A broken wall or one under attack says your privacy and personal space are being invaded. Draw boundaries firmly.

★ If walls are closing in or seem insurmountable, you should find a new way out of difficulties if you feel trapped or helpless.

★ Climbing over a wall or making a hole in it indicates the end of present restrictions through your own efforts.

★ If you dream you are building a wall, is this for protection or are you putting obstacles in your own way because of fear?

OUTCOME OF GLENN'S DREAM

Glenn went to the doctor, accompanied by his partner. Following tests, he was told his heart condition could be stabilized by medication. Glenn employed help with the heavy lifting for the conservatory. The significance of a wall, whether it is enclosing or excluding, and whether it should be left, climbed over, or knocked down, depends on your feelings in the dream.

Wasp, Hornet

Orson, eighty, dreamed he was eating jam straight from the jar in the garden. Instantly, swarms of wasps appeared, circling around the jar and his head. He rushed indoors, but some of the wasps, one with a woman's face, followed, and she stung him.

DREAM BACKGROUND AND MEANING

Orson, a widower for many years, had invited a young woman from Indonesia, who he had met on a dating site three weeks earlier, to come to live with him with a view to marriage. But when he told his family, neighbors, and friends, they said he was gullible and she was attracted only by his money and a visa.

INTERPRETATIONS AND FORTUNE-TELLING MEANINGS

★ If you dream of wasps or hornets, beware of a vicious-tongued colleague or neighbor and avoid contact where possible.

★ Dreaming of killing wasps is a good indication that you are ready to stand up to a critical relative or colleague.

★ A wasp or hornet's nest in or near your home advises caution with neighbors who may cause trouble, especially over boundary disputes.

★ Since wasps and hornets pollinate flowers and trees, a dream of wasps near flowers or greenery suggests that a sharp-tongued relative or colleague may offer help or sound advice.

★ A wasp attracted to a jam or honeypot, especially a wasp with a human face, says you may be offered instant love, but you risk the wasp's stinger in the tail.

OUTCOME OF ORSON'S DREAM

After the dream, Orson traveled to meet his prospective bride and proposed a longer courtship. She declined, and he discovered she had another, much older, boyfriend waiting in the wings. Orson still regrets not seizing happiness and ignoring the critics, but the dream wasp with the face had unsettled him. Sometimes we have to take the risk of getting hurt to enjoy the sweetness of life. Wasps pollinate orchids and so can create beauty, but only if you risk the sting. They are an ambivalent symbol, to be interpreted according to the context of the dream.

Watch (Timepiece)

Matthew, sixty-three, dreamed he was receiving the customary gold pocket watch on a chain in recognition of his forty years' service to the company. The younger men and women were getting drunk on cheap company champagne and the CEO got Matthew's name wrong. Matthew went to the harbor, pulled up his boat anchor, and set sail.

DREAM BACKGROUND AND MEANING

Matthew felt he was marking time until his retirement, and he would check his old-fashioned watch several times a day. His meticulous creative engraving skills were largely not needed anymore by the company. Though modern timepieces from Fitbits to smartphones differ from conventional timepieces, all personal-timepiece dreams alert you to the best way of using your finite time.

INTERPRETATIONS AND FORTUNE-TELLING MEANINGS

* To keep checking a watch in a dream indicates that you are worried time is passing and you need to follow your own time frame.
* If you dream you are given or buy an expensive watch like a Rolex, you will acquire wealth through trusting your inner timepiece to be in the right place at the right time.
* A tight watch strap speaks of restrictions on how you choose to spend your time that may need loosening.
* If in your dream you are given a gold pocket watch on retirement, you may feel you have wasted your time in making someone else rich.
* If you dream your watch is always fast compared with other people's, you fear you need to be one step ahead, probably due to fear of failure.
* If your watch is always slow, live at your own pace, regardless of consequences.

OUTCOME OF MATTHEW'S DREAM

Matthew retired early to sail the world in his yacht, stopping in different harbors to offer specialist engravings on board and for passengers docking on cruise ships. He traded his retirement watch for his workplace engraving tools. Personal timepieces are necessary for events but should not be allowed to rule the life cycle (see "Clocks," p. 105).

Wedding

Lauren, twenty-nine, dreamed she was at a bridal salon, trying on wedding gowns. Her mother, Constance, was highly critical of every dress Lauren tried on. Finally, Lauren chose a dress she loved, but Constance insisted, "If you wear that dress I'm not going to your wedding." Lauren left the shop still wearing the dress and eloped with her fiancé.

DREAM BACKGROUND AND MEANING

Constance had hijacked her only daughter's wedding, which she had been planning since Lauren was five. Constance's own wedding was small, as she was pregnant with Lauren. Lauren's wedding had to be perfect. Lauren loved her mother, but the wedding had turned into a nightmare. Dreams of wedding preparations, if happy, indicate a joyous union. If problematic, beware of a person dominating the preparations who may continue to interfere in the marriage.

INTERPRETATIONS AND FORTUNE-TELLING MEANINGS

* Dreaming of a wedding celebration represents a deep, lasting commitment, whether or not you and your partner are married or marrying.
* If you are not currently with a partner, wedding dreams indicate desire for a permanent relationship.
* If you are remarrying your current partner in the dream, you may need to revive romance if it has become mundane.
* If you are getting married but the dream groom or bride, known or unknown, is not your current partner, it is a warning that, consciously or unconsciously, you are attracted to someone else.
* A dream of running away from the ceremony, or a dream that one partner does not turn up, indicates uncertainty about entering a long-term relationship.
* A dream of eloping suggests you want more freedom and spontaneity in your love life.

OUTCOME OF LAUREN'S DREAM

Lauren and her fiancé took over the wedding plans and drew boundaries for Constance in their marriage, so she did not feel rejected but did not overstep the limits. Since dream wedding imagery also represents the longer-term relationship, it is important that a couple doesn't hand over major decisions in their relationship to others, however well-intentioned they may be.

Wedding Cake

Joanne, twenty-three, dreamed she was cutting her wedding cake, a small organic one she had made herself. But it would not slice. As she pressed the knife harder, the cake fell to the forest floor in small pieces, and the birds ate the crumbs. Her mother said it was the worst day of her life.

DREAM BACKGROUND AND MEANING

Joanne's family had a tradition in which an elaborate three-tiered wedding cake had been made to the same recipe design for every bride for a hundred years, but Joanne had organized a simple woodland handfasting instead of the elaborate church ceremony and reception her mother wanted. A wedding cake represents the outer expression of happiness and so is an important symbol of a united celebration if there are differences of opinion.

INTERPRETATIONS AND FORTUNE-TELLING MEANINGS

★ If you dream there is an elaborate wedding cake and everyone is eating a piece, whether at your own celebration or at that of someone close, there will be a lasting happy marriage or commitment.

★ Making your own cake indicates your current or forthcoming relationship needs to be on your terms.

★ If a wedding cake will not cut, a committed relationship needs hard work and compromise to overcome obstacles.

★ If a cake crumbles in your dream, you have serious doubts about deeper issues, concealed by superficial agreement (see "Cakes," p. 82).

★ If the cake is not big enough for everyone, you may have underestimated the demands on your time of organizing an event or project.

★ If you dream you are handing a wedding cake around, you will be central to organizing a social or family celebration.

OUTCOME OF JOANNE'S DREAM

Joanne realized her mother had set her heart on her dream wedding, symbolized by the elaborate cake. Joanne added a church blessing and allowed her mother to order a smaller version of the traditional family wedding cake for a second, more conventional reception. Joanne made her own cake for the handfasting. The design of a wedding cake in the dream and its quality reflect deeper priorities and compromises so that everyone will be happy.

Wedding Tragedy

In her dream, Daphne, twenty-four, arrived at her wedding ceremony. All the guests were watching as she slowly descended the stairs. As she neared halfway down, she tripped over her veil and tumbled, hitting her head hard on the marble floor. Daphne knew she was dead. She woke, vowing never to marry.

DREAM BACKGROUND AND MEANING

Daphne had not had much luck with her relationships. Though she had planned two weddings over the years, and had numerous proposals, neither wedding went ahead. She wondered if that dream, still vividly with her, influenced her to subconsciously call off or sabotage the weddings. A dream of death or disaster, especially at a happy event such as a wedding, never predicts death or serious injury but can make the dreamer wonder if a wedding would be the death of their identity as an independent person.

INTERPRETATIONS AND FORTUNE-TELLING MEANINGS

★ If you as the bride or groom dream of dying or being injured at the wedding, this is an anxiety dream. A wedding marks a new stage of life, and doubts should be addressed before the ceremony.

★ If you dream of a close wedding guest dying at the wedding, that person may have their own reasons for opposing the wedding, which make them unable to rejoice.

★ If in your dream the bride or groom runs from the altar or there is a reason they may not marry, the wedding ceremony may have overwhelmed the joy of getting married (see "Wedding," p. 501, and "Wedding Cake," opposite).

★ If you dream the venue is struck by lightning, catches fire, or is flooded, the couple getting married may not want an elaborate ceremony.

★ If in the dream the bride or groom falls down stairs, the dreamer may be picking up on the malice of an uninvited close relative or jealous ex-partner.

OUTCOME OF DAPHNE'S DREAM

At fifty, Daphne has now met the man of her dreams and they are talking weddings. But it feels different, and Daphne is changing every single detail of the previous dream venue. Wedding-tragedy dreams pick up doubts and angst around any wedding, but are 99 percent anxiety.

Weeds

Isla, twenty, dreamed she was weeding an overgrown garden, but the weeds were so entangled that she feared destroying the healthy plants as she removed the choking weeds. Her lover, Trudy, told her to dig the lot up and start again. But when Isla saw the bare earth and discarded petals, she knew she had made a mistake. Instead of comforting her, Trudy walked away, shutting the gate.

DREAM BACKGROUND AND MEANING

Isla accused Trudy of cheating when Trudy's college essays were found to be almost identical to hers. Isla was heartbroken, as they had been inseparable. Trudy, denying guilt, told Isla it was best not to argue and to just forget it. The worst weeds in dreams and in life are those that are beautiful and choke through love.

INTERPRETATIONS AND FORTUNE-TELLING MEANINGS

- ✷ A dream of tall weeds indicates that you have neglected a particular aspect of your life or not kept up an interest or skill you need to practice regularly.
- ✷ Choking weeds indicate unresolved issues in a relationship, which can stifle love.
- ✷ Spiky weeds choking flowers warn of a rival who appears sweet and loving but is spiteful or betrays you behind your back.
- ✷ Weeds strangling vegetable growth can represent our own fears and doubts, which hold us back from growth in business or moneymaking in our life.
- ✷ Being given flowers with weeds wrapped around them warns of a possessive lover who may use passion for control.
- ✷ Dreaming of cutting down brambly or thorny weeds indicates that freedom may not be easy, as you may keep being drawn back into a complicated relationship or situation.

OUTCOME OF ISLA'S DREAM

Isla's tutor uncovered Trudy's deviousness. Trudy was told to find somewhere else to study, and Isla returned to her studies. However, she is now wary about who she can trust. Weed dreams may identify an emotional or psychological vampire in our lives but, in removing them, we must untangle our complex emotions. It is important to not destroy the garden along with the weeds.

Weight

Leonie, twenty-eight, frequently dreamed she arrived at work and was told all the employees were being weighed as per new company policy. She was by far the heaviest, and all the others laughed and called her "Dumbo." She ran from the office, vowing never to return.

DREAM BACKGROUND AND MEANING

Leonie had battled with weight for most of her life. She suffered from hypothyroidism, resulting in weight gain. Her physician had not been helpful. Leonie was teased a lot by women in her real estate office and was not sent out to show houses to clients because of her appearance. She overate, making the problem worse, and wore shapeless black dresses.

INTERPRETATIONS AND FORTUNE-TELLING MEANINGS

- ✷ If you dream you are overweight but very glamorous and admired, you will increase your prosperity and success.
- ✷ If in the dream you are unhappy about your weight, regardless of your actual weight, you compare yourself unfairly to others, not just in appearance but in intelligence, popularity, and success.
- ✷ If you are incredibly overweight in a dream, you are trying to insulate yourself from unhappiness or from an overcritical partner.
- ✷ If in your dream you are an average weight but refuse to undress in front of a lover, you may fear letting go of your sexual inhibitions.
- ✷ If you dream you are trying to fit into an outfit two sizes too small, you are seeking to merge with others' expectations.
- ✷ If you do have weight issues, but in the dream are very slim, you are ready to stop hiding from life and reveal your authentic self.

OUTCOME OF LEONIE'S DREAM

Leonie changed her job. At her new workplace, she has started a fitness club for people of all sizes and has lost weight. She insisted on an appointment with a specialist who has new treatments for her problem. If you are excluded in a dream because of weight, start loving yourself as you are.

Welcome

Ivy, eighty-five, was having a recurring dream that when she returned home following a wartime evacuation, her mother was going out the door and told her to get her own supper. Ivy left and went to stay with her aunt around the corner, who made her welcome. Ivy woke crying.

DREAM BACKGROUND AND MEANING

The pain of her mother's indifference when Ivy had returned from evacuation during World War II still haunted Ivy. She had started having dreams of the trauma when she was planning to move in with her own daughter and family, as she was having mobility issues. She feared she would be disrupting their lives. Feeling unwelcome in a family setting is the root of many insecurity dreams.

INTERPRETATIONS AND FORTUNE-TELLING MEANINGS

★ If you are welcomed into a new family or workplace in your dream, you will fit in and find friendly faces.

★ If family or in-laws slam the door on you in your dream, rejection may be amplified by anxiety.

★ If you are returning after a long absence and dream of a welcome-home party, you are making the right decision in returning.

★ If you dream that no one is waiting to greet you at an airport or train station after an absence, former relationships may no longer exist.

★ If you are planning a welcome-home party for a friend or relative and they do not turn up, each of you may have new priorities.

★ If you dream of turning away a returning friend, partner, or family member, there may be resentments over real or imagined desertion.

OUTCOME OF IVY'S DREAM

Ivy realized by the dreams that her wartime rejection had left scars. However, she knew she would be more welcome if she regularly visited her daughter, rather than being a permanent fixture. She chose an assisted living facility. Dreams can reveal that the true depth of a welcome may depend on the people involved and where we currently fit into their lives.

Well (Water Source)

Faye, twenty-eight, dreamed she was standing by a covered overgrown well dedicated to Catherine of Alexandria. In the dream it was the eve of St. Catherine's Day, November 25. Faye was planning a traditional ritual, calling her boyfriend back from overseas as she was missing him. But well water was essential. She walked away, then saw a spring coming out of the earth close to the well. She splashed the water over her face, breasts, and wrists, calling on the saint in the old words "to send her a good husband."

DREAM BACKGROUND AND MEANING

Faye's boyfriend had gone overseas without committing himself to Faye. She intended to wait but had not heard from him. Many ancient well rituals associated with love and fertility were dedicated to the saint of the well and, in earlier times, to a goddess of a similar name.

INTERPRETATIONS AND FORTUNE-TELLING MEANINGS

★ Traditionally an archetypal symbol of life, health, and fertility, wells were called the entrance to the womb of the Mother Goddess.

★ Dreaming of taking water from a healing well suggests that you have within you the ability to heal a situation or to tap into a deep source of wisdom.

★ A dried-up, abandoned, or polluted well expresses loss of vitality, optimism, and creativity.

★ If a well is overflowing, you may be showing excessive generosity or nurturing to others and neglecting your own needs.

★ If you dream you fall into a well, you may have become overemotionally involved in others' problems.

OUTCOME OF FAYE'S DREAM

As the saint's day had not yet come, Faye went to a famous Catherine well in Dorset, England, and found a beautiful spring she could use for her ritual, as she had done in the dream. But she realized she was wasting her love and asked St. Catherine for *the right good husband.* Not long afterward, Faye and her childhood best friend fell in love. A well dream can offer a completely new perspective compared to before the dream, as it taps into unconscious awareness of the true situation.

Werewolf

Maybelline, forty-five, dreamed she was living in a cottage in the woods. The full moon shone through the windows. There was a loud commotion at the door. She thought it was her husband, home early from the tavern. There stood a huge werewolf that pushed her inside the cottage and began tearing her clothes off and biting her flesh. He staggered as though intoxicated. She seized the axe by the fire and killed him. His fur came away, and she knew she had killed her husband.

DREAM BACKGROUND AND MEANING

Maybelline's husband had severe bipolar disorder but refused to take his medicine. He could become extremely violent toward her, especially after alcohol. When he was on medication, he was very loving. But the mood swings terrified her. This was possibly a past-world dream. Werewolves can represent people with major psychological highs and lows.

INTERPRETATIONS AND FORTUNE-TELLING MEANINGS

★ If you dream that you find your werewolf under a full moon, you may discover a way to avoid trigger points in a volatile but loving relationship.

★ If you dream you are pursued by a werewolf, you may be running from your own anger or negativity rather than acknowledging and defusing it.

★ If you dream others are pursuing a werewolf, seek help with a bullying relationship whether in love or at work.

★ If you dream you are the werewolf, you may be denying a strong sexual passion out of fear.

★ Should your dream werewolf break into your home, you are accepting unreasonable behavior by a partner, family, visitor, or neighbor.

★ If you dream that the werewolf bites you, you may become absorbed by a person or situation through overwhelming emotions or suppressed desire.

OUTCOME OF MAYBELLINE'S DREAM

Maybelline realized the situation could not continue. She took out a restraining order against her husband until he took his medication regularly and stopped mixing it with alcohol. Werewolf dreams, like vampire dreams, are buried deep in the psyche and can express both unacknowledged fears and actual dangers.

Wet Paint

Penny, twenty-eight, dreamed she was trying to repaint her living room, which had been virtually destroyed at a party there the previous night. When her parents, who owned the property, arrived, she pretended she was not at home.

DREAM BACKGROUND AND MEANING

Penny had lost her job and had taken in tenants without telling her parents, who had let her live rent-free. Her parents were coming to town and always stayed with her, but her new roommates had wrecked the apartment. She had cleaned up as best she could but was too scared to tell her parents what had happened, as she feared they would not let her live there anymore.

INTERPRETATIONS AND FORTUNE-TELLING MEANINGS

★ If you dream you are covering over a dirty, faded, or graffitied wall, you may be trying to hide something you regret.

★ If you step in wet paint, you are being overhasty in making changes.

★ If paint will not dry, you may have to accept the consequences of rushing a decision that may take longer than if you allowed events to unfold naturally.

★ If you dream you get covered in wet paint, you may be feeling guilty about covering up a mistake.

★ If the new paint does not cover the old paint, consequences or feelings you thought could be left behind or denied may take longer to resolve.

★ If you dream you are repainting a picture that was not right, consider what you want to say or do rather than making an impulsive response.

OUTCOME OF PENNY'S DREAM

Penny realized she could not avoid her parents discovering the truth. They evicted the other tenants and had the apartment professionally repainted and restored to order. Penny had to move home while the work was being done. Once she found another job, her parents allowed her to move back in, but made her pay rent. Wet paint represents a new start under difficult conditions where the consequences of mistakes cannot be covered up.

Whale

Gary, twenty-eight, dreamed a mother whale and a young whale were beached on the shore. The young one would not leave the mother, although she was risking her own safety to nudge him back into deeper water. At last, the whales were caught in separate nets and towed out to sea. The young whale swam off alone.

DREAM BACKGROUND AND MEANING

Gary lived at home with his widowed mother and was very settled. His mother had remarried, but Gary resented the presence of his new stepfather and ignored hints from his mother that he might like to find a place of his own. Mother-whale dreams sometimes reveal that it can be the adult child who is unwilling to let go.

INTERPRETATIONS AND FORTUNE-TELLING MEANINGS

* Seeing whales swimming and leaping through the water in a dream represents a huge undertaking that can be successfully fulfilled, especially in commerce, accountancy, banking, or administration.
* Because whales breathe air but dive to great depths, seeing a whale blowing air through its blowhole indicates the ability and need to understand deep fears that may be holding you back.
* Dreaming of hearing a whale song heralds the growth of healing powers and a spiritual transformation.
* A mother and baby whale are a good omen for pregnancy.
* If a young whale is trying and failing to move away from the mother, this can warn of a maternal figure in the family or at work who is trying to stifle your initiative.

OUTCOME OF GARY'S DREAM

Gary realized it was time he made his own life without the security blanket and room service provided by his mother. A guy at work had asked Gary to share a luxury apartment with a gym in the city center. Gary knew he was holding his mother back as well as himself and it was time for them both to move in new directions. Whales often appear in dreams at the time of an overdue life change that will give everyone the space to grow.

Wheel of Fortune

Carrie, twenty-five, dreamed that every time she dealt the tarot cards with the question "Will I be lucky?" she picked the Wheel of Fortune. Convinced that this was a fortunate omen, she invested her savings in her best friend's beauty salon. Suddenly, Carrie was clinging to a huge revolving wheel, operated by her friend, and had to jump off before reaching the bottom to avoid being crushed.

DREAM BACKGROUND AND MEANING

Carrie had hesitated to invest in her friend's beauty salon, as the business was not thriving. Her friend had opened a luxurious salon in a working-class area where people could not afford the inflated prices. Wheel-of-fortune dreams predict luck, but with the proviso that the dreamer does not allow the wheel to carry them where they do not want to go.

INTERPRETATIONS AND FORTUNE-TELLING MEANINGS

* If you dream you win a fortune after picking the Wheel of Fortune tarot card, or dream of a big wheel turning, this is wish-fulfillment.
* If you consistently pick the Wheel of Fortune card in your dream, your luck will improve through your own decisions, rather than by someone else's.
* If you pick the Wheel of Fortune card for a friend or family member, you will be instrumental in improving their fortunes.
* If the dream wheel is spinning too fast, good luck can change suddenly. Show caution in money or relationship matters.
* If you dream you are riding on a fairground Ferris wheel, you are entering a lucky period.
* If you are riding a full-size wheel of fortune in your dream and worry about getting off, your future lies in your hands more than you realize.

OUTCOME OF CARRIE'S DREAM

Carrie realized the dream was talking about making her own luck and not handing over her fate, so she withdrew from financially supporting her friend. Wheels of fortune, whether actual dream wheels or a tarot card, warn against allowing others to dictate our future and blaming fate when it goes wrong.

Whisper, Whispering

Diana, twenty-five, had a recurring dream that she was awake in her bedroom. It was pitch-black. All around her, hissing whispers became louder, coming from the shadows. She tried to leave the room, but every time she reached for the light it would not work. The whispering moved closer and became more intense, but she could not understand what the voices were saying. At last she turned on the light, and the whispering ceased.

DREAM BACKGROUND AND MEANING

Diana was regularly experiencing sleep-paralysis dreams just before waking. She was renting a room in a basement in a dark old apartment block. The atmosphere was creepy, and she spent as little time there as possible. Diana was very psychic and so extra-sensitive to bad vibes. Whispers may be alerting us in sleep to information just outside our conscious awareness and so should be taken seriously.

INTERPRETATIONS AND FORTUNE-TELLING MEANINGS

★ Hearing whispers but not the words in a dream hints of intrigues and secrets in the daily world, which can hide factions within the family or workplace.

★ If you are whispering in your dream, you need to be careful who you share secrets with.

★ If you hear whispers and you are alone in the dream scene, unacknowledged inner fears may materialize unless you take action.

★ Colleagues or family whispering to one another in a dream suggest you are being gossiped about or excluded.

★ A whisper becoming louder contains an important message only for you.

★ If you are told to whisper, someone is trying to silence you.

OUTCOME OF DIANA'S DREAM

Diana realized they were warning whispers. On investigation, she discovered that a murder had taken place in the apartment two years earlier, and the previous tenant had been attacked by an intruder during the night. She moved out. Sinister whispering dreams with or without sleep paralysis may be paranormal voices linking with troubled souls from the past.

Whistle-Blower

Cora, fifty-six, dreamed that at the hospital where she worked she saw colleagues who had complained about dangerous practices being locked in soundproof rooms by the management. The managers who were imprisoning the staff saw Cora and tried to catch her. She ran.

DREAM BACKGROUND AND MEANING

Cora was a senior nurse at a hospital listed regularly as delivering below-standard care. She knew of neglect of patients, avoidable mortalities, and bullying by managers of personnel who complained. Anyone who raised questions was removed, on the excuse of poor performance. Cora was seriously worried about patient safety but could not afford to risk her pension. Dreaming of complaining about poor or dangerous conduct in any area of life is often a prelude to the dreamer having the courage to speak up.

INTERPRETATIONS AND FORTUNE-TELLING MEANINGS

★ If you dream of complaining about poor service or malpractice, the matter is bothering you sufficiently to intrude on your dreams and should be taken seriously.

★ If you dream of using a particular channel to complain about inefficiency or neglect, that avenue of complaint will be the most effective.

★ If you dream of a child, elderly person, or other vulnerable person being neglected, whether by family or official carers, your unconscious mind has noticed problems.

★ If you dream of being unfairly accused of malpractice, someone may be trying to wreck your career or home life.

★ If others in the dream support your whistle-blowing, it is a good sign that you will receive support.

★ If you dream of meeting a wall of silence by officialdom, you may need to go beyond internal channels to be heard.

OUTCOME OF CORA'S DREAM

Cora realized that if she complained internally, she would become another victim of the silencing process. She told the local television station, which sent in an undercover journalist. Whistle-blowing dreams usually occur when a situation is so bad that the dreamer realizes that the matter must be addressed, regardless of personal risk.

Whistling

Brian, twenty-five, dreamed he was walking through the forest, whistling. Then he heard a whistling through the trees. A black monster, attracted by Brian's whistling, backed him against a tree. Brian had heard about tree demons but had thought it was just a story. This one kept whistling, and with every whistle he grew. Brian realized that if he whistled back, he could shrink the monster until he was small enough to be overcome, so he pictured the monster as a small bird, which flew away as Brian whistled.

DREAM BACKGROUND AND MEANING

Brian had been ignoring the final notices in his mailbox and continued to build up debts. He had ignored attempts by his bank to create a payment plan. His bank froze his account, and Brian realized it was the end of the road. Dreaming of someone whistling at you means that you need to pay attention to a matter you are ignoring before it grows to insoluble proportions.

INTERPRETATIONS AND FORTUNE-TELLING MEANINGS

* For cultures from Turkey to indigenous tribes in North America, as well as people in Japan and China, whistling after dark in a forest, especially after midnight, is believed to attract bad spirits and, in a dream, can indicate fears of others threatening your lifestyle.
* If the dreamer responds to others who are whistling, the dreamer is handing over control for decision-making.
* If you are whistling on a ship in the dream, you may need to deal with confrontational people and an argument that arises out of nowhere.
* If it is daytime in the dream, someone whistling cheerfully as they approach heralds new friends and informal pleasurable gatherings.
* If you are playing a musical whistle that is in tune, harmonious times are ahead; but if out of tune, you may find that your opinions differ from others.

OUTCOME OF BRIAN'S DREAM

After the dream, Brian confronted his debt monster instead of whistling defiantly back at it. By accepting certain economies, he was able to handle his debts. "Whistling in the wind" is an expression used when problems are ignored. A dream can show how they can be reduced to size once faced.

Whitewater Rafting, Rapids

In his dream, Don, twenty-five, was at the top of a rapids as high and steep as Niagara Falls. He was riding in a rubber raft with a broken harness, holding on to a small boy left in his charge. The boy fell in and Don dove in after him. He woke, gasping for breath, and the boy was gone.

DREAM BACKGROUND AND MEANING

Don ran a whitewater rafting company with his best friend, Joe. Don was worried about safety as there had been some near-tragedies, and his partner cut corners to make extra money. Don was especially concerned about allowing young teens to ride unsupervised, and safety equipment on the rafts needed replacing. Whitewater rafting symbolizes risks with emotions as well as with physical security, and the dream outcome is significant as to the validity of the risk.

INTERPRETATIONS AND FORTUNE-TELLING MEANINGS

* If you dream you are enjoying shooting rapids, you are ready for extra excitement and activities in your life.
* If you dream your boat tips over, are you taking too many lifestyle risks?
* If you dream you are persuaded to ride dangerous rapids, beware of bad advice or temptations that may have dire consequences.
* If you dream that coins and jewels pour down the rapids, you will have the chance for a quick profit. But there is a longer-term price.
* If you dream you win a whitewater rafting race, you are heading for success and prosperity.
* If you dream you protect someone in the boat, you may need to rescue a loved one from their mistakes.

OUTCOME OF DON'S DREAM

Don talked to his friend about his concerns. Joe said he would find a new partner who would not hold him back. Don now works for an organization improving safety in extreme sports. Whitewater rafting dreams can reveal irresponsibility. Trust your instincts as to the right course.

Wildfire

Chuck, forty-seven, dreamed he was a teenager again, having a barbecue in the forest with his friends, despite dry conditions. Sparks from the barbecue set the bushes alight, and the fire rapidly spread. The boys tried to beat out the fire but could not and fled, as they did not want to be blamed. Chuck later returned and was hailed as a hero for helping extinguish the fire.

DREAM BACKGROUND AND MEANING

The dream had come back to haunt Chuck, as he had recently wrongly blamed a colleague for causing a major blackout in the company computer system, which was responsible for directing emergency rescue vehicles. Chuck knew he should admit his mistake but was worried about losing his job. Wildfire dreams often reflect panic as a relatively minor mistake escalates out of control.

INTERPRETATIONS AND FORTUNE-TELLING MEANINGS

* If you see a wildfire getting nearer in a dream, careless inflammatory words may cause a sudden flare-up that cannot be undone.
* If you dream of a wildfire in your area and the weather is unseasonably dry, you may be picking up potential danger. Ensure that your family precautions are up to date.
* If a dream wildfire spreads rapidly, beware of neighbors or colleagues spreading rumors that may spiral out of control.
* If you dream you witness someone you know starting a wildfire deliberately or carelessly, be wary of them causing trouble in your life.
* If you dream you help extinguish a wildfire, you may need to be a calming influence with hotheaded family members or colleagues.
* If you dream you are rescuing trapped people and animals from a wildfire, you may be in the front line of trouble, even if you had not intended to get involved.

OUTCOME OF CHUCK'S DREAM

Chuck offered to work through the night to put the system right, and everyone called him a hero. The other guy was demoted. Chuck did not admit his guilt and still occasionally has the dream. Wildfire dreams can mirror earlier out-of-control situations but are not always heeded.

Wildflowers

Noel, thirty, dreamed he was in a huge wildflower meadow, with acre upon acre of flowers in every color, long grasses, and tangled herbs. Noel was making wildflower bouquets and loading them into his van. His parents arrived and replaced his fields with artificial grass.

DREAM BACKGROUND AND MEANING

Noel's suburban garden had become a wildflower meadow, to the annoyance of his neighbors with their neatly trimmed gardens, who complained that seeds from his weeds were spoiling their lawns. Noel was a florist but hated the formal and sometimes artificially dyed or out-of-season cut flowers he sold in his store. He longed to share his wildflower passion. Wildflowers in dreams and life represent spontaneity, allowing life to follow its own course and unrestricted growth.

INTERPRETATIONS AND FORTUNE-TELLING MEANINGS

* If you dream you are walking through wildflower meadows, happiness lies in embracing the freedom to live by your own rules.
* Trampled wildflowers indicate that your free spirit may face opposition.
* If the wildflowers in your dream are filled with wildlife, this is a sign of fertility and natural conception, which can be encouraging if you are having difficulty becoming pregnant.
* If you dream your wildflower meadow is replaced with a neatly trimmed or artificial lawn, you will be offered approval and advancement on others' terms.
* If you are planting wildflowers, you will have the chance to help others live more authentically.
* If wildflowers will not grow, and they die in your dream garden, you may be in the wrong place to follow your own choices.

OUTCOME OF NOEL'S DREAM

Noel started offering bouquets of wildflowers and herbs for weddings and special occasions, selling wildflower seeds, and growing herbs and wildflowers in beautiful pots. Eventually he bought a house with land to grow on and space to teach visitors about wildflowers. Wildflowers represent nature running free, but some people find uncontrolled nature a threat to their ordered lives. Wildflower dreams can encourage you to follow your own path.

Willow Tree

Nesta, fifty-five, dreamed she saw a veiled woman with a willow crown who picked a small fallen willow branch by full moonlight. The woman circled the tree, and the frosts and lingering snow melted. Nesta woke at peace.

DREAM BACKGROUND AND MEANING

Nesta had returned to Ireland from America to see her dying mother, her only relative, who she had become estranged from. Her mother had been cruel to her as a child. Since she had arrived in Dublin, the roads to Nesta's childhood village had been snowbound. She was considering flying back without seeing her mother. The willow is the tree of the full moon. From Celtic times it has signified reconciliation, especially connected with mothering.

INTERPRETATIONS AND FORTUNE-TELLING MEANINGS

★ If you dream of a willow with branches trailing close to water, there are buried emotions to be released.

★ If you see a willow tree in full moonlight in a dream, mothering issues either with your own mother or as a mother require forgiveness.

★ If you are weaving or selling willow baskets, use your own experiences to guide and counsel others.

★ Dreaming of a trailing weeping willow says you should not be weighed down by old sorrows or regrets for what could not have been prevented.

★ If you see fuzzy white and gray catkins growing in your dream, new beginnings and the softening of anger will follow.

OUTCOME OF NESTA'S DREAM

Nesta discovered that the night of the dream was the festival of the Goddess Brighid, who in her maiden form melted the snows of winter to bring new life with her willow wand. This is called Candlemas in the modern tradition (see "Groundhog Day," p. 228). The weather improved, and Nesta went to see her mother, who regretted the past. Nesta stayed until her mother died. Especially if we are connected to a particular culture, we can, on the anniversary of old festivals, link to the energies if they have a message for us.

Wills, Legacy

In his dream, Albert, seventy-two, was at a lawyer's office with his wife, Margaret, discussing their wills. When Albert told the lawyer how he wanted his assets shared, Margaret totally disagreed. The lawyer tried to intervene, but Margaret stormed out of the office. Albert chased after Margaret, who insisted she was going to apply to the court to have Albert declared incapable of handling his own affairs.

DREAM BACKGROUND AND MEANING

Both Albert and Margaret had had previous marriages. Albert had two sons, and Margaret had two daughters. They had had many arguments about how their money should be split after their passing. Albert believed that because Margaret's daughters hadn't visited for some years, they should not receive as much as his sons, who remained in constant contact. Dreams about wills, while ideally representing settling the future to enjoy the present, may reveal emotional conflicts that continue after the death.

INTERPRETATIONS AND FORTUNE-TELLING MEANINGS

★ To have family disputes over a will in a dream, even if the person is still alive, suggests that family rivalries, especially over money, need resolving.

★ If in a dream a relative produces a will that the deceased apparently signed after the official one, whether the person who made the will is living or deceased in real life, beware of emotional blackmail within the family.

★ If in a dream there is no will after a death, there may be hidden liaisons and arrangements between family members of which you know nothing.

★ If you dream of making a will, you may need to resolve continuing financial demands from family members.

OUTCOME OF ALBERT'S DREAM

Albert realized he and his wife should enjoy their savings and investments themselves. To the annoyance of the children, they agreed to spend a large amount of the disputed inheritance on making their lives good in the present and started with an extended vacation in a Winnebago motor home they purchased. Dreams about wills where there are disputes at any stage suggest that the dreamer should focus on the present, as they may be postponing happiness for misguided if altruistic reasons.

Wind, Breeze

Bryan, nineteen, experienced the strangest sensation of the wind blowing from all four directions at once: chill from the north, stimulating from the east, warm from the south, and containing rain from the west. The winds were not fierce, but he was frustrated that he had to wait for them to cease.

DREAM BACKGROUND AND MEANING

Bryan, an exceptional scholar, had offers of admission from four colleges: the first, the one his father and grandfather had attended; the second, a prestigious Ivy League school; the third, one where the social life was brilliant; and the fourth, near the coast, where he could indulge his passion for windsurfing. Winds in dreams can indicate the right direction to take. If there is confusion, they may also reflect uncertainty and suggest that it may be necessary to wait for the wind to drop.

INTERPRETATIONS AND FORTUNE-TELLING MEANINGS

⋆ If you dream you are listening to the wind blowing through the trees, this is an ancient form of divination, and the rustling leaves will hold a message for you.

⋆ A breeze blowing you along indicates the blowing away of inertia and stagnation.

⋆ A warm wind promises happier and more prosperous times, travel, and/or house moves.

⋆ A breeze stirring the leaves heralds energy for change and new directions to be harnessed.

⋆ If the wind suddenly changes direction, be prepared for unexpected events to change what may have seemed permanent.

OUTCOME OF BRYAN'S DREAM

From the dream, Bryan concluded he did not have any strong preferences and decided to take a year in the working world to settle himself over the way his life should proceed. He decided to work in his uncle's ocean-sports business. If a wind turns cold in the dream, seek refuge from unfair criticism or indifference with warm, supportive friends or relatives, and use any restlessness for initiating changes of your choosing.

Windows

Mandy, sixty, dreamed she was a ghost in a darkened garden, looking through a window to where her family was having a celebration of her husband's engagement to a neighbor. Heartbroken, she faded into the darkness.

DREAM BACKGROUND AND MEANING

Mandy had heart failure. Though she was in no immediate danger, she knew the future was uncertain. Her husband vowed that he would never remarry if she did die. Their neighbor, a widow, had brought food for her husband while Mandy was in the hospital. But the neighbor still regularly turned up with food for the three of them, which intruded on their plans. Lighted windows and the dreamer standing outside looking in can bring up old fears or incidents of rejection, triggered by insecurity.

INTERPRETATIONS AND FORTUNE-TELLING MEANINGS

⋆ If you are looking out through a window, watching the world go by, you are ready to explore wider horizons.

⋆ If a window is open, new experiences and opportunities are coming.

⋆ If a window is broken or boarded up, you may be insecure in your domestic world because of intrusive people, or there may be actual household safety issues that need checking,

⋆ If you dream that a locked window will not open, an opportunity is blocked, but there may be another way to gain access.

⋆ If you are climbing in or escaping through a window, a conventional approach to a problem may not work. Investigate hidden obstacles or restrictions.

⋆ If you draw the curtains in a room, you are seeking privacy from the outside world. If they are already drawn, an older relative or friend may be unapproachable right now.

OUTCOME OF MANDY'S DREAM

Mandy was insecure about her future, as her neighbor was encroaching on her territory. She planned lots of things she still wanted to do with her husband, however long or short her life, and tactfully deterred her neighbor's unwelcome visits. Windows in dreams represent openings into the wider world as well as restrictions or unwanted intrusions, and hold a message according to the context and feelings within the dream.

Wine

Ozzie, forty, dreamed he was at a scientific awards ceremony where the wine was flowing. Ozzie was mistaken for a waiter and given a tray of drinks to offer to guests. Suddenly, his team was called to the stage to receive what was rightly his personal award for creating a vaccine against a virus. His team rushed forward to seize the reward and be photographed by the media. Ozzie slipped quietly away.

DREAM BACKGROUND AND MEANING

Ozzie was a brilliant scientist but hated wine-filled events with everyone vying for glory. However, he knew that unless he participated he would remain a backroom boy while others took credit for his work. But was the price of socializing too high? Wine evenings have become a way of networking and pushing forward those who talk the talk.

INTERPRETATIONS AND FORTUNE-TELLING MEANINGS

★ A dream of being toasted with fine wine is a sign of celebration where your achievements will be recognized.

★ Sharing wine with a lover or partner indicates deepening love and attraction.

★ If in the dream you are inebriated, you may be suppressing a problem but only postponing it.

★ If the wine is sour or vinegary, promises made will not be kept.

★ If you are in a crowded wine bar or party with people constantly topping up your glass, you may be swept along by others' excesses into acting against what is right for you.

★ If you are intimidated by someone's seemingly superior knowledge of wine, they may be relying on image to impress.

OUTCOME OF OZZIE'S DREAM

Ozzie realized that what he cared about were the results from their research. He was prepared to remain in the shadows, even if sacrificing fame and fortune. Drinking celebratory wine is an outward sign of achievement, which can overshadow the achievement. If you are filling others' glasses while no one fills yours, are you giving too much? Is that what you want?

Witch, Wise Woman

Ursula, twenty-five, had experienced disturbing dreams of being an old woman in Switzerland who was dragged to a tower and hung by her arms. She was condemned to be burned at the stake. A witch in the crowd got near enough to give her herbs to swallow so Ursula was unconscious as the flames rose. She woke screaming.

DREAM BACKGROUND AND MEANING

Ursula had recently joined a Wiccan coven, but her parents strongly disapproved and said she was pursuing the path of the Devil. Her dream was a very common past-life dream. Wise women from late medieval times through to the seventeenth century were regarded by the Church as evil. The stigma has remained among the superstitious.

INTERPRETATIONS AND FORTUNE-TELLING MEANINGS

★ Dreaming of a wise woman or witch says, "Believe in yourself and ignore prejudice or detractors."

★ A wicked witch represents deep-seated superstitious fears of our own negative side and paranormal evil.

★ A dream of a witch casting a spell says you should rely on intuition and make every earthly effort to attract what most you want.

★ A witch cursing you warns that a woman in authority may cause trouble, or an older female relative may manipulate you.

★ A dream of a wise witch or healer teaching you magick or about psychic phenomena says there is already great stored wisdom within you. Open yourself to your own inner powers.

★ Dreaming of being part of a coven at the full moon or a seasonal celebration reveals that you will come across like-minded people with whom you can develop your spirituality.

OUTCOME OF URSULA'S DREAM

Ursula discovered that what she dreamed about had happened in Lucerne, Switzerland, during the sixteenth century. She went to the tower and cast flowers on the water to honor all the witches through the centuries who had been persecuted. The dreams ceased. She moved into an apartment with a coven member. Whether you have personal past-world dreams or are tuning in to persecuted wise women throughout the ages, a simple ceremony will bring peace.

Witness

In his dream, George, fifty, was a ten-year-old, acting as lookout while his friend was stealing from the church charity box. George heard the main door opening, and the boys escaped through the vestry window, scattering coins as they ran. A boy came in and started to pick the coins up to put them back in the box. The priest heard the commotion and accused the boy of the theft. The innocent boy was punished because George did not speak out.

DREAM BACKGROUND AND MEANING

George had recently witnessed a car theft. The guy who had tried to stop it was falsely accused. George was coming out of the hotel opposite with his girlfriend, who his wife knew nothing about. George could not act as a witness without revealing his illicit affair. The wrong man was taken to court.

INTERPRETATIONS AND FORTUNE-TELLING MEANINGS

★ If you witness a crime in a dream and are intimidated or bribed by the perpetrators, you have conflicting loyalties.

★ If you dream that you see a crime and try to stop it, you are ready to speak out against an injustice at work or in the community.

★ If you dream you are a detective interviewing witnesses, you may be asked to take sides in a family or workplace dispute.

★ If you dream you are a witness in a court case who is lying to protect the accused, you are being unwillingly implicated in others' problems.

★ If you dream you are witnessing the signing of a contract, you may be offered a lucrative contract or loan on favorable terms.

★ If you are seeking a character-witness statement in a dream, note who offers a good one and who gives a bad reference for their own gain.

OUTCOME OF GEORGE'S DREAM

The dream reminded George about how his boyhood misdeeds had come back to haunt him. He admitted to the police that he had witnessed the car theft. The police did not reveal who he was with. Witness dreams are connected with conscience and justice but can contain dilemmas over divided loyalties.

Wizard

Sean, twenty-two, dreamed he was in a cave full of potions. A Merlin-type wizard was waving a wand over a cauldron of fire. Sean was his apprentice. People were coming to the cave and giving the wizard bags of gold in return for potions. Sean knew Merlin was selling people bottles of colored water over which he made strange incantations. But Sean knew no one would believe him. When Sean tried to escape, Merlin threw him in a dungeon until Sean promised to say nothing.

DREAM BACKGROUND AND MEANING

Sean was working for a company that was defrauding clients, mainly trusting elderly people, out of their pension funds. When Sean complained, he was told no one would believe him and he would be framed for embezzlement. Wizards can be masters (or mistresses) of illusion beneath a veneer of respectability and authority.

INTERPRETATIONS AND FORTUNE-TELLING MEANINGS

★ If you dream you are watching a wizard perform amazing tricks, someone at work may be claiming to be more knowledgeable than they are.

★ If you dream you are the wizard, this may indicate your own emerging magical and psychic powers.

★ An archetypal wizard teaching you magick in a dream says you should seek the advice of a wise older man or trust traditional methods.

★ If you dream that the wizard is giving you a potion, an unexpected advantage will appear in your life.

★ If you know the potion is fake, you may be falling for a scam or may be too trusting of a seemingly reliable person who intends to deceive.

★ If you dream your wizard disappears, you need to find practical solutions to problems and not expect a magical solution.

OUTCOME OF SEAN'S DREAM

Sean alerted an investigative television company, as several high-profile figures were involved in the fraud. The company was exposed, but the CEO disappeared, and it took time for Sean to prove his own innocence. Wizards should never be underestimated in their ability to transfer blame for misdeeds to others.

Wolf

Della, thirty-eight, dreamed she was standing in a clearing and saw a pack of wolves running toward her. As the wolves reached her, she became a wolf and started to run with them. They ran until they reached a circle of flattened grass. In the middle was a baby wrapped in a blanket. The pack turned into women wearing black cloaks. One of the women handed Della the baby.

DREAM BACKGROUND AND MEANING

Della was in a relationship with a man who controlled her with the promise of a baby. Della was feeling increasingly trapped, but she was desperate for a baby. Female wolves guarding or suckling a human baby are a sign of fertility, even if the baby is not yet conceived.

INTERPRETATIONS AND FORTUNE-TELLING MEANINGS

* Female wolves running together are a woman's power symbol for collective women's movements for equality, or for a woman reclaiming her confidence to overcome abuse.
* A male wolf guarding a pack says your partner is loyal and will be or will become a good parent.
* A lone male wolf running through the forest indicates desired and achievable travel and independence for men and women.
* Howling wolves warn of an outside threat in the workplace or family, to be overcome by remaining united.
* Dreaming of being attacked by a wolf or pack of wolves reflects fear of being torn apart by family or relationship conflicts.
* Becoming a wolf in a dream represents casting off fears and restrictions.

OUTCOME OF DELLA'S DREAM

The dream was triggered by Della's wise subconscious mind deciding to retake her own power. Della realized the baby was an unborn soul waiting for the right father. The dark-robed women suggest that Della once belonged to an order of priestesses or female shamans in a distant past life who knew the art of shape-shifting, changing into different creatures. Wolves are magical creatures in many cultures, beloved by the wolf clans of indigenous North Americans.

Woman on the Moon

Jean, eighteen, frequently dreamed she was in a rocket ship along with three other well-known astronauts, all women. After landing on the Moon's surface, Jean announced: "One small step for woman, one giant leap for womankind." Jean woke, hopeful that one day she would be walking on the surface of the Moon.

DREAM BACKGROUND AND MEANING

Jean was devastated when her application for a NASA internship was rejected. She attributed it to being female. Her science teacher advised Jean to take a degree in aerodynamics, specializing in space travel. Jean applied for space-program apprenticeships, despite believing the odds were stacked against women. Dreaming of the fulfillment of an ambition suggests that giving up is not an option.

INTERPRETATIONS AND FORTUNE-TELLING MEANINGS

* If you regularly have a dream unwavering in detail, it is a path in your destiny that, though not easy, is there to be tried.
* If the dream predicts a future event, you may be one of the people to change an existing trend.
* If there is prejudice through ageism, sexism, or ethnic issues that stands in the way of a major achievement, use the dream energy to break down every door and break through every glass ceiling.
* If you dream of any mentors, contact them, as they may act as role models.
* See if there are clues in your dream as to where you may find your own entry via another door, whether to space travel or to another major venture you seek.
* If the dream predicts failure, explore another role within your chosen field that could lead you back to the original path.

OUTCOME OF JEAN'S DREAM

Jean wrote to the women she recognized from the dream and was assured that space travel was slowly opening for women. One who trained in the United Kingdom pointed Jean toward an English space program taking apprentices. Jean has applied. Dreams can refocus the dreamer on what might one day be attainable.

Working in Your Sleep

Polly, forty-eight, in her dream was typing a lot of figures onto the computer screen, but the keys kept sticking. She went over and over the same piece of work again and again, but each time it added up differently. The dream seemed to last all night, and she woke exhausted and irritable.

DREAM BACKGROUND AND MEANING

Polly noticed that whenever she had a deadline and brought work home, she would dream all night of working. Although occasionally she had insights, generally the dream was a muddle and frustrating.

INTERPRETATIONS AND FORTUNE-TELLING MEANINGS

★ If you dream of a solution to a work problem or a new idea, record it as soon as you wake, as the creative mind if not overloaded can kick in.

★ If you dream of struggling under mountains of files or invoices when you leave work, this is a sign you should leave your work life at work.

★ If, however, in the dream you are powerful at work, this may be a dress rehearsal for a success, especially in an area where direct communication is important.

★ If your dreams of working all night are generally unproductive, create a switch-off transition zone before bed.

★ If your family frequently appears in your workplace in the dream, family worries may be intruding on your work life.

★ Working in your sleep followed by exhaustion the next day marks the need for a vacation or radical reassessment of unreasonable demands of time and effort in your job.

OUTCOME OF POLLY'S DREAM

Polly realized that most nights she was working till bedtime and never switching off. She took a month's sabbatical and, when she returned, delegated demands and left work worries outside the front door when home. The dreams stopped. When work intrudes into dreams, it is a certain sign that the working and life worlds are out of balance and becoming blurred.

Writers' Group

Tricia, twenty-eight, dreamed she was sitting in a wood-paneled tea room in London. It was not present-day, because the famous occult writer Dion Fortune, who died in the 1940s, was there with other, older men Tricia did not recognize. Tricia realized the group could not see her. The men, except for one with wild hair, argued that magical practices should not be revealed to the public in books. The argument became heated. Tricia tried to explain that modern writers shared all kinds of knowledge. But they could not hear her. Eventually they broke up, leaving the tea undrunk and the cakes not eaten.

DREAM BACKGROUND AND MEANING

Tricia was writing an occult novel, but the writers' group she had joined, mainly older women, totally disregarded her opinions, and Tricia felt invisible. Dreams about writers' groups refer to any form of communication where approval of others is considered necessary.

INTERPRETATIONS AND FORTUNE-TELLING MEANINGS

★ If you are amicably discussing ideas with a group of people in a dream, they may support you in everyday life.

★ If you dream of being ignored at a writers' group, you are seeking approval for your creative endeavors from the wrong people.

★ If you are sitting apart from a writers' group in your dream, it may be best to go it alone.

★ If a writers' group, known or unknown, is arguing, this suggests that an actual creative group would offer stimulating input.

★ If members of a writers' group are arguing aggressively, you may encounter jealousy or resentment for your work.

★ If you are leading a writers' group, you have ideas or creative material to share publicly.

OUTCOME OF TRICIA'S DREAM

Tricia discovered that Dion Fortune and members of the Golden Dawn magical society met regularly early in the twentieth century in the paneled British Museum tea room. After the dream, Tricia started an online forum for young writers of fantasy and occult fiction. Writers'-group dreams suggest that you seek support in your creative work from like-minded creators, rather than those with big egos.

Wrong Direction

Camilla, forty-eight, dreamed she was catching a bus to her childhood home. When she looked out of the window, she realized the bus was going in the wrong direction. She struggled to get off the crowded bus as it carried her farther away from her destination. Finally, she alighted from the bus and started walking in what she hoped was the right direction.

DREAM BACKGROUND AND MEANING

Camilla experienced many dreams of being carried in the wrong direction, by train, bus, or even by plane. Only when she walked did she seem to be going the right way, but that was so tiring. Camilla was downsizing her home, and her daughter had found her a pleasant apartment near her with a bus stop outside. Wrong-direction dreams hold clues in where we start the dream and where we want to be.

INTERPRETATIONS AND FORTUNE-TELLING MEANINGS

* Wrong-direction dreams, especially ones where the direction is determined by the transport mode, suggest that the destination chosen by others is not what we want.
* If you dream you are driving and go in the wrong direction, you may be trying to fulfill someone else's agenda.
* If you are stranded on an unfamiliar street with no obvious transport, you need to consider where you want to be.
* If you are trying to reach a childhood home, you may be uncertain about your future life plans.
* If you dream that you seek rescue by a family member but cannot reach them, it may be that you do not want to follow their advice.

OUTCOME OF CAMILLA'S DREAM

Camilla had loved her childhood home because it was in a small community where everyone knew one another. She bought a compact house in a small village where she could participate in community life. Wrong-direction dreams ask who is traveling in the wrong direction—it may not be the dreamer.

Wrong Hotel

Stefan, thirty-four, dreamed he arrived at the airport in Bali. A cab driver dropped him at his hotel. After booking in, Stefan realized that the cab driver had taken him to the wrong hotel. The room was dirty, the shower not working, and cockroaches were everywhere. Stefan tried to protest, but the receptionist had disappeared.

DREAM BACKGROUND AND MEANING

Stefan was worried that he had picked the wrong hotel on his first vacation since his separation from his wife. He needed peace and quiet, yet after booking the hotel, he learned it was surrounded by nightclubs. A dream about the wrong hotel can be a warning that a vacation hotel will not suit the dreamer.

INTERPRETATIONS AND FORTUNE-TELLING MEANINGS

* If the hotel in the dream is in the wrong location, double-check before going on vacation, despite whatever reassurances you have been given.
* If the hotel in your dream is dirty and run-down, you may be considering a bargain vacation.
* If you dream that a cab driver takes you to the wrong hotel and you discover your mistake in time, you may have handed control for your life to the wrong people.
* If you dream you are tricked into going to the wrong hotel, you may be too trusting of those who have their own agenda.
* If in the dream you start to like the hotel, though it was not what you asked for, you may have outgrown your old needs and should move on.
* If you are in the wrong hotel and are told you cannot move, you may be accepting second best in life without protest.

OUTCOME OF STEFAN'S DREAM

Stefan canceled the booking and went to another hotel. There he met a single woman his own age. Though they are taking it slowly, Stefan feels fate played a hand. Hotels are supposed to be homes away from home without the pressures. If the hotel is wrong in the dream, you may have serious questions about whether you need to move on in life generally.

YouTube Videos

Melanie, twenty-five, dreamed she was starring in a music video on YouTube and had a million views. Offers were pouring in to sign her for a recording contract and to manage her. Then the screen went blank and the video was gone, along with the positive comments, and she was feeding her young child at the kitchen table.

DREAM BACKGROUND AND MEANING

Melanie had been on the road to success as a singer and songwriter when she discovered she was pregnant. Everyone melted away, including the baby's father. Dreams of having a video on YouTube can offer encouragement to publicize talents if the dreamer feels unsupported.

INTERPRETATIONS AND FORTUNE-TELLING MEANINGS

* If you dream of being a major success with your online videos, you are clearly tuned in to current trends and should explore this way of publicizing yourself and your work, if you haven't already.
* If in the dream you are earning your living with YouTube videos, you may have a marketable product or business idea you should pursue.
* If you dream you are filming or uploading video material on YouTube, you may be ready to launch a new venture, whether a new career or activity, where you seek the approval or encouragement of others.
* If you dream that someone uploads a malicious video of you that was filmed secretly, there may be people in your life you are unconsciously insecure about sharing secrets with. Note them.
* If you are helping someone else publicize themselves on YouTube, are you happy to stay in the background, or are you feeling that you should share or stand in the limelight?

OUTCOME OF MELANIE'S DREAM

Melanie realized that YouTube subscriptions were the way to relaunch her career while she was at home with the little one. She started to receive payments and offers for her original songs. By confirming the commercial value and viability of what is being offered, YouTube dreams can give people the confidence and impetus when other avenues are closed.

Zombies

Orlando, forty-eight, dreamed that all his neighbors had turned into zombies and were walking along the road, holding flags, toward the fracking site where a beautiful forest was being dug up to explore for gas and minerals. He shouted for them to wake up, but the owner of the woodland was handing each a bag of gold in return for their flag to plant. Orlando was chased by the zombies, who wanted to bite him and turn him into a fellow zombie.

DREAM BACKGROUND AND MEANING

The owner of the local woodland was being paid a huge sum to allow fracking to rip up the land. Orlando's neighbors, who at first opposed the plan, caved in when they were offered shares in any gas or oil find. Orlando was increasingly ostracized for trying to hold up the project. Dreaming of zombies often occurs when you feel isolated because of the unwillingness of others to act or speak out against injustice.

INTERPRETATIONS AND FORTUNE-TELLING MEANINGS

* If you dream you are pursued by zombies, you may feel pressured to accept a policy or work practice you know is wrong and mindless.
* If you dream you are bitten by a zombie, you may fear being tempted to go along with what you know is unwise.
* If you dream you are a zombie, you may feel tired of fighting for your rights, but should not give up.
* If you dream you are fighting and winning a war against zombies, you will overcome unreasonable demands or pressures to conform to what you know is wrong.
* If you dream you hide from zombies, you may be avoiding dealing with a relationship or situation that no longer has life.

OUTCOME OF ORLANDO'S DREAM

Orlando called a meeting to explain the dangers of fracking to the local environment and land authority. Those who attended are starting an investigation of the facts. Zombie dreams can reflect a sense of hopelessness, especially if a partner or family member has turned into a dream zombie, but persevere in communicating before giving up.

Zoo

Jonathan, twenty-nine, dreamed he was alone in a small run-down zoo with cramped cages. He saw a bunch of keys hanging on the wall. One by one, he opened the cages. Some of the animals would not leave. Others made a bid for freedom, but soon came back to their enclosures.

DREAM BACKGROUND AND MEANING

Jonathan was opposed to all forms of animal parks and keeping animals in captivity. He believed creatures should be released back into the wild. He had been offered a position as a zoo vet working on conservation, breeding, and reproducing natural habitats, but refused on principle. Zoo dreams, especially if you dislike the principle of having animals in captivity, represent on a personal level conflict between expressing yourself freely and the need to fit in with convention.

INTERPRETATIONS AND FORTUNE-TELLING MEANINGS

★ If dream zoo enclosures are large and reflect the creatures' natural habitats, you may need to balance your natural instincts for freedom in life with accepting necessary limitations.

★ If one species makes a connection in zoo dreams, usually one you like, their powers are the strengths that will most assist you.

★ If you dream a zoo is cramped or badly run, your instincts are being restricted in your life and work, but you may fear striking out alone.

★ If you dream a fierce animal escapes, hidden aggression or repressed anger should be expressed in a controlled way.

★ If you dream you are an animal in a zoo, you may be subject to overscrutiny in your workplace or by interfering relatives or neighbors.

OUTCOME OF JONATHAN'S DREAM

After the dream, Jonathan realized that his views were as narrow as those he opposed and that some of the zoo animals could not survive right now in the wild. He took the job and went on rescue missions for mistreated wild animals overseas or those in peril of being wiped out. Zoo dreams may reveal personal dilemmas about living without boundaries.

Index

Acknowledgments

I would like to sincerely thank Sterling Ethos's Kate Zimmermann, whose professionalism, enthusiasm, and encouragement have greatly assisted in the writing of this book. Also, a huge thank-you to my agent and ultra-pedantic literary editor, John Gold, largely responsible for minimizing the publishing of my more than occasional faux pas, often written while I'm burning the midnight oil.

Picture Credits

Creative Market: ArtCreationsDesign: cover, 3, 17 (suitcase, skull, goblet, crystals, crown, snake, crystal ball, letters), 7, 16 (books), 17 (poison, lamp), 157, 346, 436, back cover; Black Aneri: cover, 3, 16 (girl, swing, flower planet, balloons, clock, ladder, castle), 5, 6, 19, 46, 485, spine, throughout (smoke)

Getty Images: *DigitalVision Vectors:* BojanMirkovic: 192; ivetavaicule: 107; saemilee: 16, 34 (blue ribbon), 72, 159 (earth), 164, 278, 290, 325; serkan6: 314; stellalevi: 256; *iStock/Getty Images Plus:* abc17: 428; Alenserart: 90; marjorie anastacio: 178, 189; AnastasiaSit: 25; andreaantunes1: 172; annwaterru: 45 (ballerina), 46; arxichtu4ki: 452; astaru: 361; Julia August: 41, 44, 54, 85, 112, 162, 200, 285, 319, 370, 383, 440, 484; Barloc: 476; Benjavisa: 56, 305, 423; Natalya Blashchinskaya: 376; Mayya Bokova: 375; Tatyana Boyko: 386; Catya_Shok: 327; cgdeaw: 461; Viktoriia Chorna: 259; chrisserbug: 182; Anastasia Chubenko: 215; Natalia Churzina: 78, 247; Color-Brush: 402; Dinkoobraz: 345; Jeanna Draw: 276, 280; Tatiana Dubin: 468; Eimizu: 34; Ekaterina Capeluck: 27; Yuliya Derbisheva: 58, 80, 231, 296; Elen11: 279; ElenaMedvedeva: 23, 202; Evgeniay_Mokeeva: 176, 517; Nadja Golubitskaya: 392; Oleg Grobachev: 33; Olya Haifisch: 60; Kateryna Holodniuk: 135, 136, 175, 227; Homunkulus28: 397; Anastasiia Iakusheva: 303, 355; iAodLeo: 147; Fumiko Inoue: 490; Inspiretta: 18; Iuliia_Zubkova: 100; Alyona Ivanova: 43, 123, 238, 331, 337, 363, 372; IvanovaJulia: 89; izumikobayashi: 79, 306; jara3000: 283; Ju-Ju: 353; jusant: 22; kameshkova: 99, 339, 357; Karisssa: 498; viktor kashin: 434, 482; katyau: 470; Khaneeros: 43, 68, 234; Dani Kingdom: 223; Katerina Koniukhova: 242, 503; Iuliia Kononenko: 479; Olga Korablev: 128; Kateryna Kovarzh: 191, 380; Ekaterina Kudriavtseva: cover, 3, 17 (compass), 268; Alena Kurianchyk: 86; Katerina Kuzmenko: 275; Ekaterina Lanbina: 121; Viktoriia Lapshyna: 348; larisa_zorina: 246; LightFieldStudios: 67; LOW FLITE: 228; luchioly: 17 (birdcage), 352; Anna Lukina: 76; Anastezia Luneva: 74; Maltiase: 322, 412; MariaSemj: 260; Maryna Maznieva: 42; m-e-l: 340; Mika_48: 53, 96, 449, 454; miko: 510; Mimomy: 65, 249, 270, 406; Nairat: 447; Nataleana: 28; natalieozog: 430; Anastasiia Nimko: 292; Anastasiia

Nishchimnykh: 40; yoko obata: 115; Olga_Bonitas: 419; Ogri: 224; Ola_Tarakanova: 411; OrPolii: 385; Milana Pavlova: 35; Plateresca: 308; Julia Poleeva: 328; ra3rn: 450; Rina_Ro: 141; Ring-ring: 312; Olga Ryabukhina: 427, 504; Jana Salnikova: 152, 364; Elena Sapegina: 506; Alena Sattarova: 16, 29 (ambulance); chihiro sawane: 139; Dinara Sharipova: 131; Margaryta Shevchyshena: 48; Elena Shirokova: 62; Nickolai Shitov: 226; Nadezhda Shoshina: 26, 155, 217; Sibiryanka: 159 (earrings); Olga Sidelnikova: 57, 350, 438; Silmairel: 110; Ekaterina Skorik: 210; Olena Slobodeniuk: 220; smodj: 45 (basketball); Mariya stupak: 218; Anna Sukhova: 236; Anna Suslina: 135; Tanya Syrytsyna: 317; tada: 117, 235; TatianaKa: 17 (chair); Olga Ternavska: 21, 193; Daria Ustiugova: 51, 369, 388, 409, 474; Olena Varavina: 61, 184; VasilisaStArt: 472; vector_ann: 92, 289 (lion), 501; vikeriya: 118; Yes: 17 (cake), 400; Yunaco: 323; Olga Zhogina: 186, 310; zzorik: 160

Shutterstock.com: alamella: 195; alenasav4: 16, 379 (cat); Natalia Alexeeva: 244; anitapol: 486; Apple Vert: 515; ArtCreationsDesign: 271, 390, 489; Art_is_mrrr: 463; artshock: 20; Astro Ann: 71; Anzhelika Belyaeva: 148; Cat_arch_angel: 82; Christina Li: 420; Cincinart: 395; Darya_Stepen: 212; DreamLoud: 496; Eisfrei: cover, 3, 16 (merry go round, keys, lighthouse, lamp and starfish), 17 (butterfly), 180; ElliVelli: 102; enra: 37; Tatyana Fedorova: 366; Yana Fefelova: 16 (suitcase); FLORABELA: 299; Natalia Hubbert: cover, 3, 17 (gambling); Inspired Vectorizator: 33, 494; Irina_Russkikh: 38; Jolliolly: 30; KHIUS: 265; Hanna Kh: 518; Victoria Ki: 300; Eva Kleinman: 199; Vilanta Klimenko: 167; Maria Kuza: 105; Anastasia Lembrik: cover, 3, 16 (dreamcatcher), 333; Lenny712: 150; likovaka: 289 (lioness); luchioly: 169; Maltiase: cover, 3, 16 (scales, gavel), 143, 297, 416; may.art: 133; mimibubu: 113, 465; mimomy: 421; Mirowatercolor: 255; Artem Musaev: 16 (ring); MyStocks: 272; nagamushi-studio: 24, 257; NadzeyaShanchuk: 359, 425; Kunrus Nakwijitpong: 31; natnatnat: 286, 414; Anastasi Nio: 512; on_cloud: 83; Alina Osadchenko: 481; Paulaparaula: 50, 95, 204, 433; PEKENBALI: 467; Plateresca: 398; Poltavska Yuliia: 493; PYRAMIS: 320, 342, 457; Rout Art: 207; runLenarun: 335; Shafran: 179; Margarita Shevchyshena: 208, 240; Slastick_Anastasia Dudnyk: 173; SLKi: 294; solarseven: 404; Steicha: 508; Anna Sukhova: 144; Supergrey: 32; SvetaArtStore: 196; TairA: 266; Olga Toshka: 126; toyotoyo: 253; Katerina Tyshkovskaya: 267; Daria Ustiiugova: 263; vector_ann: 125; Michael Viglio: 458; Vikeriya: 109; yana-viukova: 251; Yu-lya: 171

About the Author

During a writing career spanning over forty years, Cassandra Eason has become one of the most prolific and popular authors of books on all aspects of spirituality and magick, including her bestselling *1001 Spells* and *1001 Tarot Spreads*. Other bestselling titles include her entries in the Little Bit series, including *A Little Bit of Palmistry*, *A Little Bit of Auras*, *A Little Bit of Crystals*, *A Little Bit of Tarot*, *A Little Bit of Wicca*, and *A Little Bit of Runes*. Her palmistry book has been widely acclaimed for making an often unnecessarily obscure subject totally accessible to beginners. Her *New Crystal Bible*, reprinted and retitled many times over ten years, now called *The Complete Crystal Handbook*, continues to be respected by crystal sellers, experts, and newcomers alike.

Cassandra also lectures, broadcasts, and facilitates workshops throughout the world on all aspects of the paranormal. During the past forty years, Cassandra has written more than 130 titles, many of which have been translated into numerous languages, including Japanese, Chinese, Russian, Hebrew, Portuguese, German, French, Dutch, and Spanish.

Cassandra was a teacher and university lecturer for ten years. However, her life path was to change following a vision by her three-year-old son Jack, who accurately described a motorcycle accident in which his father was involved at the time of his prediction. Jack said: "Daddy's fallen off his motorbike, but he is okay," as, forty miles away, her husband's motorbike was skidding on a patch of oil. Her husband fell off but was unhurt. The motorcycle clock stopped at the time of impact and was verified as precisely the same time Jack spoke, as Cassandra had been clock-watching for her husband to return from an overnight shift.

Following a great deal of research into this phenomenon, Cassandra went on to write *Psychic Power of Children*, the first in a long list of titles that would establish her as a worldwide bestselling author. She is also now widely acknowledged as a world expert on parent–child intuitive links.

Her books have been serialized around the world including in the UK *Daily Mail*, the *Daily Mirror*, the *Daily Express*, *People*, the *Sun*, the *News of the World*, *Spirit and Destiny*, *Fate and Fortune*, *Prediction*, *Best and Bella*, *Homes and Gardens*, and *Good Housekeeping*, as well as in the *National Enquirer* many times in the United States and in *Woman's Day* and *New Idea* in Australia. She had her own psychic column in the national women's magazine *Best* and in *Writers' News* for two years, and, for eighteen months, she produced a monthly psychic master class for *Beyond* magazine.

Cassandra appeared on the NBC programs *Unsolved Mysteries* and *The Other Side* and on Paramount's *Sightings*. In the United Kingdom, she had her own weekly miniseries for several years, *Sixth Sense*, on United Artists Cable Network, moving on to Granada Breeze, where she was resident white witch for over two years on *Psychic Live Time*. She also analyzed dreams on the UK Channel 4 *Big Brother* series 3 and 4 and *Celebrity Big Brother*, using dreams to interpret the true feelings of housemates and their likelihood of surviving the next vote.

She is a mother of five children and grandmother to four, who she considers her greatest joy and achievement. She lives on the rural Isle of Wight off the South Coast of England.